"...It's a great time saver when you can't wait for an answer this book can clear up the mysteries of mortgage banking in layman's language..."
USA Today

"Author Albert Santi has put his fifteen years' experience in mortgage banking to good use by providing a handy informational resource that is a real time saver."
Mortgage Banking Magazine
Mortgage Bankers Association of America

"Santi provides one of the most extensive and pertinent treatments in book form of FHA and VA mortgages."
Kiplinger's *Changing Times, Financial Services Directory*, Issue Number 2

"Every realtor's briefcase should contain a copy, no more need to call the mortgage company daily for answers. Answers are at your fingertips, indexed and easy to find. I am extremely grateful for this long-needed publication."
Bettye I. Harrison, CRB, CRS, LTG
1986 President, Women's Council of REALTORS®
of National Association of REALTORS®

"This useful new questions and answers guide is the builder's complete resource for home financing."
National Association of Home Builders Bookstore
Washington, D.C.

"Everything you ever wanted to know about these products in a condensed reference book form."
Secondary Marketing Executive (newspaper)

"I am delighted with the book and feel it should be a must for every licensed agent selling real estate today. It would save the managers and the experienced agents a lot of time if the newer agents had a book they could refer to for their answers. Some may even stay in the business longer."

Lucille "SAM" Scott, Associate Broker
Merrill Lynch Realty, Murrysville, PA

"(Albert Santi) has written what I (and those I have shown the book) consider the best written material I have ever seen on new home financing."

Donald K. Stephens, President
Sun State Homes, American Home Mortgage and
Past National Director of the NAHB,
Lakeland, Florida

"As a mortgage banker for the past 25 years, I can only say that this book is a must for everyone involved in home sales and financing."

Tommy Thompson, Regional Vice President
Lomas & Nettleton Corporation,
Winston-Salem, North Carolina

"It is my opinion that you have done a job our industry has long needed. We are advocating that our loan officers, processors and production people have one of your books on their desks at all times."

Henry W. Ferry, Executive Vice President
American Mortgage Securities Exchange, Inc.
San Jose, CA

"...It is an excellent piece of work written in layperson's language that makes it easy to understand. The book covers questions and answers that most people, even those in real estate, would not think of until it actually happened to them."

George S. Foster, Guaranty Officer (retired)
Veterans Administration
Nashville, TN

"Your FHA/VA book is very comprehensive and very helpful. We intend to distribute these books to our loan representatives and those involved in processing/closing FHA/VA loans. Please rush our order for 50 books."

Nancy Sato, Honolulu Federal Savings & Loan
Honolulu, HI

"The processing people in our organization are using the book as an information source to assist them in their efforts and the books which we presented to realtors in the area apparently are getting good use."

Charles L. Morris, CEO, Ensign Mortgage Company
Atlanta, GA

" One of the best mortgage financing sales tools for both beginners and experienced alike."

Norman Kailo, CRB, CRS, GRI
1986 Chairman of the FHA/VA Monitoring Network of
the National Association of REALTORS®

The MORTGAGE *Manual* Q&A's

on FHA, VA and CONVENTIONAL MORTGAGE LOANS

COMPLETELY REVISED & EXPANDED

4TH EDITION

ALBERT SANTI

Probus Publishing Company
Chicago, Illinois

Library of Congress Cataloging-in-Publication Data

Santi, Albert,
     The mortgage manual.

     Rev. ed. of: Questions & answers for FHA, VA & conventional loans. Rev. 2nd ed. c1986.
     Includes index.
     1. Mortgage loans—United States. 2. Housing—United States—Finance. I. Santi, Albert. Questions & answers for FHA, VA & conventional loans. II. Title.
HG2040.5.U5S27 1989 332.7′2′0973   89-8455
ISBN 1-55738-057-0

Printed in the United States of America

1   2   3   4   5   6   7   8   9   0

Dedication

To God who gave me the idea of writing this book and the encouragement to complete the task. To my wife Connie and our children, Marc, Suzanne, and Jennifer. The success of this book is owed to Him who said: "Commit your works to the Lord, and your thoughts will be established." Proverbs 16:3.

CONTENTS

PREFACE

The purpose of this book is to provide a unique source of reference material in the shortest space possible. In writing this book the author assumes the reader's knowledge of real estate finance is at the beginning level. The "expert" reader will also gain by having an organized reference source for information about FHA, VA, and Conventional Loans.

On many occasions, authors and teachers have the choice of explaining in a simple or a sophisticated manner. On the surface, a simple manner of explanation may not impress anyone. The problem with surface impressions is they often do not stand the test of time. Most publishers classify a real estate reference book as a "success" once it has sold 5,000 copies. Based on an approximate two-year association with this book, choosing to be simple or using a "layman's language" style of writing was worthwhile. The editions of this book have now accounted for sales of more than 50,000 copies to a group of purchasers that includes all types of mortgage lenders, government agencies such as FHA, VA, GNMA, FNMA, FHLMC, FHLB, secondary market participants, REALTORS®, homebuilders, appraisers and home inspectors, home buyers, attorneys, and all major bookstores, distributors, and libraries.

For the experienced lender, a true test of a good reference book should be the amount of time it's used. Some lenders refer to their copy as their bible for the mortgage business, and many have a copy in their office and another copy in their car. The index in the back of the book is cross-referenced in such a manner that the reader should be able to find answers to questions in less than two minutes. The index in this book is the key to the use of the material in the book.

My earliest conversations about this book were in 1973, five years after the start of my mortgage banking career. Two years later the first notes began to take shape. Work on the book began by simply listing the questions most often asked by borrowers, real estate salespeople, processors, and loan officers. Over a period of time, questions were compiled and answers researched. The first edition was published in June, 1985. This first edition contained 99 pages of basic questions and answers. Later editions contained more Q & A information and additional reference information in the form of tables, sections, abbreviations, and a glossary.

The completed work has resulted in a text which is the only sourcebook of its kind. This book is an excellent teaching tool for the beginner and a great time-saver for the professional who needs a quick reference guide. The questions help the professional find information quickly rather than to challenge one for an answer. Based on notes used in compiling much of the information for this book and its updates, every one to two pages in this book correlates to roughly three to four letter-sized pages from government manuals, and letters about changes in the regulations. With the information provided in a quick reference manner, loan processing time will be reduced.

There is a condensed tax section for real estate matters or for people working in real estate-related fields. There are answers to deductions for discount points, interest, entertainment, and child care costs.

There is an Acronym and a Glossary section. There are 296 acronyms. The Glossary section is condensed from thousands of pages used as reference sources. There are 1269 terms defined in the glossary which contains 108 pages, an average of 12 terms per page. There are Monthly Principal and Interest Tables, Discount Yield Tables, and Remaining Balance Factors. People new to the business will have a better understanding by seeing the "whole picture" in a Table as opposed to an answer on the screen of a calculator. Tables are helpful in comparing different monthly payments, understanding loan amortization, and understanding how discounts affect yield.

In "Comments on Refinancing" you will read important considerations on the subject. When refinancing to a lower interest rate, your income tax liability will increase. You may be faced with choosing between loans that have different rates and points. In this section, you will also find the best and the simplest worksheet for refinancing. Completing the worksheet will give you the exact after-tax dollar savings created by refinancing.

In "Prepaying a Mortgage" there is a true story which has many readers commenting on the lessons. Some readers have said: "I didn't know you could do this," or "How long has this been available?" This section is a simple explanation of how a mortgagor may save thousands of dollars.

The section titled "Comparing 15-year and 30-year Mortgages" gives instructions on comparing the dollar savings of a 15-year versus a 30-year mortgage. Besides the additional increase in the monthly payment for a 15-year mortgage, there are other items to consider.

The "Property Inspection Checklist" will give instructions on making a professional home inspection. Practical tips in this section may save you costly repairs in the future. This section shows you how to look for defects in plumbing, electrical, heating, and other areas of the home. There is also a section for "Home Maintenance Service Agreements." The "way of the future" for home maintenance may be filled with disappointments. Read of the loopholes in some Home Maintenance Agreements that give purchasers a false sense of security.

Real estate experts can test their knowledge by taking the "Mortgage Manual Exam." The true or false exam will challenge the readers and provide a rating for their effort.

In response to requests from those readers who wish to keep the book continuously updated, we have begun an update service which we have named the Reader Service Program (RSP™). There is an explanation of RSP™ on pages 371-372.

My special thanks go to George Foster, Loan Guaranty Officer (retired) for the Veterans Administration Home Loan Division in the State of Tennessee. Mr. Foster was with the VA for twenty-eight years and was a constant help in writing of the VA section. I would like also to thank Ken Harvey, Loan Guaranty Officer, and Wayne Brindley, Chief of Loan Processing, for VA loans in Tennessee. My thanks to Keith Pedigo, Director of Loan Guaranty Service in Washington, D.C. and to Sally Younger of that office. My special thanks to Laura Westbrooks, Senior Loan Specialist of the Memphis FHA office, and to Joe Garaffa, the Director of that office. Laura has been a special help for researching some of the information in this book. Also thanks to Bud Carter and Judy Spelman of the FHA Central office in Washington, D.C. A final thanks to all my past associates and customers who help to provide some of the ideas and encouragement for this book.

I especially want to thank my copy editor, Betty Sims, and her son Doug. Betty has been an encourager, as well as a valuable copy editor, and Doug has been our computer assistant. Thanks to my wife, Connie and our neighbor, Donna Spicer, for providing the Architectural Styles.

Thanks to Dan Kelley of the Washington Freddie Mac office. My special feelings go forth to Dan and his wife, Rosemary.

This fourth edition, teaching on a national level, and secondary marketing experience have led me to write two new books. One of the new books, *The Lender's Mortgage Manual*, is an expansion of this book. In *The Lender's Manual* the reader will have answers referenced to a government source. For example, in the fourth edition of *The Mortgage Manual* there is an explanation of borrowing the downpayment for an FHA loan in Question 1.48, page 44. With the Lender's Manual there will be the same question and answer but the reader will also be able to look in the FHA Compendium for the reference source for borrowing the downpayment, which is Mortgagee Letter 87-32. *The Lender's Manual* also has a VA Compendium, and a Quality Control Plan. The new book is an outstanding reference source for the professional lender.

Another new book is *The Mortgage Workbook,* a 3-ring notebook which emphasizes the "how to" for mortgage lending. Details are given for the completion of FHA, VA and Conventional forms used in loan processing, closing, and obtaining the insurance or guaranty. This book is a seminar for loan processors, loan officers, and secondary marketing executives.

Albert Santi

FHA HOME LOANS

1.1 *In general, what is an Federal Housing Administration (FHA) loan?*

An FHA loan is a real estate mortgage insured by the Federal Housing Administration and available to anyone purchasing or refinancing property which has an appraisal acceptable to the Federal Housing Administration. In general, it is a long term, high loan-to-value ratio (LTVR), fixed- or adjustable-rate mortgage with a limited due-on-sale clause.

FHA loans in this book refer to unsubsidized first mortgage residential loans on one-to-four family dwelling units. These first mortgage loans are authorized by Title II of the 1934 National Housing Act, as amended, and as such are sometimes called Title II loans.

1.2 *Could you state the purpose of FHA and give us a brief history of that agency?*

The Federal Housing Administration is a division of the U.S. Department of Housing and Urban Development. The agency was created under the provisions of the National Housing Act of 1934. FHA does not lend money, it insures mortgages made by approved lenders. The purpose of FHA is to provide housing for low and moderate income families. Candidates for FHA loans should be people who cannot normally qualify for conventional financing.

FHA has an outstanding record of being a self-supported government agency. The Mutual Mortgage Insurance fund provides nearly all of the income for FHA by collecting insurance premiums. The most often heard acronym concerning the insurance program is MIP. This acronym stands for "mortgage insurance premium" and refers to the insurance premium paid to FHA for insuring a loan. In exchange for the premiums collected, FHA insurance will compensate a lender for a loss from a foreclosure of a FHA loan. Today we take for granted the features in a standard mortgage.

1. Low down payment.
2. Long-term amortization.
3. A fixed interest rate.
4. Loan assumability.
5. Uniform and fair loan qualification guidelines.
6. Minimum property standards.
7. Uniform property appraisals.

All the features above were FHA innovations.

Before the creation of FHA, mortgage terms were not very attractive. If you could get a home mortgage, the terms were likely to be:

1. An adjustable rate of interest.
2. A down payment of 25% or more.
3. A term of ten years or less.

Loans were made on an interest-only basis which required periodic payments to principal or a balloon payment at the end. Of course, there were no nationwide uniform guidelines for credit or property approval.

FHA has sometimes gone too far in attempting to help the public. I refer to some of the subsidized loans of the past. I have had millions of dollars of loan experience with the Section 235 loan during the "Great Society" era of the Johnson administration. This may seem shocking now, but in the early 1970s, a middle-income family in my area of the country could buy a new three- or four-bedroom house for $200 down and 1% interest with the Section 235 program. Of course, the remainder of the interest was subsidized by us, the taxpayers. Furthermore, the small down payment of $200 could come from "sweat equity" (see glossary). The intentions were good and there were a few good loans made. As one might expect, the program ran into much abuse.

Even today there are some uneasy feelings about whether FHA is serving the purpose Congress intended when the agency was created. There are two opposing views of the proper role for FHA.

The conservatives may legitimately argue that FHA makes loans to those who can afford conventional financing. This, they argue, is contrary to the intent Congress had in mind for FHA.

The moderate view is one which believes FHA can lend to anyone. The better the borrower, the lower the insurance payout for foreclosure. Decreased insurance payout creates a better operational profit which will be used to help the poor. Furthermore, if FHA didn't make loans to middle-income people, they would be operating with a deficit. Operating in the "red" may jeopardize the future of FHA. Many look at FHA as a stabilizing force in home financing.

1.3 *Where does the money come from if FHA only insures the mortgage?*

The money comes from the private sector. FHA and Veterans Administration (VA) loans are enhanced by our Government by virtue of the insurance feature for FHA loans and the guaranty feature for VA loans. The sale of GNMA securities provides almost all the funds for FHA and VA loans.

A very general and brief explanation of how GNMA helps provide capital for these loans is as follows. An approved lender will close FHA loans and gather or "warehouse" these loans until a minimum of $500,000 is reached. Once this minimum amount is achieved, the loans are placed with a custodial bank. Security dealers may sell bonds of a new pool to the public in a minimum denomination of $25,000 and in multiples of $5,000 thereafter. These bonds are backed by GNMA with the full faith and credit of the United States Government.

An investor may own a whole loan as opposed to a GNMA security. FHA, unlike VA, has restrictions on who may own an FHA loan. Refer to the glossary for definitions of "investor" and "whole loan."

1.4 *What are the advantages of an FHA mortgage?*

3

There are several advantages:

1. A high loan-to-value mortgage is available. FHA purchasers may buy a home with as little as a 3% investment.
2. The mortgagors may borrow a portion of the closing costs they pay.
3. All of the mortgage insurance premium may be financed.
4. FHA interest rates are usually comparable to VA rates. FHA/VA rates are usually better than conventional rates.
5. Various programs are available. Program types include fixed rate, adjustable rate, graduated payment, shared equity and many more programs.
6. FHA Loans are assumable. Loans originated after 1 December 1986, have a limited due-on-sale clause. Loans assumed after the December date require loan assumption approval for the purpose of evaluating the borrower's ability to repay the loan. Please refer to Questions 1.5 and 1.6 for information on loan assumptions.
7. You may refinance, and there is no prepayment penalty. If you plan on prepaying the entire loan, please refer to Question 1.68, page 59. Homeowners may take advantage of any lower rate by refinancing without penalties. Current regulations allow for a "short-cut" method of loan approval for refinancing to a lower monthly payment.
8. Other mortgages may be placed behind an FHA first mortgage, i.e., second mortgages and wrap-around mortgages.
9. In my opinion, a home has a higher market value with an FHA loan as compared to a conventional loan with a due-on-sale clause.

Beyond a doubt, the biggest advantage to the public is that the interest rate remains unchanged upon loan assumption. To understand the advantage of a limited due-on-sale clause, we need to go back in time.

I can remember, as I am sure many of my Mortgage Banking colleagues may, having an often repeated conversation in the late sixties and early seventies. REALTORS® and a few loan applicants would say, "We want to do business with you, but it's so much easier to go down to the bank or the savings and loan and get a conventional mortgage and close in one or two weeks." Until recent years, mortgage bankers made FHA and VA loans, banks and S&Ls made conventional loans. Today, mortgage bankers still have a strong leaning toward the government loans, but the banks and savings and loan associations have become more familiar with these loans. It's easy to understand how the REALTOR® wants a quick closing as a service to the person, the seller, who pays their commission. I never have understood a loan applicant's reasons for choosing a conventional loan over an FHA loan when rates and terms are even. Why do I feel this way? Let's take a look at some history of interest rates for the answer. History has a way of repeating itself.

In 1978, interest rates were 9%. Three years later, rates had skyrocketed to 18%. This doubling of the rates happened so fast that, initially, people did not understand the full impact. Most people assumed that what goes up so fast would come down at about the same speed. Another assumption was that not all home sales had to involve new financing. High rates would not affect loan assumptions. After all, there were thousands of loans made at cheaper rates. Let's go out and assume a loan with a low rate, right? Wrong! The public was in for a shock. Not only did the rates stay high for a long, long time, but people got their first real introduction to the due-on-sale clause. The reaction by the public was almost comical at times and was identical to reactions that were to come later with high payment adjustments on adjustable rate loans. By this comment I am referring to the "amnesia" the public seems to have when reality hits home about the due-on-sale clause or an adverse adjustment takes place with an ARM loan.

The following is a scenario of a typical event that would happen over and over again from late 1979 through 1985. Mr. or Mrs. Homeseller, or the REALTOR®, places a call to the mortgage company for loan assumption information. The lender would check to see if the loan assumption was for an FHA, VA, or a Conventional loan. If the loan was a conventional loan with a due-on-sale clause, the lender informed the caller that any assumption would involve an escalation of the rate to market quotes. After the lender gave a market rate quote, a typical response was, "Wait a minute. Are you telling me that the rate is going to go from 8% to 18%? This will ruin the sale!" There is nothing humorous about an escalating rate. The comical part came when every caller said: "Hey, I don't recall being told the rate would double if my loan was assumed." Of course, the caller was correct. What lender can read the future? The humorous part is the seller or REALTOR® expecting the lender to take the blame for increasing the rate on loan assumption.

In 1978 lenders did not expect rates to double in three years, but it happened. In 1981 lenders did not expect ever to see single digit fixed rate loans again, but 5 years later it happened. Real estate law gives the investor the right to exercise a due-on-sale clause. Claiming ignorance of that law by people who wanted to cut the "red tape" associated with FHA and VA loans was no excuse to blame the lender.

No doubt, the use of the due-on-sale clause was tough on the public. There were some reports of lenders who went too far by using unfair practices. Some lenders used the "double whammy," which means escalating the rate and charging a prepayment penalty if the loan refinanced. Still yet another shock to the borrowing public was an assumption fee of 1% (or higher) of the loan balance. This fee was necessary to offset the expenses of processing a new loan application for the assumption. The conventional assumption fee was very high compared with a $45 transfer fee for an FHA or VA loan.

Escalating rates on loan assumptions and high assumption fees were tough penalties to pay for a conventional loan. Some sellers paid tougher penalties when they tried to hide a sale of their property. Many sellers and purchasers tried to skirt the due-on-sale problem by using land contracts, unrecorded deeds, wrap-around mortgages, and every other method imaginable. Methods of hiding a sale became a legal

6

nightmare as unrecorded deeds ended up in fraudulent situations and buyers were left with a loss of money and property. For the most part, the "safe" ways of hiding a transfer did not work. When lenders discovered a hidden transfer they then could exercise the "acceleration clause" in the mortgage. If there is a violation of terms contained in a mortgage, a lender may "accelerate" the mortgage. An acceleration of the mortgage requires the home owner to pay the outstanding balance in full.

In my opinion, the due-on-sale clause took away some of the attraction of home ownership. It became apparent that your "castle" belonged to you and your lender. Besides the traditional restrictions of police, eminent domain, etc., the lender can restrain a home owner by dictating what will take place upon loan assumption. Terms on your conventional loan apply as long as you own the property. Some borrowers erroneously think they do not have to worry about a due-on-sale clause if they have a conventional adjustable-rate mortgage. Refer to Question 3.41, page 122.

As a predominate government lender, most of my customers had FHA and VA loans. These customers (borrowers) later became sellers in the 1979-85 market. Happiness prevailed as their homes sold quickly to a market hungry for fixed-rate assumable FHA and VA loans. Many sellers with FHA or VA loans sold their properties at premium prices. Buyers were willing to pay more for homes with loans allowing assumption without escalation of the rate. Americans began to look to FHA as a guiding light and a safe harbor for home loans.

I think the shocking experience of escalating rates on loan assumptions opened the eyes of the public to the value of FHA loans. Some eyes opened so wide that many a "get-rich-quick guru" began appearing on TV and writing books about getting rich with government financed homes. Soon, the assumability privilege began to be abused. Eventually, FHA came forth with a limited due-on-sale provision. Fortunately, what FHA did was to attack the "quick flip" scams perpetuated by investors. A "quick flip" is the phrase given an investor who purchases a property for a favorable price, makes cosmetic repairs, draws cash out by refinancing, and then sells the property on a loan assumption to an unqualified buyer. Oftentimes the property goes into foreclosure. Of course, the foreclosure creates a claim by the lender who will then ask for payment by the Mortgage Insurance Program.

Today, FHA loans are assumable with the interest rate unchanged. FHA simply requires a purchaser to pre-qualify for a loan assumption to determine the purchaser's ability to repay the loan.

1.5 *What are the guidelines for assuming an FHA loan?*

For loans originated before 1 December 1986, there are no pre-qualification requirements. Loans may be assumed without regard to the purchaser's credit worthiness.

FHA requires pre-qualification for loans assumed after the December date. There are different guidelines for owner occupants and non-owner occupants. The guidelines in this answer are effective on December, 1988. If the original loan was to an owner occupant, pre-qualification is required if the property is transferred within one year from the origination date of the loan. If the original loan was to a non-owner occupant, pre-qualification is required if the property is transferred within two years from the origination date of the loan. The one-year or two-year time limit begins with the origination of the loan. The origination and loan closing are one and the same. The time limit does not begin with the endorsement of the loan. Loans may be freely assumed after the one- or two-year time limits. The pre-qualification requirement does not remain for the remaining life of the loan.

There are some exempt property transfer types. The general rule to follow is: a purchaser must pre-qualify according to the guidelines in this answer, except when a property transfer occurs by devise, descent, or operation of the law.

1.6 *Is the seller released of liability when a purchaser pre-qualifies for the loan?*

Credit approval of the purchaser, by itself, does not release the seller of liability. The seller must ask for a release from liability. HUD form 2210.1 must be used for a release of liability.

If the seller does not ask for a release of liability or the lender refuses to provide the release, the seller will be liable for a period of 5 years. The lender can refuse to release a seller of liability, even if the credit of the assumptor is approved. The liability will be for any default caused by a foreclosure. If the purchaser assumes the debt, then both seller and buyer are liable, both individually and jointly. If the purchaser takes title subject to the mortgage, then the seller remains solely liable.

The lender may charge a processing fee for any loan assumption approval; in no event should the fee exceed $500. If the approval of the purchaser is made, but the sale does not close through no fault of the purchaser, the lender will be required to refund one-half of the collected fee.

1.7 *Will the interest rate increase for loans that require prequalification?*

Loan assumptions do not alter the terms of an FHA loan, they remain the same. There is no interest rate escalation even with the new FHA loans having a limited due-on-sale clause. FHA loans made by state housing agencies may involve an escalation of below market rates for buyers who do not qualify per income restrictions.

1.8 *In your answer to Question 1.1, you stated anyone is eligible for an FHA loan. Can a non-U.S. citizens apply for an FHA loan?*

Yes. Anyone may apply for an FHA loan for a dwelling which has an appraisal acceptable to FHA.

1.9 *Is there just one type of FHA loan?*

No. There are several types of FHA loans; identification is by section numbers. In this book you will find an explanation of each section mentioned in the index.

1.10 *Would you briefly describe the down payment requirements and maximum loan amounts?*

Loan amounts and down payments vary by section numbers. It should be noted that maximum FHA loan amounts are adapted to: new construction built with FHA or VA inspections, or to new construction insured by an acceptable homeowner warranty program, or to an existing dwelling more than one year old. If the subject property does not meet the above criteria, the maximum loan will be penalized and reduced to 90% of the total acquisition. See Question 1.12 for an explanation of total acquisition.

In penalizing the maximum loan amount to 90%, instead of a maximum of 97%, one must consider the reality of no penalty when dealing with homes in certain price ranges. In reality, there is no penalty if you are dealing with properties which have total acquisition costs more than an amount equal to the maximum FHA loan amount for your area divided by 90%. For example: assume the maximum FHA loan amount for your area is $81,000, if you divided that amount by 90%, you would get $90,000. If you are dealing with a property with a total acquisition cost more than $90,000, it will not matter if the house was built under FHA or VA inspections, is warranted by the HOW (homeowner warranty) program, or is over one year old, the maximum loan is still going to be $81,000.

1.11 *What are some of the more often used FHA sections?*

The most popular loans are the FHA 203, 221, 222, 245 and FHA/VA.

1.12 *What is an FHA 203?*

This section is most often used by the public. Since it has all the advantages as listed in Question 1.4, as do the other sections, an explanation of it and the other sections, is actually an explanation of the maximum loan amount or the minimum down payment.

There are at least four different ways to arrive at maximum loan amounts using the 203(b) formula: (1) the purchasers pay their own closing costs and prepaid items (2) the sellers pay all the purchaser's closing costs (3) the sellers pay all the purchaser's closing costs and prepaid items (4) the sellers pay a portion of the purchaser's closing costs. See Figure 6 on pages 330-331 for examples.

The maximum loan amount for a one-to-four family dwelling is determined by taking applicable percentages of the total acquisition. Once you determine total acquisition, all you need do is multiply by an applicable percentage. We will go over the applicable percentage for each section. Applications must be on an owner/occupant basis to obtain maximum loan-to-value ratio.

"Total Acquisition" refers to the lesser of (1) the "cost to the purchaser," which is the same as "the cost to acquire" and "Acquisition Cost" or (2) the FHA estimate of value plus the FHA estimate of closing costs. The "cost to the purchaser" or "the cost to acquire," normally means the sales price, any repairs the purchaser is paying for, and closing costs the purchaser pays as noted in the FHA closing cost schedule. As we will see later, cost to the purchaser can be the above, minus sales concessions or excessive buydowns. A portion of the closing costs may be financed *if* the purchasers are paying their closing costs.

You must round your loan amounts down to the nearest $50 increment if the mortgagor is paying the MIP in cash. You do not have to round down if the MIP will be financed. I repeat, you do not have to round down if the MIP is financed. A lender, as a matter of preference, may always require the loan amount to be rounded down.

If total acquisition cost is $50,000 or less, the maximum loan amount can be determined by multiplying the total acquisition by 97%. If total acquisition exceeds $50,000, the maximum loan amount would be determined by multiplying the first $25,000 by 97% and then multiplying the remainder by 95%.

Allow me to illustrate by examples: Assume both the sales price and FHA value are $48,750, and the purchasers are paying all their own closing costs, which FHA estimates to be $1,250. The formula for the maximum loan would be $48,750 + $1,250 = $50,000 x 97% = $48,500. If the total acquisition is above $50,000, say $70,000, the formula would be: $70,000 + $1,800 (FHA's estimate of closing cost) = $71,800; 97% of the first $25,000 = $24,250, 95% of the remaining $46,800 ($71,800 − $25,000 = $46,800) = $44,460; $24,250 + $44,460 = the maximum loan of $68,710 or $68,700 if rounded down to the nearest $50. See Figure 6 for examples.

11

It is important to note that the maximum loan amount can include closing costs if paid by the purchaser. A simple way to remember this rule is to think of it in terms of "one cannot borrow what one does not pay." If purchasers do not pay their closing costs, then they cannot borrow money for their closing costs. Purchasers do not have to pay all their closing costs to have them included in the loan amount. If purchasers pay half of their closing cost, then half of the closing cost can be included in the calculation to determine maximum loan amount. The dollar amount for closing costs comes from an "Estimate of Closing Cost" published by your local FHA office. Depending upon sales price and the degree of closing costs paid by the borrower, you may determine the Total Acquisition by adding the closing costs stated on the FHA estimate to the acquisition costs. A word of caution: FHA uses different closing cost estimates for different acquisition amounts, and as one might imagine, the Estimate of Closing Costs varies among different regions throughout the country. The FHA closing costs are usually listed by counties. Ask your FHA lender or your local FHA office for a copy of the Estimate of Closing Costs for your area. A publication of all the schedules would be impractical for this book and would be subject to frequent changes.

FHA Estimate of Closing Costs does not include prepaid items. Prepaid items are usually real estate taxes and hazard insurance premiums paid at closing or put into an escrow account at the time of closing. See the definition of prepaid items in the glossary.

This is one of my pet questions and answers because of its simplicity once learned compared with the complexity perceived. Granted, the maximum loan amount formula is complex in comparison with a conventional loan. In conventional financing, to determine the maximum loan, one just multiplies the LTV (loan-to-value ratio) times the lower of the sales price or appraised value. With FHA you just can't take 90% or 80% of the sales price and get the maximum loan. One may think that determining a loan amount can be basic and involve simple arithmetic. To get an idea of the nature of the problem, ask a real estate salesperson to give the maximum loan amounts based on examples in Figure 6. When you find, in most cases, a person in the profession of selling houses cannot accurately determine the FHA maximum loan amount, you will begin to understand the problem. In defense of the real estate sales-people, and in keeping with a commitment to "tell it like it is," I sympathize with the frustrations of real estate agents when they tell me, "You call four different lenders and you get four different loan amounts." Comments on this subject can be endless. A REALTOR®, who is also a high school principal, looked over Figure 6, and confessed it was the first time after ten years in the business that he can honestly say he understands FHA "total acquisition." My experiences in explaining the maximum loan amounts include teaching on a local and national level. Students in my classes, including those in the lending business, routinely give incorrect answers to some of the questions about maximum loan amounts. At a statewide direct endorsement seminar conducted by FHA, and after two days of instructions, I witnessed the head of mortgage credit becoming frustrated when professional underwriters repeatedly gave incorrect answers to test problems about maximum loan amounts.

What can be done about the problem? Can determining an FHA maximum loan amount ever be as simple as a conventional loan? Probably not. The Congressional intent for FHA is to provide financing for housing to those who cannot qualify for a conventional loan. FHA provides help in meeting a national housing policy by providing higher loan-to-value ratios than conventional loans and allowing the borrowing of closing costs, and sometimes the prepaid items. In offering the highest possible loan-to-value ratios, there are various formulas to determine the maximum loan amounts.

The reader should go over this answer very carefully and use the examples given in Figure 6. Practice with some examples of your own and check your answers with someone you trust. The key is to arrive at the correct Total Acquisition. Once you have the correct Total Acquisition, it is simply a matter of arithmetic. If you use an HP-12c, there is a method of programing your calculator to determine quickly: the cash required to close, the monthly principal and interest based on a loan amount which includes the MIP, the loan amount without MIP, the cost of prepaid items, the loan amount with MIP. The keystrokes are found on page 207.

If you think my observations on how to determine correct loan amounts are exaggerated, pick up the telephone and verify for yourself. You can start by asking someone in the industry if a seller can pay a purchaser's prepaid items.

1.13 *What are excessive buydowns?*

FHA is in the mortgage insurance business. As a mortgage insurer, it is important to insure loans based on true market values. In the way of an acknowledgement, the "TV gurus" and real estate investment authors are correct when they assert, any property can be sold for the right terms. FHA has been listening. On 8 August 1986, FHA issued guidelines for "seller buydowns" in excess of 5% of the sales price. The 5% limit was later raised to 6% on 22 October 1987. In general, FHA defines a buydown as any inducement to influence a buyer to buy when they would not do so under normal circumstances. More importantly, for insuring purposes, buydowns are abusive when they influence the buyer to accept a price higher than a true market value.

Some examples of what FHA defines as a seller buydowns are as follows:

1. Payments for discount points.
2. Any type of interest payment, i.e., 3-2-1 plans.
3. A payment of a closing cost which normally is paid by buyer, i.e., the 1% origination fee.
4. Monthly payments to principal.
5. Gifts such as: trips, maid service, any non-realty items.
6. Payments for condo or homeowner association dues.

If the seller buydowns exceed 6% of the sales price, the amount over 6% will be deducted from the sales price and the LTV will be based on the lowered sales price.

If the seller buydowns pertain to interest (3-2-1 buydown), the purchaser must qualify at no less than 2% below the note rate. If the note rate is 10%, the purchaser must qualify at a rate not less than 8%.

1.14 *What are the maximum loan amounts for Section 203?*

FHA now establishes a maximum loan amount by location and number of units:

1. The statutory limit for a single-family residence is $67,500, but may be increased to $101,250 in certain high-cost locations.
2. A two-family residence has a maximum loan of $76,000, but may be increased to $114,000 for high-cost areas.
3. A three-family residence has a maximum loan of $92,000, but may be increased to $138,000.
4. A four-family residence has a maximum loan of $107,000, but may be increased to $160,500.

The above limits may be increased an additional 1/2 of the highest amounts given if the properties are located in Alaska, Hawaii, or Guam.

FHA has maximum loan amounts for various Sections. The maximum loan amounts can be increased up to the highest amounts mentioned above, if the property is deemed to be in a high-cost location. Maximum FHA loans usually are listed by counties, a listing in this book is not practical and would be subject to frequent changes. For the maximum FHA loan in your area, check with your nearest FHA office or an approved FHA lender.

All Sections mentioned in this book have the loan amounts as explained above, except for Section 221.

1.15 *Is there a minimum loan amount?*

Lenders may not establish their own minimum loan amount. Lenders are in non-compliance with FHA regulations if they require a minimum loan amount as a condition of providing an FHA or a VA loan.

1.16 *What is FHA Section 221?*

This loan is for families of low and moderate income. The real benefit is a lower down payment requirement. Only families are eligible, with an exception for handicapped persons or an elderly person 62 years of age or older. There are no limitations on income, but there are limitations for maximum loan amounts. The maximum FHA 221 loan amount is derived by multiplying 97% of the "Total Acquisition," which can include prepaid items for Section 221. The maximum 221 loan amounts can never exceed the FHA estimate of value excluding closing costs. Displaced families applying for a 221 loan may receive a loan equal to value, closing costs, and prepaid expenses, less $200 per family dwelling unit. The $200 investment per family dwelling unit will satisfy the minimum investment required for displaced families.

Maximum loan amounts are as follows:

1. A single-family dwelling is $31,000, but may be increased to $36,000 in certain designated locations.
2. A two-family dwelling is $35,000, but may be increased to $42,000.
3. A three-family dwelling is $48,600, but may be increased to $57,600.
4. A four-family structure is $59,400, but may be increased to $68,400.

Families of five or more members are eligible for single-family dwellings with four or more bedrooms with increased limits of $36,000, which can be increased to $42,000 in certain designated locations.

1.17 *What is an FHA/VA loan?*

This loan is used mainly by reservists who have served more than 90 consecutive days on active duty for training purposes and were discharged under conditions other than dishonorable, or by veterans who have used their eligibility or want to preserve the eligibility for use at a later time. Usage of the FHA/VA loan does not involve the veteran's entitlement. Reservists or veterans can use this program as many times as they wish.

An FHA/VA loan is a Section 203 loan with a change in the formula for deriving maximum loan amount. The maximum loan amount is calculated as follows: 100% of the first $25,000 of FHA total value and 95% of the remainder. One can determine the maximum loan by taking 95% of the total acquisition and adding back $1,250. Only single-family homes are eligible. There is one supporting document all applicants must obtain, a Certificate of Veteran Status. This Certificate is furnished by request from the Veteran's Administration. A purchaser can have less than a 3% investment when buying with an FHA/VA loan.

If FHA deems an applicant to be a short-term occupant of the property, the normal FHA Section 203 down payment will be required. An example of a short-term occupant would be a serviceman subject to transfer.

Discharged veterans are eligible for this loan if there has been 90 days of active duty and if the veteran enlisted before 8 September 1980, or if the veteran was an officer enlisted before 14 October 1982. A discharged veteran who was not an officer and entered service after 7 September 1980, must have served 24 months of active duty to be eligible if enlistment was after 14 October 1982. An exception to the above would be a veteran discharged because of disability or hardship.

Reservists who served at least 90 days of active duty for training purposes continue to be eligible for this, regardless of the entry day of service.

This answer reminds me of two true and false problems usually included in a final exam I use at some of my seminars. The first is: "An FHA/VA loan is VA loan." The other is: "An individual purchasing a duplex with an FHA/VA loan was rejected. The reason for rejection had to be problems with either the appraisal, income, or credit of the purchaser." I usually put the first statement in the VA section, and many students will answer "True." Answers to the second question give me a feeling of wanting to put up a big sign reading: "YOU CAN'T GET AN FHA/VA LOAN ON ANYTHING OTHER THAN A SINGLE-FAMILY DWELLING!" Even though the book mentions this fact, many students still answer this question incorrectly.

The second true or false item has the word "rejection." To understand the importance of this problem, consider the repercussions if the error is not caught until loan submission. Based on normal situations, this occurs after the sales agent has gone through all the efforts of making the sale, after the purchaser has made a loan application, after the appraisal fee and credit report fee have been paid, and the worst part . . .

after roughly 30 days of loan processing! Now, who is going to tell whom, "Sorry, you can't get an FHA/VA loan on a duplex." This type of information should come with a warning beforehand: "The following is based on a true story except the name of the loan officer, processor, and REALTOR® have been changed to protect the innocent." Better yet, the names have been changed to protect the uninformed from the buyer.

Only single-family properties are eligible for: FHA/VA, Graduated Payment Mortgage (GPM), and Section 222.

1.18 What is FHA Section 222?

This was an often used loan in an area with a military base. There is one distinct feature of this FHA loan: payment of an FHA 1/2 of 1% monthly insurance premium by a government agency. Only single-family dwellings are eligible. Down payment guidelines are the same as for Section 203. The service person must have been on active duty for more than 2 years, and the Commanding Officer must certify that housing is required for the service person or his/her family. A Certificate of Eligibility (DD Form 802) must accompany the application to FHA. The 1/2 of 1% premium is paid by a government agency while the service person is on active duty, owns the home, and uses it for their primary residence. If the service person dies, the premium will continue to be paid for up to 2 years or until the sale of the home, whichever occurs first. A service person eligible for this section may assume an FHA loan of another section and have that loan changed to a Section 222, thereby eliminating any required monthly payment of mortgage insurance.

Today most departments of service and government agencies have not been funded for payment of the MIP. Exceptions are certain sections of the Department of Transportation and the Coast Guard.

1.19 What is a Section 245?

In comparison to the other sections mentioned, the 245 is the newest. This loan is often called a GPM loan (Graduated Payment Mortgage). There are five types of FHA GPM loans. As the name implies, a GPM begins with payments that gradually increase over a period of time. Specifically, the FHA GPM

Plans, I, II, and III graduate from years 1 through 5, then remain constant for the life of the loan. Plans IV and V increase over a period of 10 years, then remain constant. Because of Secondary Market reasons, Plans IV and V are not normally offered to the public. FHA 245 GPM loans have certain characteristics:

1. FHA will qualify the applicant on the first-year payment to determine that income is sufficient.

2. There is negative amortization. In the early years the loan balance increases instead of decreases. This will normally occur in any loan that has a payment rate in the beginning that is lower than the rate of interest or mortgage rate.

3. There is a payment rate. The monthly payment can be expressed as an interest rate percentage. For example, a 12.25% Plan III will have a monthly payment in year 1 that is equal to an interest rate equivalent to approximately 3% below the mortgage rate or, specifically, equivalent to an interest rate of 9.04%. The interest rate, however, is not 9.04%, as this is the payment rate. The interest rate is the mortgage rate or note rate, which in the above example was 12.25%

4. The mortgage rate or note rate is the actual rate of interest for the mortgage.

5. After the graduations are completed, the payment rate will be higher than the mortgage rate for the remainder of the term, (13.67% in the example above) so that amortization of the loan will occur in 30 years.

6. 245's can only be used for single-family dwellings.

7. 245's cannot be used for refinancing a permanent home mortgage, except for refinancing an existing 245 loan to a lower rate.

8. Discount points or the mortgage rate normally will be higher as compared to the other FHA Sections.

At the seminars I teach, the class seems to understand the impact of the FHA GPM program better by using some of the Figures in the book. I will attempt to prove my point in writing. Please turn to Figure 7 on pages 332-333. Take a highlighter or a pen and mark each first-year payment on Plans I, II, and III. Now turn to Figure 10 on page 338 and highlight the P & I factor for a 11.5%, 30-year loan. Turn back to Figure 7 and write this factor down at the bottom of the page, the number should be 9.9029. Now consider a loan amount of $100,000. On a Level Payment Conventional or FHA loan, the monthly Principal and Interest payment will be $990.29 (9.9029 x 100). With the FHA GPM, the first year payments will be: $906.31 for Plan I, $829.60 for Plan II, and $759.60 for Plan III. Comparing the monthly payment between a Level Payment Loan and Plan III, there is a savings of $230.69, per month! Of course, there are the negatives which are:

1. Negative amortization.
2. Once positive amortization occurs, monthly payments will end up higher compared with a Level Payment Loan.
3. An approximate 10% downpayment is required for Plan III.

1.20 *Why are discount points or the mortgage rate slightly higher for 245 loans as compared to other FHA programs?*

Normally, investors (institutions that buy mortgages) base a mortgage yield on the assumption that an FHA or VA 30-year mortgage has an average life of 12 years. FHA 245 loans have the same average life, but the payment rates are lower than the mortgage or note rate. Simply put, investors receive fewer dollars in monthly payments in the early years of a 245 loan as compared to level payment loans.

1.21 *What is the most widely used 245 plan?*

The most widely used plan was Plan III and 245(b). Because of serious foreclosure problems with 245(b), this program was discontinued in October, 1987. The principal difference between the two programs was the downpayment required. Plan (b) had eligibility requirements for the borrower and the property, but the chief difference was that one could obtain the monthly payments outlined in Plan III, with the low downpayment required in Plan I. Plan (b) could be used only for what FHA designates as new construction or substantial rehabilitation. The borrower eligibility requirements were as follows:

1. The applicant may not have held title to property within the previous three years. There could have been exceptions, such as one of two or more borrowers having owned real estate while the other borrower did not hold title to real estate.
2. The applicant's income and assets were such that qualification under other FHA programs would not have been feasible.

Plan III can be used on a new or an existing dwelling and there are no borrower eligibility requirements.

Another very good feature of Plan III, as compared to creative financing in the form of short-term or permanent buydowns, is the front end savings offered by Plan III when compared to a buydown plan. A 3-2-1 buydown can offer better front end monthly payments as compared to Plans I and II, without negative amortization. But, Plan III payments are equal to a 3-2-1 buydown without the cost of buying down the interest rate. For example: A short-term buydown of 3-2-1 (3% for the first year, 2% second year, and 1% third year) may compare with a Plan III first-year monthly payment; but the cost to the seller will be approximately 6% (3+2+1) plus the discount points. The buydown cost does not fare very well when compared to a 245 Plan III, which requires only discount points to be paid. A permanent buydown would be even more expensive as it would require buying the rate down for the life of the loan. Although the approximate 10% downpayment with a Plan III is costly, it is a downpayment and not bought down interest.

Another very important comparison, between a buydown and a GPM, is what FHA will use for the first year payment. For income analysis purposes, FHA will not allow the first year buydown payment to be less than 2% below the note rate, but as we have already seen, the first payment could be more than 3% below the note rate with a Plan III. For clarification purposes, FHA will allow a buydown of up to 3% in the first year, but for loan qualification purposes, the monthly

21

payment will be based on a rate that is not less than 2% below the note rate.

For more information on buydowns, see Question 2.83, page 105 and 3.35 through 3.38, page 120 through 121.

When FHA first began the 245 Program, I was a big believer in the advantages of this section. I still believe in the advantages of qualifying on the first year's payment rate and the savings of this section compared to buydowns. For loan qualifying purposes, a quick rule of thumb is a borrower must earn 4 times the monthly payment. Based on that assumption, a Plan III monthly payment $200 lower than a fixed rate amortized loan will result in a purchaser qualifying with $800 less monthly income. A REALTOR® can sell the same house to a buyer making $9,600 less per year compared to a buyer financing the purchase with the same loan amount, same interest rate, but with a level payment amortization. Today, the 245 Plan is not as attractive compared to when it was first introduced in 1978. When the program first began, interest rates were in the single digits (8.75-9.5%) and the values of homes were increasing in the double digits. It was possible for an individual to purchase a home in 1978 with a payment rate as low as 5.75%, and the value of the home growing at a 12%, or higher, annual rate. You don't have to be a rocket scientist to understand those numbers.

My disenchantment with Section 245 began when rates got up in the double digits and the values of homes began to appreciate in the single digits. In my opinion, with 245(b) taken away, the only attractive Plan is III. As previously noted, Plan III has a decrease of approximately 3% in the first year, but when the increases are over, the payment rate levels off at approximately 1.5% over the note rate in year six and stays that way for the duration of the loan. Furthermore, Plan III requires an approximate 10% downpayment. On the bright side, there are more people with the required downpayment than one may think, and home values in some parts of our country are increasing in double digits.

I remember originating a 245 Plan III loan for my sister when the program first started. She was a schoolteacher and wanted to buy a home in a neighborhood she really could not afford. Part of her downpayment was a gift from our parents.

I also remember my father calling each year the mortgage payments graduated. My father was an Italian immigrant. The call from my father would usually start out with him asking "Albert, how could you make such a loan *to your own sister?*" Finally the calls stopped when her payment rate leveled off at 12% and the house had increased in value by a minimum of $30,000, in just six years.

1.22 *What are the down payment requirements for all the 245 Plans?*

FHA explains these requirements in such a manner that it is much more efficient and simpler to use a factor to multiply against the Total Acquisition cost which will equal the loan amount. Figure 9, page 336 has 245 maximum loan factors, and highest outstanding balance factors.

To derive a maximum 245 loan, simply multiply the factor times the Total Acquisition. For example: For a $60,000 Total Acquisition cost, the maximum loan amount for a 13% Plan III should be $53,400 ($60,000 x .89004).

1.23 *How much do the monthly payments graduate each year for the GPM Plans?*

Plan I monthly payments graduate at 2-1/2% per year, Plan II at 5% per year, and Plan III at 7-1/2% per year, Plan IV at 2% per year (10 years) and Plan V at 3% per year (10 years).

1.24 *Does FHA have a RAM mortgage?*

In the spring of 1989 FHA should begin offering a Reverse Annuity Mortgage (RAM) and there may be some RAM mortgages with Shared Appreciation Mortgage (SAM) features. Presently, fall of 1988, the forecast is for a pilot program of three different types of RAM loans. The reverse mortgages will allow elderly home owners to convert equity into cash with guidelines different from those used for refinancing. The guidelines are presently being drafted and will soon be released for review. The three different types of RAM mortgages proposed are: tenure mortgages, term mortgages, and "line-of-credit" mortgages. The interest rates can be fixed or adjustable. Proposed guidelines call for borrowers to be at least 62 years of age, and have a large equity position in their home. The borrowers will have to undergo counseling before being permitted to close the RAM loan. The mortgage does not have to be paid off unless the borrower dies, moves, or sells the property.

1.25 *Why does FHA charge for mortgage insurance?*

When FHA was established by The National Housing Act of 1934, it was to become self-supporting by income derived primarily from a 1/2 of 1% insurance charge. The insurance charge is commonly called MIP (Mortgage Insurance Premium). In earlier days the insurance premium had been called MMI (Mutual Mortgage Insurance). Revenues and costs of FHA's permanent loan program are still accounted for in the Mutual Mortgage Fund. Throughout the history of FHA, it has been self-supporting concerning its unsubsidized programs.

FHA has altered the collection procedure for the Mortgage Insurance Premium. On most FHA Sections, the entire Mortgage Insurance Premium is collected up front at the closing. Reasons given by FHA are: (a) increased cash flow now is better than later payments, and (b) in a rather benevolent gesture, FHA wanted to lessen the paperwork burden for the lenders. A rumor gives a third reason: FHA is avoiding the gigantic task of maintaining or supervising the annual collections and balancing of the premiums for all outstanding FHA loans.

Not all FHA loans are included in the policy change. The policy change is effective for all FHA appraisals issued after 1 September 1983. The guidelines have changed since its inception, affecting FHA sections 203, 245, and 251 (adjustable rate mortgage). Also, the premium can be borrowed or paid in full. The present cost of a MIP for a 30-year loan is 3.8% of the loan amount or 3.661% if paid in cash. For a 15-year loan the MIP cost is 2.4% if financed or 2.344% if paid in cash.

This question and answer bring to mind a couple of memories. Please remember that the one-time MIP can be used only for certain sections. An experience might be the best way of relating how this fact can be overlooked. When the first edition of this book began to circulate, summer of 1985, George Foster, who is mentioned in the preface, called me to express concern over a comment by a branch manager of a major lender in the Nashville area. It seems that George had shown the book to this person and strongly recommended consideration of a large order for his branch and other branches throughout the country. After reviewing the book, the individual called George and said the book was very good but outdated. The branch manager told George "The book has monthly MIP factors and FHA has changed to a one-time MIP premium." I called this individual and he said, "It's really good, but in the Figures you have monthly MIP factors and we don't use them any more." I replied, "What are you going to do on a Section 203 loan on a condominium? You can't use the one-time premium." The reply over the phone was "Oh." Another experience involved a correspondent who closed a condo loan and collected the one-time premium. When the mistake surfaced, I called the bank and, fortunately, everyone was willing to come back and reclose.

The second thought I have on this question and answer deals with FHA being self-supporting and political efforts in the past to sell FHA to private enterprise. Besides the advantages of an FHA loan the public could lose if it were sold to the private sector, why would our government want to sell something that is generating revenues? Even when losses from foreclosures are considered, the net income for FHA has been in the millions of dollars.

A few years ago, when there was a real push on selling FHA to private enterprise, I read an editorial titled "Deal the FHA Out of the Housing Market." This article was published in a nationally distributed business newspaper. To date, this is the first supposedly non-administrative authority that I have witnessed to come out in favor of the proposal to sell FHA. My first reaction was to walk away from the source of irritation and presume that everyone else would be able to conclude that the statistics in the article were, to use the kindest word, "inaccurate." The problem I had with my initial reaction was, not everyone knows the "nuts and bolts" of home

25

financing and the article was probably read by millions. Quoting from a portion of the article:

> ...FHA has been instrumental in improving the residential mortgage market. Its standardized loan has stimulated the development of secondary markets and helped to give mortgage loans access to the securities market. In fact, these innovations were once unthinkable without FHA insurance. But conditions have greatly changed in the past few years. Currently, conventional loans are also traded actively in secondary markets, and they are used to back the securities issued by the Federal National Mortgage Association and the Federal Home Loan Mortgage Corporation or those guaranteed by the Government National Mortgage Association—the federally sponsored agencies so crucial to the supply of housing funds. In 1985, for example, the FNMA bought $12 billion of conventional loans but less than $200 million in FHA and VA mortgages.

In parts of the article, there is mention of the FHA's share of the mortgage market being 3% to 4%, and there is mention of the "present 1/2% premium." I want my readers to know the facts. If you were a lender, one of the last institutions you would sell FHA loans to would be the Federal National Mortgage Association (FNMA). The reason being that your discounts would be roughly 1% higher than those of any competitors who sell their FHA loans to the Government National Mortgage Association (GNMA). In fact, lenders sell so many FHA and VA loans to GNMA that the credit limit for that agency had to be raised to $150 billion for fiscal 1988, and $156 billion for 1989, as noted in Section 446 of the 1987 National Housing Act. Recent statistics show FHA accounting for 50% of the activity in some parts of the country.

FHA is very much alive, and in my opinion, there is no sound justification for even considering a sale of this agency to the private sector. If such a sale were ever to occur, it would take an important part away from our heritage of residential housing.

1.27 *For loans requiring the monthly payment of MIP, can you calculate the charge by simply adding 1/2% to the mortgage rate?*

No. The MIP is not amortized monthly. The 1/2% MIP is charged on the average scheduled balance of loan principal outstanding during the year. Simply stated, the MIP is based on an annual calculation, and therefore, will be slightly higher than adding 1/2% to the FHA rate.

1.28 *Is the mortgage insurance refundable?*

For the old regulation (prior to 1 September 1983), the answer would be "yes" if the following conditions exist:

1. The FHA loan was a Section 203(b).
2. Premium income has been collected for ten years or more.
3. The Mutual Mortgage Insurance fund has income in excess of expenses at the time the insurance is terminated.
4. The insurance is terminated as a result of full payment of the mortgage or a request of termination by the lender.

The new one-time MIP requirements, for certain Sections of 203, 245, and 251, have provisions for refunds. You may refer to Figure 18, page 353 to get an idea of how the one-time premium refund will apply to loans paid off before their full amortization.

I will bring out another true and false question to test what you have learned. An FHA 221 loan was paid in full for a reason other than foreclosure. "The owner of last record can expect a partial refund of the MIP premium," true or false? If you answered "true," you were like most students who answer this question incorrectly. When you refer to the original question and answer, you will see that Section 221 is not mentioned and therefore is ineligible.

1.29 *Assuming the criteria in the answer to Question 1.28 has been or will be met, what is the procedure for obtaining these funds?*

Normally Housing and Urban Development (HUD) will forward a Form HUD-2042 to an eligible party within 60 days from the termination of the FHA insurance. Disbursement is usually 45 days from HUD receipt of the completed HUD-2042. If this does not occur, contact your lender or write to:

27

U.S. Department of Housing and Urban Development
Director, Mortgage Insurance Accounting, OFA
Attn: Home Mortgage Branch
Washington, DC 20410

Include the FHA case number, property address, and the date the loan was paid in full or the date the property was sold. Any refundable insurance is payable to the last owner of record.

I inserted this information for my convenience as much as it can be for yours. This is the type of information you write down somewhere and then you can't remember where you put it. When I sometimes wear the hat of a real estate investor, the information on refunds and how to receive one has proven to be very valuable. On many occasions I have assumed FHA loans that have been in existence for many years. There have been situations where someone else paid the 1/2 of 1% MIP over a long period of time, say 22 years; I assume the loan, renovate the house, sell the home to a purchaser who finances the purchase with a new loan.

I then use the information given to you, on the MIP refund, and end up with checks from HUD ranging anywhere from $300 to $800 for a refund on the MIP I paid for a few months and someone else paid for 22 years.

1.30 *Is owner occupancy required for FHA loans?*

Yes, for certain programs such as Section 221, 245, 251, FHA/VA, but not for Section 203. One can obtain an FHA 203(b) loan on a non-occupant/owner basis. The maximum loan is restricted for a non-occupant owner, it cannot exceed 75% of the Total Acquisition.

1.31 *Is there any special restriction that would apply to loan applicants who seek to purchase a new home with an FHA loan, but who recently purchased their present home with an FHA loan and want to keep said home for rental purposes? Should they reduce the loan on their present home to a 75% LTV, since the property will be used for a non-occupant/owner purpose?*

A borrower is typically not eligible for more than one high-ratio mortgage for a principal residence at any given time. If the borrower desires to keep their principal residence for rental purposes and apply for a high-ratio loan for another principal residence, either the new loan or the old loan must be reduced to a 75% LTV.

There can be exceptions to FHA's policy. Two examples of exceptions are: a family transferred to another area due to an employment-related cause, a change in a family's income or size.

Restrictions applying to the number of FHA loans an individual may have, as discussed in Question 1.32, will apply to this question as well.

Often, students will ask, "Is there a time limit requiring one to live in the dwelling before they can apply for another FHA loan?" When I respond, "No," they then will ask, "How often can this be done?" Again, there is no limit to obtaining FHA loans providing you meet the seven units per contiguous area or subdivision. This policy will be outlined in a forthcoming question.

Some students will then ask, "Well, if there is no limit to the number of loans, except for the 7 unit rule, could an individual buy a home with the owner-occupancy high-ratio loan, live in the unit for a short time and then move out and get another home with a high-ratio FHA loan?" The answer to this type of question depends on the intent involved. As I have outlined in the second paragraph, FHA will make exceptions to having only one high-ratio at any given time. There does not have to be a law created for every conceivable situation. If your intent is to circumvent a regulation, then it is wrong and you are in danger of committing fraud which subjects you to penalties far greater than the benefits. "Circumvention of regulation" is a violation that is similar to a "dual contract."

Some students will then ask: "How can FHA find out what your intent was and how would they even know to investigate a possibly fraudulent situation?" My answer to these students is that FHA has routine audits and many other checks and balances and sources of information that act as a "red flag" to signal that a violation may have occurred and an investigation is warranted. If your intent was to live in the dwelling for which you obtained an owner-occupant loan, then due to acceptable circumstances to FHA, you have to move out in thirty days after closing, you may keep the house for rental purposes and apply for another owner-occupant high-ratio loan. If you closed your owner-occupant loan and never moved into the house, you have a real problem. Even if you moved in on a temporary basis but never made the customary change in your permanent residence address for your mail; utilities or telephone service were never placed in your name; permanent address change for your driver's license was not made, etc., your real intentions can be discovered. The key to possible fraudulent situations is the word "intent." Your home can become unsuitable for your needs with events such as: a change in your job causing you to relocate to another part of the city or the country, a sudden increase in the size of your family, or destruction of your home by natural causes. A cause which renders your newly purchased home unsuitable may allow you to apply immediately for another FHA loan on a high-ratio owner-occupied basis.

1.32 *Is there a restriction on how many FHA loans an individual may have?*

Yes, but at this time I wish to point out that for some unknown reason the interpretation of the regulations varies from region to region. The answer from FHA in Washington is that an individual may have no more than 7 non-occupant/owner units per subdivision including any adjacent or contiguous subdivisions. The limit of 7 units includes any financial interest an applicant may have in a property, regardless of the type of ownership or the type of mortgage involved in any unit. Financial interest includes any form of interest: fee simple, interest in a partnership, a corporation, or a trust. The property can be free of any liens, or financed by a VA or a conventional mortgage, it still counts in the 7 unit rule.

Over the years, I have heard answers to this question from FHA Field offices and FHA lenders that vary from no more than two loans for the whole state to seven new FHA loans per city.

There always seem to be various interpretations of the 7 unit rule. Not more than three months after the first edition was published (May '85), I was told of a mortgage company originating three investor refinances I had rejected. The investor was a friend of mine, and he explained to me that one of his partners was responsible for following up with another lender after I had rejected the loans. My friend had recently read my book and was concerned that something illegal might have taken place. I asked this investor to go back and casually enter into a conversation about the loan approval. The loan underwriter of the other mortgage company defended his action on the grounds that the three duplexes refinanced were in a corporate name and, therefore, these units were not included with the units owned in the individual names of the borrowers. To make matters more frustrating, the underwriter was a former FHA underwriter. Another incident I can recall (April '86) was one of my students who questioned me about the accuracy of the answer. The student, whose first name was Pete, was a securities dealer and a real estate investor. A Savings and Loan Association had taken Pete's application to refinance four duplexes with FHA investor loans. Of course, when we covered this material in class, Pete said, "Hey wait a minute!" In checking into the details, I was informed that the duplexes were in the same subdivision. My response to Pete was, "4 x 2 = 8" (4 duplexes with 2 units each) which means the four FHA loan applications should not be originated in your case; even if one of the duplexes were in another subdivision but said subdivision was deemed to be contiguous to the subdivision containing the three duplexes. The rule is: an investor is limited to a financial interest in no more than 7 units per subdivision, including any adjacent or contiguous subdivisions. I advised Pete to take a copy of the book to the loan officer. Pete talked to the loan officer and was told my answer was incorrect and they were processing his loans. I informed Pete that such was not the case but "let's see what happens." Approximately two weeks later, Pete's loan applications were rejected. Pete asked for his money back (money spent for a credit report and four appraisals) and the loan officer refused on the basis that the investor rules were changed while the cases were in process. I recommended that Pete have a conversation with the president of the S&L. The next time I saw Pete, he had a grin on his face as he told me that he received a refund of roughly $700 from the S&L. Approximately thirty days later, I had a grin on my face as we received an order for 30 books from the S&L Pete was dealing with; the order was placed by the president. The answer to this question is true and correct as instructed by the FHA Central Office.

Figure 16, page 350 Schedule of Real Estate, will be helpful in processing investor loan applications, particularly concerning the Contiguous Subdivision Rule.

1.33 *Is there a limitation to the number of FHA loans one can apply for?*

No. There are, however, restrictions if an individual applies for an FHA loan and has sold a property encumbered by an FHA loan within one year from date of application. The applicable restrictions have changed. In this book the old and new restrictions will be explained for a better understanding and for the sake of comparison.

1.34 *What old restrictions applied if an FHA applicant sold proper-ty encumbered by an FHA loan to an owner/occupant?*

If said property was sold to an owner/occupant on a loan assumption basis, the following restrictions applied:

1. If said property was sold within the past six months, the following restrictions applied:
   a. A credit report on the purchaser;
   b. A verification of the payment record from the mortgage company servicing the assumed mortgage.
2. If said property was sold more than six months but less than one year from the date of application, the restrictions were the same except for the credit report.

The requirements of (a) and (b) as stated above could have been waived if:

1. The assumed mortgage was verified to be 85% or less than its original balance. The local FHA office could

interpret compliance of this requirement if the assumed mortgage was less than 85% of the maximum mortgage available [in Section 203(b)] as determined by a new appraisal.

2. FHA approved the purchaser and released the seller (present applicant) from liability.

1.35 *What old restrictions applied if an FHA applicant sold property encumbered by an FHA loan to a non- occupant/owner?*

If an applicant sold a property encumbered by an FHA loan to a non-occupant/owner within one year from the date of application, the following restrictions applied:

1. If the sale to a non-occupant/owner was less than six months, the following applied:
   a. The assumed mortgage must have been 85% or less than its original balance.
   b. The mortgage must have been reduced to 85% of its original balance, or the purchaser must have placed enough funds in escrow to accomplish this reduction. If the escrow procedure was used, the funds would have been held until the property was sold to an owner/occupant or a period of eighteen months had elapsed. At the end of the eighteen month period, the funds in escrow would have been used to reduce the loan to 85% of its original balance.

2. If the sale was more than six months from date of application, the same restrictions applied as those listed in a sale to an occupant/owner less than six months from date of application.

1.36 *What are the new restrictions applicable to an FHA applicant who has sold property encumbered by an FHA mortgage within the past twelve months?*

1. Proof of sale:
   a. Submit a certified true copy of the sales agreement or a copy of the settlement statement.
   b. If the property is to be sold, the mortgagee must submit a copy of the settlement statement when

endorsement of the current HUD insured loan is requested.

c. Submit a statement from the purchaser that they intend to occupy the property as their primary residence.

2. The conditions above can be waived if one of the following documents is submitted with the application:

a. FHA Form 2210.1 showing that the purchaser has been approved by FHA;

b. A statement from the mortgagee of the assumed loan indicating that the remaining balance is no more than 75% of its original balance;

c. A current FHA appraisal which proves that the outstanding balance is no more than 75% of the FHA value plus FHA closing costs;

d. A non-owner/occupant may place into escrow an amount sufficient to lower the remaining balance to 75% of its original amount. These funds may be released if the property is sold to an owner/occupant within eighteen months; if the sale to an owner/occupant does not occur, the funds must go to reduce the remaining balance to an amount of 75% of the maximum mortgage amount available to an owner occupant.

Before closing a new FHA loan, the conditions outlined in this answer must be satisfied for any applicant who has sold property encumbered by an FHA loan within the past 12 months.

1.37 *What is a discount and what are discount points? What is the purpose of discount points?*

Long ago, I had the privilege of hearing a senior mortgage banking executive explain the theory of discount. I can still hear the words of wisdom as Bill explained how understanding discounts is completely tied to the recognition of *"all money costs the same."* Bill went on to explain that the trick to using the principle of a discount is to understand how to arrive at the same yield by taking different paths, i.e., rate +

points = yield or *cost* of the money. "All money costs the same," but you can get to the cost by taking different paths.

A discount can be defined as the difference between par and the actual bid price for said obligation. Par is 100% of the face value of a mortgage. For example, if a mortgage of $100,000 sells for $95,000, the loan discount is 5% or $5,000. The term "discount" refers to a dollar amount expressed as a percentage of the loan amount. In the above example, the discount would be $5,000. A "point" is 1% of the loan amount; two points is 2% of the loan amount, etc. In the above example, the discount can be expressed as 5% or 5 points. If you sold the loan for $100,000, you sold it sold at par.

The purpose of a discount is to increase the yield of a mortgage. Yield is the net interest a mortgagee (investor) receives from the loan. In nearly all cases, loans are sold in the secondary market and the rate of a loan must meet the yield requirement of an investor. If the rate is below the yield requirement, the loan must be discounted.

To convert a discount point into interest or yield, one can use a rule of thumb of 1.5% in discount equals 1/4% increase in yield based on a 12-year payout for a 30-year loan. For a better understanding of how discount points affect yield, refer to the Discount Yield Table beginning on page 315. Yield is controlled by laws of supply and demand in the secondary market. Discounts are seldom stagnant. One should shop lenders to arrive at a competitive discount price; don't, however, sacrifice service for points. Cheaper discount points should never be the sole reason for selecting a lender.

1.38 *Must a seller pay discount points and is the interest rate set by FHA?*

No. On 1 December 1983, FHA began allowing the buyer to pay discount points and to select the interest rate. Of course, home owners refinancing a mortgage have always been allowed to pay the discount points. The freedom to pay points and choose the rate is limited to certain FHA section loans; it is allowed for Section 203. FHA will, as will VA, allow a third party (someone other than the purchaser or seller) to pay discount points. A third party should not be someone with a financial interest in the sale, such as a real estate agent. An acceptable third party is an employer transferring an employee, who later becomes a home buyer, to another location and paying points for a home loan. A member of the buyer's family can pay points.

The sales contract should address the issue of who is to pay discount points. If the borrower is paying discount points, the points may not exceed what was disclosed to FHA when the loan was approved. The case must be reprocessed if, after loan approval, there is any increase in the points paid by the borrower.

Reprocessing a loan is also required if the interest at time of closing is more than 100 basis points (1%) higher than what was stated on the application for a firm commitment (loan approval).

1.39 *Is owner/occupancy required in obtaining an FHA refinance loan?*

No; however, the maximum loan amount to a non-occupant/owner will be limited to 75% of the total acquisition. The non-occupant/owner loan may be processed only under Section 203(b).

1.40 *What was an FHA negotiated-rate loan?*

This was an experimental program created for the free negotiation between the lender and borrower with respect to interest rates and discount points. A borrower could pay discount points and could choose to close at a higher interest rate than would be allowed by FHA.

A negotiated-rate allowed the mortgagor to pay all or any portion of the discount point. In allowing a mortgagor to close at a higher rate than permitted by FHA, discount points can be reduced. This program was used in setting present FHA policy which frees the mortgagor to select an interest rate and pay discount points.

1.41 *Was a negotiated-rate a fixed-rate loan?*

Yes, but HUD's name of the experimental program gave the public the impression that the program involved an adjustable rate; however, the FHA negotiated-rate loan was a fixed-rate loan and had all the advantages normally associated with FHA loans.

In my opinion, HUD would have been better off in naming the program "negotiated discount points" or better yet, "negotiated yield."

The major use of the negotiated-rate loan was to allow the purchaser to pay discount points; however, when the lender became involved, the negotiation was actually a negotiation of the discount points to affect the yield or actual rate of the loan. As pointed out in the explanation of discount points, these points affect the yield of the loan.

1.42 *What is an FHA refinance loan, and how much can one borrow?*

FHA will refinance acceptable properties with what will be, in most cases, a maximum loan of 85% of Total Acquisition for an owner/occupant and 75% of Total Acquisition for a non-owner/occupant. FHA Section 203(b) will be used for new loans that are refinances. Other Sections, such as 245, can be used to refinance a temporary loan to a permanent loan, or to refinance with the same Section if it is for purposes of obtaining a lower interest rate.

The 85% rule mentioned above can be exceeded if the total of the outstanding lien (loan) or liens plus the discount points and closing costs associated with the refinance surpasses the amount equivalent to 85% of Total Acquisition and if the loan is to an owner/occupant. In no event can an FHA refinance loan exceed the maximum loan amount available to an owner/occupant purchaser in which an FHA section is being used to process the loan.

On 20 May 1985, a major change was made by FHA in regard to investor refinances. Effective this date there can be no cash out to an investor except for minor adjustments to financing costs which occur at closing. It is still possible for an investor to obtain the maximum loan of 75% of Total Acquisition. Acquisition costs will be a limiting condition for all refinancing cases in which the purchase or existing liens occurred in a period of less than 12 months. Market value can be used for properties that have been owned for more than 12 months, but there can be no cash out to the investor at closing. An investor could purchase, renovate if need be, place a lien of 75% of market value and then refinance 12 months later for 75% of the FHA value plus closing costs. The author wishes to defer to your local FHA office on the matter of including renovation costs into the acquisition costs for refinancing by an investor in which the property has been owned for less than 12 months. Always remember, there can be no cash out with a refinance loan involving a non-occupant mortgagor (investor). Refer to the glossary for the two meanings of the word "investor."

There are many comments that may be made on the subject matter contained in this answer. There has been so much publicity about investor loans and the "no cash out" restriction that nearly all of my students answer the following true or false question incorrectly: "There is no cash out allowed for FHA refinance loans?" The correct answer to this question is false; one can still receive cash out if the refinance loan is to an owner/occupant.

At this point I will get a little personal in expressing my opinions or comments. It has long been advised by real estate investment experts such as Robert Allen, Albert Lowry, and others to do your mortgage business with a lender with experience as an investor, if you can find one. Although I am not advising a lender to invest so they can increase production, I am advising that a lender become more than just familiar with the guidelines for non-owner/occupant properties. The information given in the remainder of this answer will give more insight into how the FHA investor loan may be used, and it is more than what is available from government manuals and updates. The subject of real estate investments is of interest to a great many people, probably more than what the non-investor person may suspect. In terms of all-time best-seller books in print, and it may come as a surprise to some of you, there are real estate investment books ranked with other books such as dictionaries and almanacs.

For most of my seventeen years as a mortgage banker I invested in, developed, and managed property. At one time, my ownership of residential units amounted to approximately

50 units, the majority of which were single-family detached dwellings. In my opinion, the best investor loan for the middle income individual is the FHA 203 Program. Other alternatives such as set forth in Fannie Mae or Freddie Mac conventional loan guidelines just do not hold a candle to the Section 203. It is highly unlikely that I and many others like me, could have financed the purchase of rental properties had it not been for the FHA program. FHA has been very instrumental in helping the middle-income person become involved in real estate investments.

Because of public abuse of the Section 203 program for non-owner/occupant mortgages, FHA has had to severely restrain this program. The main thrust of FHA in curtailing this program is to eliminate the "quick-flips" by unscrupulous investors who buy property, make cosmetic repairs, and sell the property to an unsuspecting purchaser who is left "holding the bag" when the cosmetic repairs start to fall apart.

There is a way for investors to work within the FHA guidelines and end up with a 75% long-term amortized loan. I have nicknamed this program the "house factory." It begins as follows: a property becomes available for purchase by any number of methods such as an equity sale or a cash sale at foreclosure. Although I am no longer an "aggressive investor," for me, the best source is recommendations by the public who become acquainted with a good reputation in rental housing built by being in the business and keeping promises. Let us begin by using an example with graduating steps or stages. First we purchase Property A for $20,000. The purchase is financed by a short term loan secured by another asset, such as a house. The property is renovated as needed without cosmetic repairs of any sort. Let us assume the total cost of repairs is $6,000. An appraisal is ordered from a short term lender and the fair market value is established at $40,000. You obtain a 12-month loan based on 75% of the appraisal. At loan closing there will be approximately $4,000 (the $30,000 new loan minus $26,000 = $4,000) of new money created by the refinance transaction. The $30,000 is calculated by taking 75% of the $40,000 appraisal. The $26,000 is calculated by adding the cost of renovation to the cost to acquire the property.

Once the lien has seasoned for 12 months, you apply for an FHA investor loan, refinance and pay off the short-term loan.

These recommendations are acceptable to FHA because it (1) meets the required guidelines and (2) eliminates "quick-flips." The investor must keep the property for a minimum of 12 months. The reason for the name "house factory" is the number of times you can use this method. Providing you have adequate income, good credit, near perfect mortgage payment ratings, and meet the 7 unit rule, you can have 500, or more, FHA loans. The raw material for the "factory" is the neglected house that someone has abandoned or wants to put up for adoption. The cost of adoption and rehabilitation is the key to making the factory work. If you are not a seasoned veteran, use professionals to furnish estimates of before and after values for the property and the renovations needed. Whenever I think of factories, I think of conveyor belts or assembly lines. In the house factory, abandoned or abused houses start at the beginning of the line, they are repaired, mortgaged, and then rented. If you use the new money created from refinancing to buy houses, pay for renovations and other costs associated with running the factory; the assembly line keeps rolling and your factory is in good shape. On the other hand, if you spend the money for other purposes the assembly line slows or stops and your factory shuts down.

How is the factory connected with goals set forth in the National Housing Act? The 1987 Housing Act reaffirms the principle of decent and affordable shelter is a basic necessity for the general welfare of the nation. The health and living standards of its people require the addition of new housing units to remedy a serious shortage of housing units for all Americans, particularly for persons of low and moderate income.

Remember, the house factory takes in houses that are abandoned or abused. Any lender or FHA will testify that foreclosures are expensive. The reason foreclosure is expensive to a lender is it forces a role change. When lenders foreclose, they are forced into the house factory business. Unlike the operation of the factory for the real estate investor, the lender's house factory results in keeping the house on the assembly line "as is" until it can be dumped off to FHA. When the house arrives at the FHA factory, it is renovated then sold, or it is left in the "as is" state and sold in that condition. National statistics show the house factory business *costs* FHA roughly $20,000 per house. The real estate investor with a house factory can help eliminate claims paid by FHA through its MIP.

Does the factory eliminate the availability of houses for owner/occupants? Remember, houses normally used in the factory business are orphans or what real estate investors sometimes describe as "don't wanters." Let's face it, good buys on houses are normally not found in the upper-income part of a town. Even after the house is renovated, not everyone is ready for the responsibilities of home ownership. This is particularly true in the lower- or middle-income part of a town. Based on experience, many tenants are happier in their rented homes as compared to living in a publicly sponsored housing project or in an apartment.

What happens if a tenant wants to buy the house they are renting? My normal response to this question is: "Where do we close?" FHA loans are still assumable, even those with approval of the purchaser. As a seller you should happy if the mortgage requires approval of the assumptor. When the assumptor is approved, you may be released of liability. As a real estate investor, you should be ready to sell when a tenant offers fair market value, is ready for home ownership, and qualifies for the assumption. Selling to the tenant will usually save the investor a sales commission, advertising costs, discounts, closing costs, and the investor may end up with an annuity if a second mortgage is created per FHA guidelines.

In my career, I have seen the FHA investor loan go from obscurity to media coverage on TV and in books on real estate investments. The abuse of this program has risen along with the publicity it has received. Section 203 offers many opportunities for the lower and middle income individual. The FHA Section 203, non-owner/occupant loan, is financing available to people who cannot qualify for a similar loan from a conventional lender. Now that "everyone knows," it is my hope FHA will take steps to protect the program and not abolish it.

In my opinion, this loan is the only opportunity some have of owning rental property and it offers a better alternative than public housing.

The information provided in this answer should be preceded with a "WARNING: Information found in this answer could be hazardous to your financial health." Before starting any investment program using FHA loans, you should be aware of certain things that could go wrong. There is a possibility FHA could discontinue the non-owner/occupant program at any time. Elimination of the program could leave you without a source of long term financing to pay off the short term lender. If the program is not eliminated, adverse changes could be made while in the 12-month waiting period. Another negative is your going into debt. If you give into the temptation of personal use of money from the short term lender, you are broke before you start. Of course, there is always a risk of something happening to your financial ability to qualify for the permanent loan.

If you get in a bind while in the 12-month waiting period, you may be able to get some relief by refinancing the cost of acquisition and renovation with an FHA loan. This option will not provide you with any cash out and the loan will be limited to your costs. If you borrowed more than your costs and refinanced before the 12-month seasoning period, you will have to come up with cash at the closing to pay off the lien or liens that exceed the FHA loan.

1.43 *What is meant by an FHA investor loan?*

A loan to an owner that is neither a primary nor a secondary resident. The owner does not use the property as their personal residence or as a second home. The only types of new loans for the purchase of a property by an investor would be the Section 203(b) and Section 203(k). Investors can use other Sections, but they would be limited to refinancing for a lower rate.

1.44 *Can other FHA loans be used for refinancing?*

Yes, if the loan being refinanced is a temporary loan or a loan with a balloon payment. Also, other Sections such as 245, 221, and 222 may be used for refinancing to a lower interest rate.

1.45 *How does FHA define a second home?*

A second home is a single family dwelling that is not rented. The maximum LTV ratio is limited to 85%.

1.46 *What are the validation periods for FHA approval of credit or property, and are there any extensions available?*

The property appraisal, termed "conditional commitment," normally has a life of six months for existing dwellings and twelve months for proposed construction or substantial rehabilitation. In certain economically distressed areas, a shorter validation period is used for the appraisals. If you live in one of the "COLT" states (Colorado, Oklahoma, Louisiana, or Texas), check with your local FHA office for the validation periods for appraisals. There is no extension for existing dwellings, but if a sales contract was signed before the expiration date, the lender will be allowed 30 days to submit an application for loan approval. If the application is rejected, there will be time allowed for resubmission. If the application involves a new borrower, it must be treated as a new case. An extension for new construction or substantial rehabilitation is allowed. Refer to question 1.56, item (3), page 48.

Approval of the credit or loan is termed a "firm commitment." If a firm commitment is issued before the expiration date of the conditional commitment (appraisal), there will be a three-month term granted for the firm commitment, or the firm commitment will be valid for the remaining life of the conditional commitment, whichever is greater. There are times, however, when FHA will extend a firm commitment to allow closing. An extension of a firm commitment is discretionary and must be for good cause.

1.47 *Can a co-mortgagor's income and credit be of assistance for an FHA loan approval?*

Yes, FHA will consider the income and credit of a co-mortgagor in the same manner as the purchaser. A word of caution: a co-mortgagor's income is what is left after their housing and total obligations have been satisfied. A co-mortgagor need not be a relative.

1.48 *Can an individual apply for an FHA loan on the basis that the required down payment and closing costs will be borrowed?*

Yes; if the collateral is a secured asset, FHA is notified of the repayment provisions, and the secured asset(s) is not the applicant's household goods or principal mode of transportation. A secured asset could be real estate or stock as opposed to a personal signature loan. The lender cannot be the seller of the property or any interested third party such as the real estate broker or marketing agent.

1.49 *Can an individual borrow the down payment when the sales price exceeds FHA appraised value?*

Yes. This question came from a comparison of the answers to Questions 1.48 and 2.67. The FHA answer to this question is yes; VA's answer is no.

In answering this question, FHA's feels its only concern is the subject property. Since present guidelines allow the purchaser to pay more for the property than what the FHA estimates the property to be worth, FHA is not concerned if funds came from a loan against an acceptable secured asset and an acceptable lender.

1.50 *Can a seller pay all of the purchaser's closing costs, including prepaid items?*

Yes. The sales contract must specify that the seller is paying the closing costs and the prepaid items. Note that the purchaser must have an investment in the property equal to the minimum for each particular section as set forth in the FHA guidelines. Prepaid items are considered a sales concession by FHA, (See Figure 6-part III, page 331). Most lenders will answer this question, no, the correct answer is yes.

1.51 *Is there certain language which must be included in a sales contract or an addendum for a sale involving an FHA loan?*

Yes. If the contract is being written before an appraisal has been issued, the following amendatory language must be used for contracts written prior to issuance of an appraisal acceptable to FHA:

> It is expressly agreed that, notwithstanding any other provisions of this contract, the purchaser shall not be obligated

44

to complete the purchase of the property described herein or to incur any penalty by forfeiture of the earnest money deposits or otherwise unless the seller has delivered to the purchaser a written statement issued by the Federal Housing Commissioner setting forth the appraised value of the property (excluding closing costs) of not less than $_____ which statement the seller hereby agrees to deliver to the purchaser promptly after such appraised value statement is made available to the seller. The purchaser shall, however, have the privilege and option of proceeding with the consummation of the contract without regard to the amount of the appraised valuation made by the Federal Housing Commissioner. The appraised valuation is arrived at to determine the maximum mortgage the Department of Housing and Urban Development will insure. HUD does not warrant the value or the condition of the property. The purchaser should satisfy himself/herself that the price and condition of the property are acceptable.

FHA no longer has a prevailing rate, and discounts can be paid by the purchaser; therefore, the contract should cover the subject of rate and who will pay the points.

1.52 *Are there different types of FHA lenders?*
Yes. Two broad categories exist: supervised and non-supervised. A supervised lender is one that is subject to some type of government agency guidelines or restrictions. Non-supervised lenders can be privately owned mortgage companies as opposed to supervised lenders, such as banks or savings and loan institutions.

1.53 *Is title insurance required by FHA?*
No. The lender or the investor (actual owner of the mortgage) may require title insurance. This question has been in all my other editions and a similar question is in the VA section. I had thought about omitting this question in the new edition. The information seemed to be minor, and might not be used by the reader. The question really pertains to what FHA or VA does not require as compared to what a lender or an investor will require. My thinking changed when I taught a recent seminar in Chicago. One of the students was the Director of Consumer Affairs for Illinois. The Director told me of one case involving the president of a mortgage company who

wrote a letter in response to a complaint involving the monthly payment of taxes and insurance with the required principal and interest payments on an FHA loan. On company letterhead, the president stated FHA required the escrow of taxes and insurance and the matter was out of his control. The consumer called FHA to verify the statement. Of course, FHA had to take an opposing position when confronted with the answer given by the lender. When the consumers felt they had been lied to, they appealed to the Bureau of Consumer Affairs for help.

After hearing of this occurrence, I decided to leave the question and answer in the book. In the business world, time equals money. Of course, you can imagine the time, therefore the money, that was required of the president who incorrectly answered this small question.

1.54 *Can an agent or an individual earn a fee or a "kickback" from a lender?*

FHA prohibits payment of a fee or "kickback" to an individual if said party has received any payments in connection with a transaction involving an FHA mortgage. FHA has the right to waive the previous statement, as is customary in the case of an attorney collecting fees from other parties as well as from the mortgagee. Another example is a title company receiving payment from the lender for mortgagee's coverage and payment from the purchaser for owner's coverage.

FHA could allow a payment from the lender to a real estate agent if actual mortgage related services were performed and the agent and the property are eligible for the "rural outreach" program. The basic regulation of "rural outreach" requires the property to be located more than 50 miles from the lender's office or nearest branch office and that the person to whom the lender will pay a fee is not collecting fees from other services related to the transaction, such as a sales commission.

FHA is very watchful of business relationships between a lender and a real estate agent or real estate agency. A below-market or no-interest loan from a lender to an agent, broker, builder, or company is prohibited if the lender transacts FHA business with said parties.

1.55 *Are second mortgages permitted in conjunction with an FHA first mortgage?*

Before 8 July 1985, the answer to this question was "No, except for financing from a governmental type of institution." An example would have been a second mortgage from a utility agency for home energy-saving improvements. Effective the above date, FHA will now allow second mortgages in conjunction with the insurance of the FHA first mortgage from federal, state, or local agencies and from the private sector. Second mortgages from the private sector must meet the following guidelines:

1. The combination of the first and second mortgage cannot exceed the applicable LTVR nor the maximum loan limitation for the area.
2. Second mortgages can be used only with unsubsidized single family programs.
3. The mortgagor must show the ability to handle both mortgages, and information on the second mortgage must be included in the FHA application.
4. Monthly payments should be in substantially the same amount.
5. A balloon payment should not occur before ten years unless otherwise approved by FHA, and there is to be no prepayment penalty once the borrower has provided the second mortgage lender with a 30-day advance notice.

FHA has recently issued a ruling which states that the lender cannot be the seller of the property or any interested third party such as the real estate broker or marketing agent.

1.56 *What are some uniform guidelines for FHA appraisals?*

1. The term for an FHA appraisal is "conditional commitment."
2. An FHA appraisal on an existing dwelling is valid for six months and on new construction for twelve

months. Please refer to Question 1.46, page 43 for some exceptions.

3. An extension of a conditional commitment is available for new construction with an updated appraisal. Any extension of a conditional commitment is subject to the FHA appraiser's updating the appraisal and making a field review.

4. A requested value is necessary.

5. The eligible dwellings include detached, semi-detached, row and end-row dwellings, or an improved property deemed eligible for an FHA home loan consisting of one to four units.

6. The size of the site is a concern for FHA. The size of the lot, in most cases, is not a concern for VA. The land should be minimized in size to provide a reasonable yard for the improvements. This guideline may waiver somewhat in rural areas. If the site is too large, FHA may suggest that a reasonable site be subdivided from the tract so that the improvements have nothing more than an adequate yard or area.

   VA, on the other hand, has no objections to a veteran purchasing a home with acreage, provided the bulk of the value consists of the improvements for the home. Check with your local FHA and VA offices for their opinions on excess land.

7. To obtain the maximum FHA LTVRs, new construction must have had plans and specifications submitted for approval and have undergone periodic inspections, or have an approved extended homeowners warranty program acceptable to FHA. If, however, the above outlined procedure is not the case, the property may still be eligible, but the loan may be penalized by placing a maximum of a 90% LTVR. Of course, this is not a problem if the total value or total acquisition of the home equals or exceeds maximum FHA loan amount divided by 90%.

8. Subject to confirmation by your local FHA office, VA appraisals are acceptable to FHA.

The guidelines in this answer are general by necessity. Specific appraisal requirements such as minimum specifications for insulation, weather stripping, heating, and air conditioning will vary throughout the country due to weather conditions. The requirements for Minnesota in terms of insulation and heating will not be the same as requirements for Florida. New construction regulations are now closely tied to local building codes and inspections which vary according to weather related factors and soil conditions.

If an FHA appraisal is less than requested, you may use Figure 14 "Comparable Sales Chart" to request consideration of an increase in value. Always compare "apples to apples, oranges to oranges," meaning don't use sales on 3 bedroom houses when the subject is a 2 bedroom house. Don't compare 1 story houses to 2 story homes. Keep all comparables in a close area and have the sales dates as recent as is possible. Above all, don't get caught in what I call "square foot i-tis." A person can acquire this "disease" by comparing similar properties and coming up with a value based on square feet. For example, an appraisal on a subject property valued the property at $100,000. The real estate agent wanted a higher value and wants to request an increase in the appraised value. As justification for an increase in value, the agent submits a comparable property containing 3 bedrooms, 2 baths, a den; it has brick veneer, central heat and air, and a 2 car garage, is 1 story in height, contains 1,950 of heated livable square feet, and sold for $100,000. The real estate agent complains that their house has the same features listed in the comparable, *but* is 50 square feet larger than the comparable and therefore the appraised value should be $102,500. The lender conducts site inspections, the subject property and the comparable are similar and there are 50 additional square feet in the subject property, but the lender upholds the judgement of the appraiser and the appraisal remains unchanged. Why did the lender not recommend an increase? An increase in value is not justified on the basis of a subject property having rooms that are a few feet wider or longer than comparable properties with the same room count and components listed in Figure 15, page 349.

I have mentioned that at one time my occupation was an appraiser and it continued in a part-time role as a lender. The experience has been very useful to me and it was very helpful when I was a lender dealing with real estate agents. As a lender I was pleased with an approximate 90%, or higher, win percentage when dealing with FHA or VA in appealing appraisals. This high percentage came from a firm policy of not sending in a request for an increase in value without having on-site inspections with a completed Figure 14. After going over the information, inspecting the subject property, and driving by each comparable listed, we then decided if a request for an increase in value was warranted. In nearly all instances, the petitioner would not like my procedure. It seemed to be so much simpler to fill out some blanks and send the information for an increase in value. If the petitioner listened to me, in nearly every instance I was able to show the petitioner that FHA, or VA was correct or we were able to win an increase in value. If an appraiser did not know of my policy, I made sure they knew of this practice which was a policy I fought hard for and it was not always popular with the REALTORS.® In every case the appraiser appreciated the due diligence, and in nearly all cases, it showed in the reconsideration of value.

1.57 *Does the FHA appraisal warrant the condition of the property?*

No. The FHA appraisal is an estimate of value. Although an appraiser performs a site inspection, FHA does not warrant the condition of the appraised property. On 19 May 1988 FHA began to allow borrowing part of the cost of a professional inspection. A maximum of $200 can be added to the FHA estimate of closing costs which will result in borrowing approximately 97% of the cost. This new policy is not available for new construction inspected by FHA or VA or insured by an acceptable 10-year Homeowner Warranty program.

1.58 *Do FHA lenders have an option of approving loans such as the VA automatic approval or must all cases be submitted to a local FHA office?*

FHA has a program termed "Direct Endorsement." This program is very similar to the VA automatic approval system.

While there are some differences in the VA and FHA programs, the objective of loan approval without submission to agency is the same.

1.59 *What are the general guidelines for FHA approval of a purchaser's income and credit?*

There are no strict guidelines involved in underwriting loans. Income that may be insufficient for a family with eight members may very well be sufficient for an unmarried individual without any dependents and who has a company car and expense account. Underwriting can be defined as "an exercise in judgement." In general, some guidelines are as follows:

1. Housing expense should not exceed 38% of the purchaser's monthly net effective income. Housing expense is: principal, interest, taxes, insurance, maintenance and utilities; net effective income is: gross income minus income taxes.
2. Total obligations should not exceed 53% of net effective income; total obligations are defined as: housing expense, insurance, social security, and obligations that exceed a twelve-month repayment period. Said obligations pertain to loans or revolving credit, not telephone bills, groceries, or gas for the family automobile.
3. Credit must be acceptable for loan approval. The purchaser's credit report should reflect an ability to handle obligation in a timely manner with payment as agreed. FHA will accept letters of explanation about credit problems. FHA will review an application involved in a chapter of bankruptcy which has a method of repayment of debts. FHA will refuse to review an application involved in a completed discharge of debts until one year has elapsed from date of bankruptcy discharge. See the glossary for the different chapters of bankruptcy.

Remember, income requirements can vary with the size of the purchaser's family. FHA does use another guide based on income as it relates to the size of a family. Don't try to reject or approve an applicant on the basis of percentages. The proper use of percentages is as general guidelines.

Additionally, large cash reserves can be somewhat helpful when income is lacking. A large cash reserve can change from a status of "somewhat helpful" to a definite difference in qualifying, if the cash is in the form of a substantial down payment. *Please refer to Figure 1 for an income analysis chart.*

There is good reason to believe that FHA will soon go to a gross income ratio approach, as now used for income analysis for conventional loans.

1.60 *Do you have a checklist which can be useful in preparing an application for an FHA loan? Yes; a good checklist should include:*

1. The applicants must be ready to show a picture identity and evidence of their Social Security number. Some examples are: an unexpired driver's license, picture ID card issued by the applicant's state of residence, military ID card, alien registration receipt card—form I-151—a valid passport with photograph —issued by any country, employee ID card with picture, union card with picture. In cases where an acceptable picture identity is not possible, the lender must submit a reasonable written explanation, and also state in what manner the identity of the applicant was proven. Evidence of a Social Security number is a requirement for any person earning or receiving money in the U.S. It is possible for an applicant to have driver's licenses issued in different states, and also have several different Social Security numbers. Therefore, ask the applicant about additional driver's licenses or Social Security numbers.

2. An original sales contract or a copy with original signatures or a certified copy. The lender will check the contract for the following:

   a. Excessive earnest money or good faith deposit;

   b. The required amendatory language if the date of the contract is prior to the appraisal;

    c. Sales concessions in excess of 6% of the total acquisition;

    d. A statement as to which party will pay for any required repairs. If the sales contract does not specify who is making the repairs, the responsibility for them must be established before submission for approval. Unless stated otherwise in the contract, FHA automatically will assume the buyer is paying for repairs which will increase the settlement requirements.

3. A residence history:

    a. Where the applicant and any co-mortgagor have lived for the past 24 months,

    b. If the applicant rents,

        1. Landlord's name, address and telephone number, or

        2. Rental agency's address and phone number.

    c. If the applicant owns his or her present home,

        1. Name of lender, address, phone number and loan account number;

        2. The type of loan, i.e., FHA, VA, or conventional.

4. An employment history:

    a. The place of employment for the past 24 months, the position held and whether the employment was full-time, part-time, or temporary, and the monthly income earned upon departure. The applicant should include a history of any unemployment over the past two years. Addresses and zip codes of present and past employers should be furnished.

    b. Self-employed or fully commissioned people should be prepared to submit a complete, signed tax return for the past two calendar years, plus a year-to-date income and expense statement. The lender may require a balance sheet.

5. A list of assets:

    a. Names, addresses, and account numbers for all depositories such as banks, savings and loan associations, money market accounts, and credit unions;

b. value of your household goods and personal property;

c. Make, model, year, and market value of automobile(s);

d. Cash and face value of insurance policies;

e. Address, description, and value of real estate owned; income properties should have a spread sheet of pertinent facts (see Figure 15);

f. If a gift is the source of funds for down payment and/or closing costs, the lender will need a letter signed by the donor stating said gift is for the down payment/closing costs and is not to be repaid. A lender may require verification of funds used by the donor.

6. A list of liabilities:

a. Said list should include the creditor's name, balance, monthly payment or method of payment, and the account number. Those creditors that will not furnish above information over the phone to a credit bureau will result in requiring the applicant to prepare a list of such information along with mailing addresses and zip codes. Information usually not given over the phone normally applies to real estate loans, bank, and credit union loans.

b. If child support or alimony creates a liability, a signed copy of the divorce decree will be necessary. The signature on said decrees should be one of legal authority.

7. Additional sources of income:

   If source of income is from the following sources:

a. military retirement,

b. company pensions,

c. Social Security or Social Security benefits,

d. disability benefits,

e. child support or alimony,

then a lender will need a statement of benefits from the corresponding source of income. Child support or alimony may require a signed copy of the decree.

8. For FHA/VA or VA loans, you must furnish all of the above plus one or more of the following:
   a. Certificate of Eligibility (VA only);
   b. Copies of DD214 for all periods of service;
   c. Statement of service (VA only, active duty personnel);
   d. DD1747 off-base housing authorization (VA active duty).

9. If an application involves a sale of present home, the following will be helpful:
   a. It is important to remember that any funds received from sale of real estate will involve the net proceeds as shown on a settlement statement. Therefore, one should consider the dollar figure given at application to be the net amount after deduction of any sales commission, discount points, closing costs and any other expenses.
   b. Prior to loan closing, the lender probably will require a copy of the settlement statement and possibly a certified copy of the warranty deed.
   c. If a relocation service is acquiring your previous home, the acquisition will most likely be a "skip deed" situation instead of a true sale. If there has not been a final closing with transfer of title, then a lender will find it helpful to have a letter from the relocation service stating that all mortgage payments, taxes, insurance, maintenance, burdens, and responsibilities of subject property are removed from the present owners and assumed by the relocation service.
   d. If the applicant's relocation is due to a company transfer, and part or all their closing costs will be borne by the employer, a letter from the employer dealing directly with what costs will be paid will be much more helpful than a company manual or policy statement.

10. Last, but definitely not least, is something that might best be described as a communication gap between lenders and the general public. This gap is something lenders call "verification of settlement requirement." The term "settlement requirement" means the funds needed to acquire the property. Funds required can be the down payment, closing costs and prepaid items. The term "funds" can include balances in checking, savings, and money market accounts, stocks, bonds, real estate, and possibly a small amount of cash on hand. These funds must be verifiable. The method used to verify funds is usually a form titled "Verification of Deposit"; other methods can be used such as copies of statements, certificates, or a settlement statement for real estate. The communication gap between lenders and borrowers about this subject usually surfaces at the end of the loan application when the loan officer observes that assets listed for settlement requirement are insufficient. The typical response from the borrower is, "Oh, I'll have the money by loan closing." There have been many delays, heartaches, and much frustration created by inadequate verifiable funds for settlement requirement. One of the most important things a borrower can do in preparing for loan application is to have sufficient funds that can be verified for settlement requirement. Nothing but delays and frustration will occur when an applicant lists a total of, say $10,000, in accounts and the verification documents show $8,000, or the depository account is less than two months old. If the account is less than two months old, verification of funds used to open the account must be obtained; or applicants tell the loan officer they will net $18,000 from sale of their residence, but then forget to include sales commission or closing expenses, and the settlement statement shows a net of $16,200. Or worse yet, the house was not actually sold but disposed of by a "skip deed" process to relocation service. This section of the application

checklist is very important, because failure to comply with verification of sufficient settlement requirement can definitely delay loan approval or loan closing; yet it can easily be conquered with clear communication between lender and borrower.

This book has been advertised as containing information that will help cut processing time in half. This contention refers mainly to the information found in this answer. No matter what part of the country you are in and no matter what application form a lender uses, if you furnish the lender with the information asked for in this guideline, loan processing time will be greatly reduced. People just don't understand the importance of this information as it relates to loan processing. Credit documents are valid for ninety days. If one, just one, document is missing because of an omitted question at application, or a wrong address or account number is given, it could cause the whole loan application to be re-processed.

1.61 *If a subject property is located within 3 miles of an FHA office, but subject property is not within that FHA office's jurisdiction, must one do business with the nearest authorized FHA office which might be 300 miles away?*

The answer can now be "No," but is not a blanket "No." FHA has developed a new program called Lender Option. In certain areas of our country, situations exist where a lender's office may be within 100 miles of a property, but due to geographical boundaries (mostly state boundaries) the lender may have to deal with three different FHA offices.

FHA has now given their offices permission to deal in other FHA office jurisdictions, if the lender opts to take this course and if the property location is within certain boundaries (usually established by counties). For example, a lender in Memphis, Tennessee may be able to deal with the Memphis FHA office for properties located in certain counties in the states of: Kentucky, Missouri, Arkansas, and Mississippi; rather than dealing with the FHA offices located in: Lexington, St. Louis, Little Rock, or Jackson. Of course, we are not suggesting it is much easier for a lender to transact business operating in a somewhat different manner than the others.

1.62 *Is there a new FHA loan that can be used for rehabilitation purposes?*

The "new" loan is actually an old loan termed Section 203(k), which can be used to purchase and rehabilitate one to four-unit dwellings or to refinance existing indebtedness and rehabilitate. The LTVR and loan amounts are the same as Section 203(b), except for an investor loan. An investor can be approved for an 85% LTV under Section 203(k).

This loan is a much favored Section in the eyes of FHA. Once you become familiar with the guidelines, it is easy to appreciate how this Section helps to meet the goals of affordable housing in areas where there is need for substantial rehabilitation of the existing housing. Unfortunately, this Section is a splendid example of the answer to Question 1.86, page 68. It is sometimes difficult to find an investor for Section 203(k) mortgages.

1.63 *How may a person close a loan without having a final inspection?*

Section 203(k) is the only FHA mortgage that will allow closing without requiring a final inspection. Closing without a final inspection is a unique trait of this Section. FHA, VA, and Conventional loans normally will require a final inspection before closing, even when using an escrow for unfinished work.

1.64 *How does the lender determine how much money to distribute with a 203(k) loan?*

FHA will issue two values, an "As Is" value and a "Finished" value. Funds are disbursed in agreement with Section 203(b) guidelines for both values. Funds used for the acquisition or refinancing will be disbursed initially. Remaining funds for the rehabilitation will be placed in an escrow account and disbursed upon completion of the work. Rehabilitation (a) must begin within 60 days of closing; (b) must not stop for a period of more than 45 days; (c) will be allowed 18 months for completion; (d) can involve up to 5 draws which will include the final. Rehabilitation funds placed in escrow must draw interest at the minimum rate of 5%.

1.65 *Are there any extra costs for a 203(k) mortgage?*

Yes. The additional costs are an appraisal fee equal to 150% of the normal costs and a supplemental origination fee equal to the greater of 1-1/2% of the cost of rehabilitation or $350. The supplemental origination fee and discount applying to the rehabilitation cost may be included in the loan amount.

1.66 *How does prepayment of FHA loans apply to the mortgage?*

See page 127, *Prepaying a Mortgage*

1.67 *Is there a late charge provision for FHA loans?*

See answer to VA Question 2.84, page 106.

1.68 *Is there a 30-day interest penalty when prepaying an FHA loan in full? If so, is this a prepayment penalty?*

No. For an FHA loan insured prior to 2 August 1985, one must give a 30- day written notice to avoid a 30-day interest charge when prepaying in full. Interpreting this as a prepayment penalty is incorrect. Loans insured by FHA on or after 2 August 1985, will no longer require a 30-day written notice for prepayment in full without an interest penalty. In simple terms, a 30-day written notice is no longer required to avoid an interest penalty if full prepayment is made on the monthly due date. This change affects all mortgages insured on or after said date and is not retroactive.

Please note that a lender can refuse to credit full prepayment without including interest to the next due date, if said full payment is not received on the monthly due date. Therefore, I recommend a 30-day notice be given to the lender, even though it is not necessary in some cases. It is the obligation of the lender to notify the borrower in writing if prepayment will not be credited until the next due date. This answer can save a seller a substantial amount of money when you consider that most of a monthly house payment consists of interest.

1.69 *What are some general guidelines for the FHA adjustable rate loan?*

FHA Section 251 will follow the same guidelines as for the FHA 203(b). The only difference, of course, is the adjustable rate feature. The maximum rate change will be limited to 1% per year and a maximum rate increase or decrease of no more than 5% from the initial rate.

1.70 *Will the adjustable-rate feature apply to all FHA sections?*

No, The adjustable-rate feature is limited to FHA 203(b), 203(k) (only first mortgages), and 234(c) (condominium loans).

1.71 *Will investors be able to take advantage of the new adjustable rate mortgage?*

No. Non-occupant/owners are not eligible.

1.72 *Is a duplex an eligible property for an adjustable rate mortgage?*

Yes, if one unit is occupied by the owner. Eligible properties are one- to-four family dwellings that are owner occupied.

1.73 *Can you refinance a fixed rate mortgage with an adjustable rate mortgage?*

Yes, if you are an owner/occupant; no, if an investor. Furthermore, any approved FHA section may be refinanced to an adjustable rate provided the mortgagor is an owner/occupant.

1.74 *What is the index and margin?*

The index is the weekly average yield on United States Treasury Securities adjusted to a constant maturity of one year. FHA will not determine the margin; this item will be set by laws of "supply and demand" or, more specifically, by the GNMA mortgage-backed securities. FHA will require the margin to be constant for the life of the loan. The reader can better understand FHA's position on margin by reading an explanation of margin in the Conventional section.

1.75 *Will there be any possibility of negative amortization?*

No. The FHA adjustable mortgage has rate caps that prohibit negative amortization.

1.76 *Is the FHA adjustable mortgage assumable and does it contain a due-on-sale clause?*

The FHA adjustable loan is assumable with the FHA limited due-on-sale clause. The ARM loans have the same assumption requirements as any of the unsubsidized FHA loans.

1.77 *How is the FHA mortgage insurance premium treated for the adjustable-rate mortgage?*

One-time mortgage insurance is a requirement for the adjustable rate mortgage. Sections now eligible for one-time mortgage premium are 203(b), 245, and 251 (adjustable mortgage) insured under 203(b). Loans on condominiums still require monthly payment of the MIP.

1.78 *What is the charge for transferring title or assuming an FHA loan?*

FHA considers $45 to be a reasonable charge for recording an ownership change. This charge pertains only to what the mortgagee can charge and does not include other fees for the services of an attorney, etc.

For loans originated after 1 December 1986, the lender may charge a processing fee, see the answer to Question 1.6 on page 8.

1.79 *What is "sweat" equity?*

This term applies to labor or materials supplied by a purchaser and used as a credit for settlement requirements. The value of the sweat equity can be determined by the purchaser; however, FHA reserves the right to set a value if said value given by purchaser seems unreasonable. For example, a purchaser is short of settlement requirements by a total of $400 and the subject property is in need of painting. A purchaser could do the labor required for painting and if $400 is a figure acceptable to FHA, that amount would go towards the settlement requirements.

This answer reminds me of the truth in the statement of "time equals money." When I wrote this question, I began to write the answer without doing the research. I had made many loans involving sweat equity. Simply put, sweat equity is "sweat" from labor contributed in the completion of new construction or in fulfilling the appraisal requirements for an existing dwelling. Therefore, the simple answer was sweat equity is from labor done by the applicant. I began to wonder if sweat equity could come from materials provided by the purchaser. My first reaction to the thought on materials was, "Of course not." How would a purchaser have money to buy materials but need to "sweat" for their downpayment? I began to research the answer with an underwriter. The underwriter's answer was the same as mine, sweat equity is for sweat. In reaction to the question about the creation of sweat equity from material, the answer was: "Of course not." Shortly thereafter I met another underwriter, who used to be an underwriter with FHA, who answered the sweat equity questions in the same manner as the first underwriter. When I checked the answer with the section head of mortgage credit at FHA, the initial response from FHA was the same as my first reaction and the answers from the two underwriters. The FHA representative, however, wanted to double-check with the appraisal section since they would be involved in the valuation of the work. The reaction from the head of valuation was that he seemed to recall reading about including material in sweat equity. The appraisal chief was not sure where the guidelines were and would have to research and call back. The following day, the valuation chief called and we began to play "phone tag" for the rest of that day and the next. Finally, 3 days later, the fourth person contacted, provided the correct answer. Materials can be included in sweat equity.

This story has a few lessons: if you are selling real estate, don't stop if the buyer does not have the cash downpayment; if you are a loan officer or an underwriter, do not reject an application involving sweat equity from materials provided by the buyer; third, if you work with FHA loans and you believe "time is money," keep this book handy.

1.80 *What is shared equity?*
In general, shared equity is the use of a related co-mortgagor's income and assets so that an owner/-occupant purchaser can quality for an FHA loan. In return, the co-mortgagor receives an ownership or a share of the equity in the home. Present guidelines call for a co-mortgagor to have at least a 20% but no more than a 45% share of the equity. The percentage of

sharing in the monthly payment determines the percentage of ownership, regardless of the down payment contribution. Maximum LTVR for shared equity is the same as Section 203. Refinances cannot exceed a 75% LTVR with no cash out, except refinancing by an occupant mortgagor for the purposes of buying out an investor co-mortgagor. Some other basic guidelines are:

1. A written Shared Equity Agreement must be approved by FHA.
2. The occupant mortgagor must quality for at least 55% of the monthly payment plus any rental payments to the investor.
3. The co-mortgagor may charge a fair market rent for their share of the ownership.
4. Either party may sell their interest in the property by providing a 30-day written option to purchase to the other shared equity party.
5. The co-mortgagor must sell to the occupant mortgagor after being notified by a 30-day written notice.
6. Sales price will be determined by a HUD approved appraiser.
7. The co-mortgagor may not force a sale except to prevent foreclosure.
8. The co-mortgagor liability for loan underwriting purposes is equal to the percentage of ownership and not viewed as potentially wholly liable as in the case of a straight co-mortgagor case. Futhermore, the 7 unit rule does not apply to shared equity.
9. Co-mortgagors must be related.

I can remember watching some of the "TV real estate gurus" as they described their "get rich quick" methods with shared equity. One fellow would come on TV and talk about his former occupation as a linoleum and tile layer, as he strolled in front of several expensive cars parked in front of mansion, all which were purchased by fortunes made in shared equity. After the opening scene, the shared equity expert presented 30 or more ways you could use shared equity.

After repeated cases involving abuse of shared equity, FHA began to limit the options available to investors. Finally, on 27 June 1988 FHA issued Mortgagee Letter 88-24 which eliminated investor participation in the shared equity program. Investors are no longer eligible, only related co-mortgagors can obtain a shared equity mortgage. It would be ridiculous to blame anyone person for the action required by FHA. I do think the wholesale promotions of FHA programs to obtain financial independence helped eliminate or restrict many opportunities available through that agency.

1.81 *Referring to the last sentence in the answer to Question 1.80, what do you mean by "eliminate or restrict many opportunities available through that agency?"*

At one time, in the not too distant past, we had: cash out on refinances even if the borrower was a non-owner/occupant investor—this privilege was taken away 20 May 1985; we had unlimited assumptions of FHA and VA loans—this was taken away 1 December 1986; we could borrow the downpayment without concern as to who the lender was—this was taken away 19 October 1987; we could use some of the shared equity guidelines as stated in the answer to Question 1.79 and the shared owners could get the maximum LTV, as outlined for an owner/occupant in Section 203, even if one of the owners was an unrelated non-owner/occupant investor—this was taken away as of 1 January 1988 by lowering the maximum LTV to 75% if the loan involved an investor; shared equity was still available for an unrelated investor—this was taken away 1 September 1988 by requiring that all parties be related co-mortgagors; at one time we had higher LTV ratios for investor purchase transactions and for investor refinances—both of these were taken away on 5 February 1988 by lowering the ratio from 85% to 75%.

I believe the privileges taken away from all people related to FHA loans is another consequence of declining morals in this country. In an analogy: our sins have been forgiven, we can still assume FHA and VA loans; we can still finance and refinance investor transactions; we can still borrow the down payment; we can still have shared equity; but on every one of these programs we have paid the price for our wrongs by having the programs restricted. The recurring abuses have forced FHA to protect itself from us, the public. Of course, the innocent have suffered right along with the guilty.

1.82 *What is a dual contract?*

A dual contact is illegal and as such is subject to penalties as described by Section 1010 of Title 18, which provides for a maximum of a $5,000 fine or imprisonment for a maximum of 2 years, or both.

A dual contract is an agreement or contract that is contrary to information given to the lender by parties to the contract. A dual contract can be either written or oral.

Before 1 December 1983, the purchaser could not pay discount points on purchase transactions. Many dual contracts were discovered when the buyer reimbursed the seller for discount points the seller had to pay in compliance with FHA regulations. Contracts are very important in dual contract situations. The sales contract given the lender must be the only agreement between the parties involved. Charges on the settlement statement that conflict with the agreements in the contract is a "red flag" for the existence of a dual contract.

Several years ago a local real estate company asked me to speak to their sales agents. It is important to note that my meeting with the agents was before the FHA assumption requirement. I brought up the subject of a dual contract because my experience had shown me that many real estate agents do not know the meaning of a dual contract. I defined a dual contact and I gave examples. The broker showed me a contract recently submitted on one of her listings. The purchaser was a real estate company and the offer was submitted on a pre-printed form. According to the agent, the contract form was one of many being passed out all over town in efforts to acquire property. The basis of the offer was to have the seller refinance the subject property, and then sell by way of a loan assumption, with the seller providing a second mortgage above and beyond the sales price.

Quoting from the contract:

"THAT SELLER SHALL EXECUTE an Owner Re-Finance Loan (FHA 203-b) that can and will be assumed by _____ at closing... THE PURPOSE of 'Owner Refinance' is simply to get cash out. To qualify, owner must have ample income and credit and must occupy the property until the loan is made... THAT SELLER SHALL RECEIVE a note and deed of trust executed by _____ as a 2nd Mortgage behind the Owner Re-Finance Loan... THAT $5,300 in cash from this loan shall go to pay all costs of obtaining loan, all BUYER'S and SELLER'S closing costs, costs of any improvement (like carpets, escrowed payments, paint, etc.) planned by and all other costs NOT MENTIONED that are necessary to satisfy this contract...

NOTICE!!! MOST MORTGAGE COMPANIES WILL NOT MAKE AN OWNER RE-FINANCE LOAN IF THEY BELIEVE THE OWNER INTENDS TO SELL, OR NOT OCCUPY THE PROPERTY. HOWEVER, ONCE THE LOAN IS MADE, THE PROPERTY CAN IMMEDIATELY AND LAWFULLY BE SOLD AND THE LOAN ASSUMED."

I got depressed as I read the contract. I ask myself "how much longer will FHA stand before they take action?" I thought of what had already been taken away and what more would be if this trend does not change.

I asked for a copy of the contract and called it to the attention of the local HUD office. We have "neighborhood watch" to combat burglaries in our neighborhoods, so why not have a "fraud watch" for the FHA and VA. We are anxious to protect the neighborhoods, particularly our personal possessions. How anxious are you to protect FHA or VA? Remember, FHA and VA, in many cases, are responsible for the creation of your neighborhoods.

At the beginning of the answer I noted this incident occurred prior to FHA's taking away the right of freely assuming their insured loans. Of course, this type of contract would be of no use today if the seller wishes to be released of liability. Present guidelines require the investor to pay the loan down to 75% if the seller desires a release from liability.

1.83 *What is equity skimming?*

Equity skimming is the practice of collecting rent and not applying it to the repayment of the mortgage. Unscrupulous investors have become aware that certain FHA mortgages can be assumed without qualifying for the loan. These investors assume a non-qualifying FHA loan and then keep all the rents and make no repairs or payments on the mortgage. The new Housing Bill has an increased penalty for equity skimming, it is: five (5) years imprisonment and $250,000 in fines.

1.84 *If the applicant fails to disclose a previous foreclosure or a claim, how can a lender obtain this information?*

Before processing a loan application a lender must call for a CAIVRS clearance. CAIVRS is an acronym for Credit Alert Interactive Voice Response System. The telephone number is 301-588-2233, and the hours of operation are from 9 A.M. to 9 P.M. (Eastern time), Monday through Saturday.

The following is a sequence of the voice response system.

1. The voice will ask for the lender's 10-digit mortgagee number.
2. After verifying the mortgagee number, the voice will then ask for the borrower's Social Security number.
3. After verifying the Social Security number, the system will make a search of all files for any claims or defaults by the borrower.
4. If there are no claims or defaults found the voice will respond with "there are no claims or defaults for this borrower."
5. If the borrower has a claim or a default, the voice will recite the case number involved.
6. The voice will then recite a "Credit Alert Access Code" said code must be entered on the FHA application for loan approval, HUD-92900.

If there is a claim or default, or if the borrower disputes the information, the lender should be able to give proper consultation. CAIVRS does not apply to cases involving refinancing for a lower interest rate.

1.85 *What happens if a claim or default was caused by buyers who assumed a mortgage?*

Per Mortgagee Letter 88-4, the loan may be processed if the previous lender verifies a good payment record for the time the present applicants owned the home. The statement from the previous lender must be included with the application for loan approval, HUD-92900. The assumptor's default or claim has no effect on the applicant's eligibility for a new loan. If, however, the seller (the present applicant) was not released from liability, the good payment record will not remove the seller from any judgement caused by a foreclosure.

1.86 *Can one expect lenders throughout the country to comply with information in this book?*

I think the reader will find most lenders agree with the answers in this book. This question reminds me of an understanding I always try to impart at the beginning of my seminars. I write down the following on a blackboard or a blank transparency:

1. Agency
2. Lender
3. Investor

The Agency can refer to FHA, VA, FNMA, or FHLMC. The Lender refers to the company making the loan. The Investor refers to supplier of the money for the loan. For FHA and VA loans, the Investor is usually GNMA.

I then explain to the students how these three entities interrelate to one another. FHA or VA guidelines can state a lender can do thus and thus with a loan. The lender must comply with the minimum set forth in the guidelines formed by the agencies, but the lender can require more or the lender can refuse to participate in a program. The principal reason a lender may not offer programs or features available through FHA or VA is the absence of money available from the Investor, the Secondary Market.

I will illustrate with some examples. FHA guidelines state it is not necessary to round down to the nearest $50 in determining the loan amount, if the MIP is being financed. A Lender may require rounding down on all loans to avoid a possible mistake in not rounding down which is a requirement if the borrower is paying the MIP in cash. The Lender may not want to run the risk of having an uninsurable loan because someone in the organization forgot to round down on a loan which required rounding down. Another example is the 245 program. FHA has guidelines for Plans IV and V, but there is a lack of Investors for these two Plans. Therefore, the only Plans the public usually hears about are Plans I, II, and III. FHA encourages the 203(k) loan. Lenders have a hard time finding a good Investor for Section 203(k), many times the only way the public hears about 203(k) is when a TV "investor guru" skirts over the highlights and advertises a costly tape that will explain "this fascinating new FHA program." To understand the everyday practice of real estate finance, you must remember the relationship between: 1) the agency, 2) the lender, and 3) the investor. Avoid the trap of thinking a program is available because FHA or VA offers it, or thinking FHA or VA requires certain conditions when the investor is actually the party making the requirements.

VA HOME LOANS

2.1 *In general, what is a VA loan?*

A VA loan is a real estate mortgage available to qualified veterans for the purpose of (a) buying a single-family home, which could include condominiums, zero-lot-line housing, co-ops, and any other acceptable form of housing by the VA; (b) refinancing an existing mortgage. VA mortgages available for mobile home financing, construction loans, and second mortgage home improvement loans will not be discussed in this section.

2.2 *What are the advantages of a VA loan?*

1. A 100% loan is available, plus a seller can pay all or part of the veteran's closing costs including any escrow requirements. If the seller pays all of the veteran's closing expenses, this would allow the veteran to purchase a home with a zero investment.

2. Usually the veteran is assured a market or below market interest rate in comparison to conventional loans.

3. There are no mortgage insurance premiums charged on VA loans. FHA loans normally have a one-time premium or a 1/2 of 1% monthly premium for mortgage insurance in addition to the interest rate. Usually, conventional loans that have a LTVR higher than 80% will have a front-end premium and a mini-

mum of 1/4 of 1% private mortgage insurance added to the interest rate.

4. Compared to variable, adjustable, or renegotiable loans, a fixed interest rate loan is amortized by a level or graduated monthly payment.

5. When veterans sell their property, the original loan terms of the mortgage will remain the same and cannot be changed by loan assumption. (Note: there may be rare exceptions to the above statement, such as below market rate VA loans financed by tax-free bonds and later escalated due to income of assumptors being over statutory limits).

6. For loans closed after 1 March 1988, VA requires pre-qualification for loan assumptions. Loans originated before the March date do not require pre-qualification except as noted in the paragraph (5). The interest rate will remain unchanged regardless of the origination date, except as noted in paragraph (5).

7. Anyone can prepay part or all of a VA loan without penalty.

8. Other mortgages can be placed behind a VA first mortgage, i.e., second mortgages and wrap-around mortgages.

9. In my opinion, the marketability of a home increases with an assumable VA mortgage.

2.3 *Who is eligible for a VA loan?*

Most veterans must have served in the United States Armed Forces for more than 180 days of continuous active duty service (not as a reservist), and were not dishonorably discharged. The following is a more specific answer predicated on the veteran not being a reservist nor dishonorably discharged:

1. Veterans who served more than 90 days of continuous service during:
   a. World War II era—16 September 1940 through 25 July 1947;
   b. Korean Conflict—27 June 1950 through 31 January 1955;

    c. Vietnam Conflict—August 5, 1964 through 7 May 1975.

2. Service people not on active duty "for training purposes" and who have served for more than 180 days of continuous service, (reservists) including the "Cold War" veterans,

3. Individuals who enlisted after 7 September 1980 or entered on active duty after 16 October 1981 must have completed 24 months of active duty service or the full period for which the person was called or ordered to active duty. (Note: VA does list certain exceptions to this general guideline.)

4. A veteran discharged for a service-related injury which occurred during service other than "for training purposes" (reservist); no minimum time period required. A veteran entering service after 7 September 1980 would be eligible if discharged for disability, whether or not service connected. If the disability was service connected, it could not have been from willful misconduct or incurred during an unauthorized absence. Additionally, these veterans can be eligible if discharged for hardship.

5. Veterans entering service prior to 8 September 1980 can be considered eligible if discharged for hardship and if they completed 181 days of service.

6. Unmarried, surviving spouses. Specifically, a widow or widower of a veteran whose death was caused by a service-connected injury or ailment. To be eligible for loans, an unmarried surviving spouse cannot have acquired eligibility by reason of his or her own active military service. Eligibility as an unmarried surviving spouse is complete and distant from the eligibility of the deceased veteran, and any benefit the deceased veteran may have used in no way affects the benefits available to theeligible unmarried surviving spouse.

7. Allies. Any United States citizen who served in the Armed Forces of a country allied with the United States in World War II.

8. Hospitalized veterans. A person who has completed all the basic requirements but is hospitalized pending final discharge.

9. Spouses of Service Personnel Missing in Action or Prisoners of War. If an individual has been either missing in action, captured, or interned in the line of duty for more than 90 days, their spouse is eligible for one VA home loan.

2.4 *How does one show proof of eligibility?*

One must submit a "Certificate of Eligibility" at loan application. This is the most important document a veteran should have in applying for a VA loan.

2.5 *What is a "Certificate of Eligibility?"*

This certificate is a VA Form 26-8320 and contains the following information: name of veteran, service serial number/social security number, entitlement code, branch of service, date of birth, date issued, signature of Authorized Agent, and issuing office. The reverse side of this form shows the amount of entitlement or guaranty used and the amount available for real estate loan purposes. Refer to Figure 19.

2.6 *How does one obtain a Certificate of Eligibility?*

A certificate is obtained by completion of VA Form 26-1880, Request for Determination of Eligibility and Available Loan Guaranty Entitlement. This form must be accompanied by either a DD214, which was issued to service personnel discharged after 1 January 1950; or a Form WDAGO, Notice of Separation for veterans discharged before this date; or a computer-generated Certificate of Eligibility, which was issued to veterans who served for one period of service after approximately 1970. Many times the WDAGO, Notice of Separation, can be found on the reverse side of the Honorable Discharge. Refer to Figure 19.

2.7 *What type of information does Form DD 214 contain?*

The DD 214 contains dates of service, height, weight, color of eyes, color of hair, any distinguishing service awards or any medals awarded, what sort of occupation or specialty in the service they served, periods of service, and places served. Refer to Figure 18.

2.8 *What happens if a veteran has lost the form DD214, WDAGO, or other evidence of Military Service?*

If a veteran has lost their evidence of Military Service, a certificate in lieu of lost or destroyed discharge certificate GSA Form 6954 Certification of Military Service is acceptable. This form can be obtained by personal application of the veteran to the Service Department concerned, if an honorable discharge was originally issued. If the veteran has lost the DD 214, here are some suggested ways one might find a duplicate:

1. Obtain a VA Standard Form 180, Request Pertaining To Military Records. The 180 form should be completed and mailed to the proper custodian listed on the reverse side of form.
2. Contact the War Records Department or any similarly named department of the state where they entered service.
3. If the veteran was ever a civil service employee, a copy may have been kept by whatever agency acted as employer.
4. If the veteran ever received railroad retirement, check with the railroad.
5. Check courthouse records for a copy.
6. If the veteran was drafted, check with the local Draft Board.
7. If veteran benefits were ever used, e.g., school benefits, check with the institution that asked for proof of eligibility.
8. Check with the branch of service at time of discharge.

2.9 *What do people currently on active duty use for eligibility?*

If a veteran is currently on active duty, they can verify military service by submitting a "statement of service." For this purpose, a Form DD13 Statement of Service is acceptable, or a veteran can submit the statement in letter form on military letterhead, signed by the Personnel or the Commanding Officer of the applicant. This letter must show the applicant's active duty dates, full name, service serial number, any previous periods of service, character of service, and notation of any "time lost." Only the original is acceptable.

2.10 *After the veteran submits proof of eligibility, what copies should be kept by the veteran and what copies will be sent back to the veteran after loan closing?*

Copies of all documents submitted for loan purposes should be kept by the veteran. A veteran can submit photocopies of documents such as WDAGO or Notice of Separation, Form DD 214, or Form DD 13. The Certificate of Eligibility, however, must be the original. After loan closing, the lender will submit to the VA Regional Office a loan package for guaranty approval. If all papers are acceptable to the VA Regional Office, that office then should mail the Certificate of Eligibility directly to the veteran.

2.11 *Are there different types of Certificates of Eligibility? Yes, conditional and unconditional.*

Unconditional Certificates are issued to veterans who have not used their eligibility, or whose previously used eligibility has been restored. Unconditional Certificates will also be issued to veterans whose entitlement is reduced because the veteran retains ownership of real property acquired through use of entitlement or because a debt has been established against the veteran when VA has incurred a loss. A lender to whom an Unconditional Certificate of Eligibility is presented may rely on the amount of guaranty available.

A Conditional Certificate could be issued when a veteran has a double eligibility, derived by serving in two different time periods. A Conditional Certificate of Eligibility will be issued even though VA remains potentially liable as a guarantor and the veteran does not retain ownership of the property previously purchased. Veterans will still have their next eligibility available to receive a Conditional Certificate of Eligibility, provided there has been no claim established against this veteran from a prior VA loan. The term "conditional" should be on the face of the Certificate. The available entitlement shown on a Conditional Certificate of Eligibility will be subject to reduction in the event VA, after issuance of such Certificate, incurs actual liability or loss on the particular outstanding loans. Therefore, any lender proposing to make a loan to a veteran to whom a Conditional Certificate has been issued should not close the loan automatically. The application should be submitted for prior approval to avoid the risk of receiving reduced guaranty because of the application of reduction factors. However, once a Certificate of Commitment is issued, no reduction will be made, regardless of what happens in relation to the veteran's prior loan.

Basically, an Unconditional Certificate involves a veteran who has never used eligibility, or whose eligibility has been restored, or who has sufficient remaining eligibility to buy again, even though the previously used eligibility is in a home the veteran still owns.

2.12 *How may a veteran restore eligibility or entitlement?*

The general requirement for restoration is that the loan must be paid in full, and the real property which served as security for the loan must have either (a) been disposed of by the veteran or (b) been destroyed by fire or other natural hazard. It is important to note that besides the loan being paid in full, the property must have been disposed of by the veteran. Therefore, a veteran attempting to restore their entitlement by refinancing their home (thereby paying off the loan in full) will not receive reinstatement of eligibility, because the property had not been disposed.

A veteran's entitlement may also be restored by what is known as "substitution of entitlement." A new veteran purchaser assumes the outstanding indebtedness and (a) qualifies for the existing loan on the basis of income and credit; (b) has sufficient available entitlement to replace the amount of entitlement used by the seller in originally obtaining the loan; (c) and certifies that he or she does or will occupy the property as a home.

The VA Regional Office that originally guaranteed the loan should be contacted for details, processing, and instructions. (Note: An exception to this general guideline would be veterans who enlisted after 7 September 1980 or entered active duty after 16 October 1981. These veterans could have obtained a VA home loan while in service by completing 181 days of active duty, but without completing 2 years of service. These veterans, barring an approved exception, will not be eligible for restoration of entitlement.)

2.13 *How may a spouse of a service person Missing in Action or a Prisoner of War obtain a Certificate of Eligibility?*

The spouse should forward to the VA Regional Office: (a) a letter requesting determination of eligibility; (b) a copy of the most recent DD Form 1300, Report of Casualty; (c) a marriage certificate or other proof of marriage customarily issued in the jurisdiction where marriage occurred; (d) complete information concerning all marriages previously entered into by the spouse and service person and manner of termination. Include details as to date, place, and manner of termination.

2.14 *May a veteran who has dual periods of eligibility obtain two VA loans?*

A veteran with periods of dual eligibility will not entitle them to choose what period of service to use for the VA loan, and does not entitle the veteran to simultaneously apply for two VA loans. Unused entitlement from a previous period of qualifying service cannot be used when entitlement is obtained as a result of subsequent qualifying service. Additionally, VA loans can be obtained through the normal process of reinstatement of guaranty or by the veteran having enough remaining guaranty to quality for an additional VA loan. The term "remaining guaranty" is used in reference to a veteran who has applied for and obtains a VA home loan.

2.15 *Can a dual eligibility be beneficial to a veteran in obtaining an additional VA loan?*

Yes, if the veteran has purchased a home and qualified under the Korean eligibility, this home could have been sold, and if the old loan is current at the time of the next VA loan submission, the veteran can apply for the new VA loan under Vietnam Era eligibility. The veteran would not have to be released from liability, nor had their eligibility reinstated, but the Korean benefit must have been used to purchase a home prior to 3 March 1966.

2.16 *Is there a time limit in reference to use of veterans eligibility?*

Eligibility derived from periods of service is good until used. There are no longer any time requirements pertaining to use of a veteran's eligibility, except for dual eligibility.

2.17 *Is there a geographical limit to VA loans, and are VA loans limited to properties located within the United States?*

No. A loan may be guaranteed or insured if the property to secure the loan is located in the United States, its territories, or possessions (for example, Puerto Rico, Guam, the Virgin Islands, and American Samoa).

2.18 *Are reservists eligible for VA loans?*

If the veteran was on active duty for training purposes, the only loan associated with this type of service is an FHA loan termed "FHA/VA" loan. This type of loan is an FHA loan and is not handled or processed by the VA, except for a Certificate of Veterans Status, which is issued by the VA to the veteran or the veteran's lender to assist in processing this FHA loan. The military documents required for obtaining the Certificate of Veteran's Status are the same as those used in requesting the Certificate of Eligibility. VA Form 26-8261A, Request for Certificate of Veteran Status, must accompany the application.

2.19 *What do the words "entitlement," "eligibility," and "guaranty" imply?*

These terms are used in reference to the dollar amount of guaranty or entitlement available on each VA loan. The dollar amount of guaranty or entitlement determines the amount of VA loan available.

"Guaranty" is used more in VA's relationship with the lender; "entitlement" or "eligibility" is used in VA's relationship to the veteran.

2.20 *What is the maximum VA guaranty?*

At the time of this writing, the maximum guaranty or eligibility is 60% of the loan amount or $36,000, whichever is less.

2.21 *What were the previous maximum guaranties or entitlements?*

Originally, the maximum entitlement available for home loan purposes was $2,000. The maximum was raised to $4,000 on

28 December 1945; to $7,500 on 12 July 1950; to $12,500 on 7 May 1968; to $17,500 on 31 December 1974; to $25,000 on 1 October 1978; to $27,500 on 1 October 1980; and was further raised to the present maximum of $36,000 on 21 December 1987. If a veteran has a copy of the Certificate of Eligibility, the reverse side of said Certificate should state the available eligibility and any previously used. To determine remaining entitlement, simply subtract amount previously used from amount currently available.

Many veterans do not have a copy of their Certificate of Eligibility and are unsure of the exact entitlement previously used. A veteran can determine a minimum entitlement available by simply subtracting the maximum available at time of loan closing from the present maximum entitlement. For example, a veteran used their VA entitlement for a home loan purchase in 1971; to determine minimum remaining entitlement,subtract $12,500 (maximum entitlement at that time) from $36,000 (current maximum). The remaining entitlement would be $23,500. Of course, the remaining entitlement might be slightly more if the veteran did not use the maximum available in 1971.

In the FHA section, Question 1.86, page 68, there is an explanation of the relationship between the agency, lender, and investor. This explanation mentions VA loans are affected in the same way as FHA loans. The major investor for VA loans is GNMA.

To understand how GNMA determines a VA maximum loan amount, let us assume the following: sales price and CRV is $75,000 and the veteran's used entitlement is $20,000. Always use the lower of the sales price or the CRV (Certificate of Reasonable Value—VA appraisal). When you read, sales price and CRV, this means both have the same dollar amount.

1. We determine the remaining or unused guaranty (entitlement) as follows:

   $36,000 maximum guaranty (entitlement)
   -$20,000 used guaranty (entitlement)
   $16,000 remaining guaranty

2. We determine the percentage of guaranty as follows:
   $16,000 divided by $75,000 = 21.33% guaranty

3. GNMA requires a 25% dollar coverage. To determine the GNMA coverage required, we do the following:

    $75,000 sales price and CRV
    × .25
    $18,750 minimum dollar coverage required by GNMA

4. We meet the GNMA minimum dollar coverage as follows:

    $18,750 minimum dollar coverage required by GNMA
    $16,000 remaining guaranty
    $ 2,750 cash required to meet GNMA dollar coverage.

5. We determine the VA loan amount, eligible for purchase by GNMA, as follows:

    $75,000 sales price and CRV
    -$ 2,750 cash requirement
    $72,250 VA loan

The cash required is paid in the form of a downpayment.

To make sure we meet the 25% minimum GNMA dollar coverage for the loan, we do the following:

$16,000 divided by $75,000 = 21.33% guaranty
$ 2,750 divided by $75,000 = +3.67% downpayment
                             25.00% GNMA coverage

To obtain the maximum guaranty for this loan, you choose between the lesser of 60% of the loan amount ($43,350) or the remaining guaranty ($16,000). The guaranty for the above loan is $16,000.

The above example is the formula used by GNMA to determine the eligibility of a VA loan placed into a GNMA pool. There is a faster and easier formula to determine the loan amount acceptable to GNMA. The formula is as follows:

Sales Price and CRV × 75% + unused guaranty = loan amount

Using the numbers from the GNMA example above, determining the maximum loan amount with the shortcut formula would be as follows:

$75,000 × 75% = $56,250 + $16,000 (unused guaranty) = $72,250

Another useful formula to determine a 100% VA loan amount is as follows:

$$\text{unused guaranty} \times 4 = 100\% \text{ VA loan}$$

Using numbers from the GNMA example above, we determine the 100% VA loan as follows:

$$\$16,000 \times 4 = \$64,000$$

As you can see, for a $2,750 cash downpayment, the veterans can increase their loan amount to $72,250, an additional $8,250.

The last formula takes me back to the days when I was a loan solicitor. I was new in the business and had been calling on a real estate company ranked as one of the best in town. One day, I heard one of the top agents in the company complaining about some news she just received from another mortgage company. When I inquired about the problem, the agent told me her veteran buyer was short on guaranty required for a VA loan he needed to close a sale. She was in a bad mood because the veteran buyer did not have enough cash for a downpayment on a conventional loan and her sale was going to fall through. After getting the numbers involved with the veteran purchaser, I told her the sale could be saved and I asked for her business. She answered my solicitation by telling me I would not only get the VA loan, but would also get other loans and her recommendations to fellow agents. She gave me a stern warning that my solution had better not be a trick, after all, another mortgage company turned down the loan. With a small downpayment the veteran could easily afford, the loan closed and the agent was happy.

Many people, including lenders, think a VA loan is limited to 4 times the guaranty, and there are probably an equal amount who think VA sets the maximum loan amount. If you ask VA for the maximum loan amount, they will be quick to tell you there is no maximum VA loan. VA limits the amount of loan guaranty, not the loan amount. I have made several VA loans in the mid and upper $200,000 range.

Knowledge of real estate finance is important, it will return dividends. Another important point is not to overestimate what people know about real estate finance. The true story you just read, concerning the real estate agent, happened in the late 1960s. I can state, without hesitation, the true story is still "new news" today. Most publicity about VA loans today centers on 100% loans or having all eligibility restored if the veteran's home is sold and the loan paid in full. Imagine the new market created every time VA increases the guaranty. To help you identify the market, think of what happened to veterans in December 1987 when VA increased the guaranty from $27,500 to $36,000. The increase of $8,500 affected *all* veteran's remaining guaranty. Compare the number of veterans receiving the increase in guaranty to the number of veterans who have never used their eligibility, or had their eligibility reinstated. Of course, if you don't know about remaining entitlement or guaranty, you don't even know the market exists.

A word of caution, remember the relationship between agency, lender, and investor. Some lenders in the "COLT" states (Colorado, Oklahoma, Louisiana, and Texas) and other real estate depressed areas, may require the 25% dollar coverage to be in the form of a VA guaranty and not guaranty plus cash. Upon foreclosure, VA, unlike FHA, does not necessarily pay the loan off and accept the property. In cases where VA does not accept the property, called a "no-bid," the VA pays the guaranty to the lender who then becomes the owner. Declining real estate values and an increase in foreclosures have caused lenders in the "COLT" states to loose money on homes they own due to VA foreclosures.

2.22 *What is the purpose of the loan guaranty?*
The guaranty serves a two-fold purpose:

Guaranty primarily determines the dollar amount of a VA loan. For example, most lenders will lend at least an amount equal to four times the guaranty or entitlement.

Guaranty is additionally involved in the event of foreclosure. After foreclosure, the lender becomes owner of the foreclosed property. VA can accept the property in question from the lender by reimbursement of the outstanding loan balance plus foreclosure expenses; or VA can instruct the lender to keep title to the foreclosed property and accept a check equal to the remaining balance times the guaranty percentage originally issued when the loan was originated.

2.23 *Are VA loans limited to four times the guaranty?*

No. Actually, there is no VA maximum loan limitation. The only limitation VA makes is to the loan guaranty. A lender is free to originate a $500,000 VA loan, but the maximum loan guaranty will remain $36,000, or whatever the maximum is at time of loan origination. FNMA now has a maximum of $144,000 as the top limit for the purchase of a 100% VA loan. GNMA's limitation for a 100% VA loan placed in a GNMA pool is $144,000. It should be noted that both of the above named institutions will accept cash plus the VA guaranty as constituting a percentage of guaranty.

Although there is no maximum loan limitation of dollar amount, VA loans will not exceed the appraised value as stated by the VA appraisal or certificate of reasonable value, except by the amount financed for the funding fee.

2.24 *Since there is no maximum VA loan limitation, is there a maximum VA limitation of term or length of the loan?*

Yes. By law, VA limits their home loans to a maximum of 30 years and 32 days, or the remaining economic life of the property.

2.25 *Can a veteran purchase another home without having their eligibility reinstated?*

Yes. Provided the veteran has remaining entitlement, they may apply for and receive an additional VA home loan. Of course, the new home must be owner/occupied as the veteran's principal residence. The dollar amount of entitlement remaining will determine the maximum VA loan available.

2.26 *Is there a limitation to how many VA loans a veteran can have?*

No. Provided there is sufficient guaranty to satisfy the investor, a veteran can have an unlimited number of VA home loans.

2.27 *Is a VA home loan limited to a single-family residence for the veteran?*

No. The vast majority of VA loans originated are for single-family dwellings occupied by veterans, with fee-simple title. However, VA will also guarantee loans to veterans who purchase two to four-unit dwellings and occupy one unit as their principal residence.

2.28 *Are the loan amounts any higher for duplex, triplex, or quadruplex dwellings?*

No. There is no maximum VA loan established by VA; again, check with a prospective mortgagee for any maximum VA loan limitations.

2.29 *Is there a VA business loan, farm loan, or multi-family loan?*

No. Now the VA home loan program is limited to single-family and two to four-unit dwellings occupied by the veteran. At one time, VA had a farm and a business loan program. The closest thing a veteran can achieve in the way of a business or farm loan is to purchase a home residence on which their business or farm is located, for example, a two story building with a retail store downstairs and the veterans home upstairs, or a single-family dwelling located on a large tract of land which could be used for farming purposes. If a loan to an eligible veteran is for acquiring a residential property consisting of not more than one business unit, said unit may not exceed 25% of the total floor area of the property. If the property is to be owned by two or more eligible veterans, it may consist of four-family units and one business unit plus one additional family unit for each veteran participating in ownership. Thus, two veterans may purchase or construct a residential property consisting of up to six-family units: the basic units (four), plus one for each of the two veterans. One must be careful, however, in pursuing ideas mentioned in the above examples. VA will be looking primarily at the family dwelling for value and economic life. Secondly, one must find a mortgagee willing to originate unusual types of VA loans.

2.30 *Is VA only interested in a single-family house, or also in a duplex, triplex, or quadruplex?*

As previously mentioned above, most VA loans are for single-family dwellings occupied by the veteran. Single-family

85

dwellings can and do include condominiums, co-ops, zero-lot-line town homes, patio homes, and any other suitable dwellings approved by VA.

Additionally, two to four-unit dwellings do not necessarily mean a duplex, triplex, or quadruplex. Four single-family houses (attached or detached) on a single parcel of land that cannot be legally divided may be acceptable to VA. These houses should have separate utility meters and sewage disposal systems.

2.31 *Is a "fee-simple title" required by VA?*

No. VA will guarantee a land sale or installment contract. Contingent on prior approval, VA will guarantee the obligation of an eligible veteran for the installments payable on a land sale contract for the purchase of improved residential real property. Any installment or land sale contract guarantee must be placed on record.

2.32 *(a) Must every VA loan involve a fixed level payment? (b) Why doesn't VA have graduated, variable, or renegotiable loans?*

Unlike most people think, VA loans are not restricted to a 30-year level payment amortization. VA loans must have a fixed-rate, but payments can fluctuate according to income. For example, if a veteran is to retire from employment in 15 years, payments could be arranged for a higher amount in the first 15 years and a lower amount for the retirement years; conversely, an intern in medical school could arrange for a lower payment, then higher payment amortization. Payment variations must be prior-approved by VA, and a cooperating mortgagee must be contacted. The best procedure is to apply for a VA GPM. The VA GPM (Graduated Payment Mortgage) is identical to FHA 245 Plan III payment schedule with a minimum down payment of 2.5% of the purchase price for new homes. Existing homes require the same down payment as the FHA Plan III program. For factors to determine the monthly payment, loan amounts and highest outstanding balance, refer to Figures 7 and 9, pages 332-333 and 336-337. (Also see Questions 2.82–83, page 105).

2.33 *If a veteran cannot find a bank, mortgage company, savings and loan institution, or any other lender to originate a VA loan, can they appeal to VA for help?*

No. Therefore, a veteran must find a willing lender to originate a VA loan. There can be no VA loan for a home involving a business or land contract or a variable payment mortgage, unless the veteran can find a cooperating lender.

At one time, a veteran desiring to purchase a home in a remote area and unable to find a lender could only rely on VA for a direct loan, which may still be true for certain isolated sections within VA's lending jurisdiction.

2.34 *What is a VA refinance loan?*

Eligible veterans can refinance their homes and invest the funds for whatever reason(s) deemed worthy by the veteran. In comparing different forms of refinancing, VA has one of the best, if not the very best, programs available. The refinance loan can be equal to 100% of the appraised value if there is no cash out. If refinancing involves cash out, the loan will be limited to a 90% LTV and the veteran must occupy the property being refinanced. If there is no cash out from the refinance, the veteran does not have to occupy the property; however, the veteran must certify that he or she previously occupied the property. Investment in a business, buying a farm, acquiring rental property, educational expenses for the veteran or children, home improvement or any other worthy reason may be acceptable to VA.

Another added feature is that net proceeds to the veteran are non-taxable, since the veteran has not sold an asset, but merely refinanced real estate. Actually, the veteran could have a tax write-off if a loan discount is charged.

In February of 1977, I had the privilege of originating one of the first $100,000 VA-guaranteed mortgages to be sold in a GNMA pool from the State of Tennessee. A lucrative market quickly appeared to me for VA refinancing. An advertising campaign in newspapers and direct mailing to attorneys, CPAs, and doctors quickly resulted in many large VA refinancing loans at 8% interest. Many of the closings had net proceeds of up to $80,000 and $90,000, of which the veteran did not owe a dime in taxes; moreover, they had considerably increased the market value of the home by lowering the equity with an assumable, non-qualifying, non-escalating VA loan that could also be wrapped, second mortgaged, or paid off without penalty. There are quite a few veterans who are glad they took advantage of their VA benefits in reference to refinancing. Eligibility for VA refinancing is the same as the home loan, except there must be a lien against the property. Incidentally, if a veteran can find a willing lender, a land sale contract can be refinanced, and the veteran could receive net cash proceeds from the refinancing.

2.35 *If a veteran's home is free and clear of any liens, can the veteran place a lien on the property by borrowing money and then apply for a VA refinance loan?*

Yes.

2.36 *Can a veteran borrow the 1% funding fee?*

A veteran can add the funding fee to the maximum loan. This answer also applies to refinancing with cash out, which is limited to 90% maximum loan amount for approval.

2.37 *An advantage of an adjustable rate mortgage is the possible reduction of the interest rate charged. If rates begin to decline, would this feature be considered a disadvantage of a fixed-rate VA loan?*

No. In October of 1980, a housing benefit amendment was enacted. The portion of this amendment dealing with VA refinancing enables a veteran to take advantage of this program without the normal dollar amount of eligibility required. The following conditions must be met:

1. The veteran must own or occupy the dwelling being refinanced;
2. The interest rate of the new loan must be less than the interest rate of the loan being refinanced;
3. The new loan must be secured by the same dwelling as was the loan being refinanced;
4. The amount of the new loan may not exceed an amount equal to the sum of the balance of the loan

being refinanced and closing costs, which may include discount points;

5. The amount of guaranty on the new loan may not exceed the original guaranty amount of the loan being refinanced;

6. The term of the new loan may not exceed the original term of the loan being refinanced.

The veteran does not have to have guaranty or entitlement necessary for the refinancing. The guaranty or entitlement used for the original loan will suffice for the new refinanced loan. If a surviving spouse was used as a co-obligor or co-mortgagor on the old loan, that surviving spouse shall be deemed to be a veteran eligible for benefits under the new refinanced loan.

If rates do eventually come down, this new refinanced loan feature will be a tremendous incentive for veterans to refinance their homes. Of course, these new VA refinance loans will have all the advantages of a new VA loan, which could aid the real estate industry as a whole, as veterans eventually sell their homes, with the public being able to assume them. For more information related to refinancing refer to "Prepaying a Mortgage," page 127 "Comparing 15-Year and 30-Year Mortgages," page 135, and Figure 17 on page 350-351.

2.38 *Are VA loans available for the purchase of a farm or business without involving a permanent residence for the veteran?*

No. However, as we have learned in Question 2.34, a veteran can refinance their home and use the net proceeds for any purpose.

2.39 *Would a veteran be required to pay closing costs and discount points if the present VA loan was refinanced?*

The answer to this would be contingent upon market conditions and the lender. Although it has been rare, there have been market conditions where no discounts have had to be paid—what lenders term a quote of "par." Closing costs would most likely be charged, unless there has been some prearranged agreement with the lender or special consideration by the parties of the closing.

This feature might be viewed by some as a disadvantage of a VA loan. One needs only to consider the alternative: an adjustable rate loan will provide a lowering of the interest rate (if rates decline) without requiring refinancing; but an adjustable-rate mortgage will also allow the interest rate to go up if rates increase.

Any cost incurred in refinancing a VA loan can be considered a premium paid for having a mortgage with a fixed rate, but is open to lower interest rates by simply refinancing.

2.40 *What is a "due-on-sale clause," and how does it affect VA loans?*

In broad terms, a due-on-sale clause is an opportunity for the lender to stipulate certain things upon transfer of the property. A lender with a due-on-sale clause could (not would) require pre-qualification of an assumptor or an escalation of the interest rate, or they could demand the balance due and payable.

A U.S. Supreme Court decision (Summer 1982) upholds the right of a lender to exercise a due-on-sale clause. VA and FHA mortgages now have due-on-sale clauses, but the interest rates will remain unchanged. VA and FHA loans owned by state housing agencies or backed by housing bond issues may require a change in the interest rate if, upon loan assumption, the purchaser's income is found to be in excess of statutory income limits.

2.41 *Is owner occupancy necessary for all VA loans?*

In the earlier editions of this book this answer was: "Absolutely, if the veteran is physically able to occupy. The law requires the veteran to sign a certificate of occupancy." After 20 February 1988, the answer is the same except for VA refinances for a lower interest rate, with no cash out and with the veteran certifying they previously occupied the property.

In my seventeen years of originating VA loans, there have been many instances of veterans or their agents treating this regulation with levity. Conversations have occurred such as: "Well, he's really not going to occupy the property; it's really for his daughter and her husband"; or "The veteran wants the house for rental property." My conversations relating to this subject have also been with FBI agents investigating the possibility of fraud being committed by a veteran.

Owner/occupancy will be temporarily waived if it is impossible for a veteran to physically occupy due to active duty service. In such cases, the veteran's family must occupy the home with a certification from the veteran of plans for occupancy at the end of active duty service. A veteran's family can be construed as a dependent member of their family, which can be a parent.

As explained in Question 2.3, subparagraph (9), spouses of veterans missing in action are eligible for a VA loan.

2.42 *Is it necessary for a veteran to be present at loan application or loan closing?*

No. Loan application may be made by the veteran's spouse or a member of the veteran's immediate family. Closing and loan documents can be forwarded to a veteran for signature in front of a notary. A power of attorney can be used in the absence of a veteran. If the veteran is available to sign loan application papers, only a general power of attorney is needed. If the veteran is unable to sign the loan application, then a specific power of attorney will be required. All powers of attorney should be recorded. Power of attorney can be used for loan closing provided:

1. The donor's power of attorney is valid and legally adequate to enable the attorney in fact to act for the veteran.
2. The veteran has consented, in writing, to the specific transaction. The written consent must express a clear understanding of what is involved with the veteran's eligibility. It must also express the veteran's intention of occupying the property as a home upon the veteran's return or upon occupancy by the veteran's immediate family during the term of absence, and the veteran's signature must be attested by the Commanding Officer, Adjutant, or other person acting in a representative capacity. However, if the power of attorney expressly represents the veteran's intention of acquiring the property as a home and adequately

identifies the property and the terms of the proposed transaction, a separate written statement by the veteran is not necessary.

3. There must be an affidavit that the veteran is alive at the time of loan closing. A Certificate of Guaranty will not be issued, if at the time of loan closing, the veteran was reported as missing in action or deceased. Proof of the veteran's status can be done by letter or cable dated subsequent to the loan closing from the veteran, or by a statement from the veteran's Commanding Officer that the veteran is alive and not missing-in-action on the date of loan closing.

2.43 *Under what circumstances may a veteran pay loan discount points?*

The following circumstances allow veterans to be charged discount points:

1. Refinancing an existing loan;
2. Constructing a residence on land owned by the veteran;
3. In the purchase of a residence from a class of sellers that cannot feasibly or legally be charged discount points; e.g., a trustee for the bankruptcy court, a sheriff in a tax sale, or an executor of an estate.

2.44 *If the veteran is to be charged a loan discount, should VA be aware of the charge?*

No. In May of 1983 VA changed their regulations to allow veterans and lenders the freedom of negotiating discount points for circumstances mentioned in Question 2.43. There are written guidelines which lenders must follow in establishing the discount points. Therefore, loans involving discount points paid by the veteran may now be approved on an automatic basis.

2.45 *What are "discounts," and what are "points?"*

For an answer to this question, please refer to Question 1.37, page 34.

2.46 *If a seller refuses to pay discount points, is the veteran "out of luck" in obtaining a VA loan?*

No. VA regulations prohibit a veteran from paying the discount except as outlined in Question 2.43. However, VA regulations do not require discounts to be charged exclusively to the seller; a third party can pay the discounts.

2.47 *What is an automatic approval?*

Certain lenders designated by VA may approve or reject VA home loan applications. The advantage of being an automatic lender is a reduction in loan processing time, since the file does not have to be forwarded to the VA Regional Office for approval of the loan. The automatic authority may not apply to all loans, such as multi-family loans, joint mortgagor, or disabled veterans.

Furthermore, any VA loan sent to a Regional Office for review cannot later be approved on an automatic basis. Supervised lenders may activate automatic loans. Non-supervised lenders must apply for VA approval to act as an automatic lender.

2.48 *In general, what does VA use to qualify a veteran regarding income?*

In October of 1986, VA began using a debt-to-income ratio for loan qualification purposes. The ratio is determined by taking the sum of principal, interest, taxes and insurance (PITI), any special assessments, other expenses such as homeowner's warranty or condo fees, and monthly payments VA views as long-term obligations (monthly repayment in excess of 6 months); the sum of the debt is then divided by total income which is viewed as gross salary or earnings and other compensation or net income. The resulting ratio is then rounded up, and if it is higher than 41%, the application will most likely be rejected. VA will continue to use the Balance for Family Support as a backup for the debt-to-income ratio requirement. The Family Support chart used by VA takes into consideration social security and income taxes paid by the loan applicant(s), size of the family, maintenance and utility cost of the home being purchased. If the net balance for Family Support is higher than required by VA, the income is considered acceptable.

2.49 *Can educational or readjustment allowance income be included in a veteran's gross income?*

No, but VA retirement income or disability income can be included as gross income, and on-the-job training benefits.

2.50 *If the veteran is short on income required by VA, would a large cash reserve make a favorable difference?*

Yes and no. Large cash reserve would most likely have little or no effect if the veteran applies for a 100% loan. Cash reserves can appear or disappear as fast as it takes to complete a deposit or withdrawal slip at a local bank. On the other hand, a large cash reserve would make a favorable difference if these reserves were applied as a down payment in acquiring the home. How much of the cash reserve used as a down payment would be determined on a case-to-case basis. There are no set guidelines. Down payment would be relative to the inadequate amount of income and the loan amount requested.

2.51 *Aside from a spouse's income, may a veteran receive financial help in the way of a co-mortgagor or joint mortgagor?*

Yes. VA will consider income and credit from a non-veteran serving as a joint mortgagor, but VA will only guarantee that portion of the loan for which the veteran is obligated. This reduced guaranty may not hinder VA or the veteran, but it may be bothersome to a lender. Of course, a lender's problem will soon become the veteran's problem, or no loan—no home. Most lenders require full guaranty and will not accept a half or a proportioned guaranty.

If both the joint mortgagors are veterans and have proper eligibility, then the loan can be fully guaranteed. VA will consider both incomes and credit in qualifying the veterans for the loan. A spouse is not considered as a joint mortgagor, so his or her income and credit will normally be considered and the loan guaranteed.

All joint mortgagor loans must be sent to VA for prior approval. Co-signers are usually not considered in determining income and credit by the VA.

2.52 *What could prevent a veteran from obtaining loan approval if there is proper eligibility and sufficient income?*

Credit problems. One could easily conclude from these questions and answers that VA has one of the best, if not the best, ways of financing home ownership. VA expects the veteran to have good credit when application is made, and to pay the home payments when due after loan closing.

2.53 *If the home payments are not made and foreclosure results, isn't the loan guaranteed? Why should the lender be concerned?*

Any foreclosure is bad for both lender and borrower. The lender originates the loan for financial reasons. A foreclosure is contrary to those reasons. For the borrower, their credit will be seriously damaged, and the foreclosure could remain a part of an FHA, VA or Conventional credit report for the next seven years. Bankruptcies can be reported for up to ten years.

The above adverse circumstances may, however, only be the beginning for a veteran whose home loan has been foreclosed. The following is taken from a VA Home Loan Guaranty informational Issue:

> Under the governing law, a veteran who obtains from a private lender a loan which is guaranteed or insured by the Veterans Administration is legally obligated to indemnigy the United States Government for the net amount of any guanranty or insurance claim the VA may thereafter be required to pay to the holder of the loan. This right of indemnity has been upheld by the Supreme Court of the United States, notwithstanding that a deficiency judgement was not obtained or was not obtainable by the mortgage holder under local state law. (U.S. v. Shimer, 367 U.S. 374m 1961)

2.54 *Can a veteran apply for a VA loan if bankruptcy has ever been filed?*

There are several Chapters of Bankruptcy. One chapter (commonly known as Wage-Earner) gives the veteran a chance to eventually pay back the creditors. Other chapters would simply discharge debts.

In general, VA will refuse to review a file concerning a veteran who has filed bankruptcy, other than a wage-earner, until at least 24 months have transpired from the date of final discharge from bankruptcy and credit has been re-established. A wage-earner bankruptcy may be considered on a case-to-case basis. Three-fourths of the wage-earner's debts must have been paid in a satisfactory manner, and the trustee for the bankruptcy, as well as the bankruptcy judge, must approve the new credit. Additionally, the VA will be interested in a written explanation from the veteran on the cause of bankruptcy. In originating VA loans, many times my role has been that of a middleman between the VA and the veteran. Based on this experience, I have found that one of the biggest communication gaps between VA and the veteran is the area of credit history for a veteran discharged from bankruptcy. Considering a veteran in this situation, one of the first things VA will want to know is how much credit has been re-established along with the timely method of repayment to these new creditors. When I have previously questioned bankrupt veterans about re-establishment of new creditors, it is not unusual to hear a veteran boastfully reply: "After bankruptcy we burned all of our credit cards and have paid cash ever since; we don't owe a dime to anyone."

My advice to veterans who have had the unfortunate experience of filing bankruptcy is to re-establish credit quickly and to pay those creditors on a timely basis. Once a veteran re-establishes credit and promptly meets the obligations incurred, a proven track record can then be available for VA review.

2.55 *If VA incurs a loss from foreclosure proceedings, how can indemnification from a veteran be obtained?*

If a veteran will not indemnify VA for their loss, VA is entitled but not limited to the standard course of action our judicial system provides. Courses of action outside the courts could come from claims by the VA to the veteran's pension, social security income, or by withholding any subsequent VA benefits until the loss is paid.

2.56 *If a VA loan is assumed but later foreclosed with a loss incurred, is the original veteran-borrower liable for a loss caused by someone else?*

Yes.

2.57 *How can a veteran avoid being liable for a foreclosure loss caused by someone who assumed the veteran's home loan?*

A veteran can be set free from the obligation of a VA loan by obtaining what is called a "release of liability," which can only be granted by the VA. A real estate agent or lender can be helpful in assisting the veteran; however, the veteran is cautioned that for VA guaranteed loans, a "release of liability" can only be granted by the VA.

When application is made for the "release," the following conditions must be met:

1.   The loan must be current;
2.   The income and credit of the purchaser must be acceptable to VA;
3.   The purchaser must assume the VA loan and the indemnity obligation.

Owner occupancy is not required.

2.58 *For a veteran who doesn't want to wait for the lengthy release of liability, can they sell on a loan assumption and then later apply for a release of liability?*

Yes, if certain conditions are satisfied. For VA to grant a release of liability after a sale, the Deed transferring the property must contain an Assumption Clause, or the parties must sign an Indemnity Agreement, the instrument used must be recorded, the loan current, and the purchaser's income and credit must be acceptable to VA.

The veteran-seller should insist that an assumption clause be inserted in the deed conveying the property to the assumptor. The assumption clause will give the veteran two benefits. First, the clause will permit VA to consider a release upon the veteran's application after the property has been conveyed. Secondly, the clause will afford the veteran a right of action against the assuptor if the loan is foreclosed. The following is a sample assumption clause.

SAMPLE ASSUMPTION CLAUSE

For and in consideration of Ten Dollars ($10.00) cash in hand paid, the receipt of which is hereby acknowledged, and other good and valuable consideration, a part of which is the as-

sumption of one certain trsut deed dated _____,
198__, and filed for record _____, 19__, in
the office of the recorder of deeds of _____
County, Tennessee, in Book _____, Page ____, and note of
even date thereby secured, in the original principal amount of
$_____ payable to _____,
which debt the grantee herein assumes and agrees to pay as
part payment of the purchase price.

The grantee further hereby assumes the obligations of
_____ under the terms of the instruments
creating the loan to indemnify the Veterans Administration to
the extent of any claim payment arising from the guaranty or
insurance of the indebtedness above mentioned.

If the Assumption Clause is not incorporated in the Deed,
the veteran-seller and the assumptor may sign an Indemnity
Agreement which must be recorded. The Indemnity Agreement has wording similar to the Assumption Clause.

If neither the Assumption Clause nor the Indemnity
Agreement is executed, VA will not grant a release of liability.

2.59 *Is a "release of liability" or "substitution of entitlement" the
only way a veteran can avoid liability from VA when the
property is conveyed by loan assumption?*

Yes. There are, however, other measures a veteran could take
to prevent VA from incurring a loss caused by an assumptor:

1. The veteran is free to write the lender and ask for
    written notification of any pending foreclosure of the
    veteran's previous home loan. The veteran will want
    to make sure the lender is supplied with a current
    mailing address.
2. The veteran-seller could require a guaranty perfor-
    mance agreement to be executed by the assumptor
    and secured by a second mortgage. A guaranty agree-
    ment can serve as sufficient collateral for a second
    mortgage; money would not have to be lent by the
    veteran seller to the purchaser. Foreclosure by the
    owner of the second mortgage may occur if the
    obligations of the first mortgage are not being ful-
    filled. The veteran-owner of the second mortgage
    would then have a legal right to buy the property

back by foreclosing the second mortgage. Most state laws require the owner of a second mortgage to be put on notice of any pending foreclosure by the owner of the first mortgage.

3. The veteran may obtain a large cash equity from the assumptor. For example, a veteran could sell a home with a VA loan balance of $40,000 and accept a $15,000 cash equity from the assumptor. The numbers may vary from case-to-case, but it would be safe to assume that the larger the cash equity involved, the less a chance of foreclosure, particularly foreclosure with a loss incurred.

2.60 *Isn't the lender required to contact the endangered veteran and inform them of the possible consequences involving foreclosure of their previous home loan?*

No. There is no known VA regulation requiring a lender to "search out" a potentially liable veteran and educate that individual about what may happen. This "searching out" is a common misconception by the general public.

2.61 *Can only veterans assume VA loans?*

No.

2.62 *Can only veterans assume a VA loan and provide a release of liability for the veteran?*

No. The only time an assumptor would have to be a veteran would be when there was a substitution of entitlement for the veteran whose eligibility was used in obtaining the VA home loan.

2.63 *If the selling veteran obtains a substitution of entitlement when selling on a loan assumption basis, does this automatically mean the seller-veteran is released from liability to the VA?*

Yes. Application for release of liability is required when requesting substitution of entitlement.

2.64 *Will the pre-qualification for loans closed after 1 March 1988 provide a release of liability?*

Yes. Approval, by VA, of a loan assumption will release the veteran of liability.

2.65 *Is there be a charge for processing a loan assumption?*

For loans closed after 1 March 1988, VA will charge a 1/2% funding fee. The funding fee is based on the remaining loan balance. There are guidelines under consideration which will allow lenders to process loan assumptions and charge a fee estimated to be $300.

2.66 *Is there a time limitation for loans requiring pre- qualification?*

Yes. The time limitation is for the remaining term of the loan.

2.67 *Are second mortgages in conjunction with VA home loans limited to a home sale involving an existing VA home loan, or can a veteran-purchaser apply for a new VA loan with a second mortgage being provided by an individual or a lending institution?*

Yes and no. Yes, if the appraisal (Certificate of Reasonable Value) exceeds the VA first mortgage. A second mortgage can secure the excess portion between value and the VA first mortgage. However, most lenders will require the second mortgage term in years to match VA first mortgage; VA will allow a balloon payment on a second mortgage. Therefore, a 30-year second mortgage could become due in five years. When application is made for a VA home loan in conjunction with a second mortgage, all repayment provisions of the second must be disclosed. A second mortgage requiring a balloon payment in the very near future will probably require written explanation from the veteran of the method or source of successful performance of that obligation.

The "no" answer to this question would be in a case involving the property being sold to a veteran for more than the VA appraisal.

2.68 *Can a veteran pay more for a home than the value of the VA appraisal?*

Yes, provided the difference is paid in cash, from the veterans resources. The excess between VA value and acquisition costs cannot be borrowed, such as in a second mortgage.

2.69 *May a veteran borrow their down payment or closing costs and pledge an asset other than the residence being purchased?*

Yes, and possibly no. Yes, if the reason for the loan is to fund closing costs. Also yes, if the loan is for a down payment, provided the down payment and loan do not exceed the VA appraised value. A loan application would most likely be rejected, however, it the veteran has borrowed funds for closing costs or a down payment when the acquisition cost (sales price) exceeds the VA appraised value. Actually, a veteran borrowing funds to exceed the VA value is circumventing a regulation outlined in the answer to Question 2.67. Of course, the terms of the loan must be included in the VA application.

2.70 *How long is a VA loan approval valid, and does VA have a term for loan approval?*

A "Certificate of Commitment" is a loan approval. Certificates of Commitment are valid for six months for both existing and proposed dwellings.

2.71 *Can Certificates of Commitment be extended?*

Yes and no. No, if the property is an existing dwelling; yes, if the Certificate of Commitment involves a proposed dwelling. The extension period is six months.

2.72 *Can a real estate broker or an agent earn a fee for helping the veteran obtain VA documents, or for assisting the veteran in obtaining a Certificate of Commitment?*

No, if the real estate broker or agent is earning a fee from the transaction. A "fee" would include a commission for selling the home or selling hazard insurance for the dwelling.

2.73 *Could a below-market loan from a lender to a real estate agent be construed as a "kick-back" or illegal fee?*

Yes, if the agent and lender are involved in VA loans. It is not permissible for a mortgagee to make low-interest or no-interest loans to any person or entity from whom the mortgagee accepts proposals for VA loans.

2.74 *Are there any examples of non-conflicting services for which a lender can pay?*

Yes, for example:

1. Attorney fee.
2. Title company fees.

3. Escrow agent fees. This category could include an individual preparing VA loan packages in an area where a lender does not have a main or branch office operating within a 50 mile radius of the subject property. A lender may compensate an individual for the assistance in preparing a VA loan application, provided that the individual has no interest with the real estate broker, real estate agency, or builder. The individual must not receive a fee from any other source in connection with the transaction, excepting a commission in connection with the sale of hazard insurance at the request of the mortgagor. The fee paid by the lender must be proportionate to the amount of work done and must not exceed the allowable origination fee collected from the veteran.

4. A lender may divide fees and discounts with another lender when the parties transfer between them the mortgage loan or the VA commitment.

2.75 *What is the allowable origination fee charged for a VA loan?*
One percent.

2.76 *How much are closing costs, and are there any prohibited charges?*
The best answer to this is a referral to your closing attorney, escrow agent, or party who will close the loan. The closing agent will eventually have the exact amount for closing costs. Closing costs can vary by area, day of the month, and time of the year.

Each VA Regional Office has an established schedule of "allowable fees and charges," which should include "prohibited fees and charges." A list of some allowable charges includes:

1. Appraisal fee.
2. Recording fees or recording taxes.
3. Credit report charge.
4. Proration of taxes or assessments.
5. Hazard insurance.
6. Survey charges.

7. Title examination and title insurance premiums.
8. Loan origination fee charged by the lender of up to 1% of the loan amount.
9. Any allowable discount points.
10. A 1% funding fee charged by the veteran administration, said fee may be financed.

2.77 *Why does VA require that payments for taxes and insurance be held in escrow with the lender?*

This question comes up regularly, and the answer is surprising. VA regulations do not require lenders to collect periodic deposit for taxes and insurance, or to maintain a tax and insurance account. However, VA's viewpoint is that an establishment and maintenance of such an account is considered advantageous to all parties concerned, and a provision is made in all VA approved mortgage and Deed of Trust forms allowing the lender to hold escrow accounts. The investor (owner of mortgage) can require an escrow account.

2.78 *Does VA require fire and title insurance?*

Yes and no. Yes, VA does require fire or hazard insurance as protection for the improvements serving as collateral for the mortgage. The amount of insurance need not equal the amount of the VA loan. If requested, VA will state a value for the land portion of the appraisal. Therefore, a veteran obtaining a 100% VA loan will be required to insure improvements to the land, but not the land as well.

No, VA does not require the purchase of title insurance. However, VA requires the lender to obtain and retain title of proper dignity. Obtaining and protecting good title can be done through the purchase of title insurance. Therefore, in most cases, one will find title insurance as an investor requirement.

2.79 *Question 2.2 mentions a prepayment privilege. How are prepayments applied? Do they apply to principal, or to interest, or to both?*

(In this new edition there is a section titled "Prepaying a Mortgage." Refer to this section for a more in-depth explanation of how prepayment affects a mortgage.) Any prepayment is fully applied to a reduction in the principal loan balance. This answer also applies to FHA loans.

This question encourages me to relate a true story. An application was submitted by an army officer who was an accountant. I was asked how prepayment privilege applied to a VA loan. I answered that any prepayment would fully apply to principal. The veteran's reaction was one of surprise and disbelief. He began to reason that a prepayment of $3,000 in the first few months of the loan could skip four or five years of loan payments on an amortization schedule. The veteran's remarks concerned me, yet research proved that what the veteran thought was impossible, is possible. A remaining balance chart for a 30-year amortized loan reveals that 11-3/4% loan of $1,000 will have an outstanding balance of $996 at the end of one year and $992 at the end of the second year. Therefore, depending on the size of the loan, a substantial prepayment in the early months will have a considerable reduction in the number of payments left on a VA loan.

Now, before everyone runs out to prepay his VA loan, remember it takes a sometimes scarce commodity—cash. Furthermore, monthly payments will become due on the first of each subsequent month, regardless of any prepayments; moreover by prepaying the VA loan, more cash equity will be required of an assumptor in the event of a resale.

2.80 *Does VA have a GEM (Growing Equity Mortgage) or ERM (Early Retirement Mortgage), or any such mortgage which allows for early payment of a mortgage?*

VA has an open door to submission of proposals by lenders that call for early retirement mortgages. Basically, all a lender has to do is submit a plan to VA that completely outlines the increases in the monthly payments and the payoff date. VA will consider the plan and the ability of the veteran in fulfilling the terms of the mortgage.

GEM or ERM loans usually start with a first year payment based on a 30-year amortized mortgage. VA will usually qualify the veteran on the first year's monthly payment, particularly if it is feasible for the veteran to absorb the future increase.

A 15-1/2% VA loan with increases in the monthly payment OF 7-1/2% per year will have a maturity date of less
than 10 years. A 15% VA loan with an increase in the monthly
payments of 5% per year will mature in 12.469 years. A VA
loan at 15.1/2% with a 3% increase in the monthly payment
from years 1 through 9, then a constant payment from year 10
will mature in 14 years, 8 months.

2.81 *Can an existing VA loan be converted to a GEM method of
payment?*

Yes. VA loans can be prepaid without penalty, and the
prepayment fully applies to principal (see Question 2.79).
Therefore, if a VA loan is 5 years old, it can be paid out early
by prepaying the loan at a schedule selected by the
mortgagor. The GEM idea is a marketing idea; any loan
without a prepayment penalty may be treated as a GEM type
of amortization by prepaying the loan.

2.82 *Is a graduated payment mortgage (GPM the same as a GEM
loan, since both involve increases in the monthly payments?*

No. VA has a graduated payment mortgage (GPM) that is
identical to the FHA 245 Section III Program. The VA GPM is
a fixed-rate loan that starts at a monthly payment rate
equivalent to approximately 3% below the VA rate. For example, if the VA rate is 12.25%, the first year monthly payment would be based on a payment rate of approximately
9.04%. Each year the payment increases 7-1/2% for 5 years.
The sixth year payment will be constant for each subsequent
year until the 30-year mortgage is fully amortized. The sixth
year monthly payment will be equivalent to a payment rate of
approximately 13.67%.

2.83 *Is there any VA loan that requires a down payment?*

Yes, A GPM loan requires the same down payment for new
homes as the FHA 245(b) and for existing homes as the FHA
245(a) Plan III. Of course, it a veteran is seeking a large VA
loan, or if the veteran does not have what the lender considers
adequate eligibility, a down payment will most likely be required.

2.84 *Can a veteran buy a home with a zero investment?*

Yes. If the veteran has adequate eligibility, VA can lend 100%, and the seller is allowed to pay all closing costs, including prepaid items. This zero investment is what real estate people sometimes refer to as "zero down, zero closing."

2.85 *Is a VA GPM loan the same as a "buydown" mortgage?*

No. Buydown mortgages involve a reduction or a subsidy of the market rate of interest on either a permanent or a short-term basis. An example of a permanent buydown would be a reduction of a 15-1/2% rate to a 14-1/2% rate by paying the equivalent of anywhere from 6 to 8% in discount points in addition to whatever the market is for discounts on VA loans. The extra points are negotiable for buydowns. The above example would involve a reduction of the interest rate for the life of the loan.

A short-term or temporary buydown plan would involve funds held in escrow and used as needed for subsidizing the monthly payment. For example, a popular buydown plan is what is sometimes referred to as a "3-2-1 buydown." Here is how it works: Assuming an interest rate of 15-1/2%, a $58,000 VA loan could be bought down to 12-1/2% for the first year, 13-1/2% in the second year and 14-1/2% in the third. The arithmetic is simple. Just calculate what the purchaser would normally pay, then subtract what the purchaser will pay.The purchaser would normally pay $27,238.32, which is 36 (3 years) times a monthly payment of $756.62. Now subtract $23,923.20, which is what the purchaser will pay. Year 1 is then $619.01 × 12, year 2 is $664.34 × 12, and year 3 is $710.25 × 12.

The sum of $3,315.12 (obtained from $27,238.32 minus $23,923.20) will normally be required to be held in escrow by someone other than the lender. A shortcut formula for quick estimating is to add the reduction rates (3%-2%-1%) for a total of 6%, then multiply the loan amount by the total ($58,000 × 6% = $3,480).

2.86 *Is there a late charge provision for VA loans?*

Yes. A late charge may be collected in an amount not in excess of 4% of any installment received more than 15 days after its due date. Specifically, a late charge may not be collected unless the payment is received after the 16th of the month. No late charge will be assessed if the payment is received between the 1st and the 16th. This late charge provision also applies to FHA loans.

2.87 *Does VA have a regulation concerning a charge by the lender for transferring title?*

VA considers a charge of $45 to be reasonable for recording and changing ownership. This is a charge usually incurred with equity or loan assumption sales, and only pertains to what the mortgagee can charge and does not include other fees for the services of an attorney, etc.

2.88 *Who may qualify as a lender of VA loans?*

Any person, firm, association, corporation or governmental agency, either state or federal, may be a VA lender.

2.89 *Are there different types of VA lenders?*

Yes, supervised and non-supervised lenders. A supervised lender is usually confined to federal or state chartered banks and savings and loan institutions that are subject to review by a federal auditing agency. Non-supervised lenders consist mainly of mortgage companies. The lender's automatic authority can only apply to single-family dwelling loans. Furthermore, any VA loan sent to a Regional Office for review cannot later be approved on an automatic basis.

Supervised lenders make automatic loans. Non-supervised lenders must apply for VA approval to act as an automatic lender.

2.90 *Have you purposely avoided the issue of appraisals?*

Yes. To me the term "appraisal" implies a judgement or an opinion. We all would agree judgments and opinions may vary. It has been my experience that one may find variations in appraisals, appraisers, and appraisal policies of the various VA Regional Offices. My comments should not be misinterpreted as implying ambiguity in the VA appraisal system. Simply stated, properties are different, appraisers are different, and appraisal policies from the various VA Regional

Offices differ; however, all attempt to do what is best for the various parts of the country.

The following is a list of some uniform guidelines regarding appraisals that may be found throughout the country:

1. A VA appraisal is known as a CRV.
2. A CRV is valid for six months for existing construction, and 12 months for proposed construction.
3. A CRV may not be extended.
4. With a few exceptions, proposed construction should be prior-approved by a submission of plans and specifications to VA. Periodic inspections will then be made by VA. A few exceptions to the above would be:
   a. if the dwelling has been prior-approved and inspected by FHA;
   b. the new dwelling has been substantially completed for more than 12 months;
   c. the new dwelling will be insured by an acceptable homeowners warranty program or a similar insurance program;
   d. the home is located in a rural area, making routine inspections an impossibility or extremely difficult; and
   e. in certain cases, the VA Regional Office may consider new construction without VA or FHA inspections, if the veteran agrees in writing to waive the VA warranty required of a builder.
5. A VA Regional Office maintains a very small staff of appraisers. Appraisers are used primarily for review of appraisals done by VA designated fee appraisers. A VA designated fee appraiser is a private individual who has satisfactorily met certain VA requirements of character and experience, and is authorized to make appraisals on behalf of the VA.
6. A veteran cannot be charged for the appraisal unless the appraisal is ordered in their name.
7. A requested value is necessary.
8. A VA Regional Office may change or adjust the value or conditions outlined by the VA appraiser.

9. An appraisal cannot be made by a fee appraiser if that individual is an officer, director, trustee, employer or employee of the lender, contractor or vendor, unless the appraisal is for alterations, improvements, or repairs costing less than $2,500.

10. VA will now accept FHA appraisals.

If a VA appraisal is less than requested, Figure 14 "Comparable Sales Chart" can be utilized to request consideration for an increase in value.

2.91 *How should the veteran prepare for a loan application?*

See FHA Question 1.60, page 52.

2.92 *Is there certain language which must be included in a sales contract or an addendum for a sale involving a VA loan?*

Yes. If the contract is written prior to issuance of a VA appraisal, the following amendatory language must be included:

It is expressly agreed that notwithstanding any other provisions of this contract, the Purchaser shall not incur any penalty by forfeiture of earnest money or otherwise or be obligated to complete the purchase of the property described herein if the contract purchase price or cost exceeds the reasonable value of the property established by the VETERANS Administration. The Purchaser shall, however, have that privilege and option of proceeding with the consummation of this contract without regard to the amount of reasonable value established by the VETERANS Administration.

2.93 *If the borrower pays discount points, is it tax deductible?*

Refer to Question 10 page 177, in the tax section.

PART THREE
CONVENTIONAL LENDING

3.1 *What is generally meant by a conventional loan?*

A conventional loan is a real estate mortgage not affiliated with FHA or VA. This is not meant to imply that conventional loans are non-government related. Today many conventional loans are purchased by the Federal Home Loan Mortgage Corporation, a federally-chartered corporation. A conventional loan has simply taken on the meaning of a real estate mortgage other than an FHA or VA mortgage.

3.2 *Is anyone eligible?*

Yes. Occasionally, one may see some restrictions such as income limitations with state or municipal bond-sponsored loans. Of course, as with FHA and VA, one must be an adult or have had their minority removed for title purposes, if applicable, and be acceptable in terms of adequate income and credit requirements.

3.3 *What are conventional loan down payment requirements?*

Normally, a minimum down payment of 5% of the sales price or appraised value, whichever is less, is required. Maximum LTVRs are determined by the lender or the investor (owner of the mortgage).

3.4 *What are the maximum loan amounts?*

The answer to this question is very similar to VA circumstances. The maximum loan is dependent on the investor. FNMA or FHLMC may have maximum loan amounts while a savings and loan institution may purchase or originate a $250,000 conventional loan. As of 1 January 1989 the maximum loan amounts (for FHLMC) per units of a family dwelling will be: $187,600 for a single-family unit; $239,950 for a two-family unit; $290,000 for three-family unit; $360,000 for a four-family unit dwelling. Loan amounts will be 50% higher for Alaska, Guam, and Hawaii.

3.5 *Who are "Fannie Mae" and "Freddie Mac"?*

Believe it or not, they are not gangsters or characters in a comic strip. Fannie Mae stands for Federal National Mortgage Association (FNMA). Freddie Mac is the Federal Home Loan Mortgage Corporation (FHLMC). Fannie Mae is a publicly held corporation that purchases FHA, VA, and conventional mortgages from any financial organization authorized to sell loans to Fannie Mae. Freddie Mac is a federally chartered corporation that primarily purchases conventional mortgages from savings and loans and other financial institutions that are HUD approved.

3.6 *Who sets the interest rates for conventional loans?*

Interest rates are set by the marketplace or the laws of supply and demand. Conventional rates fluctuate freely; therefore, there are no regulated discount points or interest rates. Discount points may be charged as an optional item to reduce the interest rates and can be paid by anyone.

3.7 *What types of conventional loans are available in today's market?*

Strange as it may seem, there is a simple answer to this question. There are two types of conventional loans available in today's market: fixed and adjustable rate.

A fixed-rate loan has the interest rate set for the life of the loan. However, there are a number of variations for fixed rate loans. An Adjustable Rate Mortgage (ARM) has an interest rate that adjusts at specified periods for the life of the loan.

One can find an almost never-ending variation of these two types of mortgages in reference to terms.

3.8 *What could vary with fixed rate loan?*

The following are some possibilities:

1. The loan could amortize or involve only interest payments;
2. There could be level or graduated payments;
3. There could be a GEM provision;
4. Fixed rate loans can have negative amortization;
5. A prepayment penalty may be required;
6. A due-on-sale clause may be required.

3.9 *What terms or conditions could vary with an adjustable rate loan?*

Almost any. For a list of terms and conditions that can vary with ARM loans refer to "Comparing Adjustable Rate Mortgages" on page 125.

3.10 *What is negative amortization?*

In simple terms, negative amortization will result in your loan balance increasing instead of decreasing.

3.11 *How can negative amortization occur?*

Negative amortization can occur if you pay back the loan in level monthly payments that are lower than required to amortize a mortgage based on the note rate. Let me illustrate with a simple example: an individual obtains a $90,000 mortgage at 12-1/2% interest with a provision for payments based on 10% for the first 3 years. The negative amortization will be the sum accumulated by the difference in payments at 12-1/2% and those at 10%, plus in all probability, interest on the interest accrued at the note rate of 12 1/2%.

3.12 *Is there a limit to the extent of negative amortization?*

An industry-wide answer would be 125% of the original loan balance. Keep in mind that conventional loans are not governed comparable to FHA and VA loans. It is extremely important to read and understand the disclosure information that is normally passed out at loan application.

3.13 *Aside from the interest expense caused by negative amortization, are there other costs of negatively amortized loans as compared with regularly amortized loans?*

Yes. Since there is a possibility of a loan balance increasing to 125% of its original amount, a lender will most likely require title insurance equal to 125% of the original mortgage balance. Mortgage insurance premiums for ARM loans with the possibility of negative amortization is more costly when compared to other ARM loans. Mortgage insurance premiums are based on risk. Adjustable-rate loans with the possibility of negative amortization have a higher delinquency ratio when compared to other ARM loans without it.

Of course, if negative amortization occurs the loan balance will increase causing increases in the mortgage and hazard insurance coverage.

3.14 *Is there anything "positive" about negatively amortized loans?*

The major benefit of these loans is their ability to qualify purchasers who would normally have no chance of buying the home of their choice. Since most negatively amortized loans involve adjustable-rate mortgages, there is a possibility that one could purchase a higher priced home than what one could normally quality for, and have an improving interest rate cost by virtue of a lowering index in the future. This scenario plus the possibility of higher priced homes in the future and increasing family incomes is what lures most purchasers into negatively amortized loans. Is this type of thinking bad? Only the future will tell. Negatively amortized loans are a risk, but just as one can pull down the lever of a "one-arm bandit" in Las Vegas, one could have the following things occur: (a) loan qualification as opposed to rejection; (b) lower interest rates in the future through an adjustable-rate mortgage; (c) paper equity created by increasing value of the home; and (d) increasing family income in the future. If all of these images appear on the screen, then it's jackpot!

One final point: since there is no prepayment penalty with most of these mortgages, one can avoid negative amortization by prepaying in an amount equal to the negative amortization.

3.15 *What is private mortgage insurance?*

Commonly referred to as PMI, private mortgage insurance insures a portion of the loan against default. The amount insured depends upon the type of mortgage and the LVTR. For example, a fixed-rate loan based on a 95% LTVR could be insured on a 25% coverage basis and a 90% loan on a 20% coverage basis. This means that a purchaser's down payment plus the mortgage insurance will reduce the lender's risk down to approximately 70%.

3.16 *What does private mortgage insurance cost and how is it paid?*

The cost of PMI depends on the coverage required, type of mortgage, and the premium plan selected. Premium plans offered are usually an annual plan that is paid on a monthly basis, or a single premium plan that can be paid for a varying number of years.

3.17 *Is any part of the PMI premium refundable if there is early termination of the mortgage?*

Any premium refund will depend upon the date of loan termination and the PMI company. There are refunds available in certain situations. Due to the difference in the initial cost, a conventional mortgage premium refund will not be as high as compared to the FHA one-time premium. If one borrows the FHA one-time premium, the initial and final cost is 3.8% of the loan amount as compared to an initial cost of approximately .65% plus 1/4 of 1% per month for a 90% fixed-rate conventional loan.

3.18 *Do PMI premiums continue for the life of the loan?*

Many people assume that the premiums will automatically discontinue once the loan is amortized down to a loan-to-value ratio for which a lender does not require PMI coverage, such as 80% or less. This is an erroneous assumption. Any discontinuance of PMI will depend mostly on the investor's (owner of the mortgage) requirements and the payment record of the mortgagor. What seems surprising is that (based on my experience with the public), most applicants do not ask this question and are generally uninformed about PMI.

California has a new law about notification of when the PMI can be cancelled (Chapter 569, Laws of 1988).

3.19 *What is note rate or accrual rate?*

Note rate is the true rate of interest. The term "note rate" can be traced to the interest rate stated on the mortgage note or a similar type of instrument. "Accrual rate" is another term used to express what the term note rate means, the true interest rate or the rate of interest being accrued on the mortgage.

3.20 *What is a payment rate?*

A payment rate is one which corresponds to the actual payment, exclusive of any escrow funds for items such as taxes, insurance, association dues, etc.. A payment rate of 10% can be translated into dollars and cents by looking up the monthly principal and interest payment required for a 30-year amortized loan at 10% interest. Note that the payment rate does not indicate positive or negative amortization. The payment rate is merely an index expressed in an interest rate comparable to an amortized loan.

3.21 *Will negative amortization always occur if the payment rate is lower than the note rate?*

Usually, but not always. A growing equity mortgage could have an escrow account established by front-end discounts and annual increases in the monthly payments, so that monthly deductions for the escrow account could prevent negative amortization.

A 15-year fixed-rate mortgage requiring a yield of 15% could have a payment rate of 10% and not incur negative amortization. Here is how it can be done: A loan amount of $80,000 would require a discount or a buydown cost of 3.340% or $2,672 and require an annual monthly payment increase of 7-1/2% for 7 years. The first-year monthly payment would be $859.68; in year 2 the monthly principal and interest would increase 7-1/2% to $924.16, and the annual monthly increase would continue through year 7, then level out for the remaining term, so that complete amortization of the loan would occur in 15 years with no negative amortization at any time during the life of the loan. The discounts and 7-1/2%

116

annual monthly payment increase are placed in an escrow account. Funds in the escrow account are used to supplement the monthly payments as required in preventing negative amortization.

3.22 *Is "deferred interest" the same as negative amortization?*

Deferred interest is unpaid interest. It is negative amortization if added back to the principal; it is not, if treated as a separate obligation.

3.23 *Are there different types of deferred interest?*

Yes, deferred interest may be interest bearing or non-interest bearing.

3.24 *What is an index?*

An index is the benchmark used to adjust the interest rate at specified times in the future. For example, a one year adjustable rate mortgage may have a one-year Treasury bill as the index. If the one-year T-bill is the index, each yearly adjustment period of the rate will involve the price of a one year Treasury bill and will usually be a price determined by a weekly or monthly average over a specified time period. Refer to Figure 14 on pages 345-348 for indices most often used for adjustable rate loans. A history of the index will help determine what it may do in the future.

3.25 *What is a margin?*

One could answer by saying a margin is the lender's profit. Margin is what is added to the index to determine the interest rate for adjustable rate loans. Example: Assuming the index is 10% and the margin is 2.5%, the rate would be 12.5%. One word of caution: do not assume that the lower the margin, the lower the lender's profit. A lender may charge a low margin, but have a high measure for an index or have shorter adjustment periods. Adjustable-rate mortgages must be looked at in their entirety; what a lender gives on one feature may be more than taken back by another.

3.26 *What is a payment cap?*

A payment cap is a limit to the increase or decrease of the monthly principal and interest payments. For example,

117

monthly principal and interest payments will remain the same for the first three years, then increase by 10% in years four and five. A payment plan such as described above would work like this: assuming $1,000 per month for principal and interest, the monthly principal and interest payments for the first three years would be $1,000, year four would be $1,100, and year five would be $1,210.

3.27 *Will payment caps prevent negative amortization?*

No. Payment caps will normally create negative amortization, because these caps merely control or limit the increase or decrease in monthly payments. Rate caps prevent negative amortization.

3.28 *What are "rate caps?"*

Rate caps limit the increase or decrease in the interest rate of the mortgage. There can be rate caps for each adjustment period and rate caps for the life of the loan.

Assume an initial rate of 7%, annual rate caps of 2%, a lifetime cap of 5%, a margin of 2.75%, the one-year T-bill as the index and the T-bill is 6.5%. Assuming the T-bill rate in the second year is 7.5%, the new rate should be 10.25% (the total of the index plus the margin) but the rate is 9% because of the 2% cap limitation. Assuming a T-bill rate of 8.5% in the third year, the new rate should be 11.25 (8.5 + 2.75), but the rate is 11% because of the 2% cap. Assuming a T-bill rate of 9.5% in the fourth year, the rate should be 12.25%, but the rate is capped at 12% because of the 5% lifetime cap. Assuming a T-bill rate of 7% in the fifth year, the rate should be 9.75%, but it is 10% because of the 2% cap in the upward or downward adjustment in the rate.

The following offers a summary of the above numbers:

INDEX

Year	Rate	Margin	Rate + Margin	Rate
1	6.5%	2.75	9.25%	7%
2	7.5%	2.75	10.25%	9%
3	8.5%	2.75	11.25%	11%
4	9.5%	2.75	12.25%	12%
5	7.0%	2.75	9.75%	10%

3.29 *Why are interest rates lower on adjustable rate mortgages in comparison to fixed rate mortgages?*

An ARM loan transfers risk from the lender to the borrower. The risk comes when a lender attempts to match a fixed rate of interest received against a fluctuating interest paid for short-term money supplies. On a fixed rate mortgage the interest is set for the life of the loan. But, the lender uses short-term funds to fund a long-term investment such as a mortgage. The short-term funds come in the form of savings accounts and CDs. Since the interest received on a ARM loan can be adjusted, it becomes a safer investment for the lender. The lender is better able to match up interest received against interest paid for the use of the money. Fixed-rate lenders especially need the secondary mortgage market in selling the fixed-rate loans as fast as they are made.

3.30 *What is a teaser rate?*

A teaser rate is a secondary marketing term meaning a low initial rate on an adjustable rate mortgage. The low rate is used to attract or "tease" the borrower into accepting an ARM mortgage. Some lenders are very anxious to make ARM loans. Lenders will sometimes offer a very low rate for the first year, in hopes that the public will accept ARM loans and the rates can go up as adjustments are made.

3.31 *What is a start rate?*

The rate of interest for the initial period of an adjustable rate mortgage.

3.32 *What is a discounted rate?*

An initial interest rate for an adjustable rate mortgage that is lower than the index and the margin. The terms: discounted rate, start rate, and teaser rate can refer to the same rate.

3.33 *What is meant by payment shock?*

This term refers to a large increase in the monthly payment as a result of an adjustment period. Often times payment shock will occur with ARM loans that offer teaser or discounted rates without a rate cap.

3.34 *What is a conversion feature?*

Some ARM loans advertise an option of converting from an adjustable-rate loan to a fixed-rate loan, this option is referred to as a conversion feature. A conversion feature sounds like an answer to a prayer, but it can be an illusion. Before concluding that you can offset that risks of an ARM loan by simply getting out of it with a conversion feature you should check of the following points.

1. Is there a prepayment penalty at any time in the life of the loan?
2. Is there a charge for the conversion? If so, how much?
3. What is the formula for determining the fixed rate?

Some conversation formulas result in fixed rates that are higher then what other lenders in your area are offering. If the conversation formula results in a rate that is too high, your only alternatives may be: to swallow and pay it, to stick it out with the present ARM loan, or to refinance the loan with a new fixed-rate loan. Refinancing usually costs thousands of dollars. Many times the fixed rate at conversion is higher than a new fixed-rate loan offered by your own lender or other lenders. As noted earlier, ARM loans are less risky to the lender than fixed-rate loans. If the fixed rate at time of conversion of an ARM loan is very compatible to a new fixed-rate loan, then the lender may have originated an adjustable-rate mortgage that will probably convert into a fixed-rate loan. If the answers to the above questions and considerations are negative, then one should consider the "convertible" feature as having no value and being used for the same purpose as "teaser rates."

3.35 *Buydowns are frequently used in advertisements; what are they?*

Buydowns are normally used by builders and even lenders to attract the consumer. How many times have we all seen or heard advertisements of 7% or 8% interest or a 3-2-1 buydown?

A buydown plan involves a party "buying-down" the interest rate on either a temporary or a permanent basis.

3.36 *How does a temporary buydown work?*

The previous answer mentioned a 3-2-1 buydown; assuming a rate of 12%, a 3-2-1 buydown would result in a rate of 9% for the first year, 10% for the second year, 11% in the third year, and 12% in the fourth and remaining year.

3.37 *How do you calculate the cost of a temporary buydown?*

In the above example of a 3-2-1 buydown, the cost could be calculated in three ways:

1. The addition of 3+2+1 equaling a 6-point discount;
2. The total difference in the monthly principal and interest payments at 9%,10%, and 11% as compared to 12%;
3. A discount on the buydown for what is in effect prepaid interest. Example: A lender could give a 1.5% discount on a 3-2-1 buydown, making the total cost 4.5 percentage points instead of 6.

3.38 *How does a permanent buydown work?*

A permanent buydown is costly. The rate is brought down for the life of the loan by paying additional discount points. For example, FHA, VA or conventional loan quotes might contain the following information: 13.5% with a 1% discount, 13% with 3% discount, or 12.5% with a 6% discount.

3.39 *Can an adjustable rate mortgage be "bought-down" on a temporary or on a permanent basis?*

Yes, A temporary buydown can be calculated as in the answer to Question 3.37. A permanent buydown would involve buying down the margin for the life of the loan, which would involve calculation by basic yield requirements such as in the preceding answer.

3.40 *Do all conventional loans have due-on-sale clauses?*

The due-on-sale clause began to take on significant notoriety in the credit crunch of 1973 and 1974. During those years conventional loans (in my opinion) changed in two respects— nearly all began to add the due-on-sale clause and delete a prepayment penalty. For an explanation of due-on-sale, refer to FHA, Question 1.4, page 3.

121

3.41 *How can the due-on-sale clause affect the assumability of an adjustable-rate mortgage in terms of rate?*

Again, the nasty due-on-sale clause appears. Most people erroneously believe that since an adjustable rate changes with the influences of the market, its contents in terms of index and margin remain intact for the life of the loan. This is true for some adjustable rate mortgages, but false for those that have language in the due-on-sale clause which empowers the lender with the right to change the margin and/or index when the subject property is sold. There is a wise saying which goes like this: "everything that will change or can change in reference to your mortgage is found in the Deed of Trust" (or similar instrument for your state). Read the Deed of Trust and Disclosure Statement on all conventional mortgages. The due-on-sale clause is very powerful; in essence, this clause can mean that everything you and the lender agree upon will remain the same as long as you own the property.

3.42 *What is a typical assumption fee?*

Conventional loans have no typical transfer fee. If a conventional loan has a due-on-sale clause, the transfer fee could be comparable to an origination or application fee for a new loan (1 or 2% of the loan amount). An assumption of a conventional loan with a due-on-sale clause usually involves reprocessing the loan or obtaining the same documents as those required for a new loan origination.

3.43 *Are there ways of avoiding the due-on-sale clause?*

This author has read many answers to this question, and in my opinion, all involve substantial risk. The due-on-sale clause is so prevalent in all conventional mortgages in today's market, that (in my opinion) the only way to avoid one with an interest rate risk is to obtain an FHA or VA mortgage.

3.44 *Is there a checklist for preparation of a conventional loan applications?*

Yes; see answer to FHA Question 1.60, page 52.

3.45 *What are some general guidelines for loan approval, and how do the restraints compare to FHA and VA loans?*

In general, it is somewhat more difficult to qualify for most conventional loans as compared to the same rate and terms of an FHA or VA loan. The credit ratings are scrutinized very carefully, and there is usually not much allowance for late payments. The income guidelines usually fall into a pattern of no more than 25 to 28% of an applicant's monthly gross income spent on housing expense or PITI and no more than 33 to 36% allowed for housing expense, plus the monthly payments for obligations which have a duration of 10 months or more. Although (in my opinion) conventional guidelines are much simpler and concrete as compared to FHA and VA, it is interesting to note that even though both FHA and VA have some type of percentage guidelines regarding income vs. debt, both agencies will look at the total family income in relationship to the size of the family, whereas conventional loans usually just look at the percentages. In my opinion, this can be somewhat unfair for applicants with child support payments who have the obligation counted as a debt vs. applicants who have children, yet need not be concerned because they are not restricted by any written guidelines to the cost of dependents applied as a debit.

3.46 *If the borrower pays discount points, is it tax deductible?*
Refer to Question 10, page 177, in the tax section.

3.47 *Is there a list of underwriting guidelines for conventional loans?*

A list of underwriting guidelines for conventional loans will be inaccurate. Any investor can write their own guidelines for a conventional loan. I can, however, furnish a general guideline for FNMA and FHLMC. Together, FNMA and FHLMC comprise the largest purchasing group for conventional residential loans in the world. These two corporations (Fannie and Freddie) have such an impact on the lending industry that loans not intended for a later sale to these two giants will probably be underwritten in conformity to their guidelines. It should be noted that the guidelines listed below may differ for a lender who has negotiated a special commitment with Fannie or Freddie. The following is a list of general underwriting guidelines for Fannie Mae and Freddie Mac.

1. The borrower must pay any initial prepaid or escrow items.
2. Buyer's closing cost, buydown fees and discounts paid by a seller will be limited in relationship to the type of loan in question and the LTVR. The limitation is a percentage of the sales price or appraised value, whichever is lesser.
    a. For fixed rate loans with a LTV ratio of more than 90%, the seller cannot pay more than 3%.
    b. Fixed rate loans with a LTV ratio of 90% or less will be limited to 6%.
    c. An adjustable rate mortgage of 90% LTV ratio or less will be limited to 6%.
3. If the limits described above are exceeded, the amount of excess will be viewed as a sales concession and therefore will be deducted from the lower of sales price or appraised value in determining the maximum loan amount.
4. Buydowns for adjustable rate mortgages are not allowed.
5. The maximum LTVR for an adjustable-rate mortgage (ARM) will be 90%.
6. Qualifying ratios for fixed rate loans should be 25-28% and 35-38%, exceptions may be possible for excellent applicants—check with your lender.
7. Co-borrowers will be required to take title and occupy the property if the LTV ratio is greater than 90%. For LTV ratio of 90% or less, the co-borrowers do not have to occupy the property, but they must take title and be a family member.
8. Gifts for settlement requirements are acceptable from family members provided certain conditions are met. There must be verification that a donor has the money to give and the funds must be verified in the applicant's account. Gift letters will not be allowed for 95% loans.

PART FOUR
COMPARING ADJUSTABLE RATE MORTGAGES

U se the following checklist to make a comparison of Adjustable Rate Mortgages. I recommend you first read questions about ARM loans in the Conventional section before using the checklist below. You should also look at a "worst case" scenario prepared by your lender.

	Mortgage A	Mortgage B	Wins (A or B)
Start Rate			
Fully Indexed Rate (Index + Margin)	_____	_____	_____
Initial Monthly Payment	_____	_____	_____
Fully Indexed Payment (Index + Margin)	_____	_____	_____
Current Index Rate	_____	_____	_____
Margin	_____	_____	_____
Adjustment Period	_____	_____	_____
Type of Index	_____	_____	_____
If Index is different; which is less volatile? (refer to page 344-347)	_____	_____	_____

PART FOUR

	Mortgage A	Mortgage B	Wins (A or B)
Method used for Adjustments i.e., monthly or weekly average?	_____	_____	_____
Discounted Rate Period	_____	_____	_____
Rate Cap per Adjustment	_____	_____	_____
Life Time Rate Cap	_____	_____	_____
Cost of Buydowns	_____	_____	_____
Is Buydown Short Term or Permanent?	_____	_____	_____
Cost of Mortgage Insurance	_____	_____	_____
Cost of Title Insurance	_____	_____	_____

If ARM has a Conversion Feature, what would rate be today?

	Mortgage A	Mortgage B	Wins (A or B)
Cost for conversion	_____	_____	_____
Prepayment Feature	_____	_____	_____
Closing Costs	_____	_____	_____
Points	_____	_____	_____
Assumable?	_____	_____	_____
Can Terms change on Assumption?	_____	_____	_____
Negative Amortization	_____	_____	_____

For ARM loans with the possibility of Negative Amortization:

	Mortgage A	Mortgage B	Wins (A or B)
Payment Caps	_____	_____	_____
Cap for Negative Amortization	_____	_____	_____
If deferred interest involved, does it accumulate on a interest or non-interest bearing bases?	_____	_____	_____
Special Requirements for Mortgage, Title, Hazard Insurance	_____	_____	_____

Amount of "Wins" by: A_____ B_____

126

PREPAYING A
MORTGAGE

In the past two years, I have had much experience in teaching real estate finance. The time spent in teaching has proven to be very valuable in judging what people think they know about real estate finance and comparing it to what they do know. When I ask students if they understand prepayment of a mortgage, even the novices are quick to answer yes. I have discovered, however, whenever I tell a true story involving prepayment of mortgage, even the seasoned real estate professionals begin to rapidly take down notes and the class becomes very active with questions. I believe most people know about prepaying a mortgage, but the steps in the process are interesting to everyone.

I will now write about prepaying a mortgage, based on a true story which supplies several lessons about the subject. In 1982, an old college friend approached me about an investment opportunity. Pat said, "Albert there is a dentist I know who wants to sell me two duplexes. I believe the duplexes can be bought at a bargain, and the seller will help with the financing by carrying a second mortgage. My problem is lack of funds to buy both duplexes. If you will make the analysis of the investment, arrange the best terms, negotiate the best price and handle all the paper work, you can buy one of the duplexes."

I checked out the property, talked to the seller who was a dentist, and verified what Pat had told me was true. The dentist was in a hurry to sell, did not want to work with a real estate agent, and offered flexible terms. I offered a low price with terms providing for a $5,000 downpayment, assumption of an existing 7% first mortgage, and had the seller finance the balance of the purchase with a second mortgage. The seller accepted my offer.

I confessed to my friend, Pat, I was also short of cash and couldn't come up with the cash downpayment required. With Pat's permission, I asked a friend to become my partner on the condition of providing all the cash required. The sales price of each duplex was $19,500, we assumed a first mortgage with an outstanding balance of $8,956, the seller carried back a second mortgage for $5,543, with minor closing cost incurred. The required investment was $5,214—all of which my partner paid.

Not only was the property slightly under priced, the rent was also below market. The duplex was very small; a total of 900 square feet. On each side there was one bedroom, one bath, and a small kitchen. The property was in need of repairs and routine maintenance. In the first sixty days we spent money on basic paint up, fix up, and clean up requirements. Upon completion of the work, we increased the rent from $98 per side to $125 per side.

The increase in the rent gave us extra cash flow. At first I used the money to offset bills from the renovation. After paying all repair bills, I began to prepay the second mortgage. I'll never forget the phone call from the dentist (the seller) when he received the first check with prepayments. Dr. Smith was upset and thought I was deliberately attempting to eliminate him from receiving thousands of dollars in interest. I can still remember a statement Dr. Smith made, "so what you are saying is that you are refusing to pay the interest due me." I calmly told Dr. Smith, if the mortgage does not have a clause preventing prepayment, and I had made sure it didn't, I had the right to prepay at any time provided the mortgage was current. I tried to explain prepaying over the phone, but my attempts were to no avail. Dr. Smith consented to a meeting at his office for the purposes of clarifying the subject. At the meeting, I took out the amortization schedule of the second mortgage and I began explaining how prepayment occurs provided the required payment of principal and interest is paid each month. If the required P&I payment is made, I then could pay additional payments *without* interest.

The loan was originated at a 13% interest rate with payments of $70.14 per month based on a 15 year amortization, and there was a balloon payment at the end of 10 years. The following is a part of the amortization schedule:

Pay #	Interest	Principal	Balance
1	$60.05	$10.09	$5,533.07
2	59.94	10.20	5,522.87
3	59.83	10.31	5,512.56
4	59.72	10.42	5,502.14
5	59.61	10.53	5,491.61
6	59.49	10.65	5,480.96
7	59.38	10.76	5,470.20
8	59.26	10.88	5,459.32
9	59.14	11.00	5,448.32
10	59.02	11.12	5,437.20
11	58.90	11.24	5,425.96
12	58.78	11.36	5,414.60
13	58.66	11.48	5,403.12
14	58.53	11.61	5,391.51
15	58.41	11.73	5,379.78
16	58.28	11.86	5,367.92
17	58.15	11.99	5,355.93
18	58.02	12.12	5,343.81
19	57.89	12.25	5,331.56

If you are not familiar with an amortization schedule, please note that the numbers in the left hand column represent the number of months, and the total of principal and interest for each month will equal $70.14. As previously stated, in the beginning I used the extra cash flow to pay renovation bills, then I began to prepay the mortgage. Beginning with the

10th payment, I made a prepayment equal to the principal portion for the next three payments. My check totaled $104.59 and had a notation that it was for payment #'s 11, 12, 13, and 14. The amount of $104.59 was the sum of the principal and interest due for the month, $70.14, plus the principal payments of $11.36, $11.48, $11.61 for payments #'s 12, 13, and 14. Dr. Smith thought my check should have totaled $280.56, which is the monthly payment of $70.14 multiplied by 4 payments. While we looked at the amortization schedule, I showed Dr. Smith how the correct payment was $104.59 and I was not cheating him out of any interest. As noted in the definition of monthly amortization, a mortgagor owes interest, in my case 13%, of the outstanding balance at the time of each required payment. The outstanding balance after payment #10 was $5,437.20. If you take 13% interest on the outstanding balance, you will get $706.84, if you divide that sum by 12 months you will get $58.90, which is the required interest on payment #11. I explained that as long as the required interest is paid on the outstanding monthly balance, there was no other required interest due. Furthermore, if the mortgage did not have a clause prohibiting prepayment, the mortgagor (me) could prepay as much as desired. Dr. Smith said, "I see what you are saying, but I want to run this by my attorney." The next month I sent a check in the amount of $106.11 with a notation stating: payments #'s 15, 16, 17,and 18. Dr. Smith cashed the check without complaint.

The lessons learned from the story:

1. Financing is the *key* to real estate. Knowledge of financing can make "deals" work, and knowledge can help earn money. Eventually we increased the rent to $150 per side and I began to pay 5 payments at one time. The second mortgage was paid off in 1985, three years after we began making payments and seven years before the balloon payment was due. For a -0- cash investment, I received tax benefits from owning half of the duplex, and my net worth or equity in the investment was ever increasing. We acquired the property for $19,500, six years later I sold

my interest to my partner based on a sales price of $40,000.

2. When people ask you, "does prepaying a loan come off the "back end" or the "front end?" You now know how to answer their question; prepayment comes off the outstanding balance.

3. You can save thousands of dollars by prepaying a mortgage, particularly in the early years since most of the payment goes to interest and not to principal.

4. You now know how to calculate your prepayment according to an amortization schedule. If the mortgage does not have a prepayment penalty clause, you can structure the term to fit whatever amortization you can afford. For example, if you have a 30 year mortgage and you later desire to prepay the loan in 15 years, just have an amortization schedule made based on your outstanding balance with payments required for a 15 year pay off.

5. If you are a mortgagee, never count on receiving the full interest on your mortgage if prepayments can be made. A couple of years after we first met, and after we got to know each other, Dr. Smith told me that part of his objection to my prepayments were related to his divorce settlement. In the settlement, the wife was rewarded the mortgage asset which was described as being worth $11,567.92. The sum for the mortgage asset was determined by taking 120 (10yrs.) payments at $70.14 and adding the balloon payment of $3,151.12. When the prepayments started flowing in, it became obvious to her that she wasn't going to get anywhere near the total promised.

6. *Always* put your payment #'s on your check, and state what #'s are being prepaid. I once read a good suggestion of writing a separate check so you can have clear documentation of prepayments. Putting your payment numbers on the check or writing the prepayment on a separate check is essential if you are dealing with a mortgage company that holds your escrow account. The documentation on your check or

checks will give you proof that the prepayments should go towards reduction of the principal balance and not in a non-interest bearing escrow account for taxes and insurance. I recall a separate incident where I was prepaying a 30 year mortgage on a 15 year basis. I would be ever careful to write each payment # on the check, and then state "for a 15 year amortization." On one occasion, the mortgage company (mortgagee), without being asked, mailed me a 15 year amortization schedule and charged the cost to my escrow account. It is important to make sure the mortgagee understands what you want done with any payment exceeding the required monthly payment.

7. If you are considering a shorter term for a mortgage, you must be careful not to force yourself into a cash flow crunch. You can always prepay a long term 30 year mortgage to suit your ability to repay the loan. However, you cannot extend the term of a short term 15 year mortgage unless you go through the cost of refinancing the mortgage or your lender will allow a recasting of the mortgage at a nominal cost. In my true story, we could prepay the mortgage because of the increase in rents. If the rents had not increased, and had we been tied down to a three year mortgage, the prepayments would have had to come out of our pockets.

8. On a monthly amortized loan, the borrower must always pay the monthly payment on the due date. Prepaying several payments does not entitle the borrower to skip making the next monthly payment on the due date. Prepaying a mortgage allows you to skip payments in terms of making less monthly payments than required, but it does not allow you to skip the time payments are due. For example, at the outset of a 30 year mortgage there are 360 payments. By prepaying, you may only pay 180 payments on a mortgage scheduled for 360 payments. The borrower

is required to always pay the monthly payment on each due date until the mortgage is paid off.

Before deciding to prepaying a mortgage, I urge you to read the section titled "Comparing 15-Year and 30-Year Mortgages."

COMPARING 15-YEAR AND 30-YEAR MORTGAGES

In this section you will learn how to compare fixed rate mortgages with different amortization periods. We will compare a 30-year to a 15-year fixed-rate loan. You must compare "apples to apples, oranges to oranges," which means you should compare a fixed rate loan to a fixed rate loan.

The normal term for adjustable rate loans is 30 years. If, however, you have an ARM loan with a 15 year term or you wish to prepay on a 15 year term and you want to compare the shorter term to a longer term, you can use the information herein to make the comparison. In all cases you must name a rate for your ARM loan. If your ARM loan has a life time cap of 5% or 6%, you could take a worst case scenario and use the highest rate possible for comparison purposes.

For the purposes of illustration, we will assume the following: you need to borrow $80,000, and you have a choice of a 10%, 30-year mortgage with a 2% discount or a 15-year mortgage at a rate of 9.5% with a 1% discount, you plan on owning the property for five years, and the closing costs for the 30-year and 15-year mortgages are the same.

To make the comparison between the two loans, follow the steps outlined below.

1. Compare the total payments made over the five year period. With the 10%, 30-year mortgage, $42,123.44 will be the total of payments. You can arrive at this amount in several ways; by looking at the factor for a 10%, 30-year loan, found in Figure 10 on page 337, or by looking up the monthly payment found on page 235, or by determining the monthly payment with a HP-12c as outlined in the definition of amortization which can be found in the glossary. Of course after you determine the monthly P & I payment of $702.06, you then multiply by 60 payments (5 years).

   With the 9.5%, 15-year loan, the methods of computing the monthly payment are the same. The total of the payments will be $50,122.80 ($835.38 × 60).

   The difference between the total of payments will result in a $7,999.36 savings with a 30-year loan.

2. Let us now consider the difference in equity created by the loan amortization process. Using our Remaining Balance Factors on page 300, we see our 10%, 30-year loan will have a remaining balance of $77,256 at the end of 5 years, which creates a reduction in the outstanding balance of $2,744. We can refer to principal reduction as the creation of equity, since equity results in a lessening of the lien against the property. We can determine the remaining balance by multiplying the factor of 96.57 × 800, by taking 96.57% of the original $80,000 loan balance, or by using a HP-12c as outlined in the definition of amortization which can be found in the glossary.

   With the 9.5%, 15 year loan, the methods of computing the remaining balance are the same. The remaining balance will be $64,560 at the end of 5 years, which will create an equity build up of $15,440.

   The difference in the equity build up is a savings of $12,696 ($15,440 minus $2,744) in favor of the 15-year loan.

3. Assuming you itemize deductions for tax purposes and you are in a tax bracket of 30%, we now must determine the difference in the amount of those

deductions for the two mortgages under consideration.

We can determine the interest paid over the first five year period for the 10% loan by simply subtracting the equity build up from the total payments for five years. Using our figures from (1) and (2) above, the calculation would be: $42,123.44 minus $2,744 which would equal $39,379.44 as interest paid over the five year period. We can also determine the interest paid with a HP-12c, as outlined in the definition of amortization, which can be found in the glossary.

With the 9.5%, 15-year loan, the methods of computing the interest paid are the same. The interest paid would be $34,682.80, ($50,122.80 minus $15,440).

When we compare the interest paid on the two loans we see that the 30-year loan will cost an additional $4,696.64 ($39,379.44 minus $34,682.80). As we can see from the information given in the refinance worksheet found on pages 351-352, the after-tax savings will be $1,408.99 ($4,696.64 × 30%) in favor of the 10%, 30 year mortgage.

4. The next item of consideration is the discount points. You might be asking yourself: "if the seller is paying the points, why does this matter?" Even if the seller is paying the additional 1% discount for the 30-year loan, this item of consideration is an important point because you should attempt to negotiate a sales price adjusted by any savings in discount the seller will receive. Of course, success will depend upon you negotiating this point before the contract is written. However, there is nothing to prevent a contract price from changing after it is written, provided the changes are not viewed as an inducement to buy when the buyer would normally not buy.

Let us assume you will save the $800 difference in points between the two loans by either: paying 1% less in points at the closing (if you are paying the points), or by purchasing the house for $800 less (if the seller is paying the points). The cost savings in favor of the 15-year loan would be $800.

Now we are ready to compare the benefits in terms of savings created by the two loans in question.

	Savings 10%, 30-year loan	Savings 9.5%, 15-year loan
Difference in Payments:	$7,999.36	
Equity build up:		$12,696
Tax savings:	$1,408.99	
Difference in points:		$800
Total savings:	$9,408.35	$13,496

If you can endure the payments of a 15-year mortgage, then the savings are they will grow at a faster pace compared to the 30-year mortgage. To prove this point, look at the Remaining Balance Factors for the two loans at the end of ten years. At the end of ten years, the 10%, 30-year loan will have an outstanding balance equal to 90.94% of its' original balance, compared to 49.72% for the 9.5%, 15 year loan.

Obviously, the longer you pay the mortgage, monetary savings will be greater for a 15-year mortgage. If your goals are to live in your home for more than ten years, to save interest, and to own your home debt free in a relatively short period of time, then the 15-year loan should be your choice. Do not, however, decide for the shorter term mortgage solely on the benefit of saving money.

It is sheer fantasy to think once you have a 30-year mortgage, it must remain a 30-year mortgage. As pointed out in "Prepaying a Mortgage," provided the mortgage is without prohibitive language about prepayments, you may adjust the term of the mortgage according to your ability to repay the loan. You can tailor make a mortgage to suit your ability to pay. Your ability to pay the mortgage may change in the future. You may need the "breathing room" of a 30-year payment versus the mandatory higher payments associated with a 15-year mortgage. Your income may shrink in the future due to changes caused by adverse economic conditions, bad health, going back to school, a change in occupation, etc., you may want to consider the safety of a long term mortgage. Remember, refinancing is expensive.

Another point of consideration is the "the golden rule." Treating others as if you were in their shoes should be considered if your mortgage if you are applying for an FHA or a VA loan. What happens if you suddenly have to sell, and the buyers goals are not the same as yours? The lower monthly payments of a 30-year mortgage may be crucial to a buyer who can assume your loan. There is an old saying about the primary concern of people who buy cars and real estate; "how much down, and how much per month?" You may be thinking the answer is for the buyer to apply for a new loan. Obtaining a new loan compared to assuming a loan is expensive and your existing loan may have a low rate of interest. Remember, in nearly all situations, interest rates on FHA and VA loans do not change when upon loan assumption.

The interest rate environment should affect your decision of a 15-year versus a 30-year mortgage. When rates ran up into the high teens, Americans seemed suddenly to discover that a 15-year term will save thousands of dollars in interest without much of an increase in the monthly payment. An exciting event or discovery seems to have reruns; articles on the benefits of 15-year mortgages appear even in markets with single digit interest rates. A 15-year loan will always involve less interest than a 30-year loan at the same rate of interest. The increase in the payments, however, are different at various rates. Monthly payments on 15-year mortgages with high interest rates do not increase as much as when compared to 30 year mortgages at the same rates. For example, monthly payments on a 15-year loan at a 17% are only about 8% higher than monthly payments on a 30-year term. Monthly payments on an $80,000 loan for 30 years at a 17% rate are $1,140.55 and on a 15-year term the monthly payments are $1,231.21 which is only a 7.95% increase. If you compare the same loan at an interest rate of 9.5% the increase is a whopping 24.18%! The monthly payment on a 30-year mortgage at a 9.5% rate will be $672.69, on a 15-year term the monthly payment climbs to $835.38. You will save thousands of dollars on a short-term home mortgage, but the interest rate will determine the sacrifice.

If you choose a shorter-term mortgage you should consider the alternative use of the extra money required for the higher monthly payments. Put in simple terms, can you earn a higher return of interest for your money than what you pay on your mortgage. The alternative investment principal is also true for prepaying a mortgage. If rate of interest on a mortgage is 10%, can you earn more than 10% interest on the extra money required for a short term mortgage or prepayment of a mortgage. If you can earn more than a 10% return on your money in an investment, you should consider investing your money rather than using it to pay higher payments associated with a short term mortgage or using the money to prepay the loan. On the other hand, if your investments earn you less than 10% interest than choosing a short term loan or prepaying the mortgage would be wise.

Some people argue against choosing a 15-year mortgage and prepaying a mortgage because the equity will grow too fast and would therefore hurt an equity sale in the future. For one to decide against a 15-year loan or prepaying the mortgage solely on the bases of the equity becoming too great would be like one choosing a loan with the highest interest rate because of the greater tax deduction. Both decisions will have the same result; you will shoot yourself in the foot.

Before choosing a 15-year mortgage over a 30-year mortgage, you should consider the following points:

1. Set your financial goals for the home you are purchasing and estimate the number of years you will own the home.
2. Determine the monetary savings of the two mortgages.
3. It is nearly all cases, it is "sheer fantasy" to think you must repay a 30-year loan over a 30-year period.

4. Refinancing is expensive. If ability to repay changes and you cannot stand the "heat" associated with 15-year payments, your only alternative may be refinancing.
5. If the loan you are considering is assumable without escalating the interest rate, will the loan be attractive to others if you must sell?
6. Is the interest rate environment correct? It is less expensive to have a 15-year loan at higher rates of interest.
7. Consider an alternative investment for the extra money required to pay higher monthly payments. This advice also pertains to prepayment of a mortgage.

Some of you may wondering how I would choose between a 15- and a 30-year mortgage? For my own home, I usually choose a 30-year loan and prepay on a 15-year basis.

PROPERTY INSPECTION CHECKLIST

This checklist is intended to equip the layman with a guide for a practical inspection of a residential dwelling. The information it contains will also help a professional understand some of the things an appraiser will look for in the course of making an appraisal for FHA or VA. Although all information in this checklist will apply to almost any dwelling, it should be noted that the author is basing the information on an average-size house constructed of average quality workmanship and materials.

EXTERIOR INSPECTION

Begin by walking completely around the house, checking the condition of the roof gutters, and downspouts, the exterior veneer (wood siding, brick, etc.), paint, caulking, foundation, and drainage.

1. Roofs. The average life of a roof is based on the material used. Asphalt roofs will last 15 to 20 years; wood shingles, 30 to 35 years; and slate should last 40 or more years. Asphalt roofs that have granules missing in spots and shingles that are beginning to buckle will soon need replacing. In most cases, a good pair of binoculars will uncover these tell-tale signs as well as would climbing up on the roof. Look for inadequate flashing and tar around chimneys and vent pipes. Check for sags in the roof which can be a sign of problems with the framing structure supporting the roof. If there are any valleys in the roof, check for signs of patching caused by roof leaks. Ask the owner about roof leaks and check for any water stain marks on the ceiling. If a home has more than three layers of roofing, it is most likely in violation of a housing code. Normally FHA, VA, and housing codes stipulate that no more than three layers of roofing can be applied to a home. If you encounter a house that already has three layers of roofing, you must keep in mind the cost of having the old layer removed and hauled away before a new layer can be installed.

2. Gutters and Downspouts. Gutters should be free of rust, tightly secured to the structure, and slanted enough so that water will drain and not become stagnant. Downspouts should not empty at the base of the foundation wall but should have either splash blocks or elbow extensions to prevent basement leaks and soil erosion from the foundation walls and flower and shrub beds.

3. Foundation Walls. Check foundation walls for bowing, crumbling, and cracks. If any of these signs appear there could be serious structure problems, minor hairline cracks in the masonry wall of the foundation being a possible exception. For houses that are built on a conventional foundation (one that is not on a concrete slab), check to see if there are adequate foundation vents and an access door. You will also want to check to see what is used to cover the vents in cold weather. Look through the access door and check for any moisture problems and to see if there is a minimum ground clearance of 18 inches. In cold climates, crawl spaces should be insulated.

4. Porches. Check the porches to be sure no wood is resting on the ground. Ideally, wood should be a clearance of at least 6 inches from the ground. If a porch is enclosed down to the ground, be sure it is properly ventilated. Wood porches and decks that are too close to the ground will eventually water rot and will have to be replaced or torn down and eliminated.

5. Painting. Caulking and painting should be checked for more than just adequacy and professional workmanship. Excess caulking around sliding glass doors or windows can be an indication of a persistent problem. While examining the caulking, make sure there is adequate weather stripping. Paint that is peeling or blistered can be a sign of an inferior job due to lack of preparation, poor quality paint, or paint applied during inclement weather conditions. Curling paint can indicate a moisture problem within the walls that repainting won't resolve. Improper insulation in walls can cause paint to peel and even can cause mold on interior walls.

Houses built before 1978 (per FHA regulations) should be checked for lead-based paint. Applicable surfaces include all interior and exterior surfaces regardless of height. Lead-based paint is hazardous to your health and if found should be either washed, sanded, scraped, or wire-brushed and then replaced with two coats of non-lead based paint. Flakes from lead-based paint can get into the hands of children. The flakes have a sweet taste, similar to sweet pickles, and if eaten they can cause permanent brain damage.

6. Termites. You should check for signs of termites, and never buy without first reading a current termite clearance report.

7. Siding. The exterior veneer should be checked for its condition and the original workmanship involved in the installation. Wood siding and windows should be checked for rotting and all wood should be at least 6 to 8 inches above the ground as a precautionary measure against termite infestation and water rot. Veneer such as brick or stone should be checked for tuck-pointing and for cracks. Tuck-pointing is a term indicating the need to fill in the gaps between the brick or stone due to insufficient mortar which is normally caused by erosion. Excessive cracking in the brick, stone, or stucco can indicate settling or foundation problems.

145

8. Drainage. For ideal drainage, every house would be built on the top of a hill. Since this is not always possible, you should check all around to see that the earth slopes away from the house. If the house is located in a flood zone this fact should be disclosed to you, but always be sure to ask. If FHA, VA, or conventional financing is involved, flood insurance will be required for property in a flood zone.

INTERIOR

1. Windows and Doors. Check to see that all windows and doors work properly. Check to see if all door and window handles are tight and be sure all door and window locks are in good working condition. Doors should swing open and shut easily and interior doors should have an even gap at the bottom, and not be higher at one end than the other.

2. Electrical System. Examine the electrical service to the house. Normally the minimum requirement is a 60-amp, 3-wire, 240-volt service. Houses with central heating and air-conditioning need a minimum of 100-150 amps. The utility meter will state the volt and wire service. On the utility meter look for something such as 240V, 3W, which means 240-volt, 3-wire service. FHA will not accept a 120-volt, 2-wire service. Check the electrical panel to determine the amp service available. An electrical panel can be a clue to wiring problems. Place your hand on the panel cover. If it is extremely warm, this could be a sign of a shortage or an overload.

If you are concerned about aluminum wiring, simply take off a light switch cover plate and observe the metal used for wiring.

All light switches and receptacles should be checked for adequacy and to assure that they are secured tightly and are in working condition.

3. Heating and Air Conditioning. It usually takes a skilled technician to give an accurate opinion on the adequacy and performance of heating and air-conditioning systems. You should turn the unit on and check the heating and cooling and listen for any unusual sounds coming from the units. Of course, you will want to see the past utility bills or check with the local utility company for a history of utility bills for the house in question.

4. Hot Water Tank. Check the hot water tank for age and capacity. Hot water tanks should have a minimum capacity of 40 gallons and the normal life- expectancy is 10 years. Signs of future problems will be rust or leaks at the bottom of the tank. Check for a pressure-relief valve and be sure it is on the hot water line. Heating elements and thermostats can be checked for proper operation by filling a bathtub with hot water. An average bathtub filled to within an inch of the overflow drain will contain approximately 35 to 40 gallons of water. If the hot water tank is functioning properly, you should have continuous hot water up to the overflow drain.

5. Plumbing. The plumbing system can be checked in a number of ways. *Water pressure* can be checked by turning the kitchen faucets on full force and then going to the bathroom that is the farthest distance away and turning on the faucets. The result should be a strong flow of water and not a trickle. Check the *condition of the water* by filling the tub and sink to see if the water is clear and not rusty and then notice how fast the water drains. Check the operation of the toilets by dropping a piece of tissue in the bowl and then flushing to see if it drains completely, refills, and shuts off properly. When checking the bathroom, put your foot behind the toilet and exert pressure. If the floor gives, it is most likely rotted because of a water leak from the toilet. Plumbing *leaks* that are in the slab or under a house can be discovered by shutting off all plumbing and then observing the water meter for two to three minutes to verify that there is no water flow. *Water pipes* can be signs of age and past problems. The older houses will have brass, lead, or iron pipes, newer houses will have copper or PVC plastic piping. The type of material used in the plumbing system will indicate the age and if you notice a mixture of pipe materials, it is an indication of plumbing problems that have occurred in the past.

147

6. Kitchen and Bathroom(s) floors should be of a substance that is resistant to moisture. Normal carpeting in either of these rooms is unacceptable to FHA/VA appraisers. All kitchen and bathroom floors should be checked for signs of water-rot. Spacing and layout are important for both kitchen and bathrooms. In the bathroom, check for the relationship of the door to the vanity, the vanity to the toilet, and in general, how each fixture is located relative to the others as well as to other items such as the linen closet. In the kitchen you will want to note if cabinets, counter space, and pantry space are adequate. Any equipment such as the stove vent fan and built-in appliances should be checked for working condition. Cabinet, entry, and pantry doors should be checked to see that they will not interfere with each other or conflict with your use of the kitchen. Lighting in the kitchen should be such that you won't have to work in your own shadow. Paints in the kitchen and bathroom should be enamel or semi-gloss for easy cleaning.

7. Stairway. All stairways with four or more steps should have a handrail installed.

8. Floor. For homes built on a conventional foundation, walk across the floor to check for any give and for squeaks caused by loose flooring. Checking to see if the floors are level can be done by placing a marble on a hard floor.

9. Insulation. Check for insulation in the attic and inquire about its existence in the walls. Insulation in the wall can be identified by removing a light switch plate and probing the sides to discover the presence and type of insulation. If you discover foam insulation, it is advisable to take a sample to the Health Department to determine if the foam contains any harmful chemicals such as formaldehyde.

10. Attic. There must be access to the attic and while you are in the attic you should check for signs of structural problems with rafters and joists and to see if there is adequate ventilation.

11. Basement. If you are thinking of buying a home with a basement, be sure you check for signs of water leakage. Dampness in corners is a sign of moisture problems, and water marks along the base of walls or cabinets indicates that there is or has been some serious water leakage.

12. Radon Gas. A new checklist item is the detection of radon gas in the home. Radon is a gas trapped in a closed space, such as a house. As accumulated trapped gas inside a home, radon is believed to cause lung cancer. Radon comes from the natural breakdown of uranium. It has always been present in nature mainly in rocks containing uranium, granite, shale, phosphate and pitchblende. You can test your home for radon gas by purchasing a charcoal canister that can be bought for $10 to $25. Experts have said that lenders will soon require a home to be tested for radon gas. Some relocation companies are presently requiring homes to be tested for radon gas. The cure for radon gas can be relatively simple and inexpensive. If the house is built on a conventional foundation, the usual cure is to install a vapor proof covering in the crawl space along with a suction system that draws the air out of the area before it gets into the living spaces. The average cost to cure radon gas problems is normally between $200 to $1,000, with many homes being cured for only $100. The Environmental Protection Agency has more information on radon gas, write to: Consumer Information Center, Pueblo, CO. 81009. There are two booklets offered: *A Citizen's Guide to Radon* (item 139T, $1) and *Removal of Radon from Household Water* (item 472T, 50 cents).

This property inspection checklist should give you a good idea as to the condition of the subject property. However, the use of a professional home inspection company is strongly advised as well as a home service agreement. For information on how you can borrow part of the cost of an inspection with an FHA loan, refer to Question 1.57, page 50. For the professional, I recommend the purchase of Don Publication's *Guide to FHA Repair Requirements for Single Family Residence*. This booklet can be purchased for $12.95 with a money-back guarantee by mailing your request to: Don Publications, P.O. Box 4643, Racine, WI 53402.

HOME
MAINTENANCE
SERVICE
AGREEMENTS

Service contracts or agreements for homes are becoming a popular item. Before entering into a contract, you may want these questions answered:

1. *Where is the home office located?*
A local office location is a convenience factor.

2. *How do you get service?*
Companies that have toll-free numbers may not be as attractive as a local contact.

3. *Who performs the service work?*
Many service companies subcontract their work. Companies that have their own technicians may be available.

4. *Who inspects the equipment prior to initiation of a service contract?*
This answer will be a big shock to many homebuyers. Some of your big-name companies use real estate agents to make the home inspections. In my opinion, a home inspection should be done by licensed and bonded technicians who can render

professional evaluations of heating, air-conditioning, plumbing, and electrical systems.

5. *Does the company refuse to pay claims due to pre-existing conditions?*

Most companies will refuse to pay a claim if the repair needed is due to a pre-existing condition—one that was not picked up at the time of inspection.

6. *Does the company offer 24-hour emergency service?*

Most will, but only on a limited basis. Examples would be heating only or heating and plumbing only. Find out what qualifies for an emergency.

7. *Is there a deductible?*

Deductibles can render the contract of no benefit. You will want to avoid high deductibles or deductibles for each call.

8. *Who pays for the cost of repairs?*

Some companies pay all, other companies pay all above $100, others require the homeowner to pay all and then get reimbursed at a later date.

9. *Does the company cover: a) swimming pool, spa? b) boiler heating? c) window air-conditioning units? d) personal appliances?*

You will find the type of coverage will vary.

10. *Does the company offer total replacement of equipment that is beyond repair?*

Some companies will; others offer only equal value for worn-out parts.

11. *What is the base price?*

Shop the prices, but remember the services provided.

12. *Is the service contract transferable?*

You will find that most are not.

The home service contract business is a relatively new member of the service industry and it should have a big future. Currently, there are very few states that regulate such companies so be careful in your selection.

Roof Types

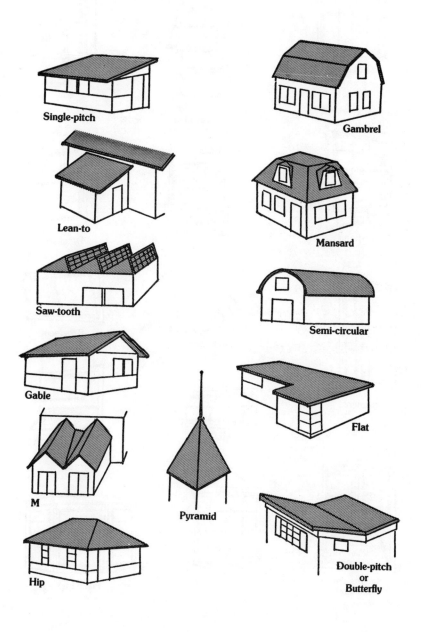

Single-pitch

Lean-to

Saw-tooth

Gable

M

Hip

Gambrel

Mansard

Semi-circular

Flat

Pyramid

Double-pitch
or
Butterfly

Window Types

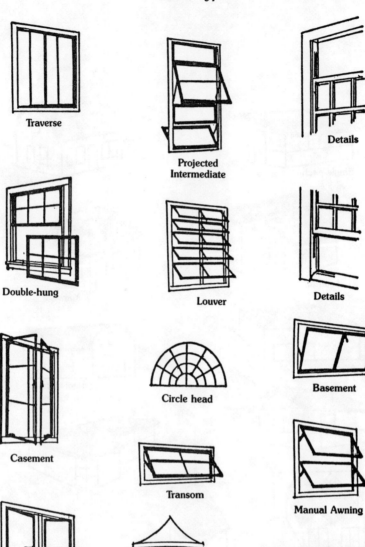

Traverse

Projected Intermediate

Details

Double-hung

Louver

Details

Casement

Circle head

Basement

Transom

Manual Awning

Intermediate Combination

Fixed bow

Fixed bay

Signs and Symbols

The reader will often encounter the following signs and symbols on blueprints and appraisals.

Symbol	Meaning	Symbol	Meaning
∺	geometrical proportion	—W—	water line
⊟	identical with	—G—	gas line
±	plus or minus	—·—·—	center line
∠	angle	—x—x—	fence line
∟	right angle	L^s	lengths
⸦ or ⟩	greater than	L^l	lineal foot
⸧ or ⟨	less than	⌀ 巾	per square foot
⊥	perpendicular	φ	diameter
⌣	difference	℞	plate
∫	integration	℄	center line
⧦	equivalent	P—	direction of pressure
∷	proportion	$\begin{array}{c} A \underline{\quad} A \\ \text{or} \\ \lfloor A \quad A \rfloor \end{array}$	{ indicates cross section of a drawing
∸	difference, excess	▨▨▨▨	{ indicates exposed surface of a section cut
∴	therefore	#	{ pounds after a number / number before a number
∵	because	▱	stadia station
∞	infinity	△	triangulation station
∞	varies as	⊙	transit traverse station
√	radical	⊕	indicates elevation point
°	degree	⊢—3½—⊣	{ dimension line. Number indicates distance between lines.
′	minute or foot	═══⌇═══	{ indicates that a section of a drawing, identical to the sections on either side of the symbol, has been omitted to reduce size.
″	second or inch	◣ 20° 5°	{ indicates dimensions of rise and span of a roof pitch.

ARCHITECTURAL STYLES

Have you ever described a house as a Colonial when it was more accurately described as a Southern Colonial? Have you ever not known what type of architectural style to describe a house? This section may help end your frustration or confusion about the correct style name for a house.

The styles are grouped together by type of design as opposed to alphabetical order. In grouping by design, the reader will be able to look at styles that are similar in design and compare the differences. For example, if you wanted to compare the difference between a Bi-Level and a Split-Level, you will find them next to each other. If the styles were in alphabetical order, several pages would separate Bi-Level from Split-Level. Not surprisingly, when the houses are grouped together by design, they often become grouped together by location in North America. The following is a list of all the styles described.

1. Queen Anne
2. Gothic
3. Eastlake
4. Victorian
5. American Mansard
6. English Tudor
7. English Tudor Ranch
8. Post Modern Victorian
9. Townhouse
10. New England Farm House
11. Cape Cod
12. Dutch Colonial
13. Salt Box Colonial
14. Southern Colonial
16. Williamsburg
17. Williamsburg Georgian
18. Farmhouse Adaption
19. Arcadian Farmhouse

20. Arcadian or Greek Revival
21. French Provincial
22. New Orleans
23. Regency
24. Log Cabin
25. "A" Frame
26. Swiss Chalet
27. Adobe
28. Spanish Ranch
29. Spanish Villa
30. Monterey Architecture

31. Italian Villa
32. California Contemporary
33. California Ranch
34. Earthen Home
35. Bi-Level
36. Split Level
37. Oriental
38. Octagon
39. Penthouse
40. Mobile Home
41. Shotgun

1. Queen Anne. A nineteenth century style home of many surface textures, materials and colors. Other characteristics are: various window designs, multi-stories, irregular in shape, turrets or towers, bay windows, projecting upper stories and much ornate fine detailing.

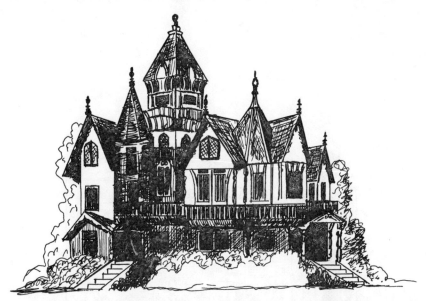

2. Gothic. A nineteenth century style house featuring: steep roofs, much gingerbread molding and trim, many different shapes and angles, ornate windows and doors, exposed framing members and extremely pointed gables.

3. Eastlake. A nineteenth century style home similar to the Queen Anne or Carpenter Gothic. The Eastlake is distinct because of the ornamentation made by the chisel gouge and lathe rather than the scroll saw. The style features a tower or turret, a single covered gable roof and an open front porch. The ornamentation resembles furniture parts.

4. Victorian. A nineteenth century style house with three different designs of window arches. It has symmetrical bays and an entrance way with columns supporting an entablature.

5. American Mansard. A nineteenth century style house mainly distinguished by the mansard roof design. There are dormers protruding through the roof. The style features french doors, much decorative iron work and massive cornice and supporting brackets.

6. English Tudor. English styled home made mostly out of stone. The exterior will feature some stucco, brick, half-timbers and a massive chimney. The house will have a fortress-like appearance, there will be molded stone trim and small leaded casement windows.

7. English Tudor Ranch. Tudor styled one-story home of brick or stone. The home will feature many of the trademarks of the English Tudor such as: stone, stucco, brick, half-timbers, small casement windows and a massive chimney.

8. Post Modern Victorian. This home is massive with many different roof angles, much gingerbread woodwork, arched windows, flat windows, decorative half timbers and a double wide chimney with a decorative cap.

9. Townhouse. Typically a two or more story unit attached to other like-units by a party wall. Most townhouses are in planned unit developments or condominium developments. Theycan also be found in cluster housing, row house, or brownstones.

10. New England Farm House. An Early American style which is usually made of clapboard siding and is box-shaped.

11. Cape Cod. A Colonial style, usually 1-1/2 in story height. The house is small and compact with a single centered front entrance. The entrance usually has one or two windows on each side of the front door and is symmetrical. The chimney is often in the center of the house, and the roof is a steep gable made of shingles. You will often see this style home with a picket fence for adornment.

12. Dutch Colonial. The home is of Early American design featuring a gambrel roof and eaves that flare outward. The chimney is off-center and there are many small pane windows.

13. Salt Box Colonial. An Early American style two-story house which is square or rectangular and features a steep gable roof extending down to the first floor in the rear.

14. Southern Colonial. A two or three-story early American style frame house with a colonnade. The roof extends over the colonnade.

15. Georgian Colonial. Colonial style with Georgian influence.
The house features two chimneys, an arch over the front entrance and decorative brick work

16. Williamsburg. English style house named after houses built in Williamsburg, VA. This house features simple exterior lines, windows with small panes, a hip or gable roof, large and high chimneys and simple front doors. It has symmetrical windows with the front door centered between the windows.

17. Williamsburg Georgian. Williamsburg style with a Georgian influence. The house will have two chimneys, arches and decorative brick work.

18. Farmhouse Adaption. Modern two-story house with wood clapboard siding, a wrap-a-round porch and a country-style door.

19. Arcadian Farmhouse. This house features the "raised cottage" architecture, wide front and rear covered porches, farmhouse-styled railings and plain square columns. The house is usually made out of clapboard siding. There will be shutters on the windows and dormers on the roof.

20. Arcadian or Greek Revival. This home is of deep southern design with columns reflecting a modified Greek Revival style. It is commonly called a "raised cottage." Usually features wide front and rear covered porches and often has dormers on roof.

21. French Provincial. A French style 1 to 2 1/2 story house that has a steep hip roof, usually a chimney in the center of the house and arched windows.

22. New Orleans. This house hugs the ground and has distinctive and varying roof planes. There will be many long windows across the front with shutters that open and close to protect the home from hurricanes. If the house has columns, they will be narrow and round. Dormers will have a French influence, being rounded at the top.

26. Swiss Chalet. A Swiss style gable roof house with much decorative wood work, large glass windows, and a natural wood look.

27. Adobe. A home made of adobe brick with projecting roof beams called "viga."

28. Spanish Ranch. A one-story ranch-style house with decorative arches, wrought iron window guards. This house is often made of stucco or brick.

29. Spanish Villa. A Spanish style house featuring stucco exterior, a tile roof and an arched entry-way.

30. Monterey Architecture. A two-story house, often made of stucco with a balcony across the front made of very plain wood or iron. The roof is usually made of tile.

31. Italian Villa. A massive 2 or 3-story Latin style house of masonry featuring: large overhanging eaves, a heavy cornice line, brackets and decorative iron work. Italian marble is often used for flooring, steps and window seals.

32. California Contemporary. A modern-styled home featuring many large windows, skylights, vaulted ceilings and sloping roof lines. The exterior is usually made of wood and there are many angles and box shapes. Often-times the gable is glassed. Most of these homes have one or more wood decks.

33. California Ranch. A one-story, ground-hugging, usually long house with a low pitched roof. There will be many contemporary styled windows.

34. Earthen Home. The approach to the front of this house is at street level, but the side walls are under the earth and the back of the house comes out to an open wall with clerestory windows for cooling purposes.

35. Bi-Level. A house built on two levels with the entrance being in between both levels. The entryway has a landing with stairs leading to the upper level and another set of stairs leading down to the lower level.

36. Split Level. A post-fifties-style house. The entry level usually consist of the living room, dining room and kitchen. There is a walk up to the bedroom level and a walk down to the den and garage level. The house usually has picture windows at the entry level and contemporary windows at the bedroom level. The garage entrance is at the street level. This style requires a sloping lot.

37. Oriental. This house is typically a long oblong design with a pagoda-styled roof.

38. Octagon. A house built in the shape of an octagon and usually made of wood with a wood shingle roof.

39. Penthouse. An expensive luxury home built atop of a high-rise building.

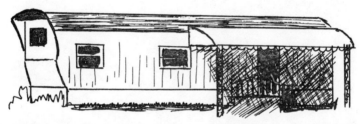

40. Mobile Home. A manufactured home which is delivered to the site and semi-permanently attached. It has a metal roof and metal siding and can be relocated to another site.

41. Shotgun. A wood frame one-story house with the front door opening into the front room. The house usually has three or four rooms stacked behind each other. You can walk from the front to the back going through each room. The back door will be in line with the front door.

QUESTIONS AND ANSWERS CONCERNING INCOME TAX REQUIREMENTS

With Emphasis on Applications to Residential Real Estate Activities

This question-and-answer section is designed to provide accurate and authoritative information in regard to income tax requirements. Most of the questions and answers pertain to real estate. The layman should note that when they read the 1986 tax law this should not be interpreted as to what applied in 1986. The end of the old tax law and the beginning of the new tax law began with the passage of the 1986 Tax Reform Act.

This material has been reviewed by a CPA, but it is published and put on sale with the understanding that the publisher is not engaged in rendering legal, accounting, financial, or other professional service. If expert assistance is required, the services of a competent professional person should be sought. The author wishes to acknowledge the assistance of Walter Lee Davis, Jr., Attorney/CPA, of Johnson City, Tennessee and Gary Howell, CPA, and Dan Tacker, CPA, of Memphis, Tennessee.

1. *Can loses from real estate investments be used to offset income from other sources?*

The *old tax law* allowed real estate expenses in excess of income to be used to offset income from non-real estate activities. The 1986 tax law (the *new tax law*) allows individual taxpayers who actively participate in rental real estate activity and own 10% (by value and for the entire taxable year) or more of rental real estate to use up to $25,000 of losses or credits to offset other income such as wages, interest, dividends, and active business income. Active participation is less stringent than "material participation" which is the requirement for other trades or businesses and requires regular continuous and substantial involvement in the operations. An owner who simply makes significant decisions (approves new tenants, decides on rental terms and approves capital or repair expenses) and provides or arranges to provide services is deemed to be actively participating in the rental property. An owner can have the services of a rental management company and still satisfies the active participation requirement so long as he makes some significant decisions.

Taxpayers who do not actively participate in the decisions concerning rental property can use losses only to offset other passive activity income or to accumulate as an offset to income in future years. Carrybacks are not allowed. The $25,000 maximum amount of passive real estate losses deductible against other income phases out for adjusted gross incomes of $100,000 to $150,000 and phases out for rehabilitation and low-income housing credit for adjusted gross incomes of $200,000 to $250,000. The phase-out rule reduces the $25,000 exception by 50 cents for every dollar of adjusted income over $100,000. The phase-out provisions apply to existing as well as future investment. Although the passive loss limitation is effective for taxable years after 1986, the legislation is phased-in over the next five years for ownership interest acquired on or prior to 22 October 1986. Passive activity losses and credit in excess of the $25,000 limitation would be disallowed according to the following format: in 1987, 35% in 1988, 60% is not allowed; in 1989, 80%; in 1990, 90%; in 1991, and thereafter 100% is disallowed. Investment losses can be used to offset gains from other investments, and they can be carried forward to offset gains from operations or from a sale.

2. *Is mortgage interest expense deductible?*

In the *old tax law*, residential-mortgage interest was fully deductible. With the new tax law, which began in 1986, interest deductions on residential mortgages are dependent on satisfying two conditions relevant to the property that secures the debt and the reason for the debt. Deduction for interest is limited to the taxpayer's principal residence plus a second home, which is also used for personal purposes at least 14 days in a year or 10% of the number of days that property is rented at fair market value, whichever is the greater. A residence for tax law requirements is a property so used which includes condominiums and cooperative units and may include a boat or motor home, an apartment or unit in a duplex or apartment building, or a time share. Use as a residence is the key. See Tax Question 24. In the case of time shares, it should be noted that only one-time share can count as a second home. The interest on the debt is deductible to the extent that the loan does not exceed the lesser of 1) the fair market value or 2) the purchase price plus the cost of improvement. One should be mindful of this rule when refinancing a house that has appreciated in value over a period of time. For example, a house that was purchased for $50,000 ten years ago may have a present value of $150,000. If the owner refinances based on 80% of the appraised value, the interest allowed would be limited to the amount paid on $50,000 even though the principal balance is $120,000 (80% of $150,000). An exception to this rule is if the debt was outstanding on 16 August 1986 or if the loan was used for qualified educational or medical expenses.

3. *What constitutes a second home?*

A second home is a residence used by the taxpayer for personal residence purposes for at least 14 days of the year or 10% of the number of days that property is rented at fair market value, whichever is the greater.

4. *Is investment interest deductible?*

The deduction of investment interest is limited to the amount of net investment income. The excess of investment interest expense over investment income can be carried forward in the succeeding year. Due to passive loss limitation phase-in, interest on rental real estate activities will be less affected as compared to other investment activities.

5. *How is construction interest treated?*

All construction interest must be capitalized on the basis of the property.

6. *How is the deduction of interest treated for a shared appreciation mortgage (SAM)?*

With a SAM mortgage, the owner pays a lower rate of fixed interest and a "contingent interest" to the lender. The contingent interest is a percentage of the appreciation in the value of the home and may be deducted in the year the SAM terminates and the contingent interest is paid. You may deduct the regular rate interest in each year that it is paid. If the home is refinanced and the contingent interest of a SAM mortgage is paid, the interest is deductible.

7. *Is the interest accrued on graduated payment mortgages (FHA-245, VA-GPM) deductible?*

No. You may deduct only the interest you pay during the year.

8. *Is personal interest no longer deductible?*

Personal interest is no longer deductible, but there is a phasing-in period. Interest on car, boat, and credit card loans and interest due to underpayment of tax are no longer deductible. The phasing in for such deductions on interest is as follows: 65% will be allowed in 1987, 40% in 1988, 20% in 1989, 10% in 1990, and none allowed in 1991 and thereafter.

9. *Is a penalty incurred for a prepayment of a mortgage deductible?*

If the penalty incurred is to obtain financing, it must be capitalized and written off over the life of the loan. On the other hand, if the prepayment penalty was incurred to extinguish an existing debt, the penalty can be deducted in the year paid.

10. *Are discount points paid by the buyer deductible?*
Discount points paid by the buyer are deductible and, depending upon the reason for the loan, can be amortized over the life of the loan or deducted in the year paid.

Discount points are fully deductible in the year you pay them if: 1) the points paid were for the purchase or renovation of your primary residence and 2) the points were paid from your own funds, and not deducted from loan proceeds.

Discount points are deductible in other situations, but they should be amortized over the life of the loan. Please remember that we are speaking of discount points and not other closing costs such as origination or service fees. Closing costs that are not deductible in the year paid should be capitalized.

11. *Are discount points paid by the seller deductible?*
No. The seller may not deduct points as interest but may include the charges as a selling expense which will reduce any gain realized.

12. *Are closing costs deductible?*
No. Closing costs, such as abstract fees, title insurance premiums, etc., must be added to the cost basis of the property. However, taxes and interest are deductible.

13. *How will the tax law changes affect what happens when you sell real estate?*
In general, the sale of real estate can be broken down into three types which have a separate effect on your personal income taxes.

The first is the sale of your principal residence and putting the gain into a new house. The 1986 tax law has no change in this area. The capital gain from a sale of your principal residence is deferred if you purchase a new residence within two years and the new residence costs as much as the old.

The second type of sale is the one-time exclusion allowed for taxpayers 55 years old or older. With the 1986 tax law,

177

these individuals continue to have a one-time exclusion from income of up to $125,000 of gain from the sale of their principal residence. The third type of sale would be the sale of real estate by an individual who does not fit into the first two types of sellers mentioned in this answer.

14. *What is long-term capital gain?*

Long-term capital gain is gain from the sale of a capital asset that is held more than six months. If the property acquired was a gift and was later sold at a gain, the time the donor owned the property is included in the holding period. The 1986 tax law provides a maximum tax of 28% of the gain from a sale in 1987. There are no longer any exclusions of capital gain from income.

15. *What happens if I sold a property using the installment-sale method?*

With the *old tax law*, you were permitted to recognize gain on installment sales in proportion to and as the proceeds were received. With the *1986 tax law*, the treatment is different if you are a dealer or if you are an individual who has sold rental property for more than $150,000. For such individuals, the installment-sale method will be limited based on the amount of outstanding debts and assets of the taxpayer. For tax purposes, a minimum installment will be imputed to the seller equal to the product of the seller's total debts-to-assets ratio times the face amount of the installment obligation. This will be the minimum installment for tax reporting purposes regardless of the actual amount received.

16. *Are real estate taxes deductible?*

Real property taxes, state and local income taxes, and personal property taxes are deductible. State and local sales taxes are not deductible after 1986.

17. *What are passive investment, passive income, and passive loss?*

Passive investment is one in which the investor does not materially participate. A real estate limited partnership and rental real estate are passive investments. Passive income or loss originates from passive investments. Passive loss can only be used to offset passive income, except as described in Tax Question 1.

18. *What is the difference between a capital expenditure and an expense?*

A capital expenditure increases the value or useful life of an asset. It is distinguished from a repair expense which is incurred to keep the building in operating condition. Capital expenditures must be added to the cost basis of the property and charged off through depreciations over their useful life whereas an expense qualifies as a current deduction.

19. *What are some examples of capital expenditures and repair expenses?*

Examples of capital expenditures are as follows: new roof, new carpets, heating and air conditioning equipment and remodeling. Generally, repair expenses are items that cannot be classified as a capital expenditures. Some examples are as follows: necessary painting and cleaning up after a tenant moves out, patching or repairing part of the roof, or minor repair of heating, plumbing, and air conditioning.

20. *How have the depreciation methods changed?*

All residential real estate placed in service after 31 December 1986 will be depreciated by using the straight-line method. Residential real estate will be depreciated over 27-1/2 years; nonresidential real estate will be depreciated over 31-1/2 years. There are two primary exceptions to the 31 December 1986 deadline. The old depreciation period of a 19-year write-off will apply for new construction if a binding contract existed prior to 1 March 1986 or if the building was self-constructed and the lesser of 5% of the total construction cost or $1,000,000 was incurred prior to 1 March 1986.

21. *Have the depreciation recapture rules changes?*

The existing rules will be in use for property sold in 1987 since there is a maximum 28% rate on capital gains in 1987 and ordinary income rates go as high as 38.5%. All gain from the sale of real property is recognized as a capital gain subject to the maximum 28% tax rate, if the property was depreciated over the straight-line method. Residential property

179

depreciated by the use of an accelerated method requires recognition of gain as ordinary income, to the extent of the depreciation claimed after 1975, in excess of that allowable under the straight-line method. If the property was placed in service prior to 1975, there are some special rules for phase-out of the ordinary income treatment of excess depreciation claimed during the period of 1969 to 1975. Non-residential properties using an accelerated method require gain recognition as ordinary income of all the post-1969 depreciation in excess of that allowable under the straight-line method. For properties sold in 1988 and beyond, all gain on a sale would be recognized as ordinary income since there will be only the 15% and 28% rates and the 5% surtax at certain income levels.

22. *Are there any tax incentives for low-income housing?*

Write-off of rehabilitation expenses under the Section 167(k) Rule is retained. The 167(k) Rule allows rehabilitation expenses of up to $20,000 ($40,000 if a certified program) to be written off over a 5-year period. Residential dwellings with Section 8 (U.S. Housing Act of 1937) rental assistance payments and properties located within target areas qualify as low-income housing.

The 1986 tax law provides new credits for low-income housing. The new rules are separated into three categories: 1) a maximum of 9% of qualified basis each year for 10 years on expenditures for new construction and rehabilitation of each qualifying unsubsidized low-income housing unit, 2) a maximum of 4% each year for 10 years on expenditures for new construction and rehabilitation financed with tax-exempt bonds or similar Federal subsidies, and 3) a maximum credit of 4% each year for 10 years on the cost of acquisition of existing over 10-year-old, low-income housing.

23. *If a taxpayer does not report a real estate transaction, how else can the IRS be informed?*

Under the 1986 tax provisions, the gross sales proceeds of all real estate transactions must now be reported on Form 1099B and the person(s) or entities responsible for the reporting are, in order of responsibility, as follows: 1) the party responsible for closing (attorney, escrow agent), 2) the mortgage lender, 3) the seller's broker, 4) the buyer's broker, and 5) any person designated by the regulations. Only one Form 1099B should be sent in for each sale.

24. *Will an owner's occupancy of a one- to four- unit single family dwelling constitute a principal residence?*

Yes, the extent of personal residential deduction, i.e., taxes and interest will be allowed in proportion to the unit occupied compared to total number of units in the building. For example, an owner occupancy of one unit in a four-unit complex will be allowed a 25% home-mortgage-interest and real-estate-tax deduction.

25. *Can investors in a cooperative apartment enjoy the privileges of special deductions?*

Stockholders in a cooperative can deduct their share of real estate taxes and interest paid for a mortgage(s). Co-ops must now also report to the IRS the tenant-stockholders proportionate share of mortgage-interest expense. The 1986 tax law allows corporations, estates, partnerships, and trusts to take advantage of the tax deductions, which heretofore were available only to individual stockholders.

26. *What is the at-risk rule?*

A limitation of a loss write-off to the amount invested in cash plus borrowed funds for which the investor is personally liable. In the past, real estate investments have been exempted from the at-risk rule. The 1986 tax law applies the at-risk rule to real estate acquired after 31 December 1986. Real estate is exempt from the at risk rule if it is purchased with borrowed funds on a non-recourse basis and the loan came from a financial institution or the government or the loan was insured by the government.

27. *Can I continue to depreciate my vehicle used for business purposes?*

Yes, but cars and light trucks have been shifted to statutory tables that have been extended from a three-year to a five-year write off. The 1986 law allows for dollar limits on the amount of annual depreciation claimed for a luxury business automobile as follows: For the first recovery year, $2,560; for

181

the second recovery year, $4,100; for the third recovery year, $2,450; and for each year thereafter in the recovery period the maximum limit is $1,475. Therefore, the 1986 law is much tougher on luxury automobiles. For example, a $20,000 luxury car used in business under the old law could have been written off in five years whereas the 1986 law would require the same car to be written off over approximately eleven years.

An auto used in a trade or business for the production of income, whether it be for 10% or 90%, is still deductible to the extent of such business use. However, there are severe limitations involved in the type of depreciation for vehicles used for less than 50% in the production of income.

28. *Are child care expenses deductible for working parents?*

Yes, and the expenses can result in a tax credit of up to $1,440 per year on IRS Form 2441. The working parent must provide more than half of the cost for maintaining a home with a dependent child under the age of 15. Expenses incurred by the use of a baby-sitter, nurse, maid, day-care center, nursery school, or summer camp may qualify for determining the child care credit. You can have a relative for a babysitter provided that person is not your dependent. If the babysitter is your child, he or she must be at least 19 by the end of the year. Expenses allowed for child care cannot exceed earned income in determining the credit. For married taxpayers, the child care expenses cannot exceed the lowest income of the couple in determining the credit. If you pay cash wages in excess of $50 in a calendar quarter for household services in your home, you must file a Payroll Tax Return Form No. 942.

29. *Can I deduct office-at-home expenses?*

Yes, if the office is used on a regular and exclusive basis as the principal place of business or as a place to deal or meet with clients or customers and for the convenience of the employer. The new tax law does not allow office expenses to be deducted if leased by an employee to his employer. Office-at-home expenses are limited to the gross income from the business activity less any deductible expenses that are not associated with the use of the home office, i.e., mortgage interest and property taxes. The new law does allow for carry forward of any deductions not allowed by the gross income limit subject to the continued use of the limit.

30. *Is health insurance cost deductible for self-employed individuals?*

The old law did not provide for any deduction for health insurance cost except as an itemized deduction. The 1986 tax law allows for a deduction on Schedule C in computing the net income or loss from a business or profession of 25% of the cost of insurance covering himself and his dependents provided the self-employed individual is not covered by a spouse's employers benefit plan and provided he pays for similar insurance for all of his employees in all unincorporated businesses in which he is a 5% owner. Self-employed persons are allowed to deduct 25% of the health insurance cost which may include the cost for a spouse and dependents. The deduction cannot exceed the self-employed individual's net earnings from self-employment. No deduction is allowed if the self-employed individual or his spouse is eligible to participate in an employer-sponsored health plan.

31. *What are some of the deductions and exclusions that have been taken away or repealed by the 1986 tax law?*

1. Deduction for two-earner married individuals.
2. Dividend exclusion of $100 ($200 for married joint returns)
3. Credit for political contributions.
4. Itemized deductions for state and local sales tax (although they can be capitalized for depreciable property used in a trade or business).
5. Expenses for travel as a form of education.
6. Expenses related to a hobby unless there has been a profit in three out of five consecutive years. (Horse breeding and racing is an exception to this rule.)
7. Expenses related to home energy items such as storm windows, insulation, etc.
8. Charitable contributions, if you do not itemize.
9. Job-related moving expenses, if you do not itemize.

10. Interest on consumer debt, i.e., cars, credit card charges.

11. The favorable tax treatment of excluding 60% on the net long-term capital gain is eliminated. (The long-term gain must be considered as ordinary income. The top tax rate for long-term capital gain is 28% for 1987 and beyond.)

12. IRA contributions if you belong to a company-funded retirement plan. You may continue to take a full deduction of up to $2,000 annually or $2,250 for a spousal IRA if: A) neither you nor your spouse is associated with a company-funded retirement plan or B) either you or your spouse belongs to a company-funded retirement plan but your adjusted gross income is less than $40,000 ($25,000 for single taxpayers). The IRA contribution is not considered as part of gross income. There is a partial deduction allowed for incomes of married taxpayers filing jointly between $40,000 to $50,000 and $25,000 to $35,000 for single taxpayers. Those above the limit are restricted to putting after-tax dollars into an IRA.

32. *What are acceptable miscellaneous itemized deductions?*

1. The cost of appraisals to determine the fair market value of capital improvements for medical expense deduction reasons, an amount of a casualty loss, or the fair market value of donated property.

2. The cost of tax return preparation and related expenditures.

3. Employee business expenses that are not reimbursed by the employer such as: Subscriptions to professional journals; dues to professional organizations; malpractice insurance premiums; union dues; work clothes or uniforms, expenses of maintaining an office at home which is used exclusively for production of business income; job-hunting expenses; medical examinations required by an employer; research expenses of a college professor; hobby or gambling losses to the extent that they equal no more than the hobby

or gambling income, certain costs of adopting hand-icapped children.

These itemized miscellaneous deductions are subject to a floor of 2% of the taxpayer's adjusted gross income.

33. *What are some miscellaneous itemized deductions that are not subject to the 2% floor?*

1. The estate tax attributable to income in respect of a decedent
2. Moving expenses
3. Impairment-related work expenses for handicapped employees
4. Certain adjustments where a taxpayer restores amounts held under a claim of right
5. Amortizable bond premiums
6. Certain costs of cooperative housing corporations
7. Deductions allowable in connection with personal property used in a short sale
8. Certain terminated annuity payments
9. Gambling losses to the extent of gambling winnings
10. Qualified home mortgage interest
11. Real estate taxes
12. Casualty and theft losses
13. Charitable contributions
14. Medical expenses in excess of 7.5 % of adjusted gross income

34. *What are examples of non-deductible expenses?*

Burial or funeral expenses, campaign expenses, capital expenses, check-writing fees, commuting expenses, fines or penalties, health spa expenses, insurance premiums for hazard and mortgage insurance on personal residence, lunches or meals while working late, personal legal expenses, professional accreditation fees, repairs to personal residence, self-improvement course fees and expenses to produce tax-exempt income.

35. *What is taxable income?*

Adjusted gross income less personal exemptions, less the standard deduction or itemized deduction.

36. *What are the new tax rates for 1989?*

All rates are based on taxable income and are as follows.

	Tax Payable	Taxable Income (TI)
Married, filing joint returns	15% of TI	$ 0 – 30,950
	4,642.50 + 28% of (TI - $30,950)	30,950 – 74,850
	$16,934.50 + 33% of (TI - $74,850)*	71,900 – 155,320
	28% of TI**	155,320 +
Heads of Household	15% of TI	0 – 24,850
	$3,727.50 + 28% of (TI - $24,850)	24,850 – 64,200
	$14,745.50 + 33% of (TI - 64,200)*	64,200 – 128,810
	28% of TI**	128,810 +
Single	15% of TI	0 – 18,550
	$2782.50 + 28% of (TI - $18,550)	18,550 – 44,900
	10,160.50 + 33% of (TI - 44,900)*	44,900 – 93,130
	28% of TI**	93,130 +
Married, filing separately	15% of TI	0 – 15,475
	28% + $2321.25 of (TI - $15,475)	15,475 – 37,425
	$8,462.25 + 33% of (TI - 37,425	37,425 – 117,895
	28% of TI**	117,895 +

* Reflects first 5% surtax
** PLUS lesser of (1) 28% of the sum of personal and dependency exemptions or (2) 5% of (TI - top taxable income in each status)

Starting in 1988 there will be only two tax rates, 15% and 28%. The benefit of the 15% tax rate and the personal exemption is phased out for high-income taxpayers, by use of a 5% surtax so for certain income levels the *marginal* tax rate would be 33%.

37. *Have the personal exemptions been changed?*

Yes, the personal exemption of $1,080 is increased to $1,900 in 1987, $1,950 in 1988, and $2,000 in 1989. It will be adjusted in accordance with the Consumer Price Index thereafter.

38. *Is income-shifting to a child still a tax-saving technique?*

No. Investment income in excess of $500 received by a child who is under age 14 is generally taxed to the child at the top marginal rate applied to the parents, even if the income source came from someone other than the parents. The Clifford Trust technique is repealed. A Clifford Trust is set up by transferring income-producing property to a trust which lasts for more than ten years. The trust income is distributed to the child each year and is taxed at the lower rate for the child and after the ten years has expired, the property reverts to the parents.

39. *Are medical expenses still deductible?*

Yes, but the floor for the itemized medical expense deduction has been increased from 5% to 7.5% of the adjusted gross income.

40. *In the case of divorced parents, how do you determine which parent gets to claim a child as a dependent for deductibility of medical expenses?*

A child of divorced parents can be claimed as a dependent of both parents for deductibility of medical expenses. It does not make any difference which parent gets the exemption deduction, and it is not necessary for the parent paying the medical expense to be required to do so by a decree or separation agreement to claim the payment for his or her medical expense deduction. Remember, only the custodial parent gets the dependency exemption unless the custodial parent has agreed for the noncustodial parent to have it and has executed Form 8332 or if a pre-1985 divorce decree granted it to the noncustodial parent who provides at least $600 per year in support.

41. *What is casualty loss?*

Something of value that you own is either stolen, damaged, or destroyed in an accident or by an act of nature which is sudden, unexpected, or unusual. The amount of loss for both business and nonbusiness is the lesser of 1) the difference between the value of the property immediately before the casualty and its value after the casualty or 2) the adjusted basis of the property immediately before the casualty. The full amount of a business casualty loss is deductible. A nonbusiness casualty loss is subject to a floor of $100 and the excess is deductible only to the extent it exceeds 10% of your adjusted gross income. After 1986, a personal casualty loss that is covered by insurance will be deductible only if the individual files a timely insurance claim for the loss.

42. *Are bad debits deductible?*

There are two types of bad debts, business and nonbusiness. A business bad debt is one created by the normal course of business. Business bad debt can be deducted from gross income to the extent of their worthlessness at any time that they become partly or totally worthless.

A nonbusiness bad debt is one that is of a personal nature. An individual can treat a nonbusiness bad debt as a short-term capital loss and can deduct up to $3,000 per year against ordinary income. There must be a true creditor-debtor relationship established, even for family members. Worthlessness must exist—it must be shown that the debtor has no way of paying back the debt. An attorney's opinion or financial statement of the debtor can help document the inability of the. debtor to repay the loan. It is important that you accumulate written evidence of worthlessness of the loan.

A loan by a taxpayer to a business, even his own corporation, results in a non-business bad debt, unless the taxpayer happened to be in the business of lending money, and then he would have a business loss.

43. *Are deductions still allowed for business expenses related to meals or entertainment?*

In general, meal and entertainment expenses will be limited to 80% of the expense. The business expense must be related to the taxpayer's trade or business and proper records and receipts must be kept. Meal expenses for the taxpayer are allowed, subject to the 80% rule, when traveling out of town for business reasons. No deduction is allowed for lavish or extravagant expenses associated with travel, meals, or beverages.

APPENDIX ONE

THE MORTGAGE MANUAL EXAM

Instructions: Circle T if the statement is completely true, F if it is false. During the test, practice using the index to help find the answers and reference each answer with a question number or numbers used as the reference source.

Example: The FHA late charge is 4%, which
applies to all payments made after the 10th
of the month   T   F
False. Reference: Question 2.84

Exam Ratings:
62-66 correct . . . Excellent
59-61 correct . . . Good
46-58 correct . . . Average

If you wish to grade yourself for just the
FHA, VA, and Conventional Parts, the Exam
Ratings are:
33-35 correct . . . Excellent
31-32 correct . . . Good
24-30 correct . . . Average

The answers to the exam begin on page 201.

PART I: FHA

1. To determine the maximum loan amount
your must start with the acquisition cost,
which is the FHA appraised value.   T   F
Reference:

2. A seller can pay the purchaser's closing
cost and prepaid items.   T   F
Reference:

3. Loan approval is referred to as a firm
commitment.   T   F
Reference:

4. Privately owned mortgage companies are
non-supervised lenders.   T   F
Reference:

5. Credit for sweat equity is limited to labor
only.   T   F
Reference:

6. To be found guilty of being a part of a
dual contract, the dual agreements must be
in writing.   T   F
Reference:

7. It is illegal to borrow the required
downpayment.   T   F
Reference:

8. An individual cannot have more than 7
FHA loans.   T   F
Reference:

9. In a shared equity ownership, the investor
must sell if the occupant mortgagor gives a
30-day written notice of intent to purchase.   T   F

Reference:

10. A FHA/VA loan is for veterans or reservists who wish to purchase a one- to four-single-family unit dwelling   T   F
Reference:

11. For any FHA loan, insurance premiums are refundable if the loan did not terminate due to foreclosure.   T   F
Reference:

12. FHA determines the margin and the index for its adjustable-rate mortgage.   T   F
Reference:

PART II VA

1. A veteran can be charged an attorney's fee at loan closing.   T   F
Reference:

2. VA loans are completely assumable without qualifying.   T   F
Reference:

3. The VA GPM monthly payment factors are identical to the FHA GPM Plan III.   T   F
Reference:

4. If a VA loan has been assumed prior to 1 March 1988, the veteran has no liability if the loan later goes into foreclosure and a deficiency results.   T   F
Reference:

5. VA loan approval is evidenced by a Certificate of Commitment   T   F
Reference:

6. The VA appraisal is known as a Certificate of Reasonable Value.   T   F
Reference:

7. Educational benefits can be included in income to assist in loan approval.   T   F
Reference:

8. VA disability income cannot be included in the veteran's income for loan qualification purposes.   T   F
Reference:

9. Provided the lender makes disclosure to VA and certain guidelines are met, second mortgages can be closed in conjunction with a VA loan.   T   F
Reference:

10. A veteran cannot apply for a VA loan on a non-owner occupant basis.   T   F
Reference:

11. A dual period of eligibility means that a veteran can choose which period of eligibility to use and can therefore automatically apply for two VA loans.   T   F
Reference:

12. A veteran can borrow any required down payment.   T   F
Reference:

13. The maximum guaranty on June 1975 was $17,500.   T   F
Reference:

14. Time restrictions no longer apply to the use of a veteran's entitlement, except as related to a dual eligibility case.　　T　　F
Reference:

15. Not remarrying is the only requirement for a surviving spouse to have eligibility.　　T　　F
Reference:

16. As a lender, I should never close a VA refinance loan with cash to the veteran in excess of 90% of the appraised value (CRV).　　T　　F
Reference:

17. There is a maximum number of loans a veteran can have.　　T　　F
Reference:

PART III CONVENTIONAL

1. The accrual rate is the note rate.　　T　　F
Reference:

2. PMI coverage automatically discontinues and the mortgagor no longer has to pay the monthly premium after the loan is amortized to less than 80% of the acquisition cost.　　T　　F
Reference:

3. Payment caps prevent negative amortization.　　T　　F
Reference:

4. Income guidelines take into consideration the size of the family.　　T　　F
Reference:

5. A 3-2-1 buydown means the interest rate is bought down 6% in the first year.　　T　　F

6. A conversion feature allows the borrower
to convert to a fixed rate loan at an interest
rate comparable to rates offered for new
fixed-rate loans by local lenders.   T   F
Reference:

PART IV TAX

1. The at-risk rule limits a loss write off
to the amount invested in cash plus
borrowed funds for which the investor
is personally liable.   T   F
Reference:

2. I am a working parent and have a dependent child under the age of 15 and I pay child
care expenses, I may be eligible for a tax
credit of up to $2,000.   T   F
Reference:

3. The new tax law prevents me from taking
advantage of deductions for interest and
taxes on a purchase of a personal residence.   T   F
Reference:

4. I can no longer deduct interest for items
such as: cars and boats.   T   F
Reference:

5. I can always deduct a prepayment penalty
in the year paid.   T   F
Reference:

6. I can no longer deduct discount points in
the year paid.   T   F
Reference:

7. I can no longer exclude capital gain from
income.   T   F
Reference:

8. For tax purposes, a second home is a
residence used by the tax payer for personal
residence purposes for at least 14 days of the
year or 10% of the number of days that
property is rented at fair market value,
whichever is the greater.   T   F
Reference:

9. I cannot deduct closing costs.   T   F
 Reference:

10. I can deduct repair expenses to
investment properties in the year paid.   T   F
Reference:

11. The new tax law will prevent me from
using deductions for my luxury automobile
used in my business.   T   F
Reference:

12. I have a $60,000 mortgage. Similar
houses in my development have sold for
$90,000 to $125,000. I may get my home
reappraised, take out a home equity loan
and buy a vehicle and the interest I pay on
the home equity loan will be tax deductible.   T   F

13. I can no longer deduct charitable
contributions.   T   F
Reference:

14. In general, I can deduct 80% of meal and
entertainment expenses.   T   F
Reference:

15. I can still use losses from my real estate investments to offset income from my non-real estate activities only if I actively participate in decisions for the investments, own 10% (by value and for the entire tax year) and manage the property without the help of a property management firm.   T   F
Reference:

_____

PART V TERMS

1. A cloud on the title refers to an existence of a claim or encumbrance that impairs the owner's claim for clear title.   T   F

2. A novation is the substitution of a debt or a debtor based on the agreement of all parties.   T   F

3. A closed-end mortgage is a fixed mortgage amount which cannot be increased.   T   F

4. The term "hypothecate" means to pledge property as collateral for a debt without giving up title or possession.   T   F

5. A subordination agreement is a clause allowing a holder of a prior encumbrance to become junior to an existing or anticipated encumbrance.   T   F

6. Regulation Z controls the APR, which is the interest rate.   T   F

_____

PART VI PROPERTY INSPECTION

1. In estimating the cost of labor and materials for installing a new roof on an existing house you need only be concerned

with the cost of the materials and the labor
costs for installing a new roof over the old
roof.   T   F

Reference:

2. The lack of foundation vents tells a person
that a house is built on a concrete slab.   T   F
Reference:

3. Peelings from lead base paint can cause
brain damage.   T   F
Reference:

4. Conventional foundations should have a
minimum of 6 to 8 inches from the ground.   T   F
Reference:

5. FHA will accept a minimum of a 120 volt,
2 wire service.   T   F
Reference:

6. The wire service can be found on the
utility meter or the electrical panel.   T   F
Reference:

7. FHA will now let a mortgagor borrow
part of the cost for a professional inspection.   T   F
Reference:

8. The normal life expectancy for a hot water
tank is 6 years.   T   F
Reference:

9. If a house is built on a slab, there is no
way to detect water leaks in the foundation.   T   F
Reference:

10. Radon gas is believed to cause lung cancer. Experts have said that lenders will soon
require a home to be tested for radon gas.　　T　　F
Reference:

PART I FHA

1. False. Reference: Question 1.12
2. True. Reference: Question 1.12
3. True. Reference: Question 1.46
4. True. Reference: Question 1.52
5. False. Reference: Question 1.79
6. False. Reference: Question 1.82
7. False. Reference: Question 1.48
8. False. Reference: Question 1.32
9. True. Reference: Question 1.80
10. False. Reference: Question 1.17
11. False. Reference: Question 1.28
12. False. Reference: Question 1.74

PART II VA

1. False. Reference: Question 2.76
2. False. Reference: Question 2.2
3. True. Reference: Question 2.32
4. False. Reference: Question 2.53
5. True. Reference: Question 2.70
6. True. Reference: Question 2.90
7. False. Reference: Question 2.49
8. False. Reference: Question 2.49
9. True. Reference: Question 2.67
10. False. Reference: Question 2.34
11. False. Reference: Question 2.14
12. False. Reference: Question 2.69
13. True. Reference: Question 2.21
14. True. Reference: Question 2.15
15. False. Reference: Question 2.3 Death of the veteran must be service connected.
16. False. Reference: Question 2.36 The loan cannot be *approved* for more than 90%, but the loan can *close* at a 91% LTV ratio.
17. False. Reference: Question 2.26

PART III CONVENTIONAL

1. True. Reference: Question 3.19
2. False. Reference: Question 3.18
3. False. Reference: Question 3.27
4. False. Reference: Question 3.45
5. False. Reference: Question 3.36
6. False. Reference: Question 3.34 (not always)

PART IV TAX

1. False. There are exceptions for real estate. Reference: Question 26.
2. False. Reference: Question 28.
3. False. Reference: Question 2.
4. False. Reference: Question 8. There is still some deductions for personal interest, 20% in 1989.
5. False. Reference: Question 9.
6. False. Reference: Question 10. There are some cases where it is possible to deduct discount points in the year paid.
7. True. Reference: Question 14.
8. True. Reference: Question 3.
9. True. Reference: Question 12.
10. True. Reference: Question 18.
11. False. Reference: Question 27.
12. False. Reference: Question 3.
13. False. Reference: Question 31.
14. True. Reference: Question 43.
15. False. Reference: Question 1. You can use the services of a property management firm.

PART V TERMS

Numbers 1 through 5 are True, number 6 is False.

*An interesting note, for any would be real estate brokers or agents, is that real estate terms constitute a large majority of the finance portion of state licensing exams.

PART VI PROPERTY INSPECTION

1. False. Reference: page 143. If it has 3 or more layers, you will need to estimate the costs for scrapping the shingles down to the decking and the cost of removing the old roofing material.
2. True. Reference: page 144.
3. True. Reference: page 145.
4. False. Reference: page 144.
5. False. Reference: page 146.
6. True. Reference: page 146.
7. True. Reference: page 149-50.
8. False. Reference: page 147.
9. False. Reference: page 147.
10. True. Reference: page 149

APPENDIX TWO

USING THE HP-12c TO SOLVE REAL ESTATE MATH PROBLEMS

This section will provide you with some easy steps to answers for real estate math problems by using your HP-12c calculator.

Monthly Principal and Interest Payments: 1) clear your calculator (press gold f then CLX and gold f then XY), 2) enter the information to obtain a monthly payment on a loan. For example, a $100,000 loan, at 10% interest, for 30 years would be entered as follows: 1) press the numbers for 100000, 2) press PV (located on top row), 3) press the numbers 10, 4) press blue g (located on bottom row), 5) press i (located on top row), 6) press the numbers 30, 7) press blue g, 8) press n (located on top row), 9) press PMT (located on top row). Your calculator will be "running," then stop with a -877.57 showing on the screen, this is your monthly principal and interest payment.

Loan Amortization: Repeat the steps in *Monthly principal and interest payments*. Do not clear your calculator. You are now ready to obtain the interest paid, the amortization or principal paid, and the remaining balance. Let us assume the loan is 10 years old. Since you have not cleared your calculator we can culator we can begin with: 1) press 120 (the number of payments made over a 10-year period), 2) press gold f (located on bottom row), 3) press n, your calculator will start running; when it is finished it should show -96,246.75, which is the interest paid over 10 years, 4) press xy (located 3rd row from top) and -$9,061.65 should show on your screen, this is the principal paid over 10 years, 5) press RCL (located on bottom row), 6) press PV and $90,938.35 will be the remaining balance for the $100,000 loan after 10 years of loan payments.

Looking at an amortization schedule gives one a better understanding of simple interest and how an unrestricted prepayment can be of value. Please see the section titled "Prepaying a Mortgage."

WAC, Weighted Average Coupon: The WAC means the weighted average coupon of mortgage loans as a group. Begin by clearing your calculator (press gold f then CLX and gold f then XY) 1) enter the interest rate, 2) enter the loan amount, 3) press E+ (the number 1 should appear on the screen), 4) continue to enter subsequent loans in the same manner as steps 1-3, 5) when all loans are entered, press RCL, 6) press the number 2, (the screen should show the total dollar amount of the loans), 7) press blue g, 8) press 6 (the screen will show the WAC). Example: you want the WAC for two loans, the first loan is at 10% interest and the loan amount is $100,000, the second loan is 11% and the loan amount is $300,000. Begin by clearing your calculator and then: 1) press the numbers 10, 2) press Enter, 3) press the numbers 100000, 4) press E+ (the screen should show 1.00), 5) press the numbers 11, 6) press Enter, 7) press the numbers 300000, 8) press E+ (the screen should show 2.00), 9) press RCL, 10) press the number 2 (the screen should show 400,000, this is the total for all loans entered), 11) press blue g, 12) press the number 6, (the screen is now showing 10.75 which is the WAC for the loans entered).

WAM, Weighted Average Maturity: The WAM is the weighted average remaining maturity of the applicable mortgage loans as a group. The steps for determining the

WAM with a HP-12C are virtually the same as used for the WAC. In calculating the WAM you start off with the number of months remaining instead of the interest rate. Using the same loan amounts as the WAC example and using a remaining maturity for the first loan of 360 months (30-year loan) and 120 months (10-year loan) for the second loan, we would use the following steps to determine the WAM: Begin by clearing your calculator (press gold f then CLX and gold f then XY) 1) press the numbers 360, 2) press enter, 3) press the numbers 100,000, 4) press E+, (screen should show 1.00), 5) press 120, 6) press Enter, 7) press 300,000, 8) press E+, (screen should show 2.00), 9) press RCL, 10) press 2, (screen should show the total of the loans, 400,000), 11) press blue g, 12) press 6, (the screen is now showing 180.00 which is the WAM for the loans entered).

Programming to Solve for the Cash Required for Closing; Monthly Principal and Interest Payment; Maximum Loan without Mip; the Prepaid Items; Maximum Loan Including Mip. Begin by setting your calculator to "Program Mode" 1) press gold f, 2) press gold letters P/R (this is the button with the white letters R/S, located on the far left side, third row from top), 3) press gold f, 4) clear program by pressing R with arrow pointing down (located third row from top), 5) enter the following keystrokes, (*Note*: do not press Enter button after entering the following keys) RCL 0; .015 (estimate for prepaid items - adjust according to your local situation) X STO 3; RCL 0; RCL 1 +; .95 X; 500 +; STO 2 (lower loan); 1.038 (3.8% premium for MIP) X PV; RCL 0; RCL 2 - (minus); RCL 1 +; RCL 3 + (cash required for closing); R/S; 30 g n; 0 FV; PMT (monthly payment for P & I); f R/S (to exit from program mode).

I suggest you write the following down on a portion of an index card small enough to tape to the back of your HP-12c. SP - STO; CC - STO 1; INT. RATE - g i; R/S - CASH REQUIRED; R/S - P & I + MIP; RCL 2 - LOWER LOAN; RCL 3 - PREPAIDS; RCL PV - TOTAL LOAN. The SP is sales price; the CC is closing costs (use the FHA estimate for your area); the INT. RATE is the interest rate; pressing R/S will give you the cash required to close; pressing R/S again will give you the monthly principal and interest payment based on the total loan amount which includes the MIP; RCL 2 will give you the loan amount without MIP; RCL 3 will give you the cost of prepaid items (remember we estimated them to be 1.5% of the loan amount, adjust for your area as needed); RCL PV will give you the total loan amount which includes the MIP.

Programming the HP-12C to Calculate FHA Total Acquisition Loans

Variables:	Selling Price	STO 0
	Closing Cost	STO 1
	Interest Rate	[g]i

Press [f] [P/R] to set calculator to "Program Mode"
Press [f] CLEAR [PRGM] to erase previous programs
Enter following sequence of keystrokes
RCL 0
.015 [×] STO [3]
RCL 0
RCL 1 [+]
.95 [×]
500 [+]
STO [2] (lower loan)
1.038 [×] PV
RCL 0
RCL 2 [−]
RCL 1 [+]
RCL 3 [+] (cash required for closing)
R/S
30 [g] n
0 FV
PMT (monthly payment P & I)
[f] R/S (to exit from program mode)

To use program, enter variables as indicated above. Then press R/S. The display will show "running" then will stop and display *Cash Required For Closing*. (Plus buyers' points)

Press R/S again. The display will show "running" then will stop and display the *Monthly Payment*.

Pressing RCL 2 will display the lower loan amount. Pressing RCL 3 will display the prepaids.

Pressing RCL PV will display the total loan amount.

APPENDIX THREE

7.00% Principal and Interest
Monthly Payment Amortization Table

Term AMOUNT	1 Year	2 Years	3 Years	4 Years	5 Years	6 Years	7 Years	8 Years	9 Years	10 Years	11 Years
50	4.33	2.24	1.55	1.20	1.00	.86	.76	.69	.63	.59	.55
100	8.66	4.48	3.09	2.40	1.99	1.71	1.51	1.37	1.26	1.17	1.09
200	17.31	8.96	6.18	4.79	3.97	3.41	3.02	2.73	2.51	2.33	2.18
300	25.96	13.44	9.27	7.19	5.95	5.12	4.53	4.10	3.76	3.49	3.27
400	34.62	17.91	12.36	9.58	7.93	6.82	6.04	5.46	5.01	4.65	4.36
500	43.27	22.39	15.44	11.98	9.91	8.53	7.55	6.82	6.26	5.81	5.45
600	51.92	26.87	18.53	14.37	11.89	10.23	9.06	8.19	7.51	6.97	6.54
700	60.57	31.35	21.62	16.77	13.87	11.94	10.57	9.55	8.76	8.13	7.62
800	69.23	35.82	24.71	19.16	15.85	13.64	12.08	10.91	10.01	9.29	8.71
900	77.88	40.30	27.79	21.56	17.83	15.35	13.59	12.28	11.26	10.45	9.80
1000	86.53	44.78	30.88	23.95	19.81	17.05	15.10	13.64	12.51	11.62	10.89
2000	173.06	89.55	61.76	47.90	39.61	34.10	30.19	27.27	25.02	23.23	21.77
3000	259.59	134.32	92.64	71.84	59.41	51.15	45.28	40.91	37.52	34.84	32.66
4000	346.11	179.10	123.51	95.79	79.21	68.20	60.38	54.54	50.03	46.45	43.54
5000	432.64	223.87	154.39	119.74	99.01	85.25	75.47	68.17	62.54	58.06	54.43
6000	519.17	268.64	185.27	143.68	118.81	102.30	90.56	81.81	75.04	69.67	65.31
7000	605.69	313.41	216.14	167.63	138.61	119.35	105.65	95.44	87.55	81.28	76.19
8000	692.22	358.19	247.02	191.57	158.41	136.40	120.75	109.07	100.06	92.89	87.08
9000	778.75	402.96	277.90	215.52	178.22	153.45	135.84	122.71	112.56	104.50	97.96
10000	865.27	447.73	308.78	239.47	198.02	170.50	150.93	136.34	125.07	116.11	108.85
11000	951.80	492.50	339.65	263.41	217.82	187.54	166.02	149.98	137.57	127.72	119.73
12000	1038.33	537.28	370.53	287.36	237.62	204.59	181.12	163.61	150.08	139.34	130.61
13000	1124.85	582.05	401.41	311.31	257.42	221.64	196.21	177.24	162.59	150.95	141.50
14000	1211.38	626.82	432.28	335.25	277.22	238.69	211.30	190.88	175.09	162.56	152.38
15000	1297.91	671.59	463.16	359.20	297.02	255.74	226.40	204.51	187.60	174.17	163.27
16000	1384.43	716.37	494.04	383.14	316.82	272.79	241.49	218.14	200.11	185.78	174.15
17000	1470.96	761.14	524.92	407.09	336.63	289.84	256.58	231.78	212.61	197.39	185.03
18000	1557.49	805.91	555.79	431.04	356.43	306.89	271.67	245.41	225.12	209.00	195.92
19000	1644.01	850.68	586.67	454.98	376.23	323.94	286.77	259.05	237.62	220.61	206.80
20000	1730.54	895.46	617.55	478.93	396.03	340.99	301.86	272.68	250.13	232.22	217.69
21000	1817.07	940.23	648.42	502.88	415.83	358.03	316.95	286.31	262.64	243.83	228.57
22000	1903.59	985.00	679.30	526.82	435.63	375.08	332.04	299.95	275.14	255.44	239.46
23000	1990.12	1029.77	710.18	550.77	455.43	392.13	347.14	313.58	287.65	267.05	250.34
24000	2076.65	1074.55	741.06	574.71	475.23	409.18	362.23	327.21	300.16	278.67	261.22
25000	2163.17	1119.32	771.93	598.66	495.03	426.23	377.32	340.85	312.66	290.28	272.11
26000	2249.70	1164.09	802.81	622.61	514.84	443.28	392.41	354.48	325.17	301.89	282.99
27000	2336.23	1208.86	833.69	646.55	534.64	460.33	407.51	368.12	337.67	313.50	293.88
28000	2422.75	1253.64	864.56	670.50	554.44	477.38	422.60	381.75	350.18	325.11	304.76
29000	2509.28	1298.41	895.44	694.45	574.24	494.43	437.69	395.38	362.69	336.72	315.64
30000	2595.81	1343.18	926.32	718.39	594.04	511.48	452.79	409.02	375.19	348.33	326.53
31000	2682.33	1387.95	957.20	742.34	613.84	528.52	467.88	422.65	387.70	359.94	337.41
32000	2768.86	1432.73	988.07	766.28	633.64	545.57	482.97	436.28	400.21	371.55	348.30
33000	2855.39	1477.50	1018.95	790.23	653.44	562.62	498.06	449.92	412.71	383.16	359.18
34000	2941.91	1522.27	1049.83	814.18	673.25	579.67	513.16	463.55	425.22	394.77	370.06
35000	3028.44	1567.05	1080.70	838.12	693.05	596.72	528.25	477.19	437.72	406.38	380.95
36000	3114.97	1611.82	1111.58	862.07	712.85	613.77	543.34	490.82	450.23	418.00	391.83
37000	3201.49	1656.59	1142.46	886.02	732.65	630.82	558.43	504.45	462.74	429.61	402.72
38000	3288.02	1701.36	1173.33	909.96	752.45	647.87	573.53	518.09	475.24	441.22	413.60
39000	3374.55	1746.14	1204.21	933.91	772.25	664.92	588.62	531.72	487.75	452.83	424.48
40000	3461.07	1790.91	1235.09	957.85	792.05	681.97	603.71	545.35	500.26	464.44	435.37
41000	3547.60	1835.68	1265.97	981.80	811.85	699.01	618.80	558.99	512.76	476.05	446.25
42000	3634.13	1880.45	1296.84	1005.75	831.66	716.06	633.90	572.62	525.27	487.66	457.14
43000	3720.66	1925.23	1327.72	1029.69	851.46	733.11	648.99	586.25	537.77	499.27	468.02
44000	3807.18	1970.00	1358.60	1053.64	871.26	750.16	664.08	599.89	550.28	510.88	478.91
45000	3893.71	2014.77	1389.47	1077.59	891.06	767.21	679.18	613.52	562.79	522.49	489.79
46000	3980.24	2059.54	1420.35	1101.53	910.86	784.26	694.27	627.16	575.29	534.10	500.67
47000	4066.76	2104.32	1451.23	1125.48	930.66	801.31	709.36	640.79	587.80	545.71	511.56
48000	4153.29	2149.09	1482.11	1149.42	950.46	818.36	724.45	654.42	600.31	557.33	522.44
49000	4239.82	2193.86	1512.98	1173.37	970.26	835.41	739.55	668.06	612.81	568.94	533.33
50000	4326.34	2238.63	1543.86	1197.32	990.06	852.46	754.64	681.69	625.32	580.55	544.21
55000	4758.98	2462.50	1698.25	1317.05	1089.07	937.70	830.10	749.86	687.85	638.60	598.63
60000	5191.61	2686.36	1852.63	1436.78	1188.08	1022.95	905.57	818.03	750.38	696.66	653.05
65000	5624.24	2910.22	2007.02	1556.51	1287.08	1108.19	981.03	886.20	812.91	754.71	707.47
70000	6056.88	3134.09	2161.40	1676.24	1386.09	1193.44	1056.49	954.37	875.44	812.77	761.89
75000	6489.51	3357.95	2315.79	1795.97	1485.09	1278.68	1131.96	1022.53	937.98	870.82	816.31
80000	6922.14	3581.81	2470.17	1915.70	1584.10	1363.93	1207.42	1090.70	1000.51	928.87	870.73
85000	7354.78	3805.67	2624.56	2035.44	1683.11	1449.17	1282.88	1158.87	1063.04	986.93	925.15
90000	7787.41	4029.54	2778.94	2155.17	1782.11	1534.42	1358.35	1227.04	1125.57	1044.98	979.57
95000	8220.05	4253.40	2933.33	2274.90	1881.12	1619.66	1433.81	1295.21	1188.10	1103.04	1033.99
100000	8652.68	4477.26	3087.71	2394.63	1980.12	1704.91	1509.27	1363.38	1250.63	1161.09	1088.42

Principal and Interest
Monthly Payment Amortization Table 7.00%

AMOUNT	12 Years	13 Years	14 Years	15 Years	16 Years	17 Years	18 Years	19 Years	20 Years	21 Years	22 Years
50	.52	.49	.47	.45	.44	.42	.41	.40	.39	.36	.34
100	1.03	.98	.94	.90	.87	.84	.82	.80	.78	.71	.67
200	2.06	1.96	1.88	1.80	1.74	1.68	1.64	1.59	1.56	1.42	1.34
300	3.09	2.94	2.81	2.70	2.61	2.52	2.45	2.39	2.33	2.13	2.00
400	4.12	3.92	3.75	3.60	3.47	3.36	3.27	3.18	3.11	2.83	2.67
500	5.15	4.90	4.68	4.50	4.34	4.20	4.08	3.98	3.88	3.54	3.33
600	6.18	5.87	5.62	5.40	5.21	5.04	4.90	4.77	4.66	4.25	4.00
700	7.20	6.85	6.55	6.30	6.08	5.88	5.71	5.56	5.43	4.95	4.66
800	8.23	7.83	7.49	7.20	6.94	6.72	6.53	6.36	6.21	5.66	5.33
900	9.26	8.81	8.42	8.09	7.81	7.56	7.34	7.15	6.98	6.37	5.99
1000	10.29	9.79	9.36	8.99	8.68	8.40	8.16	7.95	7.76	7.07	6.66
2000	20.57	19.57	18.71	17.98	17.35	16.80	16.32	15.89	15.51	14.14	13.31
3000	30.86	29.35	28.07	26.97	26.02	25.19	24.47	23.83	23.26	21.21	19.96
4000	41.14	39.13	37.42	35.96	34.69	33.59	32.63	31.77	31.02	28.28	26.62
5000	51.42	48.91	46.78	44.95	43.37	41.99	40.78	39.71	38.77	35.34	33.27
6000	61.71	58.69	56.13	53.93	52.04	50.38	48.94	47.66	46.52	42.41	39.92
7000	71.99	68.47	65.48	62.92	60.71	58.78	57.09	55.60	54.28	49.48	46.58
8000	82.28	78.25	74.84	71.91	69.38	67.18	65.25	63.54	62.03	56.55	53.23
9000	92.56	88.03	84.19	80.90	78.05	75.57	73.40	71.48	69.78	63.62	59.88
10000	102.84	97.81	93.55	89.89	86.73	83.97	81.56	79.42	77.53	70.68	66.54
11000	113.13	107.59	102.90	98.88	95.40	92.37	89.71	87.37	85.29	77.75	73.19
12000	123.41	117.37	112.25	107.86	104.07	100.76	97.87	95.31	93.04	84.82	79.84
13000	133.69	127.15	121.61	116.85	112.74	109.16	106.02	103.25	100.79	91.89	86.49
14000	143.98	136.94	130.96	125.84	121.41	117.56	114.18	111.19	108.55	98.95	93.15
15000	154.26	146.72	140.32	134.83	130.09	125.95	122.33	119.13	116.30	106.02	99.80
16000	164.55	156.50	149.67	143.82	138.76	134.35	130.49	127.08	124.05	113.09	106.45
17000	174.83	166.28	159.02	152.81	147.43	142.75	138.64	135.02	131.81	120.16	113.11
18000	185.11	176.06	168.38	161.79	156.10	151.14	146.80	142.96	139.56	127.23	119.76
19000	195.40	185.84	177.73	170.78	164.77	159.54	154.95	150.90	147.31	134.29	126.41
20000	205.68	195.62	187.09	179.77	173.45	167.94	163.11	158.84	155.06	141.36	133.07
21000	215.97	205.40	196.44	188.76	182.12	176.33	171.26	166.79	162.82	148.43	139.72
22000	226.25	215.18	205.79	197.75	190.79	184.73	179.42	174.73	170.57	155.50	146.37
23000	236.53	224.96	215.15	206.74	199.46	193.13	187.57	182.67	178.32	162.56	153.02
24000	246.82	234.74	224.50	215.72	208.13	201.52	195.73	190.61	186.08	169.63	159.68
25000	257.10	244.52	233.86	224.71	216.81	209.92	203.88	198.55	193.83	176.70	166.33
26000	267.38	254.30	243.21	233.70	225.48	218.32	212.04	206.50	201.58	183.77	172.98
27000	277.67	264.09	252.56	242.69	234.15	226.71	220.19	214.44	209.34	190.84	179.64
28000	287.95	273.87	261.92	251.68	242.82	235.11	228.35	222.38	217.09	197.90	186.29
29000	298.24	283.65	271.27	260.67	251.50	243.51	236.50	230.32	224.84	204.97	192.94
30000	308.52	293.43	280.63	269.65	260.17	251.90	244.66	238.26	232.59	212.04	199.60
31000	318.80	303.21	289.98	278.64	268.84	260.30	252.81	246.20	240.35	219.11	206.25
32000	329.09	312.99	299.33	287.63	277.51	268.70	260.97	254.15	248.10	226.17	212.90
33000	339.37	322.77	308.69	296.62	286.18	277.09	269.12	262.09	255.85	233.24	219.55
34000	349.65	332.55	318.04	305.61	294.86	285.49	277.28	270.03	263.61	240.31	226.21
35000	359.94	342.33	327.40	314.59	303.53	293.89	285.43	277.97	271.36	247.38	232.86
36000	370.22	352.11	336.75	323.58	312.20	302.28	293.59	285.91	279.11	254.45	239.51
37000	380.51	361.89	346.10	332.57	320.87	310.68	301.74	293.86	286.87	261.51	246.17
38000	390.79	371.67	355.46	341.56	329.54	319.08	309.90	301.80	294.62	268.58	252.82
39000	401.07	381.45	364.81	350.55	338.22	327.47	318.05	309.74	302.37	275.65	259.47
40000	411.36	391.23	374.17	359.54	346.89	335.87	326.21	317.68	310.12	282.72	266.13
41000	421.64	401.02	383.52	368.52	355.56	344.27	334.36	325.62	317.88	289.78	272.78
42000	431.93	410.80	392.87	377.51	364.23	352.66	342.52	333.57	325.63	296.85	279.43
43000	442.21	420.58	402.23	386.50	372.90	361.06	350.67	341.51	333.38	303.92	286.09
44000	452.49	430.36	411.58	395.49	381.58	369.46	358.83	349.45	341.14	310.99	292.74
45000	462.78	440.14	420.94	404.48	390.25	377.85	366.98	357.39	348.89	318.06	299.39
46000	473.06	449.92	430.29	413.47	398.92	386.25	375.14	365.33	356.64	325.12	306.04
47000	483.34	459.70	439.64	422.45	407.59	394.65	383.29	373.28	364.40	332.19	312.70
48000	493.63	469.48	449.00	431.44	416.26	403.04	391.45	381.22	372.15	339.26	319.35
49000	503.91	479.26	458.35	440.43	424.94	411.44	399.60	389.16	379.90	346.33	326.00
50000	514.20	489.04	467.71	449.42	433.61	419.84	407.76	397.10	387.65	353.39	332.66
55000	565.61	537.95	514.48	494.36	476.97	461.82	448.53	436.81	426.42	388.73	365.92
60000	617.03	586.85	561.25	539.30	520.33	503.80	489.31	476.52	465.18	424.07	399.19
65000	668.45	635.75	608.02	584.24	563.69	545.78	530.08	516.23	503.95	459.41	432.45
70000	719.87	684.66	654.79	629.18	607.05	587.77	570.86	555.94	542.71	494.75	465.72
75000	771.29	733.56	701.56	674.13	650.41	629.75	611.63	595.65	581.48	530.09	498.98
80000	822.71	782.46	748.33	719.07	693.77	671.73	652.41	635.36	620.24	565.43	532.25
85000	874.13	831.37	795.10	764.01	737.13	713.72	693.18	675.07	659.01	600.77	565.51
90000	925.55	880.27	841.87	808.95	780.49	755.70	733.96	714.78	697.77	636.11	598.78
95000	976.97	929.18	888.64	853.89	823.85	797.68	774.73	754.49	736.54	671.45	632.04
100000	1028.39	978.08	935.41	898.83	867.21	839.67	815.51	794.20	775.30	706.78	665.31

7.25% Principal and Interest
Monthly Payment Amortization Table

AMOUNT	1 Year	2 Years	3 Years	4 Years	5 Years	6 Years	7 Years	8 Years	9 Years	10 Years	11 Years
50	4.34	2.25	1.55	1.21	1.00	.86	.77	.69	.64	.59	.56
100	8.67	4.49	3.10	2.41	2.00	1.72	1.53	1.38	1.27	1.18	1.11
200	17.33	8.98	6.20	4.82	3.99	3.44	3.05	2.76	2.53	2.35	2.21
300	26.00	13.47	9.30	7.22	5.98	5.16	4.57	4.13	3.79	3.53	3.31
400	34.66	17.96	12.40	9.63	7.97	6.87	6.09	5.51	5.06	4.70	4.41
500	43.33	22.45	15.50	12.04	9.96	8.59	7.61	6.88	6.32	5.88	5.51
600	51.99	26.94	18.60	14.44	11.96	10.31	9.13	8.26	7.58	7.05	6.61
700	60.65	31.43	21.70	16.85	13.95	12.02	10.66	9.64	8.85	8.22	7.72
800	69.32	35.91	24.80	19.25	15.94	13.74	12.18	11.01	10.11	9.40	8.82
900	77.98	40.40	27.90	21.66	17.93	15.46	13.70	12.39	11.37	10.57	9.92
1000	86.65	44.89	31.00	24.07	19.92	17.17	15.22	13.76	12.64	11.75	11.02
2000	173.29	89.78	61.99	48.13	39.84	34.34	30.44	27.52	25.27	23.49	22.04
3000	259.93	134.66	92.98	72.19	59.76	51.51	45.65	41.28	37.90	35.23	33.05
4000	346.57	179.55	123.97	96.25	79.68	68.68	60.87	55.04	50.54	46.97	44.07
5000	433.22	224.44	154.96	120.32	99.60	85.85	76.08	68.80	63.17	58.71	55.08
6000	519.86	269.32	185.95	144.38	119.52	103.02	91.30	82.56	75.80	70.45	66.10
7000	606.50	314.21	216.95	168.44	139.44	120.19	106.51	96.31	88.44	82.19	77.11
8000	693.14	359.09	247.94	192.50	159.36	137.36	121.73	110.07	101.07	93.93	88.13
9000	779.78	403.98	278.93	216.57	179.28	154.53	136.94	123.83	113.70	105.67	99.15
10000	866.43	448.87	309.92	240.63	199.20	171.70	152.16	137.59	126.34	117.41	110.16
11000	953.07	493.75	340.91	264.69	219.12	188.87	167.37	151.35	138.97	129.15	121.18
12000	1039.71	538.64	371.90	288.75	239.04	206.04	182.59	165.11	151.60	140.89	132.19
13000	1126.35	583.52	402.89	312.82	258.96	223.21	197.80	178.86	164.24	152.63	143.21
14000	1212.99	628.41	433.89	336.88	278.88	240.38	213.02	192.62	176.87	164.37	154.22
15000	1299.64	673.30	464.88	360.94	298.80	257.54	228.23	206.38	189.50	176.11	165.24
16000	1386.28	718.18	495.87	385.00	318.71	274.71	243.45	220.14	202.14	187.85	176.25
17000	1472.92	763.07	526.86	409.07	338.63	291.88	258.66	233.90	214.77	199.59	187.27
18000	1559.56	807.95	557.85	433.13	358.55	309.05	273.88	247.66	227.40	211.33	198.29
19000	1646.20	852.84	588.84	457.19	378.47	326.22	289.09	261.42	240.04	223.07	209.30
20000	1732.85	897.73	619.84	481.25	398.39	343.39	304.31	275.17	252.67	234.81	220.32
21000	1819.49	942.61	650.83	505.32	418.31	360.56	319.52	288.93	265.30	246.55	231.33
22000	1906.13	987.50	681.82	529.38	438.23	377.73	334.74	302.69	277.94	258.29	242.35
23000	1992.77	1032.38	712.81	553.44	458.15	394.90	349.95	316.45	290.57	270.03	253.36
24000	2079.41	1077.27	743.80	577.50	478.07	412.07	365.17	330.21	303.20	281.77	264.38
25000	2166.06	1122.16	774.79	601.57	497.99	429.24	380.38	343.97	315.84	293.51	275.40
26000	2252.70	1167.04	805.78	625.63	517.91	446.41	395.60	357.72	328.47	305.25	286.41
27000	2339.34	1211.93	836.78	649.69	537.83	463.58	410.81	371.48	341.10	316.99	297.43
28000	2425.98	1256.81	867.77	673.75	557.75	480.75	426.03	385.24	353.74	328.73	308.44
29000	2512.62	1301.70	898.76	697.81	577.67	497.91	441.25	399.00	366.37	340.47	319.46
30000	2599.27	1346.59	929.75	721.88	597.59	515.08	456.46	412.76	379.00	352.21	330.47
31000	2685.91	1391.47	960.74	745.94	617.51	532.25	471.68	426.52	391.64	363.95	341.49
32000	2772.55	1436.36	991.73	770.00	637.42	549.42	486.89	440.28	404.27	375.69	352.50
33000	2859.19	1481.24	1022.73	794.06	657.34	566.59	502.11	454.03	416.90	387.43	363.52
34000	2945.83	1526.13	1053.72	818.13	677.26	583.76	517.32	467.79	429.54	399.17	374.54
35000	3032.48	1571.02	1084.71	842.19	697.18	600.93	532.54	481.55	442.17	410.91	385.55
36000	3119.12	1615.90	1115.70	866.25	717.10	618.10	547.75	495.31	454.80	422.65	396.57
37000	3205.76	1660.79	1146.69	890.31	737.02	635.27	562.97	509.07	467.44	434.39	407.58
38000	3292.40	1705.67	1177.68	914.38	756.94	652.44	578.18	522.83	480.07	446.13	418.60
39000	3379.04	1750.56	1208.67	938.44	776.86	669.61	593.40	536.58	492.70	457.87	429.61
40000	3465.69	1795.45	1239.67	962.50	796.78	686.78	608.61	550.34	505.34	469.61	440.63
41000	3552.33	1840.33	1270.66	986.56	816.70	703.95	623.83	564.10	517.97	481.35	451.64
42000	3638.97	1885.22	1301.65	1010.63	836.62	721.12	639.04	577.86	530.60	493.09	462.66
43000	3725.61	1930.10	1332.64	1034.69	856.54	738.29	654.26	591.62	543.24	504.83	473.68
44000	3812.25	1974.99	1363.63	1058.75	876.46	755.45	669.47	605.38	555.87	516.57	484.69
45000	3898.90	2019.88	1394.62	1082.81	896.38	772.62	684.69	619.14	568.50	528.31	495.71
46000	3985.54	2064.76	1425.62	1106.88	916.30	789.79	699.90	632.89	581.14	540.05	506.72
47000	4072.18	2109.65	1456.61	1130.94	936.21	806.96	715.12	646.65	593.77	551.79	517.74
48000	4158.82	2154.53	1487.60	1155.00	956.13	824.13	730.33	660.41	606.40	563.53	528.75
49000	4245.46	2199.42	1518.59	1179.06	976.05	841.30	745.55	674.17	619.04	575.27	539.77
50000	4332.11	2244.31	1549.58	1203.13	995.97	858.47	760.76	687.93	631.67	587.01	550.79
55000	4765.32	2468.74	1704.54	1323.44	1095.57	944.32	836.84	756.72	694.84	645.71	605.86
60000	5198.53	2693.17	1859.50	1443.75	1195.17	1030.16	912.92	825.51	758.00	704.41	660.94
65000	5631.74	2917.60	2014.45	1564.06	1294.76	1116.01	988.99	894.30	821.17	763.11	716.02
70000	6064.95	3142.03	2169.41	1684.37	1394.36	1201.86	1065.07	963.10	884.33	821.81	771.10
75000	6498.16	3366.46	2324.37	1804.69	1493.96	1287.70	1141.14	1031.89	947.50	880.51	826.18
80000	6931.37	3590.89	2479.33	1925.00	1593.55	1373.55	1217.22	1100.68	1010.67	939.21	881.25
85000	7364.58	3815.32	2634.29	2045.31	1693.15	1459.40	1293.30	1169.47	1073.83	997.91	936.33
90000	7797.79	4039.75	2789.24	2165.62	1792.75	1545.24	1369.37	1238.27	1137.00	1056.61	991.41
95000	8231.00	4264.18	2944.20	2285.93	1892.34	1631.09	1445.45	1307.06	1200.17	1115.31	1046.49
100000	8664.21	4488.61	3099.16	2406.25	1991.94	1716.94	1521.52	1375.85	1263.33	1174.02	1101.57

Principal and Interest
Monthly Payment Amortization Table

7.25%

Term Amount	12 Years	13 Years	14 Years	15 Years	16 Years	17 Years	18 Years	19 Years	20 Years	25 Years	30 Years
50	.53	.50	.48	.46	.45	.43	.42	.41	.40	.37	.35
100	1.05	1.00	.95	.92	.89	.86	.84	.81	.80	.73	.69
200	2.09	1.99	1.90	1.83	1.77	1.71	1.67	1.62	1.59	1.45	1.37
300	3.13	2.98	2.85	2.74	2.65	2.57	2.50	2.43	2.38	2.17	2.05
400	4.17	3.97	3.80	3.66	3.53	3.42	3.33	3.24	3.17	2.90	2.73
500	5.21	4.96	4.75	4.57	4.41	4.28	4.16	4.05	3.96	3.62	3.42
600	6.26	5.96	5.70	5.48	5.29	5.13	4.99	4.86	4.75	4.34	4.10
700	7.30	6.95	6.65	6.40	6.18	5.98	5.82	5.67	5.54	5.06	4.78
800	8.34	7.94	7.60	7.31	7.06	6.84	6.65	6.48	6.33	5.79	5.46
900	9.38	8.93	8.55	8.22	7.94	7.69	7.48	7.29	7.12	6.51	6.14
1000	10.42	9.92	9.50	9.13	8.82	8.55	8.31	8.10	7.91	7.23	6.83
2000	20.84	19.84	18.99	18.26	17.63	17.09	16.61	16.19	15.81	14.46	13.65
3000	31.26	29.76	28.48	27.39	26.45	25.63	24.91	24.28	23.72	21.69	20.47
4000	41.68	39.67	37.97	36.52	35.26	34.17	33.21	32.37	31.62	28.92	27.29
5000	52.09	49.59	47.47	45.65	44.08	42.71	41.51	40.46	39.52	36.15	34.11
6000	62.51	59.51	56.96	54.78	52.89	51.25	49.82	48.55	47.43	43.37	40.94
7000	72.93	69.42	66.45	63.91	61.71	59.79	58.12	56.64	55.33	50.60	47.76
8000	83.35	79.34	75.94	73.03	70.52	68.33	66.42	64.73	63.24	57.83	54.58
9000	93.76	89.26	85.43	82.16	79.34	76.88	74.72	72.82	71.14	65.06	61.40
10000	104.18	99.17	94.93	91.29	88.15	85.42	83.02	80.91	79.04	72.29	68.22
11000	114.60	109.09	104.42	100.42	96.97	93.96	91.32	89.00	86.95	79.51	75.04
12000	125.02	119.01	113.91	109.55	105.78	102.50	99.63	97.09	94.85	86.74	81.87
13000	135.43	128.92	123.40	118.68	114.59	111.04	107.93	105.18	102.75	93.97	88.69
14000	145.85	138.84	132.90	127.81	123.41	119.58	116.23	113.27	110.66	101.20	95.51
15000	156.27	148.76	142.39	136.93	132.22	128.12	124.53	121.37	118.56	108.43	102.33
16000	166.69	158.67	151.88	146.06	141.04	136.66	132.83	129.46	126.47	115.65	109.15
17000	177.10	168.59	161.37	155.19	149.85	145.21	141.13	137.55	134.37	122.88	115.97
18000	187.52	178.51	170.86	164.32	158.67	153.75	149.44	145.64	142.27	130.11	122.80
19000	197.94	188.42	180.36	173.45	167.48	162.29	157.74	153.73	150.18	137.34	129.62
20000	208.36	198.34	189.85	182.58	176.30	170.83	166.04	161.82	158.08	144.57	136.44
21000	218.77	208.26	199.34	191.71	185.11	179.37	174.34	169.91	165.98	151.79	143.26
22000	229.19	218.17	208.83	200.83	193.93	187.91	182.64	178.00	173.89	159.02	150.08
23000	239.61	228.09	218.33	209.96	202.74	196.45	190.94	186.09	181.79	166.25	156.91
24000	250.03	238.01	227.82	219.09	211.55	204.99	199.25	194.18	189.70	173.48	163.73
25000	260.44	247.92	237.31	228.22	220.37	213.54	207.55	202.27	197.60	180.71	170.55
26000	270.86	257.84	246.80	237.35	229.18	222.08	215.85	210.36	205.50	187.93	177.37
27000	281.28	267.76	256.29	246.48	238.00	230.62	224.15	218.45	213.41	195.16	184.19
28000	291.70	277.67	265.79	255.61	246.81	239.16	232.46	226.54	221.31	202.39	191.01
29000	302.11	287.59	275.28	264.74	255.63	247.70	240.75	234.63	229.21	209.62	197.84
30000	312.53	297.51	284.77	273.86	264.44	256.24	249.06	242.73	237.12	216.85	204.66
31000	322.95	307.42	294.26	282.99	273.26	264.78	257.36	250.82	245.02	224.08	211.48
32000	333.37	317.34	303.75	292.12	282.07	273.32	265.66	258.91	252.93	231.30	218.30
33000	343.78	327.26	313.25	301.25	290.89	281.87	273.96	267.00	260.83	238.53	225.12
34000	354.20	337.17	322.74	310.38	299.70	290.41	282.26	275.09	268.73	245.76	231.94
35000	364.62	347.09	332.23	319.51	308.52	298.95	290.57	283.18	276.64	252.99	238.77
36000	375.04	357.01	341.72	328.64	317.33	3C7.49	298.87	291.27	284.54	260.22	245.59
37000	385.45	366.92	351.22	337.76	326.14	316.03	307.17	299.36	292.44	267.44	252.41
38000	395.87	376.84	360.71	346.89	334.96	315.47	315.47	307.45	300.35	274.67	259.23
39000	406.29	386.76	370.20	356.02	343.77	333.11	323.77	315.54	308.25	281.90	266.05
40000	416.71	396.67	379.69	365.15	352.59	341.65	332.07	323.63	316.16	289.13	272.88
41000	427.12	406.59	389.18	374.28	361.40	350.20	340.38	331.72	324.06	296.36	279.70
42000	437.54	416.51	398.68	383.41	370.22	358.74	348.68	339.81	331.96	303.58	286.52
43000	447.96	426.42	408.17	392.54	379.03	367.28	356.98	347.90	339.87	310.81	293.34
44000	458.38	436.34	417.66	401.66	387.85	375.82	365.28	355.99	347.77	318.04	300.16
45000	468.80	446.26	427.15	410.79	396.66	384.36	373.58	364.09	355.67	325.27	306.98
46000	479.21	456.17	436.65	419.92	405.48	392.90	381.88	372.18	363.58	332.50	313.81
47000	489.63	466.09	446.14	429.05	414.29	401.44	390.19	380.27	371.48	339.72	320.63
48000	500.05	476.01	455.63	438.18	423.10	409.98	398.49	388.36	379.39	346.95	327.45
49000	510.47	485.92	465.12	447.31	431.92	418.52	406.79	396.45	387.29	354.18	334.27
50000	520.88	495.84	474.61	456.44	440.73	427.07	415.09	404.54	395.19	361.41	341.09
55000	572.97	545.42	522.07	502.08	484.81	469.77	456.60	444.99	434.71	397.55	375.20
60000	625.06	595.01	569.54	547.72	528.88	512.48	498.11	485.45	474.23	433.69	409.31
65000	677.15	644.59	617.00	593.37	572.95	555.18	539.62	525.90	513.75	469.83	443.42
70000	729.23	694.17	664.46	639.01	617.03	597.89	581.13	566.35	553.27	505.97	477.53
75000	781.32	743.76	711.92	684.65	661.10	640.60	622.63	606.81	592.79	542.11	511.64
80000	833.41	793.34	759.38	730.30	705.17	683.30	664.14	647.26	632.31	578.25	545.75
85000	885.50	842.93	806.84	775.94	749.24	726.01	705.65	687.71	671.82	614.39	579.85
90000	937.59	892.51	854.30	821.58	793.32	768.71	747.16	728.17	711.34	650.53	613.96
95000	989.67	942.09	901.76	867.22	837.39	811.42	788.67	768.62	750.86	686.67	648.07
100000	1041.76	991.68	949.22	912.87	881.46	854.13	830.18	809.07	790.38	722.81	682.18

7.50% Principal and Interest
Monthly Payment Amortization Table

Term Amount	1 Year	2 Years	3 Years	4 Years	5 Years	6 Years	7 Years	8 Years	9 Years	10 Years	11 Years
50	4.34	2.25	1.56	1.21	1.01	.87	.77	.70	.64	.60	.56
100	8.68	4.50	3.12	2.42	2.01	1.73	1.54	1.39	1.28	1.19	1.12
200	17.36	9.00	6.23	4.84	4.01	3.46	3.07	2.78	2.56	2.38	2.23
300	26.03	13.50	9.34	7.26	6.02	5.19	4.61	4.17	3.83	3.57	3.35
400	34.71	18.00	12.45	9.68	8.02	6.92	6.14	5.56	5.11	4.75	4.46
500	43.38	22.50	15.56	12.09	10.02	8.65	7.67	6.95	6.39	5.94	5.58
600	52.06	27.00	18.67	14.51	12.03	10.38	9.21	8.34	7.66	7.13	6.69
700	60.74	31.50	21.78	16.93	14.03	12.11	10.74	9.72	8.94	8.31	7.81
800	69.41	36.00	24.89	19.35	16.04	13.84	12.28	11.11	10.21	9.50	8.92
900	78.09	40.50	28.00	21.77	18.04	15.57	13.81	12.50	11.49	10.69	10.04
1000	86.76	45.00	31.11	24.18	20.04	17.30	15.34	13.89	12.77	11.88	11.15
2000	173.52	90.00	62.22	48.36	40.08	34.59	30.68	27.77	25.53	23.75	22.30
3000	260.28	135.00	93.32	72.54	60.12	51.88	46.02	41.66	38.29	35.62	33.45
4000	347.03	180.00	124.43	96.72	80.16	69.17	61.36	55.54	51.05	47.49	44.60
5000	433.79	225.00	155.54	120.90	100.19	86.46	76.70	69.42	63.81	59.36	55.75
6000	520.55	270.00	186.64	145.08	120.23	103.75	92.03	83.31	76.57	71.23	66.89
7000	607.31	315.00	217.75	169.26	140.27	121.04	107.37	97.19	89.33	83.10	78.04
8000	694.06	360.00	248.85	193.44	160.31	138.33	122.71	111.08	102.09	94.97	89.19
9000	780.82	405.00	279.96	217.62	180.35	155.62	138.05	124.96	114.85	106.84	100.34
10000	867.58	450.00	311.07	241.79	200.38	172.91	153.39	138.84	127.62	118.71	111.49
11000	954.34	495.00	342.17	265.97	220.42	190.20	168.73	152.73	140.38	130.58	122.63
12000	1041.09	540.00	373.28	290.15	240.46	207.49	184.06	166.61	153.14	142.45	133.78
13000	1127.85	585.00	404.39	314.33	260.50	224.78	199.40	180.50	165.90	154.32	144.93
14000	1214.61	630.00	435.49	338.51	280.54	242.07	214.74	194.38	178.66	166.19	156.08
15000	1301.37	675.00	466.60	362.69	300.57	259.36	230.08	208.26	191.42	178.06	167.23
16000	1388.12	720.00	497.70	386.87	320.61	276.65	245.42	222.15	204.18	189.93	178.37
17000	1474.88	765.00	528.81	411.05	340.65	293.94	260.76	236.03	216.94	201.80	189.52
18000	1561.64	810.00	559.92	435.23	360.69	311.23	276.09	249.91	229.70	213.67	200.67
19000	1648.40	855.00	591.02	459.40	380.73	328.52	291.43	263.80	242.46	225.54	211.82
20000	1735.15	900.00	622.13	483.58	400.76	345.81	306.77	277.68	255.23	237.41	222.97
21000	1821.91	945.00	653.24	507.76	420.80	363.10	322.11	291.57	267.99	249.28	234.11
22000	1908.67	990.00	684.34	531.94	440.84	380.39	337.45	305.45	280.75	261.15	245.26
23000	1995.43	1035.00	715.45	556.12	460.88	397.68	352.79	319.33	293.51	273.02	256.41
24000	2082.18	1080.00	746.55	580.30	480.92	414.97	368.12	333.22	306.27	284.89	267.56
25000	2168.94	1124.99	777.66	604.48	500.95	432.26	383.46	347.10	319.03	296.76	278.71
26000	2255.70	1169.99	808.77	628.66	520.99	449.55	398.80	360.99	331.79	308.63	289.85
27000	2342.46	1214.99	839.87	652.84	541.03	466.84	414.14	374.87	344.55	320.50	301.00
28000	2429.21	1259.99	870.98	677.01	561.07	484.13	429.48	388.75	357.31	332.37	312.15
29000	2515.97	1304.99	902.09	701.19	581.11	501.42	444.82	402.64	370.07	344.24	323.30
30000	2602.73	1349.99	933.19	725.37	601.14	518.71	460.15	416.52	382.84	356.11	334.45
31000	2689.48	1394.99	964.30	749.55	621.18	536.00	475.49	430.40	395.60	367.98	345.59
32000	2776.24	1439.99	995.40	773.73	641.22	553.29	490.83	444.29	408.36	379.85	356.74
33000	2863.00	1484.99	1026.51	797.91	661.26	570.58	506.17	458.17	421.12	391.72	367.89
34000	2949.76	1529.99	1057.62	822.09	681.30	587.87	521.51	472.06	433.88	403.59	379.04
35000	3036.51	1574.99	1088.72	846.27	701.33	605.16	536.84	485.94	446.64	415.46	390.19
36000	3123.27	1619.99	1119.83	870.45	721.37	622.45	552.18	499.82	459.40	427.33	401.33
37000	3210.03	1664.99	1150.94	894.62	741.41	639.74	567.52	513.71	472.16	439.20	412.48
38000	3296.79	1709.99	1182.04	918.80	761.45	657.03	582.86	527.59	484.92	451.07	423.63
39000	3383.54	1754.99	1213.15	942.98	781.48	674.32	598.20	541.48	497.68	462.94	434.78
40000	3470.30	1799.99	1244.25	967.16	801.52	691.61	613.54	555.36	510.45	474.81	445.93
41000	3557.06	1844.99	1275.36	991.34	821.56	708.90	628.87	569.24	523.21	486.68	457.07
42000	3643.82	1889.99	1306.47	1015.52	841.60	726.19	644.21	583.13	535.97	498.55	468.22
43000	3730.57	1934.99	1337.57	1039.70	861.64	743.48	659.55	597.01	548.73	510.42	479.37
44000	3817.33	1979.99	1368.68	1063.88	881.67	760.77	674.89	610.90	561.49	522.29	490.52
45000	3904.09	2024.99	1399.78	1088.06	901.71	778.06	690.23	624.78	574.25	534.16	501.67
46000	3990.85	2069.99	1430.89	1112.23	921.75	795.35	705.57	638.66	587.01	546.03	512.81
47000	4077.60	2114.99	1462.00	1136.41	941.79	812.64	720.90	652.55	599.77	557.90	523.96
48000	4164.36	2159.99	1493.10	1160.59	961.83	829.93	736.24	666.43	612.53	569.77	535.11
49000	4251.12	2204.99	1524.21	1184.77	981.86	847.22	751.58	680.31	625.29	581.64	546.26
50000	4337.88	2249.98	1555.32	1208.95	1001.90	864.51	766.92	694.20	638.06	593.51	557.41
55000	4771.66	2474.98	1710.85	1329.84	1102.09	950.96	843.61	763.62	701.86	652.86	613.15
60000	5205.45	2699.98	1866.38	1450.74	1202.28	1037.41	920.30	833.04	765.67	712.22	668.89
65000	5639.24	2924.98	2021.91	1571.63	1302.47	1123.86	996.99	902.46	829.47	771.57	724.63
70000	6073.02	3149.98	2177.44	1692.53	1402.66	1210.31	1073.68	971.88	893.28	830.92	780.37
75000	6506.81	3374.97	2332.97	1813.42	1502.85	1296.76	1150.38	1041.30	957.08	890.27	836.11
80000	6940.60	3599.97	2488.50	1934.32	1603.04	1383.21	1227.07	1110.71	1020.89	949.62	891.85
85000	7374.39	3824.97	2644.03	2055.21	1703.23	1469.66	1303.76	1180.13	1084.69	1008.97	947.59
90000	7808.17	4049.97	2799.56	2176.11	1803.42	1556.12	1380.45	1249.55	1148.50	1068.32	1003.33
95000	8241.96	4274.97	2955.10	2297.00	1903.61	1642.57	1457.14	1318.97	1212.30	1127.67	1059.07
100000	8675.75	4499.96	3110.63	2417.90	2003.80	1729.02	1533.83	1388.39	1276.11	1187.02	1114.81

Principal and Interest
Monthly Payment Amortization Table

7.50%

Term	12 Years	13 Years	14 Years	15 Years	16 Years	17 Years	18 Years	19 Years	20 Years	25 Years	30 Years
Amount											
50	.53	.51	.49	.47	.45	.44	.43	.42	.41	.37	.35
100	1.06	1.01	.97	.93	.90	.87	.85	.83	.81	.74	.70
200	2.12	2.02	1.93	1.86	1.80	1.74	1.69	1.65	1.62	1.48	1.40
300	3.17	3.02	2.89	2.79	2.69	2.61	2.54	2.48	2.42	2.22	2.10
400	4.23	4.03	3.86	3.71	3.59	3.48	3.38	3.30	3.23	2.96	2.80
500	5.28	5.03	4.82	4.64	4.48	4.35	4.23	4.13	4.03	3.70	3.50
600	6.34	6.04	5.78	5.57	5.38	5.22	5.07	4.95	4.84	4.44	4.20
700	7.39	7.04	6.75	6.49	6.28	6.09	5.92	5.77	5.64	5.18	4.90
800	8.45	8.05	7.71	7.42	7.17	6.95	6.76	6.60	6.45	5.92	5.60
900	9.50	9.05	8.67	8.35	8.07	7.82	7.61	7.42	7.26	6.66	6.30
1000	10.56	10.06	9.64	9.28	8.96	8.69	8.45	8.25	8.06	7.39	7.00
2000	21.11	20.11	19.27	18.55	17.92	17.38	16.90	16.49	16.12	14.78	13.99
3000	31.66	30.17	28.90	27.82	26.88	26.07	25.35	24.73	24.17	22.17	20.98
4000	42.21	40.22	38.53	37.09	35.84	34.75	33.80	32.97	32.23	29.56	27.97
5000	52.77	50.27	48.16	46.36	44.80	43.44	42.25	41.21	40.28	36.95	34.97
6000	63.32	60.33	57.79	55.63	53.75	52.13	50.70	49.45	48.34	44.34	41.96
7000	73.87	70.38	67.43	64.90	62.71	60.81	59.15	57.69	56.40	51.73	48.95
8000	84.42	80.43	77.06	74.17	71.67	69.50	67.60	65.93	64.45	59.12	55.94
9000	94.98	90.49	86.69	83.44	80.63	78.19	76.05	74.17	72.51	66.51	62.93
10000	105.53	100.54	96.32	92.71	89.59	86.88	84.50	82.41	80.56	73.90	69.93
11000	116.08	110.60	105.95	101.98	98.55	95.56	92.95	90.65	88.62	81.29	76.92
12000	126.63	120.65	115.58	111.25	107.50	104.25	101.40	98.89	96.68	88.68	83.91
13000	137.18	130.70	125.21	120.52	116.46	112.94	109.85	107.14	104.73	96.07	90.90
14000	147.74	140.76	134.85	129.79	125.42	121.62	118.30	115.38	112.79	103.46	97.90
15000	158.29	150.81	144.48	139.06	134.38	130.31	126.75	123.62	120.84	110.85	104.89
16000	168.84	160.86	154.11	148.33	143.34	139.00	135.20	131.86	128.90	118.24	111.88
17000	179.39	170.92	163.74	157.60	152.30	147.69	143.65	140.10	136.96	125.63	118.87
18000	189.95	180.97	173.37	166.87	161.25	156.37	152.10	148.34	145.01	133.02	125.86
19000	200.50	191.03	183.00	176.14	170.21	165.06	160.55	156.58	153.07	140.41	132.86
20000	211.05	201.08	192.63	185.41	179.17	173.75	169.00	164.82	161.12	147.80	139.85
21000	221.60	211.13	202.27	194.68	188.13	182.43	177.45	173.06	169.18	155.19	146.84
22000	232.15	221.19	211.90	203.95	197.09	191.12	185.90	181.30	177.24	162.58	153.83
23000	242.71	231.24	221.53	213.22	206.05	199.81	194.35	189.54	185.29	169.97	160.82
24000	253.26	241.29	231.16	222.49	215.00	208.50	202.80	197.78	193.35	177.36	167.82
25000	263.81	251.35	240.79	231.76	223.96	217.18	211.25	206.02	201.40	184.75	174.81
26000	274.36	261.40	250.42	241.03	232.92	225.87	219.70	214.27	209.46	192.14	181.80
27000	284.92	271.46	260.05	250.30	241.88	234.56	228.15	222.51	217.52	199.53	188.79
28000	295.47	281.51	269.69	259.57	250.84	243.24	236.60	230.75	225.57	206.92	195.79
29000	306.02	291.56	279.32	268.84	259.80	251.93	245.05	238.99	233.63	214.31	202.78
30000	316.57	301.62	288.95	278.11	268.75	260.62	253.50	247.23	241.68	221.70	209.77
31000	327.13	311.67	298.58	287.38	277.71	269.30	261.95	255.47	249.74	229.09	216.76
32000	337.68	321.72	308.21	296.65	286.67	277.99	270.40	263.71	257.79	236.48	223.75
33000	348.23	331.78	317.84	305.92	295.63	286.68	278.85	271.95	265.85	243.87	230.75
34000	358.78	341.83	327.47	315.19	304.59	295.37	287.30	280.19	273.91	251.26	237.74
35000	369.33	351.88	337.11	324.46	313.54	304.05	295.75	288.43	281.96	258.65	244.73
36000	379.89	361.94	346.74	333.73	322.50	312.74	304.20	296.67	290.02	266.04	251.72
37000	390.44	371.99	356.37	343.00	331.46	321.43	312.65	304.91	298.07	273.43	258.71
38000	400.99	382.05	366.00	352.27	340.42	330.11	321.09	313.15	306.13	280.82	265.71
39000	411.54	392.10	375.63	361.54	349.38	338.80	329.54	321.40	314.19	288.21	272.70
40000	422.10	402.15	385.26	370.81	358.34	347.49	337.99	329.64	322.24	295.60	279.69
41000	432.65	412.21	394.89	380.08	367.29	356.18	346.44	337.88	330.30	302.99	286.68
42000	443.20	422.26	404.53	389.35	376.25	364.86	354.89	346.12	338.35	310.38	293.68
43000	453.75	432.31	414.16	398.62	385.21	373.55	363.34	354.36	346.41	317.77	300.67
44000	464.30	442.37	423.79	407.89	394.17	382.24	371.79	362.60	354.47	325.16	307.66
45000	474.86	452.42	433.42	417.16	403.13	390.92	380.24	370.84	362.52	332.55	314.65
46000	485.41	462.48	443.05	426.43	412.09	399.61	388.69	379.08	370.58	339.94	321.64
47000	495.96	472.53	452.68	435.70	421.04	408.30	397.14	387.32	378.63	347.33	328.64
48000	506.51	482.58	462.31	444.97	430.00	416.99	405.59	395.56	386.69	354.72	335.63
49000	517.07	492.64	471.95	454.24	438.96	425.67	414.04	403.80	394.75	362.11	342.62
50000	527.62	502.69	481.58	463.51	447.92	434.36	422.49	412.04	402.80	369.50	349.61
55000	580.38	552.96	529.73	509.86	492.71	477.80	464.74	453.25	443.08	406.45	384.57
60000	633.14	603.23	577.89	556.21	537.50	521.23	506.99	494.45	483.36	443.40	419.53
65000	685.90	653.50	626.05	602.56	582.29	564.67	549.24	535.66	523.64	480.35	454.49
70000	738.66	703.76	674.21	648.91	627.08	608.10	591.49	576.86	563.92	517.30	489.46
75000	791.42	754.03	722.36	695.26	671.88	651.54	633.73	618.06	604.20	554.25	524.42
80000	844.19	804.30	770.52	741.61	716.67	694.97	675.98	659.27	644.48	591.20	559.38
85000	896.95	854.57	818.68	787.97	761.46	738.41	718.23	700.47	684.76	628.15	594.34
90000	949.71	904.84	866.83	834.32	806.25	781.84	760.48	741.68	725.04	665.10	629.30
95000	1002.47	955.11	914.99	880.67	851.04	825.28	802.73	782.88	765.32	702.05	664.26
100000	1055.23	1005.38	963.15	927.02	895.83	868.71	844.98	824.08	805.60	739.00	699.22

7.75% Principal and Interest
Monthly Payment Amortization Table

Term Amount	1 Year	2 Years	3 Years	4 Years	5 Years	6 Years	7 Years	8 Years	9 Years	10 Years	11 Years
50	4.35	2.26	1.57	1.22	1.01	.88	.78	.71	.65	.61	.57
100	8.69	4.52	3.13	2.43	2.02	1.75	1.55	1.41	1.29	1.21	1.13
200	17.38	9.03	6.25	4.86	4.04	3.49	3.10	2.81	2.58	2.41	2.26
300	26.07	13.54	9.37	7.29	6.05	5.23	4.64	4.21	3.87	3.61	3.39
400	34.75	18.05	12.49	9.72	8.07	6.97	6.19	5.61	5.16	4.81	4.52
500	43.44	22.56	15.62	12.15	10.08	8.71	7.74	7.01	6.45	6.01	5.65
600	52.13	27.07	18.74	14.58	12.10	10.45	9.28	8.41	7.74	7.21	6.77
700	60.82	31.58	21.86	17.01	14.11	12.19	10.83	9.81	9.03	8.41	7.90
800	69.50	36.10	24.98	19.44	16.13	13.93	12.37	11.21	10.32	9.61	9.03
900	78.19	40.61	28.10	21.87	18.15	15.68	13.92	12.61	11.61	10.81	10.16
1000	86.88	45.12	31.23	24.30	20.16	17.42	15.47	14.01	12.89	12.01	11.29
2000	173.75	90.23	62.45	48.60	40.32	34.83	30.93	28.02	25.78	24.01	22.57
3000	260.62	135.35	93.67	72.89	60.48	52.24	46.39	42.03	38.67	36.01	33.85
4000	347.50	180.46	124.89	97.19	80.63	69.65	61.85	56.04	51.56	48.01	45.13
5000	434.37	225.57	156.11	121.48	100.79	87.06	77.31	70.05	64.45	60.01	56.41
6000	521.24	270.69	187.33	145.78	120.95	104.47	92.78	84.06	77.34	72.01	67.69
7000	608.12	315.80	218.55	170.08	141.10	121.88	108.24	98.07	90.23	84.01	78.97
8000	694.99	360.91	249.77	194.37	161.26	139.30	123.70	112.08	103.12	96.01	90.26
9000	781.86	406.03	281.00	218.67	181.42	156.71	139.16	126.09	116.01	108.01	101.54
10000	868.73	451.14	312.22	242.96	201.57	174.12	154.62	140.10	128.90	120.02	112.82
11000	955.61	496.25	343.44	267.26	221.73	191.53	170.09	154.11	141.79	132.02	124.10
12000	1042.48	541.37	374.66	291.55	241.89	208.94	185.55	168.12	154.68	144.02	135.38
13000	1129.35	586.48	405.88	315.85	262.05	226.35	201.01	182.13	167.57	156.02	146.66
14000	1216.23	631.59	437.10	340.15	282.20	243.76	216.47	196.14	180.46	168.02	157.94
15000	1303.10	676.71	468.32	364.44	302.36	261.18	231.93	210.15	193.35	180.02	169.22
16000	1389.97	721.82	499.54	388.74	322.52	278.59	247.40	224.16	206.24	192.02	180.51
17000	1476.84	766.93	530.76	413.03	342.67	296.00	262.86	238.17	219.13	204.02	191.79
18000	1563.72	812.05	561.99	437.33	362.83	313.41	278.32	252.18	232.02	216.02	203.07
19000	1650.59	857.16	593.21	461.62	382.99	330.82	293.78	266.19	244.91	228.03	214.35
20000	1737.46	902.27	624.43	485.92	403.14	348.23	309.24	280.20	257.79	240.03	225.63
21000	1824.34	947.39	655.65	510.22	423.30	365.64	324.71	294.21	270.68	252.03	236.91
22000	1911.21	992.50	686.87	534.51	443.46	383.06	340.17	308.22	283.57	264.03	248.19
23000	1998.08	1037.61	718.09	558.81	463.62	400.47	355.63	322.23	296.46	276.03	259.47
24000	2084.95	1082.73	749.31	583.10	483.77	417.88	371.09	336.24	309.35	288.03	270.76
25000	2171.83	1127.84	780.53	607.40	503.93	435.29	386.55	350.25	322.24	300.03	282.04
26000	2258.70	1172.95	811.76	631.69	524.09	452.70	402.02	364.26	335.13	312.03	293.32
27000	2345.57	1218.07	842.98	655.99	544.24	470.11	417.48	378.27	348.02	324.03	304.60
28000	2432.45	1263.18	874.20	680.29	564.40	487.52	432.94	392.28	360.91	336.03	315.88
29000	2519.32	1308.29	905.42	704.58	584.56	504.94	448.40	406.29	373.80	348.04	327.16
30000	2606.19	1353.41	936.64	728.88	604.71	522.35	463.86	420.30	386.69	360.04	338.44
31000	2693.06	1398.52	967.86	753.17	624.87	539.76	479.33	434.31	399.58	372.04	349.72
32000	2779.94	1443.63	999.08	777.47	645.03	557.17	494.79	448.32	412.47	384.04	361.01
33000	2866.81	1488.75	1030.30	801.76	665.18	574.58	510.25	462.33	425.36	396.04	372.29
34000	2953.68	1533.86	1061.52	826.06	685.34	591.99	525.71	476.34	438.25	408.04	383.57
35000	3040.56	1578.97	1092.75	850.36	705.50	609.40	541.17	490.35	451.14	420.04	394.85
36000	3127.43	1624.09	1123.97	874.65	725.66	626.82	556.64	504.36	464.03	432.04	406.13
37000	3214.30	1669.20	1155.19	898.95	745.81	644.23	572.10	518.37	476.92	444.04	417.41
38000	3301.17	1714.31	1186.41	923.24	765.97	661.64	587.56	532.38	489.81	456.05	428.69
39000	3388.05	1759.43	1217.63	947.54	786.13	679.05	603.02	546.39	502.70	468.05	439.98
40000	3474.92	1804.54	1248.85	971.83	806.28	696.46	618.48	560.40	515.58	480.05	451.26
41000	3561.79	1849.65	1280.07	996.13	826.44	713.87	633.95	574.41	528.47	492.05	462.54
42000	3648.67	1894.77	1311.29	1020.43	846.60	731.28	649.41	588.42	541.36	504.05	473.82
43000	3735.54	1939.88	1342.52	1044.72	866.75	748.70	664.87	602.43	554.25	516.05	485.10
44000	3822.41	1984.99	1373.74	1069.02	886.91	766.11	680.33	616.44	567.14	528.05	496.38
45000	3909.28	2030.11	1404.96	1093.31	907.07	783.52	695.79	630.45	580.03	540.05	507.66
46000	3996.16	2075.22	1436.18	1117.61	927.23	800.93	711.25	644.46	592.92	552.05	518.94
47000	4083.03	2120.33	1467.40	1141.90	947.38	818.34	726.72	658.47	605.81	564.05	530.23
48000	4169.90	2165.45	1498.62	1166.20	967.54	835.75	742.18	672.48	618.70	576.06	541.51
49000	4256.78	2210.56	1529.84	1190.50	987.70	853.16	757.64	686.49	631.59	588.06	552.79
50000	4343.65	2255.67	1561.06	1214.79	1007.85	870.58	773.10	700.50	644.48	600.06	564.07
55000	4778.01	2481.24	1717.17	1336.27	1108.64	957.63	850.41	770.55	708.93	660.06	620.48
60000	5212.38	2706.81	1873.27	1457.75	1209.42	1044.69	927.72	840.60	773.37	720.07	676.88
65000	5646.74	2932.37	2029.38	1579.23	1310.21	1131.75	1005.03	910.65	837.82	780.07	733.29
70000	6081.11	3157.94	2185.49	1700.71	1410.99	1218.80	1082.34	980.70	902.27	840.08	789.70
75000	6515.47	3383.51	2341.59	1822.19	1511.78	1305.86	1159.65	1050.75	966.72	900.08	846.10
80000	6949.84	3609.07	2497.70	1943.66	1612.56	1392.92	1236.96	1120.80	1031.16	960.09	902.51
85000	7384.20	3834.64	2653.80	2065.14	1713.35	1479.98	1314.27	1190.85	1095.61	1020.10	958.91
90000	7818.56	4060.21	2809.91	2186.62	1814.13	1567.03	1391.58	1260.90	1160.06	1080.10	1015.32
95000	8252.93	4285.77	2966.02	2308.10	1914.92	1654.09	1468.89	1330.95	1224.51	1140.11	1071.73
100000	8687.29	4511.34	3122.12	2429.58	2015.70	1741.15	1546.20	1401.00	1288.95	1200.11	1128.13

Principal and Interest
Monthly Payment Amortization Table

7.75%

Term Amount	12 Years	13 Years	14 Years	15 Years	16 Years	17 Years	18 Years	19 Years	20 Years	25 Years	30 Years
50	.54	.51	.49	.48	.46	.45	.43	.42	.42	.38	.36
100	1.07	1.02	.98	.95	.92	.89	.86	.84	.83	.76	.72
200	2.14	2.04	1.96	1.89	1.83	1.77	1.72	1.68	1.65	1.52	1.44
300	3.21	3.06	2.94	2.83	2.74	2.66	2.58	2.52	2.47	2.27	2.15
400	4.28	4.08	3.91	3.77	3.65	3.54	3.44	3.36	3.29	3.03	2.87
500	5.35	5.10	4.89	4.71	4.56	4.42	4.30	4.20	4.11	3.78	3.59
600	6.42	6.12	5.87	5.65	5.47	5.31	5.16	5.04	4.93	4.54	4.30
700	7.49	7.14	6.85	6.59	6.38	6.19	6.02	5.88	5.75	5.29	5.02
800	8.56	8.16	7.82	7.54	7.29	7.07	6.88	6.72	6.57	6.05	5.74
900	9.62	9.18	8.80	8.48	8.20	7.96	7.74	7.56	7.39	6.80	6.45
1000	10.69	10.20	9.78	9.42	9.11	8.84	8.60	8.40	8.21	7.56	7.17
2000	21.38	20.39	19.55	18.83	18.21	17.67	17.20	16.79	16.42	15.11	14.33
3000	32.07	30.58	29.32	28.24	27.31	26.51	25.80	25.18	24.63	22.66	21.50
4000	42.76	40.77	39.09	37.66	36.42	35.34	34.40	33.57	32.84	30.22	28.66
5000	53.44	50.96	48.86	47.07	45.52	44.18	43.00	41.97	41.05	37.77	35.83
6000	64.13	61.16	58.64	56.48	54.62	53.01	51.60	50.36	49.26	45.32	42.99
7000	74.82	71.35	68.41	65.89	63.73	61.84	60.20	58.75	57.47	52.88	50.15
8000	85.51	81.54	78.18	75.31	72.83	70.68	68.80	67.14	65.68	60.43	57.32
9000	96.20	91.73	87.95	84.72	81.93	79.51	77.40	75.54	73.89	67.98	64.48
10000	106.88	101.92	97.72	94.13	91.04	88.35	86.00	83.93	82.10	75.54	71.65
11000	117.57	112.11	107.49	103.55	100.14	97.18	94.59	92.32	90.31	83.09	78.81
12000	128.26	122.31	117.27	112.96	109.24	106.02	103.19	100.71	98.52	90.64	85.97
13000	138.95	132.50	127.04	122.37	118.35	114.85	111.79	109.10	106.73	98.20	93.14
14000	149.64	142.69	136.81	131.78	127.45	123.68	120.39	117.50	114.94	105.75	100.30
15000	160.32	152.88	146.58	141.20	136.55	132.52	128.99	125.89	123.15	113.30	107.47
16000	171.01	163.07	156.35	150.61	145.66	141.35	137.59	134.28	131.36	120.86	114.63
17000	181.70	173.26	166.13	160.02	154.76	150.19	146.19	142.67	139.57	128.41	121.80
18000	192.39	183.46	175.90	169.43	163.86	159.02	154.79	151.07	147.78	135.96	128.96
19000	203.08	193.65	185.67	178.85	172.97	167.86	163.39	159.46	155.99	143.52	136.12
20000	213.76	203.84	195.44	188.26	182.07	176.69	171.99	167.85	164.19	151.07	143.29
21000	224.45	214.03	205.21	197.67	191.17	185.52	180.58	176.24	172.40	158.62	150.45
22000	235.14	224.22	214.98	207.09	200.27	194.36	189.18	184.63	180.61	166.18	157.62
23000	245.83	234.41	224.76	216.50	209.38	203.19	197.78	193.03	188.82	173.73	164.78
24000	256.52	244.61	234.53	225.91	218.48	212.03	206.38	201.42	197.03	181.28	171.94
25000	267.20	254.80	244.30	235.32	227.58	220.86	214.98	209.81	205.24	188.84	179.11
26000	277.89	264.99	254.07	244.74	236.69	229.69	223.58	218.20	213.45	196.39	186.27
27000	288.58	275.18	263.84	254.15	245.79	238.53	232.18	226.60	221.66	203.94	193.44
28000	299.27	285.37	273.61	263.56	254.89	247.36	240.78	234.99	229.87	211.50	200.60
29000	309.95	295.56	283.39	272.97	264.00	256.20	249.38	243.38	238.08	219.05	207.76
30000	320.64	305.76	293.16	282.39	273.10	265.03	257.98	251.77	246.29	226.60	214.93
31000	331.33	315.95	302.93	291.80	282.20	273.87	266.58	260.16	254.50	234.16	222.09
32000	342.02	326.14	312.70	301.21	291.31	282.70	275.17	268.56	262.71	241.71	229.26
33000	352.71	336.33	322.47	310.63	300.41	291.53	283.77	276.95	270.92	249.26	236.42
34000	363.39	346.52	332.25	320.04	309.51	300.37	292.37	285.34	279.13	256.82	243.59
35000	374.08	356.72	342.02	329.45	318.62	309.20	300.97	293.73	287.34	264.37	250.75
36000	384.77	366.91	351.79	338.86	327.72	318.04	309.57	302.13	295.55	271.92	257.91
37000	395.46	377.10	361.56	348.28	336.82	326.87	318.17	310.52	303.76	279.48	265.08
38000	406.15	387.29	371.33	357.69	345.93	335.71	326.77	318.91	311.97	287.03	272.24
39000	416.83	397.48	381.10	367.10	355.03	344.54	335.37	327.30	320.17	294.58	279.41
40000	427.52	407.67	390.88	376.52	364.13	353.37	343.97	335.69	328.38	302.14	286.57
41000	438.21	417.87	400.65	385.93	373.24	362.21	352.57	344.09	336.59	309.69	293.73
42000	448.90	428.06	410.42	395.34	382.34	371.04	361.16	352.48	344.80	317.24	300.90
43000	459.59	438.25	420.19	404.75	391.44	379.88	369.76	360.87	353.01	324.80	308.06
44000	470.27	448.44	429.96	414.17	400.54	388.71	378.36	369.26	361.22	332.35	315.23
45000	480.96	458.63	439.73	423.58	409.65	397.54	386.96	377.66	369.43	339.90	322.39
46000	491.65	468.82	449.51	432.99	418.75	406.38	395.56	386.05	377.64	347.46	329.55
47000	502.34	479.02	459.28	442.40	427.85	415.21	404.16	394.44	385.85	355.01	336.72
48000	513.03	489.21	469.05	451.82	436.96	424.05	412.76	402.83	394.06	362.56	343.88
49000	523.71	499.40	478.82	461.23	446.06	432.88	421.36	411.22	402.27	370.12	351.05
50000	534.40	509.59	488.59	470.64	455.16	441.72	429.96	419.62	410.48	377.67	358.21
55000	587.84	560.55	537.45	517.71	500.68	485.89	472.95	461.58	451.53	415.44	394.03
60000	641.28	611.51	586.31	564.77	546.20	530.06	515.95	503.54	492.57	453.20	429.85
65000	694.72	662.47	635.17	611.83	591.71	574.23	558.94	545.50	533.62	490.97	465.67
70000	748.16	713.43	684.03	658.90	637.23	618.40	601.94	587.46	574.67	528.74	501.49
75000	801.60	764.38	732.89	705.96	682.74	662.57	644.93	629.42	615.72	566.50	537.31
80000	855.04	815.34	781.75	753.03	728.26	706.74	687.93	671.38	656.76	604.27	573.13
85000	908.48	866.30	830.61	800.09	773.77	750.91	730.92	713.35	697.81	642.03	608.96
90000	961.92	917.26	879.46	847.15	819.29	795.08	773.92	755.31	738.86	679.80	644.78
95000	1015.36	968.22	928.32	894.22	864.81	839.26	816.91	797.27	779.91	717.57	680.60
100000	1068.80	1019.18	977.18	941.28	910.32	883.43	859.91	839.23	820.95	755.33	716.42

8.00% Principal and Interest
Monthly Payment Amortization Table

Term Amount	1 Year	2 Years	3 Years	4 Years	5 Years	6 Years	7 Years	8 Years	9 Years	10 Years	11 Years
50	4.35	2.27	1.57	1.23	1.02	.88	.78	.71	.66	.61	.58
100	8.70	4.53	3.14	2.45	2.03	1.76	1.56	1.42	1.31	1.22	1.15
200	17.40	9.05	6.27	4.89	4.06	3.51	3.12	2.83	2.61	2.43	2.29
300	26.10	13.57	9.41	7.33	6.09	5.26	4.68	4.25	3.91	3.64	3.43
400	34.80	18.10	12.54	9.77	8.12	7.02	6.24	5.66	5.21	4.86	4.57
500	43.50	22.62	15.67	12.21	10.14	8.77	7.80	7.07	6.51	6.07	5.71
600	52.20	27.14	18.81	14.65	12.17	10.52	9.36	8.49	7.82	7.28	6.85
700	60.90	31.66	21.94	17.09	14.20	12.28	10.92	9.90	9.12	8.50	8.00
800	69.60	36.19	25.07	19.54	16.23	14.03	12.47	11.31	10.42	9.71	9.14
900	78.29	40.71	28.21	21.98	18.25	15.78	14.03	12.73	11.72	10.92	10.28
1000	86.99	45.23	31.34	24.42	20.28	17.54	15.59	14.14	13.02	12.14	11.42
2000	173.98	90.46	62.68	48.83	40.56	35.07	31.18	28.28	26.04	24.27	22.84
3000	260.97	135.69	94.01	73.24	60.83	52.60	46.76	42.42	39.06	36.40	34.25
4000	347.96	180.91	125.35	97.66	81.11	70.14	62.35	56.55	52.08	48.54	45.67
5000	434.95	226.14	156.69	122.07	101.39	87.67	77.94	70.69	65.10	60.67	57.08
6000	521.94	271.37	188.02	146.48	121.66	105.20	93.52	84.83	78.12	72.80	68.50
7000	608.92	316.60	219.36	170.90	141.94	122.74	109.11	98.96	91.14	84.93	79.91
8000	695.91	361.82	250.70	195.31	162.22	140.27	124.69	113.10	104.15	97.07	91.33
9000	782.90	407.05	282.03	219.72	182.49	157.80	140.28	127.24	117.17	109.20	102.74
10000	869.89	452.28	313.37	244.13	202.77	175.34	155.87	141.37	130.19	121.33	114.16
11000	956.88	497.51	344.71	268.55	223.05	192.87	171.45	155.51	143.21	133.47	125.57
12000	1043.87	542.73	376.04	292.96	243.32	210.40	187.04	169.65	156.23	145.60	136.99
13000	1130.85	587.96	407.38	317.37	263.60	227.94	202.63	183.78	169.25	157.73	148.41
14000	1217.84	633.19	438.71	341.79	283.87	245.47	218.21	197.92	182.27	169.86	159.82
15000	1304.83	678.41	470.05	366.20	304.15	263.00	233.80	212.06	195.29	182.00	171.24
16000	1391.82	723.64	501.39	390.61	324.43	280.54	249.38	226.19	208.30	194.13	182.65
17000	1478.81	768.87	532.72	415.02	344.70	298.07	264.97	240.33	221.32	206.26	194.07
18000	1565.80	814.10	564.06	439.44	364.98	315.60	280.56	254.47	234.34	218.39	205.48
19000	1652.79	859.32	595.40	463.85	385.26	333.14	296.14	268.60	247.36	230.53	216.90
20000	1739.77	904.55	626.73	488.26	405.53	350.67	311.73	282.74	260.38	242.66	228.31
21000	1826.76	949.78	658.07	512.68	425.81	368.20	327.32	296.88	273.40	254.79	239.73
22000	1913.75	995.01	689.41	537.09	446.09	385.74	342.90	311.01	286.42	266.93	251.14
23000	2000.74	1040.23	720.74	561.50	466.36	403.27	358.49	325.15	299.44	279.06	262.56
24000	2087.73	1085.46	752.08	585.92	486.64	420.80	374.07	339.29	312.45	291.19	273.98
25000	2174.72	1130.69	783.41	610.33	506.92	438.34	389.66	353.42	325.47	303.32	285.39
26000	2261.70	1175.91	814.75	634.74	527.19	455.87	405.25	367.56	338.49	315.46	296.81
27000	2348.69	1221.14	846.09	659.15	547.47	473.40	420.83	381.70	351.51	327.59	308.22
28000	2435.68	1266.37	877.42	683.57	567.74	490.94	436.42	395.83	364.53	339.72	319.64
29000	2522.67	1311.60	908.76	707.98	588.02	508.47	452.01	409.97	377.55	351.86	331.05
30000	2609.66	1356.82	940.10	732.39	608.30	526.00	467.59	424.11	390.57	363.99	342.47
31000	2696.65	1402.05	971.43	756.81	628.57	543.54	483.18	438.24	403.59	376.12	353.88
32000	2783.63	1447.28	1002.77	781.22	648.85	561.07	498.76	452.38	416.60	388.25	365.30
33000	2870.62	1492.51	1034.11	805.63	669.13	578.60	514.35	466.52	429.62	400.39	376.71
34000	2957.61	1537.73	1065.44	830.04	689.40	596.14	529.94	480.65	442.64	412.52	388.13
35000	3044.60	1582.96	1096.78	854.46	709.68	613.67	545.52	494.79	455.66	424.65	399.55
36000	3131.59	1628.19	1128.11	878.87	729.96	631.20	561.11	508.93	468.68	436.78	410.96
37000	3218.58	1673.41	1159.45	903.28	750.23	648.73	576.69	523.06	481.70	448.92	422.38
38000	3305.57	1718.64	1190.79	927.70	770.51	666.27	592.28	537.20	494.72	461.05	433.79
39000	3392.55	1763.87	1222.12	952.11	790.78	683.80	607.87	551.34	507.73	473.18	445.21
40000	3479.54	1809.10	1253.46	976.52	811.06	701.33	623.45	565.47	520.75	485.32	456.62
41000	3566.53	1854.32	1284.80	1000.93	831.34	718.87	639.04	579.61	533.77	497.45	468.04
42000	3653.52	1899.55	1316.13	1025.35	851.61	736.40	654.63	593.75	546.79	509.58	479.45
43000	3740.51	1944.78	1347.47	1049.76	871.89	753.93	670.21	607.88	559.81	521.71	490.87
44000	3827.50	1990.01	1378.81	1074.17	892.17	771.47	685.80	622.02	572.83	533.85	502.28
45000	3914.48	2035.23	1410.14	1098.59	912.44	789.00	701.38	636.16	585.85	545.98	513.70
46000	4001.47	2080.46	1441.48	1123.00	932.72	806.53	716.97	650.29	598.87	558.11	525.12
47000	4088.46	2125.69	1472.81	1147.41	953.00	824.07	732.56	664.43	611.88	570.24	536.53
48000	4175.45	2170.92	1504.15	1171.83	973.27	841.60	748.14	678.57	624.90	582.38	547.95
49000	4262.44	2216.14	1535.49	1196.24	993.55	859.13	763.73	692.70	637.92	594.51	559.36
50000	4349.43	2261.37	1566.82	1220.65	1013.82	876.67	779.32	706.84	650.94	606.64	570.78
55000	4784.37	2487.51	1723.51	1342.72	1115.21	964.33	857.25	777.52	716.03	667.31	627.85
60000	5219.31	2713.64	1880.19	1464.78	1216.59	1052.00	935.18	848.21	781.13	727.97	684.93
65000	5654.25	2939.78	2036.87	1586.84	1317.97	1139.67	1013.11	918.89	846.22	788.63	742.01
70000	6089.20	3165.92	2193.55	1708.91	1419.35	1227.33	1091.04	989.57	911.32	849.30	799.09
75000	6524.14	3392.05	2350.23	1830.97	1520.73	1315.00	1168.97	1060.26	976.41	909.96	856.16
80000	6959.08	3618.19	2506.91	1953.04	1622.12	1402.66	1246.90	1130.94	1041.50	970.63	913.24
85000	7394.02	3844.32	2663.60	2075.10	1723.50	1490.33	1324.83	1201.62	1106.60	1031.29	970.32
90000	7828.96	4070.46	2820.28	2197.17	1824.88	1578.00	1402.76	1272.31	1171.69	1091.95	1027.40
95000	8263.91	4296.60	2976.96	2319.23	1926.26	1665.66	1480.70	1342.99	1236.78	1152.62	1084.47
100000	8698.85	4522.73	3133.64	2441.30	2027.64	1753.33	1558.63	1413.67	1301.88	1213.28	1141.55

Principal and Interest
Monthly Payment Amortization Table

8.00%

Term / Amount	12 Years	13 Years	14 Years	15 Years	16 Years	17 Years	18 Years	19 Years	20 Years	25 Years	30 Years
50	.55	.52	.50	.48	.47	.45	.44	.43	.42	.39	.37
100	1.09	1.04	1.00	.96	.93	.90	.88	.86	.84	.78	.74
200	2.17	2.07	1.99	1.92	1.85	1.80	1.75	1.71	1.68	1.55	1.47
300	3.25	3.10	2.98	2.87	2.78	2.70	2.63	2.57	2.51	2.32	2.21
400	4.33	4.14	3.97	3.83	3.70	3.60	3.50	3.42	3.35	3.09	2.94
500	5.42	5.17	4.96	4.78	4.63	4.50	4.38	4.28	4.19	3.86	3.67
600	6.50	6.20	5.95	5.74	5.55	5.39	5.25	5.13	5.02	4.64	4.41
700	7.58	7.24	6.94	6.69	6.48	6.29	6.13	5.99	5.86	5.41	5.14
800	8.66	8.27	7.94	7.65	7.40	7.19	7.00	6.84	6.70	6.18	5.88
900	9.75	9.30	8.93	8.61	8.33	8.09	7.88	7.70	7.53	6.95	6.61
1000	10.83	10.34	9.92	9.56	9.25	8.99	8.75	8.55	8.37	7.72	7.34
2000	21.65	20.67	19.83	19.12	18.50	17.97	17.50	17.10	16.73	15.44	14.68
3000	32.48	31.00	29.74	28.67	27.75	26.95	26.25	25.64	25.10	23.16	22.02
4000	43.30	41.33	39.66	38.23	37.00	35.94	35.00	34.19	33.46	30.88	29.36
5000	54.13	51.66	49.57	47.79	46.25	44.92	43.75	42.73	41.83	38.60	36.69
6000	64.95	61.99	59.48	57.34	55.50	53.90	52.50	51.28	50.19	46.31	44.03
7000	75.78	72.32	69.40	66.90	64.75	62.88	61.25	59.82	58.56	54.03	51.37
8000	86.60	82.65	79.31	76.46	74.00	71.87	70.00	68.37	66.92	61.75	58.71
9000	97.43	92.98	89.22	86.01	83.25	80.85	78.75	76.91	75.28	69.47	66.04
10000	108.25	103.31	99.14	95.57	92.50	89.83	87.50	85.46	83.65	77.19	73.38
11000	119.07	113.64	109.05	105.13	101.75	98.81	96.25	94.00	92.01	84.90	80.72
12000	129.90	123.97	118.96	114.68	111.00	107.80	105.00	102.55	100.38	92.62	88.06
13000	140.72	134.30	128.88	124.24	120.25	116.78	113.75	111.09	108.74	100.34	95.39
14000	151.55	144.64	138.79	133.80	129.49	125.76	122.50	119.64	117.11	108.06	102.73
15000	162.37	154.97	148.70	143.35	138.74	134.74	131.25	128.18	125.47	115.78	110.07
16000	173.20	165.30	158.62	152.91	147.99	143.73	140.00	136.73	133.84	123.50	117.41
17000	184.02	175.63	168.53	162.47	157.24	152.71	148.75	145.27	142.20	131.21	124.74
18000	194.85	185.96	178.44	172.02	166.49	161.69	157.50	153.82	150.56	138.93	132.08
19000	205.67	196.29	188.36	181.58	175.74	170.67	166.25	162.36	158.93	146.65	139.42
20000	216.50	206.62	198.27	191.14	184.99	179.66	175.00	170.91	167.29	154.37	146.76
21000	227.32	216.95	208.18	200.69	194.24	188.64	183.75	179.45	175.66	162.09	154.10
22000	238.14	227.28	218.10	210.25	203.49	197.62	192.50	188.00	184.02	169.80	161.43
23000	248.97	237.61	228.01	219.80	212.74	206.60	201.25	196.54	192.39	177.52	168.77
24000	259.79	247.94	237.92	229.36	221.99	215.59	210.00	205.09	200.75	185.24	176.11
25000	270.62	258.27	247.83	238.92	231.24	224.57	218.75	213.63	209.12	192.96	183.45
26000	281.44	268.60	257.75	248.47	240.49	233.55	227.50	222.18	217.48	200.68	190.78
27000	292.27	278.93	267.66	258.03	249.73	242.53	236.24	230.72	225.84	208.40	198.12
28000	303.09	289.27	277.57	267.59	258.98	251.52	244.99	239.27	234.21	216.11	205.46
29000	313.92	299.60	287.49	277.14	268.23	260.50	253.74	247.81	242.57	223.83	212.80
30000	324.74	309.93	297.40	286.70	277.48	269.48	262.49	256.36	250.94	231.55	220.13
31000	335.57	320.26	307.31	296.26	286.73	278.46	271.24	264.90	259.30	239.27	227.47
32000	346.39	330.59	317.23	305.81	295.98	287.45	279.99	273.45	267.67	246.99	234.81
33000	357.21	340.92	327.14	315.37	305.23	296.43	288.74	281.99	276.03	254.70	242.15
34000	368.04	351.25	337.05	324.93	314.48	305.41	297.49	290.54	284.39	262.42	249.48
35000	378.86	361.58	346.97	334.48	323.73	314.39	306.24	299.08	292.76	270.14	256.82
36000	389.69	371.91	356.88	344.04	332.98	323.38	314.99	307.63	301.12	277.86	264.16
37000	400.51	382.24	366.79	353.60	342.23	332.36	323.74	316.17	309.49	285.58	271.50
38000	411.34	392.57	376.71	363.15	351.48	341.34	332.49	324.72	317.85	293.30	278.84
39000	422.16	402.90	386.62	372.71	360.73	350.33	341.24	333.26	326.22	301.01	286.17
40000	432.99	413.23	396.53	382.27	369.98	359.31	349.99	341.81	334.58	308.73	293.51
41000	443.81	423.57	406.45	391.82	379.22	368.29	358.74	350.35	342.95	316.45	300.85
42000	454.64	433.90	416.36	401.38	388.47	377.27	367.49	358.90	351.31	324.17	308.19
43000	465.46	444.23	426.27	410.94	397.72	386.26	376.24	367.44	359.67	331.89	315.52
44000	476.28	454.56	436.19	420.49	406.97	395.24	384.99	375.99	368.04	339.60	322.86
45000	487.11	464.89	446.10	430.05	416.22	404.22	393.74	384.53	376.40	347.32	330.20
46000	497.93	475.22	456.01	439.60	425.47	413.20	402.49	393.08	384.77	355.04	337.54
47000	508.76	485.55	465.92	449.16	434.72	422.19	411.24	401.62	393.13	362.76	344.87
48000	519.58	495.88	475.84	458.72	443.97	431.17	419.99	410.17	401.50	370.48	352.21
49000	530.41	506.21	485.75	468.27	453.22	440.15	428.74	418.71	409.86	378.19	359.55
50000	541.23	516.54	495.66	477.83	462.47	449.13	437.49	427.26	418.23	385.91	366.89
55000	595.35	568.20	545.23	525.61	508.71	494.05	481.23	469.98	460.05	424.50	403.58
60000	649.48	619.85	594.80	573.40	554.96	538.96	524.98	512.71	501.87	463.09	440.26
65000	703.60	671.50	644.36	621.18	601.21	583.87	568.73	555.43	543.69	501.69	476.95
70000	757.72	723.16	693.93	668.96	647.45	628.78	612.48	598.16	585.51	540.28	513.64
75000	811.84	774.81	743.49	716.74	693.70	673.70	656.23	640.88	627.34	578.87	550.33
80000	865.97	826.46	793.06	764.53	739.55	718.61	699.98	683.61	669.16	617.46	587.02
85000	920.09	878.12	842.63	812.31	786.19	763.52	743.72	726.33	710.98	656.05	623.70
90000	974.21	929.77	892.19	860.09	832.44	808.44	787.47	769.06	752.80	694.64	660.39
95000	1028.33	981.43	941.76	907.87	878.68	853.35	831.22	811.78	794.62	733.23	697.08
100000	1082.46	1033.08	991.32	955.66	924.93	898.26	874.97	854.51	836.45	771.82	733.77

8.25% Principal and Interest
Monthly Payment Amortization Table

Term Amount	1 Year	2 Years	3 Years	4 Years	5 Years	6 Years	7 Years	8 Years	9 Years	10 Years	11 Years
50	4.36	2.27	1.58	1.23	1.02	.89	.79	.72	.66	.62	.58
100	8.72	4.54	3.15	2.46	2.04	1.77	1.58	1.43	1.32	1.23	1.16
200	17.43	9.07	6.30	4.91	4.08	3.54	3.15	2.86	2.63	2.46	2.32
300	26.14	13.61	9.44	7.36	6.12	5.30	4.72	4.28	3.95	3.68	3.47
400	34.85	18.14	12.59	9.82	8.16	7.07	6.29	5.71	5.26	4.91	4.63
500	43.56	22.68	15.73	12.27	10.20	8.83	7.86	7.14	6.58	6.14	5.78
600	52.27	27.21	18.88	14.72	12.24	10.60	9.43	8.56	7.89	7.36	6.94
700	60.98	31.74	22.02	17.18	14.28	12.36	11.00	9.99	9.21	8.59	8.09
800	69.69	36.28	25.17	19.63	16.32	14.13	12.57	11.42	10.52	9.82	9.25
900	78.40	40.81	28.31	22.08	18.36	15.90	14.14	12.84	11.84	11.04	10.40
1000	87.11	45.35	31.46	24.54	20.40	17.66	15.72	14.27	13.15	12.27	11.56
2000	174.21	90.69	62.91	49.07	40.80	35.32	31.43	28.53	26.30	24.54	23.11
3000	261.32	136.03	94.36	73.60	61.19	52.97	47.14	42.80	39.45	36.80	34.66
4000	348.42	181.37	125.81	98.13	81.59	70.63	62.85	57.06	52.60	49.07	46.21
5000	435.53	226.71	157.26	122.66	101.99	88.28	78.56	71.33	65.75	61.33	57.76
6000	522.63	272.05	188.72	147.19	122.38	105.94	94.27	85.59	78.90	73.60	69.31
7000	609.73	317.39	220.17	171.72	142.78	123.59	109.98	99.85	92.05	85.86	80.86
8000	696.84	362.74	251.62	196.25	163.18	141.25	125.69	114.12	105.19	98.13	92.41
9000	783.94	408.08	283.07	220.78	183.57	158.91	141.40	128.38	118.34	110.39	103.96
10000	871.05	453.42	314.52	245.31	203.97	176.56	157.12	142.65	131.49	122.66	115.51
11000	958.15	498.76	345.98	269.84	224.36	194.22	172.83	156.91	144.64	134.92	127.06
12000	1045.25	544.10	377.43	294.37	244.76	211.87	188.54	171.17	157.79	147.19	138.61
13000	1132.36	589.44	408.88	318.90	265.16	229.53	204.25	185.44	170.94	159.45	150.16
14000	1219.46	634.78	440.33	343.43	285.55	247.18	219.96	199.70	184.09	171.72	161.71
15000	1306.57	680.13	471.78	367.96	305.95	264.84	235.67	213.97	197.24	183.98	173.26
16000	1393.67	725.47	503.23	392.49	326.35	282.49	251.38	228.23	210.38	196.25	184.81
17000	1480.77	770.81	534.69	417.02	346.74	300.15	267.09	242.49	223.53	208.51	196.36
18000	1567.88	816.15	566.14	441.55	367.14	317.81	282.80	256.76	236.68	220.78	207.91
19000	1654.98	861.49	597.59	466.08	387.53	335.46	298.52	271.02	249.83	233.04	219.46
20000	1742.09	906.83	629.04	490.61	407.93	353.12	314.23	285.29	262.98	245.31	231.01
21000	1829.19	952.17	660.49	515.14	428.33	370.77	329.94	299.55	276.13	257.58	242.57
22000	1916.29	997.52	691.95	539.67	448.72	388.43	345.65	313.81	289.28	269.84	254.12
23000	2003.40	1042.86	723.40	564.21	469.12	406.08	361.36	328.08	302.42	282.11	265.67
24000	2090.50	1088.20	754.85	588.74	489.52	423.74	377.07	342.34	315.57	294.37	277.22
25000	2177.61	1133.54	786.30	613.27	509.91	441.39	392.78	356.61	328.72	306.64	288.77
26000	2264.71	1178.88	817.75	637.80	530.31	459.05	408.49	370.87	341.87	318.90	300.32
27000	2351.81	1224.22	849.20	662.33	550.70	476.71	424.20	385.14	355.02	331.17	311.87
28000	2438.92	1269.56	880.66	686.86	571.10	494.36	439.91	399.40	368.17	343.43	323.42
29000	2526.02	1314.91	912.11	711.39	591.50	512.02	455.63	413.66	381.32	355.70	334.97
30000	2613.13	1360.25	943.56	735.92	611.89	529.67	471.34	427.93	394.47	367.96	346.52
31000	2700.23	1405.59	975.01	760.45	632.29	547.33	487.05	442.19	407.61	380.23	358.07
32000	2787.34	1450.93	1006.46	784.98	652.69	564.98	502.76	456.46	420.76	392.49	369.62
33000	2874.44	1496.27	1037.92	809.51	673.08	582.64	518.47	470.72	433.91	404.76	381.17
34000	2961.54	1541.61	1069.37	834.04	693.48	600.29	534.18	484.98	447.06	417.02	392.72
35000	3048.65	1586.95	1100.82	858.57	713.87	617.95	549.89	499.25	460.21	429.29	404.27
36000	3135.75	1632.30	1132.27	883.10	734.27	635.61	565.60	513.51	473.36	441.55	415.82
37000	3222.86	1677.64	1163.72	907.63	754.67	653.26	581.31	527.78	486.51	453.82	427.37
38000	3309.96	1722.98	1195.17	932.16	775.06	670.92	597.03	542.04	499.65	466.08	438.92
39000	3397.06	1768.32	1226.63	956.69	795.46	688.57	612.74	556.30	512.80	478.35	450.47
40000	3484.17	1813.66	1258.08	981.22	815.86	706.23	628.45	570.57	525.95	490.62	462.02
41000	3571.27	1859.00	1289.53	1005.75	836.25	723.88	644.16	584.83	539.10	502.88	473.57
42000	3658.38	1904.34	1320.98	1030.28	856.65	741.54	659.87	599.10	552.25	515.15	485.13
43000	3745.48	1949.69	1352.43	1054.81	877.04	759.19	675.58	613.36	565.40	527.41	496.68
44000	3832.58	1995.03	1383.89	1079.34	897.44	776.85	691.29	627.62	578.55	539.68	508.23
45000	3919.69	2040.37	1415.34	1103.87	917.84	794.51	707.00	641.89	591.70	551.94	519.78
46000	4006.79	2085.71	1446.79	1128.41	938.23	812.16	722.71	656.15	604.84	564.21	531.33
47000	4093.90	2131.05	1478.24	1152.94	958.63	829.82	738.42	670.42	617.99	576.47	542.88
48000	4181.00	2176.39	1509.69	1177.47	979.03	847.47	754.14	684.68	631.14	588.74	554.43
49000	4268.10	2221.73	1541.14	1202.00	999.42	865.13	769.85	698.94	644.29	601.00	565.98
50000	4355.21	2267.07	1572.60	1226.53	1019.82	882.78	785.56	713.21	657.44	613.27	577.53
55000	4790.73	2493.78	1729.86	1349.18	1121.80	971.06	864.11	784.53	723.18	674.59	635.28
60000	5226.25	2720.49	1887.11	1471.83	1223.78	1059.34	942.67	855.85	788.93	735.92	693.03
65000	5661.77	2947.20	2044.37	1594.48	1325.76	1147.62	1021.22	927.17	854.67	797.25	750.79
70000	6097.29	3173.90	2201.63	1717.14	1427.74	1235.89	1099.78	998.49	920.41	858.57	808.54
75000	6532.81	3400.61	2358.89	1839.79	1529.72	1324.17	1178.33	1069.81	986.16	919.90	866.29
80000	6968.33	3627.32	2516.15	1962.44	1631.71	1412.45	1256.89	1141.13	1051.90	981.23	924.04
85000	7403.85	3854.02	2673.41	2085.09	1733.69	1500.73	1335.45	1212.45	1117.64	1042.55	981.80
90000	7839.37	4080.73	2830.67	2207.74	1835.67	1589.01	1414.00	1283.77	1183.39	1103.88	1039.55
95000	8274.89	4307.44	2987.93	2330.40	1937.65	1677.28	1492.56	1355.09	1249.13	1165.20	1097.30
100000	8710.41	4534.14	3145.19	2453.05	2039.63	1765.56	1571.11	1426.41	1314.87	1226.53	1155.05

Principal and Interest
Monthly Payment Amortization Table

8.25%

Term / Amount	12 Years	13 Years	14 Years	15 Years	16 Years	17 Years	18 Years	19 Years	20 Years	25 Years	30 Years
50	.55	.53	.51	.49	.47	.46	.45	.44	.43	.40	.38
100	1.10	1.05	1.01	.98	.94	.92	.90	.87	.86	.79	.76
200	2.20	2.10	2.02	1.95	1.88	1.83	1.79	1.74	1.71	1.58	1.51
300	3.29	3.15	3.02	2.92	2.82	2.74	2.68	2.61	2.56	2.37	2.26
400	4.39	4.19	4.03	3.89	3.76	3.66	3.57	3.48	3.41	3.16	3.01
500	5.49	5.24	5.03	4.86	4.70	4.57	4.46	4.35	4.27	3.95	3.76
600	6.58	6.29	6.04	5.83	5.64	5.48	5.35	5.22	5.12	4.74	4.51
700	7.68	7.33	7.04	6.80	6.58	6.40	6.24	6.09	5.97	5.52	5.26
800	8.77	8.38	8.05	7.77	7.52	7.31	7.13	6.96	6.82	6.31	6.02
900	9.87	9.43	9.06	8.74	8.46	8.22	8.02	7.83	7.67	7.10	6.77
1000	10.97	10.48	10.06	9.71	9.40	9.14	8.91	8.70	8.53	7.89	7.52
2000	21.93	20.95	20.12	19.41	18.80	18.27	17.81	17.40	17.05	15.77	15.03
3000	32.89	31.42	30.17	29.11	28.19	27.40	26.71	26.10	25.57	23.66	22.54
4000	43.85	41.89	40.23	38.81	37.59	36.53	35.61	34.80	34.09	31.54	30.06
5000	54.82	52.36	50.28	48.51	46.99	45.67	44.51	43.50	42.61	39.43	37.57
6000	65.78	62.83	60.34	58.21	56.38	54.80	53.41	52.20	51.13	47.31	45.08
7000	76.74	73.30	70.39	67.91	65.78	63.93	62.32	60.90	59.65	55.20	52.59
8000	87.70	83.77	80.45	77.62	75.18	73.06	71.22	69.60	68.17	63.08	60.11
9000	98.66	94.24	90.51	87.32	84.57	82.19	80.12	78.30	76.69	70.97	67.62
10000	109.63	104.71	100.56	97.02	93.97	91.33	89.02	87.00	85.21	78.85	75.13
11000	120.59	115.18	110.62	106.72	103.37	100.46	97.92	95.70	93.73	86.73	82.64
12000	131.55	125.65	120.67	116.42	112.76	109.59	106.82	104.39	102.25	94.62	90.16
13000	142.51	136.12	130.73	126.12	122.16	118.72	115.72	113.09	110.77	102.50	97.67
14000	153.47	146.60	140.78	135.82	131.55	127.85	124.63	121.79	119.29	110.39	105.18
15000	164.44	157.07	150.84	145.53	140.95	136.99	133.53	130.49	127.81	118.27	112.69
16000	175.40	167.54	160.90	155.23	150.35	146.12	142.43	139.19	136.34	126.16	120.21
17000	186.36	178.01	170.95	164.93	159.75	155.25	151.33	147.89	144.86	134.04	127.72
18000	197.32	188.48	181.01	174.63	169.14	164.38	160.23	156.59	153.38	141.93	135.23
19000	208.28	198.95	191.06	184.33	178.54	173.52	169.13	165.29	161.90	149.81	142.75
20000	219.25	209.42	201.12	194.03	187.94	182.65	178.03	173.99	170.42	157.70	150.26
21000	230.21	219.89	211.17	203.73	197.33	191.78	186.94	182.69	178.94	165.58	157.77
22000	241.17	230.36	221.23	213.44	206.73	200.91	195.84	191.39	187.46	173.46	165.28
23000	252.13	240.83	231.29	223.14	216.12	210.04	204.74	200.08	195.98	181.35	172.80
24000	263.09	251.30	241.34	232.84	225.52	219.18	213.66	208.78	204.50	189.23	180.31
25000	274.06	261.77	251.40	242.54	234.92	228.31	222.54	217.48	213.02	197.12	187.82
26000	285.02	272.24	261.45	252.24	244.31	237.44	231.44	226.18	221.54	205.00	195.33
27000	295.98	282.72	271.51	261.94	253.71	246.57	240.34	234.88	230.06	212.89	202.85
28000	306.94	293.19	281.56	271.64	263.11	255.70	249.25	243.58	238.58	220.77	210.36
29000	317.91	303.66	291.62	281.35	272.50	264.84	258.15	252.28	247.10	228.66	217.87
30000	328.87	314.13	301.67	291.05	281.90	273.97	267.05	260.98	255.62	236.54	225.38
31000	339.83	324.60	311.73	300.75	291.30	283.10	275.95	269.68	264.15	244.42	232.90
32000	350.79	335.07	321.79	310.45	300.69	292.23	284.85	278.38	272.67	252.31	240.41
33000	361.75	345.54	331.84	320.15	310.09	301.37	293.75	287.08	281.19	260.19	247.92
34000	372.72	356.01	341.90	329.85	319.49	310.50	302.66	295.77	289.71	268.08	255.44
35000	383.68	366.48	351.95	339.55	328.88	319.63	311.56	304.47	298.23	275.96	262.95
36000	394.64	376.95	362.01	349.26	338.28	328.76	320.46	313.17	306.75	283.85	270.46
37000	405.60	387.42	372.06	358.96	347.68	337.89	329.36	321.87	315.27	291.73	277.97
38000	416.56	397.89	382.12	368.66	357.07	347.03	338.26	330.57	323.79	299.62	285.49
39000	427.53	408.36	392.18	378.36	366.47	356.16	347.16	339.27	332.31	307.50	293.00
40000	438.49	418.84	402.23	388.06	375.87	365.29	356.06	347.97	340.83	315.39	300.51
41000	449.45	429.31	412.29	397.76	385.26	374.42	364.97	356.67	349.35	323.27	308.02
42000	460.41	439.78	422.34	407.46	394.66	383.55	373.87	365.37	357.87	331.15	315.54
43000	471.37	450.25	432.40	417.17	404.05	392.69	382.77	374.07	366.39	339.04	323.05
44000	482.34	460.72	442.45	426.87	413.45	401.82	391.67	382.77	374.91	346.92	330.56
45000	493.30	471.19	452.51	436.57	422.85	410.95	400.57	391.46	383.43	354.81	338.07
46000	504.26	481.66	462.57	446.27	432.24	420.08	409.47	400.16	391.96	362.69	345.59
47000	515.22	492.13	472.62	455.97	441.64	429.22	418.37	408.86	400.48	370.58	353.10
48000	526.18	502.60	482.68	465.67	451.04	438.35	427.28	417.56	409.00	378.46	360.61
49000	537.15	513.07	492.73	475.37	460.43	447.48	436.18	426.26	417.52	386.35	368.13
50000	548.11	523.54	502.79	485.08	469.83	456.61	445.08	434.96	426.04	394.23	375.64
55000	602.92	575.90	553.07	533.58	516.81	502.27	489.59	478.46	468.64	433.65	413.20
60000	657.73	628.25	603.34	582.09	563.80	547.93	534.09	521.95	511.24	473.08	450.76
65000	712.54	680.60	653.62	610.78	610.78	593.59	578.60	565.45	553.85	512.50	488.33
70000	767.35	732.96	703.90	679.10	657.76	639.25	623.11	608.94	596.45	551.92	525.89
75000	822.16	785.31	754.18	727.61	704.74	684.92	667.62	652.44	639.05	591.34	563.45
80000	876.97	837.67	804.46	776.12	751.73	730.58	712.12	695.93	681.66	630.77	601.02
85000	931.78	890.02	854.74	824.62	798.71	776.24	756.63	739.43	724.26	670.19	638.58
90000	986.59	942.37	905.01	873.13	845.69	821.90	801.14	782.92	766.86	709.61	676.14
95000	1041.40	994.73	955.29	921.64	892.67	867.56	845.65	826.42	809.47	749.03	713.71
100000	1096.21	1047.08	1005.57	970.15	939.66	913.22	890.15	869.91	852.07	788.46	751.27

8.50% Principal and Interest
Monthly Payment Amortization Table

Term Amount	1 Year	2 Years	3 Years	4 Years	5 Years	6 Years	7 Years	8 Years	9 Years	10 Years	11 Years
50	4.37	2.28	1.58	1.24	1.03	.89	.80	.72	.67	.62	.59
100	8.73	4.55	3.16	2.47	2.06	1.78	1.59	1.44	1.33	1.24	1.17
200	17.45	9.10	6.32	4.93	4.11	3.56	3.17	2.88	2.66	2.48	2.34
300	26.17	13.64	9.48	7.40	6.16	5.34	4.76	4.32	3.99	3.72	3.51
400	34.89	18.19	12.63	9.86	8.21	7.12	6.34	5.76	5.32	4.96	4.68
500	43.61	22.73	15.79	12.33	10.26	8.89	7.92	7.20	6.64	6.20	5.85
600	52.34	27.28	18.95	14.79	12.31	10.67	9.51	8.64	7.97	7.44	7.02
700	61.06	31.82	22.10	17.26	14.37	12.45	11.09	10.08	9.30	8.68	8.19
800	69.78	36.37	25.26	19.72	16.42	14.23	12.67	11.52	10.63	9.92	9.35
900	78.50	40.92	28.42	22.19	18.47	16.01	14.26	12.96	11.96	11.16	10.52
1000	87.22	45.46	31.57	24.65	20.52	17.78	15.84	14.40	13.28	12.40	11.69
2000	174.44	90.92	63.14	49.30	41.04	35.56	31.68	28.79	26.56	24.80	23.38
3000	261.66	136.37	94.71	73.95	61.55	53.34	47.51	43.18	39.84	37.20	35.06
4000	348.88	181.83	126.28	98.60	82.07	71.12	63.35	57.57	53.12	49.60	46.75
5000	436.10	227.28	157.84	123.25	102.59	88.90	79.19	71.97	66.40	62.00	58.44
6000	523.32	272.74	189.41	147.89	123.10	106.68	95.02	86.36	79.68	74.40	70.12
7000	610.54	318.19	220.98	172.54	143.62	124.45	110.86	100.75	92.96	86.79	81.81
8000	697.76	363.65	252.55	197.19	164.14	142.23	126.70	115.14	106.24	99.19	93.50
9000	784.98	409.11	284.11	221.84	184.65	160.01	142.53	129.53	119.52	111.59	105.18
10000	872.20	454.56	315.68	246.49	205.17	177.79	158.37	143.93	132.80	123.99	116.87
11000	959.42	500.02	347.25	271.14	225.69	195.57	174.21	158.32	146.08	136.39	128.56
12000	1046.64	545.47	378.82	295.78	246.20	213.35	190.04	172.71	159.36	148.79	140.24
13000	1133.86	590.93	410.38	320.43	266.72	231.12	205.88	187.10	172.64	161.19	151.93
14000	1221.08	636.38	441.95	345.08	287.24	248.90	221.72	201.49	185.92	173.58	163.61
15000	1308.30	681.84	473.52	369.73	307.75	266.68	237.55	215.89	199.20	185.98	175.30
16000	1395.52	727.30	505.09	394.38	328.27	284.46	253.39	230.28	212.47	198.38	186.99
17000	1482.74	772.75	536.65	419.03	348.79	302.24	269.23	244.67	225.75	210.78	198.67
18000	1569.96	818.21	568.22	443.67	369.30	320.02	285.06	259.06	239.03	223.18	210.36
19000	1657.18	863.66	599.79	468.32	389.82	337.79	300.90	273.46	252.31	235.58	222.05
20000	1744.40	909.12	631.36	492.97	410.34	355.57	316.73	287.85	265.59	247.98	233.73
21000	1831.62	954.57	662.92	517.62	430.85	373.35	332.57	302.24	278.87	260.37	245.42
22000	1918.84	1000.03	694.49	542.27	451.37	391.13	348.41	316.63	292.15	272.77	257.11
23000	2006.06	1045.49	726.06	566.92	471.89	408.91	364.24	331.02	305.43	285.17	268.79
24000	2093.28	1090.94	757.63	591.56	492.40	426.69	380.08	345.42	318.71	297.57	280.48
25000	2180.50	1136.40	789.19	616.21	512.92	444.46	395.92	359.81	331.99	309.97	292.16
26000	2267.72	1181.85	820.76	640.86	533.43	462.24	411.75	374.20	345.27	322.37	303.85
27000	2354.94	1227.31	852.33	665.51	553.95	480.02	427.59	388.59	358.55	334.77	315.54
28000	2442.16	1272.76	883.90	690.16	574.47	497.80	443.43	402.98	371.83	347.16	327.22
29000	2529.38	1318.22	915.46	714.81	594.98	515.58	459.26	417.38	385.11	359.56	338.91
30000	2616.60	1363.68	947.03	739.45	615.50	533.36	475.10	431.77	398.39	371.96	350.60
31000	2703.82	1409.13	978.60	764.10	636.02	551.13	490.94	446.16	411.66	384.36	362.28
32000	2791.04	1454.59	1010.17	788.75	656.53	568.91	506.77	460.55	424.94	396.76	373.97
33000	2878.26	1500.04	1041.73	813.40	677.05	586.69	522.61	474.95	438.22	409.16	385.66
34000	2965.48	1545.50	1073.30	838.05	697.57	604.47	538.45	489.34	451.50	421.56	397.34
35000	3052.70	1590.95	1104.87	862.70	718.08	622.25	554.28	503.73	464.78	433.95	409.03
36000	3139.92	1636.41	1136.44	887.34	738.60	640.03	570.12	518.12	478.06	446.35	420.72
37000	3227.14	1681.87	1168.00	911.99	759.12	657.81	585.95	532.51	491.34	458.75	432.40
38000	3314.36	1727.32	1199.57	936.64	779.63	675.58	601.79	546.91	504.62	471.15	444.09
39000	3401.58	1772.78	1231.14	961.29	800.15	693.36	617.63	561.30	517.90	483.55	455.77
40000	3488.80	1818.23	1262.71	985.94	820.67	711.14	633.46	575.69	531.18	495.95	467.46
41000	3576.02	1863.69	1294.27	1010.59	841.18	728.92	649.30	590.08	544.46	508.35	479.15
42000	3663.24	1909.14	1325.84	1035.23	861.70	746.70	665.14	604.47	557.74	520.74	490.83
43000	3750.46	1954.60	1357.41	1059.88	882.22	764.48	680.97	618.87	571.02	533.14	502.52
44000	3837.68	2000.05	1388.98	1084.53	902.73	782.25	696.81	633.26	584.30	545.54	514.21
45000	3924.90	2045.51	1420.54	1109.18	923.25	800.03	712.65	647.65	597.58	557.94	525.89
46000	4012.12	2090.97	1452.11	1133.83	943.77	817.81	728.48	662.04	610.86	570.34	537.58
47000	4099.33	2136.42	1483.68	1158.48	964.28	835.59	744.32	676.44	624.13	582.74	549.27
48000	4186.55	2181.88	1515.25	1183.12	984.80	853.37	760.16	690.83	637.41	595.14	560.95
49000	4273.77	2227.33	1546.81	1207.77	1005.32	871.15	775.99	705.22	650.69	607.53	572.64
50000	4360.99	2272.79	1578.38	1232.42	1025.83	888.92	791.83	719.61	663.97	619.93	584.32
55000	4797.09	2500.07	1736.22	1355.66	1128.41	977.82	871.01	791.57	730.37	681.93	642.76
60000	5233.19	2727.35	1894.06	1478.90	1231.00	1066.71	950.19	863.53	796.77	743.92	701.19
65000	5669.29	2954.62	2051.89	1602.14	1333.58	1155.60	1029.38	935.49	863.16	805.91	759.62
70000	6105.39	3181.90	2209.73	1725.39	1436.16	1244.49	1108.56	1007.45	929.56	867.90	818.05
75000	6541.49	3409.18	2367.57	1848.63	1538.74	1333.38	1187.74	1079.41	995.96	929.90	876.48
80000	6977.59	3636.46	2525.41	1971.87	1641.33	1422.28	1266.92	1151.38	1062.35	991.89	934.92
85000	7413.69	3863.74	2683.25	2095.11	1743.91	1511.17	1346.11	1223.34	1128.75	1053.88	993.35
90000	7849.79	4091.02	2841.08	2218.35	1846.49	1600.06	1425.29	1295.30	1195.15	1115.88	1051.78
95000	8285.88	4318.29	2998.92	2341.59	1949.08	1688.95	1504.47	1367.26	1261.54	1177.87	1110.21
100000	8721.98	4545.57	3156.76	2464.84	2051.66	1777.84	1583.65	1439.22	1327.94	1239.86	1168.64

Principal and Interest
Monthly Payment Amortization Table

8.50%

Term Amount	12 Years	13 Years	14 Years	15 Years	16 Years	17 Years	18 Years	19 Years	20 Years	25 Years	30 Years
50	.56	.54	.51	.50	.48	.47	.46	.45	.44	.41	.39
100	1.12	1.07	1.02	.99	.96	.93	.91	.89	.87	.81	.77
200	2.23	2.13	2.04	1.97	1.91	1.86	1.82	1.78	1.74	1.62	1.54
300	3.34	3.19	3.06	2.96	2.87	2.79	2.72	2.66	2.61	2.42	2.31
400	4.45	4.25	4.08	3.94	3.82	3.72	3.63	3.55	3.48	3.23	3.08
500	5.56	5.31	5.10	4.93	4.78	4.65	4.53	4.43	4.34	4.03	3.85
600	6.67	6.37	6.12	5.91	5.73	5.57	5.44	5.32	5.21	4.84	4.62
700	7.78	7.43	7.14	6.90	6.69	6.50	6.34	6.20	6.08	5.64	5.39
800	8.89	8.49	8.16	7.88	7.64	7.43	7.25	7.09	6.95	6.45	6.16
900	10.00	9.56	9.18	8.87	8.60	8.36	8.15	7.97	7.82	7.25	6.93
1000	11.11	10.62	10.20	9.85	9.55	9.29	9.06	8.86	8.68	8.06	7.69
2000	22.21	21.23	20.40	19.70	19.09	18.57	18.11	17.71	17.36	16.11	15.38
3000	33.31	31.84	30.60	29.55	28.64	27.85	27.17	26.57	26.04	24.16	23.07
4000	44.41	42.45	40.80	39.39	38.18	37.14	36.22	35.42	34.72	32.21	30.76
5000	55.51	53.06	51.00	49.24	47.73	46.42	45.28	44.28	43.40	40.27	38.45
6000	66.61	63.68	61.20	59.09	57.27	55.70	54.33	53.13	52.07	48.32	46.14
7000	77.71	74.29	71.40	68.94	66.82	64.99	63.39	61.99	60.75	56.37	53.83
8000	88.81	84.90	81.60	78.78	76.36	74.27	72.44	70.84	69.43	64.42	61.52
9000	99.91	95.51	91.80	88.63	85.91	83.55	81.50	79.70	78.11	72.48	69.21
10000	111.01	106.12	102.00	98.48	95.45	92.83	90.55	88.55	86.79	80.53	76.90
11000	122.11	116.73	112.20	108.33	105.00	102.12	99.61	97.40	95.47	88.58	84.59
12000	133.21	127.35	122.40	118.17	114.54	111.40	108.66	106.26	104.14	96.63	92.27
13000	144.31	137.96	132.59	128.02	124.09	120.68	117.71	115.11	112.82	104.68	99.96
14000	155.41	148.57	142.79	137.87	133.63	129.97	126.77	123.97	121.50	112.74	107.65
15000	166.51	159.18	152.99	147.72	143.18	139.25	135.82	132.82	130.18	120.79	115.34
16000	177.61	169.79	163.19	157.56	152.72	148.53	144.88	141.68	138.86	128.84	123.03
17000	188.71	180.41	173.39	167.41	162.27	157.81	153.93	150.53	147.53	136.89	130.72
18000	199.82	191.02	183.59	177.26	171.81	167.10	162.99	159.39	156.21	144.95	138.41
19000	210.92	201.63	193.79	187.11	181.36	176.38	172.04	168.24	164.89	153.00	146.10
20000	222.02	212.24	203.99	196.95	190.90	185.66	181.10	177.09	173.57	161.05	153.79
21000	233.12	222.85	214.19	206.80	200.45	194.95	190.15	185.95	182.25	169.10	161.48
22000	244.22	233.46	224.39	216.65	209.99	204.23	199.21	194.80	190.93	177.15	169.17
23000	255.32	244.08	234.59	226.50	219.54	213.51	208.26	203.66	199.60	185.21	176.86
24000	266.42	254.69	244.79	236.34	229.08	222.80	217.31	212.51	208.28	193.26	184.54
25000	277.52	265.30	254.98	246.19	238.63	232.08	226.37	221.37	216.96	201.31	192.23
26000	288.62	275.91	265.18	256.04	248.17	241.36	235.42	230.22	225.64	209.36	199.92
27000	299.72	286.52	275.38	265.88	257.72	250.64	244.48	239.08	234.32	217.42	207.61
28000	310.82	297.14	285.58	275.73	267.26	259.93	253.53	247.93	243.00	225.47	215.30
29000	321.92	307.75	295.78	285.58	276.81	269.21	262.59	256.78	251.67	233.52	222.99
30000	333.02	318.36	305.98	295.43	286.35	278.49	271.64	265.64	260.35	241.57	230.68
31000	344.12	328.97	316.18	305.27	295.90	287.78	280.70	274.49	269.03	249.63	238.37
32000	355.22	339.58	326.38	315.12	305.44	297.06	289.75	283.35	277.71	257.68	246.06
33000	366.32	350.19	336.58	324.97	314.99	306.34	298.81	292.20	286.39	265.73	253.75
34000	377.42	360.81	346.78	334.82	324.53	315.62	307.86	301.06	295.06	273.78	261.44
35000	388.52	371.42	356.98	344.66	334.08	324.91	316.92	309.91	303.74	281.83	269.12
36000	399.63	382.03	367.18	354.51	343.62	334.19	325.97	318.77	312.42	289.89	276.81
37000	410.73	392.64	377.37	364.36	353.17	343.47	335.02	327.62	321.10	297.94	284.50
38000	421.83	403.25	387.57	374.21	362.71	352.76	344.08	336.47	329.78	305.99	292.19
39000	432.93	413.86	397.77	384.05	372.26	362.04	353.13	345.33	338.46	314.04	299.88
40000	444.03	424.48	407.97	393.90	381.80	371.32	362.19	354.18	347.13	322.10	307.57
41000	455.13	435.09	418.17	403.75	391.35	380.60	371.24	363.04	355.81	330.15	315.26
42000	466.23	445.70	428.37	413.60	400.89	389.89	380.30	371.89	364.49	338.20	322.95
43000	477.33	456.31	438.57	423.44	410.44	399.17	389.35	380.75	373.17	346.25	330.64
44000	488.43	466.92	448.77	433.29	419.98	408.45	398.41	389.60	381.85	354.30	338.33
45000	499.53	477.54	458.97	443.14	429.53	417.74	407.46	398.46	390.53	362.36	346.02
46000	510.63	488.15	469.17	452.99	439.07	427.02	416.52	407.31	399.20	370.41	353.71
47000	521.73	498.76	479.37	462.83	448.62	436.30	425.57	416.16	407.88	378.46	361.39
48000	532.83	509.37	489.57	472.68	458.16	445.59	434.62	425.02	416.56	386.51	369.08
49000	543.93	519.98	499.77	482.53	467.71	454.87	443.68	433.87	425.24	394.57	376.77
50000	555.03	530.59	509.96	492.37	477.25	464.15	452.73	442.73	433.92	402.62	384.46
55000	610.54	583.65	560.96	541.61	524.98	510.57	498.01	487.00	477.31	442.88	422.91
60000	666.04	636.71	611.96	590.85	572.70	556.98	543.28	531.27	520.70	483.14	461.35
65000	721.54	689.77	662.95	640.09	620.42	603.39	588.55	575.54	564.09	523.40	499.80
70000	777.04	742.83	713.95	689.32	668.15	649.81	633.83	619.82	607.48	563.66	538.24
75000	832.55	795.89	764.94	738.56	715.87	696.22	679.10	664.09	650.87	603.93	576.69
80000	888.05	848.95	815.94	787.80	763.60	742.64	724.37	708.36	694.26	644.19	615.14
85000	943.55	902.01	866.94	837.03	811.32	789.05	769.64	752.63	737.65	684.45	653.58
90000	999.06	955.07	917.93	886.27	859.05	835.47	814.92	796.91	781.05	724.71	692.03
95000	1054.56	1008.13	968.93	935.51	906.77	881.88	860.19	841.18	824.44	764.97	730.47
100000	1110.06	1061.18	1019.92	984.74	954.50	928.30	905.46	885.45	867.83	805.23	768.92

8.75%   Principal and Interest
Monthly Payment Amortization Table

Term Amount	1 Year	2 Years	3 Years	4 Years	5 Years	6 Years	7 Years	8 Years	9 Years	10 Years	11 Years
50	4.37	2.28	1.59	1.24	1.04	.90	.80	.73	.68	.63	.60
100	8.74	4.56	3.17	2.48	2.07	1.80	1.60	1.46	1.35	1.26	1.19
200	17.47	9.12	6.34	4.96	4.13	3.59	3.20	2.91	2.69	2.51	2.37
300	26.21	13.68	9.51	7.43	6.20	5.38	4.79	4.36	4.03	3.76	3.55
400	34.94	18.23	12.68	9.91	8.26	7.17	6.39	5.81	5.37	5.02	4.73
500	43.67	22.79	15.85	12.39	10.32	8.96	7.99	7.27	6.71	6.27	5.92
600	52.41	27.35	19.02	14.86	12.39	10.75	9.58	8.72	8.05	7.52	7.10
700	61.14	31.90	22.18	17.34	14.45	12.54	11.18	10.17	9.39	8.78	8.28
800	69.87	36.46	25.35	19.82	16.51	14.33	12.77	11.62	10.73	10.03	9.46
900	78.61	41.02	28.52	22.29	18.58	16.12	14.37	13.07	12.07	11.28	10.65
1000	87.34	45.58	31.69	24.77	20.64	17.91	15.97	14.53	13.42	12.54	11.83
2000	174.68	91.15	63.37	49.54	41.28	35.81	31.93	29.05	26.83	25.07	23.65
3000	262.01	136.72	95.06	74.30	61.92	53.71	47.89	43.57	40.24	37.60	35.47
4000	349.35	182.29	126.74	99.07	82.55	71.61	63.85	58.09	53.65	50.14	47.30
5000	436.68	227.86	158.42	123.84	103.19	89.51	79.82	72.61	67.06	62.67	59.12
6000	524.02	273.43	190.11	148.60	123.83	107.42	95.78	87.13	80.47	75.20	70.94
7000	611.35	319.00	221.79	173.37	144.47	125.32	111.74	101.65	93.88	87.73	82.77
8000	698.69	364.57	253.47	198.14	165.10	143.22	127.70	116.17	107.29	100.27	94.59
9000	786.03	410.14	285.16	222.90	185.74	161.12	143.67	130.69	120.70	112.80	106.41
10000	873.36	455.71	316.84	247.67	206.38	179.02	159.63	145.21	134.11	125.33	118.24
11000	960.70	501.28	348.52	272.44	227.01	196.92	175.59	159.73	147.52	137.86	130.06
12000	1048.03	546.85	380.21	297.20	247.65	214.83	191.55	174.26	160.93	150.40	141.88
13000	1135.37	592.42	411.89	321.97	268.29	232.73	207.52	188.78	174.34	162.93	153.71
14000	1222.70	637.99	443.57	346.74	288.92	250.63	223.48	203.30	187.76	175.46	165.53
15000	1310.04	683.56	475.26	371.50	309.56	268.53	239.44	217.82	201.17	188.00	177.35
16000	1397.37	729.13	506.94	396.27	330.20	286.43	255.40	232.34	214.58	200.53	189.18
17000	1484.71	774.70	538.62	421.04	350.84	304.33	271.37	246.86	227.99	213.06	201.00
18000	1572.05	820.27	570.31	445.80	371.48	322.24	287.33	261.38	241.40	225.59	212.82
19000	1659.38	865.84	601.99	470.57	392.11	340.14	303.29	275.90	254.81	238.13	224.65
20000	1746.72	911.41	633.68	495.34	412.75	358.04	319.25	290.42	268.22	250.66	236.47
21000	1834.05	956.98	665.36	520.10	433.39	375.94	335.22	304.94	281.63	263.19	248.29
22000	1921.39	1002.55	697.04	544.87	454.02	393.84	351.18	319.46	295.04	275.72	260.11
23000	2008.72	1048.12	728.73	569.63	474.66	411.74	367.14	333.98	308.45	288.26	271.94
24000	2096.06	1093.69	760.41	594.40	495.30	429.65	383.10	348.51	321.86	300.79	283.76
25000	2183.39	1139.26	792.09	619.17	515.94	447.55	399.07	363.03	335.27	313.32	295.58
26000	2270.73	1184.83	823.78	643.93	536.57	465.45	415.03	377.55	348.68	325.85	307.41
27000	2358.07	1230.40	855.46	668.70	557.21	483.35	430.99	392.07	362.10	338.39	319.23
28000	2445.40	1275.97	887.14	693.47	577.85	501.25	446.95	406.59	375.51	350.92	331.05
29000	2532.74	1321.54	918.83	718.23	598.48	519.15	462.92	421.11	388.92	363.45	342.88
30000	2620.07	1367.11	950.51	743.00	619.12	537.06	478.88	435.63	402.33	375.99	354.70
31000	2707.41	1412.68	982.19	767.77	639.76	554.96	494.84	450.15	415.74	388.52	366.52
32000	2794.74	1458.25	1013.88	792.53	660.40	572.86	510.80	464.67	429.15	401.05	378.35
33000	2882.08	1503.82	1045.56	817.30	681.03	590.76	526.77	479.19	442.56	413.58	390.17
34000	2969.41	1549.39	1077.24	842.07	701.67	608.66	542.73	493.71	455.97	426.12	401.99
35000	3056.75	1594.96	1108.93	866.83	722.31	626.56	558.69	508.23	469.38	438.65	413.82
36000	3144.09	1640.53	1140.61	891.60	742.95	644.47	574.65	522.76	482.79	451.18	425.64
37000	3231.42	1686.10	1172.29	916.37	763.58	662.37	590.62	537.28	496.20	463.71	437.46
38000	3318.76	1731.67	1203.98	941.13	784.22	680.27	606.58	551.80	509.61	476.25	449.29
39000	3406.09	1777.24	1235.66	965.90	804.86	698.17	622.54	566.32	523.02	488.78	461.11
40000	3493.43	1822.81	1267.35	990.67	825.49	716.07	638.50	580.84	536.44	501.31	472.93
41000	3580.76	1868.38	1299.03	1015.43	846.13	733.98	654.47	595.36	549.85	513.84	484.75
42000	3668.10	1913.95	1330.71	1040.20	866.77	751.88	670.43	609.88	563.26	526.38	496.58
43000	3755.44	1959.52	1362.40	1064.96	887.41	769.78	686.39	624.40	576.67	538.91	508.40
44000	3842.77	2005.09	1394.08	1089.73	908.04	787.68	702.35	638.92	590.08	551.44	520.22
45000	3930.11	2050.66	1425.76	1114.50	928.68	805.58	718.32	653.44	603.49	563.98	532.05
46000	4017.44	2096.23	1457.45	1139.26	949.32	823.48	734.28	667.96	616.90	576.51	543.87
47000	4104.78	2141.80	1489.13	1164.03	969.95	841.39	750.24	682.48	630.31	589.04	555.69
48000	4192.11	2187.37	1520.81	1188.80	990.59	859.29	766.20	697.01	643.72	601.57	567.52
49000	4279.45	2232.94	1552.50	1213.56	1011.23	877.19	782.17	711.53	657.13	614.11	579.34
50000	4366.78	2278.51	1584.18	1238.33	1031.87	895.09	798.13	726.05	670.54	626.64	591.16
55000	4803.46	2506.36	1742.60	1362.16	1135.05	984.60	877.94	798.65	737.60	689.30	650.28
60000	5240.14	2734.21	1901.02	1486.00	1238.24	1074.11	957.75	871.26	804.65	751.97	709.40
65000	5676.82	2962.06	2059.43	1609.83	1341.43	1163.62	1037.57	943.86	871.70	814.63	768.51
70000	6113.50	3189.91	2217.85	1733.66	1444.61	1253.12	1117.38	1016.46	938.76	877.29	827.63
75000	6550.17	3417.76	2376.27	1857.49	1547.80	1342.63	1197.19	1089.07	1005.81	939.96	886.74
80000	6986.85	3645.61	2534.69	1981.33	1650.98	1432.14	1277.00	1161.67	1072.87	1002.62	945.86
85000	7423.53	3873.47	2693.10	2105.16	1754.17	1521.65	1356.82	1234.28	1139.92	1065.28	1004.97
90000	7860.21	4101.32	2851.52	2228.99	1857.36	1611.16	1436.63	1306.88	1206.97	1127.95	1064.09
95000	8296.89	4329.17	3009.94	2352.82	1960.54	1700.67	1516.44	1379.48	1274.03	1190.61	1123.21
100000	8733.56	4557.02	3168.36	2476.66	2063.73	1790.18	1596.25	1452.09	1341.08	1253.27	1182.32

Principal and Interest
Monthly Payment Amortization Table

8.75%

Term Amount	12 Years	13 Years	14 Years	15 Years	16 Years	17 Years	18 Years	19 Years	20 Years	25 Years	30 Years
50	.57	.54	.52	.50	.49	.48	.47	.46	.45	.42	.40
100	1.13	1.08	1.04	1.00	.97	.95	.93	.91	.89	.83	.79
200	2.25	2.16	2.07	2.00	1.94	1.89	1.85	1.81	1.77	1.65	1.58
300	3.38	3.23	3.11	3.00	2.91	2.84	2.77	2.71	2.66	2.47	2.37
400	4.50	4.31	4.14	4.00	3.88	3.78	3.69	3.61	3.54	3.29	3.15
500	5.62	5.38	5.18	5.00	4.85	4.72	4.61	4.51	4.42	4.12	3.94
600	6.75	6.46	6.21	6.00	5.82	5.67	5.53	5.41	5.31	4.94	4.73
700	7.87	7.53	7.25	7.00	6.79	6.61	6.45	6.31	6.19	5.76	5.51
800	9.00	8.61	8.28	8.00	7.76	7.55	7.37	7.21	7.07	6.58	6.30
900	10.12	9.68	9.31	9.00	8.73	8.50	8.29	8.11	7.96	7.40	7.09
1000	11.24	10.76	10.35	10.00	9.70	9.44	9.21	9.02	8.84	8.23	7.87
2000	22.48	21.51	20.69	19.99	19.39	18.87	18.42	18.03	17.68	16.45	15.74
3000	33.72	32.27	31.04	29.99	29.09	28.31	27.63	27.04	26.52	24.67	23.61
4000	44.96	43.02	41.38	39.98	38.78	37.74	36.84	36.05	35.35	32.89	31.47
5000	56.20	53.77	51.72	49.98	48.48	47.18	46.05	45.06	44.19	41.11	39.34
6000	67.44	64.53	62.07	59.97	58.17	56.61	55.26	54.07	53.03	49.33	47.21
7000	78.68	75.28	72.41	69.97	67.87	66.05	64.47	63.08	61.86	57.56	55.07
8000	89.92	86.04	82.76	79.96	77.56	75.48	73.68	72.09	70.70	65.78	62.94
9000	101.16	96.79	93.10	89.96	87.26	84.92	82.89	81.10	79.54	74.00	70.81
10000	112.40	107.54	103.44	99.95	96.95	94.35	92.09	90.12	88.38	82.22	78.68
11000	123.64	118.30	113.79	109.94	106.64	103.79	101.30	99.13	97.21	90.44	86.54
12000	134.88	129.05	124.13	119.94	116.34	113.22	110.51	108.14	106.05	98.66	94.41
13000	146.12	139.80	134.47	129.93	126.03	122.66	119.72	117.15	114.89	106.88	102.28
14000	157.36	150.56	144.82	139.93	135.73	132.09	128.93	126.16	123.72	115.11	110.14
15000	168.60	161.31	155.16	149.92	145.42	141.53	138.14	135.17	132.56	123.33	118.01
16000	179.84	172.07	165.51	159.92	155.12	150.96	147.35	144.18	141.40	131.55	125.88
17000	191.08	182.82	175.85	169.91	164.81	160.40	156.56	153.19	150.24	139.77	133.74
18000	202.32	193.57	186.19	179.91	174.51	169.83	165.77	162.20	159.07	147.99	141.61
19000	213.56	204.33	196.54	189.90	184.20	179.27	174.97	171.22	167.91	156.21	149.48
20000	224.80	215.08	206.88	199.89	193.89	188.70	184.18	180.23	176.75	164.43	157.35
21000	236.04	225.83	217.22	209.89	203.59	198.14	193.39	189.24	185.58	172.66	165.21
22000	247.28	236.59	227.57	219.88	213.28	207.57	202.60	198.25	194.42	180.88	173.08
23000	258.52	247.34	237.91	229.88	222.98	217.01	211.81	207.26	203.26	189.10	180.95
24000	269.76	258.10	248.26	239.87	232.67	226.44	221.02	216.27	212.10	197.32	188.81
25000	281.00	268.85	258.60	249.87	242.37	235.88	230.23	225.28	220.93	205.54	196.68
26000	292.24	279.60	268.94	259.86	252.06	245.31	239.44	234.29	229.77	213.76	204.55
27000	303.48	290.36	279.29	269.86	261.76	254.75	248.65	243.30	238.61	221.98	212.41
28000	314.72	301.11	289.63	279.85	271.45	264.18	257.85	252.32	247.44	230.21	220.28
29000	325.96	311.87	299.97	289.85	281.14	273.62	267.06	261.33	256.28	238.43	228.15
30000	337.20	322.62	310.32	299.84	290.84	283.05	276.27	270.34	265.12	246.65	236.02
31000	348.44	333.37	320.66	309.83	300.53	292.49	285.48	279.35	273.96	254.87	243.88
32000	359.68	344.13	331.01	319.83	310.23	301.92	294.69	288.36	282.79	263.09	251.75
33000	370.92	354.88	341.35	329.82	319.92	311.36	303.90	297.37	291.63	271.31	259.62
34000	382.16	365.63	351.69	339.82	329.62	320.79	313.11	306.38	300.47	279.53	267.48
35000	393.40	376.39	362.04	349.81	339.31	330.23	322.32	315.39	309.30	287.76	275.35
36000	404.64	387.14	372.38	359.81	349.01	339.66	331.53	324.40	318.14	295.98	283.22
37000	415.88	397.90	382.72	369.80	358.70	349.10	340.73	333.42	326.98	304.20	291.08
38000	427.12	408.65	393.07	379.80	368.39	358.53	349.94	342.43	335.82	312.42	298.95
39000	438.36	419.40	403.41	389.79	378.09	367.97	359.15	351.44	344.65	320.64	306.82
40000	449.60	430.16	413.76	399.78	387.78	377.40	368.36	360.45	353.49	328.86	314.69
41000	460.84	440.91	424.10	409.78	397.48	386.84	377.57	369.46	362.33	337.08	322.55
42000	472.08	451.66	434.44	419.77	407.17	396.27	386.78	378.47	371.16	345.31	330.42
43000	483.32	462.42	444.79	429.77	416.87	405.71	395.99	387.48	380.00	353.53	338.29
44000	494.56	473.17	455.13	439.76	426.56	415.14	405.20	396.49	388.84	361.75	346.15
45000	505.80	483.93	465.47	449.76	436.26	424.58	414.41	405.50	397.67	369.97	354.02
46000	517.04	494.68	475.82	459.75	445.95	434.01	423.61	414.52	406.51	378.19	361.89
47000	528.28	505.43	486.16	469.75	455.64	443.44	432.82	423.53	415.35	386.41	369.75
48000	539.52	516.19	496.51	479.74	465.34	452.88	442.03	432.54	424.19	394.63	377.62
49000	550.76	526.94	506.85	489.73	475.03	462.31	451.24	441.55	433.02	402.86	385.49
50000	562.00	537.70	517.19	499.73	484.73	471.75	460.45	450.56	441.86	411.08	393.36
55000	618.20	591.46	568.91	549.70	533.20	518.92	506.49	495.61	486.05	452.18	432.69
60000	674.40	645.23	620.63	599.67	581.67	566.10	552.54	540.67	530.23	493.29	472.03
65000	730.60	699.00	672.35	649.65	630.15	613.27	598.58	585.73	574.42	534.40	511.36
70000	786.80	752.77	724.07	699.62	678.62	660.45	644.63	630.78	618.60	575.51	550.70
75000	843.00	806.54	775.79	749.59	727.09	707.62	690.67	675.84	662.79	616.61	590.03
80000	899.20	860.31	827.51	799.56	775.56	754.80	736.72	720.89	706.97	657.72	629.37
85000	955.40	914.08	879.22	849.54	824.03	801.97	782.76	765.95	751.16	698.83	668.70
90000	1011.60	967.85	930.94	899.51	872.51	849.15	828.81	811.00	795.34	739.93	708.04
95000	1067.80	1021.62	982.66	949.48	920.98	896.32	874.85	856.06	839.53	781.04	747.37
100000	1124.00	1075.39	1034.38	999.45	969.45	943.49	920.90	901.11	883.72	822.15	786.71

9.00%   Principal and Interest
Monthly Payment Amortization Table

Term Amount	1 Year	2 Years	3 Years	4 Years	5 Years	6 Years	7 Years	8 Years	9 Years	10 Years	11 Years
50	4.38	2.29	1.59	1.25	1.04	.91	.81	.74	.68	.64	.60
100	8.75	4.57	3.18	2.49	2.08	1.81	1.61	1.47	1.36	1.27	1.20
200	17.50	9.14	6.36	4.98	4.16	3.61	3.22	2.94	2.71	2.54	2.40
300	26.24	13.71	9.54	7.47	6.23	5.41	4.83	4.40	4.07	3.81	3.59
400	34.99	18.28	12.72	9.96	8.31	7.22	6.44	5.87	5.42	5.07	4.79
500	43.73	22.85	15.90	12.45	10.38	9.02	8.05	7.33	6.78	6.34	5.99
600	52.48	27.42	19.08	14.94	12.46	10.82	9.66	8.80	8.13	7.61	7.18
700	61.22	31.98	22.26	17.42	14.54	12.62	11.27	10.26	9.49	8.87	8.38
800	69.97	36.55	25.44	19.91	16.61	14.43	12.88	11.73	10.84	10.14	9.57
900	78.71	41.12	28.62	22.40	18.69	16.23	14.49	13.19	12.19	11.41	10.77
1000	87.46	45.69	31.80	24.89	20.76	18.03	16.09	14.66	13.55	12.67	11.97
2000	174.91	91.37	63.60	49.78	41.52	36.06	32.18	29.31	27.09	25.34	23.93
3000	262.36	137.06	95.40	74.66	62.28	54.08	48.27	43.96	40.63	38.01	35.89
4000	349.81	182.74	127.20	99.55	83.04	72.11	64.36	58.61	54.18	50.68	47.85
5000	437.26	228.43	159.00	124.43	103.80	90.13	80.45	73.26	67.72	63.34	59.81
6000	524.71	274.11	190.80	149.32	124.56	108.16	96.54	87.91	81.26	76.01	71.77
7000	612.17	319.80	222.60	174.20	145.31	126.18	112.63	102.56	94.81	88.68	83.73
8000	699.62	365.48	254.40	199.09	166.07	144.21	128.72	117.21	108.35	101.35	95.69
9000	787.07	411.17	286.20	223.97	186.83	162.23	144.81	131.86	121.89	114.01	107.65
10000	874.52	456.85	318.00	248.86	207.59	180.26	160.90	146.51	135.43	126.68	119.61
11000	961.97	502.54	349.80	273.74	228.35	198.29	176.98	161.16	148.98	139.35	131.57
12000	1049.42	548.22	381.60	298.63	249.11	216.31	193.07	175.81	162.52	152.02	143.53
13000	1136.87	593.91	413.40	323.51	269.86	234.34	209.16	190.46	176.06	164.68	155.50
14000	1224.33	639.59	445.20	348.40	290.62	252.36	225.25	205.11	189.61	177.35	167.46
15000	1311.78	685.28	477.00	373.28	311.38	270.39	241.34	219.76	203.15	190.02	179.42
16000	1399.23	730.96	508.80	398.17	332.14	288.41	257.43	234.41	216.69	202.69	191.38
17000	1486.68	776.65	540.60	423.05	352.90	306.44	273.52	249.06	230.23	215.35	203.34
18000	1574.13	822.33	572.40	447.94	373.66	324.46	289.61	263.71	243.78	228.02	215.30
19000	1661.58	868.02	604.20	472.82	394.41	342.49	305.70	278.36	257.32	240.69	227.26
20000	1749.03	913.70	636.00	497.71	415.17	360.52	321.79	293.01	270.86	253.36	239.22
21000	1836.49	959.38	667.80	522.59	435.93	378.54	337.88	307.66	284.41	266.02	251.18
22000	1923.94	1005.07	699.60	547.48	456.69	396.57	353.96	322.31	297.95	278.69	263.14
23000	2011.39	1050.75	731.40	572.36	477.45	414.59	370.05	336.96	311.49	291.36	275.10
24000	2098.84	1096.44	763.20	597.25	498.21	432.62	386.14	351.61	325.03	304.03	287.06
25000	2186.29	1142.12	795.00	622.13	518.96	450.64	402.23	366.26	338.58	316.69	299.03
26000	2273.74	1187.81	826.80	647.02	539.72	468.67	418.32	380.91	352.12	329.36	310.99
27000	2361.19	1233.49	858.60	671.90	560.48	486.69	434.41	395.56	365.66	342.03	322.95
28000	2448.65	1279.18	890.40	696.79	581.24	504.72	450.50	410.21	379.21	354.70	334.91
29000	2536.10	1324.86	922.20	721.67	602.00	522.75	466.59	424.86	392.75	367.36	346.87
30000	2623.55	1370.55	954.00	746.56	622.76	540.77	482.68	439.51	406.29	380.03	358.83
31000	2711.00	1416.23	985.80	771.44	643.51	558.80	498.77	454.15	419.84	392.70	370.79
32000	2798.45	1461.92	1017.60	796.33	664.27	576.82	514.86	468.81	433.38	405.37	382.75
33000	2885.90	1507.60	1049.40	821.21	685.03	594.85	530.94	483.46	446.93	418.04	394.71
34000	2973.36	1553.29	1081.20	846.10	705.79	612.87	547.03	498.11	460.46	430.70	406.67
35000	3060.81	1598.97	1113.00	870.98	726.55	630.90	563.12	512.76	474.01	443.37	418.63
36000	3148.26	1644.66	1144.80	895.87	747.31	648.92	579.21	527.41	487.55	456.04	430.59
37000	3235.71	1690.34	1176.60	920.75	768.06	666.95	595.30	542.06	501.09	468.71	442.55
38000	3323.16	1736.03	1208.39	945.64	788.82	684.98	611.39	556.71	514.64	481.37	454.52
39000	3410.61	1781.71	1240.19	970.52	809.58	703.00	627.48	571.36	528.18	494.04	466.48
40000	3498.06	1827.39	1271.99	995.41	830.34	721.03	643.57	586.01	541.72	506.71	478.44
41000	3585.52	1873.08	1303.79	1020.29	851.10	739.05	659.66	600.66	555.26	519.38	490.40
42000	3672.97	1918.76	1335.59	1045.18	871.86	757.08	675.75	615.31	568.81	532.04	502.36
43000	3760.42	1964.45	1367.39	1070.06	892.61	775.10	691.84	629.96	582.35	544.71	514.32
44000	3847.87	2010.13	1399.19	1094.95	913.37	793.13	707.92	644.61	595.89	557.38	526.28
45000	3935.32	2055.82	1430.99	1119.83	934.13	811.15	724.01	659.26	609.44	570.05	538.24
46000	4022.77	2101.50	1462.79	1144.72	954.89	829.18	740.10	673.91	622.98	582.71	550.20
47000	4110.22	2147.19	1494.59	1169.60	975.65	847.21	756.19	688.56	636.52	595.38	562.16
48000	4197.68	2192.87	1526.39	1194.49	996.41	865.23	772.28	703.21	650.06	608.05	574.12
49000	4285.13	2238.56	1558.19	1219.37	1017.16	883.26	788.37	717.86	663.61	620.72	586.08
50000	4372.58	2284.24	1589.99	1244.26	1037.92	901.28	804.46	732.52	677.15	633.38	598.05
55000	4809.84	2512.67	1748.99	1368.68	1141.71	991.41	884.90	805.77	744.86	696.72	657.85
60000	5247.09	2741.09	1907.99	1493.11	1245.51	1081.54	965.35	879.02	812.58	760.06	717.65
65000	5684.35	2969.51	2066.99	1617.53	1349.30	1171.66	1045.80	952.27	880.29	823.40	777.46
70000	6121.61	3197.94	2225.99	1741.96	1453.09	1261.79	1126.24	1025.52	948.01	886.74	837.26
75000	6558.87	3426.36	2384.98	1866.38	1556.88	1351.92	1206.69	1098.77	1015.72	950.07	897.07
80000	6996.12	3654.78	2543.98	1990.81	1660.67	1442.05	1287.13	1172.02	1083.44	1013.41	956.87
85000	7433.38	3883.21	2702.98	2115.23	1764.47	1532.18	1367.58	1245.27	1151.15	1076.75	1016.67
90000	7870.64	4111.63	2861.98	2239.66	1868.26	1622.30	1448.02	1318.52	1218.87	1140.09	1076.48
95000	8307.90	4340.06	3020.98	2364.08	1972.05	1712.43	1528.47	1391.77	1286.58	1203.42	1136.28
100000	8745.15	4568.48	3179.98	2488.51	2075.84	1802.56	1608.91	1465.03	1354.30	1266.76	1196.09

Principal and Interest
Monthly Payment Amortization Table

9.00%

Term Amount	12 Years	13 Years	14 Years	15 Years	16 Years	17 Years	18 Years	19 Years	20 Years	25 Years	30 Years
50	.57	.55	.53	.51	.50	.48	.47	.46	.45	.42	.41
100	1.14	1.09	1.05	1.02	.99	.96	.94	.92	.90	.84	.81
200	2.28	2.18	2.10	2.03	1.97	1.92	1.88	1.84	1.80	1.68	1.61
300	3.42	3.27	3.15	3.05	2.96	2.88	2.81	2.76	2.70	2.52	2.42
400	4.56	4.36	4.20	4.06	3.94	3.84	3.75	3.67	3.60	3.36	3.22
500	5.70	5.45	5.25	5.08	4.93	4.80	4.69	4.59	4.50	4.20	4.03
600	6.83	6.54	6.30	6.09	5.91	5.76	5.62	5.51	5.40	5.04	4.83
700	7.97	7.63	7.35	7.10	6.90	6.72	6.56	6.42	6.30	5.88	5.64
800	9.11	8.72	8.40	8.12	7.88	7.68	7.50	7.34	7.20	6.72	6.44
900	10.25	9.81	9.45	9.13	8.87	8.63	8.43	8.26	8.10	7.56	7.25
1000	11.39	10.90	10.49	10.15	9.85	9.59	9.37	9.17	9.00	8.40	8.05
2000	22.77	21.80	20.98	20.29	19.70	19.18	18.73	18.34	18.00	16.79	16.10
3000	34.15	32.70	31.47	30.43	29.54	28.77	28.10	27.51	27.00	25.18	24.14
4000	45.53	43.59	41.96	40.58	39.39	38.36	37.46	36.68	35.99	33.57	32.19
5000	56.91	54.49	52.45	50.72	49.23	47.95	46.83	45.85	44.99	41.96	40.24
6000	68.29	65.39	62.94	60.86	59.08	57.53	56.19	55.02	53.99	50.36	48.28
7000	79.67	76.28	73.43	71.00	68.92	67.12	65.56	64.19	62.99	58.75	56.33
8000	91.05	87.18	83.92	81.15	78.77	76.71	74.92	73.36	71.98	67.14	64.37
9000	102.43	98.08	94.41	91.29	88.61	86.30	84.29	82.53	80.98	75.53	72.42
10000	113.81	108.97	104.90	101.43	98.46	95.89	93.65	91.69	89.98	83.92	80.47
11000	125.19	119.87	115.39	111.57	108.30	105.47	103.01	100.86	98.97	92.32	88.51
12000	136.57	130.77	125.88	121.72	118.15	115.06	112.38	110.03	107.97	100.71	96.56
13000	147.95	141.66	136.37	131.86	127.99	124.65	121.74	119.20	116.97	109.10	104.61
14000	159.33	152.56	146.86	142.00	137.84	134.24	131.11	128.37	125.97	117.49	112.65
15000	170.71	163.46	157.35	152.14	147.68	143.83	140.47	137.54	134.96	125.88	120.70
16000	182.09	174.35	167.84	162.29	157.53	153.41	149.84	146.71	143.96	134.28	128.74
17000	193.47	185.25	178.32	172.43	167.37	163.00	159.20	155.88	152.96	142.67	136.79
18000	204.85	196.15	188.81	182.57	177.22	172.59	168.57	165.05	161.96	151.06	144.84
19000	216.23	207.04	199.30	192.72	187.06	182.18	177.93	174.22	170.95	159.45	152.88
20000	227.61	217.94	209.79	202.86	196.91	191.77	187.29	183.38	179.95	167.84	160.93
21000	238.99	228.84	220.28	213.00	206.75	201.35	196.66	192.55	188.95	176.24	168.98
22000	250.37	239.73	230.77	223.14	216.60	210.94	206.02	201.72	197.94	184.63	177.02
23000	261.75	250.63	241.26	233.29	226.44	220.53	215.39	210.89	206.94	193.02	185.07
24000	273.13	261.53	251.75	243.43	236.29	230.12	224.75	220.06	215.94	201.41	193.11
25000	284.51	272.43	262.24	253.57	246.13	239.71	234.12	229.23	224.94	209.80	201.16
26000	295.89	283.32	272.73	263.71	255.98	249.29	243.48	238.40	233.93	218.20	209.21
27000	307.27	294.22	283.22	273.86	265.82	258.88	252.85	247.57	242.93	226.59	217.25
28000	318.65	305.12	293.71	284.00	275.67	268.47	262.21	256.74	251.93	234.98	225.30
29000	330.03	316.01	304.20	294.14	285.51	278.06	271.57	265.91	260.93	243.37	233.35
30000	341.41	326.91	314.69	304.28	295.36	287.65	280.94	275.07	269.92	251.76	241.39
31000	352.79	337.81	325.18	314.43	305.20	297.23	290.30	284.24	278.92	260.16	249.44
32000	364.17	348.70	335.67	324.57	315.05	306.82	299.67	293.41	287.92	268.55	257.48
33000	375.56	359.60	346.15	334.71	324.90	316.41	309.03	302.58	296.91	276.94	265.53
34000	386.94	370.50	356.64	344.86	334.74	326.00	318.40	311.75	305.91	285.33	273.58
35000	398.32	381.39	367.13	355.00	344.59	335.59	327.76	320.92	314.91	293.72	281.62
36000	409.70	392.29	377.62	365.14	354.43	345.17	337.13	330.09	323.91	302.12	289.67
37000	421.08	403.19	388.11	375.28	364.28	354.76	346.49	339.26	332.90	310.51	297.72
38000	432.46	414.08	398.60	385.43	374.12	364.35	355.85	348.43	341.90	318.90	305.76
39000	443.84	424.98	409.09	395.57	383.97	373.94	365.22	357.60	350.90	327.29	313.81
40000	455.22	435.88	419.58	405.71	393.81	383.53	374.58	366.76	359.90	335.68	321.85
41000	466.60	446.77	430.07	415.85	403.66	393.11	383.95	375.93	368.89	344.08	329.90
42000	477.98	457.67	440.56	426.00	413.50	402.70	393.31	385.10	377.89	352.47	337.95
43000	489.36	468.57	451.05	436.14	423.35	412.29	402.68	394.27	386.89	360.86	345.99
44000	500.74	479.46	461.54	446.28	433.19	421.88	412.04	403.44	395.88	369.25	354.04
45000	512.12	490.36	472.03	456.42	443.04	431.47	421.41	412.61	404.88	377.64	362.09
46000	523.50	501.26	482.52	466.57	452.88	441.05	430.77	421.78	413.88	386.04	370.13
47000	534.88	512.15	493.01	476.71	462.73	450.64	440.13	430.95	422.88	394.43	378.18
48000	546.26	523.05	503.50	486.85	472.57	460.23	449.50	440.12	431.87	402.82	386.22
49000	557.64	533.95	513.98	497.00	482.42	469.82	458.86	449.28	440.87	411.21	394.27
50000	569.02	544.85	524.47	507.14	492.26	479.41	468.23	458.45	449.87	419.60	402.32
55000	625.92	599.33	576.92	557.85	541.49	527.35	515.05	504.30	494.85	461.56	442.55
60000	682.82	653.81	629.37	608.56	590.71	575.29	561.87	550.14	539.84	503.52	482.78
65000	739.72	708.30	681.81	659.28	639.94	623.23	608.69	595.99	584.83	545.48	523.01
70000	796.63	762.78	734.26	709.99	689.17	671.17	655.52	641.83	629.81	587.44	563.24
75000	853.53	817.27	786.71	760.70	738.39	719.11	702.34	687.68	674.80	629.40	603.47
80000	910.43	871.75	839.16	811.42	787.62	767.05	749.16	733.52	719.79	671.36	643.70
85000	967.33	926.23	891.60	862.13	836.84	814.99	795.98	779.37	764.77	713.32	683.93
90000	1024.23	980.72	944.05	912.84	886.07	862.93	842.81	825.21	809.76	755.28	724.17
95000	1081.13	1035.20	996.50	963.56	935.30	910.87	889.63	871.06	854.74	797.24	764.40
100000	1138.04	1089.69	1048.94	1014.27	984.52	958.81	936.45	916.90	899.73	839.20	804.63

9.25% Principal and Interest
Monthly Payment Amortization Table

Term Amount	1 Year	2 Years	3 Years	4 Years	5 Years	6 Years	7 Years	8 Years	9 Years	10 Years	11 Years
50	4.38	2.29	1.60	1.26	1.05	.91	.82	.74	.69	.65	.61
100	8.76	4.58	3.20	2.51	2.09	1.82	1.63	1.48	1.37	1.29	1.21
200	17.52	9.16	6.39	5.01	4.18	3.63	3.25	2.96	2.74	2.57	2.42
300	26.28	13.74	9.58	7.51	6.27	5.45	4.87	4.44	4.11	3.85	3.63
400	35.03	18.32	12.77	10.01	8.36	7.26	6.49	5.92	5.48	5.13	4.84
500	43.79	22.90	15.96	12.51	10.44	9.08	8.11	7.40	6.84	6.41	6.05
600	52.55	27.48	19.15	15.01	12.53	10.89	9.73	8.87	8.21	7.69	7.26
700	61.30	32.06	22.35	17.51	14.62	12.71	11.36	10.35	9.58	8.97	8.47
800	70.06	36.64	25.54	20.01	16.71	14.52	12.98	11.83	10.95	10.25	9.68
900	78.82	41.22	28.73	22.51	18.80	16.34	14.60	13.31	12.31	11.53	10.89
1000	87.57	45.80	31.92	25.01	20.88	18.15	16.22	14.79	13.68	12.81	12.10
2000	175.14	91.60	63.84	50.01	41.76	36.30	32.44	29.57	27.36	25.61	24.20
3000	262.71	137.40	95.75	75.02	62.64	54.45	48.65	44.35	41.03	38.41	36.30
4000	350.27	183.20	127.67	100.02	83.52	72.60	64.87	59.13	54.71	51.22	48.40
5000	437.84	229.00	159.59	125.02	104.40	90.75	81.09	73.91	68.38	64.02	60.50
6000	525.41	274.80	191.50	150.03	125.28	108.90	97.30	88.69	82.06	76.82	72.60
7000	612.98	320.60	223.42	175.03	146.16	127.05	113.52	103.47	95.74	89.63	84.70
8000	700.54	366.40	255.33	200.04	167.04	145.20	129.73	118.25	109.41	102.43	96.80
9000	788.11	412.20	287.25	225.04	187.92	163.35	145.95	133.03	123.09	115.23	108.90
10000	875.68	458.00	319.17	250.04	208.80	181.50	162.17	147.81	136.76	128.04	121.00
11000	963.25	503.80	351.08	275.05	229.68	199.65	178.38	162.59	150.44	140.84	133.10
12000	1050.81	549.60	383.00	300.05	250.56	217.80	194.60	177.37	164.11	153.64	145.20
13000	1138.38	595.40	414.92	325.06	271.44	235.95	210.82	192.15	177.79	166.45	157.30
14000	1225.95	641.20	446.83	350.06	292.32	254.10	227.03	206.93	191.47	179.25	169.40
15000	1313.52	687.00	478.75	375.06	313.20	272.25	243.25	221.71	205.14	192.05	181.49
16000	1401.08	732.80	510.66	400.07	334.08	290.40	259.46	236.49	218.82	204.86	193.59
17000	1488.65	778.60	542.58	425.07	354.96	308.55	275.68	251.27	232.49	217.66	205.69
18000	1576.22	824.40	574.50	450.08	375.84	326.70	291.90	266.05	246.17	230.46	217.79
19000	1663.79	870.20	606.41	475.08	396.72	344.85	308.11	280.83	259.84	243.27	229.89
20000	1751.35	916.00	638.33	500.08	417.60	363.00	324.33	295.61	273.52	256.07	241.99
21000	1838.92	961.80	670.25	525.09	438.48	381.15	340.55	310.39	287.20	268.87	254.09
22000	1926.49	1007.59	702.16	550.09	459.36	399.30	356.76	325.17	300.87	281.68	266.19
23000	2014.06	1053.39	734.08	575.10	480.24	417.45	372.98	339.95	314.55	294.48	278.29
24000	2101.62	1099.19	765.99	600.10	501.12	435.60	389.19	354.73	328.22	307.28	290.39
25000	2189.19	1144.99	797.91	625.10	522.00	453.75	405.41	369.51	341.90	320.09	302.49
26000	2276.76	1190.79	829.83	650.11	542.88	471.90	421.63	384.29	355.58	332.89	314.59
27000	2364.33	1236.59	861.74	675.11	563.76	490.05	437.84	399.07	369.25	345.69	326.69
28000	2451.89	1282.39	893.66	700.11	584.64	508.20	454.06	413.85	382.93	358.50	338.79
29000	2539.46	1328.19	925.58	725.12	605.52	526.35	470.28	428.63	396.60	371.30	350.88
30000	2627.03	1373.99	957.49	750.12	626.40	544.50	486.49	443.41	410.28	384.10	362.98
31000	2714.60	1419.79	989.41	775.13	647.28	562.65	502.71	458.19	423.95	396.91	375.08
32000	2802.16	1465.59	1021.32	800.13	668.16	580.80	518.92	472.97	437.63	409.71	387.18
33000	2889.73	1511.39	1053.24	825.13	689.04	598.95	535.14	487.75	451.31	422.51	399.28
34000	2977.30	1557.19	1085.16	850.14	709.92	617.10	551.36	502.53	464.98	435.32	411.38
35000	3064.87	1602.99	1117.07	875.14	730.80	635.25	567.57	517.31	478.66	448.12	423.48
36000	3152.43	1648.79	1146.99	900.15	751.68	653.40	583.79	532.09	492.33	460.92	435.58
37000	3240.00	1694.59	1180.90	925.15	772.56	671.55	600.01	546.87	506.01	473.73	447.68
38000	3327.57	1740.39	1212.82	950.15	793.44	689.70	616.22	561.65	519.68	486.53	459.78
39000	3415.14	1786.19	1244.74	975.16	814.32	707.85	632.44	576.43	533.36	499.33	471.88
40000	3502.70	1831.99	1276.65	1000.16	835.20	726.00	648.65	591.21	547.04	512.14	483.98
41000	3590.27	1877.79	1308.57	1025.17	856.08	744.15	664.87	605.99	560.71	524.94	496.08
42000	3677.84	1923.59	1340.49	1050.17	876.96	762.30	681.09	620.77	574.39	537.74	508.18
43000	3765.41	1969.38	1372.40	1075.17	897.84	780.45	697.30	635.55	588.06	550.55	520.27
44000	3852.97	2015.18	1404.32	1100.18	918.72	798.60	713.52	650.33	601.74	563.35	532.37
45000	3940.54	2060.98	1436.23	1125.18	939.60	816.75	729.74	665.11	615.41	576.15	544.47
46000	4028.11	2106.78	1468.15	1150.19	960.48	834.90	745.95	679.90	629.09	588.96	556.57
47000	4115.68	2152.58	1500.07	1175.19	981.36	853.05	762.17	694.68	642.77	601.76	568.67
48000	4203.24	2198.38	1531.98	1200.19	1002.24	871.20	778.38	709.46	656.44	614.56	580.77
49000	4290.81	2244.18	1563.90	1225.20	1023.12	889.35	794.60	724.24	670.12	627.37	592.87
50000	4378.38	2289.98	1595.82	1250.20	1044.00	907.50	810.82	739.02	683.79	640.17	604.97
55000	4816.21	2518.98	1755.40	1375.22	1148.40	998.25	891.90	812.92	752.17	704.18	665.47
60000	5254.05	2747.98	1914.98	1500.24	1252.80	1089.00	972.98	886.82	820.55	768.20	725.96
65000	5691.89	2976.97	2074.56	1625.26	1357.20	1179.75	1054.06	960.72	888.93	832.22	786.46
70000	6129.73	3205.97	2234.14	1750.28	1461.60	1270.50	1135.14	1034.62	957.31	896.23	846.96
75000	6567.56	3434.97	2393.72	1875.30	1566.00	1361.24	1216.22	1108.52	1025.69	960.25	907.45
80000	7005.40	3663.97	2553.30	2000.31	1670.40	1451.99	1297.30	1182.42	1094.07	1024.27	967.95
85000	7443.24	3892.97	2712.88	2125.34	1774.80	1542.74	1378.39	1256.32	1162.45	1088.28	1028.45
90000	7881.08	4121.96	2872.46	2250.36	1879.20	1633.49	1459.47	1330.22	1230.82	1152.30	1088.94
95000	8318.91	4350.96	3032.05	2375.38	1983.60	1724.24	1540.55	1404.13	1299.20	1216.32	1149.44
100000	8756.75	4579.96	3191.63	2500.40	2087.99	1814.99	1621.63	1478.03	1367.58	1280.33	1209.93

Principal and Interest Monthly Payment Amortization Table   9.25%

Term / Amount	12 Years	13 Years	14 Years	15 Years	16 Years	17 Years	18 Years	19 Years	20 Years	25 Years	30 Years
50	.58	.56	.54	.52	.50	.49	.48	.47	.46	.43	.42
100	1.16	1.11	1.07	1.03	1.00	.98	.96	.94	.92	.86	.83
200	2.31	2.21	2.13	2.06	2.00	1.95	1.91	1.87	1.84	1.72	1.65
300	3.46	3.32	3.20	3.09	3.00	2.93	2.86	2.80	2.75	2.57	2.47
400	4.61	4.42	4.26	4.12	4.00	3.90	3.81	3.74	3.67	3.43	3.30
500	5.77	5.53	5.32	5.15	5.00	4.88	4.77	4.67	4.58	4.29	4.12
600	6.92	6.63	6.39	6.18	6.00	5.85	5.72	5.60	5.50	5.14	4.94
700	8.07	7.73	7.45	7.21	7.00	6.82	6.67	6.53	6.42	6.00	5.76
800	9.22	8.84	8.51	8.24	8.00	7.80	7.62	7.47	7.33	6.86	6.59
900	10.37	9.94	9.58	9.27	9.00	8.77	8.57	8.40	8.25	7.71	7.41
1000	11.53	11.05	10.64	10.30	10.00	9.75	9.53	9.33	9.16	8.57	8.23
2000	23.05	22.09	21.28	20.59	20.00	19.49	19.05	18.66	18.32	17.13	16.46
3000	34.57	33.13	31.91	30.88	30.00	29.23	28.57	27.99	27.48	25.70	24.69
4000	46.09	44.17	42.55	41.17	39.99	38.97	38.09	37.32	36.64	34.26	32.91
5000	57.61	55.21	53.19	51.46	49.99	48.72	47.61	46.65	45.80	42.82	41.14
6000	69.13	66.25	63.82	61.76	59.99	58.46	57.13	55.97	54.96	51.39	49.37
7000	80.66	77.29	74.46	72.05	69.98	68.20	66.65	65.30	64.12	59.95	57.59
8000	92.18	88.33	85.09	82.34	79.98	77.94	76.17	74.63	73.27	68.52	65.82
9000	103.70	99.37	95.73	92.63	89.98	87.69	85.70	83.96	82.43	77.08	74.05
10000	115.22	110.41	106.37	102.92	99.97	97.43	95.22	93.29	91.59	85.64	82.27
11000	126.74	121.45	117.00	113.22	109.97	107.17	104.74	102.61	100.75	94.21	90.50
12000	138.26	132.49	127.64	123.51	119.97	116.91	114.26	111.94	109.91	102.77	98.73
13000	149.79	143.54	138.27	133.80	129.97	126.66	123.78	121.27	119.07	111.33	106.95
14000	161.31	154.58	148.91	144.09	139.96	136.40	133.30	130.60	128.23	119.90	115.18
15000	172.83	165.62	159.55	154.38	149.96	146.14	142.82	139.93	137.39	128.46	123.41
16000	184.35	176.66	170.18	164.68	159.96	155.88	152.34	149.25	146.54	137.03	131.63
17000	195.87	187.70	180.82	174.97	169.95	165.62	161.87	158.58	155.70	145.59	139.86
18000	207.39	198.74	191.45	185.26	179.95	175.37	171.39	167.91	164.86	154.15	148.09
19000	218.91	209.78	202.09	195.55	189.95	185.11	180.91	177.24	174.02	162.72	156.31
20000	230.44	220.82	212.73	205.84	199.94	194.85	190.43	186.57	183.18	171.28	164.54
21000	241.96	231.86	223.36	216.14	209.94	204.59	199.95	195.89	192.34	179.85	172.77
22000	253.48	242.90	234.00	226.43	219.94	214.34	209.47	205.22	201.50	188.41	180.99
23000	265.00	253.94	244.63	236.72	229.94	224.08	218.99	214.55	210.65	196.97	189.22
24000	276.52	264.98	255.27	247.01	239.93	233.82	228.51	223.88	219.81	205.54	197.45
25000	288.04	276.02	265.91	257.30	249.93	243.56	238.03	233.21	228.97	214.10	205.67
26000	299.57	287.07	276.54	267.59	259.93	253.31	247.56	242.54	238.13	222.66	213.90
27000	311.09	298.11	287.18	277.89	269.92	263.05	257.08	251.86	247.29	231.23	222.13
28000	322.61	309.15	297.81	288.18	279.92	272.79	266.60	261.19	256.45	239.79	230.35
29000	334.13	320.19	308.45	298.47	289.92	282.53	276.12	270.52	265.61	248.36	238.58
30000	345.65	331.23	319.09	308.76	299.91	292.28	285.64	279.85	274.77	256.92	246.81
31000	357.17	342.27	329.72	319.05	309.91	302.02	295.16	289.18	283.92	265.48	255.03
32000	368.70	353.31	340.36	329.35	319.91	311.76	304.68	298.50	293.08	274.05	263.26
33000	380.22	364.35	350.99	339.64	329.91	321.50	314.20	307.83	302.24	282.61	271.49
34000	391.74	375.39	361.63	349.93	339.90	331.24	323.73	317.16	311.40	291.17	279.71
35000	403.26	386.43	372.27	360.22	349.90	340.99	333.25	326.49	320.56	299.74	287.94
36000	414.78	397.47	382.90	370.51	359.90	350.73	342.77	335.82	329.72	308.30	296.17
37000	426.30	408.51	393.54	380.81	369.89	360.47	352.29	345.14	338.88	316.87	304.39
38000	437.82	419.55	404.17	391.10	379.89	370.21	361.81	354.47	348.03	325.43	312.62
39000	449.35	430.60	414.81	401.39	389.89	379.96	371.33	363.80	357.19	333.99	320.85
40000	460.87	441.64	425.45	411.68	399.88	389.70	380.85	373.13	366.35	342.56	329.08
41000	472.39	452.68	436.08	421.97	409.88	399.44	390.37	382.46	375.51	351.12	337.30
42000	483.91	463.72	446.72	432.27	419.88	409.18	399.90	391.78	384.67	359.69	345.53
43000	495.43	474.76	457.35	442.56	429.87	418.93	409.42	401.11	393.83	368.25	353.76
44000	506.95	485.80	467.99	452.85	439.87	428.67	418.94	410.44	402.99	376.81	361.98
45000	518.48	496.84	478.63	463.14	449.87	438.41	428.46	419.77	412.15	385.38	370.21
46000	530.00	507.88	489.26	473.43	459.87	448.15	437.98	429.10	421.30	393.94	378.44
47000	541.52	518.92	499.90	483.73	469.86	457.90	447.50	438.42	430.46	402.50	386.66
48000	553.04	529.96	510.53	494.02	479.86	467.64	457.02	447.75	439.62	411.07	394.89
49000	564.56	541.00	521.17	504.31	489.86	477.38	466.54	457.08	448.78	419.63	403.12
50000	576.08	552.04	531.81	514.60	499.85	487.12	476.06	466.41	457.94	428.20	411.34
55000	633.69	607.25	584.99	566.06	549.84	535.83	523.67	513.05	503.73	471.02	452.48
60000	691.30	662.45	638.17	617.52	599.82	584.55	571.28	559.69	549.53	513.83	493.61
65000	748.91	717.66	691.35	668.98	649.81	633.26	618.88	606.33	595.32	556.65	534.74
70000	806.51	772.86	744.53	720.44	699.79	681.97	666.49	652.97	641.11	599.47	575.88
75000	864.12	828.06	797.71	771.90	749.78	730.68	714.09	699.61	686.91	642.29	617.01
80000	921.73	883.27	850.89	823.36	799.76	779.39	761.70	746.25	732.70	685.11	658.15
85000	979.34	938.47	904.07	874.82	849.75	828.10	809.31	792.89	778.49	727.93	699.28
90000	1036.95	993.68	957.25	926.28	899.73	876.82	856.91	839.53	824.29	770.75	740.41
95000	1094.55	1048.88	1010.43	977.74	949.72	925.53	904.52	886.17	870.08	813.57	781.55
100000	1152.16	1104.08	1063.61	1029.20	999.70	974.24	952.12	932.81	915.87	856.39	822.68

9.50% Principal and Interest
Monthly Payment Amortization Table

Term	1 Year	2 Years	3 Years	4 Years	5 Years	6 Years	7 Years	8 Years	9 Years	10 Years	11 Years
Amount											
50	4.39	2.30	1.61	1.26	1.06	.92	.82	.75	.70	.65	.62
100	8.77	4.60	3.21	2.52	2.11	1.83	1.64	1.50	1.39	1.30	1.23
200	17.54	9.19	6.41	5.03	4.21	3.66	3.27	2.99	2.77	2.59	2.45
300	26.31	13.78	9.61	7.54	6.31	5.49	4.91	4.48	4.15	3.89	3.68
400	35.08	18.37	12.82	10.05	8.41	7.31	6.54	5.97	5.53	5.18	4.90
500	43.85	22.96	16.02	12.57	10.51	9.14	8.18	7.46	6.91	6.47	6.12
600	52.62	27.55	19.22	15.08	12.61	10.97	9.81	8.95	8.29	7.77	7.35
700	61.38	32.15	22.43	17.59	14.71	12.80	11.45	10.44	9.67	9.06	8.57
800	70.15	36.74	25.63	20.10	16.81	14.62	13.08	11.93	11.05	10.36	9.80
900	78.92	41.33	28.83	22.62	18.91	16.45	14.71	13.42	12.43	11.65	11.02
1000	87.69	45.92	32.04	25.13	21.01	18.28	16.35	14.92	13.81	12.94	12.24
2000	175.37	91.83	64.07	50.25	42.01	36.55	32.69	29.83	27.62	25.88	24.48
3000	263.06	137.75	96.10	75.37	63.01	54.83	49.04	44.74	41.43	38.82	36.72
4000	350.74	183.66	128.14	100.50	84.01	73.10	65.38	59.65	55.24	51.76	48.96
5000	438.42	229.58	160.17	125.62	105.01	91.38	81.72	74.56	69.05	64.70	61.20
6000	526.11	275.49	192.20	150.74	126.02	109.65	98.07	89.47	82.86	77.64	73.44
7000	613.79	321.41	224.24	175.87	147.02	127.93	114.41	104.38	96.67	90.58	85.68
8000	701.47	367.32	256.27	200.99	168.02	146.20	130.76	119.29	110.48	103.52	97.91
9000	789.16	413.24	288.30	226.11	189.02	164.48	147.10	134.20	124.29	116.46	110.15
10000	876.84	459.15	320.33	251.24	210.02	182.75	163.44	149.11	138.10	129.40	122.39
11000	964.52	505.06	352.37	276.36	231.03	201.03	179.79	164.02	151.91	142.34	134.63
12000	1052.21	550.98	384.40	301.48	252.03	219.30	196.13	178.94	165.72	155.28	146.87
13000	1139.89	596.89	416.43	326.61	273.03	237.58	212.48	193.85	179.53	168.22	159.11
14000	1227.57	642.81	448.47	351.73	294.03	255.85	228.82	208.76	193.34	181.16	171.35
15000	1315.26	688.72	480.50	376.85	315.03	274.13	245.16	223.67	207.15	194.10	183.58
16000	1402.94	734.64	512.53	401.98	336.03	292.40	261.51	238.58	220.95	207.04	195.82
17000	1490.62	780.55	544.57	427.10	357.04	310.67	277.85	253.49	234.76	219.98	208.06
18000	1578.31	826.47	576.60	452.22	378.04	328.95	294.20	268.40	248.57	232.92	220.30
19000	1665.99	872.38	608.63	477.34	399.04	347.22	310.54	283.31	262.38	245.86	232.54
20000	1753.68	918.29	640.66	502.47	420.04	365.50	326.88	298.22	276.19	258.80	244.78
21000	1841.36	964.21	672.70	527.59	441.04	383.77	343.23	313.13	290.00	271.74	257.02
22000	1929.04	1010.12	704.73	552.71	462.05	402.05	359.57	328.04	303.81	284.68	269.26
23000	2016.73	1056.04	736.76	577.84	483.05	420.32	375.92	342.96	317.62	297.62	281.49
24000	2104.41	1101.95	768.80	602.96	504.05	438.60	392.26	357.87	331.43	310.56	293.73
25000	2192.09	1147.87	800.83	628.08	525.05	456.87	408.60	372.78	345.24	323.50	305.97
26000	2279.78	1193.78	832.86	653.21	546.05	475.15	424.95	387.69	359.05	336.44	318.21
27000	2367.46	1239.70	864.89	678.33	567.06	493.42	441.29	402.60	372.86	349.38	330.45
28000	2455.14	1285.61	896.93	703.45	588.06	511.70	457.64	417.51	386.67	362.32	342.69
29000	2542.83	1331.53	928.96	728.58	609.06	529.97	473.98	432.42	400.48	375.26	354.93
30000	2630.51	1377.44	960.99	753.70	630.06	548.25	490.32	447.33	414.29	388.20	367.16
31000	2718.19	1423.35	993.03	778.82	651.06	566.52	506.67	462.24	428.10	401.14	379.40
32000	2805.88	1469.27	1025.06	803.95	672.06	584.80	523.01	477.15	441.90	414.08	391.64
33000	2893.56	1515.18	1057.09	829.07	693.07	603.07	539.36	492.06	455.71	427.02	403.88
34000	2981.24	1561.10	1089.13	854.19	714.07	621.34	555.70	506.98	469.52	439.96	416.12
35000	3068.93	1607.01	1121.16	879.31	735.07	639.62	572.04	521.89	483.33	452.90	428.36
36000	3156.61	1652.93	1153.19	904.44	756.07	657.89	588.39	536.80	497.14	465.84	440.60
37000	3244.29	1698.84	1185.22	929.56	777.07	676.17	604.73	551.71	510.95	478.78	452.83
38000	3331.98	1744.76	1217.26	954.68	798.08	694.44	621.08	566.62	524.76	491.72	465.07
39000	3419.66	1790.67	1249.29	979.81	819.08	712.72	637.42	581.53	538.57	504.66	477.31
40000	3507.35	1836.58	1281.32	1004.93	840.08	730.99	653.76	596.44	552.38	517.60	489.55
41000	3595.03	1882.50	1313.36	1030.05	861.08	749.27	670.11	611.35	566.19	530.53	501.79
42000	3682.71	1928.41	1345.39	1055.18	882.08	767.54	686.45	626.26	580.00	543.47	514.03
43000	3770.40	1974.33	1377.42	1080.30	903.09	785.82	702.80	641.17	593.81	556.41	526.27
44000	3858.08	2020.24	1409.45	1105.42	924.09	804.09	719.14	656.08	607.62	569.35	538.51
45000	3945.76	2066.16	1441.49	1130.55	945.09	822.37	735.48	670.99	621.43	582.29	550.74
46000	4033.45	2112.07	1473.52	1155.67	966.09	840.64	751.83	685.91	635.24	595.23	562.98
47000	4121.13	2157.99	1505.55	1180.79	987.09	858.92	768.17	700.82	649.04	608.17	575.22
48000	4208.81	2203.90	1537.59	1205.92	1008.09	877.19	784.52	715.73	662.85	621.11	587.46
49000	4296.50	2249.82	1569.62	1231.04	1029.10	895.46	800.86	730.64	676.66	634.05	599.70
50000	4384.18	2295.73	1601.65	1256.16	1050.10	913.74	817.20	745.55	690.47	646.99	611.94
55000	4822.60	2525.30	1761.82	1381.78	1155.11	1005.11	898.92	820.10	759.52	711.69	673.13
60000	5261.02	2754.87	1921.98	1507.39	1260.12	1096.49	980.64	894.66	828.57	776.39	734.32
65000	5699.43	2984.45	2082.15	1633.01	1365.13	1187.86	1062.36	969.21	897.61	841.09	795.52
70000	6137.85	3214.02	2242.31	1758.62	1470.14	1279.23	1144.08	1043.77	966.66	905.79	856.71
75000	6576.27	3443.59	2402.48	1884.24	1575.14	1370.61	1225.80	1118.32	1035.71	970.49	917.90
80000	7014.69	3673.16	2562.64	2009.86	1680.15	1461.98	1307.52	1192.88	1104.75	1035.19	979.10
85000	7453.10	3902.74	2722.81	2135.47	1785.16	1553.35	1389.24	1267.43	1173.80	1099.88	1040.29
90000	7891.52	4132.31	2882.97	2261.09	1890.17	1644.73	1470.96	1341.98	1242.85	1164.58	1101.48
95000	8329.94	4361.88	3043.14	2386.70	1995.18	1736.10	1552.68	1416.54	1311.89	1229.28	1162.68
100000	8768.36	4591.45	3203.30	2512.32	2100.19	1827.47	1634.40	1491.09	1380.94	1293.98	1223.87

Principal and Interest
Monthly Payment Amortization Table

9.50%

Term Amount	12 Years	13 Years	14 Years	15 Years	16 Years	17 Years	18 Years	19 Years	20 Years	25 Years	30 Years
50	.59	.56	.54	.53	.51	.50	.49	.48	.47	.44	.43
100	1.17	1.12	1.08	1.05	1.02	.99	.97	.95	.94	.88	.85
200	2.34	2.24	2.16	2.09	2.03	1.98	1.94	1.90	1.87	1.75	1.69
300	3.50	3.36	3.24	3.14	3.05	2.97	2.91	2.85	2.80	2.63	2.53
400	4.67	4.48	4.32	4.18	4.06	3.96	3.88	3.80	3.73	3.50	3.37
500	5.84	5.60	5.40	5.23	5.08	4.95	4.84	4.75	4.67	4.37	4.21
600	7.00	6.72	6.48	6.27	6.09	5.94	5.81	5.70	5.60	5.25	5.05
700	8.17	7.84	7.55	7.31	7.11	6.93	6.78	6.65	6.53	6.12	5.89
800	9.34	8.95	8.63	8.36	8.12	7.92	7.75	7.60	7.46	6.99	6.73
900	10.50	10.07	9.71	9.40	9.14	8.91	8.72	8.54	8.39	7.87	7.57
1000	11.67	11.19	10.79	10.45	10.15	9.90	9.68	9.49	9.33	8.74	8.41
2000	23.33	22.38	21.57	20.89	20.30	19.80	19.36	18.98	18.65	17.48	16.82
3000	35.00	33.56	32.36	31.33	30.45	29.70	29.04	28.47	27.97	26.22	25.23
4000	46.66	44.75	43.14	41.77	40.60	39.60	38.72	37.96	37.29	34.95	33.64
5000	58.32	55.93	53.92	52.22	50.75	49.49	48.40	47.45	46.61	43.69	42.05
6000	69.99	67.12	64.71	62.66	60.90	59.39	58.08	56.94	55.93	52.43	50.46
7000	81.65	78.31	75.49	73.10	71.05	69.29	67.76	66.42	65.25	61.16	58.86
8000	93.31	89.49	86.27	83.54	81.20	79.19	77.44	75.91	74.58	69.90	67.27
9000	104.98	100.68	97.06	93.99	91.35	89.09	87.12	85.40	83.90	78.64	75.68
10000	116.64	111.86	107.84	104.43	101.50	98.98	96.80	94.89	93.22	87.37	84.09
11000	128.31	123.05	118.63	114.87	111.65	108.88	106.48	104.38	102.54	96.11	92.50
12000	139.97	134.23	129.41	125.31	121.80	118.78	116.15	113.87	111.86	104.85	100.91
13000	151.63	145.42	140.19	135.75	131.95	128.68	125.83	123.35	121.18	113.59	109.32
14000	163.30	156.61	150.98	146.20	142.10	138.57	135.51	132.84	130.50	122.32	117.72
15000	174.96	167.79	161.76	156.64	152.25	148.47	145.19	142.33	139.82	131.06	126.13
16000	186.62	178.98	172.54	167.08	162.40	158.37	154.87	151.82	149.15	139.80	134.54
17000	198.29	190.16	183.33	177.52	172.55	168.27	164.55	161.31	158.47	148.53	142.95
18000	209.95	201.35	194.11	187.97	182.70	178.17	174.23	170.80	167.79	157.27	151.36
19000	221.62	212.53	204.89	198.41	192.85	188.06	183.91	180.28	177.11	166.01	159.77
20000	233.28	223.72	215.68	208.85	203.00	197.96	193.59	189.77	186.43	174.74	168.18
21000	244.94	234.91	226.46	219.29	213.15	207.86	203.27	199.26	195.75	183.48	176.58
22000	256.61	246.09	237.25	229.73	223.30	217.76	212.95	208.75	205.07	192.22	184.99
23000	268.27	257.28	248.03	240.18	233.45	227.65	222.62	218.24	214.40	200.96	193.40
24000	279.93	268.46	258.81	250.62	243.60	237.55	232.30	227.73	223.72	209.69	201.81
25000	291.60	279.65	269.60	261.06	253.75	247.45	241.98	237.21	233.04	218.43	210.22
26000	303.26	290.83	280.38	271.50	263.90	257.35	251.66	246.70	242.36	227.17	218.63
27000	314.93	302.02	291.16	281.95	274.05	267.25	261.34	256.19	251.68	235.90	227.04
28000	326.59	313.21	301.95	292.39	284.20	277.14	271.02	265.68	261.00	244.64	235.44
29000	338.25	324.39	312.73	302.83	294.35	287.04	280.70	275.17	270.32	253.38	243.85
30000	349.92	335.58	323.52	313.27	304.50	296.94	290.38	284.66	279.64	262.11	252.26
31000	361.58	346.76	334.30	323.71	314.65	306.84	300.06	294.15	288.97	270.85	260.67
32000	373.24	357.95	345.08	334.16	324.80	316.73	309.74	303.63	298.29	279.59	269.08
33000	384.91	369.13	355.87	344.60	334.95	326.63	319.42	313.12	307.61	288.32	277.49
34000	396.57	380.32	366.65	355.04	345.10	336.53	329.09	322.61	316.93	297.06	285.90
35000	408.24	391.51	377.43	365.48	355.25	346.43	338.77	332.10	326.25	305.80	294.30
36000	419.90	402.69	388.22	375.93	365.40	356.33	348.45	341.59	335.57	314.54	302.71
37000	431.56	413.88	399.00	386.37	375.55	366.22	358.13	351.08	344.89	323.27	311.12
38000	443.23	425.06	409.78	396.81	385.70	376.12	367.81	360.56	354.21	332.01	319.53
39000	454.89	436.25	420.57	407.25	395.85	386.02	377.49	370.05	363.54	340.75	327.94
40000	466.55	447.43	431.35	417.69	406.00	395.92	387.17	379.54	372.86	349.48	336.35
41000	478.22	458.62	442.14	428.14	416.15	405.82	396.85	389.03	382.18	358.22	344.76
42000	489.88	469.81	452.92	438.58	426.30	415.71	406.53	398.52	391.50	366.96	353.16
43000	501.55	480.99	463.70	449.02	436.45	425.61	416.21	408.01	400.82	375.69	361.57
44000	513.21	492.18	474.49	459.46	446.60	435.51	425.89	417.49	410.14	384.43	369.98
45000	524.87	503.36	485.27	469.91	456.75	445.41	435.57	426.98	419.46	393.17	378.39
46000	536.54	514.55	496.05	480.35	466.90	455.30	445.24	436.47	428.79	401.91	386.80
47000	548.20	525.73	506.84	490.79	477.05	465.20	454.92	445.96	438.11	410.64	395.21
48000	559.86	536.92	517.62	501.23	487.20	475.10	464.60	455.45	447.43	419.38	403.62
49000	571.53	548.11	528.41	511.68	497.35	485.00	474.28	464.94	456.75	428.12	412.02
50000	583.19	559.29	539.19	522.12	507.50	494.90	483.96	474.42	466.07	436.85	420.43
55000	641.51	615.22	593.11	574.33	558.25	544.38	532.36	521.87	512.68	480.54	462.47
60000	699.83	671.15	647.03	626.54	609.00	593.87	580.75	569.31	559.28	524.22	504.52
65000	758.15	727.08	700.94	678.75	659.75	643.36	629.15	616.75	605.89	567.91	546.56
70000	816.47	783.01	754.86	730.96	710.50	692.85	677.54	664.19	652.50	611.59	588.60
75000	874.78	838.93	808.78	783.17	761.25	742.34	725.94	711.63	699.10	655.28	630.65
80000	933.10	894.86	862.70	835.38	812.00	791.83	774.33	759.08	745.71	698.96	672.69
85000	991.42	950.79	916.62	887.60	862.75	841.32	822.73	806.52	792.32	742.65	714.73
90000	1049.74	1006.72	970.54	939.81	913.50	890.81	871.13	853.96	838.92	786.33	756.77
95000	1108.06	1062.65	1024.45	992.02	964.25	940.30	919.52	901.40	885.53	830.02	798.82
100000	1166.38	1118.58	1078.37	1044.23	1014.99	989.79	967.92	948.84	932.14	873.70	840.86

9.75% Principal and Interest
Monthly Payment Amortization Table

Term	1 Year	2 Years	3 Years	4 Years	5 Years	6 Years	7 Years	8 Years	9 Years	10 Years	11 Years
Amount											
50	4.39	2.31	1.61	1.27	1.06	.93	.83	.76	.70	.66	.62
100	8.78	4.61	3.22	2.53	2.12	1.85	1.65	1.51	1.40	1.31	1.24
200	17.56	9.21	6.43	5.05	4.23	3.69	3.30	3.01	2.79	2.62	2.48
300	26.34	13.81	9.65	7.58	6.34	5.53	4.95	4.52	4.19	3.93	3.72
400	35.12	18.42	12.86	10.10	8.45	7.37	6.59	6.02	5.58	5.24	4.96
500	43.90	23.02	16.08	12.63	10.57	9.21	8.24	7.53	6.98	6.54	6.19
600	52.68	27.62	19.29	15.15	12.68	11.05	9.89	9.03	8.37	7.85	7.43
700	61.46	32.23	22.51	17.67	14.79	12.89	11.54	10.53	9.77	9.16	8.67
800	70.24	36.83	25.72	20.20	16.90	14.73	13.18	12.04	11.16	10.47	9.91
900	79.02	41.43	28.94	22.72	19.02	16.57	14.83	13.54	12.55	11.77	11.15
1000	87.80	46.03	32.15	25.25	21.13	18.41	16.48	15.05	13.95	13.08	12.38
2000	175.60	92.06	64.30	50.49	42.25	36.81	32.95	30.09	27.89	26.16	24.76
3000	263.40	138.09	96.45	75.73	63.38	55.21	49.42	45.13	41.84	39.24	37.14
4000	351.20	184.12	128.60	100.98	84.50	73.61	65.89	60.17	55.78	52.31	49.52
5000	439.00	230.15	160.75	126.22	105.63	92.01	82.37	75.22	69.72	65.39	61.90
6000	526.80	276.18	192.90	151.46	126.75	110.41	98.84	90.26	83.67	78.47	74.28
7000	614.60	322.21	225.05	176.70	147.87	128.81	115.31	105.30	97.61	91.54	86.66
8000	702.40	368.24	257.20	201.95	169.00	147.21	131.78	120.34	111.55	104.62	99.04
9000	790.20	414.27	289.35	227.19	190.12	165.61	148.26	135.38	125.50	117.70	111.41
10000	878.00	460.30	321.50	252.43	211.25	184.01	164.73	150.43	139.44	130.78	123.79
11000	965.80	506.33	353.65	277.67	232.37	202.41	181.20	165.47	153.39	143.85	136.17
12000	1053.60	552.36	385.80	302.92	253.50	220.81	197.67	180.51	167.33	156.93	148.55
13000	1141.40	598.39	417.95	328.16	274.62	239.21	214.14	195.55	181.27	170.01	160.93
14000	1229.20	644.42	450.10	353.40	295.74	257.61	230.62	210.60	195.22	183.08	173.31
15000	1317.00	690.45	482.25	378.65	316.87	276.01	247.09	225.64	209.16	196.16	185.69
16000	1404.80	736.48	514.40	403.89	337.99	294.41	263.56	240.68	223.10	209.24	198.07
17000	1492.60	782.51	546.55	429.13	359.12	312.81	280.03	255.72	237.05	222.31	210.45
18000	1580.40	828.54	578.70	454.37	380.24	331.21	296.51	270.76	250.99	235.39	222.82
19000	1668.20	874.57	610.85	479.62	401.37	349.61	312.98	285.81	264.93	248.47	235.20
20000	1756.00	920.60	643.00	504.86	422.49	368.01	329.45	300.85	278.88	261.55	247.58
21000	1843.80	966.63	675.15	530.10	443.61	386.41	345.92	315.89	292.82	274.62	259.96
22000	1931.60	1012.66	707.30	555.34	464.74	404.81	362.40	330.93	306.77	287.70	272.34
23000	2019.40	1058.69	739.45	580.59	485.86	423.21	378.87	345.98	320.71	300.78	284.72
24000	2107.20	1104.72	771.60	605.83	506.99	441.61	395.34	361.02	334.65	313.85	297.10
25000	2195.00	1150.75	803.75	631.07	528.11	460.01	411.81	376.06	348.60	326.93	309.48
26000	2282.80	1196.78	835.90	656.31	549.24	478.41	428.28	391.10	362.54	340.01	321.85
27000	2370.60	1242.80	868.05	681.56	570.36	496.81	444.76	406.14	376.48	353.08	334.23
28000	2458.40	1288.83	900.20	706.80	591.48	515.21	461.23	421.19	390.43	366.16	346.61
29000	2546.20	1334.86	932.35	732.04	612.61	533.61	477.70	436.23	404.37	379.24	358.99
30000	2633.99	1380.89	964.50	757.29	633.73	552.01	494.17	451.27	418.31	392.32	371.37
31000	2721.79	1426.92	996.65	782.53	654.86	570.41	510.65	466.31	432.26	405.39	383.75
32000	2809.59	1472.95	1028.80	807.77	675.98	588.81	527.12	481.36	446.20	418.47	396.13
33000	2897.39	1518.98	1060.95	833.01	697.11	607.21	543.59	496.40	460.15	431.55	408.51
34000	2985.19	1565.01	1093.10	858.26	718.23	625.61	560.06	511.44	474.09	444.62	420.89
35000	3072.99	1611.04	1125.25	883.50	739.35	644.01	576.54	526.48	488.03	457.70	433.26
36000	3160.79	1657.07	1157.40	908.74	760.48	662.41	593.01	541.52	501.98	470.78	445.64
37000	3248.59	1703.10	1189.55	933.98	781.60	680.81	609.48	556.57	515.92	483.85	458.02
38000	3336.39	1749.13	1221.70	959.23	802.73	699.21	625.95	571.61	529.86	496.93	470.40
39000	3424.19	1795.16	1253.85	984.47	823.85	717.61	642.42	586.65	543.81	510.01	482.78
40000	3511.99	1841.19	1286.00	1009.71	844.97	736.01	658.90	601.69	557.75	523.09	495.16
41000	3599.79	1887.22	1318.15	1034.96	866.10	754.41	675.37	616.74	571.70	536.16	507.54
42000	3687.59	1933.25	1350.30	1060.20	887.22	772.81	691.84	631.78	585.64	549.24	519.92
43000	3775.39	1979.28	1382.45	1085.44	908.35	791.21	708.31	646.82	599.58	562.32	532.30
44000	3863.19	2025.31	1414.60	1110.68	929.47	809.61	724.79	661.86	613.53	575.39	544.67
45000	3950.99	2071.34	1446.75	1135.93	950.60	828.01	741.26	676.90	627.47	588.47	557.05
46000	4038.79	2117.37	1478.90	1161.17	971.72	846.41	757.73	691.95	641.41	601.55	569.43
47000	4126.59	2163.40	1511.05	1186.41	992.84	864.81	774.20	706.99	655.36	614.63	581.81
48000	4214.39	2209.43	1543.20	1211.65	1013.97	883.21	790.68	722.03	669.30	627.70	594.19
49000	4302.19	2255.46	1575.35	1236.90	1035.09	901.61	807.15	737.07	683.24	640.78	606.57
50000	4389.99	2301.49	1607.50	1262.14	1056.22	920.01	823.62	752.12	697.19	653.86	618.95
55000	4828.99	2531.63	1768.25	1388.35	1161.84	1012.01	905.98	827.33	766.91	719.24	680.84
60000	5267.98	2761.78	1929.00	1514.57	1267.46	1104.01	988.34	902.54	836.62	784.63	742.74
65000	5706.98	2991.93	2089.75	1640.78	1373.08	1196.01	1070.70	977.75	906.34	850.01	804.63
70000	6145.98	3222.08	2250.50	1766.99	1478.70	1288.01	1153.07	1052.96	976.06	915.40	866.52
75000	6584.98	3452.23	2411.25	1893.21	1584.32	1380.01	1235.43	1128.17	1045.78	980.78	928.42
80000	7023.98	3682.37	2572.00	2019.42	1689.94	1472.01	1317.79	1203.38	1115.50	1046.17	990.31
85000	7462.98	3912.52	2732.75	2145.63	1795.57	1564.01	1400.15	1278.59	1185.22	1111.55	1052.21
90000	7901.97	4142.67	2893.50	2271.85	1901.19	1656.01	1482.51	1353.80	1254.93	1176.94	1114.10
95000	8340.97	4372.82	3054.25	2398.06	2006.81	1748.01	1564.87	1429.01	1324.65	1242.32	1175.99
100000	8779.97	4602.97	3215.00	2524.27	2112.43	1840.01	1647.23	1504.23	1394.37	1307.71	1237.89

Principal and Interest
Monthly Payment Amortization Table

9.75%

Term	12 Years	13 Years	14 Years	15 Years	16 Years	17 Years	18 Years	19 Years	20 Years	25 Years	30 Years
Amount											
50	.60	.57	.55	.53	.52	.51	.50	.49	.48	.45	.43
100	1.19	1.14	1.10	1.06	1.04	1.01	.99	.97	.95	.90	.86
200	2.37	2.27	2.19	2.12	2.07	2.02	1.97	1.93	1.90	1.79	1.72
300	3.55	3.40	3.28	3.18	3.10	3.02	2.96	2.90	2.85	2.68	2.58
400	4.73	4.54	4.38	4.24	4.13	4.03	3.94	3.86	3.80	3.57	3.44
500	5.91	5.67	5.47	5.30	5.16	5.04	4.92	4.83	4.75	4.46	4.30
600	7.09	6.80	6.56	6.36	6.19	6.04	5.91	5.79	5.70	5.35	5.16
700	8.27	7.94	7.66	7.42	7.22	7.04	6.89	6.76	6.64	6.24	6.02
800	9.45	9.07	8.75	8.48	8.25	8.05	7.88	7.72	7.59	7.13	6.88
900	10.63	10.20	9.84	9.54	9.28	9.05	8.86	8.69	8.54	8.03	7.74
1000	11.81	11.34	10.94	10.60	10.31	10.06	9.84	9.65	9.49	8.92	8.60
2000	23.62	22.67	21.87	21.19	20.61	20.11	19.68	19.30	18.98	17.83	17.19
3000	35.43	34.00	32.80	31.79	30.92	30.17	29.52	28.95	28.46	26.74	25.78
4000	47.23	45.33	43.73	42.38	41.22	40.22	39.36	38.60	37.95	35.65	34.37
5000	59.04	56.66	54.67	52.97	51.52	50.28	49.20	48.25	47.43	44.56	42.96
6000	70.85	67.99	65.60	63.57	61.83	60.33	59.03	57.90	56.92	53.47	51.55
7000	82.65	79.33	76.53	74.16	72.13	70.39	68.87	67.55	66.40	62.38	60.15
8000	94.46	90.66	87.46	84.75	82.44	80.44	78.71	77.20	75.89	71.30	68.74
9000	106.27	101.99	98.40	95.35	92.74	90.49	88.55	86.85	85.37	80.21	77.33
10000	118.07	113.32	109.33	105.94	103.04	100.55	98.39	96.50	94.86	89.12	85.92
11000	129.88	124.65	120.26	116.53	113.35	110.60	108.23	106.15	104.34	98.03	94.51
12000	141.69	135.98	131.19	127.13	123.65	120.66	118.06	115.80	113.83	106.94	103.10
13000	153.49	147.32	142.13	137.72	133.96	130.71	127.90	125.45	123.31	115.85	111.70
14000	165.30	158.65	153.06	148.32	144.26	140.77	137.74	135.10	132.80	124.76	120.29
15000	177.11	169.98	163.99	158.91	154.56	150.82	147.58	144.75	142.28	133.68	128.88
16000	188.91	181.31	174.92	169.50	164.87	160.88	157.42	154.40	151.77	142.59	137.47
17000	200.72	192.64	185.86	180.10	175.17	170.93	167.25	164.05	161.25	151.50	146.06
18000	212.53	203.97	196.79	190.69	185.48	180.98	177.09	173.70	170.74	160.41	154.65
19000	224.33	215.31	207.72	201.28	195.78	191.04	186.93	183.35	180.22	169.32	163.24
20000	236.14	226.64	218.65	211.88	206.08	201.09	196.77	193.00	189.71	178.23	171.84
21000	247.95	237.97	229.58	222.47	216.39	211.15	206.61	202.65	199.19	187.14	180.43
22000	259.75	249.30	240.52	233.06	226.69	221.20	216.45	212.30	208.68	196.06	189.02
23000	271.56	260.63	251.45	243.66	237.00	231.26	226.28	221.95	218.16	204.97	197.61
24000	283.37	271.96	262.38	254.25	247.30	241.31	236.12	231.60	227.65	213.88	206.20
25000	295.18	283.30	273.31	264.85	257.60	251.36	245.96	241.25	237.13	222.79	214.79
26000	306.98	294.63	284.25	275.44	267.91	261.42	255.80	250.90	246.62	231.70	223.39
27000	318.79	305.96	295.18	286.03	278.21	271.47	265.64	260.55	256.10	240.61	231.98
28000	330.60	317.29	306.11	296.63	288.51	281.53	275.47	270.20	265.59	249.52	240.57
29000	342.40	328.62	317.04	307.22	298.82	291.58	285.31	279.85	275.07	258.43	249.16
30000	354.21	339.95	327.98	317.81	309.12	301.64	295.15	289.50	284.56	267.35	257.75
31000	366.02	351.29	338.91	328.41	319.43	311.69	304.99	299.15	294.05	276.26	266.34
32000	377.82	362.62	349.84	339.00	329.73	321.75	314.83	308.80	303.53	285.17	274.93
33000	389.63	373.95	360.77	349.59	340.03	331.80	324.67	318.45	313.02	294.08	283.53
34000	401.44	385.28	371.70	360.19	350.34	341.85	334.50	328.10	322.50	302.99	292.12
35000	413.24	396.61	382.64	370.78	360.64	351.91	344.34	337.75	331.99	311.90	300.71
36000	425.05	407.94	393.57	381.38	370.95	361.96	354.18	347.40	341.47	320.81	309.30
37000	436.86	419.28	404.50	391.97	381.25	372.02	364.02	357.05	350.96	329.73	317.89
38000	448.66	430.61	415.43	402.56	391.55	382.07	373.86	366.70	360.44	338.64	326.48
39000	460.47	441.94	426.37	413.16	401.86	392.13	383.69	376.35	369.93	347.55	335.08
40000	472.28	453.27	437.30	423.75	412.16	402.18	393.53	386.00	379.41	356.46	343.67
41000	484.08	464.60	448.23	434.34	422.47	412.24	403.37	395.65	388.90	365.37	352.26
42000	495.89	475.93	459.16	444.94	432.77	422.29	413.21	405.30	398.38	374.28	360.85
43000	507.70	487.26	470.10	455.53	443.07	432.34	423.05	414.95	407.87	383.19	369.44
44000	519.50	498.60	481.03	466.12	453.38	442.40	432.89	424.60	417.35	392.11	378.03
45000	531.31	509.93	491.96	476.72	463.68	452.45	442.72	434.25	426.84	401.02	386.62
46000	543.12	521.26	502.89	487.31	473.99	462.51	452.56	443.90	436.32	409.93	395.22
47000	554.92	532.59	513.83	497.91	484.29	472.56	462.40	453.55	445.81	418.84	403.81
48000	566.73	543.92	524.76	508.50	494.59	482.62	472.24	463.20	455.29	427.75	412.40
49000	578.54	555.25	535.69	519.09	504.90	492.67	482.08	472.85	464.78	436.66	420.99
50000	590.35	566.59	546.62	529.69	515.20	502.72	491.92	482.50	474.26	445.57	429.58
55000	649.38	623.24	601.28	582.65	566.72	553.00	541.11	530.75	521.69	490.13	472.54
60000	708.41	679.90	655.95	635.62	618.24	603.27	590.30	579.00	569.12	534.69	515.50
65000	767.45	736.56	710.61	688.59	669.76	653.54	639.49	627.25	616.54	579.24	558.46
70000	826.48	793.22	765.27	741.56	721.28	703.81	688.68	675.50	663.97	623.80	601.41
75000	885.52	849.88	819.93	794.53	772.80	754.08	737.87	723.75	711.39	668.36	644.37
80000	944.55	906.54	874.59	847.50	824.32	804.36	787.06	772.00	758.82	712.91	687.33
85000	1003.58	963.19	929.25	900.46	875.84	854.63	836.25	820.25	806.24	757.47	730.29
90000	1062.62	1019.85	983.92	953.43	927.36	904.90	885.44	868.50	853.67	802.03	773.24
95000	1121.65	1076.51	1038.58	1006.40	978.88	955.17	934.63	916.75	901.10	846.59	816.20
100000	1180.69	1133.17	1093.24	1059.37	1030.40	1005.44	983.83	965.00	948.52	891.14	859.16

10.00% Principal and Interest
Monthly Payment Amortization Table

Term / Amount	1 Year	2 Years	3 Years	4 Years	5 Years	6 Years	7 Years	8 Years	9 Years	10 Years	11 Years
50	4.40	2.31	1.62	1.27	1.07	.93	.84	.76	.71	.67	.63
100	8.80	4.62	3.23	2.54	2.13	1.86	1.67	1.52	1.41	1.33	1.26
200	17.59	9.23	6.46	5.08	4.25	3.71	3.33	3.04	2.82	2.65	2.51
300	26.38	13.85	9.69	7.61	6.38	5.56	4.99	4.56	4.23	3.97	3.76
400	35.17	18.46	12.91	10.15	8.50	7.42	6.65	6.07	5.64	5.29	5.01
500	43.96	23.08	16.14	12.69	10.63	9.27	8.31	7.59	7.04	6.61	6.26
600	52.75	27.69	19.37	15.22	12.75	11.12	9.97	9.11	8.45	7.93	7.52
700	61.55	32.31	22.59	17.76	14.88	12.97	11.63	10.63	9.86	9.26	8.77
800	70.34	36.92	25.82	20.30	17.00	14.83	13.29	12.14	11.27	10.58	10.02
900	79.13	41.54	29.05	22.83	19.13	16.68	14.95	13.66	12.68	11.90	11.27
1000	87.92	46.15	32.27	25.37	21.25	18.53	16.61	15.18	14.08	13.22	12.52
2000	175.84	92.29	64.54	50.73	42.50	37.06	33.21	30.35	28.16	26.44	25.04
3000	263.75	138.44	96.81	76.09	63.75	55.58	49.81	45.53	42.24	39.65	37.56
4000	351.67	184.58	129.07	101.46	84.99	74.11	66.41	60.70	56.32	52.87	50.08
5000	439.58	230.73	161.34	126.82	106.24	92.63	83.01	75.88	70.40	66.08	62.60
6000	527.50	276.87	193.61	152.18	127.49	111.16	99.61	91.05	84.48	79.30	75.12
7000	615.42	323.02	225.88	177.54	148.73	129.69	116.21	106.22	98.56	92.51	87.64
8000	703.33	369.16	258.14	202.91	169.98	148.21	132.81	121.40	112.63	105.73	100.16
9000	791.25	415.31	290.41	228.27	191.23	166.74	149.42	136.57	126.71	118.94	112.68
10000	879.16	461.45	322.68	253.63	212.48	185.26	166.02	151.75	140.79	132.16	125.20
11000	967.08	507.60	354.94	278.99	233.72	203.79	182.62	166.92	154.87	145.37	137.72
12000	1055.00	553.74	387.21	304.36	254.97	222.32	199.22	182.09	168.95	158.59	150.24
13000	1142.91	599.89	419.48	329.72	276.22	240.84	215.82	197.27	183.03	171.80	162.76
14000	1230.83	646.03	451.75	355.08	297.46	259.37	232.42	212.44	197.11	185.02	175.28
15000	1318.74	692.18	484.01	380.44	318.71	277.89	249.02	227.62	211.19	198.23	187.80
16000	1406.66	738.32	516.28	405.81	339.96	296.42	265.62	242.79	225.26	211.45	200.32
17000	1494.58	784.47	548.55	431.17	361.20	314.94	282.23	257.97	239.34	224.66	212.84
18000	1582.49	830.61	580.81	456.53	382.45	333.47	298.83	273.14	253.42	237.88	225.36
19000	1670.41	876.76	613.08	481.89	403.70	352.00	315.43	288.31	267.50	251.09	237.88
20000	1758.32	922.90	645.35	507.26	424.95	370.52	332.03	303.49	281.58	264.31	250.40
21000	1846.24	969.05	677.62	532.62	446.19	389.05	348.63	318.66	295.66	277.52	262.92
22000	1934.15	1015.19	709.88	557.98	467.44	407.57	365.23	333.84	309.74	290.74	275.44
23000	2022.07	1061.34	742.15	583.34	488.69	426.10	381.83	349.01	323.81	303.95	287.96
24000	2109.99	1107.48	774.42	608.71	509.93	444.63	398.43	364.18	337.89	317.17	300.48
25000	2197.90	1153.63	806.68	634.07	531.18	463.15	415.03	379.36	351.97	330.38	313.00
26000	2285.82	1199.77	838.95	659.43	552.43	481.68	431.64	394.53	366.05	343.60	325.52
27000	2373.73	1245.92	871.22	684.79	573.68	500.20	448.24	409.71	380.13	356.81	338.04
28000	2461.65	1292.06	903.49	710.16	594.92	518.73	464.84	424.88	394.21	370.03	350.56
29000	2549.57	1338.21	935.75	735.52	616.17	537.25	481.44	440.06	408.29	383.24	363.08
30000	2637.48	1384.35	968.02	760.88	637.42	555.78	498.04	455.23	422.37	396.46	375.60
31000	2725.40	1430.50	1000.29	786.25	658.66	574.31	514.64	470.40	436.44	409.67	388.12
32000	2813.31	1476.64	1032.56	811.61	679.91	592.83	531.24	485.58	450.52	422.89	400.64
33000	2901.23	1522.79	1064.82	836.97	701.16	611.36	547.84	500.75	464.60	436.10	413.16
34000	2989.15	1568.93	1097.09	862.33	722.40	629.88	564.45	515.93	478.68	449.32	425.68
35000	3077.06	1615.08	1129.36	887.70	743.65	648.41	581.05	531.10	492.76	462.53	438.20
36000	3164.98	1661.22	1161.62	913.06	764.90	666.94	597.65	546.27	506.84	475.75	450.72
37000	3252.89	1707.37	1193.89	938.42	786.15	685.46	614.25	561.45	520.92	488.96	463.24
38000	3340.81	1753.51	1226.16	963.78	807.39	703.99	630.85	576.62	535.00	502.18	475.76
39000	3428.72	1799.66	1258.43	989.15	828.64	722.51	647.45	591.80	549.07	515.39	488.28
40000	3516.64	1845.80	1290.69	1014.51	849.89	741.04	664.05	606.97	563.15	528.61	500.80
41000	3604.56	1891.95	1322.96	1039.87	871.13	759.56	680.65	622.15	577.23	541.82	513.32
42000	3692.47	1938.09	1355.23	1065.23	892.38	778.09	697.25	637.32	591.31	555.04	525.84
43000	3780.39	1984.24	1387.49	1090.60	913.63	796.62	713.86	652.49	605.39	568.25	538.36
44000	3868.30	2030.38	1419.76	1115.96	934.87	815.14	730.46	667.67	619.47	581.47	550.88
45000	3956.22	2076.53	1452.03	1141.32	956.12	833.67	747.06	682.84	633.55	594.68	563.40
46000	4044.14	2122.67	1484.30	1166.68	977.37	852.19	763.66	698.02	647.62	607.90	575.92
47000	4132.05	2168.82	1516.56	1192.05	998.62	870.72	780.26	713.19	661.70	621.11	588.44
48000	4219.97	2214.96	1548.83	1217.41	1019.86	889.25	796.86	728.36	675.78	634.33	600.96
49000	4307.88	2261.11	1581.10	1242.77	1041.11	907.77	813.46	743.54	689.86	647.54	613.48
50000	4395.80	2307.25	1613.36	1268.13	1062.36	926.30	830.06	758.71	703.94	660.76	626.00
55000	4835.38	2537.98	1774.70	1394.95	1168.59	1018.93	913.07	834.58	774.33	726.83	688.60
60000	5274.96	2768.70	1936.04	1521.76	1274.83	1111.56	996.08	910.45	844.73	792.91	751.20
65000	5714.54	2999.43	2097.37	1648.57	1381.06	1204.18	1079.08	986.33	915.12	858.98	813.80
70000	6154.12	3230.15	2258.71	1775.39	1487.30	1296.81	1162.09	1062.20	985.51	925.06	876.40
75000	6593.70	3460.87	2420.04	1902.20	1593.53	1389.44	1245.09	1138.07	1055.91	991.14	939.00
80000	7033.28	3691.60	2581.38	2029.01	1699.77	1482.07	1328.10	1213.94	1126.30	1057.21	1001.60
85000	7472.86	3922.32	2742.72	2155.82	1806.00	1574.70	1411.11	1289.81	1196.69	1123.29	1064.19
90000	7912.43	4153.05	2904.05	2282.64	1912.24	1667.33	1494.11	1365.68	1267.09	1189.36	1126.79
95000	8352.01	4383.77	3065.39	2409.45	2018.47	1759.96	1577.12	1441.55	1337.48	1255.44	1189.39
100000	8791.59	4614.50	3226.72	2536.26	2124.71	1852.59	1660.12	1517.42	1407.87	1321.51	1251.99

Principal and Interest
Monthly Payment Amortization Table
10.00%

Term / Amount	12 Years	13 Years	14 Years	15 Years	16 Years	17 Years	18 Years	19 Years	20 Years	25 Years	30 Years
50	.60	.58	.56	.54	.53	.52	.50	.50	.49	.46	.44
100	1.20	1.15	1.11	1.08	1.05	1.03	1.00	.99	.97	.91	.88
200	2.40	2.30	2.22	2.15	2.10	2.05	2.00	1.97	1.94	1.82	1.76
300	3.59	3.45	3.33	3.23	3.14	3.07	3.00	2.95	2.90	2.73	2.64
400	4.79	4.60	4.44	4.30	4.19	4.09	4.00	3.93	3.87	3.64	3.52
500	5.98	5.74	5.55	5.38	5.23	5.11	5.00	4.91	4.83	4.55	4.39
600	7.18	6.89	6.65	6.45	6.28	6.13	6.00	5.89	5.80	5.46	5.27
700	8.37	8.04	7.76	7.53	7.33	7.15	7.00	6.87	6.76	6.37	6.15
800	9.57	9.19	8.87	8.60	8.37	8.17	8.00	7.86	7.73	7.27	7.03
900	10.76	10.34	9.98	9.68	9.42	9.20	9.00	8.84	8.69	8.18	7.90
1000	11.96	11.48	11.09	10.75	10.46	10.22	10.00	9.82	9.66	9.09	8.78
2000	23.91	22.96	22.17	21.50	20.92	20.43	20.00	19.63	19.31	18.18	17.56
3000	35.86	34.44	33.25	32.24	31.38	30.64	30.00	29.44	28.96	27.27	26.33
4000	47.81	45.92	44.33	42.99	41.84	40.85	40.00	39.26	38.61	36.35	35.11
5000	59.76	57.40	55.42	53.74	52.30	51.07	50.00	49.07	48.26	45.44	43.88
6000	71.71	68.88	66.50	64.48	62.76	61.28	60.00	58.88	57.91	54.53	52.66
7000	83.66	80.35	77.58	75.23	73.22	71.49	69.99	68.69	67.56	63.61	61.44
8000	95.61	91.83	88.66	85.97	83.68	81.70	79.99	78.51	77.21	72.70	70.21
9000	107.56	103.31	99.74	96.72	94.14	91.91	89.99	88.32	86.86	81.79	78.99
10000	119.51	114.79	110.83	107.47	104.60	102.13	99.99	98.13	96.51	90.88	87.76
11000	131.46	126.27	121.91	118.21	115.05	112.34	109.99	107.94	106.16	99.96	96.54
12000	143.41	137.75	132.99	128.96	125.51	122.55	119.99	117.76	115.81	109.05	105.31
13000	155.37	149.23	144.07	139.70	135.97	132.76	129.98	127.57	125.46	118.14	114.09
14000	167.32	160.70	155.15	150.45	146.43	142.97	139.98	137.38	135.11	127.22	122.87
15000	179.27	172.18	166.24	161.20	156.89	153.19	149.98	147.19	144.76	136.31	131.64
16000	191.22	183.66	177.32	171.94	167.35	163.40	159.98	157.01	154.41	145.40	140.42
17000	203.17	195.14	188.40	182.69	177.81	173.61	169.98	166.82	164.06	154.48	149.19
18000	215.12	206.62	199.48	193.43	188.27	183.82	179.98	176.63	173.71	163.57	157.97
19000	227.07	218.10	210.56	204.18	198.73	194.03	189.98	186.44	183.36	172.66	166.74
20000	239.02	229.57	221.65	214.93	209.19	204.25	199.97	196.26	193.01	181.75	175.52
21000	250.97	241.05	232.73	225.67	219.64	214.46	209.97	206.07	202.66	190.83	184.30
22000	262.92	252.53	243.81	236.42	230.10	224.67	219.97	215.88	212.31	199.92	193.07
23000	274.87	264.01	254.89	247.16	240.56	234.88	229.97	225.69	221.96	209.01	201.85
24000	286.82	275.49	265.97	257.91	251.02	245.10	239.97	235.51	231.61	218.09	210.62
25000	298.77	286.97	277.06	268.66	261.48	255.31	249.97	245.32	241.26	227.18	219.40
26000	310.73	298.45	288.14	279.40	271.94	265.52	259.96	255.13	250.91	236.27	228.17
27000	322.68	309.92	299.22	290.15	282.40	275.73	269.96	264.94	260.56	245.35	236.95
28000	334.63	321.40	310.30	300.89	292.86	285.94	279.96	274.76	270.21	254.44	245.73
29000	346.58	332.88	321.38	311.64	303.32	296.16	289.96	284.57	279.86	263.53	254.50
30000	358.53	344.36	332.47	322.39	313.78	306.37	299.96	294.38	289.51	272.62	263.28
31000	370.48	355.84	343.55	333.13	324.23	316.58	309.96	304.20	299.16	281.70	272.05
32000	382.43	367.32	354.63	343.88	334.69	326.79	319.95	314.01	308.81	290.79	280.83
33000	394.38	378.79	365.71	354.62	345.15	337.00	329.95	323.82	318.46	299.88	289.60
34000	406.33	390.27	376.79	365.37	355.61	347.22	339.95	333.63	328.11	308.96	298.38
35000	418.28	401.75	387.88	376.12	366.07	357.43	349.95	343.45	337.76	318.05	307.16
36000	430.23	413.23	398.96	386.86	376.53	367.64	359.95	353.26	347.41	327.14	315.93
37000	442.18	424.71	410.04	397.61	386.99	377.85	369.95	363.07	357.06	336.22	324.71
38000	454.13	436.19	421.12	408.35	397.45	388.06	379.95	372.88	366.71	345.31	333.48
39000	466.09	447.67	432.20	419.10	407.91	398.28	389.94	382.70	376.36	354.40	342.26
40000	478.04	459.14	443.29	429.85	418.37	408.49	399.94	392.51	386.01	363.49	351.03
41000	489.99	470.62	454.37	440.59	428.82	418.70	409.94	402.32	395.66	372.57	359.81
42000	501.94	482.10	465.45	451.34	439.28	428.91	419.94	412.13	405.31	381.66	368.59
43000	513.89	493.58	476.53	462.09	449.74	439.13	429.94	421.95	414.96	390.75	377.36
44000	525.84	505.06	487.61	472.83	460.20	449.34	439.94	431.76	424.61	399.83	386.14
45000	537.79	516.54	498.70	483.58	470.66	459.55	449.93	441.57	434.26	408.92	394.91
46000	549.74	528.02	509.78	494.32	481.12	469.76	459.93	451.38	443.91	418.01	403.69
47000	561.69	539.49	520.86	505.07	491.58	479.97	469.93	461.20	453.57	427.09	412.46
48000	573.64	550.97	531.94	515.82	502.04	490.19	479.93	471.01	463.22	436.18	421.24
49000	585.59	562.45	543.02	526.56	512.50	500.40	489.93	480.82	472.87	445.27	430.02
50000	597.54	573.93	554.11	537.31	522.96	510.61	499.93	490.63	482.52	454.36	438.79
55000	657.30	631.32	609.52	591.04	575.25	561.67	549.92	539.70	530.77	499.79	482.67
60000	717.05	688.71	664.93	644.77	627.55	612.73	599.91	588.76	579.02	545.23	526.55
65000	776.81	746.11	720.34	698.50	679.84	663.79	649.90	637.82	627.27	590.66	570.43
70000	836.56	803.50	775.75	752.23	732.14	714.85	699.90	686.89	675.52	636.10	614.31
75000	896.31	860.89	831.16	805.96	784.43	765.91	749.89	735.95	723.77	681.53	658.18
80000	956.07	918.28	886.57	859.69	836.73	816.97	799.88	785.01	772.02	726.97	702.06
85000	1015.82	975.68	941.98	913.42	889.02	868.03	849.87	834.08	820.27	772.40	745.94
90000	1075.58	1033.07	997.39	967.15	941.32	919.09	899.86	883.14	868.52	817.84	789.82
95000	1135.33	1090.46	1052.80	1020.88	993.61	970.15	949.86	932.20	916.78	863.27	833.70
100000	1195.08	1147.85	1108.21	1074.61	1045.91	1021.22	999.85	981.26	965.03	908.71	877.58

10.25% Principal and Interest
Monthly Payment Amortization Table

Term / Amount	1 Year	2 Years	3 Years	4 Years	5 Years	6 Years	7 Years	8 Years	9 Years	10 Years	11 Years
50	4.41	2.32	1.62	1.28	1.07	.94	.84	.77	.72	.67	.64
100	8.81	4.63	3.24	2.55	2.14	1.87	1.68	1.54	1.43	1.34	1.27
200	17.61	9.26	6.48	5.10	4.28	3.74	3.35	3.07	2.85	2.68	2.54
300	26.41	13.88	9.72	7.65	6.42	5.60	5.02	4.60	4.27	4.01	3.80
400	35.22	18.51	12.96	10.20	8.55	7.47	6.70	6.13	5.69	5.35	5.07
500	44.02	23.14	16.20	12.75	10.69	9.33	8.37	7.66	7.11	6.68	6.34
600	52.82	27.76	19.44	15.29	12.83	11.20	10.04	9.19	8.53	8.02	7.60
700	61.63	32.39	22.67	17.84	14.96	13.06	11.72	10.72	9.96	9.35	8.87
800	70.43	37.01	25.91	20.39	17.10	14.93	13.39	12.25	11.38	10.69	10.13
900	79.23	41.64	29.15	22.94	19.24	16.79	15.06	13.78	12.80	12.02	11.40
1000	88.04	46.27	32.39	25.49	21.38	18.66	16.74	15.31	14.22	13.36	12.67
2000	176.07	92.53	64.77	50.97	42.75	37.31	33.47	30.62	28.43	26.71	25.33
3000	264.10	138.79	97.16	76.45	64.12	55.96	50.20	45.93	42.65	40.07	37.99
4000	352.13	185.05	129.54	101.94	85.49	74.61	66.93	61.23	56.86	53.42	50.65
5000	440.17	231.31	161.93	127.42	106.86	93.27	83.66	76.54	71.08	66.77	63.31
6000	528.20	277.57	194.31	152.90	128.23	111.92	100.39	91.85	85.29	80.13	75.98
7000	616.23	323.83	226.70	178.38	149.60	130.57	117.12	107.15	99.51	93.48	88.64
8000	704.26	370.09	259.08	203.87	170.97	149.22	133.85	122.46	113.72	106.84	101.30
9000	792.29	416.35	291.47	229.35	192.34	167.87	150.58	137.77	127.93	120.19	113.96
10000	880.33	462.61	323.85	254.83	213.71	186.53	167.31	153.07	142.15	133.54	126.62
11000	968.36	508.87	356.24	280.32	235.08	205.18	184.04	168.38	156.36	146.90	139.28
12000	1056.39	555.13	388.62	305.80	256.45	223.83	200.77	183.69	170.58	160.25	151.95
13000	1144.42	601.39	421.01	331.28	277.82	242.48	217.50	198.99	184.79	173.61	164.61
14000	1232.46	647.65	453.39	356.76	299.19	261.14	234.23	214.30	199.01	186.96	177.27
15000	1320.49	693.91	485.78	382.25	320.56	279.79	250.96	229.61	213.22	200.31	189.93
16000	1408.52	740.17	518.16	407.73	341.93	298.44	267.70	244.91	227.44	213.67	202.59
17000	1496.55	786.43	550.54	433.21	363.30	317.09	284.43	260.22	241.65	227.02	215.25
18000	1584.58	832.69	582.93	458.70	384.67	335.74	301.16	275.53	255.86	240.38	227.92
19000	1672.62	878.95	615.31	484.18	406.04	354.40	317.89	290.83	270.08	253.73	240.58
20000	1760.65	925.21	647.70	509.66	427.41	373.05	334.62	306.14	284.29	267.08	253.24
21000	1848.68	971.47	680.08	535.14	448.78	391.70	351.35	321.45	298.51	280.44	265.90
22000	1936.71	1017.73	712.47	560.63	470.15	410.35	368.08	336.75	312.72	293.79	278.56
23000	2024.75	1063.99	744.85	586.11	491.52	429.00	384.81	352.06	326.94	307.14	291.23
24000	2112.78	1110.25	777.24	611.59	512.89	447.66	401.54	367.37	341.15	320.50	303.89
25000	2200.81	1156.52	809.62	637.08	534.26	466.31	418.27	382.67	355.37	333.85	316.55
26000	2288.84	1202.78	842.01	662.56	555.63	484.96	435.00	397.98	369.58	347.21	329.21
27000	2376.87	1249.04	874.39	688.04	577.00	503.61	451.73	413.29	383.79	360.56	341.87
28000	2464.91	1295.30	906.78	713.52	598.37	522.27	468.46	428.59	398.01	373.91	354.53
29000	2552.94	1341.56	939.16	739.01	619.74	540.92	485.19	443.90	412.22	387.27	367.20
30000	2640.97	1387.82	971.55	764.49	641.11	559.57	501.92	459.21	426.44	400.62	379.86
31000	2729.00	1434.08	1003.93	789.97	662.48	578.22	518.65	474.51	440.65	413.98	392.52
32000	2817.04	1480.34	1036.32	815.46	683.85	596.87	535.39	489.82	454.87	427.33	405.18
33000	2905.07	1526.60	1068.70	840.94	705.22	615.53	552.12	505.13	469.08	440.68	417.84
34000	2993.10	1572.86	1101.08	866.42	726.59	634.18	568.85	520.44	483.30	454.04	430.50
35000	3081.13	1619.12	1133.47	891.90	747.96	652.83	585.58	535.74	497.51	467.39	443.17
36000	3169.16	1665.38	1165.85	917.39	769.33	671.48	602.31	551.05	511.72	480.75	455.83
37000	3257.20	1711.64	1198.24	942.87	790.70	690.13	619.04	566.36	525.94	494.10	468.49
38000	3345.23	1757.90	1230.62	968.35	812.08	708.79	635.77	581.66	540.15	507.45	481.15
39000	3433.26	1804.16	1263.01	993.83	833.45	727.44	652.50	596.97	554.37	520.81	493.81
40000	3521.29	1850.42	1295.39	1019.32	854.82	746.09	669.23	612.28	568.58	534.16	506.48
41000	3609.33	1896.68	1327.78	1044.80	876.19	764.74	685.96	627.58	582.80	547.51	519.14
42000	3697.36	1942.94	1360.16	1070.28	897.56	783.40	702.69	642.89	597.01	560.87	531.80
43000	3785.39	1989.20	1392.55	1095.77	918.93	802.05	719.42	658.20	611.23	574.22	544.46
44000	3873.42	2035.46	1424.93	1121.25	940.30	820.70	736.15	673.50	625.44	587.58	557.12
45000	3961.45	2081.72	1457.32	1146.73	961.67	839.35	752.88	688.81	639.65	600.93	569.78
46000	4049.49	2127.98	1489.70	1172.21	983.04	858.00	769.61	704.12	653.87	614.28	582.45
47000	4137.52	2174.24	1522.09	1197.70	1004.41	876.66	786.35	719.42	668.08	627.64	595.11
48000	4225.55	2220.50	1554.47	1223.18	1025.78	895.31	803.08	734.73	682.30	640.99	607.77
49000	4313.58	2266.76	1586.85	1248.66	1047.15	913.96	819.81	750.04	696.51	654.35	620.43
50000	4401.62	2313.02	1619.24	1274.15	1068.52	932.61	836.54	765.34	710.73	667.70	633.09
55000	4841.78	2544.33	1781.16	1401.56	1175.37	1025.87	920.19	841.88	781.80	734.47	696.40
60000	5281.94	2775.63	1943.09	1528.97	1282.22	1119.13	1003.84	918.41	852.87	801.24	759.71
65000	5722.10	3006.93	2105.01	1656.39	1389.07	1212.40	1087.50	994.95	923.94	868.01	823.02
70000	6162.26	3238.23	2266.93	1783.80	1495.92	1305.66	1171.15	1071.48	995.01	934.78	886.33
75000	6602.42	3469.53	2428.86	1911.22	1602.77	1398.92	1254.80	1148.01	1066.09	1001.55	949.64
80000	7042.58	3700.84	2590.78	2038.63	1709.63	1492.18	1338.46	1224.55	1137.16	1068.32	1012.95
85000	7482.74	3932.14	2752.70	2166.04	1816.48	1585.44	1422.11	1301.08	1208.23	1135.09	1076.25
90000	7922.90	4163.44	2914.63	2293.46	1923.33	1678.70	1505.76	1377.61	1279.30	1201.86	1139.56
95000	8363.06	4394.74	3076.55	2420.87	2030.18	1771.96	1589.42	1454.15	1350.37	1268.63	1202.87
100000	8803.23	4626.04	3238.47	2548.29	2137.03	1865.22	1673.07	1530.68	1421.45	1335.40	1266.18

Principal and Interest
Monthly Payment Amortization Table

10.25%

Term Amount	12 Years	13 Years	14 Years	15 Years	16 Years	17 Years	18 Years	19 Years	20 Years	25 Years	30 Years
50	.61	.59	.57	.55	.54	.52	.51	.50	.50	.47	.45
100	1.21	1.17	1.13	1.09	1.07	1.04	1.02	1.00	.99	.93	.90
200	2.42	2.33	2.25	2.18	2.13	2.08	2.04	2.00	1.97	1.86	1.80
300	3.63	3.49	3.37	3.27	3.19	3.12	3.05	3.00	2.95	2.78	2.69
400	4.84	4.66	4.50	4.36	4.25	4.15	4.07	4.00	3.93	3.71	3.59
500	6.05	5.82	5.62	5.45	5.31	5.19	5.08	4.99	4.91	4.64	4.49
600	7.26	6.98	6.74	6.54	6.37	6.23	6.10	5.99	5.89	5.56	5.38
700	8.47	8.14	7.87	7.63	7.44	7.26	7.12	6.99	6.88	6.49	6.28
800	9.68	9.31	8.99	8.72	8.50	8.30	8.13	7.99	7.86	7.42	7.17
900	10.89	10.47	10.11	9.81	9.56	9.34	9.15	8.98	8.84	8.34	8.07
1000	12.10	11.63	11.24	10.90	10.62	10.38	10.16	9.98	9.82	9.27	8.97
2000	24.20	23.26	22.47	21.80	21.24	20.75	20.32	19.96	19.64	18.53	17.93
3000	36.29	34.88	33.70	32.70	31.85	31.12	30.48	29.93	29.45	27.80	26.89
4000	48.39	46.51	44.94	43.60	42.47	41.49	40.64	39.91	39.27	37.06	35.85
5000	60.48	58.14	56.17	54.50	53.08	51.86	50.80	49.89	49.09	46.32	44.81
6000	72.58	69.76	67.40	65.40	63.70	62.23	60.96	59.86	58.90	55.59	53.77
7000	84.67	81.39	78.63	76.30	74.31	72.60	71.12	69.84	68.72	64.85	62.73
8000	96.77	93.02	89.87	87.20	84.93	82.97	81.28	79.82	78.54	74.12	71.69
9000	108.87	104.64	101.10	98.10	95.54	93.34	91.44	89.79	88.35	83.38	80.65
10000	120.96	116.27	112.33	109.00	106.16	103.71	101.60	99.77	98.17	92.64	89.62
11000	133.06	127.89	123.56	119.90	116.77	114.09	111.76	109.75	107.99	101.91	98.58
12000	145.15	139.52	134.80	130.80	127.39	124.46	121.92	119.72	117.80	111.17	107.54
13000	157.25	151.15	146.03	141.70	138.00	134.83	132.08	129.70	127.62	120.43	116.50
14000	169.34	162.77	157.26	152.60	148.62	145.20	142.24	139.67	137.44	129.70	125.46
15000	181.44	174.40	168.50	163.50	159.23	155.57	152.40	149.65	147.25	138.96	134.42
16000	193.54	186.03	179.73	174.40	169.85	165.94	162.56	159.63	157.07	148.23	143.38
17000	205.63	197.65	190.96	185.30	180.46	176.31	172.72	169.60	166.88	157.49	152.34
18000	217.73	209.28	202.19	196.20	191.08	186.68	182.88	179.58	176.70	166.75	161.30
19000	229.82	220.90	213.43	207.10	201.69	197.05	193.04	189.56	186.52	176.02	170.26
20000	241.92	232.53	224.66	218.00	212.31	207.42	203.20	199.53	196.33	185.28	179.23
21000	254.01	244.16	235.89	228.89	222.92	217.79	213.36	209.51	206.15	194.55	188.19
22000	266.11	255.78	247.12	239.79	233.54	228.17	223.52	219.49	215.97	203.81	197.15
23000	278.20	267.41	258.36	250.69	244.15	238.54	233.68	229.46	225.78	213.07	206.11
24000	290.30	279.04	269.59	261.59	254.77	248.91	243.84	239.44	235.60	222.34	215.07
25000	302.40	290.66	280.82	272.49	265.38	259.28	254.00	249.42	245.42	231.60	224.03
26000	314.49	302.29	292.06	283.39	276.00	269.65	264.16	259.39	255.23	240.86	232.99
27000	326.59	313.91	303.29	294.29	286.62	280.02	274.32	269.37	265.05	250.13	241.95
28000	338.68	325.54	314.52	305.19	297.23	290.39	284.48	279.34	274.87	259.39	250.91
29000	350.78	337.17	325.75	316.09	307.85	300.76	294.64	289.32	284.68	268.66	259.87
30000	362.87	348.79	336.99	326.99	318.46	311.13	304.80	299.30	294.50	277.92	268.84
31000	374.97	360.42	348.22	337.89	329.08	321.50	314.96	309.27	304.31	287.18	277.80
32000	387.07	372.05	359.45	348.79	339.69	331.87	325.12	319.25	314.13	296.45	286.76
33000	399.16	383.67	370.68	359.69	350.31	342.25	335.28	329.23	323.95	305.71	295.72
34000	411.26	395.30	381.92	370.59	360.92	352.62	345.44	339.20	333.76	314.98	304.68
35000	423.35	406.92	393.15	381.49	371.54	362.99	355.60	349.18	343.58	324.24	313.64
36000	435.45	418.55	404.38	392.39	382.15	373.36	365.76	359.16	353.40	333.50	322.60
37000	447.54	430.18	415.61	403.29	392.77	383.73	375.92	369.13	363.21	342.77	331.56
38000	459.64	441.80	426.85	414.19	403.38	394.10	386.08	379.11	373.03	352.03	340.52
39000	471.74	453.43	438.08	425.09	414.00	404.47	396.24	389.09	382.85	361.29	349.48
40000	483.83	465.06	449.31	435.99	424.61	414.84	406.40	399.06	392.66	370.56	358.45
41000	495.93	476.68	460.55	446.88	435.23	425.21	416.56	409.04	402.48	379.82	367.41
42000	508.02	488.31	471.78	457.78	445.84	435.58	426.72	419.01	412.30	389.09	376.37
43000	520.12	499.94	483.01	468.68	456.46	445.95	436.88	428.99	422.11	398.35	385.33
44000	532.21	511.56	494.24	479.58	467.07	456.33	447.04	438.97	431.93	407.61	394.29
45000	544.31	523.19	505.48	490.48	477.69	466.70	457.20	448.94	441.74	416.88	403.25
46000	556.40	534.81	516.71	501.38	488.30	477.07	467.36	458.92	451.56	426.14	412.21
47000	568.50	546.44	527.94	512.28	498.92	487.44	477.52	468.90	461.38	435.41	421.17
48000	580.60	558.07	539.17	523.18	509.53	497.81	487.68	478.87	471.19	444.67	430.13
49000	592.69	569.69	550.41	534.08	520.15	508.18	497.84	488.85	481.01	453.93	439.09
50000	604.79	581.32	561.64	544.98	530.76	518.55	508.00	498.83	490.83	463.20	448.06
55000	665.27	639.45	617.80	599.48	583.84	570.41	558.79	548.71	539.91	509.52	492.86
60000	725.74	697.58	673.97	653.98	636.92	622.26	609.59	598.59	588.99	555.83	537.67
65000	786.22	755.71	730.13	708.47	689.99	674.11	660.39	648.47	638.07	602.15	582.47
70000	846.70	813.84	786.29	762.97	743.07	725.97	711.19	698.35	687.16	648.47	627.28
75000	907.18	871.98	842.46	817.47	796.14	777.82	761.99	748.24	736.24	694.79	672.08
80000	967.66	930.11	898.62	871.97	849.22	829.68	812.79	798.12	785.32	741.11	716.89
85000	1028.14	988.24	954.78	926.46	902.30	881.53	863.59	848.00	834.40	787.43	761.69
90000	1088.61	1046.37	1010.95	980.96	955.37	933.39	914.39	897.88	883.48	833.75	806.50
95000	1149.09	1104.50	1067.11	1035.46	1008.45	985.24	965.19	947.77	932.57	880.07	851.30
100000	1209.57	1162.63	1123.27	1089.96	1061.52	1037.10	1015.99	997.65	981.65	926.39	896.11

10.50% Principal and Interest
Monthly Payment Amortization Table

Term Amount	1 Year	2 Years	3 Years	4 Years	5 Years	6 Years	7 Years	8 Years	9 Years	10 Years	11 Years
50	4.41	2.32	1.63	1.29	1.08	.94	.85	.78	.72	.68	.65
100	8.82	4.64	3.26	2.57	2.15	1.88	1.69	1.55	1.44	1.35	1.29
200	17.63	9.28	6.51	5.13	4.30	3.76	3.38	3.09	2.88	2.70	2.57
300	26.45	13.92	9.76	7.69	6.45	5.64	5.06	4.64	4.31	4.05	3.85
400	35.26	18.56	13.01	10.25	8.60	7.52	6.75	6.18	5.75	5.40	5.13
500	44.08	23.19	16.26	12.81	10.75	9.39	8.44	7.73	7.18	6.75	6.41
600	52.89	27.83	19.51	15.37	12.90	11.27	10.12	9.27	8.62	8.10	7.69
700	61.71	32.47	22.76	17.93	15.05	13.15	11.81	10.81	10.05	9.45	8.97
800	70.52	37.11	26.01	20.49	17.20	15.03	13.49	12.36	11.49	10.80	10.25
900	79.34	41.74	29.26	23.05	19.35	16.91	15.18	13.90	12.92	12.15	11.53
1000	88.15	46.38	32.51	25.61	21.50	18.78	16.87	15.45	14.36	13.50	12.81
2000	176.30	92.76	65.01	51.21	42.99	37.56	33.73	30.89	28.71	26.99	25.61
3000	264.45	139.13	97.51	76.82	64.49	56.34	50.59	46.33	43.06	40.49	38.42
4000	352.60	185.51	130.01	102.42	85.98	75.12	67.45	61.77	57.41	53.98	51.22
5000	440.75	231.89	162.52	128.02	107.47	93.90	84.31	77.21	71.76	67.47	64.03
6000	528.90	278.26	195.02	153.63	128.97	112.68	101.17	92.65	86.11	80.97	76.83
7000	617.05	324.64	227.52	179.23	150.46	131.46	118.03	108.09	100.46	94.46	89.64
8000	705.19	371.01	260.02	204.83	171.96	150.24	134.89	123.53	114.81	107.95	102.44
9000	793.34	417.39	292.53	230.44	193.45	169.02	151.75	138.97	129.16	121.45	115.25
10000	881.49	463.77	325.03	256.04	214.94	187.79	168.61	154.41	143.51	134.94	128.05
11000	969.64	510.14	357.53	281.64	236.44	206.57	185.47	169.85	157.86	148.43	140.85
12000	1057.79	556.52	390.03	307.25	257.93	225.35	202.33	185.29	172.22	161.93	153.66
13000	1145.94	602.89	422.54	332.85	279.43	244.13	219.19	200.73	186.57	175.42	166.46
14000	1234.09	649.27	455.04	358.45	300.92	262.91	236.05	216.17	200.92	188.91	179.27
15000	1322.23	695.65	487.54	384.06	322.41	281.69	252.92	231.61	215.27	202.41	192.07
16000	1410.38	742.02	520.04	409.66	343.91	300.47	269.78	247.05	229.62	215.90	204.88
17000	1498.53	788.40	552.55	435.26	365.40	319.25	286.64	262.49	243.97	229.39	217.68
18000	1586.68	834.77	585.05	460.87	386.90	338.03	303.50	277.93	258.32	242.89	230.49
19000	1674.83	881.15	617.55	486.47	408.39	356.81	320.36	293.37	272.67	256.38	243.29
20000	1762.98	927.53	650.05	512.07	429.88	375.58	337.22	308.81	287.02	269.87	256.09
21000	1851.13	973.90	682.56	537.68	451.38	394.36	354.08	324.25	301.37	283.37	268.90
22000	1939.27	1020.28	715.06	563.28	472.87	413.14	370.94	339.69	315.72	296.86	281.70
23000	2027.42	1066.65	747.56	588.88	494.36	431.92	387.80	355.13	330.07	310.36	294.51
24000	2115.57	1113.03	780.06	614.49	515.86	450.70	404.66	370.57	344.43	323.85	307.31
25000	2203.72	1159.41	812.57	640.09	537.35	469.48	421.52	386.01	358.78	337.34	320.12
26000	2291.87	1205.78	845.07	665.69	558.85	488.26	438.38	401.45	373.13	350.84	332.92
27000	2380.02	1252.16	877.57	691.30	580.34	507.04	455.24	416.89	387.48	364.33	345.73
28000	2468.17	1298.53	910.07	716.90	601.83	525.82	472.10	432.33	401.83	377.82	358.53
29000	2556.31	1344.91	942.58	742.50	623.33	544.60	488.96	447.77	416.18	391.32	371.33
30000	2644.46	1391.29	975.08	768.11	644.82	563.37	505.83	463.21	430.53	404.81	384.14
31000	2732.61	1437.66	1007.58	793.71	666.32	582.15	522.69	478.65	444.88	418.30	396.94
32000	2820.76	1484.04	1040.08	819.31	687.81	600.93	539.55	494.09	459.23	431.80	409.75
33000	2908.91	1530.41	1072.59	844.92	709.30	619.71	556.41	509.53	473.58	445.29	422.55
34000	2997.06	1576.79	1105.09	870.52	730.80	638.49	573.27	524.97	487.93	458.78	435.36
35000	3085.21	1623.17	1137.59	896.12	752.29	657.27	590.13	540.41	502.29	472.28	448.16
36000	3173.35	1669.54	1170.09	921.73	773.79	676.05	606.99	555.85	516.64	485.77	460.97
37000	3261.50	1715.92	1202.60	947.33	795.28	694.83	623.85	571.29	530.99	499.26	473.77
38000	3349.65	1762.29	1235.10	972.93	816.77	713.61	640.71	586.73	545.34	512.76	486.57
39000	3437.80	1808.67	1267.60	998.54	838.27	732.38	657.57	602.17	559.69	526.25	499.38
40000	3525.95	1855.05	1300.10	1024.14	859.76	751.16	674.43	617.61	574.04	539.74	512.18
41000	3614.10	1901.42	1332.61	1049.74	881.25	769.94	691.29	633.05	588.39	553.24	524.99
42000	3702.25	1947.80	1365.11	1075.35	902.75	788.72	708.15	648.49	602.74	566.73	537.79
43000	3790.39	1994.17	1397.61	1100.95	924.24	807.50	725.01	663.93	617.09	580.23	550.60
44000	3878.54	2040.55	1430.11	1126.55	945.74	826.28	741.87	679.37	631.44	593.72	563.40
45000	3966.69	2086.93	1462.61	1152.16	967.23	845.06	758.74	694.81	645.79	607.21	576.21
46000	4054.84	2133.30	1495.12	1177.76	988.72	863.84	775.60	710.25	660.14	620.71	589.01
47000	4142.99	2179.68	1527.62	1203.36	1010.22	882.62	792.46	725.69	674.50	634.20	601.81
48000	4231.14	2226.06	1560.12	1228.97	1031.71	901.40	809.32	741.13	688.85	647.69	614.62
49000	4319.29	2272.43	1592.62	1254.57	1053.21	920.17	826.18	756.57	703.20	661.19	627.42
50000	4407.44	2318.81	1625.13	1280.17	1074.70	938.95	843.04	772.01	717.55	674.68	640.23
55000	4848.18	2550.69	1787.64	1408.19	1182.17	1032.85	927.34	849.21	789.30	742.15	704.25
60000	5288.92	2782.57	1950.15	1536.21	1289.64	1126.74	1011.65	926.41	861.06	809.61	768.27
65000	5729.66	3014.45	2112.66	1664.22	1397.11	1220.64	1095.95	1003.61	932.81	877.08	832.29
70000	6170.41	3246.33	2275.18	1792.24	1504.58	1314.53	1180.25	1080.81	1004.57	944.55	896.32
75000	6611.15	3478.21	2437.69	1920.26	1612.05	1408.43	1264.56	1158.01	1076.32	1012.02	960.34
80000	7051.89	3710.09	2600.20	2048.28	1719.52	1502.32	1348.86	1235.21	1148.07	1079.49	1024.36
85000	7492.64	3941.97	2762.71	2176.29	1826.99	1596.22	1433.16	1312.41	1219.83	1146.95	1088.38
90000	7933.38	4173.85	2925.22	2304.31	1934.46	1690.11	1517.47	1389.61	1291.58	1214.42	1152.41
95000	8374.12	4405.73	3087.74	2432.33	2041.93	1784.01	1601.77	1466.81	1363.34	1281.89	1216.43
100000	8814.87	4637.61	3250.25	2560.34	2149.40	1877.90	1686.07	1544.01	1435.09	1349.36	1280.45

Principal and Interest
Monthly Payment Amortization Table

10.50%

Term / Amount	12 Years	13 Years	14 Years	15 Years	16 Years	17 Years	18 Years	19 Years	20 Years	25 Years	30 Years
50	.62	.59	.57	.56	.54	.53	.52	.51	.50	.48	.46
100	1.23	1.18	1.14	1.11	1.08	1.06	1.04	1.02	1.00	.95	.92
200	2.45	2.36	2.28	2.22	2.16	2.11	2.07	2.03	2.00	1.89	1.83
300	3.68	3.54	3.42	3.32	3.24	3.16	3.10	3.05	3.00	2.84	2.75
400	4.90	4.72	4.56	4.43	4.31	4.22	4.13	4.06	4.00	3.78	3.66
500	6.13	5.89	5.70	5.53	5.39	5.27	5.17	5.08	5.00	4.73	4.58
600	7.35	7.07	6.84	6.64	6.47	6.32	6.20	6.09	6.00	5.67	5.49
700	8.57	8.25	7.97	7.74	7.55	7.38	7.23	7.10	6.99	6.61	6.41
800	9.80	9.43	9.11	8.85	8.62	8.43	8.26	8.12	7.99	7.56	7.32
900	11.02	10.60	10.25	9.95	9.70	9.48	9.30	9.13	8.99	8.50	8.24
1000	12.25	11.78	11.39	11.06	10.78	10.54	10.33	10.15	9.99	9.45	9.15
2000	24.49	23.56	22.77	22.11	21.55	21.07	20.65	20.29	19.97	18.89	18.30
3000	36.73	35.33	34.16	33.17	32.32	31.60	30.97	30.43	29.96	28.33	27.45
4000	48.97	47.11	45.54	44.22	43.09	42.13	41.29	40.57	39.94	37.77	36.59
5000	61.21	58.88	56.93	55.27	53.87	52.66	51.62	50.71	49.92	47.21	45.74
6000	73.45	70.66	68.31	66.33	64.64	63.19	61.94	60.85	59.91	56.66	54.89
7000	85.69	82.43	79.70	77.38	75.41	73.72	72.26	70.99	69.89	66.10	64.04
8000	97.94	94.21	91.08	88.44	86.18	84.25	82.58	81.14	79.88	75.54	73.18
9000	110.18	105.98	102.46	99.49	96.96	94.78	92.91	91.28	89.86	84.98	82.33
10000	122.42	117.76	113.85	110.54	107.73	105.31	103.23	101.42	99.84	94.42	91.48
11000	134.66	129.53	125.23	121.60	118.50	115.84	113.55	111.56	109.83	103.86	100.63
12000	146.90	141.31	136.62	132.65	129.27	126.37	123.87	121.70	119.81	113.31	109.77
13000	159.14	153.08	148.00	143.71	140.05	136.91	134.19	131.84	129.79	122.75	118.92
14000	171.38	164.86	159.39	154.76	150.82	147.44	144.52	141.98	139.78	132.19	128.07
15000	183.63	176.63	170.77	165.81	161.59	157.97	154.84	152.13	149.76	141.63	137.22
16000	195.87	188.41	182.15	176.87	172.36	168.50	165.16	162.27	159.75	151.07	146.36
17000	208.11	200.18	193.54	187.92	183.14	179.03	175.48	172.41	169.73	160.52	155.51
18000	220.35	211.96	204.92	198.98	193.91	189.56	185.81	182.55	179.71	169.96	164.66
19000	232.59	223.73	216.31	210.03	204.68	200.09	196.13	192.69	189.70	179.40	173.81
20000	244.83	235.51	227.69	221.08	215.45	210.62	206.45	202.83	199.68	188.84	182.95
21000	257.07	247.28	239.08	232.14	226.23	221.15	216.77	212.97	209.66	198.28	192.10
22000	269.32	259.06	250.46	243.19	237.00	231.68	227.10	223.12	219.65	207.72	201.25
23000	281.56	270.83	261.84	254.25	247.77	242.21	237.42	233.26	229.63	217.17	210.40
24000	293.80	282.61	273.23	265.30	258.54	252.74	247.74	243.40	239.62	226.61	219.54
25000	306.04	294.38	284.61	276.35	269.32	263.28	258.06	253.54	249.60	236.05	228.69
26000	318.28	306.16	296.00	287.41	280.09	273.81	268.38	263.68	259.58	245.49	237.84
27000	330.52	317.93	307.38	298.46	290.86	284.34	278.71	273.82	269.57	254.93	246.98
28000	342.76	329.71	318.77	309.52	301.63	294.87	289.03	283.96	279.55	264.38	256.13
29000	355.01	341.48	330.15	320.57	312.41	305.40	299.35	294.11	289.54	273.82	265.28
30000	367.25	353.26	341.54	331.62	323.18	315.93	309.67	304.25	299.52	283.26	274.43
31000	379.49	365.03	352.92	342.68	333.95	326.46	320.00	314.39	309.50	292.70	283.57
32000	391.73	376.81	364.30	353.73	344.72	336.99	330.32	324.53	319.49	302.14	292.72
33000	403.97	388.58	375.69	364.79	355.50	347.52	340.64	334.67	329.47	311.58	301.87
34000	416.21	400.36	387.07	375.84	366.27	358.05	350.96	344.81	339.45	321.03	311.02
35000	428.45	412.13	398.46	386.89	377.04	368.58	361.28	354.95	349.44	330.47	320.16
36000	440.70	423.91	409.84	397.95	387.81	379.11	371.61	365.10	359.42	339.91	329.31
37000	452.94	435.68	421.23	409.00	398.58	389.65	381.93	375.24	369.41	349.35	338.46
38000	465.18	447.46	432.61	420.06	409.36	400.18	392.25	385.38	379.39	358.79	347.61
39000	477.42	459.23	443.99	431.11	420.13	410.71	402.57	395.52	389.37	368.24	356.75
40000	489.66	471.01	455.38	442.16	430.90	421.24	412.90	405.66	399.36	377.68	365.90
41000	501.90	482.78	466.76	453.22	441.67	431.77	423.22	415.80	409.34	387.12	375.05
42000	514.14	494.56	478.15	464.27	452.45	442.30	433.54	425.94	419.32	396.56	384.20
43000	526.39	506.33	489.53	475.33	463.22	452.83	443.86	436.08	429.31	406.00	393.34
44000	538.63	518.11	500.92	486.38	473.99	463.36	454.19	446.23	439.29	415.44	402.49
45000	550.87	529.88	512.30	497.43	484.76	473.89	464.51	456.37	449.28	424.89	411.64
46000	563.11	541.66	523.68	508.49	495.54	484.42	474.83	466.51	459.26	434.33	420.79
47000	575.35	553.43	535.07	519.54	506.31	494.95	485.15	476.65	469.24	443.77	429.93
48000	587.59	565.21	546.45	530.60	517.08	505.48	495.47	486.79	479.23	453.21	439.08
49000	599.83	576.98	557.84	541.65	527.85	516.01	505.80	496.93	489.21	462.65	448.23
50000	612.08	588.76	569.22	552.70	538.63	526.55	516.12	507.07	499.19	472.10	457.37
55000	673.28	647.63	626.14	607.97	592.49	579.20	567.73	557.78	549.11	519.30	503.11
60000	734.49	706.51	683.07	663.24	646.35	631.85	619.34	608.49	599.03	566.51	548.85
65000	795.70	765.38	739.99	718.51	700.21	684.51	670.95	659.20	648.95	613.72	594.59
70000	856.90	824.26	796.91	773.78	754.07	737.16	722.56	709.90	698.87	660.93	640.32
75000	918.11	883.13	853.83	829.05	807.94	789.82	774.18	760.61	748.79	708.14	686.06
80000	979.32	942.01	910.75	884.32	861.80	842.47	825.79	811.32	798.71	755.35	731.80
85000	1040.52	1000.88	967.67	939.59	915.66	895.12	877.40	862.02	848.63	802.56	777.53
90000	1101.73	1059.76	1024.60	994.86	969.52	947.78	929.01	912.73	898.55	849.77	823.27
95000	1162.94	1118.63	1081.52	1050.13	1023.39	1000.43	980.62	963.44	948.47	896.98	869.01
100000	1224.15	1177.51	1138.44	1105.40	1077.25	1053.09	1032.23	1014.14	998.38	944.19	914.74

10.75% Principal and Interest
Monthly Payment Amortization Table

Term	1 Year	2 Years	3 Years	4 Years	5 Years	6 Years	7 Years	8 Years	9 Years	10 Years	11 Years
Amount											
50	4.42	2.33	1.64	1.29	1.09	.95	.85	.78	.73	.69	.65
100	8.83	4.65	3.27	2.58	2.17	1.90	1.70	1.56	1.45	1.37	1.30
200	17.66	9.30	6.53	5.15	4.33	3.79	3.40	3.12	2.90	2.73	2.59
300	26.48	13.95	9.79	7.72	6.49	5.68	5.10	4.68	4.35	4.10	3.89
400	35.31	18.60	13.05	10.29	8.65	7.57	6.80	6.23	5.80	5.46	5.18
500	44.14	23.25	16.32	12.87	10.81	9.46	8.50	7.79	7.25	6.82	6.48
600	52.96	27.90	19.58	15.44	12.98	11.35	10.20	9.35	8.70	8.19	7.77
700	61.79	32.55	22.84	18.01	15.14	13.24	11.90	10.91	10.15	9.55	9.07
800	70.62	37.20	26.10	20.58	17.30	15.13	13.60	12.46	11.60	10.91	10.36
900	79.44	41.85	29.36	23.16	19.46	17.02	15.30	14.02	13.04	12.28	11.66
1000	88.27	46.50	32.63	25.73	21.62	18.91	17.00	15.58	14.49	13.64	12.95
2000	176.54	92.99	65.25	51.45	43.24	37.82	33.99	31.15	28.98	27.27	25.90
3000	264.80	139.48	97.87	77.18	64.86	56.72	50.98	46.73	43.47	40.91	38.85
4000	353.07	185.97	130.49	102.90	86.48	75.63	67.97	62.30	57.96	54.54	51.80
5000	441.33	232.46	163.11	128.63	108.09	94.54	84.96	77.87	72.45	68.17	64.74
6000	529.60	278.96	195.73	154.35	129.71	113.44	101.95	93.45	86.93	81.81	77.69
7000	617.86	325.45	228.35	180.07	151.33	132.35	118.94	109.02	101.42	95.44	90.64
8000	706.13	371.94	260.97	205.80	172.95	151.26	135.94	124.60	115.91	109.08	103.59
9000	794.39	418.43	293.59	231.52	194.57	170.16	152.93	140.17	130.40	122.71	116.54
10000	882.66	464.92	326.21	257.25	216.18	189.07	169.92	155.74	144.89	136.34	129.48
11000	970.92	511.42	358.83	282.97	237.80	207.97	186.91	171.32	159.37	149.98	142.43
12000	1059.19	557.91	391.45	308.70	259.42	226.88	203.90	186.89	173.86	163.61	155.38
13000	1147.45	604.40	424.07	334.42	281.04	245.79	220.89	202.47	188.35	177.25	168.33
14000	1235.72	650.89	456.69	360.14	302.66	264.69	237.88	218.04	202.84	190.88	181.28
15000	1323.98	697.38	489.31	385.87	324.27	283.60	254.87	233.61	217.33	204.51	194.22
16000	1412.25	743.87	521.93	411.59	345.89	302.51	271.87	249.19	231.81	218.15	207.17
17000	1500.51	790.37	554.55	437.32	367.51	321.41	288.86	264.76	246.30	231.78	220.12
18000	1588.78	836.86	587.17	463.04	389.13	340.32	305.85	280.34	260.79	245.41	233.07
19000	1677.04	883.35	619.79	488.77	410.75	359.22	322.84	295.91	275.28	259.05	246.02
20000	1765.31	929.84	652.41	514.49	432.36	378.13	339.83	311.48	289.77	272.68	258.96
21000	1853.57	976.33	685.03	540.21	453.98	397.04	356.82	327.06	304.25	286.32	271.91
22000	1941.84	1022.83	717.65	565.94	475.60	415.94	373.81	342.63	318.74	299.95	284.86
23000	2030.10	1069.32	750.28	591.66	497.22	434.85	390.80	358.20	333.23	313.58	297.81
24000	2118.37	1115.81	782.90	617.39	518.84	453.76	407.80	373.78	347.72	327.22	310.76
25000	2206.63	1162.30	815.52	643.11	540.45	472.66	424.79	389.35	362.21	340.85	323.70
26000	2294.90	1208.79	848.14	668.84	562.07	491.57	441.78	404.93	376.69	354.49	336.65
27000	2383.16	1255.29	880.76	694.56	583.69	510.47	458.77	420.50	391.18	368.12	349.60
28000	2471.43	1301.78	913.38	720.28	605.31	529.38	475.76	436.07	405.67	381.75	362.55
29000	2559.69	1348.27	946.00	746.01	626.93	548.29	492.75	451.65	420.16	395.39	375.50
30000	2647.96	1394.76	978.62	771.73	648.54	567.19	509.74	467.22	434.65	409.02	388.44
31000	2736.22	1441.25	1011.24	797.46	670.16	586.10	526.73	482.80	449.13	422.65	401.39
32000	2824.49	1487.74	1043.86	823.18	691.78	605.01	543.73	498.37	463.62	436.29	414.34
33000	2912.75	1534.24	1076.48	848.91	713.40	623.91	560.72	513.94	478.11	449.92	427.29
34000	3001.02	1580.73	1109.10	874.63	735.02	642.82	577.71	529.52	492.60	463.56	440.24
35000	3089.28	1627.22	1141.72	900.35	756.63	661.72	594.70	545.09	507.09	477.19	453.18
36000	3177.55	1673.71	1174.34	926.08	778.25	680.63	611.69	560.67	521.57	490.82	466.13
37000	3265.81	1720.20	1206.96	951.80	799.87	699.54	628.68	576.24	536.06	504.46	479.08
38000	3354.08	1766.70	1239.58	977.53	821.49	718.44	645.67	591.81	550.55	518.09	492.03
39000	3442.34	1813.19	1272.20	1003.25	843.11	737.35	662.66	607.39	565.04	531.73	504.98
40000	3530.61	1859.68	1304.82	1028.98	864.72	756.26	679.66	622.96	579.53	545.36	517.92
41000	3618.87	1906.17	1337.44	1054.70	886.34	775.16	696.65	638.54	594.01	558.99	530.87
42000	3707.14	1952.66	1370.06	1080.42	907.96	794.07	713.64	654.11	608.50	572.63	543.82
43000	3795.40	1999.15	1402.68	1106.15	929.58	812.97	730.63	669.68	622.99	586.26	556.77
44000	3883.67	2045.65	1435.30	1131.87	951.19	831.88	747.62	685.26	637.48	599.90	569.72
45000	3971.93	2092.14	1467.93	1157.60	972.81	850.79	764.61	700.83	651.97	613.53	582.66
46000	4060.20	2138.63	1500.55	1183.32	994.43	869.69	781.60	716.40	666.45	627.16	595.61
47000	4148.46	2185.12	1533.17	1209.05	1016.05	888.60	798.59	731.98	680.94	640.80	608.56
48000	4236.73	2231.61	1565.79	1234.77	1037.67	907.51	815.59	747.55	695.43	654.43	621.51
49000	4324.99	2278.11	1598.41	1260.49	1059.28	926.41	832.58	763.13	709.92	668.06	634.46
50000	4413.26	2324.60	1631.03	1286.22	1080.90	945.32	849.57	778.70	724.41	681.70	647.40
55000	4854.58	2557.06	1794.13	1414.84	1188.99	1039.85	934.52	856.57	796.85	749.87	712.14
60000	5295.91	2789.52	1957.23	1543.46	1297.08	1134.38	1019.48	934.44	869.29	818.04	776.88
65000	5737.24	3021.98	2120.33	1672.08	1405.17	1228.91	1104.44	1012.31	941.73	886.21	841.62
70000	6178.56	3254.43	2283.44	1800.70	1513.26	1323.44	1189.39	1090.18	1014.17	954.38	906.36
75000	6619.89	3486.89	2446.54	1929.33	1621.35	1417.98	1274.35	1168.05	1086.61	1022.55	971.10
80000	7061.21	3719.35	2609.64	2057.95	1729.44	1512.51	1359.31	1245.92	1159.05	1090.71	1035.84
85000	7502.54	3951.81	2772.74	2186.57	1837.53	1607.04	1444.26	1323.79	1231.49	1158.88	1100.58
90000	7943.86	4184.27	2935.85	2315.19	1945.62	1701.57	1529.22	1401.66	1303.93	1227.05	1165.32
95000	8385.19	4416.73	3098.95	2443.81	2053.71	1796.10	1614.18	1479.53	1376.37	1295.22	1230.06
100000	8826.51	4649.19	3262.05	2572.43	2161.80	1890.63	1699.13	1557.40	1448.81	1363.39	1294.80

Principal and Interest
Monthly Payment Amortization Table

10.75%

Term Amount	12 Years	13 Years	14 Years	15 Years	16 Years	17 Years	18 Years	19 Years	20 Years	25 Years	30 Years
50	.62	.60	.58	.57	.55	.54	.53	.52	.51	.49	.47
100	1.24	1.20	1.16	1.13	1.10	1.07	1.05	1.04	1.02	.97	.94
200	2.48	2.39	2.31	2.25	2.19	2.14	2.10	2.07	2.04	1.93	1.87
300	3.72	3.58	3.47	3.37	3.28	3.21	3.15	3.10	3.05	2.89	2.81
400	4.96	4.77	4.62	4.49	4.38	4.28	4.20	4.13	4.07	3.85	3.74
500	6.20	5.97	5.77	5.61	5.47	5.35	5.25	5.16	5.08	4.82	4.67
600	7.44	7.16	6.93	6.73	6.56	6.42	6.30	6.19	6.10	5.78	5.61
700	8.68	8.35	8.08	7.85	7.66	7.49	7.35	7.22	7.11	6.74	6.54
800	9.92	9.54	9.23	8.97	8.75	8.56	8.39	8.25	8.13	7.70	7.47
900	11.15	10.74	10.39	10.09	9.84	9.63	9.44	9.28	9.14	8.66	8.41
1000	12.39	11.93	11.54	11.21	10.94	10.70	10.49	10.31	10.16	9.63	9.34
2000	24.78	23.85	23.08	22.42	21.87	21.39	20.98	20.62	20.31	19.25	18.67
3000	37.17	35.78	34.62	33.63	32.80	32.08	31.46	30.93	30.46	28.87	28.01
4000	49.56	47.70	46.15	44.84	43.73	42.77	41.95	41.23	40.61	38.49	37.34
5000	61.95	59.63	57.69	56.05	54.66	53.46	52.43	51.54	50.77	48.11	46.68
6000	74.33	71.55	69.23	67.26	65.59	64.16	62.92	61.85	60.92	57.73	56.01
7000	86.72	83.48	80.76	78.47	76.52	74.85	73.41	72.16	71.07	67.35	65.35
8000	99.11	95.40	92.30	89.68	87.45	85.54	83.89	82.46	81.22	76.97	74.68
9000	111.50	107.33	103.84	100.89	98.38	96.23	94.38	92.77	91.38	86.59	84.02
10000	123.89	119.25	115.37	112.10	109.31	106.92	104.86	103.08	101.53	96.21	93.35
11000	136.27	131.18	126.91	123.31	120.24	117.61	115.35	113.39	111.68	105.84	102.69
12000	148.66	143.10	138.45	134.52	131.17	128.31	125.84	123.69	121.83	115.46	112.02
13000	161.05	155.03	149.99	145.73	142.10	139.00	136.32	134.00	131.98	125.08	121.36
14000	173.44	166.95	161.52	156.94	153.03	149.69	146.81	144.31	142.14	134.70	130.69
15000	185.83	178.88	173.06	168.15	163.97	160.38	157.29	154.62	152.29	144.32	140.03
16000	198.21	190.80	184.60	179.36	174.90	171.07	167.78	164.92	162.44	153.94	149.36
17000	210.60	202.72	196.13	190.57	185.83	181.77	178.26	175.23	172.59	163.56	158.70
18000	222.99	214.65	207.67	201.78	196.76	192.46	188.75	185.54	182.75	173.18	168.03
19000	235.38	226.57	219.21	212.99	207.69	203.15	199.24	195.85	192.90	182.80	177.37
20000	247.77	238.50	230.74	224.19	218.62	213.84	209.72	206.15	203.05	192.42	186.70
21000	260.15	250.42	242.28	235.40	229.55	224.53	220.21	216.46	213.20	202.04	196.04
22000	272.54	262.35	253.82	246.61	240.48	235.22	230.69	226.77	223.36	211.67	205.37
23000	284.93	274.27	265.36	257.82	251.41	245.92	241.18	237.08	233.51	221.29	214.71
24000	297.32	286.20	276.89	269.03	262.34	256.61	251.67	247.38	243.66	230.91	224.04
25000	309.71	298.12	288.43	280.24	273.27	267.30	262.15	257.69	253.81	240.53	233.38
26000	322.09	310.05	299.97	291.45	284.20	277.99	272.64	268.00	263.96	250.15	242.71
27000	334.48	321.97	311.50	302.66	295.13	288.68	283.12	278.31	274.12	259.77	252.04
28000	346.87	333.90	323.04	313.87	306.06	299.37	293.61	288.61	284.27	269.39	261.38
29000	359.26	345.82	334.58	325.08	317.00	310.07	304.09	298.92	294.42	279.01	270.71
30000	371.65	357.75	346.11	336.29	327.93	320.76	314.58	309.23	304.57	288.63	280.05
31000	384.03	369.67	357.65	347.50	338.86	331.45	325.07	319.54	314.73	298.25	289.38
32000	396.42	381.59	369.19	358.71	349.79	342.14	335.55	329.84	324.88	307.87	298.72
33000	408.81	393.52	380.72	369.92	360.72	352.83	346.04	340.15	335.03	317.50	308.05
34000	421.20	405.44	392.26	381.13	371.65	363.53	356.52	350.46	345.18	327.12	317.39
35000	433.59	417.37	403.80	392.34	382.58	374.22	367.01	360.77	355.34	336.74	326.72
36000	445.97	429.29	415.34	403.55	393.51	384.91	377.50	371.07	365.49	346.36	336.06
37000	458.36	441.22	426.87	414.76	404.44	395.60	387.98	381.38	375.64	355.98	345.39
38000	470.75	453.14	438.41	425.97	415.37	406.29	398.47	391.69	385.79	365.60	354.73
39000	483.14	465.07	449.95	437.17	426.30	416.98	408.95	402.00	395.94	375.22	364.06
40000	495.53	476.99	461.48	448.38	437.23	427.68	419.44	412.30	406.10	384.84	373.40
41000	507.91	488.92	473.02	459.59	448.16	438.37	429.92	422.61	416.25	394.46	382.73
42000	520.30	500.84	484.56	470.80	459.09	449.06	440.41	432.92	426.40	404.08	392.07
43000	532.69	512.77	496.09	482.01	470.03	459.75	450.90	443.23	436.55	413.70	401.40
44000	545.08	524.69	507.63	493.22	480.96	470.44	461.38	453.53	446.71	423.33	410.74
45000	557.47	536.62	519.17	504.43	491.89	481.14	471.87	463.84	456.86	432.95	420.07
46000	569.85	548.54	530.71	515.64	502.82	491.83	482.35	474.15	467.01	442.57	429.41
47000	582.24	560.47	542.24	526.85	513.75	502.52	492.84	484.46	477.16	452.19	438.74
48000	594.63	572.39	553.78	538.06	524.68	513.21	503.33	494.76	487.31	461.81	448.08
49000	607.02	584.31	565.32	549.27	535.61	523.90	513.81	505.07	497.47	471.43	457.41
50000	619.41	596.24	576.85	560.48	546.54	534.59	524.30	515.38	507.62	481.05	466.75
55000	681.35	655.86	634.54	616.53	601.19	588.05	576.73	566.92	558.38	529.16	513.42
60000	743.29	715.49	692.22	672.57	655.85	641.51	629.16	618.45	609.14	577.26	560.09
65000	805.23	775.11	749.91	728.62	710.50	694.97	681.59	669.99	659.90	625.37	606.77
70000	867.17	834.73	807.59	784.67	765.15	748.43	734.01	721.53	710.67	673.47	653.44
75000	929.11	894.36	865.28	840.72	819.81	801.89	786.44	773.07	761.43	721.57	700.12
80000	991.05	953.98	922.96	896.76	874.46	855.35	838.87	824.60	812.19	769.68	746.79
85000	1052.99	1013.60	980.65	952.81	929.11	908.81	891.30	876.14	862.95	817.78	793.46
90000	1114.93	1073.23	1038.33	1008.86	983.77	962.27	943.73	927.68	913.71	865.89	840.14
95000	1176.87	1132.85	1096.02	1064.91	1038.42	1015.72	996.16	979.21	964.47	913.99	886.81
100000	1238.81	1192.47	1153.70	1120.95	1093.07	1069.18	1048.59	1030.75	1015.23	962.10	933.49

11.00% Principal and Interest
Monthly Payment Amortization Table

Term Amount	1 Year	2 Years	3 Years	4 Years	5 Years	6 Years	7 Years	8 Years	9 Years	10 Years	11 Years
50	4.42	2.34	1.64	1.30	1.09	.96	.86	.79	.74	.69	.66
100	8.84	4.67	3.28	2.59	2.18	1.91	1.72	1.58	1.47	1.38	1.31
200	17.68	9.33	6.55	5.17	4.35	3.81	3.43	3.15	2.93	2.76	2.62
300	26.52	13.99	9.83	7.76	6.53	5.72	5.14	4.72	4.39	4.14	3.93
400	35.36	18.65	13.10	10.34	8.70	7.62	6.85	6.29	5.86	5.52	5.24
500	44.20	23.31	16.37	12.93	10.88	9.52	8.57	7.86	7.32	6.89	6.55
600	53.03	27.97	19.65	15.51	13.05	11.43	10.28	9.43	8.78	8.27	7.86
700	61.87	32.63	22.92	18.10	15.22	13.33	11.99	11.00	10.24	9.65	9.17
800	70.71	37.29	26.20	20.68	17.40	15.23	13.70	12.57	11.71	11.03	10.48
900	79.55	41.95	29.47	23.27	19.57	17.14	15.42	14.14	13.17	12.40	11.79
1000	88.39	46.61	32.74	25.85	21.75	19.04	17.13	15.71	14.63	13.78	13.10
2000	176.77	93.22	65.48	51.70	43.49	38.07	34.25	31.42	29.26	27.56	26.19
3000	265.15	139.83	98.22	77.54	65.23	57.11	51.37	47.13	43.88	41.33	39.28
4000	353.53	186.44	130.96	103.39	86.97	76.14	68.49	62.84	58.51	55.11	52.37
5000	441.91	233.04	163.70	129.23	108.72	95.18	85.62	78.55	73.13	68.88	65.47
6000	530.29	279.65	196.44	155.08	130.46	114.21	102.74	94.26	87.76	82.66	78.56
7000	618.68	326.26	229.18	180.92	152.20	133.24	119.86	109.96	102.39	96.43	91.65
8000	707.06	372.87	261.91	206.77	173.94	152.28	136.98	125.67	117.01	110.21	104.74
9000	795.44	419.48	294.65	232.61	195.69	171.31	154.11	141.38	131.64	123.98	117.84
10000	883.82	466.08	327.39	258.46	217.43	190.35	171.23	157.09	146.26	137.76	130.93
11000	972.20	512.69	360.13	284.31	239.17	209.38	188.35	172.80	160.89	151.53	144.02
12000	1060.58	559.30	392.87	310.15	260.91	228.41	205.47	188.51	175.52	165.31	157.11
13000	1148.97	605.91	425.61	336.00	282.66	247.45	222.60	204.21	190.14	179.08	170.21
14000	1237.35	652.51	458.35	361.84	304.40	266.48	239.72	219.92	204.77	192.86	183.30
15000	1325.73	699.12	491.09	387.69	326.14	285.52	256.84	235.63	219.39	206.63	196.39
16000	1414.11	745.73	523.82	413.53	347.88	304.55	273.96	251.34	234.02	220.41	209.48
17000	1502.49	792.34	556.56	439.38	369.63	323.58	291.09	267.05	248.64	234.18	222.57
18000	1590.87	838.95	589.30	465.22	391.37	342.62	308.21	282.76	263.27	247.96	235.67
19000	1679.26	885.55	622.04	491.07	413.11	361.65	325.33	298.47	277.90	261.73	248.76
20000	1767.64	932.16	654.78	516.92	434.85	380.69	342.45	314.17	292.52	275.51	261.85
21000	1856.02	978.77	687.52	542.76	456.60	399.72	359.58	329.88	307.15	289.28	274.94
22000	1944.40	1025.38	720.26	568.61	478.34	418.75	376.70	345.59	321.77	303.06	288.04
23000	2032.78	1071.99	753.00	594.45	500.08	437.79	393.82	361.30	336.40	316.83	301.13
24000	2121.16	1118.59	785.73	620.30	521.82	456.82	410.94	377.01	351.03	330.61	314.22
25000	2209.55	1165.20	818.47	646.14	543.57	475.86	428.07	392.72	365.65	344.38	327.31
26000	2297.93	1211.81	851.21	671.99	565.31	494.89	445.19	408.42	380.28	358.16	340.41
27000	2386.31	1258.42	883.95	697.83	587.05	513.93	462.31	424.13	394.90	371.93	353.50
28000	2474.69	1305.02	916.69	723.68	608.79	532.96	479.43	439.84	409.53	385.71	366.59
29000	2563.07	1351.63	949.43	749.53	630.54	551.99	496.56	455.55	424.15	399.48	379.68
30000	2651.45	1398.24	982.17	775.37	652.28	571.03	513.68	471.26	438.78	413.26	392.78
31000	2739.84	1444.85	1014.91	801.22	674.02	590.06	530.80	486.97	453.41	427.03	405.87
32000	2828.22	1491.46	1047.64	827.06	695.76	609.10	547.92	502.67	468.03	440.81	418.96
33000	2916.60	1538.06	1080.38	852.91	717.50	628.13	565.05	518.38	482.66	454.58	432.05
34000	3004.98	1584.67	1113.12	878.75	739.25	647.16	582.17	534.09	497.28	468.36	445.14
35000	3093.36	1631.28	1145.86	904.60	760.99	666.20	599.29	549.80	511.91	482.13	458.24
36000	3181.74	1677.89	1178.60	930.44	782.73	685.23	616.41	565.51	526.54	495.91	471.33
37000	3270.13	1724.50	1211.34	956.29	804.47	704.27	633.54	581.22	541.16	509.68	484.42
38000	3358.51	1771.10	1244.08	982.13	826.22	723.30	650.66	596.93	555.79	523.46	497.51
39000	3446.89	1817.71	1276.82	1007.98	847.96	742.33	667.78	612.63	570.41	537.23	510.61
40000	3535.27	1864.32	1309.55	1033.83	869.70	761.37	684.90	628.34	585.04	551.01	523.70
41000	3623.65	1910.93	1342.29	1059.67	891.44	780.40	702.02	644.05	599.67	564.78	536.79
42000	3712.03	1957.53	1375.03	1085.52	913.19	799.44	719.15	659.76	614.29	578.56	549.88
43000	3800.42	2004.14	1407.77	1111.36	934.93	818.47	736.27	675.47	628.92	592.33	562.98
44000	3888.80	2050.75	1440.51	1137.21	956.67	837.50	753.39	691.18	643.54	606.11	576.07
45000	3977.18	2097.36	1473.25	1163.05	978.41	856.54	770.51	706.88	658.17	619.88	589.16
46000	4065.56	2143.97	1505.99	1188.90	1000.16	875.57	787.64	722.59	672.79	633.66	602.25
47000	4153.94	2190.57	1538.72	1214.74	1021.90	894.61	804.76	738.30	687.42	647.43	615.35
48000	4242.32	2237.18	1571.46	1240.59	1043.64	913.64	821.88	754.01	702.05	661.21	628.44
49000	4330.71	2283.79	1604.20	1266.44	1065.38	932.67	839.00	769.72	716.67	674.98	641.53
50000	4419.09	2330.40	1636.94	1292.28	1087.13	951.71	856.13	785.43	731.30	688.76	654.62
55000	4861.00	2563.44	1800.63	1421.51	1195.84	1046.88	941.74	863.97	804.43	757.63	720.08
60000	5302.90	2796.48	1964.33	1550.74	1304.55	1142.05	1027.35	942.51	877.56	826.51	785.55
65000	5744.81	3029.51	2128.02	1679.96	1413.26	1237.22	1112.96	1021.05	950.69	895.38	851.01
70000	6186.72	3262.55	2291.72	1809.19	1521.97	1332.39	1198.58	1099.59	1023.82	964.26	916.47
75000	6628.63	3495.59	2455.41	1938.42	1630.69	1427.56	1284.19	1178.14	1096.94	1033.13	981.93
80000	7070.54	3728.63	2619.10	2067.65	1739.40	1522.73	1369.80	1256.68	1170.07	1102.01	1047.39
85000	7512.45	3961.67	2782.80	2196.87	1848.11	1617.90	1455.41	1335.22	1243.20	1170.88	1112.85
90000	7954.35	4194.71	2946.49	2326.10	1956.82	1713.07	1541.02	1413.76	1316.33	1239.76	1178.32
95000	8396.26	4427.75	3110.18	2455.33	2065.54	1808.24	1626.64	1492.31	1389.46	1308.63	1243.78
100000	8838.17	4660.79	3273.88	2584.56	2174.25	1903.41	1712.25	1570.85	1462.59	1377.51	1309.24

Principal and Interest
Monthly Payment Amortization Table

11.00%

Term Amount	12 Years	13 Years	14 Years	15 Years	16 Years	17 Years	18 Years	19 Years	20 Years	25 Years	30 Years
50	.63	.61	.59	.57	.56	.55	.54	.53	.52	.50	.48
100	1.26	1.21	1.17	1.14	1.11	1.09	1.07	1.05	1.04	.99	.96
200	2.51	2.42	2.34	2.28	2.22	2.18	2.14	2.10	2.07	1.97	1.91
300	3.77	3.63	3.51	3.41	3.33	3.26	3.20	3.15	3.10	2.95	2.86
400	5.02	4.84	4.68	4.55	4.44	4.35	4.27	4.19	4.13	3.93	3.81
500	6.27	6.04	5.85	5.69	5.55	5.43	5.33	5.24	5.17	4.91	4.77
600	7.53	7.25	7.02	6.82	6.66	6.52	6.40	6.29	6.20	5.89	5.72
700	8.78	8.46	8.19	7.96	7.77	7.60	7.46	7.34	7.23	6.87	6.67
800	10.03	9.67	9.36	9.10	8.88	8.69	8.53	8.38	8.26	7.85	7.62
900	11.29	10.87	10.53	10.23	9.99	9.77	9.59	9.43	9.29	8.83	8.58
1000	12.54	12.08	11.70	11.37	11.10	10.86	10.66	10.48	10.33	9.81	9.53
2000	25.08	24.16	23.39	22.74	22.19	21.71	21.31	20.95	20.65	19.61	19.05
3000	37.61	36.23	35.08	34.10	33.28	32.57	31.96	31.43	30.97	29.41	28.57
4000	50.15	48.31	46.77	45.47	44.37	43.42	42.61	41.90	41.29	39.21	38.10
5000	62.68	60.38	58.46	56.83	55.46	54.27	53.26	52.38	51.61	49.01	47.62
6000	75.22	72.46	70.15	68.20	66.55	65.13	63.91	62.85	61.94	58.81	57.14
7000	87.75	84.53	81.84	79.57	77.64	75.98	74.56	73.33	72.26	68.61	66.67
8000	100.29	96.61	93.53	90.93	88.73	86.84	85.21	83.80	82.58	78.41	76.19
9000	112.82	108.68	105.22	102.30	99.82	97.69	95.86	94.28	92.90	88.22	85.71
10000	125.36	120.76	116.91	113.66	110.91	108.54	106.51	104.75	103.22	98.02	95.24
11000	137.90	132.83	128.60	125.03	122.00	119.40	117.16	115.23	113.55	107.82	104.76
12000	150.43	144.91	140.29	136.40	133.09	130.25	127.81	125.70	123.87	117.62	114.28
13000	162.97	156.98	151.98	147.76	144.18	141.10	138.46	136.18	134.19	127.42	123.81
14000	175.50	169.06	163.67	159.13	155.27	151.96	149.11	146.65	144.51	137.22	133.33
15000	188.04	181.13	175.36	170.49	166.36	162.81	159.76	157.12	154.83	147.02	142.85
16000	200.57	193.21	187.05	181.86	177.45	173.67	170.41	167.60	165.16	156.82	152.38
17000	213.11	205.28	198.74	193.23	188.54	184.52	181.06	178.07	175.48	166.62	161.90
18000	225.64	217.36	210.43	204.59	199.63	195.37	191.71	188.55	185.80	176.43	171.42
19000	238.18	229.44	222.13	215.96	210.72	206.23	202.36	199.02	196.12	186.23	180.95
20000	250.72	241.51	233.82	227.32	221.81	217.08	213.01	209.50	206.44	196.03	190.47
21000	263.25	253.59	245.51	238.69	232.90	227.93	223.67	219.97	216.76	205.83	199.99
22000	275.79	265.66	257.20	250.06	243.99	238.79	230.45	230.45	227.09	215.63	209.52
23000	288.32	277.74	268.89	261.42	255.08	249.64	244.97	240.92	237.41	225.43	219.04
24000	300.86	289.81	280.58	272.79	266.17	260.50	255.62	251.40	247.73	235.23	228.56
25000	313.39	301.89	292.27	284.15	277.26	271.35	266.27	261.87	258.05	245.03	238.09
26000	325.93	313.96	303.96	295.52	288.35	282.20	276.92	272.35	268.37	254.83	247.61
27000	338.46	326.04	315.65	306.89	299.44	293.06	287.57	282.82	278.70	264.64	257.13
28000	351.00	338.11	327.34	318.25	310.53	303.91	298.22	293.29	289.02	274.44	266.66
29000	363.54	350.19	339.03	329.62	321.62	314.77	308.87	303.77	299.34	284.24	276.18
30000	376.07	362.26	350.72	340.98	332.71	325.62	319.52	314.24	309.66	294.04	285.70
31000	388.61	374.34	362.41	352.35	343.80	336.47	330.17	324.72	319.98	303.84	295.23
32000	401.14	386.41	374.10	363.72	354.89	347.33	340.82	335.19	330.31	313.64	304.75
33000	413.68	398.49	385.79	375.08	365.98	358.18	351.47	345.67	340.63	323.44	314.27
34000	426.21	410.56	397.48	386.45	377.07	369.03	362.12	356.14	350.95	333.24	323.79
35000	438.75	422.64	409.17	397.81	388.16	379.89	372.77	366.62	361.27	343.04	333.32
36000	451.28	434.71	420.86	409.18	399.25	390.74	383.42	377.09	371.59	352.85	342.84
37000	463.82	446.79	432.56	420.55	410.34	401.60	394.07	387.57	381.91	362.65	352.36
38000	476.36	458.87	444.25	431.91	421.43	412.45	404.72	398.04	392.24	372.45	361.89
39000	488.89	470.94	455.94	443.28	432.52	423.30	415.37	408.52	402.56	382.25	371.41
40000	501.43	483.02	467.63	454.64	443.61	434.16	426.02	418.99	412.88	392.05	380.93
41000	513.96	495.09	479.32	466.01	454.70	445.01	436.68	429.47	423.20	401.85	390.46
42000	526.50	507.17	491.01	477.38	465.79	455.86	447.33	439.94	433.52	411.65	399.98
43000	539.03	519.24	502.70	488.74	476.88	466.72	457.98	450.41	443.85	421.45	409.50
44000	551.57	531.32	514.39	500.11	487.97	477.57	468.63	460.89	454.17	431.25	419.03
45000	564.10	543.39	526.08	511.47	499.06	488.43	479.28	471.36	464.49	441.06	428.55
46000	576.64	555.47	537.77	522.84	510.15	499.28	489.93	481.84	474.81	450.86	438.07
47000	589.18	567.54	549.46	534.21	521.24	510.13	500.58	492.31	485.13	460.66	447.60
48000	601.71	579.62	561.15	545.57	532.33	520.99	511.23	502.79	495.46	470.46	457.12
49000	614.25	591.69	572.84	556.94	543.42	531.84	521.88	513.26	505.78	480.26	466.64
50000	626.78	603.77	584.53	568.30	554.51	542.70	532.53	523.74	516.10	490.06	476.17
55000	689.46	664.15	642.98	625.13	609.96	596.96	585.78	576.11	567.71	539.07	523.78
60000	752.14	724.52	701.44	681.96	665.41	651.23	639.03	628.48	619.32	588.07	571.40
65000	814.82	784.90	759.89	738.79	720.86	705.50	692.29	680.86	670.93	637.08	619.02
70000	877.49	845.27	818.34	795.62	776.31	759.77	745.54	733.23	722.54	686.08	666.63
75000	940.17	905.65	876.80	852.45	831.76	814.04	798.79	785.60	774.15	735.09	714.25
80000	1002.85	966.03	935.25	909.28	887.21	868.31	852.04	837.98	825.76	784.10	761.86
85000	1065.53	1026.40	993.70	966.11	942.66	922.58	905.30	890.35	877.37	833.10	809.48
90000	1128.20	1086.78	1052.15	1022.94	998.11	976.85	958.55	942.72	928.97	882.11	857.10
95000	1190.88	1147.16	1110.61	1079.77	1053.56	1031.12	1011.80	995.10	980.58	931.11	904.71
100000	1253.56	1207.53	1169.06	1136.60	1109.01	1085.39	1065.05	1047.47	1032.19	980.12	952.33

11.25% Principal and Interest
Monthly Payment Amortization Table

Term Amount	1 Year	2 Years	3 Years	4 Years	5 Years	6 Years	7 Years	8 Years	9 Years	10 Years	11 Years
50	4.43	2.34	1.65	1.30	1.10	.96	.87	.80	.74	.70	.67
100	8.85	4.68	3.29	2.60	2.19	1.92	1.73	1.59	1.48	1.40	1.33
200	17.70	9.35	6.58	5.20	4.38	3.84	3.46	3.17	2.96	2.79	2.65
300	26.55	14.02	9.86	7.80	6.57	5.75	5.18	4.76	4.43	4.18	3.98
400	35.40	18.69	13.15	10.39	8.75	7.67	6.91	6.34	5.91	5.57	5.30
500	44.25	23.37	16.43	12.99	10.94	9.59	8.63	7.93	7.39	6.96	6.62
600	53.10	28.04	19.72	15.59	13.13	11.50	10.36	9.51	8.86	8.36	7.95
700	61.95	32.71	23.01	18.18	15.31	13.42	12.08	11.10	10.34	9.75	9.27
800	70.80	37.38	26.29	20.78	17.50	15.33	13.81	12.68	11.82	11.14	10.60
900	79.65	42.06	29.58	23.38	19.69	17.25	15.53	14.26	13.29	12.53	11.92
1000	88.50	46.73	32.86	25.97	21.87	19.17	17.26	15.85	14.77	13.92	13.24
2000	177.00	93.45	65.72	51.94	43.74	38.33	34.51	31.69	29.53	27.84	26.48
3000	265.50	140.18	98.58	77.91	65.61	57.49	51.77	47.54	44.30	41.76	39.72
4000	354.00	186.90	131.43	103.87	87.47	76.65	69.02	63.38	59.06	55.67	52.96
5000	442.50	233.62	164.29	129.84	109.34	95.82	86.28	79.22	73.83	69.59	66.19
6000	530.99	280.35	197.15	155.81	131.21	114.98	103.53	95.07	88.59	83.51	79.43
7000	619.49	327.07	230.01	181.77	153.08	134.14	120.78	110.91	103.36	97.42	92.67
8000	707.99	373.80	262.86	207.74	174.94	153.30	138.04	126.75	118.12	111.34	105.91
9000	796.49	420.52	295.72	233.71	196.81	172.47	155.29	142.60	132.88	125.26	119.14
10000	884.99	467.24	328.58	259.68	218.68	191.63	172.55	158.44	147.65	139.17	132.38
11000	973.49	513.97	361.43	285.64	240.55	210.79	189.80	174.28	162.41	153.09	145.62
12000	1061.98	560.69	394.29	311.61	262.41	229.95	207.06	190.13	177.18	167.01	158.86
13000	1150.48	607.42	427.15	337.58	284.28	249.12	224.31	205.97	191.94	180.92	172.09
14000	1238.98	654.14	460.01	363.54	306.15	268.28	241.56	221.82	206.71	194.84	185.33
15000	1327.48	700.86	492.86	389.51	328.01	287.44	258.82	237.66	221.47	208.76	198.57
16000	1415.98	747.59	525.72	415.48	349.88	306.60	276.07	253.50	236.24	222.68	211.81
17000	1504.48	794.31	558.58	441.45	371.75	325.77	293.33	269.35	251.00	236.59	225.04
18000	1592.97	841.04	591.44	467.41	393.62	344.93	310.58	285.19	265.76	250.51	238.28
19000	1681.47	887.76	624.29	493.38	415.48	364.09	327.83	301.03	280.53	264.43	251.52
20000	1769.97	934.48	657.15	519.35	437.35	383.25	345.09	316.88	295.29	278.34	264.76
21000	1858.47	981.21	690.01	545.31	459.22	402.41	362.34	332.72	310.06	292.26	277.99
22000	1946.97	1027.93	722.86	571.28	481.09	421.58	379.60	348.56	324.82	306.18	291.23
23000	2035.47	1074.66	755.72	597.25	502.95	440.74	396.85	364.41	339.59	320.09	304.47
24000	2123.96	1121.38	788.58	623.22	524.82	459.90	414.11	380.25	354.35	334.01	317.71
25000	2212.46	1168.10	821.44	649.18	546.69	479.06	431.36	396.09	369.12	347.93	330.94
26000	2300.96	1214.83	854.29	675.15	568.56	498.23	448.61	411.94	383.88	361.84	344.18
27000	2389.46	1261.55	887.15	701.12	590.42	517.39	465.87	427.78	398.64	375.76	357.42
28000	2477.96	1308.28	920.01	727.08	612.29	536.55	483.12	443.63	413.41	389.68	370.66
29000	2566.46	1355.00	952.86	753.05	634.16	555.71	500.38	459.47	428.17	403.59	383.89
30000	2654.95	1401.72	985.72	779.02	656.02	574.88	517.63	475.31	442.94	417.51	397.13
31000	2743.45	1448.45	1018.58	804.99	677.89	594.04	534.88	491.16	457.70	431.43	410.37
32000	2831.95	1495.17	1051.44	830.95	699.76	613.20	552.14	507.00	472.47	445.35	423.61
33000	2920.45	1541.90	1084.29	856.92	721.63	632.36	569.39	522.84	487.23	459.26	436.84
34000	3008.95	1588.62	1117.15	882.89	743.49	651.53	586.65	538.69	502.00	473.18	450.08
35000	3097.45	1635.34	1150.01	908.85	765.36	670.69	603.90	554.53	516.76	487.10	463.32
36000	3185.94	1682.07	1182.87	934.82	787.23	689.85	621.16	570.37	531.52	501.01	476.56
37000	3274.44	1728.79	1215.72	960.79	809.10	709.01	638.41	586.22	546.29	514.93	489.79
38000	3362.94	1775.52	1248.58	986.75	830.96	728.18	655.66	602.06	561.05	528.85	503.03
39000	3451.44	1822.24	1281.44	1012.72	852.83	747.34	672.92	617.90	575.82	542.76	516.27
40000	3539.94	1868.96	1314.29	1038.69	874.70	766.50	690.17	633.75	590.58	556.68	529.51
41000	3628.44	1915.69	1347.15	1064.66	896.56	785.66	707.43	649.59	605.35	570.60	542.74
42000	3716.93	1962.41	1380.01	1090.62	918.43	804.82	724.68	665.44	620.11	584.51	555.98
43000	3805.43	2009.14	1412.87	1116.59	940.30	823.99	741.93	681.28	634.87	598.43	569.22
44000	3893.93	2055.86	1445.72	1142.56	962.17	843.15	759.19	697.12	649.64	612.35	582.46
45000	3982.43	2102.58	1478.58	1168.52	984.03	862.31	776.44	712.97	664.40	626.27	595.69
46000	4070.93	2149.31	1511.44	1194.49	1005.90	881.47	793.70	728.81	679.17	640.18	608.93
47000	4159.43	2196.03	1544.30	1220.46	1027.77	900.64	810.95	744.65	693.93	654.10	622.17
48000	4247.92	2242.76	1577.15	1246.43	1049.64	919.80	828.21	760.50	708.70	668.02	635.41
49000	4336.42	2289.48	1610.01	1272.39	1071.50	938.96	845.46	776.34	723.46	681.93	648.64
50000	4424.92	2336.20	1642.87	1298.36	1093.37	958.12	862.71	792.18	738.23	695.85	661.88
55000	4867.41	2569.82	1807.15	1428.20	1202.71	1053.94	948.98	871.40	812.05	765.43	728.07
60000	5309.90	2803.44	1971.44	1558.03	1312.04	1149.75	1035.26	950.62	885.87	835.02	794.26
65000	5752.40	3037.06	2135.73	1687.87	1421.38	1245.56	1121.53	1029.84	959.69	904.60	860.44
70000	6194.89	3270.68	2300.01	1817.70	1530.72	1341.37	1207.80	1109.06	1033.51	974.19	926.63
75000	6637.38	3504.30	2464.30	1947.54	1640.05	1437.18	1294.07	1188.27	1107.34	1043.77	992.82
80000	7079.87	3737.92	2628.58	2077.37	1749.39	1532.99	1380.34	1267.49	1181.16	1113.36	1059.01
85000	7522.36	3971.54	2792.87	2207.21	1858.73	1628.81	1466.61	1346.71	1254.98	1182.94	1125.19
90000	7964.85	4205.16	2957.16	2337.04	1968.06	1724.62	1552.88	1425.93	1328.80	1252.53	1191.38
95000	8407.35	4438.78	3121.44	2466.88	2077.40	1820.43	1639.15	1505.15	1402.62	1322.11	1257.57
100000	8849.84	4672.40	3285.73	2596.71	2186.74	1916.24	1725.42	1584.36	1476.45	1391.69	1323.76

Principal and Interest
Monthly Payment Amortization Table

11.25%

Term Amount	12 Years	13 Years	14 Years	15 Years	16 Years	17 Years	18 Years	19 Years	20 Years	25 Years	30 Years
50	.64	.62	.60	.58	.57	.56	.55	.54	.53	.50	.49
100	1.27	1.23	1.19	1.16	1.13	1.11	1.09	1.07	1.05	1.00	.98
200	2.54	2.45	2.37	2.31	2.26	2.21	2.17	2.13	2.10	2.00	1.95
300	3.81	3.67	3.56	3.46	3.38	3.31	3.25	3.20	3.15	3.00	2.92
400	5.08	4.90	4.74	4.61	4.51	4.41	4.33	4.26	4.20	4.00	3.89
500	6.35	6.12	5.93	5.77	5.63	5.51	5.41	5.33	5.25	5.00	4.86
600	7.62	7.34	7.11	6.92	6.76	6.62	6.49	6.39	6.30	5.99	5.83
700	8.88	8.56	8.30	8.07	7.88	7.72	7.58	7.46	7.35	6.99	6.80
800	10.15	9.79	9.48	9.22	9.01	8.82	8.66	8.52	8.40	7.99	7.78
900	11.42	11.01	10.67	10.38	10.13	9.92	9.74	9.58	9.45	8.99	8.75
1000	12.69	12.23	11.85	11.53	11.26	11.02	10.82	10.65	10.50	9.99	9.72
2000	25.37	24.46	23.70	23.05	22.51	22.04	21.64	21.29	20.99	19.97	19.43
3000	38.06	36.69	35.54	34.58	33.76	33.06	32.45	31.93	31.48	29.95	29.14
4000	50.74	48.91	47.39	46.10	45.01	44.07	43.27	42.58	41.98	39.93	38.86
5000	63.42	61.14	59.23	57.62	56.26	55.09	54.09	53.22	52.47	49.92	48.57
6000	76.11	73.37	71.08	69.15	67.51	66.11	64.90	63.86	62.96	59.90	58.28
7000	88.79	85.59	82.92	80.67	78.76	77.12	75.72	74.51	73.45	69.88	67.99
8000	101.48	97.82	94.77	92.19	90.01	88.14	86.53	85.15	83.95	79.86	77.71
9000	114.16	110.05	106.61	103.72	101.26	99.16	97.35	95.79	94.44	89.85	87.42
10000	126.84	122.27	118.46	115.24	112.51	110.17	108.17	106.43	104.93	99.83	97.13
11000	139.53	134.50	130.30	126.76	123.76	121.19	118.98	117.08	115.42	109.81	106.84
12000	152.21	146.73	142.15	138.29	135.01	132.21	129.80	127.72	125.92	119.79	116.56
13000	164.90	158.95	153.99	149.81	146.26	143.22	140.62	138.36	136.41	129.78	126.27
14000	177.58	171.18	165.84	161.33	157.51	154.24	151.43	149.01	146.90	139.76	135.98
15000	190.26	183.41	177.68	172.86	168.76	165.26	162.25	159.65	157.39	149.74	145.69
16000	202.95	195.63	189.53	184.38	180.01	176.27	173.06	170.29	167.89	159.72	155.41
17000	215.63	207.86	201.37	195.90	191.26	187.29	183.88	180.93	178.38	169.71	165.12
18000	228.32	220.09	213.22	207.43	202.51	198.31	194.70	191.58	188.87	179.69	174.83
19000	241.00	232.31	225.06	218.95	213.76	209.33	205.51	202.22	199.36	189.67	184.54
20000	253.68	244.54	236.91	230.47	225.01	220.34	216.33	212.86	209.86	199.65	194.26
21000	266.37	256.77	248.75	242.00	236.26	231.36	227.15	223.51	220.35	209.64	203.97
22000	279.05	268.99	260.60	253.52	247.51	242.38	237.96	234.15	230.84	219.62	213.68
23000	291.74	281.22	272.44	265.04	258.76	253.39	248.78	244.79	241.33	229.60	223.40
24000	304.42	293.45	284.29	276.57	270.01	264.41	259.59	255.43	251.83	239.58	233.11
25000	317.10	305.67	296.13	288.09	281.26	275.43	270.41	266.08	262.32	249.56	242.82
26000	329.79	317.90	307.98	299.61	292.51	286.44	281.23	276.72	272.81	259.55	252.53
27000	342.47	330.13	319.82	311.14	303.76	297.46	292.04	287.36	283.30	269.53	262.25
28000	355.16	342.35	331.67	322.66	315.01	308.48	302.86	298.01	293.80	279.51	271.96
29000	367.84	354.58	343.51	334.18	326.26	319.49	313.67	308.65	304.29	289.49	281.67
30000	380.52	366.81	355.36	345.71	337.51	330.51	324.49	319.29	314.78	299.48	291.38
31000	393.21	379.03	367.20	357.23	348.77	341.53	335.31	329.93	325.27	309.46	301.10
32000	405.89	391.26	379.05	368.76	360.02	352.54	346.12	340.58	335.77	319.44	310.81
33000	418.57	403.49	390.89	380.28	371.27	363.56	356.94	351.22	346.26	329.42	320.52
34000	431.26	415.72	402.74	391.80	382.52	374.58	367.76	361.86	356.75	339.41	330.23
35000	443.94	427.94	414.58	403.33	393.77	385.60	378.57	372.51	367.24	349.39	339.95
36000	456.63	440.17	426.43	414.85	405.02	396.61	389.39	383.15	377.74	359.37	349.66
37000	469.31	452.40	438.27	426.37	416.27	407.63	400.20	393.79	388.23	369.35	359.37
38000	481.99	464.62	450.12	437.90	427.52	418.65	411.02	404.43	398.72	379.34	369.08
39000	494.68	476.85	461.96	449.42	438.77	429.66	421.84	415.08	409.21	389.32	378.80
40000	507.36	489.08	473.81	460.94	450.02	440.68	432.65	425.72	419.71	399.30	388.51
41000	520.05	501.30	485.65	472.47	461.27	451.70	443.47	436.36	430.20	409.28	398.22
42000	532.73	513.53	497.50	483.99	472.52	462.71	454.29	447.01	440.69	419.27	407.93
43000	545.41	525.76	509.34	495.51	483.77	473.73	465.10	457.65	451.19	429.25	417.65
44000	558.10	537.98	521.19	507.04	495.02	484.75	475.92	468.29	461.68	439.23	427.36
45000	570.78	550.21	533.03	518.56	506.27	495.76	486.73	478.93	472.17	449.21	437.07
46000	583.47	562.44	544.88	530.08	517.52	506.78	497.55	489.58	482.66	459.20	446.79
47000	596.15	574.66	556.72	541.61	528.77	517.80	508.37	500.22	493.16	469.18	456.50
48000	608.83	586.89	568.57	553.13	540.02	528.81	519.18	510.86	503.65	479.16	466.21
49000	621.52	599.12	580.41	564.65	551.27	539.83	530.00	521.51	514.14	489.14	475.92
50000	634.20	611.34	592.26	576.18	562.52	550.85	540.81	532.15	524.63	499.12	485.64
55000	697.62	672.48	651.48	633.79	618.77	605.93	594.90	585.36	577.10	549.04	534.20
60000	761.04	733.61	710.71	691.41	675.02	661.02	648.98	638.58	629.56	598.95	582.76
65000	824.46	794.75	769.94	749.03	731.28	716.10	703.06	691.79	682.02	648.86	631.32
70000	887.88	855.88	829.16	806.65	787.53	771.19	757.14	745.01	734.48	698.77	679.89
75000	951.30	917.01	888.39	864.26	843.78	826.27	811.22	798.22	786.95	748.68	728.45
80000	1014.72	978.15	947.61	921.88	900.03	881.35	865.30	851.44	839.41	798.60	777.01
85000	1078.14	1039.28	1006.84	979.50	956.28	936.44	919.38	904.65	891.87	848.51	825.58
90000	1141.56	1100.41	1066.06	1037.12	1012.53	991.52	973.46	957.86	944.34	898.42	874.14
95000	1204.98	1161.55	1125.29	1094.73	1068.79	1046.61	1027.54	1011.08	996.80	948.33	922.70
100000	1268.40	1222.68	1184.51	1152.35	1125.04	1101.69	1081.63	1064.29	1049.26	998.24	971.27

11.50% Principal and Interest
Monthly Payment Amortization Table

Term Amount	1 Year	2 Years	3 Years	4 Years	5 Years	6 Years	7 Years	8 Years	9 Years	10 Years	11 Years
50	4.44	2.35	1.65	1.31	1.10	.97	.87	.80	.75	.71	.67
100	8.87	4.69	3.30	2.61	2.20	1.93	1.74	1.60	1.50	1.41	1.34
200	17.73	9.37	6.60	5.22	4.40	3.86	3.48	3.20	2.99	2.82	2.68
300	26.59	14.06	9.90	7.83	6.60	5.79	5.22	4.80	4.48	4.22	4.02
400	35.45	18.74	13.20	10.44	8.80	7.72	6.96	6.40	5.97	5.63	5.36
500	44.31	23.43	16.49	13.05	11.00	9.65	8.70	7.99	7.46	7.03	6.70
600	53.17	28.11	19.79	15.66	13.20	11.58	10.44	9.59	8.95	8.44	8.04
700	62.04	32.79	23.09	18.27	15.40	13.51	12.18	11.19	10.44	9.85	9.37
800	70.90	37.48	26.39	20.88	17.60	15.44	13.91	12.79	11.93	11.25	10.71
900	79.76	42.16	29.68	23.49	19.80	17.37	15.65	14.39	13.42	12.66	12.05
1000	88.62	46.85	32.98	26.09	22.00	19.30	17.39	15.98	14.91	14.06	13.39
2000	177.24	93.69	65.96	52.18	43.99	38.59	34.78	31.96	29.81	28.12	26.77
3000	265.85	140.53	98.93	78.27	65.98	57.88	52.16	47.94	44.72	42.18	40.16
4000	354.47	187.37	131.91	104.36	87.98	77.17	69.55	63.92	59.62	56.24	53.54
5000	443.08	234.21	164.89	130.45	109.97	96.46	86.94	79.90	74.52	70.30	66.92
6000	531.70	281.05	197.86	156.54	131.96	115.75	104.32	95.88	89.43	84.36	80.31
7000	620.31	327.89	230.84	182.63	153.95	135.04	121.71	111.86	104.33	98.42	93.69
8000	708.93	374.73	263.81	208.72	175.95	154.33	139.10	127.84	119.23	112.48	107.07
9000	797.54	421.57	296.79	234.81	197.94	173.63	156.48	143.82	134.14	126.54	120.46
10000	886.16	468.41	329.77	260.90	219.93	192.92	173.87	159.80	149.04	140.60	133.84
11000	974.77	515.25	362.74	286.98	241.92	212.21	191.26	175.78	163.95	154.66	147.22
12000	1063.39	562.09	395.72	313.07	263.92	231.50	208.64	191.76	178.85	168.72	160.61
13000	1152.00	608.93	428.69	339.16	285.91	250.79	226.03	207.74	193.75	182.78	173.99
14000	1240.62	655.77	461.67	365.25	307.90	270.08	243.42	223.72	208.66	196.84	187.37
15000	1329.23	702.61	494.65	391.34	329.89	289.37	260.80	239.70	223.56	210.90	200.76
16000	1417.85	749.45	527.62	417.43	351.89	308.66	278.19	255.67	238.46	224.96	214.14
17000	1506.46	796.29	560.60	443.52	373.88	327.95	295.57	271.65	253.37	239.02	227.52
18000	1595.08	843.13	593.57	469.61	395.87	347.25	312.96	287.63	268.27	253.08	240.91
19000	1683.69	889.97	626.55	495.70	417.86	366.54	330.35	303.61	283.17	267.14	254.29
20000	1772.31	936.81	659.53	521.79	439.86	385.83	347.73	319.59	298.08	281.20	267.68
21000	1860.92	983.65	692.50	547.87	461.85	405.12	365.12	335.57	312.98	295.26	281.06
22000	1949.54	1030.49	725.48	573.96	483.84	424.41	382.51	351.55	327.89	309.31	294.44
23000	2038.15	1077.33	758.45	600.05	505.83	443.70	399.89	367.53	342.79	323.37	307.83
24000	2126.77	1124.17	791.43	626.14	527.83	462.99	417.28	383.51	357.69	337.43	321.21
25000	2215.38	1171.01	824.41	652.23	549.82	482.28	434.67	399.49	372.60	351.49	334.59
26000	2304.00	1217.85	857.38	678.32	571.81	501.58	452.05	415.47	387.50	365.55	347.98
27000	2392.61	1264.69	890.36	704.41	593.81	520.87	469.44	431.45	402.40	379.61	361.36
28000	2481.23	1311.53	923.33	730.50	615.80	540.16	486.83	447.43	417.31	393.67	374.74
29000	2569.84	1358.37	956.31	756.59	637.79	559.45	504.21	463.41	432.21	407.73	388.13
30000	2658.46	1405.21	989.29	782.68	659.78	578.74	521.60	479.39	447.11	421.79	401.51
31000	2747.07	1452.05	1022.26	808.76	681.78	598.03	538.99	495.37	462.02	435.85	414.89
32000	2835.69	1498.90	1055.24	834.85	703.77	617.32	556.37	511.34	476.92	449.91	428.28
33000	2924.30	1545.74	1088.21	860.94	725.76	636.61	573.76	527.32	491.83	463.97	441.66
34000	3012.92	1592.58	1121.19	887.03	747.75	655.90	591.14	543.30	506.73	478.03	455.04
35000	3101.53	1639.42	1154.17	913.12	769.75	675.20	608.53	559.28	521.63	492.09	468.43
36000	3190.15	1686.26	1187.14	939.21	791.74	694.49	625.92	575.26	536.54	506.15	481.81
37000	3278.76	1733.10	1220.12	965.30	813.73	713.78	643.30	591.24	551.44	520.21	495.19
38000	3367.38	1779.94	1253.09	991.39	835.72	733.07	660.69	607.22	566.34	534.27	508.58
39000	3455.99	1826.78	1286.07	1017.48	857.72	752.36	678.08	623.20	581.25	548.33	521.96
40000	3544.61	1873.62	1319.05	1043.57	879.71	771.65	695.46	639.18	596.15	562.39	535.35
41000	3633.22	1920.46	1352.02	1069.65	901.70	790.94	712.85	655.16	611.06	576.45	548.73
42000	3721.84	1967.30	1385.00	1095.74	923.69	810.23	730.24	671.14	625.96	590.51	562.11
43000	3810.45	2014.14	1417.97	1121.83	945.69	829.52	747.62	687.12	640.86	604.57	575.50
44000	3899.07	2060.98	1450.95	1147.92	967.68	848.82	765.01	703.10	655.77	618.62	588.88
45000	3987.68	2107.82	1483.93	1174.01	989.67	868.11	782.40	719.08	670.67	632.68	602.26
46000	4076.30	2154.66	1516.90	1200.10	1011.66	887.40	799.78	735.06	685.57	646.74	615.65
47000	4164.91	2201.50	1549.88	1226.19	1033.66	906.69	817.17	751.04	700.48	660.80	629.03
48000	4253.53	2248.34	1582.85	1252.28	1055.65	925.98	834.56	767.01	715.38	674.86	642.41
49000	4342.14	2295.18	1615.83	1278.37	1077.64	945.27	851.94	782.99	730.28	688.92	655.80
50000	4430.76	2342.02	1648.81	1304.46	1099.64	964.56	869.33	798.97	745.19	702.98	669.18
55000	4873.83	2576.22	1813.69	1434.90	1209.60	1061.02	956.26	878.87	819.71	773.28	736.10
60000	5316.91	2810.42	1978.57	1565.35	1319.56	1157.47	1043.19	958.77	894.22	843.58	803.02
65000	5759.98	3044.63	2143.45	1695.79	1429.52	1253.93	1130.12	1038.66	968.74	913.88	869.93
70000	6203.06	3278.83	2308.33	1826.24	1539.49	1350.39	1217.06	1118.56	1043.26	984.17	936.85
75000	6646.13	3513.03	2473.21	1956.68	1649.45	1446.84	1303.99	1198.46	1117.78	1054.47	1003.77
80000	7089.21	3747.23	2638.09	2087.13	1759.41	1543.30	1390.92	1278.35	1192.30	1124.77	1070.69
85000	7532.28	3981.43	2802.97	2217.57	1869.38	1639.75	1477.85	1358.25	1266.82	1195.07	1137.60
90000	7975.36	4215.63	2967.85	2348.02	1979.34	1736.21	1564.79	1438.15	1341.33	1265.36	1204.52
95000	8418.44	4449.83	3132.73	2478.46	2089.30	1832.66	1651.72	1518.05	1415.85	1335.66	1271.44
100000	8861.51	4684.04	3297.61	2608.91	2199.27	1929.12	1738.65	1597.94	1490.37	1405.96	1338.36

Principal and Interest
Monthly Payment Amortization Table
11.50%

Term Amount	12 Years	13 Years	14 Years	15 Years	16 Years	17 Years	18 Years	19 Years	20 Years	25 Years	30 Years
50	.65	.62	.61	.59	.58	.56	.55	.55	.54	.51	.50
100	1.29	1.24	1.21	1.17	1.15	1.12	1.10	1.09	1.07	1.02	1.00
200	2.57	2.48	2.41	2.34	2.29	2.24	2.20	2.17	2.14	2.04	1.99
300	3.85	3.72	3.61	3.51	3.43	3.36	3.30	3.25	3.20	3.05	2.98
400	5.14	4.96	4.81	4.68	4.57	4.48	4.40	4.33	4.27	4.07	3.97
500	6.42	6.19	6.01	5.85	5.71	5.60	5.50	5.41	5.34	5.09	4.96
600	7.70	7.43	7.21	7.01	6.85	6.71	6.59	6.49	6.40	6.10	5.95
700	8.99	8.67	8.41	8.18	7.99	7.83	7.69	7.57	7.47	7.12	6.94
800	10.27	9.91	9.61	9.35	9.13	8.95	8.79	8.65	8.54	8.14	7.93
900	11.55	11.15	10.81	10.52	10.28	10.07	9.89	9.74	9.60	9.15	8.92
1000	12.84	12.38	12.01	11.69	11.42	11.19	10.99	10.82	10.67	10.17	9.91
2000	25.67	24.76	24.01	23.37	22.83	22.37	21.97	21.63	21.33	20.33	19.81
3000	38.50	37.14	36.01	35.05	34.24	33.55	32.95	32.44	32.00	30.50	29.71
4000	51.34	49.52	48.01	46.73	45.65	44.73	43.94	43.25	42.66	40.66	39.62
5000	64.17	61.90	60.01	58.41	57.06	55.91	54.92	54.07	53.33	50.83	49.52
6000	77.00	74.28	72.01	70.10	68.47	67.09	65.90	64.88	63.99	60.99	59.42
7000	89.84	86.66	84.01	81.78	79.89	78.27	76.89	75.69	74.66	71.16	69.33
8000	102.67	99.04	96.01	93.46	91.30	89.45	87.87	86.50	85.32	81.32	79.23
9000	115.50	111.42	108.01	105.14	102.71	100.63	98.85	97.31	95.98	91.49	89.13
10000	128.34	123.80	120.01	116.82	114.12	111.81	109.83	108.13	106.65	101.65	99.03
11000	141.17	136.18	132.01	128.51	125.53	123.00	120.82	118.94	117.31	111.82	108.94
12000	154.00	148.56	144.01	140.19	136.94	134.18	131.80	129.75	127.98	121.98	118.84
13000	166.84	160.93	156.01	151.87	148.36	145.36	142.78	140.56	138.64	132.15	128.74
14000	179.67	173.31	168.01	163.55	159.77	156.54	153.77	151.38	149.31	142.31	138.65
15000	192.50	185.69	180.01	175.23	171.18	167.72	164.75	162.19	159.97	152.48	148.55
16000	205.34	198.07	192.01	186.92	182.59	178.90	175.73	173.00	170.63	162.64	158.45
17000	218.17	210.45	204.01	198.60	194.00	190.08	186.72	183.81	181.30	172.80	168.35
18000	231.00	222.83	216.01	210.28	205.41	201.26	197.70	194.62	191.96	182.97	178.26
19000	243.84	235.21	228.02	221.96	216.83	212.44	208.68	205.44	202.63	193.13	188.16
20000	256.67	247.59	240.02	233.64	228.24	223.62	219.66	216.25	213.29	203.30	198.06
21000	269.50	259.97	252.02	245.32	239.65	234.81	230.65	227.06	223.96	213.46	207.97
22000	282.33	272.35	264.02	257.01	251.06	245.99	241.63	237.87	234.62	223.63	217.87
23000	295.17	284.73	276.02	268.69	262.47	257.17	252.61	248.69	245.28	233.79	227.77
24000	308.00	297.11	288.02	280.37	273.88	268.35	263.60	259.50	255.95	243.96	237.67
25000	320.83	309.48	300.02	292.05	285.30	279.53	274.58	270.31	266.61	254.12	247.58
26000	333.67	321.86	312.02	303.73	296.71	290.71	285.56	281.12	277.28	264.29	257.48
27000	346.50	334.24	324.02	315.42	308.12	301.89	296.54	291.93	287.94	274.45	267.38
28000	359.33	346.62	336.02	327.10	319.53	313.07	307.53	302.75	298.61	284.62	277.29
29000	372.17	359.00	348.02	338.78	330.94	324.25	318.51	313.56	309.27	294.78	287.19
30000	385.00	371.38	360.02	350.46	342.35	335.43	329.49	324.37	319.93	304.95	297.09
31000	397.83	383.76	372.02	362.14	353.77	346.61	340.48	335.18	330.60	315.11	307.00
32000	410.67	396.14	384.02	373.83	365.18	357.80	351.46	345.99	341.26	325.28	316.90
33000	423.50	408.52	396.02	385.51	376.59	368.98	362.44	356.81	351.93	335.44	326.80
34000	436.33	420.90	408.02	397.19	388.00	380.16	373.43	367.62	362.59	345.60	336.70
35000	449.17	433.28	420.02	408.87	399.41	391.34	384.41	378.43	373.26	355.77	346.61
36000	462.00	445.66	432.02	420.55	410.82	402.52	395.39	389.24	383.92	365.93	356.51
37000	474.83	458.03	444.03	432.24	422.24	413.70	406.37	400.06	394.58	376.10	366.41
38000	487.67	470.41	456.03	443.92	433.65	424.88	417.36	410.87	405.25	386.26	376.32
39000	500.50	482.79	468.03	455.60	445.06	436.06	428.34	421.68	415.91	396.43	386.22
40000	513.33	495.17	480.03	467.28	456.47	447.24	439.32	432.49	426.58	406.59	396.12
41000	526.16	507.55	492.03	478.96	467.88	458.42	450.31	443.30	437.24	416.76	406.02
42000	539.00	519.93	504.03	490.64	479.29	469.61	461.29	454.12	447.91	426.92	415.93
43000	551.83	532.31	516.03	502.33	490.71	480.79	472.27	464.93	458.57	437.09	425.83
44000	564.66	544.69	528.03	514.01	502.12	491.97	483.25	475.74	469.23	447.25	435.73
45000	577.50	557.07	540.03	525.69	513.53	503.15	494.24	486.55	479.90	457.42	445.64
46000	590.33	569.45	552.03	537.37	524.94	514.33	505.22	497.37	490.56	467.58	455.54
47000	603.16	581.83	564.03	549.05	536.35	525.51	516.20	508.18	501.23	477.75	465.44
48000	616.00	594.21	576.03	560.74	547.76	536.69	527.19	518.99	511.89	487.91	475.34
49000	628.83	606.58	588.03	572.42	559.18	547.87	538.17	529.80	522.56	498.07	485.25
50000	641.66	618.96	600.03	584.10	570.59	559.05	549.15	540.61	533.22	508.24	495.15
55000	705.83	680.86	660.04	642.51	627.65	614.96	604.07	594.67	586.54	559.06	544.67
60000	769.99	742.76	720.04	700.92	684.70	670.86	658.98	648.74	639.86	609.89	594.18
65000	834.16	804.65	780.04	759.33	741.76	726.77	713.90	702.80	693.18	660.71	643.69
70000	898.33	866.55	840.04	817.74	798.82	782.67	768.81	756.86	746.51	711.53	693.21
75000	962.49	928.44	900.05	876.15	855.88	838.58	823.73	810.92	799.83	762.36	742.72
80000	1026.66	990.34	960.05	934.56	912.94	894.48	878.64	864.98	853.15	813.18	792.24
85000	1090.82	1052.24	1020.05	992.97	970.00	950.39	933.56	919.04	906.47	864.00	841.75
90000	1154.99	1114.13	1080.05	1051.38	1027.05	1006.29	988.47	973.10	959.79	914.83	891.27
95000	1219.16	1176.03	1140.06	1109.79	1084.11	1062.20	1043.39	1027.16	1013.11	965.65	940.78
100000	1283.32	1237.92	1200.06	1168.19	1141.17	1118.10	1098.30	1081.22	1066.43	1016.47	990.30

11.75% Principal and Interest
Monthly Payment Amortization Table

Term Amount	1 Year	2 Years	3 Years	4 Years	5 Years	6 Years	7 Years	8 Years	9 Years	10 Years	11 Years
50	4.44	2.35	1.66	1.32	1.11	.98	.88	.81	.76	.72	.68
100	8.88	4.70	3.31	2.63	2.22	1.95	1.76	1.62	1.51	1.43	1.36
200	17.75	9.40	6.62	5.25	4.43	3.89	3.51	3.23	3.01	2.85	2.71
300	26.62	14.09	9.93	7.87	6.64	5.83	5.26	4.84	4.52	4.27	4.06
400	35.50	18.79	13.24	10.49	8.85	7.77	7.01	6.45	6.02	5.69	5.42
500	44.37	23.48	16.55	13.11	11.06	9.72	8.76	8.06	7.53	7.11	6.77
600	53.24	28.18	19.86	15.73	13.28	11.66	10.52	9.67	9.03	8.53	8.12
700	62.12	32.87	23.17	18.35	15.49	13.60	12.27	11.29	10.54	9.95	9.48
800	70.99	37.57	26.48	20.97	17.70	15.54	14.02	12.90	12.04	11.37	10.83
900	79.86	42.27	29.79	23.60	19.91	17.48	15.77	14.51	13.54	12.79	12.18
1000	88.74	46.96	33.10	26.22	22.12	19.43	17.52	16.12	15.05	14.21	13.54
2000	177.47	93.92	66.20	52.43	44.24	38.85	35.04	32.24	30.09	28.41	27.07
3000	266.20	140.88	99.29	78.64	66.36	58.27	52.56	48.35	45.14	42.61	40.60
4000	354.93	187.83	132.39	104.85	88.48	77.69	70.08	64.47	60.18	56.82	54.13
5000	443.66	234.79	165.48	131.06	110.60	97.11	87.60	80.58	75.22	71.02	67.66
6000	532.40	281.75	198.58	157.27	132.71	116.53	105.12	96.70	90.27	85.22	81.19
7000	621.13	328.70	231.67	183.48	154.83	135.95	122.64	112.82	105.31	99.43	94.72
8000	709.86	375.66	264.77	209.70	176.95	155.37	140.16	128.93	120.35	113.63	108.25
9000	798.59	422.62	297.86	235.91	199.07	174.79	157.68	145.05	135.40	127.83	121.78
10000	887.32	469.57	330.96	262.12	221.19	194.21	175.20	161.16	150.44	142.03	135.31
11000	976.06	516.53	364.05	288.33	243.31	213.63	192.72	177.28	165.48	156.24	148.84
12000	1064.79	563.49	397.15	314.54	265.42	233.05	210.24	193.39	180.53	170.44	162.37
13000	1153.52	610.44	430.24	340.75	287.54	252.47	227.76	209.51	195.57	184.64	175.90
14000	1242.25	657.40	463.34	366.96	309.66	271.89	245.28	225.63	210.62	198.85	189.43
15000	1330.98	704.36	496.43	393.17	331.78	291.31	262.79	241.74	225.66	213.05	202.96
16000	1419.72	751.31	529.53	419.39	353.90	310.73	280.31	257.86	240.70	227.25	216.49
17000	1508.45	798.27	562.62	445.60	376.02	330.15	297.83	273.97	255.75	241.46	230.02
18000	1597.18	845.23	595.72	471.81	398.13	349.57	315.35	290.09	270.79	255.66	243.55
19000	1685.91	892.18	628.81	498.02	420.25	368.99	332.87	306.21	285.83	269.86	257.08
20000	1774.64	939.14	661.91	524.23	442.37	388.41	350.39	322.32	300.88	284.06	270.61
21000	1863.37	986.10	695.00	550.44	464.49	407.83	367.91	338.44	315.92	298.27	284.14
22000	1952.11	1033.05	728.10	576.65	486.61	427.25	385.43	354.55	330.96	312.47	297.67
23000	2040.84	1080.01	761.19	602.86	508.73	446.67	402.95	370.67	346.01	326.67	311.20
24000	2129.57	1126.97	794.29	629.08	530.84	466.10	420.47	386.78	361.05	340.88	324.73
25000	2218.30	1173.93	827.38	655.29	552.96	485.52	437.99	402.90	376.10	355.08	338.26
26000	2307.03	1220.88	860.48	681.50	575.08	504.94	455.51	419.02	391.14	369.28	351.79
27000	2395.77	1267.84	893.57	707.71	597.20	524.36	473.03	435.13	406.18	383.48	365.32
28000	2484.50	1314.80	926.67	733.92	619.32	543.78	490.55	451.25	421.23	397.69	378.85
29000	2573.23	1361.75	959.76	760.13	641.44	563.20	508.07	467.36	436.27	411.89	392.38
30000	2661.96	1408.71	992.86	786.34	663.55	582.62	525.58	483.48	451.31	426.09	405.91
31000	2750.69	1455.67	1025.95	812.55	685.67	602.04	543.10	499.59	466.36	440.30	419.44
32000	2839.43	1502.62	1059.05	838.77	707.79	621.46	560.62	515.71	481.40	454.50	432.97
33000	2928.16	1549.58	1092.14	864.98	729.91	640.88	578.14	531.83	496.44	468.70	446.50
34000	3016.89	1596.54	1125.24	891.19	752.03	660.30	595.66	547.94	511.49	482.91	460.03
35000	3105.62	1643.49	1158.33	917.40	774.15	679.72	613.18	564.06	526.53	497.11	473.57
36000	3194.35	1690.45	1191.40	943.61	796.26	699.14	630.70	580.17	541.57	511.31	487.10
37000	3283.08	1737.41	1224.52	969.82	818.38	718.56	648.22	596.29	556.62	525.51	500.63
38000	3371.82	1784.36	1257.62	996.03	840.50	737.98	665.74	612.41	571.66	539.72	514.16
39000	3460.55	1831.32	1290.71	1022.24	862.62	757.40	683.26	628.52	586.71	553.92	527.69
40000	3549.28	1878.28	1323.81	1048.46	884.74	776.82	700.78	644.64	601.75	568.12	541.22
41000	3638.01	1925.23	1356.90	1074.67	906.86	796.24	718.30	660.75	616.79	582.33	554.75
42000	3726.74	1972.19	1390.00	1100.88	928.97	815.66	735.82	676.87	631.84	596.53	568.28
43000	3815.48	2019.15	1423.09	1127.09	951.09	835.08	753.34	692.98	646.88	610.73	581.81
44000	3904.21	2066.10	1456.19	1153.30	973.21	854.50	770.85	709.10	661.92	624.93	595.34
45000	3992.94	2113.06	1489.28	1179.51	995.33	873.92	788.37	725.22	676.97	639.14	608.87
46000	4081.67	2160.02	1522.38	1205.72	1017.45	893.34	805.89	741.33	692.01	653.34	622.40
47000	4170.40	2206.98	1555.47	1231.93	1039.57	912.77	823.41	757.45	707.05	667.54	635.93
48000	4259.14	2253.93	1588.57	1258.15	1061.68	932.19	840.93	773.56	722.10	681.75	649.46
49000	4347.87	2300.89	1621.66	1284.36	1083.80	951.61	858.45	789.68	737.14	695.95	662.99
50000	4436.60	2347.85	1654.76	1310.57	1105.92	971.03	875.97	805.79	752.19	710.15	676.52
55000	4880.26	2582.63	1820.23	1441.62	1216.51	1068.13	963.57	886.37	827.40	781.17	744.17
60000	5323.92	2817.41	1985.71	1572.68	1327.10	1165.23	1051.16	966.95	902.62	852.18	811.82
65000	5767.58	3052.20	2151.18	1703.74	1437.70	1262.33	1138.76	1047.53	977.84	923.20	879.47
70000	6211.24	3286.98	2316.66	1834.79	1548.29	1359.44	1226.36	1128.11	1053.06	994.21	947.13
75000	6654.90	3521.77	2482.13	1965.85	1658.88	1456.54	1313.95	1208.69	1128.28	1065.23	1014.78
80000	7098.56	3756.55	2647.61	2096.91	1769.47	1553.64	1401.55	1289.27	1203.49	1136.24	1082.43
85000	7542.21	3991.33	2813.08	2227.96	1880.06	1650.74	1489.15	1369.85	1278.71	1207.26	1150.08
90000	7985.87	4226.12	2978.56	2359.02	1990.65	1747.84	1576.74	1450.43	1353.93	1278.27	1217.73
95000	8429.53	4460.90	3144.03	2490.07	2101.25	1844.95	1664.34	1531.01	1429.15	1349.28	1285.38
100000	8873.19	4695.69	3309.51	2621.13	2211.84	1942.05	1751.94	1611.58	1504.37	1420.30	1353.03

Principal and Interest
Monthly Payment Amortization Table **11.75%**

Term Amount	12 Years	13 Years	14 Years	15 Years	16 Years	17 Years	18 Years	19 Years	20 Years	25 Years	30 Years
50	.65	.63	.61	.60	.58	.57	.56	.55	.55	.52	.51
100	1.30	1.26	1.22	1.19	1.16	1.14	1.12	1.10	1.09	1.04	1.01
200	2.60	2.51	2.44	2.37	2.32	2.27	2.24	2.20	2.17	2.07	2.02
300	3.90	3.76	3.65	3.56	3.48	3.41	3.35	3.30	3.26	3.11	3.03
400	5.20	5.02	4.87	4.74	4.63	4.54	4.47	4.40	4.34	4.14	4.04
500	6.50	6.27	6.08	5.93	5.79	5.68	5.58	5.50	5.42	5.18	5.05
600	7.79	7.52	7.30	7.11	6.95	6.81	6.70	6.59	6.51	6.21	6.06
700	9.09	8.78	8.51	8.29	8.11	7.95	7.81	7.69	7.59	7.25	7.07
800	10.39	10.03	9.73	9.48	9.26	9.08	8.93	8.79	8.67	8.28	8.08
900	11.69	11.28	10.95	10.66	10.42	10.22	10.04	9.89	9.76	9.32	9.09
1000	12.99	12.54	12.16	11.85	11.58	11.35	11.16	10.99	10.84	10.35	10.10
2000	25.97	25.07	24.32	23.69	23.15	22.70	22.31	21.97	21.68	20.70	20.19
3000	38.95	37.60	36.48	35.53	34.73	34.04	33.46	32.95	32.52	31.05	30.29
4000	51.94	50.13	48.63	47.37	46.30	45.39	44.61	43.94	43.35	41.40	40.38
5000	64.92	62.67	60.79	59.21	57.87	56.74	55.76	54.92	54.19	51.74	50.48
6000	77.90	75.20	72.95	71.05	69.45	68.08	66.91	65.90	65.03	62.09	60.57
7000	90.89	87.73	85.10	82.89	81.02	79.43	78.06	76.88	75.86	72.44	70.66
8000	103.87	100.26	97.26	94.74	92.60	90.77	89.21	87.87	86.70	82.79	80.76
9000	116.85	112.80	109.42	106.58	104.17	102.12	100.36	98.85	97.54	93.14	90.85
10000	129.84	125.33	121.57	118.42	115.74	113.47	111.51	109.83	108.38	103.48	100.95
11000	142.82	137.86	133.73	130.26	127.32	124.81	122.66	120.81	119.21	113.83	111.04
12000	155.80	150.39	145.89	142.10	138.89	136.16	133.81	131.80	130.05	124.18	121.13
13000	168.79	162.93	158.05	153.94	150.47	147.50	144.96	142.78	140.89	134.53	131.23
14000	181.77	175.46	170.20	165.78	162.04	158.85	156.12	153.76	151.72	144.88	141.32
15000	194.75	187.99	182.36	177.62	173.61	170.20	167.27	164.74	162.56	155.22	151.42
16000	207.74	200.52	194.52	189.47	185.19	181.54	178.42	175.73	173.40	165.57	161.51
17000	220.72	213.06	206.67	201.31	196.76	192.89	189.57	186.71	184.24	175.92	171.60
18000	233.70	225.59	218.83	213.15	208.34	204.23	200.72	197.69	195.07	186.27	181.70
19000	246.69	238.12	230.99	224.99	219.91	215.58	211.87	208.67	205.91	196.62	191.79
20000	259.67	250.65	243.14	236.83	231.48	226.93	223.02	219.66	216.75	206.96	201.89
21000	272.65	263.19	255.30	248.67	243.06	238.27	234.17	230.64	227.58	217.31	211.98
22000	285.64	275.72	267.46	260.51	254.63	249.62	245.32	241.62	238.42	227.66	222.08
23000	298.62	288.25	279.62	272.36	266.21	260.96	256.47	252.60	249.26	238.01	232.17
24000	311.60	300.78	291.77	284.20	277.78	272.31	267.62	263.59	260.09	248.36	242.26
25000	324.59	313.32	303.93	296.04	289.35	283.66	278.77	274.57	270.93	258.70	252.36
26000	337.57	325.85	316.09	307.88	300.93	295.00	289.92	285.55	281.77	269.05	262.45
27000	350.55	338.38	328.24	319.72	312.50	306.35	301.07	296.53	292.61	279.40	272.55
28000	363.54	350.91	340.40	331.56	324.08	317.69	312.23	307.52	303.44	289.75	282.64
29000	376.52	363.45	352.56	343.40	335.65	329.04	323.38	318.50	314.28	300.10	292.73
30000	389.50	375.98	364.71	355.24	347.22	340.39	334.53	329.48	325.12	310.44	302.83
31000	402.49	388.51	376.87	367.09	358.80	351.73	345.68	340.46	335.95	320.79	312.92
32000	415.47	401.04	389.03	378.93	370.37	363.08	356.83	351.45	346.79	331.14	323.02
33000	428.45	413.58	401.18	390.77	381.95	374.43	367.98	362.43	357.63	341.49	333.11
34000	441.44	426.11	413.34	402.61	393.52	385.77	379.13	373.41	368.47	351.84	343.20
35000	454.42	438.64	425.50	414.45	405.09	397.12	390.28	384.39	379.30	362.18	353.30
36000	467.40	451.17	437.66	426.29	416.67	408.46	401.43	395.38	390.14	372.53	363.39
37000	480.39	463.71	449.81	438.13	428.24	419.81	412.58	406.36	400.98	382.88	373.49
38000	493.37	476.24	461.97	449.97	439.82	431.16	423.73	417.34	411.81	393.23	383.58
39000	506.35	488.77	474.13	461.82	451.39	442.50	434.88	428.32	422.65	403.58	393.67
40000	519.34	501.30	486.28	473.66	462.96	453.85	446.03	439.31	433.49	413.92	403.77
41000	532.32	513.84	498.44	485.50	474.54	465.19	457.18	450.29	444.32	424.27	413.86
42000	545.30	526.37	510.60	497.34	486.11	476.54	468.33	461.27	455.16	434.62	423.96
43000	558.28	538.90	522.75	509.18	497.69	487.89	479.49	472.25	466.00	444.97	434.05
44000	571.27	551.43	534.91	521.02	509.26	499.23	490.64	483.24	476.84	455.32	444.15
45000	584.25	563.97	547.07	532.86	520.83	510.58	501.79	494.22	487.67	465.66	454.24
46000	597.23	576.50	559.23	544.71	532.41	521.92	512.94	505.20	498.51	476.01	464.33
47000	610.22	589.03	571.38	556.55	543.98	533.27	524.09	516.18	509.35	486.36	474.43
48000	623.20	601.56	583.54	568.39	555.56	544.62	535.24	527.17	520.18	496.71	484.52
49000	636.18	614.10	595.70	580.23	567.13	555.96	546.39	538.15	531.02	507.06	494.62
50000	649.17	626.63	607.85	592.07	578.70	567.31	557.54	549.13	541.86	517.40	504.71
55000	714.08	689.29	668.64	651.28	636.57	624.04	613.29	604.04	596.04	569.14	555.18
60000	779.00	751.95	729.42	710.48	694.44	680.77	669.05	658.96	650.23	620.88	605.65
65000	843.92	814.62	790.21	769.69	752.31	737.50	724.80	713.87	704.41	672.62	656.12
70000	908.83	877.28	850.99	828.90	810.18	794.23	780.56	768.78	758.60	724.36	706.59
75000	973.75	939.94	911.78	888.10	868.05	850.96	836.31	823.69	812.79	776.10	757.06
80000	1038.67	1002.60	972.56	947.31	925.92	907.69	892.06	878.61	866.97	827.84	807.53
85000	1103.58	1065.27	1033.35	1006.52	983.79	964.42	947.82	933.52	921.16	879.58	858.00
90000	1168.50	1127.93	1094.13	1065.72	1041.66	1021.15	1003.57	988.43	975.34	931.32	908.47
95000	1233.41	1190.60	1154.92	1124.93	1099.53	1077.88	1059.32	1043.34	1029.53	983.06	958.94
100000	1298.33	1253.25	1215.70	1184.14	1157.40	1134.61	1115.08	1098.26	1083.71	1034.80	1009.41

12.00% Principal and Interest
Monthly Payment Amortization Table

Term Amount	1 Year	2 Years	3 Years	4 Years	5 Years	6 Years	7 Years	8 Years	9 Years	10 Years	11 Years
50	4.45	2.36	1.67	1.32	1.12	.98	.89	.82	.76	.72	.69
100	8.89	4.71	3.33	2.64	2.23	1.96	1.77	1.63	1.52	1.44	1.37
200	17.77	9.42	6.65	5.27	4.45	3.92	3.54	3.26	3.04	2.87	2.74
300	26.66	14.13	9.97	7.91	6.68	5.87	5.30	4.88	4.56	4.31	4.11
400	35.54	18.83	13.29	10.54	8.90	7.83	7.07	6.51	6.08	5.74	5.48
500	44.43	23.54	16.61	13.17	11.13	9.78	8.83	8.13	7.60	7.18	6.84
600	53.31	28.25	19.93	15.81	13.35	11.74	10.60	9.76	9.12	8.61	8.21
700	62.20	32.96	23.26	18.44	15.58	13.69	12.36	11.38	10.63	10.05	9.58
800	71.08	37.66	26.58	21.07	17.80	15.65	14.13	13.01	12.15	11.48	10.95
900	79.97	42.37	29.90	23.71	20.03	17.60	15.89	14.63	13.67	12.92	12.32
1000	88.85	47.08	33.22	26.34	22.25	19.56	17.66	16.26	15.19	14.35	13.68
2000	177.70	94.15	66.43	52.67	44.49	39.11	35.31	32.51	30.37	28.70	27.36
3000	266.55	141.23	99.65	79.01	66.74	58.66	52.96	48.76	45.56	43.05	41.04
4000	355.40	188.30	132.86	105.34	88.98	78.21	70.62	65.02	60.74	57.39	54.72
5000	444.25	235.37	166.08	131.67	111.23	97.76	88.27	81.27	75.93	71.74	68.39
6000	533.10	282.45	199.29	158.01	133.47	117.31	105.92	97.52	91.11	86.09	82.07
7000	621.95	329.52	232.51	184.34	155.72	136.86	123.57	113.77	106.29	100.43	95.75
8000	710.80	376.59	265.72	210.68	177.96	156.41	141.23	130.03	121.48	114.78	109.43
9000	799.64	423.67	298.93	237.01	200.21	175.96	158.88	146.28	136.66	129.13	123.11
10000	888.49	470.74	332.15	263.34	222.45	195.51	176.53	162.53	151.85	143.48	136.78
11000	977.34	517.81	365.36	289.68	244.69	215.06	194.19	178.79	167.03	157.82	150.46
12000	1066.19	564.89	398.58	316.01	266.94	234.61	211.84	195.04	182.22	172.17	164.14
13000	1155.04	611.96	431.79	342.34	289.18	254.16	229.49	211.29	197.40	186.52	177.82
14000	1243.89	659.03	465.01	368.68	311.43	273.71	247.14	227.54	212.58	200.86	191.50
15000	1332.74	706.11	498.22	395.01	333.67	293.26	264.80	243.80	227.77	215.21	205.17
16000	1421.59	753.18	531.43	421.35	355.92	312.81	282.45	260.05	242.95	229.56	218.85
17000	1510.43	800.25	564.65	447.68	378.16	332.36	300.10	276.30	258.14	243.91	232.53
18000	1599.28	847.33	597.86	474.01	400.41	351.91	317.75	292.56	273.32	258.25	246.21
19000	1688.13	894.40	631.08	500.35	422.65	371.46	335.41	308.81	288.51	272.60	259.88
20000	1776.98	941.47	664.29	526.68	444.89	391.01	353.06	325.06	303.69	286.95	273.56
21000	1865.83	988.55	697.51	553.02	467.14	410.56	370.71	341.31	318.87	301.29	287.24
22000	1954.68	1035.62	730.72	579.35	489.38	430.11	388.37	357.57	334.06	315.64	300.92
23000	2043.53	1082.69	763.93	605.68	511.63	449.66	406.02	373.82	349.24	329.99	314.60
24000	2132.38	1129.77	797.15	632.02	533.87	469.21	423.67	390.07	364.43	344.34	328.27
25000	2221.22	1176.84	830.36	658.35	556.12	488.76	441.32	406.33	379.61	358.68	341.95
26000	2310.07	1223.92	863.58	684.68	578.36	508.31	458.98	422.58	394.80	373.03	355.63
27000	2398.92	1270.99	896.79	711.02	600.61	527.86	476.63	438.83	409.98	387.38	369.31
28000	2487.77	1318.06	930.01	737.35	622.85	547.41	494.28	455.08	425.16	401.72	382.99
29000	2576.62	1365.14	963.22	763.69	645.09	566.96	511.93	471.34	440.35	416.07	396.66
30000	2665.47	1412.21	996.43	790.02	667.34	586.51	529.59	487.59	455.53	430.42	410.34
31000	2754.32	1459.28	1029.65	816.35	689.58	606.06	547.24	503.84	470.72	444.76	424.02
32000	2843.17	1506.36	1062.86	842.69	711.83	625.61	564.89	520.10	485.90	459.11	437.70
33000	2932.02	1553.43	1096.08	869.02	734.07	645.16	582.55	536.35	501.08	473.46	451.38
34000	3020.86	1600.50	1129.29	895.36	756.32	664.71	600.20	552.60	516.27	487.81	465.05
35000	3109.71	1647.58	1162.51	921.69	778.56	684.26	617.85	568.85	531.45	502.15	478.73
36000	3198.56	1694.65	1195.72	948.02	800.81	703.81	635.50	585.11	546.64	516.50	492.41
37000	3287.41	1741.72	1228.93	974.36	823.05	723.36	653.16	601.36	561.82	530.85	506.09
38000	3376.26	1788.80	1262.15	1000.69	845.29	742.91	670.81	617.61	577.01	545.19	519.76
39000	3465.11	1835.87	1295.36	1027.02	867.54	762.46	688.46	633.87	592.19	559.54	533.44
40000	3553.96	1882.94	1328.58	1053.36	889.78	782.01	706.11	650.12	607.37	573.89	547.12
41000	3642.81	1930.02	1361.79	1079.69	912.03	801.56	723.77	666.37	622.56	588.24	560.80
42000	3731.65	1977.09	1395.01	1106.03	934.27	821.11	741.42	682.62	637.74	602.58	574.48
43000	3820.50	2024.16	1428.22	1132.36	956.52	840.66	759.07	698.88	652.93	616.93	588.15
44000	3909.35	2071.24	1461.43	1158.69	978.76	860.21	776.73	715.13	668.11	631.28	601.83
45000	3998.20	2118.31	1494.65	1185.03	1001.01	879.76	794.38	731.38	683.30	645.62	615.51
46000	4087.05	2165.38	1527.86	1211.36	1023.25	899.31	812.03	747.64	698.48	659.97	629.19
47000	4175.90	2212.46	1561.08	1237.70	1045.49	918.86	829.68	763.89	713.66	674.32	642.87
48000	4264.75	2259.53	1594.29	1264.03	1067.74	938.41	847.34	780.14	728.85	688.67	656.54
49000	4353.60	2306.61	1627.51	1290.36	1089.98	957.96	864.99	796.39	744.03	703.01	670.22
50000	4442.44	2353.68	1660.72	1316.70	1112.23	977.51	882.64	812.65	759.22	717.36	683.90
55000	4886.69	2589.05	1826.79	1448.37	1223.45	1075.27	970.91	893.91	835.14	789.10	752.29
60000	5330.93	2824.41	1992.86	1580.04	1334.67	1173.02	1059.17	975.18	911.06	860.83	820.68
65000	5775.18	3059.78	2158.94	1711.70	1445.89	1270.77	1147.43	1056.44	986.98	932.57	889.07
70000	6219.42	3295.15	2325.01	1843.37	1557.12	1368.52	1235.70	1137.70	1062.90	1004.30	957.46
75000	6663.66	3530.52	2491.08	1975.04	1668.34	1466.27	1323.96	1218.97	1138.82	1076.04	1025.85
80000	7107.91	3765.88	2657.15	2106.71	1779.56	1564.02	1412.22	1300.23	1214.74	1147.77	1094.24
85000	7552.15	4001.25	2823.22	2238.38	1890.78	1661.77	1500.49	1381.50	1290.66	1219.51	1162.62
90000	7996.40	4236.62	2989.29	2370.05	2002.01	1759.52	1588.75	1462.76	1366.59	1291.24	1231.01
95000	8440.64	4471.98	3155.36	2501.72	2113.23	1857.27	1677.01	1544.02	1442.51	1362.98	1299.40
100000	8884.88	4707.35	3321.44	2633.39	2224.45	1955.02	1765.28	1625.29	1518.43	1434.71	1367.79

Principal and Interest
Monthly Payment Amortization Table

12.00%

Term Amount	12 Years	13 Years	14 Years	15 Years	16 Years	17 Years	18 Years	19 Years	20 Years	25 Years	30 Years
50	.66	.64	.62	.61	.59	.58	.57	.56	.56	.53	.52
100	1.32	1.27	1.24	1.21	1.18	1.16	1.14	1.12	1.11	1.06	1.03
200	2.63	2.54	2.47	2.41	2.35	2.31	2.27	2.24	2.21	2.11	2.06
300	3.95	3.81	3.70	3.61	3.53	3.46	3.40	3.35	3.31	3.16	3.09
400	5.26	5.08	4.93	4.81	4.70	4.61	4.53	4.47	4.41	4.22	4.12
500	6.57	6.35	6.16	6.01	5.87	5.76	5.66	5.58	5.51	5.27	5.15
600	7.89	7.62	7.39	7.21	7.05	6.91	6.80	6.70	6.61	6.32	6.18
700	9.20	8.89	8.63	8.41	8.22	8.06	7.93	7.81	7.71	7.38	7.21
800	10.51	10.15	9.86	9.61	9.39	9.21	9.06	8.93	8.81	8.43	8.23
900	11.83	11.42	11.09	10.81	10.57	10.37	10.19	10.04	9.91	9.48	9.26
1000	13.14	12.69	12.32	12.01	11.74	11.52	11.32	11.16	11.02	10.54	10.29
2000	26.27	25.38	24.63	24.01	23.48	23.03	22.64	22.31	22.03	21.07	20.58
3000	39.41	38.06	36.95	36.01	35.22	34.54	33.96	33.47	33.04	31.60	30.86
4000	52.54	50.75	49.26	48.01	46.95	46.05	45.28	44.62	44.05	42.13	41.15
5000	65.68	63.44	61.58	60.01	58.69	57.57	56.60	55.77	55.06	52.67	51.44
6000	78.81	76.12	73.89	72.02	70.43	69.08	67.92	66.93	66.07	63.20	61.72
7000	91.94	88.81	86.21	84.02	82.17	80.59	79.24	78.08	77.08	73.73	72.01
8000	105.08	101.50	98.52	96.02	93.90	92.10	90.56	89.24	88.09	84.26	82.29
9000	118.21	114.18	110.83	108.02	105.64	103.61	101.88	100.39	99.10	94.80	92.58
10000	131.35	126.87	123.15	120.02	117.38	115.13	113.20	111.54	110.11	105.33	102.87
11000	144.48	139.56	135.46	132.02	129.11	126.64	124.52	122.70	121.12	115.86	113.15
12000	157.62	152.24	147.78	144.03	140.85	138.15	135.84	133.85	132.14	126.39	123.44
13000	170.75	164.93	160.09	156.03	152.59	149.66	147.16	145.01	143.15	136.92	133.72
14000	183.88	177.62	172.41	168.03	164.33	161.18	158.48	156.16	154.16	147.46	144.01
15000	197.02	190.30	184.72	180.03	176.06	172.69	169.80	167.31	165.17	157.99	154.30
16000	210.15	202.99	197.03	192.03	187.80	184.20	181.12	178.47	176.18	168.52	164.58
17000	223.29	215.68	209.35	204.03	199.54	195.71	192.44	189.62	187.19	179.05	174.87
18000	236.42	228.36	221.66	216.04	211.28	207.22	203.76	200.77	198.20	189.59	185.16
19000	249.55	241.05	233.98	228.04	223.01	218.74	215.08	211.93	209.21	200.12	195.44
20000	262.69	253.74	246.29	240.04	234.75	230.25	226.40	223.08	220.22	210.65	205.73
21000	275.82	266.42	258.61	252.04	246.49	241.76	237.71	234.24	231.23	221.18	216.01
22000	288.96	279.11	270.92	264.04	258.22	253.27	249.03	245.39	242.24	231.71	226.30
23000	302.09	291.80	283.23	276.04	269.96	264.78	260.35	256.54	253.25	242.25	236.59
24000	315.23	304.48	295.55	288.05	281.70	276.30	271.67	267.70	264.27	252.78	246.87
25000	328.36	317.17	307.86	300.05	293.44	287.81	282.99	278.85	275.28	263.31	257.16
26000	341.49	329.86	320.18	312.05	305.17	299.32	294.31	290.01	286.29	273.84	267.44
27000	354.63	342.54	332.49	324.05	316.91	310.83	305.63	301.16	297.30	284.38	277.73
28000	367.76	355.23	344.81	336.05	328.65	322.35	316.95	312.31	308.31	294.91	288.02
29000	380.90	367.92	357.12	348.05	340.39	333.86	328.27	323.47	319.32	305.44	298.30
30000	394.03	380.60	369.43	360.06	352.12	345.37	339.59	334.62	330.33	315.97	308.59
31000	407.16	393.29	381.75	372.06	363.86	356.88	350.91	345.77	341.34	326.50	318.87
32000	420.30	405.98	394.06	384.06	375.60	368.39	362.23	356.93	352.35	337.04	329.16
33000	433.43	418.66	406.38	396.06	387.33	379.91	373.55	368.08	363.36	347.57	339.45
34000	446.57	431.35	418.69	408.06	399.07	391.42	384.87	379.24	374.37	358.10	349.73
35000	459.70	444.04	431.01	420.06	410.81	402.93	396.19	390.39	385.39	368.63	360.02
36000	472.84	456.72	443.32	432.07	422.55	414.44	4C7.51	401.54	396.40	379.17	370.31
37000	485.97	469.41	455.63	444.07	434.28	425.95	418.83	412.70	407.41	389.70	380.59
38000	499.10	482.10	467.95	456.07	446.02	437.47	430.15	423.85	418.42	400.23	390.88
39000	512.24	494.78	480.26	468.07	457.76	448.98	441.47	435.01	429.43	410.76	401.16
40000	525.37	507.47	492.58	480.07	469.50	460.49	452.79	446.16	440.44	421.29	411.45
41000	538.51	520.16	504.89	492.07	481.23	472.00	464.10	457.31	451.45	431.83	421.74
42000	551.64	532.84	517.21	504.08	492.97	483.52	475.42	468.47	462.46	442.36	432.02
43000	564.78	545.53	529.52	516.08	504.71	495.03	486.74	479.62	473.47	452.89	442.31
44000	577.91	558.22	541.83	528.08	516.44	506.54	498.06	490.77	484.48	463.42	452.60
45000	591.04	570.90	554.15	540.08	528.18	518.05	509.38	501.93	495.49	473.96	462.88
46000	604.18	583.59	566.46	552.08	539.92	529.56	520.70	513.08	506.50	484.49	473.17
47000	617.31	596.28	578.78	564.08	551.66	541.08	532.02	524.24	517.52	495.02	483.45
48000	630.45	608.96	591.09	576.09	563.39	552.59	543.34	535.39	528.53	505.55	493.74
49000	643.58	621.65	603.41	588.09	575.13	564.10	554.66	546.54	539.54	516.08	504.03
50000	656.71	634.34	615.72	600.09	586.87	575.61	565.98	557.70	550.55	526.62	514.31
55000	722.39	697.77	677.29	660.10	645.55	633.17	622.58	613.47	605.60	579.28	565.74
60000	788.06	761.20	738.86	720.11	704.24	690.73	679.18	669.24	660.66	631.94	617.17
65000	853.73	824.64	800.43	780.11	762.93	748.30	735.77	725.01	715.71	684.60	668.60
70000	919.40	888.07	862.01	840.12	821.61	805.86	792.37	780.77	770.77	737.26	720.03
75000	985.07	951.50	923.58	900.13	880.30	863.42	848.97	836.54	825.82	789.92	771.46
80000	1050.74	1014.94	985.15	960.14	938.99	920.98	905.57	892.31	880.87	842.58	822.90
85000	1116.41	1078.37	1046.72	1020.15	997.67	978.54	962.16	948.08	935.93	895.25	874.33
90000	1182.08	1141.80	1108.29	1080.16	1056.36	1036.11	1018.76	1003.85	990.98	947.91	925.76
95000	1247.75	1205.24	1169.86	1140.16	1115.04	1093.66	1075.36	1059.62	1046.04	1000.57	977.19
100000	1313.42	1268.67	1231.43	1200.17	1173.73	1151.22	1131.96	1115.39	1101.09	1053.23	1028.62

12.25% Principal and Interest
Monthly Payment Amortization Table

Term Amount	1 Year	2 Years	3 Years	4 Years	5 Years	6 Years	7 Years	8 Years	9 Years	10 Years	11 Years
50	4.45	2.36	1.67	1.33	1.12	.99	.89	.82	.77	.73	.70
100	8.90	4.72	3.34	2.65	2.24	1.97	1.78	1.64	1.54	1.45	1.39
200	17.80	9.44	6.67	5.30	4.48	3.94	3.56	3.28	3.07	2.90	2.77
300	26.69	14.16	10.01	7.94	6.72	5.91	5.34	4.92	4.60	4.35	4.15
400	35.59	18.88	13.34	10.59	8.95	7.88	7.12	6.56	6.14	5.80	5.54
500	44.49	23.60	16.67	13.23	11.19	9.85	8.90	8.20	7.67	7.25	6.92
600	53.38	28.32	20.01	15.88	13.43	11.81	10.68	9.84	9.20	8.70	8.30
700	62.28	33.04	23.34	18.52	15.66	13.78	12.46	11.48	10.73	10.15	9.68
800	71.18	37.76	26.67	21.17	17.90	15.75	14.23	13.12	12.27	11.60	11.07
900	80.07	42.48	30.01	23.82	20.14	17.72	16.01	14.76	13.80	13.05	12.45
1000	88.97	47.20	33.34	26.46	22.38	19.69	17.79	16.40	15.33	14.50	13.83
2000	177.94	94.39	66.67	52.92	44.75	39.37	35.58	32.79	30.66	28.99	27.66
3000	266.90	141.58	100.01	79.38	67.12	59.05	53.37	49.18	45.98	43.48	41.48
4000	355.87	188.77	133.34	105.83	89.49	78.73	71.15	65.57	61.31	57.97	55.31
5000	444.83	235.96	166.67	132.29	111.86	98.41	88.94	81.96	76.63	72.46	69.14
6000	533.80	283.15	200.01	158.75	134.23	118.09	106.73	98.35	91.96	86.96	82.96
7000	622.77	330.34	233.34	185.20	156.60	137.77	124.51	114.74	107.28	101.45	96.79
8000	711.73	377.53	266.68	211.66	178.97	157.45	142.30	131.13	122.61	115.94	110.62
9000	800.70	424.72	300.01	238.12	201.34	177.13	160.09	147.52	137.93	130.43	124.44
10000	889.66	471.91	333.34	264.57	223.71	196.81	177.87	163.91	153.26	144.92	138.27
11000	978.63	519.10	366.68	291.03	246.09	216.49	195.66	180.30	168.59	159.42	152.09
12000	1067.59	566.29	400.01	317.49	268.46	236.17	213.45	196.69	183.91	173.91	165.92
13000	1156.56	613.48	433.34	343.94	290.83	255.85	231.23	213.08	199.24	188.40	179.75
14000	1245.53	660.67	466.68	370.40	313.20	275.53	249.02	229.47	214.56	202.89	193.57
15000	1334.49	707.86	500.01	396.86	335.57	295.21	266.81	245.86	229.89	217.38	207.40
16000	1423.46	755.05	533.35	423.31	357.94	314.89	284.59	262.25	245.21	231.88	221.23
17000	1512.42	802.24	566.68	449.77	380.31	334.57	302.38	278.64	260.54	246.37	235.05
18000	1601.39	849.43	600.01	476.23	402.68	354.25	320.17	295.03	275.86	260.86	248.88
19000	1690.35	896.62	633.35	502.68	425.05	373.93	337.95	311.42	291.19	275.35	262.70
20000	1779.32	943.81	666.68	529.14	447.42	393.61	355.74	327.82	306.52	289.84	276.53
21000	1868.29	991.00	700.02	555.60	469.80	413.29	373.53	344.21	321.84	304.34	290.36
22000	1957.25	1038.19	733.35	582.05	492.17	432.97	391.31	360.60	337.17	318.83	304.18
23000	2046.22	1085.38	766.68	608.51	514.54	452.66	409.10	376.99	352.49	333.32	318.01
24000	2135.18	1132.57	800.02	634.97	536.91	472.34	426.89	393.38	367.82	347.81	331.84
25000	2224.15	1179.76	833.35	661.42	559.28	492.02	444.67	409.77	383.14	362.30	345.66
26000	2313.12	1226.95	866.68	687.88	581.65	511.70	462.46	426.16	398.47	376.80	359.49
27000	2402.08	1274.14	900.02	714.34	604.02	531.38	480.25	442.55	413.79	391.29	373.31
28000	2491.05	1321.33	933.35	740.79	626.39	551.06	498.03	458.94	429.12	405.78	387.14
29000	2580.01	1368.52	966.69	767.25	648.76	570.74	515.82	475.33	444.45	420.27	400.97
30000	2668.98	1415.71	1000.02	793.71	671.13	590.42	533.61	491.72	459.77	434.76	414.79
31000	2757.94	1462.90	1033.35	820.16	693.51	610.10	551.39	508.11	475.10	449.26	428.62
32000	2846.91	1510.09	1066.69	846.62	715.88	629.78	569.18	524.50	490.42	463.75	442.45
33000	2935.88	1557.29	1100.02	873.08	738.25	649.46	586.97	540.89	505.75	478.24	456.27
34000	3024.84	1604.48	1133.36	899.53	760.62	669.14	604.75	557.28	521.07	492.73	470.10
35000	3113.81	1651.67	1166.69	925.99	782.99	688.82	622.54	573.67	536.40	507.22	483.92
36000	3202.77	1698.86	1200.02	952.45	805.36	708.50	640.33	590.06	551.72	521.72	497.75
37000	3291.74	1746.05	1233.36	978.90	827.73	728.18	658.11	606.45	567.05	536.21	511.58
38000	3380.70	1793.24	1266.69	1005.36	850.10	747.86	675.90	622.84	582.38	550.70	525.40
39000	3469.67	1840.43	1300.02	1031.82	872.47	767.54	693.69	639.24	597.70	565.19	539.23
40000	3558.64	1887.62	1333.36	1058.28	894.84	787.22	711.47	655.63	613.03	579.68	553.06
41000	3647.60	1934.81	1366.69	1084.73	917.22	806.90	729.26	672.02	628.35	594.18	566.88
42000	3736.57	1982.00	1400.03	1111.19	939.59	826.58	747.05	688.41	643.68	608.67	580.71
43000	3825.53	2029.19	1433.36	1137.65	961.96	846.26	764.83	704.80	659.00	623.16	594.53
44000	3914.50	2076.38	1466.69	1164.10	984.33	865.94	782.62	721.19	674.33	637.65	608.36
45000	4003.47	2123.57	1500.03	1190.56	1006.70	885.62	800.41	737.58	689.65	652.14	622.19
46000	4092.43	2170.76	1533.36	1217.02	1029.07	905.31	818.19	753.97	704.98	666.64	636.01
47000	4181.40	2217.95	1566.70	1243.47	1051.44	924.99	835.98	770.36	720.31	681.13	649.84
48000	4270.36	2265.14	1600.03	1269.93	1073.81	944.67	853.77	786.75	735.63	695.62	663.67
49000	4359.33	2312.33	1633.36	1296.39	1096.18	964.35	871.55	803.14	750.96	710.11	677.49
50000	4448.29	2359.52	1666.70	1322.84	1118.55	984.03	889.34	819.53	766.28	724.60	691.32
55000	4893.12	2595.47	1833.37	1455.13	1230.41	1082.43	978.27	901.48	842.91	797.06	760.45
60000	5337.95	2831.42	2000.04	1587.41	1342.26	1180.83	1067.21	983.44	919.54	869.52	829.58
65000	5782.78	3067.37	2166.70	1719.69	1454.12	1279.23	1156.14	1065.39	996.17	941.98	898.71
70000	6227.61	3303.33	2333.37	1851.98	1565.97	1377.64	1245.07	1147.34	1072.79	1014.44	967.84
75000	6672.44	3539.28	2500.04	1984.26	1677.83	1476.04	1334.01	1229.29	1149.42	1086.90	1036.97
80000	7117.27	3775.23	2666.71	2116.55	1789.68	1574.44	1422.94	1311.25	1226.05	1159.36	1106.11
85000	7562.10	4011.18	2833.38	2248.83	1901.54	1672.84	1511.88	1393.20	1302.68	1231.82	1175.24
90000	8006.93	4247.13	3000.05	2381.11	2013.39	1771.24	1600.81	1475.15	1379.30	1304.28	1244.37
95000	8451.75	4483.08	3166.72	2513.40	2125.25	1869.65	1689.74	1557.10	1455.93	1376.74	1313.50
100000	8896.58	4719.04	3333.39	2645.68	2237.10	1968.05	1778.68	1639.06	1532.56	1449.20	1382.63

Principal and Interest
Monthly Payment Amortization Table

12.25%

Term / Amount	12 Years	13 Years	14 Years	15 Years	16 Years	17 Years	18 Years	19 Years	20 Years	25 Years	30 Years
50	.67	.65	.63	.61	.60	.59	.58	.57	.56	.54	.53
100	1.33	1.29	1.25	1.22	1.20	1.17	1.15	1.14	1.12	1.08	1.05
200	2.66	2.57	2.50	2.44	2.39	2.34	2.30	2.27	2.24	2.15	2.10
300	3.99	3.86	3.75	3.65	3.58	3.51	3.45	3.40	3.36	3.22	3.15
400	5.32	5.14	4.99	4.87	4.77	4.68	4.60	4.54	4.48	4.29	4.20
500	6.65	6.43	6.24	6.09	5.96	5.84	5.75	5.67	5.60	5.36	5.24
600	7.98	7.71	7.49	7.30	7.15	7.01	6.90	6.80	6.72	6.44	6.29
700	9.31	8.99	8.74	8.52	8.34	8.18	8.05	7.93	7.83	7.51	7.34
800	10.63	10.28	9.98	9.74	9.53	9.35	9.20	9.07	8.95	8.58	8.39
900	11.96	11.56	11.23	10.95	10.72	10.52	10.35	10.20	10.07	9.65	9.44
1000	13.29	12.85	12.48	12.17	11.91	11.68	11.49	11.33	11.19	10.72	10.48
2000	26.58	25.69	24.95	24.33	23.81	23.36	22.98	22.66	22.38	21.44	20.96
3000	39.86	38.53	37.42	36.49	35.71	35.04	34.47	33.98	33.56	32.16	31.44
4000	53.15	51.37	49.90	48.66	47.61	46.72	45.96	45.31	44.75	42.87	41.92
5000	66.43	64.21	62.37	60.82	59.51	58.40	57.45	56.64	55.93	53.59	52.40
6000	79.72	77.06	74.84	72.98	71.41	70.08	68.94	67.96	67.12	64.31	62.88
7000	93.01	89.90	87.31	85.15	83.32	81.76	80.43	79.29	78.30	75.03	73.36
8000	106.29	102.74	99.79	97.31	95.22	93.44	91.92	90.61	89.49	85.74	83.84
9000	119.58	115.58	112.26	109.47	107.12	105.12	103.41	101.94	100.68	96.46	94.32
10000	132.86	128.42	124.73	121.63	119.02	116.80	114.90	113.27	111.86	107.18	104.79
11000	146.15	141.26	137.20	133.80	130.92	128.48	126.39	124.59	123.05	117.90	115.27
12000	159.44	154.11	149.68	145.96	142.82	140.16	137.88	135.92	134.23	128.61	125.75
13000	172.72	166.95	162.15	158.12	154.72	151.83	149.37	147.25	145.42	139.33	136.23
14000	186.01	179.79	174.62	170.29	166.63	163.51	160.85	158.57	156.60	150.05	146.71
15000	199.29	192.63	187.09	182.45	178.53	175.19	172.34	169.90	167.79	160.77	157.19
16000	212.58	205.47	199.57	194.61	190.43	186.87	183.83	181.22	178.98	171.48	167.67
17000	225.87	218.31	212.04	206.78	202.33	198.55	195.32	192.55	190.16	182.20	178.15
18000	239.15	231.16	224.51	218.94	214.23	210.23	206.81	203.88	201.35	192.92	188.63
19000	252.44	244.00	236.98	231.10	226.13	221.91	218.30	215.20	212.53	203.64	199.11
20000	265.72	256.84	249.46	243.26	238.04	233.59	229.79	226.53	223.72	214.35	209.58
21000	279.01	269.68	261.93	255.43	249.94	245.27	241.28	237.86	234.90	225.07	220.06
22000	292.30	282.52	274.40	267.59	261.84	256.95	252.77	249.18	246.09	235.79	230.54
23000	305.58	295.36	286.87	279.75	273.74	268.63	264.26	260.51	257.27	246.51	241.02
24000	318.87	308.21	299.35	291.92	285.64	280.31	275.75	271.83	268.46	257.22	251.50
25000	332.15	321.05	311.82	304.08	297.54	291.99	287.24	283.16	279.65	267.94	261.98
26000	345.44	333.89	324.29	316.24	309.44	303.66	298.73	294.49	290.83	278.66	272.46
27000	358.73	346.73	336.76	328.41	321.35	315.34	310.22	305.81	302.02	289.38	282.94
28000	372.01	359.57	349.24	340.57	333.25	327.02	321.70	317.14	313.20	300.09	293.42
29000	385.30	372.42	361.71	352.73	345.15	338.70	333.19	328.46	324.39	310.81	303.89
30000	398.58	385.26	374.18	364.89	357.05	350.38	344.68	339.79	335.57	321.53	314.37
31000	411.87	398.10	386.65	377.06	368.95	362.06	356.17	351.12	346.76	332.25	324.85
32000	425.16	410.94	399.13	389.22	380.85	373.74	367.66	362.44	357.95	342.96	335.33
33000	438.44	423.78	411.60	401.38	392.75	385.42	379.15	373.77	369.13	353.68	345.81
34000	451.73	436.62	424.07	413.55	404.66	397.10	390.64	385.10	380.32	364.40	356.29
35000	465.01	449.47	436.54	425.71	416.56	408.78	402.13	396.42	391.50	375.12	366.77
36000	478.30	462.31	449.02	437.87	428.46	420.46	413.62	407.75	402.69	385.83	377.25
37000	491.59	475.15	461.49	450.04	440.36	432.14	425.11	419.07	413.87	396.55	387.73
38000	504.87	487.99	473.96	462.20	452.26	443.82	436.60	430.40	425.06	407.27	398.21
39000	518.16	500.83	486.43	474.36	464.16	455.49	448.09	441.73	436.25	417.99	408.68
40000	531.44	513.67	498.91	486.52	476.07	467.17	459.58	453.05	447.43	428.70	419.16
41000	544.73	526.52	511.38	498.69	487.97	478.85	471.07	464.38	458.62	439.42	429.64
42000	558.02	539.36	523.85	510.85	499.87	490.53	482.55	475.71	469.80	450.14	440.12
43000	571.30	552.20	536.32	523.01	511.77	502.21	494.04	487.03	480.99	460.85	450.60
44000	584.59	565.04	548.80	535.18	523.67	513.89	505.53	498.36	492.17	471.57	461.08
45000	597.87	577.88	561.27	547.34	535.57	525.57	517.02	509.68	503.36	482.29	471.56
46000	611.16	590.72	573.74	559.50	547.47	537.25	528.51	521.01	514.54	493.01	482.04
47000	624.45	603.57	586.21	571.67	559.38	548.93	540.00	532.34	525.73	503.72	492.52
48000	637.73	616.41	598.69	583.83	571.28	560.61	551.49	543.66	536.92	514.44	503.00
49000	651.02	629.25	611.16	595.99	583.18	572.29	562.98	554.99	548.10	525.16	513.47
50000	664.30	642.09	623.63	608.15	595.08	583.97	574.47	566.31	559.29	535.88	523.95
55000	730.73	706.30	685.99	668.97	654.59	642.36	631.91	622.95	615.22	589.46	576.35
60000	797.16	770.51	748.36	729.78	714.10	700.76	689.36	679.58	671.14	643.05	628.74
65000	863.59	834.72	810.72	790.60	773.60	759.15	746.81	736.21	727.07	696.64	681.14
70000	930.02	898.93	873.08	851.41	833.11	817.55	804.25	792.84	783.00	750.23	733.53
75000	996.45	963.13	935.45	912.23	892.62	875.95	861.70	849.47	838.93	803.81	785.93
80000	1062.88	1027.34	997.81	973.04	952.13	934.34	919.15	906.10	894.86	857.40	838.32
85000	1129.31	1091.55	1060.17	1033.86	1011.63	992.74	976.59	962.73	950.78	910.99	890.72
90000	1195.74	1155.76	1122.53	1094.67	1071.14	1051.14	1034.04	1019.36	1006.71	964.57	943.11
95000	1262.17	1219.97	1184.90	1155.49	1130.65	1109.53	1091.49	1075.99	1062.64	1018.16	995.51
100000	1328.60	1284.18	1247.26	1216.30	1190.16	1167.93	1148.93	1132.62	1118.57	1071.75	1047.90

12.50% Principal and Interest
Monthly Payment Amortization Table

Term / Amount	1 Year	2 Years	3 Years	4 Years	5 Years	6 Years	7 Years	8 Years	9 Years	10 Years	11 Years
50	4.46	2.37	1.68	1.33	1.13	1.00	.90	.83	.78	.74	.70
100	8.91	4.74	3.35	2.66	2.25	1.99	1.80	1.66	1.55	1.47	1.40
200	17.82	9.47	6.70	5.32	4.50	3.97	3.59	3.31	3.10	2.93	2.80
300	26.73	14.20	10.04	7.98	6.75	5.95	5.38	4.96	4.65	4.40	4.20
400	35.64	18.93	13.39	10.64	9.00	7.93	7.17	6.62	6.19	5.86	5.60
500	44.55	23.66	16.73	13.29	11.25	9.91	8.97	8.27	7.74	7.32	6.99
600	53.45	28.39	20.08	15.95	13.50	11.89	10.76	9.92	9.29	8.79	8.39
700	62.36	33.12	23.42	18.61	15.75	13.87	12.55	11.58	10.83	10.25	9.79
800	71.27	37.85	26.77	21.27	18.00	15.85	14.34	13.23	12.38	11.72	11.19
900	80.18	42.58	30.11	23.93	20.25	17.84	16.13	14.88	13.93	13.18	12.58
1000	89.09	47.31	33.46	26.58	22.50	19.82	17.93	16.53	15.47	14.64	13.98
2000	178.17	94.62	66.91	53.16	45.00	39.63	35.85	33.06	30.94	29.28	27.96
3000	267.25	141.93	100.37	79.74	67.50	59.44	53.77	49.59	46.41	43.92	41.93
4000	356.34	189.23	133.82	106.32	90.00	79.25	71.69	66.12	61.88	58.56	55.91
5000	445.42	236.54	167.27	132.90	112.49	99.06	89.61	82.65	77.34	73.19	69.88
6000	534.50	283.85	200.73	159.48	134.99	118.87	107.53	99.18	92.81	87.83	83.86
7000	623.59	331.16	234.18	186.06	157.49	138.68	125.45	115.71	108.28	102.47	97.83
8000	712.67	378.46	267.63	212.64	179.99	158.49	143.37	132.24	123.75	117.11	111.81
9000	801.75	425.77	301.09	239.22	202.49	178.31	161.30	148.76	139.21	131.74	125.78
10000	890.83	473.08	334.54	265.80	224.99	198.12	179.22	165.29	154.68	146.38	139.76
11000	979.92	520.39	367.99	292.38	247.48	217.93	197.14	181.82	170.15	161.02	153.73
12000	1069.00	567.69	401.45	318.96	269.98	237.74	215.06	198.35	185.62	175.66	167.71
13000	1158.08	615.00	434.90	345.54	292.48	257.55	232.98	214.88	201.08	190.29	181.69
14000	1247.17	662.31	468.36	372.12	314.97	277.36	250.90	231.41	216.55	204.93	195.66
15000	1336.25	709.61	501.81	398.70	337.47	297.17	268.82	247.94	232.02	219.57	209.64
16000	1425.33	756.92	535.26	425.28	359.97	316.98	286.74	264.47	247.49	234.21	223.61
17000	1514.41	804.23	568.72	451.86	382.47	336.80	304.67	280.99	262.95	248.84	237.59
18000	1603.50	851.54	602.17	478.44	404.97	356.61	322.59	297.52	278.42	263.48	251.56
19000	1692.58	898.84	635.62	505.02	427.47	376.42	340.51	314.05	293.89	278.12	265.54
20000	1781.66	946.15	669.08	531.60	449.96	396.23	358.43	330.58	309.36	292.76	279.51
21000	1870.75	993.46	702.53	558.18	472.46	416.04	376.35	347.11	324.82	307.39	293.49
22000	1959.83	1040.77	735.98	584.76	494.96	435.85	394.27	363.64	340.29	322.03	307.46
23000	2048.91	1088.07	769.44	611.34	517.46	455.66	412.19	380.17	355.76	336.67	321.44
24000	2137.99	1135.38	802.89	637.92	539.96	475.47	430.11	396.70	371.23	351.31	335.42
25000	2227.08	1182.69	836.35	664.50	562.45	495.28	448.04	413.23	386.69	365.95	349.39
26000	2316.16	1230.00	869.80	691.08	584.95	515.10	465.96	429.75	402.16	380.58	363.37
27000	2405.24	1277.30	903.25	717.66	607.45	534.91	483.88	446.28	417.63	395.22	377.34
28000	2494.33	1324.61	936.71	744.24	629.95	554.72	501.80	462.81	433.10	409.86	391.32
29000	2583.41	1371.92	970.16	770.82	652.45	574.53	519.72	479.34	448.56	424.50	405.29
30000	2672.49	1419.22	1003.61	797.40	674.94	594.34	537.64	495.87	464.03	439.13	419.27
31000	2761.57	1466.53	1037.07	823.98	697.44	614.15	555.56	512.40	479.50	453.77	433.24
32000	2850.66	1513.84	1070.52	850.56	719.94	633.96	573.48	528.93	494.97	468.41	447.22
33000	2939.74	1561.15	1103.97	877.14	742.44	653.77	591.41	545.46	510.43	483.05	461.19
34000	3028.82	1608.45	1137.43	903.72	764.93	673.59	609.33	561.98	525.90	497.68	475.17
35000	3117.91	1655.76	1170.88	930.30	787.43	693.40	627.25	578.51	541.37	512.32	489.15
36000	3206.99	1703.07	1204.34	956.88	809.93	713.21	645.17	595.04	556.84	526.96	503.12
37000	3296.07	1750.38	1237.79	983.46	832.43	733.02	663.09	611.57	572.30	541.60	517.10
38000	3385.15	1797.68	1271.24	1010.04	854.93	752.83	681.01	628.10	587.77	556.23	531.07
39000	3474.24	1844.99	1304.70	1036.63	877.42	772.64	698.93	644.63	603.24	570.87	545.05
40000	3563.32	1892.30	1338.15	1063.20	899.92	792.45	716.85	661.16	618.71	585.51	559.02
41000	3652.40	1939.60	1371.60	1089.78	922.42	812.26	734.78	677.69	634.17	600.15	573.00
42000	3741.49	1986.91	1405.06	1116.36	944.92	832.07	752.70	694.21	649.64	614.78	586.97
43000	3830.57	2034.22	1438.51	1142.94	967.42	851.89	770.62	710.74	665.11	629.42	600.95
44000	3919.65	2081.53	1471.96	1169.52	989.91	871.70	788.54	727.27	680.58	644.06	614.92
45000	4008.73	2128.83	1505.42	1196.10	1012.41	891.51	806.46	743.80	696.05	658.70	628.90
46000	4097.82	2176.14	1538.87	1222.68	1034.91	911.32	824.38	760.33	711.51	673.34	642.87
47000	4186.90	2223.45	1572.33	1249.26	1057.41	931.13	842.30	776.86	726.98	687.97	656.85
48000	4275.98	2270.76	1605.78	1275.84	1079.91	950.94	860.22	793.39	742.45	702.61	670.83
49000	4365.07	2318.06	1639.23	1302.42	1102.40	970.75	878.15	809.92	757.91	717.25	684.80
50000	4454.15	2365.37	1672.69	1329.00	1124.90	990.56	896.07	826.45	773.38	731.89	698.78
55000	4899.56	2601.91	1839.95	1461.90	1237.39	1089.62	985.67	909.09	850.72	805.07	768.65
60000	5344.98	2838.44	2007.22	1594.80	1349.88	1188.68	1075.28	991.73	928.06	878.26	838.53
65000	5790.39	3074.98	2174.49	1727.70	1462.37	1287.73	1164.89	1074.38	1005.40	951.45	908.41
70000	6235.81	3311.52	2341.76	1860.60	1574.86	1386.79	1254.49	1157.02	1082.73	1024.64	978.29
75000	6681.22	3548.05	2509.03	1993.50	1687.35	1485.84	1344.10	1239.67	1160.07	1097.83	1048.16
80000	7126.63	3784.59	2676.30	2126.40	1799.84	1584.90	1433.70	1322.31	1237.41	1171.01	1118.04
85000	7572.05	4021.13	2843.56	2259.30	1912.33	1683.96	1523.31	1404.95	1314.75	1244.20	1187.92
90000	8017.46	4257.66	3010.83	2392.20	2024.82	1783.01	1612.92	1487.60	1392.08	1317.39	1257.79
95000	8462.88	4494.20	3178.10	2525.10	2137.31	1882.07	1702.52	1570.24	1469.42	1390.58	1327.67
100000	8908.29	4730.74	3345.37	2658.00	2249.80	1981.12	1792.13	1652.89	1546.76	1463.77	1397.55

Principal and Interest
Monthly Payment Amortization Table   12.50%

Term / Amount	12 Years	13 Years	14 Years	15 Years	16 Years	17 Years	18 Years	19 Years	20 Years	25 Years	30 Years
50	.68	.65	.64	.62	.61	.60	.59	.58	.57	.55	.54
100	1.35	1.30	1.27	1.24	1.21	1.19	1.17	1.15	1.14	1.10	1.07
200	2.69	2.60	2.53	2.47	2.42	2.37	2.34	2.30	2.28	2.19	2.14
300	4.04	3.90	3.79	3.70	3.63	3.56	3.50	3.45	3.41	3.28	3.21
400	5.38	5.20	5.06	4.94	4.83	4.74	4.67	4.60	4.55	4.37	4.27
500	6.72	6.50	6.32	6.17	6.04	5.93	5.84	5.75	5.69	5.46	5.34
600	8.07	7.80	7.58	7.40	7.25	7.11	7.00	6.90	6.82	6.55	6.41
700	9.41	9.10	8.85	8.63	8.45	8.30	8.17	8.05	7.96	7.64	7.48
800	10.76	10.40	10.11	9.87	9.66	9.48	9.33	9.20	9.09	8.73	8.54
900	12.10	11.70	11.37	11.10	10.87	10.67	10.50	10.35	10.23	9.82	9.61
1000	13.44	13.00	12.64	12.33	12.07	11.85	11.67	11.50	11.37	10.91	10.68
2000	26.88	26.00	25.27	24.66	24.14	23.70	23.33	23.00	22.73	21.81	21.35
3000	40.32	39.00	37.90	36.98	36.21	35.55	34.99	34.50	34.09	32.72	32.02
4000	53.76	52.00	50.53	49.31	48.27	47.39	46.65	46.00	45.45	43.62	42.70
5000	67.20	64.99	63.16	61.63	60.34	59.24	58.31	57.50	56.81	54.52	53.37
6000	80.64	77.99	75.80	73.96	72.41	71.09	69.97	69.00	68.17	65.43	64.04
7000	94.08	90.99	88.43	86.28	84.47	82.94	81.63	80.50	79.53	76.33	74.71
8000	107.51	103.99	101.06	98.61	96.54	94.78	93.29	92.00	90.90	87.23	85.39
9000	120.95	116.98	113.69	110.93	108.61	106.63	104.95	103.50	102.26	98.14	96.06
10000	134.39	129.98	126.32	123.26	120.67	118.48	116.61	115.00	113.62	109.04	106.73
11000	147.83	142.98	138.95	135.58	132.74	130.32	128.27	126.50	124.98	119.94	117.40
12000	161.27	155.98	151.59	147.91	144.81	142.17	139.93	138.00	136.34	130.85	128.08
13000	174.71	168.97	164.22	160.23	156.87	154.02	151.59	149.50	147.70	141.75	138.75
14000	188.15	181.97	176.85	172.56	168.94	165.87	163.25	161.00	159.06	152.65	149.42
15000	201.58	194.97	189.48	184.88	181.01	177.71	174.91	172.50	170.43	163.56	160.09
16000	215.02	207.97	202.11	197.21	193.07	189.56	186.57	184.00	181.79	174.46	170.77
17000	228.46	220.97	214.74	209.53	205.14	201.41	198.23	195.50	193.15	185.37	181.44
18000	241.90	233.96	227.38	221.86	217.21	213.26	209.89	207.00	204.51	196.27	192.11
19000	255.34	246.96	240.01	234.18	229.27	225.10	221.55	218.50	215.87	207.17	202.78
20000	268.78	259.96	252.64	246.51	241.34	236.95	233.21	230.00	227.23	218.08	213.46
21000	282.22	272.96	265.27	258.83	253.41	248.80	244.87	241.49	238.59	228.98	224.13
22000	295.65	285.95	277.90	271.16	265.47	260.64	256.53	252.99	249.96	239.88	234.80
23000	309.09	298.95	290.53	283.49	277.54	272.49	268.19	264.49	261.32	250.79	245.47
24000	322.53	311.95	303.17	295.81	289.61	284.34	279.85	275.99	272.68	261.69	256.15
25000	335.97	324.95	315.80	308.14	301.67	296.19	291.51	287.49	284.04	272.59	266.82
26000	349.41	337.94	328.43	320.46	313.74	308.03	303.17	298.99	295.40	283.50	277.49
27000	362.85	350.94	341.06	332.79	325.81	319.88	314.83	310.49	306.76	294.40	288.16
28000	376.29	363.94	353.69	345.11	337.87	331.73	326.49	321.99	318.12	305.30	298.84
29000	389.72	376.94	366.32	357.44	349.94	343.58	338.15	333.49	329.49	316.21	309.51
30000	403.16	389.93	378.96	369.76	362.01	355.42	349.81	344.99	340.85	327.11	320.18
31000	416.60	402.93	391.59	382.09	374.07	367.27	361.47	356.49	352.21	338.01	330.85
32000	430.04	415.93	404.22	394.41	386.14	379.12	373.13	367.99	363.57	348.92	341.53
33000	443.48	428.93	416.85	406.74	398.21	390.96	384.79	379.49	374.93	359.82	352.20
34000	456.92	441.93	429.48	419.06	410.27	402.81	396.45	390.99	386.29	370.73	362.87
35000	470.36	454.92	442.11	431.39	422.34	414.66	408.11	402.49	397.65	381.63	373.55
36000	483.79	467.92	454.75	443.71	434.41	426.51	419.77	413.99	409.02	392.53	384.22
37000	497.23	480.92	467.38	456.04	446.47	438.35	431.43	425.49	420.38	403.44	394.89
38000	510.67	493.92	480.01	468.36	458.54	450.20	443.09	436.99	431.74	414.34	405.56
39000	524.11	506.91	492.64	480.69	470.61	462.05	454.75	448.49	443.10	425.24	416.24
40000	537.55	519.91	505.27	493.01	482.67	473.90	466.41	459.99	454.46	436.15	426.91
41000	550.99	532.91	517.90	505.34	494.74	485.74	478.07	471.48	465.82	447.05	437.58
42000	564.43	545.91	530.54	517.66	506.81	497.59	489.73	482.98	477.18	457.95	448.25
43000	577.86	558.90	543.17	529.99	518.87	509.44	501.39	494.48	488.55	468.86	458.93
44000	591.30	571.90	555.80	542.31	530.94	521.28	513.05	505.98	499.91	479.76	469.60
45000	604.74	584.90	568.43	554.64	543.01	533.13	524.71	517.48	511.27	490.66	480.27
46000	618.18	597.90	581.06	566.97	555.07	544.98	536.37	528.98	522.63	501.57	490.94
47000	631.62	610.90	593.69	579.29	567.14	556.83	548.03	540.48	533.99	512.47	501.62
48000	645.06	623.89	606.33	591.62	579.21	568.67	559.69	551.98	545.35	523.37	512.29
49000	658.50	636.89	618.96	603.94	591.27	580.52	571.35	563.48	556.71	534.28	522.96
50000	671.93	649.89	631.59	616.27	603.34	592.37	583.01	574.98	568.08	545.18	533.63
55000	739.13	714.88	694.75	677.89	663.67	651.60	641.31	632.48	624.88	599.70	587.00
60000	806.32	779.86	757.91	739.52	724.01	710.84	699.61	689.98	681.69	654.22	640.36
65000	873.51	844.85	821.06	801.14	784.34	770.08	757.91	747.47	738.50	708.74	693.72
70000	940.71	909.84	884.22	862.77	844.67	829.31	816.21	804.97	795.30	763.25	747.09
75000	1007.90	974.83	947.38	924.40	905.01	888.55	874.51	862.47	852.11	817.77	800.45
80000	1075.09	1039.82	1010.54	986.02	965.34	947.79	932.81	919.97	908.92	872.29	853.81
85000	1142.28	1104.81	1073.70	1047.65	1025.67	1007.02	991.11	977.46	965.72	926.81	907.17
90000	1209.48	1169.79	1136.86	1109.27	1086.01	1066.26	1049.41	1034.96	1022.53	981.32	960.54
95000	1276.67	1234.78	1200.01	1170.90	1146.34	1125.49	1107.71	1092.46	1079.34	1035.84	1013.90
100000	1343.86	1299.77	1263.17	1232.53	1206.67	1184.73	1166.01	1149.96	1136.15	1090.36	1067.26

12.75% Principal and Interest
Monthly Payment Amortization Table

Term Amount	1 Year	2 Years	3 Years	4 Years	5 Years	6 Years	7 Years	8 Years	9 Years	10 Years	11 Years
50	4.47	2.38	1.68	1.34	1.14	1.00	.91	.84	.79	.74	.71
100	8.93	4.75	3.36	2.68	2.27	2.00	1.81	1.67	1.57	1.48	1.42
200	17.85	9.49	6.72	5.35	4.53	3.99	3.62	3.34	3.13	2.96	2.83
300	26.77	14.23	10.08	8.02	6.79	5.99	5.42	5.01	4.69	4.44	4.24
400	35.69	18.97	13.43	10.69	9.06	7.98	7.23	6.67	6.25	5.92	5.66
500	44.61	23.72	16.79	13.36	11.32	9.98	9.03	8.34	7.81	7.40	7.07
600	53.53	28.46	20.15	16.03	13.58	11.97	10.84	10.01	9.37	8.88	8.48
700	62.45	33.20	23.51	18.70	15.84	13.96	12.64	11.67	10.93	10.35	9.89
800	71.37	37.94	26.86	21.37	18.11	15.96	14.45	13.34	12.49	11.83	11.31
900	80.29	42.69	30.22	24.04	20.37	17.95	16.26	15.01	14.05	13.31	12.72
1000	89.21	47.43	33.58	26.71	22.63	19.95	18.06	16.67	15.62	14.79	14.13
2000	178.41	94.85	67.15	53.41	45.26	39.89	36.12	33.34	31.23	29.57	28.26
3000	267.61	142.28	100.73	80.12	67.88	59.83	54.17	50.01	46.84	44.36	42.38
4000	356.81	189.70	134.30	106.82	90.51	79.77	72.23	66.68	62.45	59.14	56.51
5000	446.01	237.13	167.87	133.52	113.13	99.72	90.29	83.34	78.06	73.92	70.63
6000	535.21	284.55	201.45	160.23	135.76	119.66	108.34	100.01	93.67	88.71	84.76
7000	624.41	331.98	235.02	186.93	158.38	139.60	126.40	116.68	109.28	103.49	98.88
8000	713.61	379.40	268.59	213.63	181.01	159.54	144.46	133.35	124.89	118.28	113.01
9000	802.81	426.83	302.17	240.34	203.63	179.49	162.51	150.01	140.50	133.06	127.13
10000	892.01	474.25	335.74	267.04	226.26	199.43	180.57	166.68	156.11	147.84	141.26
11000	981.21	521.67	369.32	293.74	248.88	219.37	198.62	183.35	171.72	162.63	155.38
12000	1070.41	569.10	402.89	320.45	271.51	239.31	216.68	200.02	187.33	177.41	169.51
13000	1159.61	616.52	436.46	347.15	294.13	259.26	234.74	216.69	202.94	192.20	183.63
14000	1248.81	663.95	470.04	373.86	316.76	279.20	252.79	233.35	218.55	206.98	197.76
15000	1338.01	711.37	503.61	400.56	339.38	299.14	270.85	250.02	234.16	221.76	211.89
16000	1427.21	758.80	537.18	427.26	362.01	319.08	288.91	266.69	249.77	236.55	226.01
17000	1516.41	806.22	570.76	453.97	384.64	339.03	306.96	283.36	265.38	251.33	240.14
18000	1605.61	853.65	604.33	480.67	407.26	358.97	325.02	300.02	280.99	266.12	254.26
19000	1694.81	901.07	637.90	507.37	429.89	378.91	343.08	316.69	296.60	280.90	268.39
20000	1784.01	948.49	671.48	534.08	452.51	398.85	361.13	333.36	312.21	295.68	282.51
21000	1873.21	995.92	705.05	560.78	475.14	418.80	379.19	350.03	327.82	310.47	296.64
22000	1962.41	1043.34	738.63	587.48	497.76	438.74	397.24	366.69	343.43	325.25	310.76
23000	2051.61	1090.77	772.20	614.19	520.39	458.68	415.30	383.36	359.04	340.04	324.89
24000	2140.81	1138.19	805.77	640.89	543.01	478.62	433.36	400.03	374.65	354.82	339.01
25000	2230.01	1185.62	839.35	667.59	565.64	498.57	451.41	416.70	390.26	369.60	353.14
26000	2319.21	1233.04	872.92	694.30	588.26	518.51	469.47	433.37	405.87	384.39	367.26
27000	2408.41	1280.47	906.49	721.00	610.89	538.45	487.53	450.03	421.48	399.17	381.39
28000	2497.61	1327.89	940.07	747.71	633.51	558.39	505.58	466.70	437.09	413.96	395.52
29000	2586.81	1375.31	973.64	774.41	656.14	578.33	523.64	483.37	452.70	428.74	409.64
30000	2676.01	1422.74	1007.21	801.11	678.76	598.28	541.69	500.04	468.31	443.52	423.77
31000	2765.21	1470.16	1040.79	827.82	701.39	618.22	559.75	516.70	483.92	458.31	437.89
32000	2854.41	1517.59	1074.36	854.52	724.01	638.16	577.81	533.37	499.53	473.09	452.02
33000	2943.61	1565.01	1107.94	881.22	746.64	658.10	595.86	550.04	515.14	487.88	466.14
34000	3032.81	1612.44	1141.51	907.93	769.27	678.05	613.92	566.71	530.75	502.66	480.27
35000	3122.01	1659.86	1175.08	934.63	791.89	697.99	631.98	583.38	546.36	517.44	494.39
36000	3211.21	1707.29	1208.66	961.33	814.52	717.93	650.03	600.04	561.97	532.23	508.52
37000	3300.41	1754.71	1242.23	988.04	837.14	737.87	668.09	616.71	577.58	547.01	522.64
38000	3389.61	1802.14	1275.80	1014.74	859.77	757.82	686.15	633.38	593.19	561.80	536.77
39000	3478.81	1849.56	1309.38	1041.44	882.39	777.76	704.20	650.05	608.80	576.58	550.89
40000	3568.01	1896.98	1342.95	1068.15	905.02	797.70	722.26	666.71	624.41	591.36	565.02
41000	3657.21	1944.41	1376.53	1094.85	927.64	817.64	740.31	683.38	640.02	606.15	579.15
42000	3746.41	1991.83	1410.10	1121.56	950.27	837.59	758.37	700.05	655.63	620.93	593.27
43000	3835.61	2039.26	1443.67	1148.26	972.89	857.53	776.43	716.72	671.24	635.72	607.40
44000	3924.81	2086.68	1477.25	1174.96	995.52	877.47	794.48	733.38	686.86	650.50	621.52
45000	4014.01	2134.11	1510.82	1201.67	1018.14	897.41	812.54	750.05	702.47	665.28	635.65
46000	4103.21	2181.53	1544.39	1228.37	1040.77	917.36	830.60	766.72	718.08	680.07	649.77
47000	4192.41	2228.96	1577.97	1255.07	1063.39	937.30	848.65	783.39	733.69	694.85	663.90
48000	4281.61	2276.38	1611.54	1281.78	1086.02	957.24	866.71	800.06	749.30	709.64	678.02
49000	4370.81	2323.80	1645.11	1308.48	1108.64	977.18	884.76	816.72	764.91	724.42	692.15
50000	4460.01	2371.23	1678.69	1335.18	1131.27	997.13	902.82	833.39	780.52	739.20	706.27
55000	4906.01	2608.35	1846.56	1468.70	1244.40	1096.84	993.10	916.73	858.57	813.12	776.90
60000	5352.01	2845.47	2014.42	1602.22	1357.52	1196.55	1083.38	1000.07	936.62	887.04	847.53
65000	5798.01	3082.60	2182.29	1735.74	1470.65	1296.26	1173.67	1083.41	1014.67	960.96	918.15
70000	6244.01	3319.72	2350.16	1869.26	1583.78	1395.97	1263.95	1166.75	1092.72	1034.88	988.78
75000	6690.01	3556.84	2518.03	2002.77	1696.90	1495.69	1354.23	1250.08	1170.77	1108.80	1059.41
80000	7136.01	3793.96	2685.90	2136.29	1810.03	1595.40	1444.51	1333.42	1248.82	1182.72	1130.04
85000	7582.01	4031.09	2853.77	2269.81	1923.16	1695.11	1534.79	1416.76	1326.87	1256.64	1200.66
90000	8028.01	4268.21	3021.63	2403.33	2036.28	1794.82	1625.07	1500.10	1404.93	1330.56	1271.29
95000	8474.01	4505.33	3189.50	2536.85	2149.41	1894.53	1715.36	1583.44	1482.98	1404.48	1341.92
100000	8920.01	4742.45	3357.37	2670.36	2262.54	1994.25	1805.64	1666.78	1561.03	1478.40	1412.54

Principal and Interest
Monthly Payment Amortization Table

12.75%

Term Amount	12 Years	13 Years	14 Years	15 Years	16 Years	17 Years	18 Years	19 Years	20 Years	25 Years	30 Years
50	.68	.66	.64	.63	.62	.61	.60	.59	.58	.56	.55
100	1.36	1.32	1.28	1.25	1.23	1.21	1.19	1.17	1.16	1.11	1.09
200	2.72	2.64	2.56	2.50	2.45	2.41	2.37	2.34	2.31	2.22	2.18
300	4.08	3.95	3.84	3.75	3.67	3.61	3.55	3.51	3.47	3.33	3.27
400	5.44	5.27	5.12	5.00	4.90	4.81	4.74	4.67	4.62	4.44	4.35
500	6.80	6.58	6.40	6.25	6.12	6.01	5.92	5.84	5.77	5.55	5.44
600	8.16	7.90	7.68	7.50	7.34	7.21	7.10	7.01	6.93	6.66	6.53
700	9.52	9.21	8.96	8.75	8.57	8.42	8.29	8.18	8.08	7.77	7.61
800	10.88	10.53	10.24	10.00	9.79	9.62	9.47	9.34	9.24	8.88	8.70
900	12.24	11.84	11.52	11.24	11.01	10.82	10.65	10.51	10.39	9.99	9.79
1000	13.60	13.16	12.80	12.49	12.24	12.02	11.84	11.68	11.54	11.10	10.87
2000	27.19	26.31	25.59	24.98	24.47	24.04	23.67	23.35	23.08	22.19	21.74
3000	40.78	39.47	38.38	37.47	36.70	36.05	35.50	35.03	34.62	33.28	32.61
4000	54.37	52.62	51.17	49.96	48.94	48.07	47.33	46.70	46.16	44.37	43.47
5000	67.97	65.78	63.96	62.45	61.17	60.09	59.16	58.37	57.70	55.46	54.34
6000	81.56	78.93	76.76	74.94	73.40	72.10	71.00	70.05	69.23	66.55	65.21
7000	95.15	92.09	89.55	87.42	85.63	84.12	82.83	81.72	80.77	77.64	76.07
8000	108.74	105.24	102.34	99.91	97.87	96.13	94.66	93.40	92.31	88.73	86.94
9000	122.33	118.40	115.13	112.40	110.10	108.15	106.49	105.07	103.85	99.82	97.81
10000	135.93	131.55	127.92	124.89	122.33	120.17	118.32	116.74	115.39	110.91	108.67
11000	149.52	144.70	140.71	137.38	134.57	132.18	130.15	128.42	126.92	122.00	119.64
12000	163.11	157.86	153.51	149.87	146.80	144.20	141.99	140.09	138.46	133.09	130.41
13000	176.70	171.01	166.30	162.35	159.03	156.22	153.82	151.76	150.00	144.18	141.28
14000	190.29	184.17	179.09	174.84	171.26	168.23	165.65	163.44	161.54	155.27	152.14
15000	203.89	197.32	191.88	187.33	183.50	180.25	177.48	175.11	173.08	166.36	163.01
16000	217.48	210.48	204.67	199.82	195.73	192.26	189.31	186.79	184.61	177.45	173.88
17000	231.07	223.63	217.46	212.31	207.96	204.28	201.14	198.46	196.15	188.54	184.74
18000	244.66	236.79	230.26	224.80	220.20	216.30	212.98	210.13	207.69	199.63	195.61
19000	258.25	249.94	243.05	237.28	232.43	228.31	224.81	221.81	219.23	210.72	206.48
20000	271.85	263.09	255.84	249.77	244.66	240.33	236.64	233.48	230.77	221.82	217.34
21000	285.44	276.25	268.63	262.26	256.89	252.35	248.47	245.15	242.31	232.91	228.21
22000	299.03	289.40	281.42	274.75	269.13	264.36	260.30	256.83	253.84	244.00	239.08
23000	312.62	302.56	294.21	287.24	281.36	276.38	272.13	268.50	265.38	255.09	249.94
24000	326.21	315.71	307.01	299.73	293.59	288.39	283.97	280.18	276.92	266.18	260.81
25000	339.81	328.87	319.80	312.21	305.83	300.41	295.80	291.85	288.46	277.27	271.68
26000	353.40	342.02	332.59	324.70	318.06	312.43	307.63	303.52	300.00	288.36	282.55
27000	366.99	355.18	345.38	337.19	330.29	324.44	319.46	315.20	311.53	299.45	293.41
28000	380.58	368.33	358.17	349.68	342.52	336.46	331.29	326.87	323.07	310.54	304.28
29000	394.17	381.48	370.96	362.17	354.76	348.48	343.12	338.54	334.61	321.63	315.15
30000	407.77	394.64	383.76	374.66	366.99	360.49	354.96	350.22	346.15	332.72	326.01
31000	421.36	407.79	396.55	387.14	379.22	372.51	366.79	361.89	357.69	343.81	336.88
32000	434.95	420.95	409.34	399.63	391.46	384.52	378.62	373.57	369.22	354.90	347.75
33000	448.54	434.10	422.13	412.12	403.69	396.54	390.45	385.24	380.76	365.99	358.61
34000	462.13	447.26	434.92	424.61	415.92	408.56	402.28	396.91	392.30	377.08	369.48
35000	475.73	460.41	447.72	437.10	428.15	420.57	414.11	408.59	403.84	388.17	380.35
36000	489.32	473.57	460.51	449.59	440.39	432.59	425.95	420.26	415.38	399.26	391.21
37000	502.91	486.72	473.30	462.07	452.62	444.61	437.78	431.93	426.92	410.35	402.08
38000	516.50	499.87	486.09	474.56	464.85	456.62	449.61	443.61	438.45	421.44	412.95
39000	530.09	513.03	498.88	487.05	477.09	468.64	461.44	455.28	449.99	432.54	423.82
40000	543.69	526.18	511.67	499.54	489.32	480.65	473.27	466.96	461.53	443.63	434.68
41000	557.28	539.34	524.47	512.03	501.55	492.67	485.10	478.63	473.07	454.72	445.55
42000	570.87	552.49	537.26	524.52	513.78	504.69	496.94	490.30	484.61	465.81	456.42
43000	584.46	565.65	550.05	537.00	526.02	516.70	508.77	501.98	496.14	476.90	467.28
44000	598.05	578.80	562.84	549.49	538.25	528.72	520.60	513.65	507.68	487.99	478.15
45000	611.65	591.96	575.63	561.98	550.48	540.74	532.43	525.32	519.22	499.08	489.02
46000	625.24	605.11	588.42	574.47	562.72	552.75	544.26	537.00	530.76	510.17	499.88
47000	638.83	618.26	601.22	586.96	574.95	564.77	556.09	548.67	542.30	521.26	510.75
48000	652.42	631.42	614.01	599.45	587.18	576.78	567.93	560.35	553.83	532.35	521.62
49000	666.01	644.57	626.80	611.94	599.41	588.80	579.76	572.02	565.37	543.44	532.48
50000	679.61	657.73	639.59	624.42	611.65	600.82	591.59	583.69	576.91	554.53	543.35
55000	747.57	723.50	703.55	686.87	672.81	660.90	650.75	642.06	634.60	609.98	597.69
60000	815.53	789.27	767.51	749.31	733.97	720.98	709.91	700.43	692.29	665.44	652.02
65000	883.49	855.04	831.47	811.75	795.14	781.06	769.07	758.80	749.98	720.89	706.36
70000	951.45	920.82	895.43	874.19	856.30	841.14	828.22	817.17	807.67	776.34	760.69
75000	1019.41	986.59	959.38	936.63	917.47	901.22	887.38	875.54	865.36	831.79	815.02
80000	1087.37	1052.36	1023.34	999.07	978.63	961.30	946.54	933.91	923.05	887.25	869.36
85000	1155.33	1118.13	1087.30	1061.52	1039.80	1021.39	1005.70	992.28	980.74	942.70	923.69
90000	1223.29	1183.91	1151.26	1123.96	1100.96	1081.47	1064.86	1050.64	1038.44	998.15	978.03
95000	1291.25	1249.68	1215.22	1186.40	1162.12	1141.55	1124.02	1109.01	1096.13	1053.60	1032.36
100000	1359.21	1315.45	1279.18	1248.84	1223.29	1201.63	1183.17	1167.38	1153.82	1109.06	1086.70

13.00% Principal and Interest
Monthly Payment Amortization Table

Term / Amount	1 Year	2 Years	3 Years	4 Years	5 Years	6 Years	7 Years	8 Years	9 Years	10 Years	11 Years
50	4.47	2.38	1.69	1.35	1.14	1.01	.91	.85	.79	.75	.72
100	8.94	4.76	3.37	2.69	2.28	2.01	1.82	1.69	1.58	1.50	1.43
200	17.87	9.51	6.74	5.37	4.56	4.02	3.64	3.37	3.16	2.99	2.86
300	26.80	14.27	10.11	8.05	6.83	6.03	5.46	5.05	4.73	4.48	4.29
400	35.73	19.02	13.48	10.74	9.11	8.03	7.28	6.73	6.31	5.98	5.72
500	44.66	23.78	16.85	13.42	11.38	10.04	9.10	8.41	7.88	7.47	7.14
600	53.60	28.53	20.22	16.10	13.66	12.05	10.92	10.09	9.46	8.96	8.57
700	62.53	33.28	23.59	18.78	15.93	14.06	12.74	11.77	11.03	10.46	10.00
800	71.46	38.04	26.96	21.47	18.21	16.06	14.56	13.45	12.61	11.95	11.43
900	80.39	42.79	30.33	24.15	20.48	18.07	16.38	15.13	14.18	13.44	12.85
1000	89.32	47.55	33.70	26.83	22.76	20.08	18.20	16.81	15.76	14.94	14.28
2000	178.64	95.09	67.39	53.66	45.51	40.15	36.39	33.62	31.51	29.87	28.56
3000	267.96	142.63	101.09	80.49	68.26	60.23	54.58	50.43	47.27	44.80	42.83
4000	357.27	190.17	134.78	107.31	91.02	80.30	72.77	67.23	63.02	59.73	57.11
5000	446.59	237.71	168.47	134.14	113.77	100.38	90.96	84.04	78.77	74.66	71.39
6000	535.91	285.26	202.17	160.97	136.52	120.45	109.16	100.85	94.53	89.59	85.66
7000	625.23	332.80	235.86	187.80	159.28	140.52	127.35	117.66	110.28	104.52	99.94
8000	714.54	380.34	269.56	214.62	182.03	160.60	145.54	134.46	126.03	119.45	114.21
9000	803.86	427.88	303.25	241.45	204.78	180.67	163.73	151.27	141.79	134.38	128.49
10000	893.18	475.42	336.94	268.28	227.54	200.75	181.92	168.08	157.54	149.32	142.77
11000	982.50	522.97	370.64	295.11	250.29	220.82	200.12	184.88	173.29	164.25	157.04
12000	1071.81	570.51	404.33	321.93	273.04	240.89	218.31	201.69	189.05	179.18	171.32
13000	1161.13	618.05	438.03	348.76	295.79	260.97	236.50	218.50	204.80	194.11	185.59
14000	1250.45	665.59	471.72	375.59	318.55	281.04	254.69	235.31	220.56	209.04	199.87
15000	1339.76	713.13	505.41	402.42	341.30	301.12	272.88	252.11	236.31	223.97	214.15
16000	1429.08	760.67	539.11	429.24	364.05	321.19	291.08	268.92	252.06	238.90	228.42
17000	1518.40	808.22	572.80	456.07	386.81	341.26	309.27	285.73	267.82	253.83	242.70
18000	1607.72	855.76	606.50	482.90	409.56	361.34	327.46	302.54	283.57	268.76	256.97
19000	1697.03	903.30	640.19	509.73	432.31	381.41	345.65	319.34	299.32	283.70	271.25
20000	1786.35	950.84	673.88	536.55	455.07	401.49	363.84	336.15	315.08	298.63	285.53
21000	1875.67	998.38	707.58	563.38	477.82	421.56	382.04	352.96	330.83	313.56	299.80
22000	1964.99	1045.93	741.27	590.21	500.57	441.64	400.23	369.76	346.58	328.49	314.08
23000	2054.30	1093.47	774.97	617.04	523.33	461.71	418.42	386.57	362.34	343.42	328.36
24000	2143.62	1141.01	808.66	643.86	546.08	481.78	436.61	403.38	378.09	358.35	342.63
25000	2232.94	1188.55	842.35	670.69	568.83	501.86	454.80	420.19	393.84	373.28	356.91
26000	2322.25	1236.09	876.05	697.52	591.58	521.93	473.00	436.99	409.60	388.21	371.18
27000	2411.57	1283.63	909.74	724.35	614.34	542.01	491.19	453.80	425.35	403.14	385.46
28000	2500.89	1331.18	943.44	751.17	637.09	562.08	509.38	470.61	441.11	418.08	399.74
29000	2590.21	1378.72	977.13	778.00	659.84	582.15	527.57	487.42	456.86	433.01	414.01
30000	2679.52	1426.26	1010.82	804.83	682.60	602.23	545.76	504.22	472.61	447.94	428.29
31000	2768.84	1473.80	1044.52	831.66	705.35	622.30	563.96	521.03	488.37	462.87	442.56
32000	2858.16	1521.34	1078.21	858.48	728.10	642.38	582.15	537.84	504.12	477.80	456.84
33000	2947.48	1568.89	1111.91	885.31	750.86	662.45	600.34	554.64	519.87	492.73	471.12
34000	3036.79	1616.43	1145.60	912.14	773.61	682.52	618.53	571.45	535.63	507.66	485.39
35000	3126.11	1663.97	1179.29	938.97	796.36	702.60	636.72	588.26	551.38	522.59	499.67
36000	3215.43	1711.51	1212.99	965.79	819.12	722.67	654.92	605.07	567.13	537.52	513.94
37000	3304.74	1759.05	1246.68	992.62	841.87	742.75	673.11	621.87	582.89	552.45	528.22
38000	3394.06	1806.59	1280.38	1019.45	864.62	762.82	691.30	638.68	598.64	567.39	542.50
39000	3483.38	1854.14	1314.07	1046.28	887.37	782.90	709.49	655.49	614.39	582.32	556.77
40000	3572.70	1901.68	1347.76	1073.10	910.13	802.97	727.68	672.30	630.15	597.25	571.05
41000	3662.01	1949.22	1381.46	1099.93	932.88	823.04	745.88	689.10	645.90	612.18	585.33
42000	3751.33	1996.76	1415.15	1126.76	955.63	843.12	764.07	705.91	661.66	627.11	599.60
43000	3840.65	2044.30	1448.84	1153.59	978.39	863.19	782.26	722.72	677.41	642.04	613.88
44000	3929.97	2091.85	1482.54	1180.41	1001.14	883.27	800.45	739.52	693.16	656.97	628.15
45000	4019.28	2139.39	1516.23	1207.24	1023.89	903.34	818.64	756.33	708.92	671.90	642.43
46000	4108.60	2186.93	1549.93	1234.07	1046.65	923.41	836.84	773.14	724.67	686.83	656.71
47000	4197.92	2234.47	1583.62	1260.90	1069.40	943.49	855.03	789.95	740.42	701.77	670.98
48000	4287.23	2282.01	1617.31	1287.72	1092.15	963.56	873.22	806.75	756.18	716.70	685.26
49000	4376.55	2329.55	1651.01	1314.55	1114.91	983.64	891.41	823.56	771.93	731.63	699.53
50000	4465.87	2377.10	1684.70	1341.38	1137.66	1003.71	909.60	840.37	787.68	746.56	713.81
55000	4912.46	2614.81	1853.17	1475.52	1251.42	1104.08	1000.56	924.40	866.45	821.21	785.19
60000	5359.04	2852.52	2021.64	1609.65	1365.19	1204.45	1091.52	1008.44	945.22	895.87	856.57
65000	5805.63	3090.22	2190.11	1743.79	1478.95	1304.82	1182.48	1092.48	1023.99	970.52	927.95
70000	6252.21	3327.93	2358.58	1877.93	1592.72	1405.19	1273.44	1176.51	1102.76	1045.18	999.33
75000	6698.80	3565.64	2527.05	2012.07	1706.49	1505.56	1364.40	1260.55	1181.52	1119.84	1070.71
80000	7145.39	3803.35	2695.52	2146.20	1820.25	1605.93	1455.36	1344.59	1260.29	1194.49	1142.09
85000	7591.97	4041.06	2863.99	2280.34	1934.02	1706.30	1546.32	1428.62	1339.06	1269.15	1213.47
90000	8038.56	4278.77	3032.46	2414.48	2047.78	1806.67	1637.28	1512.66	1417.83	1343.80	1284.85
95000	8485.15	4516.48	3200.93	2548.62	2161.55	1907.05	1728.24	1596.69	1496.60	1418.46	1356.24
100000	8931.73	4754.19	3369.40	2682.75	2275.31	2007.42	1819.20	1680.73	1575.36	1493.11	1427.62

Principal and Interest
Monthly Payment Amortization Table

13.00%

Term / Amount	12 Years	13 Years	14 Years	15 Years	16 Years	17 Years	18 Years	19 Years	20 Years	25 Years	30 Years
50	.69	.67	.65	.64	.62	.61	.61	.60	.59	.57	.56
100	1.38	1.34	1.30	1.27	1.24	1.22	1.21	1.19	1.18	1.13	1.11
200	2.75	2.67	2.60	2.54	2.48	2.44	2.41	2.37	2.35	2.26	2.22
300	4.13	4.00	3.89	3.80	3.72	3.66	3.61	3.56	3.52	3.39	3.32
400	5.50	5.33	5.19	5.07	4.96	4.88	4.81	4.74	4.69	4.52	4.43
500	6.88	6.66	6.48	6.33	6.20	6.10	6.01	5.93	5.86	5.64	5.54
600	8.25	7.99	7.78	7.60	7.44	7.32	7.21	7.11	7.03	6.77	6.64
700	9.63	9.32	9.07	8.86	8.68	8.54	8.41	8.30	8.21	7.90	7.75
800	11.00	10.65	10.37	10.13	9.92	9.75	9.61	9.48	9.38	9.03	8.85
900	12.38	11.99	11.66	11.39	11.16	10.97	10.81	10.67	10.55	10.16	9.96
1000	13.75	13.32	12.96	12.66	12.40	12.19	12.01	11.85	11.72	11.28	11.07
2000	27.50	26.63	25.91	25.31	24.80	24.38	24.01	23.70	23.44	22.56	22.13
3000	41.24	39.94	38.86	37.96	37.20	36.56	36.02	35.55	35.15	33.84	33.19
4000	54.99	53.25	51.82	50.61	49.60	48.75	48.02	47.40	46.87	45.12	44.25
5000	68.74	66.57	64.77	63.27	62.00	60.94	60.03	59.25	58.58	56.40	55.31
6000	82.48	79.88	77.72	75.92	74.40	73.12	72.03	71.10	70.30	67.68	66.38
7000	96.23	93.19	90.67	88.57	86.80	85.31	84.04	82.95	82.02	78.95	77.44
8000	109.98	106.50	103.63	101.22	99.20	97.49	96.04	94.80	93.73	90.23	88.50
9000	123.72	119.81	116.58	113.88	111.60	109.68	108.04	106.65	105.45	101.51	99.56
10000	137.47	133.13	129.53	126.53	124.00	121.87	120.05	118.49	117.16	112.79	110.62
11000	151.21	146.44	142.48	139.18	136.40	134.05	132.05	130.34	128.88	124.07	121.69
12000	164.96	159.75	155.44	151.83	148.80	146.24	144.06	142.19	140.59	135.35	132.75
13000	178.71	173.06	168.39	164.49	161.20	158.42	156.06	154.04	152.31	146.62	143.81
14000	192.45	186.37	181.34	177.14	173.60	170.61	168.07	165.89	164.03	157.90	154.87
15000	206.20	199.69	194.29	189.79	186.00	182.80	180.07	177.74	175.74	169.18	165.93
16000	219.95	213.00	207.25	202.44	198.40	194.98	192.07	189.59	187.46	180.46	177.00
17000	233.69	226.31	220.20	215.10	210.80	207.17	204.08	201.44	199.17	191.74	188.06
18000	247.44	239.62	233.15	227.75	223.20	219.36	216.08	213.29	210.89	203.02	199.12
19000	261.18	252.93	246.11	240.40	235.60	231.54	228.09	225.14	222.60	214.29	210.18
20000	274.93	266.25	259.06	253.05	248.00	243.73	240.09	236.98	234.32	225.57	221.24
21000	288.68	279.56	272.01	265.71	260.40	255.91	252.10	248.83	246.04	236.85	232.31
22000	302.42	292.87	284.96	278.36	272.80	268.10	264.10	260.68	257.75	248.13	243.37
23000	316.17	306.18	297.92	291.01	285.20	280.29	276.10	272.53	269.47	259.41	254.43
24000	329.92	319.50	310.87	303.66	297.60	292.47	288.11	284.38	281.18	270.69	265.49
25000	343.66	332.81	323.82	316.32	310.00	304.66	300.11	296.23	292.90	281.96	276.55
26000	357.41	346.12	336.77	328.97	322.40	316.84	312.12	308.08	304.61	293.24	287.62
27000	371.15	359.43	349.73	341.62	334.80	329.03	324.12	319.93	316.33	304.52	298.68
28000	384.90	372.74	362.68	354.27	347.20	341.22	336.13	331.78	328.05	315.80	309.74
29000	398.65	386.06	375.63	366.93	359.60	353.40	348.13	343.63	339.76	327.08	320.80
30000	412.39	399.37	388.58	379.58	372.00	365.59	360.13	355.47	351.48	338.36	331.86
31000	426.14	412.68	401.54	392.23	384.40	377.78	372.14	367.32	363.19	349.63	342.93
32000	439.89	425.99	414.49	404.88	396.80	389.96	384.14	379.17	374.91	360.91	353.99
33000	453.63	439.30	427.44	417.53	409.20	402.15	396.15	391.02	386.62	372.19	365.05
34000	467.38	452.62	440.39	430.19	421.60	414.33	408.15	402.87	398.34	383.47	376.11
35000	481.12	465.93	453.35	442.84	434.00	426.52	420.16	414.72	410.06	394.75	387.17
36000	494.87	479.24	466.30	455.49	446.40	438.71	432.16	426.57	421.77	406.03	398.24
37000	508.62	492.55	479.25	468.14	458.80	450.89	444.17	438.42	433.49	417.30	409.30
38000	522.36	505.86	492.21	480.80	471.20	463.08	456.17	450.27	445.20	428.58	420.36
39000	536.11	519.18	505.16	493.45	483.60	475.26	468.17	462.12	456.92	439.86	431.42
40000	549.86	532.49	518.11	506.10	496.00	487.45	480.18	473.96	468.64	451.14	442.48
41000	563.60	545.80	531.06	518.75	508.40	499.64	492.18	485.81	480.35	462.42	453.55
42000	577.35	559.11	544.02	531.41	520.80	511.82	504.19	497.66	492.07	473.70	464.61
43000	591.09	572.43	556.97	544.06	533.20	524.01	516.19	509.51	503.78	484.97	475.67
44000	604.84	585.74	569.92	556.71	545.60	536.20	528.20	521.36	515.50	496.25	486.73
45000	618.59	599.05	582.87	569.36	558.00	548.38	540.20	533.21	527.21	507.53	497.79
46000	632.33	612.36	595.83	582.02	570.40	560.57	552.20	545.06	538.93	518.81	508.86
47000	646.08	625.67	608.78	594.67	582.80	572.75	564.21	556.91	550.65	530.09	519.92
48000	659.83	638.99	621.73	607.32	595.20	584.94	576.21	568.76	562.36	541.37	530.98
49000	673.57	652.30	634.68	619.97	607.60	597.13	588.22	580.61	574.08	552.64	542.04
50000	687.32	665.61	647.64	632.63	620.00	609.31	600.22	592.45	585.79	563.92	553.10
55000	756.05	732.17	712.40	695.89	682.00	670.24	660.24	651.70	644.37	620.31	608.41
60000	824.78	798.73	777.16	759.15	744.00	731.17	720.26	710.94	702.95	676.71	663.72
65000	893.51	865.29	841.93	822.41	806.00	792.10	780.29	770.19	761.53	733.10	719.03
70000	962.24	931.85	906.69	885.67	868.00	853.04	840.31	829.43	820.11	789.49	774.34
75000	1030.97	998.41	971.45	948.94	930.00	913.97	900.33	888.68	878.69	845.88	829.65
80000	1099.71	1064.97	1036.22	1012.20	992.00	974.90	960.35	947.92	937.27	902.27	884.96
85000	1168.44	1131.53	1100.98	1075.46	1053.99	1035.83	1020.37	1007.17	995.84	958.67	940.27
90000	1237.17	1198.09	1165.74	1138.72	1115.99	1096.76	1080.39	1066.41	1054.42	1015.06	995.58
95000	1305.90	1264.65	1230.51	1201.99	1177.99	1157.69	1140.42	1125.66	1113.00	1071.45	1050.89
100000	1374.63	1331.22	1295.27	1265.25	1239.99	1218.62	1200.44	1184.90	1171.58	1127.84	1106.20

13.25% Principal and Interest
Monthly Payment Amortization Table

Term Amount	1 Year	2 Years	3 Years	4 Years	5 Years	6 Years	7 Years	8 Years	9 Years	10 Years	11 Years
50	4.48	2.39	1.70	1.35	1.15	1.02	.92	.85	.80	.76	.73
100	8.95	4.77	3.39	2.70	2.29	2.03	1.84	1.70	1.59	1.51	1.45
200	17.89	9.54	6.77	5.40	4.58	4.05	3.67	3.39	3.18	3.02	2.89
300	26.84	14.30	10.15	8.09	6.87	6.07	5.50	5.09	4.77	4.53	4.33
400	35.78	19.07	13.53	10.79	9.16	8.09	7.34	6.78	6.36	6.04	5.78
500	44.72	23.83	16.91	13.48	11.45	10.11	9.17	8.48	7.95	7.54	7.22
600	53.67	28.60	20.29	16.18	13.73	12.13	11.00	10.17	9.54	9.05	8.66
700	62.61	33.37	23.68	18.87	16.02	14.15	12.83	11.87	11.13	10.56	10.10
800	71.55	38.13	27.06	21.57	18.31	16.17	14.67	13.56	12.72	12.07	11.55
900	80.50	42.90	30.44	24.26	20.60	18.19	16.50	15.26	14.31	13.58	12.99
1000	89.44	47.66	33.82	26.96	22.89	20.21	18.33	16.95	15.90	15.08	14.43
2000	178.87	95.32	67.63	53.91	45.77	40.42	36.66	33.90	31.80	30.16	28.86
3000	268.31	142.98	101.45	80.86	68.65	60.62	54.99	50.85	47.70	45.24	43.29
4000	357.74	190.64	135.26	107.81	91.53	80.83	73.32	67.79	63.60	60.32	57.72
5000	447.18	238.30	169.08	134.76	114.41	101.04	91.65	84.74	79.49	75.40	72.14
6000	536.61	285.96	202.89	161.72	137.29	121:24	109.97	101.69	95.39	90.48	86.57
7000	626.05	333.62	236.71	188.67	160.17	141.45	128.30	118.64	111.29	105.56	101.00
8000	715.48	381.28	270.52	215.62	183.06	161.66	146.63	135.58	127.19	120.64	115.43
9000	804.92	428.94	304.34	242.57	205.94	181.86	164.96	152.53	143.08	135.72	129.85
10000	894.35	476.60	338.15	269.52	228.82	202.07	183.29	169.48	158.98	150.79	144.28
11000	983.79	524.26	371.96	296.47	251.70	222.27	201.61	186.43	174.88	165.87	158.71
12000	1073.22	571.92	405.78	323.43	274.58	242.48	219.94	203.37	190.78	180.95	173.14
13000	1162.65	619.58	439.59	350.38	297.46	262.69	238.27	220.32	206.67	196.03	187.56
14000	1252.09	667.24	473.41	377.33	320.34	282.89	256.60	237.27	222.57	211.11	201.99
15000	1341.52	714.90	507.22	404.28	343.22	303.10	274.93	254.22	238.47	226.19	216.42
16000	1430.96	762.55	541.04	431.23	366.11	323.31	293.26	271.16	254.37	241.27	230.85
17000	1520.39	810.21	574.85	458.18	388.99	343.51	311.58	288.11	270.26	256.35	245.27
18000	1609.83	857.87	608.67	485.14	411.87	363.72	329.91	305.06	286.16	271.43	259.70
19000	1699.26	905.53	642.48	512.09	434.75	383.92	348.24	322.01	302.06	286.50	274.13
20000	1788.70	953.19	676.29	539.04	457.63	404.13	366.57	338.95	317.96	301.58	288.56
21000	1878.13	1000.85	710.11	565.99	480.51	424.34	384.90	355.90	333.85	316.66	302.98
22000	1967.57	1048.51	743.92	592.94	503.39	444.54	403.22	372.85	349.75	331.74	317.41
23000	2057.00	1096.17	777.74	619.90	526.27	464.75	421.55	389.80	365.65	346.82	331.84
24000	2146.44	1143.83	811.55	646.85	549.16	484.96	439.88	406.74	381.55	361.90	346.27
25000	2235.87	1191.49	845.37	673.80	572.04	505.16	458.21	423.69	397.45	376.98	360.70
26000	2325.30	1239.15	879.18	700.75	594.92	525.37	476.54	440.64	413.34	392.06	375.12
27000	2414.74	1286.81	913.00	727.70	617.80	545.57	494.87	457.58	429.24	407.14	389.55
28000	2504.17	1334.47	946.81	754.65	640.68	565.78	513.19	474.53	445.14	422.21	403.98
29000	2593.61	1382.13	980.63	781.61	663.56	585.99	531.52	491.48	461.04	437.29	418.41
30000	2683.04	1429.79	1014.44	808.56	686.44	606.19	549.85	508.43	476.93	452.37	432.83
31000	2772.48	1477.44	1048.25	835.51	709.32	626.40	568.18	525.37	492.83	467.45	447.26
32000	2861.91	1525.10	1082.07	862.46	732.21	646.61	586.51	542.32	508.73	482.53	461.69
33000	2951.35	1572.76	1115.88	889.41	755.09	666.81	604.83	559.27	524.63	497.61	476.12
34000	3040.78	1620.42	1149.70	916.36	777.97	687.02	623.16	576.22	540.52	512.69	490.54
35000	3130.22	1668.08	1183.51	943.32	800.85	707.23	641.49	593.16	556.42	527.77	504.97
36000	3219.65	1715.74	1217.33	970.27	823.73	727.43	659.82	610.11	572.32	542.85	519.40
37000	3309.09	1763.40	1251.14	997.22	846.61	747.64	678.15	627.06	588.22	557.92	533.83
38000	3398.52	1811.06	1284.96	1024.17	869.49	767.84	696.47	644.01	604.11	573.00	548.25
39000	3487.95	1858.72	1318.77	1051.12	892.37	788.05	714.80	660.95	620.01	588.08	562.68
40000	3577.39	1906.38	1352.58	1078.07	915.26	808.26	733.13	677.90	635.91	603.16	577.11
41000	3666.82	1954.04	1386.40	1105.03	938.14	828.46	751.46	694.85	651.81	618.24	591.54
42000	3756.26	2001.70	1420.21	1131.98	961.02	848.67	769.79	711.80	667.70	633.32	605.96
43000	3845.69	2049.36	1454.03	1158.93	983.90	868.88	788.12	728.74	683.60	648.40	620.39
44000	3935.13	2097.02	1487.84	1185.88	1006.78	889.08	806.44	745.69	699.50	663.48	634.82
45000	4024.56	2144.68	1521.66	1212.83	1029.66	909.29	824.77	762.64	715.40	678.56	649.25
46000	4114.00	2192.33	1555.47	1239.79	1052.54	929.49	843.10	779.59	731.30	693.63	663.67
47000	4203.43	2239.99	1589.29	1266.74	1075.42	949.70	861.43	796.53	747.19	708.71	678.10
48000	4292.87	2287.65	1623.10	1293.69	1098.31	969.91	879.76	813.48	763.09	723.79	692.53
49000	4382.30	2335.31	1656.92	1320.64	1121.19	990.11	898.08	830.43	778.99	738.87	706.96
50000	4471.74	2382.97	1690.73	1347.59	1144.07	1010.32	916.41	847.38	794.89	753.95	721.39
55000	4918.91	2621.27	1859.80	1482.35	1258.47	1111.35	1008.05	932.11	874.37	829.34	793.52
60000	5366.08	2859.57	2028.87	1617.11	1372.88	1212.38	1099.69	1016.85	953.86	904.74	865.66
65000	5813.25	3097.86	2197.95	1751.87	1487.29	1313.41	1191.34	1101.59	1033.35	980.13	937.80
70000	6260.43	3336.16	2367.02	1886.63	1601.69	1414.45	1282.98	1186.32	1112.84	1055.53	1009.94
75000	6707.60	3574.46	2536.09	2021.39	1716.10	1515.48	1374.62	1271.06	1192.33	1130.92	1082.08
80000	7154.77	3812.75	2705.16	2156.14	1830.51	1616.51	1466.26	1355.80	1271.81	1206.32	1154.21
85000	7601.95	4051.05	2874.24	2290.90	1944.91	1717.54	1557.90	1440.53	1351.30	1281.71	1226.35
90000	8049.12	4289.35	3043.31	2425.66	2059.32	1818.57	1649.54	1525.27	1430.79	1357.11	1298.49
95000	8496.29	4527.64	3212.38	2560.42	2173.72	1919.60	1741.18	1610.01	1510.28	1432.50	1370.63
100000	8943.47	4765.94	3381.45	2695.18	2288.13	2020.63	1832.82	1694.75	1589.77	1507.89	1442.77

Principal and Interest   13.25%
Monthly Payment Amortization Table

Term Amount	12 Years	13 Years	14 Years	15 Years	16 Years	17 Years	18 Years	19 Years	20 Years	25 Years	30 Years
50	.70	.68	.66	.65	.63	.62	.61	.61	.60	.58	.57
100	1.40	1.35	1.32	1.29	1.26	1.24	1.22	1.21	1.19	1.15	1.13
200	2.79	2.70	2.63	2.57	2.52	2.48	2.44	2.41	2.38	2.30	2.26
300	4.18	4.05	3.94	3.85	3.78	3.71	3.66	3.61	3.57	3.45	3.38
400	5.57	5.39	5.25	5.13	5.03	4.95	4.88	4.82	4.76	4.59	4.51
500	6.96	6.74	6.56	6.41	6.29	6.18	6.09	6.02	5.95	5.74	5.63
600	8.35	8.09	7.87	7.70	7.55	7.42	7.31	7.22	7.14	6.89	6.76
700	9.74	9.43	9.19	8.98	8.80	8.65	8.53	8.42	8.33	8.03	7.89
800	11.13	10.78	10.50	10.26	10.06	9.89	9.75	9.63	9.52	9.18	9.01
900	12.52	12.13	11.81	11.54	11.32	11.13	10.97	10.83	10.71	10.33	10.14
1000	13.91	13.48	13.12	12.82	12.57	12.36	12.18	12.03	11.90	11.47	11.26
2000	27.81	26.95	26.23	25.64	25.14	24.72	24.36	24.06	23.79	22.94	22.52
3000	41.71	40.42	39.35	38.46	37.71	37.08	36.54	36.08	35.69	34.41	33.78
4000	55.61	53.89	52.46	51.27	50.28	49.43	48.72	48.11	47.58	45.87	45.04
5000	69.51	67.36	65.58	64.09	62.84	61.79	60.89	60.13	59.48	57.34	56.29
6000	83.41	80.83	78.69	76.91	75.41	74.15	73.07	72.16	71.37	68.81	67.55
7000	97.31	94.30	91.81	89.73	67.98	86.50	85.25	84.18	83.27	80.27	78.81
8000	111.22	107.77	104.92	102.54	100.55	98.86	97.43	96.21	95.16	91.74	90.07
9000	125.12	121.24	118.03	115.36	113.12	111.22	109.61	108.23	107.05	103.21	101.32
10000	139.02	134.71	131.15	128.18	125.68	123.57	121.78	120.26	118.95	114.68	112.58
11000	152.92	148.18	144.26	141.00	138.25	135.93	133.96	132.28	130.84	126.14	123.84
12000	166.82	161.65	157.38	153.81	150.82	148.29	146.14	144.31	142.74	137.61	135.10
13000	180.72	175.12	170.49	166.63	163.39	160.65	158.32	156.33	154.63	149.08	146.36
14000	194.62	188.59	183.61	179.45	175.95	173.00	170.50	168.36	166.53	160.54	157.61
15000	208.52	202.06	196.72	192.27	188.52	185.36	182.67	180.38	178.42	172.01	168.87
16000	222.43	215.53	209.84	205.08	201.09	197.72	194.85	192.41	190.31	183.48	180.13
17000	236.33	229.01	222.95	217.90	213.66	210.07	207.03	204.43	202.21	194.94	191.39
18000	250.23	242.48	236.06	230.72	226.23	222.43	219.21	216.46	214.10	206.41	202.64
19000	264.13	255.95	249.18	243.53	238.79	234.79	231.38	228.48	226.00	217.88	213.90
20000	278.03	269.42	262.29	256.35	251.36	247.14	243.56	240.51	237.89	229.35	225.16
21000	291.93	282.89	275.41	269.17	263.93	259.50	255.74	252.53	249.79	240.81	236.42
22000	305.83	296.36	288.52	281.99	276.50	271.86	267.92	264.56	261.68	252.28	247.68
23000	319.74	309.83	301.64	294.80	289.07	284.22	280.10	276.58	273.57	263.75	258.93
24000	333.64	323.30	314.75	307.62	301.63	296.57	292.27	288.61	285.47	275.21	270.19
25000	347.54	336.77	327.87	320.44	314.20	308.93	304.45	300.63	297.36	286.68	281.45
26000	361.44	350.24	340.98	333.26	326.77	321.29	316.63	312.66	309.26	298.15	292.71
27000	375.34	363.71	354.09	346.07	339.34	333.64	328.81	324.68	321.15	309.61	303.96
28000	389.24	377.18	367.21	358.89	351.90	346.00	340.99	336.71	333.05	321.08	315.22
29000	403.14	390.65	380.32	371.71	364.47	358.36	353.16	348.73	344.94	332.55	326.48
30000	417.04	404.12	393.44	384.53	377.04	370.71	365.34	360.76	356.83	344.02	337.74
31000	430.95	417.59	406.55	397.34	389.61	383.07	377.52	372.78	368.73	355.48	348.99
32000	444.85	431.06	419.67	410.16	402.18	395.43	389.70	384.81	380.62	366.95	360.25
33000	458.75	444.53	432.78	422.98	414.74	407.78	401.87	396.83	392.52	378.42	371.51
34000	472.65	458.01	445.90	435.80	427.31	420.14	414.05	408.86	404.41	389.88	382.77
35000	486.55	471.48	459.01	448.61	439.88	432.50	426.23	420.88	416.31	401.35	394.03
36000	500.45	484.95	472.12	461.43	452.45	444.86	438.41	432.91	428.20	412.82	405.28
37000	514.35	498.42	485.24	474.25	465.01	457.21	450.59	444.93	440.09	424.28	416.54
38000	528.25	511.89	498.35	487.06	477.58	469.57	462.76	456.96	451.99	435.75	427.80
39000	542.16	525.36	511.47	499.88	490.15	481.93	474.94	468.98	463.88	447.22	439.06
40000	556.06	538.83	524.58	512.70	502.72	494.28	487.12	481.01	475.78	458.69	450.31
41000	569.96	552.30	537.70	525.52	515.29	506.64	499.30	493.03	487.67	470.15	461.57
42000	583.86	565.77	550.81	538.33	527.85	519.00	511.48	505.06	499.57	481.62	472.83
43000	597.76	579.24	563.93	551.15	540.42	531.35	523.65	517.08	511.46	493.09	484.09
44000	611.66	592.71	577.04	563.97	552.99	543.71	535.83	529.11	523.35	504.55	495.35
45000	625.56	606.18	590.15	576.79	565.56	556.07	548.01	541.13	535.25	516.02	506.60
46000	639.47	619.65	603.27	589.60	578.13	568.43	560.19	553.16	547.14	527.49	517.86
47000	653.37	633.12	616.38	602.42	590.69	580.78	572.36	565.18	559.04	538.95	529.12
48000	667.27	646.59	629.50	615.24	603.26	593.14	584.54	577.21	570.93	550.42	540.38
49000	681.17	660.06	642.61	628.06	615.83	605.50	596.72	589.23	582.83	561.89	551.63
50000	695.07	673.53	655.73	640.87	628.40	617.86	608.90	601.26	594.72	573.36	562.89
55000	764.58	740.89	721.30	704.96	691.24	679.64	669.79	661.39	654.19	630.69	619.18
60000	834.08	808.24	786.87	769.05	754.08	741.42	730.68	721.51	713.66	688.03	675.47
65000	903.59	875.59	852.44	833.13	816.91	803.21	791.57	781.64	773.13	745.36	731.76
70000	973.10	942.95	918.01	897.22	879.75	864.99	852.46	841.76	832.61	802.70	788.05
75000	1042.60	1010.30	983.59	961.31	942.59	926.78	913.35	901.89	892.08	860.03	844.34
80000	1112.11	1077.65	1049.16	1025.39	1005.43	988.56	974.23	962.01	951.55	917.37	900.62
85000	1181.62	1145.01	1114.73	1089.48	1068.27	1050.35	1035.12	1022.14	1011.02	974.70	956.91
90000	1251.12	1212.36	1180.30	1153.57	1131.11	1112.13	1096.01	1082.26	1070.49	1032.04	1013.20
95000	1320.63	1279.71	1245.88	1217.65	1193.95	1173.92	1156.90	1142.39	1129.96	1089.37	1069.49
100000	1390.14	1347.06	1311.45	1281.74	1256.79	1235.70	1217.79	1202.51	1189.44	1146.71	1125.78

13.50% Principal and Interest
Monthly Payment Amortization Table

Term Amount	1 Year	2 Years	3 Years	4 Years	5 Years	6 Years	7 Years	8 Years	9 Years	10 Years	11 Years
50	4.48	2.39	1.70	1.36	1.16	1.02	.93	.86	.81	.77	.73
100	8.96	4.78	3.40	2.71	2.31	2.04	1.85	1.71	1.61	1.53	1.46
200	17.92	9.56	6.79	5.42	4.61	4.07	3.70	3.42	3.21	3.05	2.92
300	26.87	14.34	10.19	8.13	6.91	6.11	5.54	5.13	4.82	4.57	4.38
400	35.83	19.12	13.58	10.84	9.21	8.14	7.39	6.84	6.42	6.10	5.84
500	44.78	23.89	16.97	13.54	11.51	10.17	9.24	8.55	8.03	7.62	7.29
600	53.74	28.67	20.37	16.25	13.81	12.21	11.08	10.26	9.63	9.14	8.75
700	62.69	33.45	23.76	18.96	16.11	14.24	12.93	11.97	11.23	10.66	10.21
800	71.65	38.23	27.15	21.67	18.41	16.28	14.78	13.68	12.84	12.19	11.67
900	80.60	43.00	30.55	24.37	20.71	18.31	16.62	15.38	14.44	13.71	13.13
1000	89.56	47.78	33.94	27.08	23.01	20.34	18.47	17.09	16.05	15.23	14.58
2000	179.11	95.56	67.88	54.16	46.02	40.68	36.93	34.18	32.09	30.46	29.16
3000	268.66	143.34	101.81	81.23	69.03	61.02	55.40	51.27	48.13	45.69	43.74
4000	358.21	191.11	135.75	108.31	92.04	81.36	73.86	68.36	64.17	60.91	58.32
5000	447.77	238.89	169.68	135.39	115.05	101.70	92.33	85.45	80.22	76.14	72.90
6000	537.32	286.67	203.62	162.46	138.06	122.04	110.79	102.53	96.26	91.37	87.48
7000	626.87	334.44	237.55	189.54	161.07	142.38	129.26	119.62	112.30	106.60	102.06
8000	716.42	382.22	271.49	216.62	184.08	162.72	147.72	136.71	128.34	121.82	116.64
9000	805.97	430.00	305.42	243.69	207.09	183.06	166.19	153.80	144.39	137.05	131.22
10000	895.53	477.78	339.36	270.77	230.10	203.39	184.65	170.89	160.43	152.28	145.80
11000	985.08	525.55	373.29	297.84	253.11	223.73	203.12	187.97	176.47	167.51	160.38
12000	1074.63	573.33	407.23	324.92	276.12	244.07	221.58	205.06	192.51	182.73	174.96
13000	1164.18	621.11	441.16	352.00	299.13	264.41	240.05	222.15	208.56	197.96	189.54
14000	1253.73	668.88	475.10	379.07	322.14	284.75	258.51	239.24	224.60	213.19	204.12
15000	1343.29	716.66	509.03	406.15	345.15	305.09	276.98	256.33	240.64	228.42	218.70
16000	1432.84	764.44	542.97	433.23	368.16	325.43	295.44	273.42	256.68	243.64	233.28
17000	1522.39	812.21	576.90	460.30	391.17	345.77	313.91	290.50	272.72	258.87	247.86
18000	1611.94	859.99	610.84	487.38	414.18	366.11	332.37	307.59	288.77	274.10	262.44
19000	1701.49	907.77	644.78	514.46	437.19	386.45	350.84	324.68	304.81	289.33	277.02
20000	1791.05	955.55	678.71	541.53	460.20	406.78	369.30	341.77	320.85	304.55	291.60
21000	1880.60	1003.32	712.65	568.61	483.21	427.12	387.77	358.86	336.89	319.78	306.18
22000	1970.15	1051.10	746.58	595.68	506.22	447.46	406.23	375.94	352.94	335.01	320.76
23000	2059.70	1098.88	780.52	622.76	529.23	467.80	424.70	393.03	368.98	350.24	335.34
24000	2149.25	1146.65	814.45	649.84	552.24	488.14	443.16	410.12	385.02	365.46	349.92
25000	2238.81	1194.43	848.39	676.91	575.25	508.48	461.63	427.21	401.06	380.69	364.50
26000	2328.36	1242.21	882.32	703.99	598.26	528.82	480.09	444.30	417.11	395.92	379.08
27000	2417.91	1289.98	916.26	731.07	621.27	549.16	498.56	461.39	433.15	411.15	393.66
28000	2507.46	1337.76	950.19	758.14	644.28	569.50	517.02	478.47	449.19	426.37	408.24
29000	2597.01	1385.54	984.13	785.22	667.29	589.83	535.49	495.56	465.23	441.60	422.82
30000	2686.57	1433.32	1018.06	812.29	690.30	610.17	553.95	512.65	481.27	456.83	437.40
31000	2776.12	1481.09	1052.00	839.37	713.31	630.51	572.42	529.74	497.32	472.06	451.98
32000	2865.67	1528.87	1085.93	866.45	736.32	650.85	590.88	546.83	513.36	487.28	466.56
33000	2955.22	1576.65	1119.87	893.52	759.33	671.19	609.35	563.91	529.40	502.51	481.14
34000	3044.77	1624.42	1153.80	920.60	782.34	691.53	627.81	581.00	545.44	517.74	495.72
35000	3134.33	1672.20	1187.74	947.68	805.35	711.87	646.28	598.09	561.49	532.97	510.30
36000	3223.88	1719.98	1221.68	974.75	828.36	732.21	664.74	615.18	577.53	548.19	524.88
37000	3313.43	1767.75	1255.61	1001.83	851.37	752.55	683.21	632.27	593.57	563.42	539.46
38000	3402.98	1815.53	1289.55	1028.91	874.38	772.89	701.67	649.36	609.61	578.65	554.04
39000	3492.53	1863.31	1323.48	1055.98	897.39	793.22	720.14	666.44	625.66	593.87	568.62
40000	3582.09	1911.09	1357.42	1083.06	920.40	813.56	738.60	683.53	641.70	609.10	583.20
41000	3671.64	1958.86	1391.35	1110.13	943.41	833.90	757.07	700.62	657.74	624.33	597.78
42000	3761.19	2006.64	1425.29	1137.21	966.42	854.24	775.53	717.71	673.78	639.56	612.36
43000	3850.74	2054.42	1459.22	1164.29	989.43	874.58	794.00	734.80	689.82	654.78	626.94
44000	3940.29	2102.19	1493.16	1191.36	1012.44	894.92	812.46	751.88	705.87	670.01	641.52
45000	4029.85	2149.97	1527.09	1218.44	1035.45	915.26	830.93	768.97	721.91	685.24	656.10
46000	4119.40	2197.75	1561.03	1245.52	1058.46	935.60	849.39	786.06	737.95	700.47	670.68
47000	4208.95	2245.52	1594.96	1272.59	1081.47	955.94	867.85	803.15	753.99	715.69	685.26
48000	4298.50	2293.30	1628.90	1299.67	1104.48	976.28	886.32	820.24	770.04	730.92	699.84
49000	4388.05	2341.08	1662.83	1326.74	1127.49	996.61	904.78	837.32	786.08	746.15	714.42
50000	4477.61	2388.86	1696.77	1353.82	1150.50	1016.95	923.25	854.41	802.12	761.38	729.00
55000	4925.37	2627.74	1866.45	1489.20	1265.55	1118.65	1015.57	939.85	882.33	837.51	801.90
60000	5373.13	2866.63	2036.12	1624.58	1380.60	1220.34	1107.90	1025.29	962.54	913.65	874.80
65000	5820.89	3105.51	2205.80	1759.97	1495.65	1322.04	1200.22	1110.74	1042.76	989.79	947.70
70000	6268.65	3344.40	2375.48	1895.35	1610.69	1423.73	1292.55	1196.18	1122.97	1065.93	1020.60
75000	6716.41	3583.28	2545.15	2030.73	1725.74	1525.43	1384.87	1281.62	1203.18	1142.06	1093.50
80000	7164.17	3822.17	2714.83	2166.11	1840.79	1627.12	1477.20	1367.06	1283.39	1218.20	1166.39
85000	7611.93	4061.05	2884.50	2301.49	1955.84	1728.82	1569.52	1452.50	1363.60	1294.34	1239.29
90000	8059.69	4299.94	3054.18	2436.87	2070.89	1830.51	1661.85	1537.94	1443.81	1370.47	1312.19
95000	8507.45	4538.82	3223.86	2572.26	2185.94	1932.21	1754.17	1623.38	1524.02	1446.61	1385.09
100000	8955.21	4777.71	3393.53	2707.64	2300.99	2033.90	1846.49	1708.82	1604.24	1522.75	1457.99

Principal and Interest 13.50%
Monthly Payment Amortization Table

Term Amount	12 Years	13 Years	14 Years	15 Years	16 Years	17 Years	18 Years	19 Years	20 Years	25 Years	30 Years
50	.71	.69	.67	.65	.64	.63	.62	.62	.61	.59	.58
100	1.41	1.37	1.33	1.30	1.28	1.26	1.24	1.23	1.21	1.17	1.15
200	2.82	2.73	2.66	2.60	2.55	2.51	2.48	2.45	2.42	2.34	2.30
300	4.22	4.09	3.99	3.90	3.83	3.76	3.71	3.67	3.63	3.50	3.44
400	5.63	5.46	5.32	5.20	5.10	5.02	4.95	4.89	4.83	4.67	4.59
500	7.03	6.82	6.64	6.50	6.37	6.27	6.18	6.11	6.04	5.83	5.73
600	8.44	8.18	7.97	7.79	7.65	7.52	7.42	7.33	7.25	7.00	6.88
700	9.85	9.55	9.30	9.09	8.92	8.78	8.65	8.55	8.46	8.16	8.02
800	11.25	10.91	10.63	10.39	10.19	10.03	9.89	9.77	9.66	9.33	9.17
900	12.66	12.27	11.95	11.69	11.47	11.28	11.12	10.99	10.87	10.50	10.31
1000	14.06	13.63	13.28	12.99	12.74	12.53	12.36	12.21	12.08	11.66	11.46
2000	28.12	27.26	26.56	25.97	25.48	25.06	24.71	24.41	24.15	23.32	22.91
3000	42.18	40.89	39.84	38.95	38.22	37.59	37.06	36.61	36.23	34.97	34.37
4000	56.23	54.52	53.11	51.94	50.95	50.12	49.41	48.81	48.30	46.63	45.82
5000	70.29	68.15	66.39	64.92	63.69	62.65	61.77	61.02	60.37	58.29	57.28
6000	84.35	81.78	79.67	77.90	76.43	75.18	74.12	73.22	72.45	69.94	68.73
7000	98.41	95.41	92.94	90.89	89.16	87.71	86.47	85.42	84.52	81.60	80.18
8000	112.46	109.04	106.22	103.87	101.90	100.23	98.82	97.62	96.59	93.26	91.64
9000	126.52	122.67	119.50	116.85	114.64	112.76	111.18	109.82	108.67	104.91	103.09
10000	140.58	136.30	132.78	129.84	127.37	125.29	123.53	122.03	120.74	116.57	114.55
11000	154.63	149.93	146.05	142.82	140.11	137.82	135.88	134.23	132.82	128.23	126.00
12000	168.69	163.56	159.33	155.80	152.85	150.35	148.23	146.43	144.89	139.88	137.45
13000	182.75	177.19	172.61	168.79	165.58	162.88	160.59	158.63	156.96	151.54	148.91
14000	196.81	190.82	185.88	181.77	178.32	175.41	172.94	170.83	169.04	163.20	160.36
15000	210.86	204.45	199.16	194.75	191.06	187.94	185.29	183.04	181.11	174.85	171.82
16000	224.92	218.08	212.44	207.74	203.79	200.46	197.64	195.24	193.18	186.51	183.27
17000	238.98	231.71	225.72	220.72	216.53	212.99	209.99	207.44	205.26	198.16	194.73
18000	253.03	245.34	238.99	233.70	229.27	225.52	222.35	219.64	217.33	209.82	206.18
19000	267.09	258.97	252.27	246.69	242.00	238.05	234.70	231.85	229.41	221.48	217.63
20000	281.15	272.60	265.55	259.67	254.74	250.58	247.05	244.05	241.48	233.13	229.09
21000	295.21	286.23	278.82	272.65	267.48	263.11	259.40	256.25	253.55	244.79	240.54
22000	309.26	299.86	292.10	285.64	280.21	275.64	271.76	268.45	265.63	256.45	252.00
23000	323.32	313.49	305.38	298.62	292.95	288.16	284.11	280.65	277.70	268.10	263.45
24000	337.38	327.12	318.65	311.60	305.69	300.69	296.46	292.86	289.77	279.76	274.90
25000	351.43	340.75	331.93	324.58	318.42	313.22	308.81	305.06	301.85	291.42	286.36
26000	365.49	354.38	345.21	337.57	331.16	325.75	321.17	317.26	313.92	303.07	297.81
27000	379.55	368.01	358.49	350.55	343.90	338.28	333.52	329.46	326.00	314.73	309.27
28000	393.61	381.64	371.76	363.53	356.63	350.81	345.87	341.66	338.07	326.39	320.72
29000	407.66	395.27	385.04	376.52	369.37	363.34	358.22	353.87	350.14	338.04	332.17
30000	421.72	408.90	398.32	389.50	382.11	375.87	370.57	366.07	362.22	349.70	343.63
31000	435.78	422.53	411.59	402.48	394.84	388.39	382.93	378.27	374.29	361.35	355.08
32000	449.83	436.16	424.87	415.47	407.58	400.92	395.28	390.47	386.36	373.01	366.54
33000	463.89	449.79	438.15	428.45	420.32	413.45	407.63	402.67	398.44	384.67	377.99
34000	477.95	463.42	451.43	441.43	433.05	425.98	419.98	414.88	410.51	396.32	389.45
35000	492.01	477.05	464.70	454.42	445.79	438.51	432.34	427.08	422.59	407.98	400.90
36000	506.06	490.68	477.98	467.40	458.53	451.04	444.69	439.28	434.66	419.64	412.35
37000	520.12	504.31	491.26	480.38	471.26	463.57	457.04	451.48	446.73	431.29	423.81
38000	534.18	517.94	504.53	493.37	484.00	476.10	469.39	463.69	458.81	442.95	435.26
39000	548.23	531.57	517.81	506.35	496.74	488.62	481.75	475.89	470.88	454.61	446.72
40000	562.29	545.20	531.09	519.33	509.47	501.15	494.10	488.09	482.95	466.26	458.17
41000	576.35	558.83	544.36	532.32	522.21	513.68	506.45	500.29	495.03	477.92	469.62
42000	590.41	572.46	557.64	545.30	534.95	526.21	518.80	512.49	507.10	489.58	481.08
43000	604.46	586.09	570.92	558.28	547.68	538.74	531.15	524.70	519.18	501.23	492.53
44000	618.52	599.72	584.20	571.27	560.42	551.27	543.51	536.90	531.25	512.89	503.99
45000	632.58	613.35	597.47	584.25	573.16	563.80	555.86	549.10	543.32	524.55	515.44
46000	646.63	626.98	610.75	597.23	585.89	576.32	568.21	561.30	555.40	536.20	526.89
47000	660.69	640.61	624.03	610.21	598.63	588.85	580.56	573.50	567.47	547.86	538.35
48000	674.75	654.24	637.30	623.20	611.37	601.38	592.92	585.71	579.54	559.51	549.80
49000	688.81	667.87	650.58	636.18	624.10	613.91	605.27	597.91	591.62	571.17	561.26
50000	702.86	681.50	663.86	649.16	636.84	626.44	617.62	610.11	603.69	582.83	572.71
55000	773.15	749.65	730.24	714.08	700.52	689.08	679.38	671.12	664.06	641.11	629.98
60000	843.44	817.80	796.63	779.00	764.21	751.73	741.14	732.13	724.43	699.39	687.25
65000	913.72	885.95	863.01	843.91	827.89	814.37	802.91	793.14	784.80	757.67	744.52
70000	984.01	954.10	929.40	908.83	891.57	877.01	864.67	854.15	845.17	815.96	801.79
75000	1054.29	1022.25	995.79	973.74	955.26	939.66	926.43	915.16	905.54	874.24	859.06
80000	1124.58	1090.40	1062.17	1038.66	1018.94	1002.30	988.19	976.17	965.90	932.52	916.33
85000	1194.86	1158.55	1128.56	1103.58	1082.62	1064.94	1049.95	1037.18	1026.27	990.80	973.61
90000	1265.15	1226.70	1194.94	1168.49	1146.31	1127.59	1111.71	1098.20	1086.64	1049.09	1030.88
95000	1335.44	1294.85	1261.33	1233.41	1209.99	1190.23	1173.47	1159.21	1147.01	1107.37	1088.15
100000	1405.72	1363.00	1327.71	1298.32	1273.67	1252.87	1235.24	1220.22	1207.38	1165.65	1145.42

13.75%   Principal and Interest
Monthly Payment Amortization Table

Term Amount	1 Year	2 Years	3 Years	4 Years	5 Years	6 Years	7 Years	8 Years	9 Years	10 Years	11 Years
50	4.49	2.40	1.71	1.37	1.16	1.03	.94	.87	.81	.77	.74
100	8.97	4.79	3.41	2.73	2.32	2.05	1.87	1.73	1.62	1.54	1.48
200	17.94	9.58	6.82	5.45	4.63	4.10	3.73	3.45	3.24	3.08	2.95
300	26.91	14.37	10.22	8.17	6.95	6.15	5.59	5.17	4.86	4.62	4.42
400	35.87	19.16	13.63	10.89	9.26	8.19	7.45	6.90	6.48	6.16	5.90
500	44.84	23.95	17.03	13.61	11.57	10.24	9.31	8.62	8.10	7.69	7.37
600	53.81	28.74	20.44	16.33	13.89	12.29	11.17	10.34	9.72	9.23	8.84
700	62.77	33.53	23.84	19.05	16.20	14.34	13.03	12.07	11.34	10.77	10.32
800	71.74	38.32	27.25	21.77	18.52	16.38	14.89	13.79	12.96	12.31	11.79
900	80.71	43.11	30.66	24.49	20.83	18.43	16.75	15.51	14.57	13.84	13.26
1000	89.67	47.90	34.06	27.21	23.14	20.48	18.61	17.23	16.19	15.38	14.74
2000	179.34	95.79	68.12	54.41	46.28	40.95	37.21	34.46	32.38	30.76	29.47
3000	269.01	143.69	102.17	81.61	69.42	61.42	55.81	51.69	48.57	46.14	44.20
4000	358.68	191.58	136.23	108.81	92.56	81.89	74.41	68.92	64.76	61.51	58.94
5000	448.35	239.48	170.29	136.01	115.70	102.37	93.02	86.15	80.94	76.89	73.67
6000	538.02	287.37	204.34	163.21	138.84	122.84	111.62	103.38	97.13	92.27	88.40
7000	627.69	335.27	238.40	190.41	161.98	143.31	130.22	120.61	113.32	107.64	103.14
8000	717.36	383.16	272.46	217.61	185.12	163.78	148.82	137.84	129.51	123.02	117.87
9000	807.03	431.06	306.51	244.82	208.25	184.25	167.42	155.07	145.69	138.40	132.60
10000	896.70	478.95	340.57	272.02	231.39	204.73	186.03	172.30	161.88	153.77	147.33
11000	986.37	526.85	374.62	299.22	254.53	225.20	204.63	189.53	178.07	169.15	162.07
12000	1076.04	574.74	408.68	326.42	277.67	245.67	223.23	206.76	194.26	184.53	176.80
13000	1165.71	622.64	442.74	353.62	300.81	266.14	241.83	223.99	210.44	199.90	191.53
14000	1255.38	670.53	476.79	380.82	323.95	286.61	260.44	241.22	226.63	215.28	206.27
15000	1345.05	718.43	510.85	408.02	347.09	307.09	279.04	258.45	242.82	230.66	221.00
16000	1434.72	766.32	544.91	435.22	370.23	327.56	297.64	275.68	259.01	246.03	235.73
17000	1524.39	814.22	578.96	462.43	393.37	348.03	316.24	292.91	275.20	261.41	250.46
18000	1614.06	862.11	613.02	489.63	416.50	368.50	334.84	310.14	291.38	276.79	265.20
19000	1703.73	910.01	647.08	516.83	439.64	388.98	353.45	327.37	307.57	292.16	279.93
20000	1793.40	957.90	681.13	544.03	462.78	409.45	372.05	344.60	323.76	307.54	294.66
21000	1883.07	1005.80	715.19	571.23	485.92	429.92	390.65	361.83	339.95	322.92	309.40
22000	1972.73	1053.69	749.24	598.43	509.06	450.39	409.25	379.05	356.13	338.29	324.13
23000	2062.40	1101.59	783.30	625.63	532.20	470.86	427.85	396.28	372.32	353.67	338.86
24000	2152.07	1149.48	817.36	652.83	555.34	491.34	446.46	413.51	388.51	369.05	353.59
25000	2241.74	1197.38	851.41	680.04	578.48	511.81	465.06	430.74	404.70	384.42	368.33
26000	2331.41	1245.27	885.47	707.24	601.61	532.28	483.66	447.97	420.88	399.80	383.06
27000	2421.08	1293.17	919.53	734.44	624.75	552.75	502.26	465.20	437.07	415.18	397.79
28000	2510.75	1341.06	953.58	761.64	647.89	573.22	520.87	482.43	453.26	430.55	412.53
29000	2600.42	1388.96	987.64	788.84	671.03	593.70	539.47	499.66	469.45	445.93	427.26
30000	2690.09	1436.85	1021.69	816.04	694.17	614.17	558.07	516.89	485.64	461.31	441.99
31000	2779.76	1484.75	1055.75	843.24	717.31	634.64	576.67	534.12	501.82	476.68	456.72
32000	2869.43	1532.64	1089.81	870.44	740.45	655.11	595.27	551.35	518.01	492.06	471.46
33000	2959.10	1580.54	1123.86	897.65	763.59	675.58	613.88	568.58	534.20	507.44	486.19
34000	3048.77	1628.43	1157.92	924.85	786.73	696.06	632.48	585.81	550.39	522.81	500.92
35000	3138.44	1676.33	1191.98	952.05	809.86	716.53	651.08	603.04	566.57	538.19	515.66
36000	3228.11	1724.22	1226.03	979.25	833.00	737.00	669.68	620.27	582.76	553.57	530.39
37000	3317.78	1772.12	1260.09	1006.45	856.14	757.47	688.29	637.50	598.95	568.94	545.12
38000	3407.45	1820.01	1294.15	1033.65	879.28	777.95	706.89	654.73	615.14	584.32	559.85
39000	3497.12	1867.90	1328.20	1060.85	902.42	798.42	725.49	671.96	631.32	599.70	574.59
40000	3586.79	1915.80	1362.26	1088.05	925.56	818.89	744.09	689.19	647.51	615.07	589.32
41000	3676.46	1963.69	1396.31	1115.26	948.70	839.36	762.69	706.42	663.70	630.45	604.05
42000	3766.13	2011.59	1430.37	1142.46	971.84	859.83	781.30	723.65	679.89	645.83	618.79
43000	3855.79	2059.48	1464.43	1169.66	994.98	880.31	799.90	740.87	696.08	661.20	633.52
44000	3945.46	2107.38	1498.48	1196.86	1018.11	900.78	818.50	758.10	712.26	676.58	648.25
45000	4035.13	2155.27	1532.54	1224.06	1041.25	921.25	837.10	775.33	728.45	691.96	662.98
46000	4124.80	2203.17	1566.60	1251.26	1064.39	941.72	855.71	792.56	744.64	707.33	677.72
47000	4214.47	2251.06	1600.65	1278.46	1087.53	962.19	874.31	809.79	760.83	722.71	692.45
48000	4304.14	2298.96	1634.71	1305.66	1110.67	982.67	892.91	827.02	777.01	738.09	707.18
49000	4393.81	2346.85	1668.77	1332.87	1133.81	1003.14	911.51	844.25	793.20	753.46	721.92
50000	4483.48	2394.75	1702.82	1360.07	1156.95	1023.61	930.11	861.48	809.39	768.84	736.65
55000	4931.83	2634.22	1873.10	1496.07	1272.64	1125.97	1023.12	947.63	890.33	845.72	810.31
60000	5380.18	2873.70	2043.39	1632.08	1388.34	1228.33	1116.14	1033.78	971.27	922.61	883.98
65000	5828.52	3113.17	2213.67	1768.09	1504.03	1330.69	1209.15	1119.92	1052.20	999.49	957.64
70000	6276.87	3352.65	2383.95	1904.09	1619.72	1433.05	1302.16	1206.07	1133.14	1076.37	1031.31
75000	6725.22	3592.12	2554.23	2040.10	1735.42	1535.41	1395.17	1292.22	1214.08	1153.26	1104.97
80000	7173.57	3831.59	2724.51	2176.10	1851.11	1637.77	1488.18	1378.37	1295.02	1230.14	1178.64
85000	7621.92	4071.07	2894.79	2312.11	1966.81	1740.13	1581.19	1464.51	1375.96	1307.02	1252.30
90000	8070.26	4310.54	3065.07	2448.12	2082.50	1842.50	1674.20	1550.66	1456.90	1383.91	1325.97
95000	8518.61	4550.02	3235.36	2584.12	2198.20	1944.86	1767.21	1636.81	1537.83	1460.79	1399.63
100000	8966.96	4789.49	3405.64	2720.13	2313.89	2047.22	1860.22	1722.96	1618.77	1537.67	1473.29

Principal and Interest
Monthly Payment Amortization Table   13.75%

Term / Amount	12 Years	13 Years	14 Years	15 Years	16 Years	17 Years	18 Years	19 Years	20 Years	25 Years	30 Years
50	.72	.69	.68	.66	.65	.64	.63	.62	.62	.60	.59
100	1.43	1.38	1.35	1.32	1.30	1.28	1.26	1.24	1.23	1.19	1.17
200	2.85	2.76	2.69	2.63	2.59	2.55	2.51	2.48	2.46	2.37	2.34
300	4.27	4.14	4.04	3.95	3.88	3.82	3.76	3.72	3.68	3.56	3.50
400	5.69	5.52	5.38	5.26	5.17	5.09	5.02	4.96	4.91	4.74	4.67
500	7.11	6.90	6.73	6.58	6.46	6.36	6.27	6.20	6.13	5.93	5.83
600	8.53	8.28	8.07	7.89	7.75	7.63	7.52	7.43	7.36	7.11	7.00
700	9.95	9.66	9.41	9.21	9.04	8.90	8.77	8.67	8.58	8.30	8.16
800	11.38	11.04	10.76	10.52	10.33	10.17	10.03	9.91	9.81	9.48	9.33
900	12.80	12.42	12.10	11.84	11.62	11.44	11.28	11.15	11.03	10.67	10.49
1000	14.22	13.80	13.45	13.15	12.91	12.71	12.53	12.39	12.26	11.85	11.66
2000	28.43	27.59	26.89	26.30	25.82	25.41	25.06	24.77	24.51	23.70	23.31
3000	42.65	41.38	40.33	39.45	38.72	38.11	37.59	37.15	36.77	35.54	34.96
4000	56.86	55.17	53.77	52.60	51.63	50.81	50.12	49.53	49.02	47.39	46.61
5000	71.07	68.96	67.21	65.75	64.54	63.51	62.64	61.91	61.28	59.24	58.26
6000	85.29	82.75	80.65	78.90	77.44	76.21	75.17	74.29	73.53	71.08	69.91
7000	99.50	96.54	94.09	92.05	90.35	88.91	87.70	86.67	85.78	82.93	81.56
8000	113.72	110.33	107.53	105.20	103.26	101.62	100.23	99.05	98.04	94.78	93.21
9000	127.93	124.12	120.97	118.35	116.16	114.32	112.75	111.43	110.29	106.62	104.87
10000	142.14	137.91	134.41	131.50	129.07	127.02	125.28	123.81	122.55	118.47	116.52
11000	156.36	151.70	147.85	144.65	141.98	139.72	137.81	136.19	134.80	130.32	128.17
12000	170.57	165.49	161.29	157.80	154.88	152.42	150.34	148.57	147.05	142.16	139.82
13000	184.78	179.28	174.73	170.95	167.79	165.12	162.86	160.95	159.31	154.01	151.47
14000	199.00	193.07	188.17	184.10	180.69	177.82	175.39	173.33	171.56	165.86	163.12
15000	213.21	206.86	201.61	197.25	193.60	190.52	187.92	185.71	183.82	177.70	174.77
16000	227.43	220.65	215.05	210.40	206.51	203.23	200.45	198.09	196.07	189.55	186.42
17000	241.64	234.44	228.49	223.55	219.41	215.93	212.97	210.47	208.32	201.40	198.07
18000	255.85	248.23	241.94	236.70	232.32	228.63	225.50	222.85	220.58	213.24	209.73
19000	270.07	262.02	255.38	249.85	245.23	241.33	238.03	235.23	232.83	225.09	221.38
20000	284.28	275.81	268.82	263.00	258.13	254.03	250.56	247.61	245.09	236.94	233.03
21000	298.50	289.60	282.26	276.15	271.04	266.73	263.09	259.99	257.34	248.78	244.68
22000	312.71	303.39	295.70	289.30	283.95	279.43	275.61	272.37	269.59	260.63	256.33
23000	326.92	317.18	309.14	302.45	296.85	292.13	288.14	284.75	281.85	272.48	267.98
24000	341.14	330.97	322.58	315.60	309.76	304.84	300.67	297.13	294.10	284.32	279.63
25000	355.35	344.76	336.02	328.75	322.67	317.54	313.20	309.51	306.36	296.17	291.28
26000	369.56	358.55	349.46	341.90	335.57	330.24	325.72	321.89	318.61	308.02	302.93
27000	383.78	372.34	362.90	355.05	348.48	342.94	338.25	334.27	330.86	319.86	314.59
28000	397.99	386.13	376.34	368.20	361.38	355.64	350.78	346.65	343.12	331.71	326.24
29000	412.21	399.92	389.78	381.35	374.29	368.34	363.31	359.03	355.37	343.56	337.89
30000	426.42	413.71	403.22	394.50	387.20	381.04	375.83	371.41	367.63	355.40	349.54
31000	440.63	427.50	416.66	407.65	400.10	393.75	388.36	383.79	379.88	367.25	361.19
32000	454.85	441.29	430.10	420.80	413.01	406.45	400.89	396.17	392.13	379.10	372.84
33000	469.06	455.08	443.54	433.95	425.92	419.15	413.42	408.55	404.39	390.94	384.49
34000	483.28	468.87	456.98	447.10	438.82	431.85	425.94	420.93	416.64	402.79	396.14
35000	497.49	482.66	470.42	460.25	451.73	444.55	438.47	433.31	428.90	414.64	407.79
36000	511.70	496.45	483.87	473.40	464.64	457.25	451.00	445.69	441.15	426.48	419.45
37000	525.92	510.24	497.31	486.55	477.54	469.95	463.53	458.07	453.40	438.33	431.10
38000	540.13	524.03	510.75	499.70	490.45	482.65	476.06	470.45	465.66	450.18	442.75
39000	554.34	537.82	524.19	512.85	503.35	495.36	488.58	482.83	477.91	462.02	454.40
40000	568.56	551.61	537.63	526.00	516.26	508.06	501.11	495.21	490.17	473.87	466.05
41000	582.77	565.40	551.07	539.15	529.17	520.76	513.64	507.59	502.42	485.72	477.70
42000	596.99	579.19	564.51	552.30	542.07	533.46	526.17	519.97	514.68	497.56	489.35
43000	611.20	592.98	577.95	565.45	554.98	546.16	538.69	532.35	526.93	509.41	501.00
44000	625.41	606.77	591.39	578.60	567.89	558.86	551.22	544.73	539.18	521.26	512.65
45000	639.63	620.56	604.83	591.75	580.79	571.56	563.75	557.11	551.44	533.10	524.31
46000	653.84	634.35	618.27	604.90	593.70	584.26	576.28	569.49	563.69	544.95	535.96
47000	668.05	648.14	631.71	618.05	606.61	596.97	588.80	581.87	575.95	556.80	547.61
48000	682.27	661.93	645.15	631.20	619.51	609.67	601.33	594.25	588.20	568.64	559.26
49000	696.48	675.72	658.59	644.35	632.42	622.37	613.86	606.63	600.45	580.49	570.91
50000	710.70	689.51	672.03	657.50	645.33	635.07	626.39	619.01	612.71	592.34	582.56
55000	781.77	758.46	739.24	723.25	709.86	698.58	689.03	680.91	673.98	651.57	640.82
60000	852.83	827.41	806.44	789.00	774.39	762.08	751.66	742.81	735.25	710.80	699.07
65000	923.90	896.36	873.64	854.75	838.92	825.59	814.30	804.71	796.52	770.04	757.33
70000	994.97	965.31	940.84	920.50	903.45	889.10	876.94	866.61	857.79	829.27	815.58
75000	1066.04	1034.26	1008.05	986.25	967.99	952.60	939.58	928.51	919.06	888.50	873.84
80000	1137.11	1103.21	1075.25	1051.99	1032.52	1016.11	1002.22	990.41	980.33	947.74	932.10
85000	1208.18	1172.16	1142.45	1117.74	1097.05	1079.61	1064.85	1052.31	1041.60	1006.97	990.35
90000	1279.25	1241.11	1209.66	1183.49	1161.58	1143.12	1127.49	1114.21	1102.87	1066.20	1048.61
95000	1350.32	1310.06	1276.86	1249.24	1226.11	1206.63	1190.13	1176.11	1164.14	1125.44	1106.86
100000	1421.39	1379.01	1344.06	1314.99	1290.65	1270.13	1252.77	1238.01	1225.41	1184.67	1165.12

14.00% Principal and Interest
Monthly Payment Amortization Table

Term Amount	1 Year	2 Years	3 Years	4 Years	5 Years	6 Years	7 Years	8 Years	9 Years	10 Years	11 Years
50	4.49	2.41	1.71	1.37	1.17	1.04	.94	.87	.82	.78	.75
100	8.98	4.81	3.42	2.74	2.33	2.07	1.88	1.74	1.64	1.56	1.49
200	17.96	9.61	6.84	5.47	4.66	4.13	3.75	3.48	3.27	3.11	2.98
300	26.94	14.41	10.26	8.20	6.99	6.19	5.63	5.22	4.91	4.66	4.47
400	35.92	19.21	13.68	10.94	9.31	8.25	7.50	6.95	6.54	6.22	5.96
500	44.90	24.01	17.09	13.67	11.64	10.31	9.38	8.69	8.17	7.77	7.45
600	53.88	28.81	20.51	16.40	13.97	12.37	11.25	10.43	9.81	9.32	8.94
700	62.86	33.61	23.93	19.13	16.29	14.43	13.12	12.17	11.44	10.37	10.43
800	71.83	38.42	27.35	21.87	18.62	16.49	15.00	13.90	13.07	12.43	11.91
900	80.81	43.22	30.76	24.60	20.95	18.55	16.87	15.64	14.71	13.98	13.40
1000	89.79	48.02	34.18	27.33	23.27	20.61	18.75	17.38	16.34	15.53	14.89
2000	179.58	96.03	68.36	54.66	46.54	41.22	37.49	34.75	32.67	31.06	29.78
3000	269.37	144.04	102.54	81.98	69.81	61.82	56.23	52.12	49.01	46.58	44.66
4000	359.15	192.06	136.72	109.31	93.08	82.43	74.97	69.49	65.34	62.11	59.55
5000	448.94	240.07	170.89	136.64	116.35	103.03	93.71	86.86	81.67	77.64	74.44
6000	538.73	288.08	205.07	163.96	139.61	123.64	112.45	104.23	98.01	93.16	89.32
7000	628.51	336.10	239.25	191.29	162.88	144.25	131.19	121.61	114.34	108.69	104.21
8000	718.30	384.11	273.43	218.62	186.15	164.85	149.93	138.98	130.67	124.22	119.10
9000	808.09	432.12	307.60	245.94	209.42	185.46	168.67	156.35	147.01	139.74	133.98
10000	897.88	480.13	341.78	273.27	232.69	206.06	187.41	173.72	163.34	155.27	148.87
11000	987.66	528.15	375.96	300.60	255.96	226.67	206.15	191.09	179.68	170.80	163.76
12000	1077.45	576.16	410.14	327.92	279.22	247.27	224.89	208.46	196.01	186.32	178.64
13000	1167.24	624.17	444.31	355.25	302.49	267.88	243.63	225.83	212.34	201.85	193.53
14000	1257.02	672.19	478.49	382.58	325.76	288.49	262.37	243.21	228.68	217.38	208.42
15000	1346.81	720.20	512.67	409.90	349.03	309.09	281.11	260.58	245.01	232.90	223.30
16000	1436.60	768.21	546.85	437.23	372.30	329.70	299.85	277.95	261.34	248.43	238.19
17000	1526.39	816.22	581.02	464.56	395.57	350.30	318.59	295.32	277.68	263.96	253.08
18000	1616.17	864.24	615.20	491.88	418.83	370.91	337.33	312.69	294.01	279.48	267.96
19000	1705.96	912.25	649.38	519.21	442.10	391.51	356.07	330.06	310.35	295.01	282.85
20000	1795.75	960.26	683.56	546.53	465.37	412.12	374.81	347.44	326.68	310.54	297.74
21000	1885.53	1008.28	717.74	573.86	488.64	432.73	393.55	364.81	343.01	326.06	312.62
22000	1975.32	1056.29	751.91	601.19	511.91	453.33	412.29	382.18	359.35	341.59	327.51
23000	2065.11	1104.30	786.09	628.51	535.17	473.94	431.03	399.55	375.68	357.12	342.40
24000	2154.90	1152.31	820.27	655.84	558.44	494.54	449.77	416.92	392.01	372.64	357.28
25000	2244.68	1200.33	854.45	683.17	581.71	515.15	468.51	434.29	408.35	388.17	372.17
26000	2334.47	1248.34	888.62	710.49	604.98	535.75	487.25	451.66	424.68	403.70	387.06
27000	2424.26	1296.35	922.80	737.82	628.25	556.36	505.99	469.04	441.01	419.22	401.94
28000	2514.04	1344.37	956.98	765.15	651.52	576.97	524.73	486.41	457.35	434.75	416.83
29000	2603.83	1392.38	991.16	792.47	674.78	597.57	543.47	503.78	473.68	450.28	431.72
30000	2693.62	1440.39	1025.33	819.80	698.05	618.18	562.21	521.15	490.02	465.80	446.60
31000	2783.41	1488.40	1059.51	847.13	721.32	638.78	580.95	538.52	506.35	481.33	461.49
32000	2873.19	1536.42	1093.69	874.45	744.59	659.39	599.69	555.89	522.68	496.86	476.38
33000	2962.98	1584.43	1127.87	901.78	767.86	679.99	618.43	573.26	539.02	512.38	491.26
34000	3052.77	1632.44	1162.04	929.11	791.13	700.60	637.17	590.64	555.35	527.91	506.15
35000	3142.55	1680.46	1196.22	956.43	814.39	721.21	655.91	608.01	571.68	543.44	521.04
36000	3232.34	1728.47	1230.40	983.76	837.66	741.81	674.65	625.38	588.02	558.96	535.92
37000	3322.13	1776.48	1264.58	1011.08	860.93	762.42	693.39	642.75	604.35	574.49	550.81
38000	3411.92	1824.49	1298.75	1038.41	884.20	783.02	712.13	660.12	620.69	590.02	565.70
39000	3501.70	1872.51	1332.93	1065.74	907.47	803.63	730.87	677.49	637.02	605.54	580.58
40000	3591.49	1920.52	1367.11	1093.06	930.74	824.23	749.61	694.87	653.35	621.07	595.47
41000	3681.28	1968.53	1401.29	1120.39	954.00	844.84	768.35	712.24	669.69	636.60	610.36
42000	3771.06	2016.55	1435.47	1147.72	977.27	865.45	787.09	729.61	686.02	652.12	625.24
43000	3860.85	2064.56	1469.64	1175.04	1000.54	886.05	805.83	746.98	702.35	667.65	640.13
44000	3950.64	2112.57	1503.82	1202.37	1023.81	906.66	824.57	764.35	718.69	683.18	655.02
45000	4040.43	2160.58	1538.00	1229.70	1047.08	927.26	843.31	781.72	735.02	698.70	669.90
46000	4130.21	2208.60	1572.18	1257.02	1070.34	947.87	862.05	799.09	751.36	714.23	684.79
47000	4220.00	2256.61	1606.35	1284.35	1093.61	968.47	880.79	816.47	767.69	729.76	699.68
48000	4309.79	2304.62	1640.53	1311.68	1116.88	989.08	899.53	833.84	784.02	745.28	714.56
49000	4399.57	2352.64	1674.71	1339.00	1140.15	1009.69	918.27	851.21	800.36	760.81	729.45
50000	4489.36	2400.65	1708.89	1366.33	1163.42	1030.29	937.01	868.58	816.69	776.34	744.34
55000	4938.30	2640.71	1879.77	1502.96	1279.76	1133.32	1030.71	955.44	898.36	853.97	818.77
60000	5387.23	2880.78	2050.66	1639.59	1396.10	1236.35	1124.41	1042.30	980.03	931.60	893.20
65000	5836.17	3120.84	2221.55	1776.23	1512.44	1339.38	1218.11	1129.15	1061.70	1009.24	967.64
70000	6285.10	3360.91	2392.44	1912.86	1628.78	1442.41	1311.81	1216.01	1143.36	1086.87	1042.07
75000	6734.04	3600.97	2563.33	2049.49	1745.12	1545.44	1405.51	1302.87	1225.03	1164.50	1116.50
80000	7182.97	3841.04	2734.22	2186.12	1861.47	1648.46	1499.21	1389.73	1306.70	1242.14	1190.94
85000	7631.91	4081.10	2905.10	2322.76	1977.81	1751.49	1592.91	1476.58	1388.37	1319.77	1265.37
90000	8080.85	4321.16	3075.99	2459.39	2094.15	1854.52	1686.61	1563.44	1470.04	1397.40	1339.80
95000	8529.78	4561.23	3246.88	2596.02	2210.49	1957.55	1780.31	1650.30	1551.71	1475.04	1414.24
100000	8978.72	4801.29	3417.77	2732.65	2326.83	2060.58	1874.01	1737.16	1633.38	1552.67	1488.67

Principal and Interest
Monthly Payment Amortization Table

14.00%

Term Amount	12 Years	13 Years	14 Years	15 Years	16 Years	17 Years	18 Years	19 Years	20 Years	25 Years	30 Years
50	.72	.70	.69	.67	.66	.65	.64	.63	.63	.61	.60
100	1.44	1.40	1.37	1.34	1.31	1.29	1.28	1.26	1.25	1.21	1.19
200	2.88	2.80	2.73	2.67	2.62	2.58	2.55	2.52	2.49	2.41	2.37
300	4.32	4.19	4.09	4.00	3.93	3.87	3.82	3.77	3.74	3.62	3.56
400	5.75	5.59	5.45	5.33	5.24	5.15	5.09	5.03	4.98	4.82	4.74
500	7.19	6.98	6.81	6.66	6.54	6.44	6.36	6.28	6.22	6.02	5.93
600	8.63	8.38	8.17	8.00	7.85	7.73	7.63	7.54	7.47	7.23	7.11
700	10.06	9.77	9.53	9.33	9.16	9.02	8.90	8.80	8.71	8.43	8.30
800	11.50	11.17	10.89	10.66	10.47	10.30	10.17	10.05	9.95	9.64	9.48
900	12.94	12.56	12.25	11.99	11.77	11.59	11.44	11.31	11.20	10.84	10.67
1000	14.38	13.96	13.61	13.32	13.08	12.88	12.71	12.56	12.44	12.04	11.85
2000	28.75	27.91	27.21	26.64	26.16	25.75	25.41	25.12	24.88	24.08	23.70
3000	43.12	41.86	40.82	39.96	39.24	38.63	38.12	37.68	37.31	36.12	35.55
4000	57.49	55.81	54.42	53.27	52.31	51.50	50.82	50.24	49.75	48.16	47.40
5000	71.86	69.76	68.03	66.59	65.39	64.38	63.52	62.80	62.18	60.19	59.25
6000	86.23	83.71	81.63	79.91	78.47	77.25	76.23	75.36	74.62	72.23	71.10
7000	100.60	97.66	95.24	93.23	91.54	90.13	88.93	87.92	87.05	84.27	82.95
8000	114.98	111.61	108.84	106.54	104.62	103.00	101.64	100.48	99.49	96.31	94.79
9000	129.35	125.56	122.45	119.86	117.70	115.88	114.34	113.03	111.92	108.34	106.64
10000	143.72	139.52	136.05	133.18	130.77	128.75	127.04	125.59	124.36	120.38	118.49
11000	158.09	153.47	149.66	146.50	143.85	141.63	139.75	138.15	136.79	132.42	130.34
12000	172.46	167.42	163.26	159.81	156.93	154.50	152.45	150.71	149.23	144.46	142.19
13000	186.83	181.37	176.87	173.13	170.01	167.38	165.15	163.27	161.66	156.49	154.04
14000	201.20	195.32	190.47	186.45	183.08	180.25	177.86	175.83	174.10	168.53	165.89
15000	215.57	209.27	204.08	199.77	196.16	193.13	190.56	188.39	186.53	180.57	177.74
16000	229.95	223.22	217.68	213.08	209.24	206.00	203.27	200.95	198.97	192.61	189.58
17000	244.32	237.17	231.29	226.40	222.31	218.88	215.97	213.50	211.40	204.64	201.43
18000	258.69	251.12	244.89	239.72	235.39	231.75	228.67	226.06	223.84	216.68	213.28
19000	273.06	265.07	258.50	253.04	248.47	244.63	241.38	238.62	236.27	228.72	225.13
20000	287.43	279.03	272.10	266.35	261.54	257.50	254.08	251.18	248.71	240.76	236.98
21000	301.80	292.98	285.71	279.67	274.62	270.38	266.79	263.74	261.14	252.79	248.83
22000	316.17	306.93	299.31	292.99	287.70	283.25	279.49	276.30	273.58	264.83	260.68
23000	330.54	320.88	312.92	306.31	300.78	296.12	292.19	288.86	286.01	276.87	272.53
24000	344.92	334.83	326.52	319.62	313.85	309.00	304.90	301.42	298.45	288.91	284.37
25000	359.29	348.78	340.13	332.94	326.93	321.87	317.60	313.97	310.89	300.95	296.22
26000	373.66	362.73	353.73	346.26	340.01	334.75	330.30	326.53	323.32	312.98	308.07
27000	388.03	376.68	367.34	359.58	353.08	347.62	343.01	339.09	335.76	325.02	319.92
28000	402.40	390.63	380.94	372.89	366.16	360.50	355.71	351.65	348.19	337.06	331.77
29000	416.77	404.58	394.55	386.21	379.24	373.37	368.42	364.21	360.63	349.10	343.62
30000	431.14	418.54	408.15	399.53	392.31	386.25	381.12	376.77	373.06	361.13	355.47
31000	445.51	432.49	421.76	412.84	405.39	399.12	393.82	389.33	385.50	373.17	367.32
32000	459.89	446.44	435.36	426.16	418.47	412.00	406.53	401.89	397.93	385.21	379.16
33000	474.26	460.39	448.97	439.48	431.55	424.87	419.23	414.44	410.37	397.25	391.01
34000	488.63	474.34	462.57	452.80	444.62	437.75	431.94	427.00	422.80	409.28	402.86
35000	503.00	488.29	476.18	466.11	457.70	450.62	444.64	439.56	435.24	421.32	414.71
36000	517.37	502.24	489.78	479.43	470.78	463.50	457.34	452.12	447.67	433.36	426.56
37000	531.74	516.19	503.39	492.75	483.85	476.37	470.05	464.68	460.11	445.40	438.41
38000	546.11	530.14	516.99	506.07	496.93	489.25	482.75	477.24	472.54	457.43	450.26
39000	560.48	544.10	530.60	519.38	510.01	502.12	495.45	489.80	484.98	469.47	462.10
40000	574.86	558.05	544.20	532.70	523.08	515.00	508.16	502.36	497.41	481.51	473.95
41000	589.23	572.00	557.81	546.02	536.16	527.87	520.86	514.91	509.85	493.55	485.80
42000	603.60	585.95	571.41	559.34	549.24	540.75	533.57	527.47	522.28	505.58	497.65
43000	617.97	599.90	585.02	572.65	562.32	553.62	546.27	540.03	534.72	517.62	509.50
44000	632.34	613.85	598.62	585.97	575.39	566.49	558.97	552.59	547.15	529.66	521.35
45000	646.71	627.80	612.23	599.29	588.47	579.37	571.68	565.15	559.59	541.70	533.20
46000	661.08	641.75	625.83	612.61	601.55	592.24	584.38	577.71	572.02	553.74	545.05
47000	675.45	655.70	639.44	625.92	614.62	605.12	597.09	590.27	584.46	565.77	556.89
48000	689.83	669.65	653.04	639.24	627.70	617.99	609.79	602.83	596.89	577.81	568.74
49000	704.20	683.61	666.64	652.56	640.78	630.87	622.49	615.38	609.33	589.85	580.59
50000	718.57	697.56	680.25	665.88	653.85	643.74	635.20	627.94	621.77	601.89	592.44
55000	790.42	767.31	748.27	732.46	719.24	708.12	698.72	690.74	683.94	662.07	651.68
60000	862.28	837.07	816.30	799.05	784.62	772.49	762.23	753.53	746.12	722.26	710.93
65000	934.14	906.82	884.32	865.64	850.01	836.86	825.75	816.32	808.29	782.45	770.17
70000	1005.99	976.58	952.35	932.22	915.39	901.24	889.27	879.12	870.47	842.64	829.42
75000	1077.85	1046.33	1020.37	998.81	980.78	965.61	952.79	941.91	932.65	902.83	888.66
80000	1149.71	1116.09	1088.40	1065.40	1046.16	1029.99	1016.31	1004.71	994.82	963.01	947.90
85000	1221.56	1185.84	1156.42	1131.99	1111.55	1094.36	1079.83	1067.50	1057.00	1023.20	1007.15
90000	1293.42	1255.60	1224.45	1198.57	1176.93	1158.73	1143.35	1130.29	1119.17	1083.39	1066.39
95000	1365.28	1325.35	1292.47	1265.16	1242.32	1223.11	1206.87	1193.09	1181.35	1143.58	1125.63
100000	1437.13	1395.11	1360.49	1331.75	1307.70	1287.48	1270.39	1255.88	1243.53	1203.77	1184.88

14.25% Principal and Interest
Monthly Payment Amortization Table

Term Amount	1 Year	2 Years	3 Years	4 Years	5 Years	6 Years	7 Years	8 Years	9 Years	10 Years	11 Years
50	4.50	2.41	1.72	1.38	1.17	1.04	.95	.88	.83	.79	.76
100	9.00	4.82	3.43	2.75	2.34	2.08	1.89	1.76	1.65	1.57	1.51
200	17.99	9.63	6.86	5.50	4.68	4.15	3.78	3.51	3.30	3.14	3.01
300	26.98	14.44	10.29	8.24	7.02	6.23	5.67	5.26	4.95	4.71	4.52
400	35.97	19.26	13.72	10.99	9.36	8.30	7.56	7.01	6.60	6.28	6.02
500	44.96	24.07	17.15	13.73	11.70	10.37	9.44	8.76	8.25	7.84	7.53
600	53.95	28.88	20.58	16.48	14.04	12.45	11.33	10.51	9.89	9.41	9.03
700	62.94	33.70	24.01	19.22	16.38	14.52	13.22	12.26	11.54	10.98	10.53
800	71.93	38.51	27.44	21.97	18.72	16.60	15.11	14.02	13.19	12.55	12.04
900	80.92	43.32	30.87	24.71	21.06	18.67	17.00	15.77	14.84	14.11	13.54
1000	89.91	48.14	34.30	27.46	23.40	20.74	18.88	17.52	16.49	15.68	15.05
2000	179.81	96.27	68.60	54.91	46.80	41.48	37.76	35.03	32.97	31.36	30.09
3000	269.72	144.40	102.90	82.36	70.20	62.22	56.64	52.55	49.45	47.04	45.13
4000	359.62	192.53	137.20	109.81	93.60	82.96	75.52	70.06	65.93	62.71	60.17
5000	449.53	240.66	171.50	137.27	117.00	103.70	94.40	87.58	82.41	78.39	75.21
6000	539.43	288.79	205.80	164.72	140.39	124.44	113.28	105.09	98.89	94.07	90.25
7000	629.34	336.92	240.10	192.17	163.79	145.18	132.15	122.60	115.37	109.75	105.29
8000	719.24	385.05	274.40	219.62	187.19	165.92	151.03	140.12	131.85	125.42	120.33
9000	809.15	433.18	308.70	247.07	210.59	186.66	169.91	157.63	148.33	141.10	135.38
10000	899.05	481.32	343.00	274.53	233.99	207.40	188.79	175.15	164.81	156.78	150.42
11000	988.96	529.45	377.30	301.98	257.38	228.14	207.67	192.66	181.29	172.46	165.46
12000	1078.86	577.58	411.60	329.43	280.78	248.88	226.55	210.17	197.77	188.13	180.50
13000	1168.77	625.71	445.89	356.88	304.18	269.62	245.42	227.69	214.25	203.81	195.54
14000	1258.67	673.84	480.19	384.33	327.58	290.36	264.30	245.20	230.73	219.49	210.58
15000	1348.58	721.97	514.49	411.79	350.98	311.10	283.18	262.72	247.21	235.16	225.62
16000	1438.48	770.10	548.79	439.24	374.37	331.84	302.06	280.23	263.69	250.84	240.66
17000	1528.39	818.23	583.09	466.69	397.77	352.58	320.94	297.74	280.17	266.52	255.71
18000	1618.29	866.36	617.39	494.14	421.17	373.32	339.82	315.26	296.65	282.20	270.75
19000	1708.20	914.50	651.69	521.59	444.57	394.06	358.69	332.77	313.13	297.87	285.79
20000	1798.10	962.63	685.99	549.05	467.97	414.80	377.57	350.29	329.61	313.55	300.83
21000	1888.01	1010.76	720.29	576.50	491.36	435.54	396.45	367.80	346.09	329.23	315.87
22000	1977.91	1058.89	754.59	603.95	514.76	456.28	415.33	385.31	362.57	344.91	330.91
23000	2067.82	1107.02	788.89	631.40	538.16	477.02	434.21	402.83	379.05	360.58	345.95
24000	2157.72	1155.15	823.19	658.85	561.56	497.76	453.09	420.34	395.53	376.26	360.99
25000	2247.62	1203.28	857.48	686.31	584.96	518.50	471.96	437.86	412.01	391.94	376.03
26000	2337.53	1251.41	891.78	713.76	608.35	539.24	490.84	455.37	428.49	407.62	391.08
27000	2427.43	1299.54	926.08	741.21	631.75	559.98	509.72	472.89	444.98	423.29	406.12
28000	2517.34	1347.68	960.38	768.66	655.15	580.72	528.60	490.40	461.46	438.97	421.16
29000	2607.24	1395.81	994.68	796.11	678.55	601.46	547.48	507.91	477.94	454.65	436.20
30000	2697.15	1443.94	1028.98	823.57	701.95	622.20	566.36	525.43	494.42	470.32	451.24
31000	2787.05	1492.07	1063.28	851.02	725.34	642.94	585.24	542.94	510.90	486.00	466.28
32000	2876.96	1540.20	1097.58	878.47	748.74	663.68	604.11	560.46	527.38	501.68	481.32
33000	2966.86	1588.33	1131.88	905.92	772.14	684.42	622.99	577.97	543.86	517.36	496.36
34000	3056.77	1636.46	1166.18	933.37	795.54	705.16	641.87	595.48	560.34	533.03	511.41
35000	3146.67	1684.59	1200.48	960.83	818.94	725.90	660.75	613.00	576.82	548.71	526.45
36000	3236.58	1732.72	1234.78	988.28	842.34	746.64	679.63	630.51	593.30	564.39	541.49
37000	3326.48	1780.85	1269.07	1015.73	865.73	767.38	698.51	648.03	609.78	580.07	556.53
38000	3416.39	1828.99	1303.37	1043.18	889.13	788.12	717.38	665.54	626.26	595.74	571.57
39000	3506.29	1877.12	1337.67	1070.63	912.53	808.86	736.26	683.05	642.74	611.42	586.61
40000	3596.20	1925.25	1371.97	1098.09	935.93	829.60	755.14	700.57	659.22	627.10	601.65
41000	3686.10	1973.38	1406.27	1125.54	959.33	850.34	774.02	718.08	675.70	642.77	616.69
42000	3776.01	2021.51	1440.57	1152.99	982.72	871.08	792.90	735.60	692.18	658.45	631.73
43000	3865.91	2069.64	1474.87	1180.44	1006.12	891.82	811.78	753.11	708.66	674.13	646.78
44000	3955.82	2117.77	1509.17	1207.90	1029.52	912.56	830.65	770.62	725.14	689.81	661.82
45000	4045.72	2165.90	1543.47	1235.35	1052.92	933.30	849.53	788.14	741.62	705.48	676.86
46000	4135.63	2214.03	1577.77	1262.80	1076.32	954.04	868.41	805.65	758.10	721.16	691.90
47000	4225.53	2262.17	1612.07	1290.25	1099.71	974.78	887.29	823.17	774.58	736.84	706.94
48000	4315.43	2310.30	1646.37	1317.70	1123.11	995.52	906.17	840.68	791.06	752.52	721.98
49000	4405.34	2358.43	1680.66	1345.16	1146.51	1016.26	925.05	858.19	807.54	768.19	737.02
50000	4495.24	2406.56	1714.96	1372.61	1169.91	1037.00	943.92	875.71	824.02	783.87	752.06
55000	4944.77	2647.21	1886.46	1509.87	1286.90	1140.70	1038.32	963.28	906.43	862.26	827.27
60000	5394.29	2887.87	2057.96	1647.13	1403.89	1244.40	1132.71	1050.85	988.83	940.64	902.48
65000	5843.82	3128.52	2229.45	1784.39	1520.88	1348.09	1227.10	1138.42	1071.23	1019.03	977.68
70000	6293.34	3369.18	2400.95	1921.65	1637.87	1451.79	1321.49	1225.99	1153.63	1097.42	1052.89
75000	6742.86	3609.84	2572.44	2058.91	1754.86	1555.49	1415.88	1313.56	1236.03	1175.80	1128.09
80000	7192.39	3850.49	2743.94	2196.17	1871.85	1659.19	1510.28	1401.13	1318.44	1254.19	1203.30
85000	7641.91	4091.15	2915.44	2333.43	1988.84	1762.89	1604.67	1488.70	1400.84	1332.58	1278.51
90000	8091.44	4331.80	3086.93	2470.69	2105.83	1866.59	1699.06	1576.27	1483.24	1410.96	1353.71
95000	8540.96	4572.46	3258.43	2607.95	2222.82	1970.29	1793.45	1663.84	1565.64	1489.35	1428.92
100000	8990.48	4813.11	3429.92	2745.21	2339.81	2073.99	1887.84	1751.41	1648.04	1567.74	1504.12

Principal and Interest
Monthly Payment Amortization Table

14.25%

Term Amount	12 Years	13 Years	14 Years	15 Years	16 Years	17 Years	18 Years	19 Years	20 Years	25 Years	30 Years
50	.73	.71	.69	.68	.67	.66	.65	.64	.64	.62	.61
100	1.46	1.42	1.38	1.35	1.33	1.31	1.29	1.28	1.27	1.23	1.21
200	2.91	2.83	2.76	2.70	2.65	2.61	2.58	2.55	2.53	2.45	2.41
300	4.36	4.24	4.14	4.05	3.98	3.92	3.87	3.83	3.79	3.67	3.62
400	5.82	5.65	5.51	5.40	5.30	5.22	5.16	5.10	5.05	4.90	4.82
500	7.27	7.06	6.89	6.75	6.63	6.53	6.45	6.37	6.31	6.12	6.03
600	8.72	8.47	8.27	8.10	7.95	7.83	7.73	7.65	7.58	7.34	7.23
700	10.18	9.88	9.64	9.45	9.28	9.14	9.02	8.92	8.84	8.57	8.44
800	11.63	11.30	11.02	10.79	10.60	10.44	10.31	10.20	10.10	9.79	9.64
900	13.08	12.71	12.40	12.14	11.93	11.75	11.60	11.47	11.36	11.01	10.85
1000	14.53	14.12	13.78	13.49	13.25	13.05	12.89	12.74	12.62	12.23	12.05
2000	29.06	28.23	27.55	26.98	26.50	26.10	25.77	25.48	25.24	24.46	24.10
3000	43.59	42.34	41.32	40.46	39.75	39.15	38.65	38.22	37.86	36.69	36.15
4000	58.12	56.46	55.09	53.95	53.00	52.20	51.53	50.96	50.47	48.92	48.19
5000	72.65	70.57	68.86	67.43	66.25	65.25	64.41	63.70	63.09	61.15	60.24
6000	87.18	84.68	82.63	80.92	79.50	78.30	77.29	76.44	75.71	73.38	72.29
7000	101.71	98.79	96.40	94.41	92.74	91.35	90.17	89.17	88.33	85.61	84.33
8000	116.24	112.91	110.17	107.89	105.99	104.40	103.05	101.91	100.94	97.84	96.38
9000	130.77	127.02	123.94	121.38	119.24	117.45	115.93	114.65	113.56	110.07	108.43
10000	145.30	141.13	137.71	134.86	132.49	130.50	128.81	127.39	126.18	122.30	120.47
11000	159.83	155.25	151.48	148.35	145.74	143.54	141.69	140.13	138.79	134.53	132.52
12000	174.36	169.36	165.25	161.83	158.99	156.59	154.58	152.87	151.41	146.76	144.57
13000	188.89	183.47	179.02	175.32	172.23	169.64	167.46	165.60	164.03	158.99	156.61
14000	203.42	197.58	192.79	188.81	185.48	182.69	180.34	178.34	176.65	171.21	168.66
15000	217.95	211.70	206.56	202.29	198.73	195.74	193.22	191.08	189.26	183.44	180.71
16000	232.48	225.81	220.33	215.78	211.98	208.79	206.10	203.82	201.88	195.67	192.75
17000	247.01	239.92	234.10	229.26	225.23	221.84	218.98	216.56	214.50	207.90	204.80
18000	261.54	254.04	247.87	242.75	238.48	234.89	231.86	229.30	227.11	220.13	216.85
19000	276.07	268.15	261.64	256.24	251.73	247.94	244.74	242.03	239.73	232.36	228.90
20000	290.59	282.26	275.41	269.72	264.97	260.99	257.62	254.77	252.35	244.59	240.94
21000	305.12	296.37	289.18	283.21	278.22	274.04	270.50	267.51	264.97	256.82	252.99
22000	319.65	310.49	302.95	296.69	291.47	287.08	283.38	280.25	277.58	269.05	265.04
23000	334.18	324.60	316.72	310.18	304.72	300.13	296.27	292.99	290.20	281.28	277.08
24000	348.71	338.71	330.49	323.66	317.97	313.18	309.15	305.73	302.82	293.51	289.13
25000	363.24	352.83	344.26	337.15	331.22	326.23	322.03	318.46	315.43	305.74	301.18
26000	377.77	366.94	358.03	350.64	344.46	339.28	334.91	331.20	328.05	317.97	313.22
27000	392.30	381.05	371.80	364.12	357.71	352.33	347.79	343.94	340.67	330.20	325.27
28000	406.83	395.16	385.57	377.61	370.96	365.38	360.67	356.68	353.29	342.42	337.32
29000	421.36	409.28	399.34	391.09	384.21	378.43	373.55	369.42	365.90	354.65	349.36
30000	435.89	423.39	413.11	404.58	397.46	391.48	386.43	382.16	378.52	366.88	361.41
31000	450.42	437.50	426.88	418.06	410.71	404.53	399.31	394.89	391.14	379.11	373.46
32000	464.95	451.61	440.65	431.55	423.95	417.58	412.19	407.63	403.76	391.34	385.50
33000	479.48	465.73	454.42	445.04	437.20	430.62	425.07	420.37	416.37	403.57	397.55
34000	494.01	479.84	468.19	458.52	450.45	443.67	437.95	433.11	428.99	415.80	409.60
35000	508.54	493.95	481.96	472.01	463.70	456.72	450.84	445.85	441.61	428.03	421.65
36000	523.07	508.07	495.73	485.49	476.95	469.77	463.72	458.59	454.22	440.26	433.69
37000	537.60	522.18	509.50	498.98	490.20	482.82	476.60	471.32	466.84	452.49	445.74
38000	552.13	536.29	523.27	512.47	503.45	495.87	489.48	484.06	479.46	464.72	457.79
39000	566.66	550.40	537.04	525.95	516.69	508.92	502.36	496.80	492.08	476.95	469.83
40000	581.18	564.52	550.81	539.44	529.94	521.97	515.24	509.54	504.69	489.18	481.88
41000	595.71	578.63	564.58	552.92	543.19	535.02	528.12	522.28	517.31	501.41	493.93
42000	610.24	592.74	578.35	566.41	556.44	548.07	541.00	535.02	529.93	513.63	505.97
43000	624.77	606.86	592.12	579.89	569.69	561.12	553.88	547.75	542.54	525.86	518.02
44000	639.30	620.97	605.89	593.38	582.94	574.16	566.76	560.49	555.16	538.09	530.07
45000	653.83	635.08	619.66	606.87	596.18	587.21	579.64	573.23	567.78	550.32	542.11
46000	668.36	649.19	633.43	620.35	609.43	600.26	592.53	585.97	580.40	562.55	554.16
47000	682.89	663.31	647.20	633.84	622.68	613.31	605.41	598.71	593.01	574.78	566.21
48000	697.42	677.42	660.97	647.32	635.93	626.36	618.29	611.45	605.63	587.01	578.25
49000	711.95	691.53	674.74	660.81	649.18	639.41	631.17	624.18	618.25	599.24	590.30
50000	726.48	705.65	688.51	674.29	662.43	652.46	644.05	636.92	630.86	611.47	602.35
55000	799.13	776.21	757.36	741.72	728.67	717.70	708.45	700.61	693.95	672.62	662.58
60000	871.77	846.77	826.21	809.15	794.91	782.95	772.86	764.31	757.04	733.76	722.82
65000	944.42	917.34	895.06	876.58	861.15	848.20	837.26	828.00	820.12	794.91	783.05
70000	1017.07	987.90	963.91	944.01	927.40	913.44	901.67	891.69	883.21	856.05	843.29
75000	1089.72	1058.47	1032.76	1011.44	993.64	978.69	966.07	955.38	946.29	917.20	903.52
80000	1162.36	1129.03	1101.61	1078.87	1059.88	1043.93	1030.47	1019.07	1009.38	978.35	963.75
85000	1235.01	1199.59	1170.46	1146.30	1126.12	1109.18	1094.88	1082.76	1072.47	1039.49	1023.99
90000	1307.66	1270.16	1239.31	1213.73	1192.36	1174.42	1159.28	1146.46	1135.55	1100.64	1084.22
95000	1380.31	1340.72	1308.16	1281.16	1258.61	1239.67	1223.69	1210.15	1198.64	1161.79	1144.46
100000	1452.95	1411.29	1377.01	1348.58	1324.85	1304.91	1288.09	1273.84	1261.72	1222.93	1204.69

14.50% Principal and Interest
Monthly Payment Amortization Table

Term / Amount	1 Year	2 Years	3 Years	4 Years	5 Years	6 Years	7 Years	8 Years	9 Years	10 Years	11 Years
50	4.51	2.42	1.73	1.38	1.18	1.05	.96	.89	.84	.80	.76
100	9.01	4.83	3.45	2.76	2.36	2.09	1.91	1.77	1.67	1.59	1.52
200	18.01	9.65	6.89	5.52	4.71	4.18	3.81	3.54	3.33	3.17	3.04
300	27.01	14.48	10.33	8.28	7.06	6.27	5.71	5.30	4.99	4.75	4.56
400	36.01	19.30	13.77	11.04	9.42	8.35	7.61	7.07	6.66	6.34	6.08
500	45.02	24.13	17.22	13.79	11.77	10.44	9.51	8.83	8.32	7.92	7.60
600	54.02	28.95	20.66	16.55	14.12	12.53	11.42	10.60	9.98	9.50	9.12
700	63.02	33.78	24.10	19.31	16.47	14.62	13.32	12.37	11.64	11.09	10.64
800	72.02	38.60	27.54	22.07	18.83	16.70	15.22	14.13	13.31	12.67	12.16
900	81.03	43.43	30.98	24.83	21.18	18.79	17.12	15.90	14.97	14.25	13.68
1000	90.03	48.25	34.43	27.58	23.53	20.88	19.02	17.66	16.63	15.83	15.20
2000	180.05	96.50	68.85	55.16	47.06	41.75	38.04	35.32	33.26	31.66	30.40
3000	270.07	144.75	103.27	82.74	70.59	62.63	57.06	52.98	49.89	47.49	45.59
4000	360.10	193.00	137.69	110.32	94.12	83.50	76.07	70.63	66.52	63.32	60.79
5000	450.12	241.25	172.11	137.89	117.65	104.38	95.09	88.29	83.14	79.15	75.99
6000	540.14	289.50	206.53	165.47	141.17	125.25	114.11	105.95	99.77	94.98	91.18
7000	630.16	337.75	240.95	193.05	164.70	146.13	133.13	123.61	116.40	110.81	106.38
8000	720.19	386.00	275.37	220.63	188.23	167.00	152.14	141.26	133.03	126.63	121.58
9000	810.21	434.25	309.79	248.21	211.76	187.87	171.16	158.92	149.65	142.46	136.77
10000	900.23	482.50	344.21	275.78	235.29	208.75	190.18	176.58	166.28	158.29	151.97
11000	990.25	530.75	378.64	303.36	258.82	229.62	209.20	194.23	182.91	174.12	167.17
12000	1080.28	579.00	413.06	330.94	282.34	250.50	228.21	211.89	199.54	189.95	182.36
13000	1170.30	627.25	447.48	358.52	305.87	271.37	247.23	229.55	216.17	205.78	197.56
14000	1260.32	675.50	481.90	386.10	329.40	292.25	266.25	247.21	232.79	221.61	212.76
15000	1350.34	723.75	516.32	413.67	352.93	313.12	285.26	264.86	249.42	237.44	227.95
16000	1440.37	772.00	550.74	441.25	376.46	334.00	304.28	282.52	266.05	253.26	243.15
17000	1530.39	820.25	585.16	468.83	399.99	354.87	323.30	300.18	282.68	269.09	258.34
18000	1620.41	868.49	619.58	496.41	423.51	375.74	342.32	317.84	299.30	284.92	273.54
19000	1710.43	916.74	654.00	523.99	447.04	396.62	361.33	335.49	315.93	300.75	288.74
20000	1800.46	964.99	688.42	551.56	470.57	417.49	380.35	353.15	332.56	316.58	303.93
21000	1890.48	1013.24	722.85	579.14	494.10	438.37	399.37	370.81	349.19	332.41	319.13
22000	1980.50	1061.49	757.27	606.72	517.63	459.24	418.39	388.46	365.81	348.24	334.33
23000	2070.52	1109.74	791.69	634.30	541.16	480.12	437.40	406.12	382.44	364.06	349.52
24000	2160.55	1157.99	826.11	661.88	564.68	500.99	456.42	423.78	399.07	379.89	364.72
25000	2250.57	1206.24	860.53	689.45	588.21	521.87	475.44	441.44	415.70	395.72	379.92
26000	2340.59	1254.49	894.95	717.03	611.74	542.74	494.45	459.09	432.33	411.55	395.11
27000	2430.61	1302.74	929.37	744.61	635.27	563.61	513.47	476.75	448.95	427.38	410.31
28000	2520.64	1350.99	963.79	772.19	658.80	584.49	532.49	494.41	465.58	443.21	425.51
29000	2610.66	1399.24	998.21	799.77	682.33	605.36	551.51	512.07	482.21	459.04	440.70
30000	2700.68	1447.50	1032.63	827.34	705.85	626.24	570.52	529.72	498.84	474.87	455.90
31000	2790.70	1495.74	1067.06	854.92	729.38	647.11	589.54	547.38	515.46	490.69	471.09
32000	2880.73	1543.99	1101.48	882.50	752.91	667.99	608.56	565.04	532.09	506.52	486.29
33000	2970.75	1592.24	1135.90	910.08	776.44	688.86	627.58	582.69	548.72	522.35	501.49
34000	3060.77	1640.49	1170.32	937.66	799.97	709.74	646.59	600.35	565.35	538.18	516.68
35000	3150.79	1688.74	1204.74	965.23	823.49	730.61	665.61	618.01	581.98	554.01	531.88
36000	3240.82	1736.98	1239.16	992.81	847.02	751.48	684.63	635.67	598.60	569.84	547.08
37000	3330.84	1785.23	1273.58	1020.39	870.55	772.36	703.65	653.32	615.23	585.67	562.27
38000	3420.86	1833.48	1308.00	1047.97	894.08	793.23	722.66	670.98	631.86	601.49	577.47
39000	3510.88	1881.73	1342.42	1075.55	917.61	814.11	741.68	688.64	648.49	617.32	592.67
40000	3600.91	1929.98	1376.84	1103.12	941.14	834.98	760.70	706.30	665.11	633.15	607.86
41000	3690.93	1978.23	1411.27	1130.70	964.66	855.86	779.71	723.95	681.74	648.98	623.06
42000	3780.95	2026.48	1445.69	1158.28	988.19	876.73	798.73	741.61	698.37	664.81	638.26
43000	3870.97	2074.73	1480.11	1185.86	1011.72	897.61	817.75	759.27	715.00	680.64	653.45
44000	3961.00	2122.98	1514.53	1213.43	1035.25	918.48	836.77	776.92	731.62	696.47	668.65
45000	4051.02	2171.23	1548.95	1241.01	1058.77	939.35	855.78	794.58	748.25	712.30	683.84
46000	4141.04	2219.48	1583.37	1268.59	1082.31	960.23	874.80	812.24	764.88	728.12	699.04
47000	4231.06	2267.73	1617.79	1296.17	1105.83	981.10	893.82	829.90	781.51	743.95	714.24
48000	4321.09	2315.98	1652.21	1323.75	1129.36	1001.98	912.84	847.55	798.14	759.78	729.43
49000	4411.11	2364.23	1686.63	1351.32	1152.89	1022.85	931.85	865.21	814.76	775.61	744.63
50000	4501.13	2412.48	1721.05	1378.90	1176.42	1043.73	950.87	882.87	831.39	791.44	759.83
55000	4951.25	2653.72	1893.16	1516.79	1294.06	1148.10	1045.96	971.15	914.53	870.58	835.81
60000	5401.36	2894.97	2065.26	1654.68	1411.70	1252.47	1141.04	1059.44	997.67	949.73	911.79
65000	5851.47	3136.22	2237.37	1792.57	1529.34	1356.84	1236.13	1147.73	1080.81	1028.87	987.77
70000	6301.58	3377.46	2409.47	1930.46	1646.98	1461.21	1331.22	1236.01	1163.95	1108.01	1063.76
75000	6751.70	3618.71	2581.58	2068.35	1764.63	1565.59	1426.30	1324.30	1247.08	1187.16	1139.74
80000	7201.81	3859.96	2753.68	2206.24	1882.27	1669.96	1521.39	1412.59	1330.22	1266.30	1215.72
85000	7651.92	4101.21	2925.79	2344.13	1999.91	1774.33	1616.48	1500.87	1413.36	1345.44	1291.70
90000	8102.03	4342.45	3097.89	2482.02	2117.55	1878.70	1711.56	1589.16	1496.50	1424.59	1367.68
95000	8552.15	4583.70	3270.00	2619.91	2235.19	1983.08	1806.65	1677.44	1579.64	1503.73	1443.67
100000	9002.26	4824.95	3442.10	2757.80	2352.83	2087.45	1901.74	1765.73	1662.78	1582.87	1519.65

Principal and Interest
Monthly Payment Amortization Table

14.50%

Term Amount	12 Years	13 Years	14 Years	15 Years	16 Years	17 Years	18 Years	19 Years	20 Years	25 Years	30 Years
50	.74	.72	.70	.69	.68	.67	.66	.65	.64	.63	.62
100	1.47	1.43	1.40	1.37	1.35	1.33	1.31	1.30	1.28	1.25	1.23
200	2.94	2.86	2.79	2.74	2.69	2.65	2.62	2.59	2.56	2.49	2.45
300	4.41	4.29	4.19	4.10	4.03	3.97	3.92	3.88	3.84	3.73	3.68
400	5.88	5.72	5.58	5.47	5.37	5.29	5.23	5.17	5.12	4.97	4.90
500	7.35	7.14	6.97	6.83	6.72	6.62	6.53	6.46	6.40	6.22	6.13
600	8.82	8.57	8.37	8.20	8.06	7.94	7.84	7.76	7.68	7.46	7.35
700	10.29	10.00	9.76	9.56	9.40	9.26	9.15	9.05	8.96	8.70	8.58
800	11.76	11.43	11.15	10.93	10.74	10.58	10.45	10.34	10.24	9.94	9.80
900	13.22	12.85	12.55	12.29	12.08	11.91	11.76	11.63	11.52	11.18	11.03
1000	14.69	14.28	13.94	13.66	13.43	13.23	13.06	12.92	12.80	12.43	12.25
2000	29.38	28.56	27.88	27.32	26.85	26.45	26.12	25.84	25.60	24.85	24.50
3000	44.07	42.83	41.81	40.97	40.27	39.68	39.18	38.76	38.40	37.27	36.74
4000	58.76	57.11	55.75	54.63	53.69	52.90	52.24	51.68	51.20	49.69	48.99
5000	73.45	71.38	69.69	68.28	67.11	66.13	65.30	64.60	64.00	62.11	61.23
6000	88.14	85.66	83.62	81.94	80.53	79.35	78.36	77.52	76.80	74.53	73.48
7000	102.82	99.93	97.56	95.59	93.95	92.57	91.42	90.44	89.60	86.96	85.72
8000	117.51	114.21	111.49	109.25	107.37	105.80	104.47	103.36	102.40	99.38	97.97
9000	132.20	128.48	125.43	122.90	120.79	119.02	117.53	116.27	115.20	111.80	110.22
10000	146.89	142.76	139.37	136.56	134.21	132.25	130.59	129.19	128.00	124.22	122.46
11000	161.58	157.03	153.30	150.21	147.63	145.47	143.65	142.11	140.80	136.64	134.71
12000	176.27	171.31	167.24	163.87	161.05	158.70	156.71	155.03	153.60	149.06	146.95
13000	190.96	185.58	181.17	177.52	174.47	171.92	169.77	167.95	166.40	161.49	159.20
14000	205.64	199.86	195.11	191.18	187.89	185.14	182.83	180.87	179.20	173.91	171.44
15000	220.33	214.14	209.05	204.83	201.32	198.37	195.89	193.79	192.00	186.33	183.69
16000	235.02	228.41	222.98	218.49	214.74	211.59	208.94	206.71	204.80	198.75	195.93
17000	249.71	242.69	236.92	232.14	228.16	224.82	222.00	219.62	217.60	211.17	208.18
18000	264.40	256.96	250.85	245.80	241.58	238.04	235.06	232.54	230.40	223.59	220.43
19000	279.09	271.24	264.79	259.45	255.00	251.27	248.12	245.46	243.20	236.02	232.67
20000	293.77	285.51	278.73	273.11	268.42	264.49	261.18	258.38	256.00	248.44	244.92
21000	308.46	299.79	292.66	286.76	281.84	277.71	274.24	271.30	268.80	260.86	257.16
22000	323.15	314.06	306.60	300.42	295.26	290.94	287.30	284.22	281.60	273.28	269.41
23000	337.84	328.34	320.53	314.07	308.68	304.16	300.36	297.14	294.40	285.70	281.65
24000	352.53	342.61	334.47	327.73	322.10	317.39	313.41	310.06	307.20	298.12	293.90
25000	367.22	356.89	348.41	341.38	335.52	330.61	326.47	322.97	320.00	310.55	306.14
26000	381.91	371.16	362.34	355.04	348.94	343.84	339.53	335.89	332.80	322.97	318.39
27000	396.59	385.44	376.28	368.69	362.36	357.06	352.59	348.81	345.60	335.39	330.64
28000	411.28	399.72	390.21	382.35	375.78	370.28	365.65	361.73	358.40	347.81	342.88
29000	425.97	413.99	404.15	396.00	389.21	383.51	378.71	374.65	371.20	360.23	355.13
30000	440.66	428.27	418.09	409.66	402.63	396.73	391.77	387.57	384.00	372.65	367.37
31000	455.35	442.54	432.02	423.31	416.05	409.96	404.83	400.49	396.80	385.08	379.62
32000	470.04	456.82	445.96	436.97	429.47	423.18	417.88	413.41	409.60	397.50	391.86
33000	484.73	471.09	459.89	450.62	442.89	436.41	430.94	426.32	422.40	409.92	404.11
34000	499.41	485.37	473.83	464.28	456.31	449.63	444.00	439.24	435.20	422.34	416.35
35000	514.10	499.64	487.77	477.93	469.73	462.85	457.06	452.16	448.00	434.76	428.60
36000	528.79	513.92	501.70	491.59	483.15	476.08	470.12	465.08	460.80	447.18	440.85
37000	543.48	528.19	515.64	505.24	496.57	489.30	483.18	478.00	473.60	459.61	453.09
38000	558.17	542.47	529.57	518.90	509.99	502.53	496.24	490.92	486.40	472.03	465.34
39000	572.86	556.74	543.51	532.55	523.41	515.75	509.30	503.84	499.20	484.45	477.58
40000	587.54	571.02	557.45	546.21	536.83	528.97	522.35	516.76	512.00	496.87	489.83
41000	602.23	585.30	571.38	559.86	550.25	542.20	535.41	529.67	524.80	509.29	502.07
42000	616.92	599.57	585.32	573.52	563.67	555.42	548.47	542.59	537.60	521.71	514.32
43000	631.61	613.85	599.25	587.17	577.10	568.65	561.53	555.51	550.40	534.13	526.56
44000	646.30	628.12	613.19	600.83	590.52	581.87	574.59	568.43	563.20	546.56	538.81
45000	660.99	642.40	627.13	614.48	603.94	595.10	587.65	581.35	576.00	558.98	551.06
46000	675.68	656.67	641.06	628.14	617.36	608.32	600.71	594.27	588.80	571.40	563.30
47000	690.36	670.95	655.00	641.79	630.78	621.54	613.77	607.19	601.60	583.82	575.55
48000	705.05	685.22	668.93	655.45	644.20	634.77	626.82	620.11	614.40	596.24	587.79
49000	719.74	699.50	682.87	669.10	657.62	647.99	639.88	633.02	627.20	608.66	600.04
50000	734.43	713.77	696.81	682.76	671.04	661.22	652.94	645.94	640.00	621.09	612.28
55000	807.87	785.15	766.49	751.03	738.14	727.34	718.24	710.54	704.00	683.19	673.51
60000	881.31	856.53	836.17	819.31	805.25	793.46	783.53	775.13	768.00	745.30	734.74
65000	954.76	927.90	905.85	887.58	872.35	859.58	848.82	839.72	832.00	807.41	795.97
70000	1028.20	999.28	975.53	955.86	939.45	925.70	914.12	904.32	896.00	869.52	857.19
75000	1101.64	1070.66	1045.21	1024.13	1006.56	991.82	979.41	968.91	960.00	931.63	918.42
80000	1175.08	1142.04	1114.89	1092.41	1073.66	1057.94	1044.70	1033.51	1024.00	993.74	979.65
85000	1248.53	1213.41	1184.57	1160.68	1140.76	1124.07	1110.00	1098.10	1088.00	1055.84	1040.88
90000	1321.97	1284.79	1254.25	1228.96	1207.87	1190.19	1175.29	1162.69	1152.00	1117.95	1102.11
95000	1395.41	1356.17	1323.93	1297.23	1274.97	1256.31	1240.59	1227.29	1216.00	1180.06	1163.33
100000	1468.85	1427.54	1393.61	1365.51	1342.08	1322.43	1305.88	1291.88	1280.00	1242.17	1224.56

14.75% Principal and Interest
Monthly Payment Amortization Table

Term Amount	1 Year	2 Years	3 Years	4 Years	5 Years	6 Years	7 Years	8 Years	9 Years	10 Years	11 Years
50	4.51	2.42	1.73	1.39	1.19	1.06	.96	.90	.84	.80	.77
100	9.02	4.84	3.46	2.78	2.37	2.11	1.92	1.79	1.68	1.60	1.54
200	18.03	9.68	6.91	5.55	4.74	4.21	3.84	3.57	3.36	3.20	3.08
300	27.05	14.52	10.37	8.32	7.10	6.31	5.75	5.35	5.04	4.80	4.61
400	36.06	19.35	13.82	11.09	9.47	8.41	7.67	7.13	6.72	6.40	6.15
500	45.08	24.19	17.28	13.86	11.83	10.51	9.58	8.91	8.39	8.00	7.68
600	54.09	29.03	20.73	16.63	14.20	12.61	11.50	10.69	10.07	9.59	9.22
700	63.10	33.86	24.19	19.40	16.57	14.71	13.41	12.47	11.75	11.19	10.75
800	72.12	38.70	27.64	22.17	18.93	16.81	15.33	14.25	13.43	12.79	12.29
900	81.13	43.54	31.09	24.94	21.30	18.91	17.25	16.03	15.10	14.39	13.82
1000	90.15	48.37	34.55	27.71	23.66	21.01	19.16	17.81	16.78	15.99	15.36
2000	180.29	96.74	69.09	55.41	47.32	42.02	38.32	35.61	33.56	31.97	30.71
3000	270.43	145.11	103.63	83.12	70.98	63.03	57.48	53.41	50.33	47.95	46.06
4000	360.57	193.48	138.18	110.82	94.64	84.04	76.63	71.21	67.11	63.93	61.41
5000	450.71	241.84	172.72	138.53	118.30	105.05	95.79	89.01	83.88	79.91	76.77
6000	540.85	290.21	207.26	166.23	141.96	126.06	114.95	106.81	100.66	95.89	92.12
7000	630.99	338.58	241.81	193.93	165.62	147.07	134.10	124.61	117.43	111.87	107.47
8000	721.13	386.95	276.35	221.64	189.28	168.08	153.26	142.41	134.21	127.85	122.82
9000	811.27	435.32	310.89	249.34	212.94	189.09	172.42	160.21	150.99	143.83	138.18
10000	901.41	483.68	345.44	277.05	236.59	210.10	191.57	178.02	167.76	159.81	153.53
11000	991.55	532.05	379.98	304.75	260.25	231.11	210.73	195.82	184.54	175.79	168.88
12000	1081.69	580.42	414.52	332.46	283.91	252.12	229.89	213.62	201.31	191.77	184.23
13000	1171.83	628.79	449.06	360.16	307.57	273.13	249.04	231.42	218.09	207.75	199.59
14000	1261.97	677.16	483.61	387.86	331.23	294.14	268.20	249.22	234.86	223.74	214.94
15000	1352.11	725.52	518.15	415.57	354.89	315.15	287.36	267.02	251.64	239.72	230.29
16000	1442.25	773.89	552.69	443.27	378.55	336.16	306.51	284.82	268.42	255.70	245.64
17000	1532.39	822.26	587.24	470.98	402.21	357.17	325.67	302.62	285.19	271.68	261.00
18000	1622.53	870.63	621.78	498.68	425.87	378.18	344.83	320.42	301.97	287.66	276.35
19000	1712.67	919.00	656.32	526.38	449.52	399.19	363.98	338.22	318.74	303.64	291.70
20000	1802.81	967.36	690.87	554.09	473.18	420.19	383.14	356.03	335.52	319.62	307.05
21000	1892.95	1015.73	725.41	581.79	496.84	441.20	402.30	373.83	352.29	335.60	322.41
22000	1983.09	1064.10	759.95	609.50	520.50	462.21	421.45	391.63	369.07	351.58	337.76
23000	2073.23	1112.47	794.49	637.20	544.16	483.22	440.61	409.43	385.85	367.56	353.11
24000	2163.37	1160.84	829.04	664.91	567.82	504.23	459.77	427.23	402.62	383.54	368.46
25000	2253.51	1209.20	863.58	692.61	591.48	525.24	478.92	445.03	419.40	399.52	383.82
26000	2343.66	1257.57	898.12	720.31	615.14	546.25	498.08	462.83	436.17	415.50	399.17
27000	2433.80	1305.94	932.67	748.02	638.80	567.26	517.24	480.63	452.95	431.49	414.52
28000	2523.94	1354.31	967.21	775.72	662.45	588.27	536.39	498.43	469.72	447.47	429.87
29000	2614.08	1402.68	1001.75	803.43	686.11	609.28	555.55	516.23	486.50	463.45	445.23
30000	2704.22	1451.04	1036.30	831.13	709.77	630.29	574.71	534.04	503.28	479.43	460.58
31000	2794.36	1499.41	1070.84	858.83	733.43	651.30	593.86	551.84	520.05	495.41	475.93
32000	2884.50	1547.78	1105.38	886.54	757.09	672.31	613.02	569.64	536.83	511.39	491.28
33000	2974.64	1596.15	1139.92	914.24	780.75	693.32	632.18	587.44	553.60	527.37	506.64
34000	3064.78	1644.52	1174.47	941.95	804.41	714.33	651.33	605.24	570.38	543.35	521.99
35000	3154.92	1692.88	1209.01	969.65	828.07	735.34	670.49	623.04	587.15	559.33	537.34
36000	3245.06	1741.25	1243.55	997.36	851.73	756.35	689.65	640.84	603.93	575.31	552.69
37000	3335.20	1789.62	1278.10	1025.06	875.38	777.36	708.80	658.64	620.71	591.29	568.04
38000	3425.34	1837.99	1312.64	1052.76	899.04	798.37	727.96	676.44	637.48	607.27	583.40
39000	3515.48	1886.36	1347.18	1080.47	922.70	819.37	747.12	694.25	654.26	623.25	598.75
40000	3605.62	1934.72	1381.73	1108.17	946.36	840.38	766.28	712.05	671.03	639.23	614.10
41000	3695.76	1983.09	1416.27	1135.88	970.02	861.39	785.43	729.85	687.81	655.22	629.45
42000	3785.90	2031.46	1450.81	1163.58	993.68	882.40	804.59	747.65	704.58	671.20	644.81
43000	3876.04	2079.83	1485.36	1191.29	1017.34	903.41	823.75	765.45	721.36	687.18	660.16
44000	3966.18	2128.19	1519.90	1218.99	1041.00	924.42	842.90	783.25	738.14	703.16	675.51
45000	4056.32	2176.56	1554.44	1246.69	1064.66	945.43	862.06	801.05	754.91	719.14	690.86
46000	4146.46	2224.93	1588.98	1274.40	1088.31	966.44	881.22	818.85	771.69	735.12	706.22
47000	4236.60	2273.30	1623.53	1302.10	1111.97	987.45	900.37	836.65	788.46	751.10	721.57
48000	4326.74	2321.67	1658.07	1329.81	1135.63	1008.46	919.53	854.45	805.24	767.08	736.92
49000	4416.88	2370.03	1692.61	1357.51	1159.29	1029.47	938.69	872.26	822.01	783.06	752.27
50000	4507.02	2418.40	1727.16	1385.21	1182.95	1050.48	957.84	890.06	838.79	799.04	767.63
55000	4957.73	2660.24	1899.87	1523.74	1301.24	1155.53	1053.63	979.06	922.67	878.95	844.39
60000	5408.43	2902.08	2072.59	1662.26	1419.54	1260.57	1149.41	1068.07	1006.55	958.85	921.15
65000	5859.13	3143.92	2245.30	1800.78	1537.83	1365.62	1245.19	1157.07	1090.43	1038.75	997.91
70000	6309.83	3385.76	2418.02	1939.30	1656.13	1470.67	1340.98	1246.08	1174.30	1118.66	1074.68
75000	6760.53	3627.60	2590.73	2077.82	1774.42	1575.72	1436.76	1335.08	1258.18	1198.56	1151.44
80000	7211.24	3869.44	2763.45	2216.34	1892.72	1680.76	1532.55	1424.09	1342.06	1278.46	1228.20
85000	7661.94	4111.28	2936.16	2354.86	2011.01	1785.81	1628.33	1513.09	1425.94	1358.37	1304.96
90000	8112.64	4353.12	3108.88	2493.38	2129.31	1890.86	1724.11	1602.10	1509.82	1438.27	1381.72
95000	8563.34	4594.96	3281.59	2631.90	2247.60	1995.91	1819.90	1691.10	1593.70	1518.18	1458.49
100000	9014.04	4836.80	3454.31	2770.42	2365.90	2100.95	1915.68	1780.11	1677.58	1598.08	1535.25

Principal and Interest
Monthly Payment Amortization Table

14.75%

Term Amount	12 Years	13 Years	14 Years	15 Years	16 Years	17 Years	18 Years	19 Years	20 Years	25 Years	30 Years
50	.75	.73	.71	.70	.68	.68	.67	.66	.65	.64	.63
100	1.49	1.45	1.42	1.39	1.36	1.35	1.33	1.31	1.30	1.27	1.25
200	2.97	2.89	2.83	2.77	2.72	2.69	2.65	2.62	2.60	2.53	2.49
300	4.46	4.34	4.24	4.15	4.08	4.03	3.98	3.93	3.90	3.79	3.74
400	5.94	5.78	5.65	5.54	5.44	5.37	5.30	5.24	5.20	5.05	4.98
500	7.43	7.22	7.06	6.92	6.80	6.71	6.62	6.55	6.50	6.31	6.23
600	8.91	8.67	8.47	8.30	8.16	8.05	7.95	7.86	7.80	7.57	7.47
700	10.40	10.11	9.88	9.68	9.52	9.39	9.27	9.17	9.09	8.84	8.72
800	11.88	11.56	11.29	11.07	10.88	10.73	10.59	10.48	10.39	10.10	9.96
900	13.37	13.00	12.70	12.45	12.24	12.07	11.92	11.79	11.69	11.36	11.21
1000	14.85	14.44	14.11	13.83	13.60	13.41	13.24	13.10	12.99	12.62	12.45
2000	29.70	28.88	28.21	27.66	27.19	26.81	26.48	26.20	25.97	25.23	24.89
3000	44.55	43.32	42.31	41.48	40.79	40.21	39.72	39.30	38.96	37.85	37.34
4000	59.40	57.76	56.42	55.31	54.38	53.61	52.95	52.40	51.94	50.46	49.78
5000	74.25	72.20	70.52	69.13	67.97	67.01	66.19	65.50	64.92	63.08	62.23
6000	89.09	86.64	84.62	82.96	81.57	80.41	79.43	78.60	77.91	75.69	74.67
7000	103.94	101.08	98.72	96.78	95.16	93.81	92.67	91.70	90.89	88.31	87.12
8000	118.79	115.51	112.83	110.61	108.76	107.21	105.90	104.80	103.87	100.92	99.56
9000	133.64	129.95	126.93	124.43	122.35	120.61	119.14	117.90	116.86	113.54	112.01
10000	148.49	144.39	141.03	138.26	135.94	134.01	132.38	131.00	129.84	126.15	124.45
11000	163.34	158.83	155.14	152.08	149.54	147.41	145.62	144.10	142.82	138.77	136.90
12000	178.18	173.27	169.24	165.91	163.13	160.81	158.85	157.20	155.81	151.38	149.34
13000	193.03	187.71	183.34	179.73	176.72	174.21	172.09	170.30	168.79	164.00	161.79
14000	207.88	202.15	197.44	193.56	190.32	187.61	185.33	183.40	181.77	176.61	174.23
15000	222.73	216.59	211.55	207.38	203.91	201.01	198.57	196.50	194.76	189.22	186.68
16000	237.58	231.02	225.65	221.21	217.51	214.41	211.80	209.60	207.74	201.84	199.12
17000	252.43	245.46	239.75	235.03	231.10	227.81	225.04	222.70	220.73	214.45	211.57
18000	267.27	259.90	253.86	248.86	244.69	241.21	238.28	235.80	233.71	227.07	224.01
19000	282.12	274.34	267.96	262.68	258.29	254.61	251.52	248.90	246.69	239.68	236.46
20000	296.97	288.78	282.06	276.51	271.88	268.01	264.75	262.00	259.68	252.30	248.90
21000	311.82	303.22	296.16	290.33	285.47	281.41	277.99	275.10	272.66	264.91	261.34
22000	326.67	317.66	310.27	304.16	299.07	294.81	291.23	288.20	285.64	277.53	273.79
23000	341.51	332.10	324.37	317.98	312.66	308.21	304.47	301.30	298.63	290.14	286.23
24000	356.36	346.53	338.47	331.81	326.26	321.61	317.70	314.40	311.61	302.76	298.68
25000	371.21	360.97	352.58	345.63	339.85	335.01	330.94	327.50	324.59	315.37	311.12
26000	386.06	375.41	366.68	359.46	353.44	348.41	344.18	340.60	337.58	327.99	323.57
27000	400.91	389.85	380.78	373.28	367.04	361.81	357.42	353.70	350.56	340.60	336.01
28000	415.76	404.29	394.88	387.11	380.63	375.21	370.65	366.80	363.54	353.22	348.46
29000	430.60	418.73	408.99	400.93	394.23	388.61	383.89	379.90	376.53	365.83	360.90
30000	445.45	433.17	423.09	414.76	407.82	402.01	397.13	393.00	389.51	378.44	373.35
31000	460.30	447.61	437.19	428.58	421.41	415.41	410.37	406.10	402.50	391.06	385.79
32000	475.15	462.04	451.30	442.41	435.01	428.81	423.60	419.20	415.48	403.67	398.24
33000	490.00	476.48	465.40	456.23	448.60	442.21	436.84	432.30	428.46	416.29	410.68
34000	504.85	490.92	479.50	470.06	462.19	455.61	450.08	445.40	441.45	428.90	423.13
35000	519.69	505.36	493.60	483.88	475.79	469.01	463.31	458.50	454.43	441.52	435.57
36000	534.54	519.80	507.71	497.71	489.38	482.41	476.55	471.60	467.41	454.13	448.02
37000	549.39	534.24	521.81	511.53	502.98	495.81	489.79	484.70	480.40	466.75	460.46
38000	564.24	548.68	535.91	525.36	516.57	509.21	503.03	497.80	493.38	479.36	472.91
39000	579.09	563.12	550.01	539.18	530.16	522.61	516.26	510.90	506.36	491.98	485.35
40000	593.94	577.55	564.12	553.01	543.76	536.01	529.50	524.00	519.35	504.59	497.80
41000	608.78	591.99	578.22	566.83	557.35	549.41	542.74	537.10	532.33	517.21	510.24
42000	623.63	606.43	592.32	580.66	570.94	562.81	555.98	550.20	545.31	529.82	522.68
43000	638.48	620.87	606.43	594.48	584.54	576.21	569.21	563.30	558.30	542.43	535.13
44000	653.33	635.31	620.53	608.31	598.13	589.61	582.45	576.40	571.28	555.05	547.57
45000	668.18	649.75	634.63	622.13	611.73	603.01	595.69	589.50	584.26	567.66	560.02
46000	683.02	664.19	648.73	635.96	625.32	616.42	608.93	602.60	597.25	580.28	572.46
47000	697.87	678.63	662.84	649.78	638.91	629.82	622.16	615.70	610.23	592.89	584.91
48000	712.72	693.06	676.94	663.61	652.51	643.22	635.40	628.80	623.22	605.51	597.35
49000	727.57	707.50	691.04	677.43	666.10	656.62	648.64	641.90	636.20	618.12	609.80
50000	742.42	721.94	705.15	691.26	679.69	670.02	661.88	655.00	649.18	630.74	622.24
55000	816.66	794.14	775.66	760.38	747.66	737.02	728.06	720.50	714.10	693.81	684.47
60000	890.90	866.33	846.17	829.51	815.63	804.02	794.25	786.00	779.02	756.88	746.69
65000	965.14	938.52	916.69	898.63	883.60	871.02	860.44	851.50	843.94	819.96	808.91
70000	1039.38	1010.72	987.20	967.76	951.57	938.02	926.62	917.00	908.85	883.03	871.14
75000	1113.62	1082.91	1057.72	1036.88	1019.54	1005.02	992.81	982.50	973.77	946.10	933.36
80000	1187.87	1155.10	1128.23	1106.01	1087.51	1072.02	1059.00	1048.00	1038.69	1009.18	995.59
85000	1262.11	1227.30	1198.74	1175.13	1155.48	1139.02	1125.19	1113.50	1103.61	1072.25	1057.81
90000	1336.35	1299.49	1269.26	1244.26	1223.45	1206.02	1191.37	1179.00	1168.52	1135.32	1120.03
95000	1410.59	1371.68	1339.77	1313.38	1291.42	1273.03	1257.56	1244.50	1233.44	1198.40	1182.26
100000	1484.83	1443.88	1410.29	1382.51	1359.38	1340.03	1323.75	1310.00	1298.36	1261.47	1244.48

15.00% Principal and Interest
Monthly Payment Amortization Table

Term Amount	1 Year	2 Years	3 Years	4 Years	5 Years	6 Years	7 Years	8 Years	9 Years	10 Years	11 Years
50	4.52	2.43	1.74	1.40	1.19	1.06	.97	.90	.85	.81	.78
100	9.03	4.85	3.47	2.79	2.38	2.12	1.93	1.80	1.70	1.62	1.56
200	18.06	9.70	6.94	5.57	4.76	4.23	3.86	3.59	3.39	3.23	3.11
300	27.08	14.55	10.40	8.35	7.14	6.35	5.79	5.39	5.08	4.85	4.66
400	36.11	19.40	13.87	11.14	9.52	8.46	7.72	7.18	6.77	6.46	6.21
500	45.13	24.25	17.34	13.92	11.90	10.58	9.65	8.98	8.47	8.07	7.76
600	54.16	29.10	20.80	16.70	14.28	12.69	11.58	10.77	10.16	9.69	9.31
700	63.19	33.95	24.27	19.49	16.66	14.81	13.51	12.57	11.85	11.30	10.86
800	72.21	38.79	27.74	22.27	19.04	16.92	15.44	14.36	13.54	12.91	12.41
900	81.24	43.64	31.20	25.05	21.42	19.04	17.37	16.16	15.24	14.53	13.96
1000	90.26	48.49	34.67	27.84	23.79	21.15	19.30	17.95	16.93	16.14	15.51
2000	180.52	96.98	69.34	55.67	47.58	42.30	38.60	35.90	33.85	32.27	31.02
3000	270.78	145.46	104.00	83.50	71.37	63.44	57.90	53.84	50.78	48.41	46.53
4000	361.04	193.95	138.67	111.33	95.16	84.59	77.19	71.79	67.70	64.54	62.04
5000	451.30	242.44	173.33	139.16	118.95	105.73	96.49	89.73	84.63	80.67	77.55
6000	541.55	290.92	208.00	166.99	142.74	126.88	115.79	107.68	101.55	96.81	93.06
7000	631.81	339.41	242.66	194.82	166.53	148.02	135.08	125.62	118.48	112.94	108.57
8000	722.07	387.90	277.33	222.65	190.32	169.17	154.38	143.57	135.40	129.07	124.08
9000	812.33	436.38	311.99	250.48	214.11	190.31	173.68	161.51	152.32	145.21	139.59
10000	902.59	484.87	346.66	278.31	237.90	211.46	192.97	179.46	169.25	161.34	155.10
11000	992.85	533.36	381.32	306.14	261.69	232.60	212.27	197.40	186.17	177.47	170.61
12000	1083.10	581.84	415.99	333.97	285.48	253.75	231.57	215.35	203.10	193.61	186.11
13000	1173.36	630.33	450.65	361.80	309.27	274.89	250.86	233.30	220.02	209.74	201.62
14000	1263.62	678.82	485.32	389.64	333.06	296.04	270.16	251.24	236.95	225.87	217.13
15000	1353.88	727.30	519.98	417.47	356.85	317.18	289.46	269.19	253.87	242.01	232.64
16000	1444.14	775.79	554.65	445.30	380.64	338.33	308.75	287.13	270.79	258.14	248.15
17000	1534.40	824.28	589.32	473.13	404.43	359.47	328.05	305.08	287.72	274.27	263.66
18000	1624.65	872.76	623.98	500.96	428.22	380.62	347.35	323.02	304.64	290.41	279.17
19000	1714.91	921.25	658.65	528.79	452.01	401.76	366.64	340.97	321.57	306.54	294.68
20000	1805.17	969.74	693.31	556.62	475.80	422.91	385.94	358.91	338.49	322.67	310.19
21000	1895.43	1018.22	727.98	584.45	499.59	444.05	405.24	376.86	355.42	338.81	325.70
22000	1985.69	1066.71	762.64	612.28	523.38	465.20	424.53	394.80	372.34	354.94	341.21
23000	2075.95	1115.20	797.31	640.11	547.17	486.34	443.83	412.75	389.26	371.08	356.72
24000	2166.20	1163.68	831.97	667.94	570.96	507.49	463.13	430.69	406.19	387.21	372.22
25000	2256.46	1212.17	866.64	695.77	594.75	528.63	482.42	448.64	423.11	403.34	387.73
26000	2346.72	1260.66	901.30	723.60	618.54	549.78	501.72	466.59	440.04	419.48	403.24
27000	2436.98	1309.14	935.97	751.44	642.33	570.92	521.02	484.53	456.96	435.61	418.75
28000	2527.24	1357.63	970.63	779.27	666.12	592.07	540.31	502.48	473.89	451.74	434.26
29000	2617.50	1406.12	1005.30	807.10	689.91	613.21	559.61	520.42	490.81	467.88	449.77
30000	2707.75	1454.60	1039.96	834.93	713.70	634.36	578.91	538.37	507.74	484.01	465.28
31000	2798.01	1503.09	1074.63	862.76	737.49	655.50	598.20	556.31	524.66	500.14	480.79
32000	2888.27	1551.58	1109.30	890.59	761.28	676.65	617.50	574.26	541.58	516.28	496.30
33000	2978.53	1600.06	1143.96	918.42	785.07	697.79	636.80	592.20	558.51	532.41	511.81
34000	3068.79	1648.55	1178.63	946.25	808.86	718.94	656.09	610.15	575.43	548.54	527.32
35000	3159.05	1697.04	1213.29	974.08	832.65	740.08	675.39	628.09	592.36	564.68	542.83
36000	3249.30	1745.52	1247.96	1001.91	856.44	761.23	694.69	646.04	609.28	580.81	558.33
37000	3339.56	1794.01	1282.62	1029.74	880.23	782.37	713.98	663.98	626.21	596.94	573.84
38000	3429.82	1842.50	1317.29	1057.57	904.02	803.52	733.28	681.93	643.13	613.08	589.35
39000	3520.08	1890.98	1351.95	1085.40	927.81	824.66	752.58	699.88	660.05	629.21	604.86
40000	3610.34	1939.47	1386.62	1113.23	951.60	845.81	771.88	717.82	676.98	645.34	620.37
41000	3700.60	1987.96	1421.28	1141.07	975.39	866.95	791.17	735.77	693.90	661.48	635.88
42000	3790.85	2036.44	1455.95	1168.90	999.18	888.10	810.47	753.71	710.83	677.61	651.39
43000	3881.11	2084.93	1490.61	1196.73	1022.97	909.24	829.77	771.66	727.75	693.75	666.90
44000	3971.37	2133.42	1525.28	1224.56	1046.76	930.39	849.06	789.60	744.68	709.88	682.41
45000	4061.63	2181.90	1559.94	1252.39	1070.55	951.53	868.36	807.55	761.60	726.01	697.92
46000	4151.89	2230.39	1594.61	1280.22	1094.34	972.68	887.66	825.49	778.52	742.15	713.43
47000	4242.15	2278.88	1629.28	1308.05	1118.13	993.82	906.95	843.44	795.45	758.28	728.94
48000	4332.40	2327.36	1663.94	1335.88	1141.92	1014.97	926.25	861.38	812.37	774.41	744.44
49000	4422.66	2375.85	1698.61	1363.71	1165.71	1036.11	945.55	879.33	829.30	790.55	759.95
50000	4512.92	2424.34	1733.27	1391.54	1189.50	1057.26	964.84	897.28	846.22	806.68	775.46
55000	4964.21	2666.77	1906.60	1530.70	1308.45	1162.98	1061.33	987.00	930.84	887.35	853.01
60000	5415.50	2909.20	2079.92	1669.85	1427.40	1268.71	1157.81	1076.73	1015.47	968.01	930.55
65000	5866.80	3151.64	2253.25	1809.00	1546.35	1374.43	1254.29	1166.46	1100.09	1048.68	1008.10
70000	6318.09	3394.07	2426.58	1948.16	1665.30	1480.16	1350.78	1256.18	1184.71	1129.35	1085.65
75000	6769.38	3636.50	2599.90	2087.31	1784.25	1585.88	1447.26	1345.91	1269.33	1210.02	1163.19
80000	7220.67	3878.94	2773.23	2226.46	1903.20	1691.61	1543.75	1435.64	1353.95	1290.68	1240.74
85000	7671.96	4121.37	2946.56	2365.62	2022.15	1797.33	1640.23	1525.36	1438.57	1371.35	1318.28
90000	8123.25	4363.80	3119.88	2504.77	2141.10	1903.06	1736.71	1615.09	1523.20	1452.02	1395.83
95000	8574.55	4606.24	3293.21	2643.93	2260.05	2008.78	1833.20	1704.82	1607.82	1532.69	1473.37
100000	9025.84	4848.67	3466.54	2783.08	2379.00	2114.51	1929.68	1794.55	1692.44	1613.35	1550.92

Principal and Interest Monthly Payment Amortization Table

15.00%

Term / Amount	12 Years	13 Years	14 Years	15 Years	16 Years	17 Years	18 Years	19 Years	20 Years	25 Years	30 Years
50	.76	.74	.72	.70	.69	.68	.68	.67	.66	.65	.64
100	1.51	1.47	1.43	1.40	1.38	1.36	1.35	1.33	1.32	1.29	1.27
200	3.01	2.93	2.86	2.80	2.76	2.72	2.69	2.66	2.64	2.57	2.53
300	4.51	4.39	4.29	4.20	4.14	4.08	4.03	3.99	3.96	3.85	3.80
400	6.01	5.85	5.71	5.60	5.51	5.44	5.37	5.32	5.27	5.13	5.06
500	7.51	7.31	7.14	7.00	6.89	6.79	6.71	6.65	6.59	6.41	6.33
600	9.01	8.77	8.57	8.40	8.27	8.15	8.06	7.97	7.91	7.69	7.59
700	10.51	10.23	9.99	9.80	9.64	9.51	9.40	9.30	9.22	8.97	8.86
800	12.01	11.69	11.42	11.20	11.02	10.87	10.74	10.63	10.54	10.25	10.12
900	13.51	13.15	12.85	12.60	12.40	12.22	12.08	11.96	11.86	11.53	11.38
1000	15.01	14.61	14.28	14.00	13.77	13.58	13.42	13.29	13.17	12.81	12.65
2000	30.02	29.21	28.55	28.00	27.54	27.16	26.84	26.57	26.34	25.62	25.29
3000	45.03	43.81	42.82	41.99	41.31	40.74	40.26	39.85	39.51	38.43	37.94
4000	60.04	58.42	57.09	55.99	55.08	54.31	53.67	53.13	52.68	51.24	50.58
5000	75.05	73.02	71.36	69.98	68.84	67.89	67.09	66.41	65.84	64.05	63.23
6000	90.06	87.62	85.63	83.98	82.61	81.47	80.51	79.70	79.01	76.85	75.87
7000	105.07	102.23	99.90	97.98	96.38	95.04	93.92	92.98	92.18	89.66	88.52
8000	120.08	116.83	114.17	111.97	110.15	108.62	107.34	106.26	105.35	102.47	101.16
9000	135.08	131.43	128.44	125.97	123.91	122.20	120.76	119.54	118.52	115.28	113.80
10000	150.09	146.03	142.71	139.96	137.68	135.78	134.17	132.82	131.68	128.09	126.45
11000	165.10	160.64	156.98	153.96	151.45	149.35	147.59	146.11	144.85	140.90	139.09
12000	180.11	175.24	171.25	167.96	165.22	162.93	161.01	159.39	158.02	153.70	151.74
13000	195.12	189.84	185.52	181.95	178.99	176.51	174.42	172.67	171.19	166.51	164.38
14000	210.13	204.45	199.79	195.95	192.75	190.08	187.84	185.95	184.36	179.32	177.03
15000	225.14	219.05	214.06	209.94	206.52	203.66	201.26	199.23	197.52	192.13	189.67
16000	240.15	233.65	228.33	223.94	220.29	217.24	214.68	212.52	210.69	204.94	202.32
17000	255.15	248.25	242.60	237.93	234.06	230.81	228.09	225.80	223.86	217.75	214.96
18000	270.16	262.86	256.87	251.93	247.82	244.39	241.51	239.08	237.03	230.55	227.60
19000	285.17	277.46	271.14	265.93	261.59	257.97	254.93	252.36	250.20	243.36	240.25
20000	300.18	292.06	285.41	279.92	275.36	271.55	268.34	265.64	263.36	256.17	252.89
21000	315.19	306.67	299.68	293.92	289.13	285.12	281.76	278.93	276.53	268.98	265.54
22000	330.20	321.27	313.95	307.91	302.89	298.70	295.18	292.21	289.70	281.79	278.18
23000	345.21	335.87	328.22	321.91	316.66	312.28	308.59	305.49	302.87	294.60	290.83
24000	360.22	350.47	342.49	335.91	330.43	325.85	322.01	318.77	316.03	307.40	303.47
25000	375.22	365.08	356.76	349.90	344.20	339.43	335.43	332.05	329.20	320.21	316.12
26000	390.23	379.68	371.04	363.90	357.97	353.01	348.84	345.34	342.37	333.02	328.76
27000	405.24	394.28	385.31	377.89	371.73	366.58	362.26	358.62	355.54	345.83	341.40
28000	420.25	408.89	399.58	391.89	385.50	380.16	375.68	371.90	368.71	358.64	354.05
29000	435.26	423.49	413.85	405.89	399.27	393.74	389.10	385.18	381.87	371.45	366.69
30000	450.27	438.09	428.12	419.88	413.04	407.32	402.51	398.46	395.04	384.25	379.34
31000	465.28	452.69	442.39	433.88	426.80	420.89	415.93	411.75	408.21	397.06	391.98
32000	480.29	467.30	456.66	447.87	440.57	434.47	429.35	425.03	421.38	409.87	404.63
33000	495.29	481.90	470.93	461.87	454.34	448.05	442.76	438.31	434.55	422.68	417.27
34000	510.30	496.50	485.20	475.86	468.11	461.62	456.18	451.59	447.71	435.49	429.92
35000	525.31	511.11	499.47	489.86	481.87	475.20	469.60	464.87	460.88	448.30	442.56
36000	540.32	525.71	513.74	503.86	495.64	488.78	483.01	478.16	474.05	461.10	455.20
37000	555.33	540.31	528.01	517.85	509.41	502.35	496.43	491.44	487.22	473.91	467.85
38000	570.34	554.91	542.28	531.85	523.18	515.93	509.85	504.72	500.39	486.72	480.49
39000	585.35	569.52	556.55	545.84	536.95	529.51	523.26	518.00	513.55	499.53	493.14
40000	600.36	584.12	570.82	559.84	550.71	543.09	536.68	531.28	526.72	512.34	505.78
41000	615.36	598.72	585.09	573.84	564.48	556.66	550.10	544.57	539.89	525.15	518.43
42000	630.37	613.33	599.36	587.83	578.25	570.24	563.52	557.85	553.06	537.95	531.07
43000	645.38	627.93	613.63	601.83	592.02	583.82	576.93	571.13	566.22	550.76	543.72
44000	660.39	642.53	627.90	615.82	605.78	597.39	590.35	584.41	579.39	563.57	556.36
45000	675.40	657.13	642.17	629.82	619.55	610.97	603.77	597.69	592.56	576.38	569.00
46000	690.41	671.74	656.44	643.82	633.32	624.55	617.18	610.98	605.73	589.19	581.65
47000	705.42	686.34	670.71	657.81	647.09	638.12	630.60	624.26	618.90	602.00	594.29
48000	720.43	700.94	684.98	671.81	660.85	651.70	644.02	637.54	632.06	614.80	606.94
49000	735.43	715.55	699.25	685.80	674.62	665.28	657.43	650.82	645.23	627.61	619.58
50000	750.44	730.15	713.52	699.80	688.39	678.86	670.85	664.10	658.40	640.42	632.23
55000	825.49	803.16	784.88	769.78	757.23	746.74	737.93	730.51	724.24	704.46	695.45
60000	900.53	876.18	856.23	839.76	826.07	814.63	805.02	796.92	790.08	768.50	758.67
65000	975.57	949.19	927.58	909.74	894.91	882.51	872.10	863.33	855.92	832.54	821.89
70000	1050.62	1022.21	998.93	979.72	963.74	950.40	939.19	929.74	921.76	896.59	885.12
75000	1125.66	1095.22	1070.28	1049.70	1032.58	1018.28	1006.27	996.15	987.60	960.63	948.34
80000	1200.71	1168.24	1141.64	1119.67	1101.42	1086.17	1073.36	1062.56	1053.44	1024.67	1011.56
85000	1275.75	1241.25	1212.99	1189.65	1170.26	1154.05	1140.44	1128.97	1119.28	1088.71	1074.78
90000	1350.79	1314.26	1284.34	1259.63	1239.10	1221.94	1207.53	1195.38	1185.12	1152.75	1138.00
95000	1425.84	1387.28	1355.69	1329.61	1307.94	1289.82	1274.61	1261.79	1250.96	1216.79	1201.23
100000	1500.88	1460.29	1427.04	1399.59	1376.77	1357.71	1341.70	1328.20	1316.79	1280.84	1264.45

15.25% Principal and Interest
Monthly Payment Amortization Table

Term Amount	1 Year	2 Years	3 Years	4 Years	5 Years	6 Years	7 Years	8 Years	9 Years	10 Years	11 Years
50	4.52	2.44	1.74	1.40	1.20	1.07	.98	.91	.86	.82	.79
100	9.04	4.87	3.48	2.80	2.40	2.13	1.95	1.81	1.71	1.63	1.57
200	18.08	9.73	6.96	5.60	4.79	4.26	3.89	3.62	3.42	3.26	3.14
300	27.12	14.59	10.44	8.39	7.18	6.39	5.84	5.43	5.13	4.89	4.70
400	36.16	19.45	13.92	11.19	9.57	8.52	7.78	7.24	6.83	6.52	6.27
500	45.19	24.31	17.40	13.98	11.97	10.65	9.72	9.05	8.54	8.15	7.84
600	54.23	29.17	20.88	16.78	14.36	12.77	11.67	10.86	10.25	9.78	9.40
700	63.27	34.03	24.36	19.58	16.75	14.90	13.61	12.67	11.96	11.41	10.97
800	72.31	38.89	27.84	22.37	19.14	17.03	15.55	14.48	13.66	13.03	12.54
900	81.34	43.75	31.31	25.17	21.53	19.16	17.50	16.29	15.37	14.66	14.10
1000	90.38	48.61	34.79	27.96	23.93	21.29	19.44	18.10	17.08	16.29	15.67
2000	180.76	97.22	69.58	55.92	47.85	42.57	38.88	36.19	34.15	32.58	31.34
3000	271.13	145.82	104.37	83.88	71.77	63.85	58.32	54.28	51.23	48.87	47.00
4000	361.51	194.43	139.16	111.84	95.69	85.13	77.75	72.37	68.30	65.15	62.67
5000	451.89	243.03	173.94	139.79	119.61	106.41	97.19	90.46	85.37	81.44	78.34
6000	542.26	291.64	208.73	167.75	143.53	127.69	116.63	108.55	102.45	97.73	94.00
7000	632.64	340.24	243.52	195.71	167.45	148.97	136.07	126.64	119.52	114.01	109.67
8000	723.02	388.85	278.31	223.67	191.38	170.25	155.50	144.73	136.59	130.30	125.34
9000	813.39	437.45	313.10	251.62	215.30	191.53	174.94	162.82	153.67	146.59	141.00
10000	903.77	486.06	347.88	279.58	239.22	212.82	194.38	180.91	170.74	162.87	156.67
11000	994.14	534.67	382.67	307.54	263.14	234.10	213.82	199.00	187.81	179.16	172.34
12000	1084.52	583.27	417.46	335.50	287.06	255.38	233.25	217.09	204.89	195.45	188.00
13000	1174.90	631.88	452.25	363.45	310.98	276.66	252.69	235.18	221.96	211.74	203.67
14000	1265.27	680.48	487.04	391.41	334.90	297.94	272.13	253.27	239.04	228.02	219.34
15000	1355.65	729.09	521.82	419.37	358.83	319.22	291.56	271.36	256.11	244.31	235.00
16000	1446.03	777.69	556.61	447.33	382.75	340.50	311.00	289.45	273.18	260.60	250.67
17000	1536.40	826.30	591.40	475.28	406.67	361.78	330.44	307.54	290.26	276.88	266.34
18000	1626.78	874.90	626.19	503.24	430.59	383.06	349.88	325.63	307.33	293.17	282.00
19000	1717.16	923.51	660.97	531.20	454.51	404.34	369.31	343.72	324.40	309.46	297.67
20000	1807.53	972.12	695.76	559.16	478.43	425.63	388.75	361.81	341.48	325.74	313.34
21000	1897.91	1020.72	730.55	587.12	502.35	446.91	408.19	379.90	358.55	342.03	329.00
22000	1988.28	1069.33	765.34	615.07	526.27	468.19	427.63	397.99	375.62	358.32	344.67
23000	2078.66	1117.93	800.13	643.03	550.20	489.47	447.06	416.08	392.70	374.60	360.34
24000	2169.04	1166.54	834.91	670.99	574.12	510.75	466.50	434.17	409.77	390.89	376.00
25000	2259.41	1215.14	869.70	698.95	598.04	532.03	485.94	452.26	426.85	407.18	391.67
26000	2349.79	1263.75	904.49	726.90	621.96	553.31	505.37	470.35	443.92	423.47	407.34
27000	2440.17	1312.35	939.28	754.86	645.88	574.59	524.81	488.44	460.99	439.75	423.00
28000	2530.54	1360.96	974.07	782.82	669.80	595.87	544.25	506.54	478.07	456.04	438.67
29000	2620.92	1409.56	1008.85	810.78	693.72	617.15	563.69	524.63	495.14	472.33	454.34
30000	2711.29	1458.17	1043.64	838.73	717.65	638.44	583.12	542.72	512.21	488.61	470.00
31000	2801.67	1506.78	1078.43	866.69	741.57	659.72	602.56	560.81	529.29	504.90	485.67
32000	2892.05	1555.38	1113.22	894.65	765.49	681.00	622.00	578.90	546.36	521.19	501.34
33000	2982.42	1603.99	1148.01	922.61	789.41	702.28	641.44	596.99	563.43	537.47	517.00
34000	3072.80	1652.59	1182.79	950.56	813.33	723.56	660.87	615.08	580.51	553.76	532.67
35000	3163.18	1701.20	1217.58	978.52	837.25	744.84	680.31	633.17	597.58	570.05	548.34
36000	3253.55	1749.80	1252.37	1006.48	861.17	766.12	699.75	651.26	614.66	586.33	564.00
37000	3343.93	1798.41	1287.16	1034.44	885.10	787.40	719.18	669.35	631.73	602.62	579.67
38000	3434.31	1847.01	1321.94	1062.40	909.02	808.68	738.62	687.44	648.80	618.91	595.34
39000	3524.68	1895.62	1356.73	1090.35	932.94	829.96	758.06	705.53	665.88	635.20	611.00
40000	3615.06	1944.23	1391.52	1118.31	956.86	851.25	777.50	723.62	682.95	651.48	626.67
41000	3705.43	1992.83	1426.31	1146.27	980.78	872.53	796.93	741.71	700.02	667.77	642.34
42000	3795.81	2041.44	1461.10	1174.23	1004.70	893.81	816.37	759.80	717.10	684.06	658.00
43000	3886.19	2090.04	1495.88	1202.18	1028.62	915.09	835.81	777.89	734.17	700.34	673.67
44000	3976.56	2138.65	1530.67	1230.14	1052.54	936.37	855.25	795.98	751.24	716.63	689.33
45000	4066.94	2187.25	1565.46	1258.10	1076.47	957.65	874.68	814.07	768.32	732.92	705.00
46000	4157.32	2235.86	1600.25	1286.06	1100.39	978.93	894.12	832.16	785.39	749.20	720.67
47000	4247.69	2284.46	1635.04	1314.01	1124.31	1000.21	913.56	850.25	802.46	765.49	736.33
48000	4338.07	2333.07	1669.82	1341.97	1148.23	1021.49	932.99	868.34	819.54	781.78	752.00
49000	4428.44	2381.68	1704.61	1369.93	1172.15	1042.77	952.43	886.43	836.61	798.06	767.67
50000	4518.82	2430.28	1739.40	1397.89	1196.07	1064.06	971.87	904.52	853.69	814.35	783.33
55000	4970.70	2673.31	1913.34	1537.68	1315.68	1170.46	1069.06	994.98	939.05	895.79	861.67
60000	5422.58	2916.34	2087.28	1677.46	1435.29	1276.87	1166.24	1085.43	1024.42	977.22	940.00
65000	5874.47	3159.36	2261.22	1817.25	1554.89	1383.27	1263.43	1175.88	1109.79	1058.66	1018.33
70000	6326.35	3402.39	2435.16	1957.04	1674.50	1489.68	1360.61	1266.33	1195.16	1140.09	1096.67
75000	6778.23	3645.42	2609.10	2096.83	1794.11	1596.08	1457.80	1356.78	1280.53	1221.53	1175.00
80000	7230.11	3888.45	2783.04	2236.62	1913.71	1702.49	1554.99	1447.23	1365.89	1302.96	1253.33
85000	7681.99	4131.47	2956.97	2376.40	2033.32	1808.89	1652.17	1537.69	1451.26	1384.39	1331.67
90000	8133.87	4374.50	3130.91	2516.19	2152.93	1915.30	1749.36	1628.14	1536.63	1465.83	1410.00
95000	8585.76	4617.53	3304.85	2655.98	2272.53	2021.70	1846.55	1718.59	1622.00	1547.26	1488.33
100000	9037.64	4860.56	3478.79	2795.77	2392.14	2128.11	1943.73	1809.04	1707.37	1628.70	1566.66

Principal and Interest
Monthly Payment Amortization Table

15.25%

Term Amount	12 Years	13 Years	14 Years	15 Years	16 Years	17 Years	18 Years	19 Years	20 Years	25 Years	30 Years
50	.76	.74	.73	.71	.70	.69	.68	.68	.67	.66	.65
100	1.52	1.48	1.45	1.42	1.40	1.38	1.36	1.35	1.34	1.31	1.29
200	3.04	2.96	2.89	2.84	2.79	2.76	2.72	2.70	2.68	2.61	2.57
300	4.56	4.44	4.34	4.26	4.19	4.13	4.08	4.04	4.01	3.91	3.86
400	6.07	5.91	5.78	5.67	5.58	5.51	5.44	5.39	5.35	5.21	5.14
500	7.59	7.39	7.22	7.09	6.98	6.88	6.80	6.74	6.68	6.51	6.43
600	9.11	8.87	8.67	8.51	8.37	8.26	8.16	8.08	8.02	7.81	7.71
700	10.62	10.34	10.11	9.92	9.76	9.63	9.52	9.43	9.35	9.11	9.00
800	12.14	11.82	11.56	11.34	11.16	11.01	10.88	10.78	10.69	10.41	10.28
900	13.66	13.30	13.00	12.76	12.55	12.38	12.24	12.12	12.02	11.71	11.57
1000	15.18	14.77	14.44	14.17	13.95	13.76	13.60	13.47	13.36	13.01	12.85
2000	30.35	29.54	28.88	28.34	27.89	27.51	27.20	26.93	26.71	26.01	25.69
3000	45.52	44.31	43.32	42.51	41.83	41.27	40.80	40.40	40.06	39.01	38.54
4000	60.69	59.08	57.76	56.67	55.77	55.02	54.39	53.86	53.42	52.02	51.38
5000	75.86	73.84	72.20	70.84	69.72	68.78	67.99	67.33	66.77	65.02	64.23
6000	91.03	88.61	86.64	85.01	83.66	82.53	81.59	80.79	80.12	78.02	77.07
7000	106.20	103.38	101.08	99.18	97.60	96.29	95.19	94.26	93.48	91.02	89.92
8000	121.37	118.15	115.52	113.34	111.54	110.04	108.78	107.72	106.83	104.03	102.76
9000	136.54	132.92	129.95	127.51	125.49	123.80	122.38	121.19	120.18	117.03	115.61
10000	151.71	147.68	144.39	141.68	139.43	137.55	135.98	134.65	133.53	130.03	128.45
11000	166.88	162.45	158.83	155.85	153.37	151.31	149.57	148.12	146.89	143.03	141.30
12000	182.05	177.22	173.27	170.01	167.31	165.06	163.17	161.58	160.24	156.04	154.14
13000	197.22	191.99	187.71	184.18	181.26	178.81	176.77	175.05	173.59	169.04	166.98
14000	212.39	206.75	202.15	198.35	195.20	192.57	190.37	188.51	186.95	182.04	179.83
15000	227.56	221.52	216.59	212.52	209.14	206.32	203.96	201.98	200.30	195.04	192.67
16000	242.73	236.29	231.03	226.68	223.08	220.08	217.56	215.44	213.65	208.05	205.52
17000	257.90	251.06	245.46	240.85	237.03	233.83	231.16	228.91	227.01	221.05	218.36
18000	273.07	265.83	259.90	255.02	250.97	247.59	244.75	242.37	240.36	234.05	231.21
19000	288.24	280.59	274.34	269.19	264.91	261.34	258.35	255.84	253.71	247.05	244.05
20000	303.41	295.36	288.78	283.35	278.85	275.10	271.95	269.30	267.06	260.06	256.90
21000	318.58	310.13	303.22	297.52	292.80	288.85	285.55	282.76	280.42	273.06	269.74
22000	333.75	324.90	317.66	311.69	306.74	302.61	299.14	296.23	293.77	286.06	282.59
23000	348.92	339.66	332.10	325.86	320.68	316.36	312.74	309.69	307.12	299.06	295.43
24000	364.09	354.43	346.54	340.02	334.62	330.11	326.34	323.16	320.48	312.07	308.28
25000	379.26	369.20	360.97	354.19	348.56	343.87	339.93	336.62	333.83	325.07	321.12
26000	394.43	383.97	375.41	368.36	362.51	357.62	353.53	350.09	347.18	338.07	333.96
27000	409.60	398.74	389.85	382.53	376.45	371.38	367.13	363.55	360.54	351.07	346.81
28000	424.77	413.50	404.29	396.69	390.39	385.13	380.73	377.02	373.89	364.08	359.65
29000	439.94	428.27	418.73	410.86	404.33	398.89	394.32	390.48	387.24	377.08	372.50
30000	455.11	443.04	433.17	425.03	418.28	412.64	407.92	403.95	400.59	390.08	385.34
31000	470.28	457.81	447.61	439.20	432.22	426.40	421.52	417.41	413.95	403.09	398.19
32000	485.45	472.57	462.05	453.36	446.16	440.15	435.11	430.88	427.30	416.09	411.03
33000	500.62	487.34	476.48	467.53	460.10	453.91	448.71	444.34	440.65	429.09	423.88
34000	515.79	502.11	490.92	481.70	474.05	467.66	462.31	457.81	454.01	442.09	436.72
35000	530.96	516.88	505.36	495.87	487.99	481.42	475.91	471.27	467.36	455.10	449.57
36000	546.13	531.65	519.80	510.03	501.93	495.17	489.50	484.74	480.71	468.10	462.41
37000	561.30	546.41	534.24	524.20	515.87	508.93	503.10	498.20	494.07	481.10	475.25
38000	576.47	561.18	548.68	538.37	529.82	522.68	516.70	511.67	507.42	494.10	488.10
39000	591.64	575.95	563.12	552.54	543.76	536.43	530.29	525.13	520.77	507.11	500.94
40000	606.81	590.72	577.56	566.70	557.70	550.19	543.89	538.59	534.12	520.11	513.79
41000	621.98	605.48	591.99	580.87	571.64	563.94	557.49	552.06	547.48	533.11	526.63
42000	637.15	620.25	606.43	595.04	585.59	577.70	571.09	565.52	560.83	546.11	539.48
43000	652.32	635.02	620.87	609.21	599.53	591.45	584.68	578.99	574.18	559.12	552.32
44000	667.49	649.79	635.31	623.37	613.47	605.21	598.28	592.45	587.54	572.12	565.17
45000	682.66	664.56	649.75	637.54	627.41	618.96	611.88	605.92	600.89	585.12	578.01
46000	697.83	679.32	664.19	651.71	641.36	632.72	625.47	619.38	614.24	598.12	590.86
47000	713.00	694.09	678.63	665.88	655.30	646.47	639.07	632.85	627.60	611.13	603.70
48000	728.17	708.86	693.07	680.04	669.24	660.22	652.67	646.31	640.95	624.13	616.55
49000	743.34	723.63	707.50	694.21	683.18	673.98	666.27	659.78	654.30	637.13	629.39
50000	758.51	738.39	721.94	708.38	697.12	687.73	679.86	673.24	667.65	650.13	642.23
55000	834.36	812.23	794.14	779.22	766.84	756.51	747.85	740.57	734.42	715.15	706.46
60000	910.21	886.07	866.33	850.05	836.55	825.28	815.84	807.89	801.18	780.16	770.68
65000	986.06	959.91	938.52	920.89	906.26	894.05	883.82	875.21	867.95	845.17	834.90
70000	1061.91	1033.75	1010.72	991.73	975.97	962.83	951.81	942.54	934.71	910.19	899.13
75000	1137.76	1107.59	1082.91	1062.57	1045.68	1031.60	1019.79	1009.86	1001.48	975.20	963.35
80000	1213.61	1181.43	1155.11	1133.40	1115.40	1100.37	1087.78	1077.18	1068.24	1040.21	1027.57
85000	1289.46	1255.27	1227.30	1204.24	1185.11	1169.14	1155.76	1144.51	1135.01	1105.22	1091.79
90000	1365.31	1329.11	1299.49	1275.08	1254.82	1237.92	1223.75	1211.83	1201.77	1170.24	1156.02
95000	1441.16	1402.94	1371.69	1345.92	1324.53	1306.69	1291.74	1279.16	1268.54	1235.25	1220.24
100000	1517.01	1476.78	1443.88	1416.75	1394.24	1375.46	1359.72	1346.48	1335.30	1300.26	1284.46

15.50%   Principal and Interest
Monthly Payment Amortization Table

Term Amount	1 Year	2 Years	3 Years	4 Years	5 Years	6 Years	7 Years	8 Years	9 Years	10 Years	11 Years
50	4.53	2.44	1.75	1.41	1.21	1.08	.98	.92	.87	.83	.80
100	9.05	4.88	3.50	2.81	2.41	2.15	1.96	1.83	1.73	1.65	1.59
200	18.10	9.75	6.99	5.62	4.82	4.29	3.92	3.65	3.45	3.29	3.17
300	27.15	14.62	10.48	8.43	7.22	6.43	5.88	5.48	5.17	4.94	4.75
400	36.20	19.49	13.97	11.24	9.63	8.57	7.84	7.30	6.89	6.58	6.33
500	45.25	24.37	17.46	14.05	12.03	10.71	9.79	9.12	8.62	8.23	7.92
600	54.30	29.24	20.95	16.86	14.44	12.86	11.75	10.95	10.34	9.87	9.50
700	63.35	34.11	24.44	19.66	16.84	15.00	13.71	12.77	12.06	11.51	11.08
800	72.40	38.98	27.93	22.47	19.25	17.14	15.67	14.59	13.78	13.16	12.66
900	81.45	43.86	31.42	25.28	21.65	19.28	17.63	16.42	15.51	14.80	14.25
1000	90.50	48.73	34.92	28.09	24.06	21.42	19.58	18.24	17.23	16.45	15.83
2000	180.99	97.45	69.83	56.17	48.11	42.84	39.16	36.48	34.45	32.89	31.65
3000	271.49	146.18	104.74	84.26	72.16	64.26	58.74	54.71	51.68	49.33	47.48
4000	361.98	194.90	139.65	112.34	96.22	85.67	78.32	72.95	68.90	65.77	63.30
5000	452.48	243.63	174.56	140.43	120.27	107.09	97.90	91.18	86.12	82.21	79.13
6000	542.97	292.35	209.47	168.51	144.32	128.51	117.48	109.42	103.35	98.65	94.95
7000	633.47	341.08	244.38	196.60	168.38	149.93	137.05	127.66	120.57	115.09	110.78
8000	723.96	389.80	279.29	224.68	192.43	171.34	156.63	145.89	137.79	131.53	126.60
9000	814.45	438.53	314.20	252.77	216.48	192.76	176.21	164.13	155.02	147.97	142.43
10000	904.95	487.25	349.11	280.85	240.54	214.18	195.79	182.36	172.24	164.42	158.25
11000	995.44	535.97	384.02	308.94	264.59	235.60	215.37	200.60	189.46	180.86	174.08
12000	1085.94	584.70	418.93	337.02	288.64	257.01	234.95	218.84	206.69	197.30	189.90
13000	1176.43	633.42	453.84	365.11	312.70	278.43	254.52	237.07	223.91	213.74	205.73
14000	1266.93	682.15	488.75	393.19	336.75	299.85	274.10	255.31	241.13	230.18	221.55
15000	1357.42	730.87	523.67	421.28	360.80	321.27	293.68	273.54	258.36	246.62	237.38
16000	1447.92	779.60	558.58	449.36	384.86	342.68	313.26	291.78	275.58	263.06	253.20
17000	1538.41	828.32	593.49	477.45	408.91	364.10	332.84	310.02	292.80	279.50	269.03
18000	1628.90	877.05	628.40	505.53	432.96	385.52	352.42	328.25	310.03	295.94	284.85
19000	1719.40	925.77	663.31	533.62	457.02	406.94	371.99	346.49	327.25	312.39	300.68
20000	1809.89	974.50	698.22	561.70	481.07	428.35	391.57	364.72	344.48	328.83	316.50
21000	1900.39	1023.22	733.13	589.79	505.12	449.77	411.15	382.96	361.70	345.27	332.32
22000	1990.88	1071.94	768.04	617.87	529.18	471.19	430.73	401.20	378.92	361.71	348.15
23000	2081.38	1120.67	802.95	645.96	553.23	492.61	450.31	419.43	396.15	378.15	363.97
24000	2171.87	1169.39	837.86	674.04	577.28	514.02	469.89	437.67	413.37	394.59	379.80
25000	2262.37	1218.12	872.77	702.13	601.33	535.44	489.46	455.90	430.59	411.03	395.62
26000	2352.86	1266.84	907.68	730.21	625.39	556.86	509.04	474.14	447.82	427.47	411.45
27000	2443.35	1315.57	942.59	758.30	649.44	578.28	528.62	492.37	465.04	443.91	427.27
28000	2533.85	1364.29	977.50	786.38	673.49	599.69	548.20	510.61	482.26	460.35	443.10
29000	2624.34	1413.02	1012.41	814.47	697.55	621.11	567.78	528.85	499.49	476.80	458.92
30000	2714.84	1461.74	1047.33	842.55	721.60	642.53	587.36	547.08	516.71	493.24	474.75
31000	2805.33	1510.47	1082.24	870.64	745.65	663.95	606.93	565.32	533.93	509.68	490.57
32000	2895.83	1559.19	1117.15	898.72	769.71	685.36	626.51	583.55	551.16	526.12	506.40
33000	2986.32	1607.91	1152.06	926.81	793.76	706.78	646.09	601.79	568.38	542.56	522.22
34000	3076.82	1656.64	1186.97	954.89	817.81	728.20	665.67	620.03	585.60	559.00	538.05
35000	3167.31	1705.36	1221.88	982.98	841.87	749.62	685.25	638.26	602.83	575.44	553.87
36000	3257.80	1754.09	1256.79	1011.06	865.92	771.03	704.83	656.50	620.05	591.88	569.70
37000	3348.30	1802.81	1291.70	1039.14	889.97	792.45	724.40	674.73	637.28	608.32	585.52
38000	3438.79	1851.54	1326.61	1067.23	914.03	813.87	743.98	692.97	654.50	624.77	601.35
39000	3529.29	1900.26	1361.52	1095.31	938.08	835.29	763.56	711.21	671.72	641.21	617.17
40000	3619.78	1948.99	1396.43	1123.40	962.13	856.70	783.14	729.44	688.95	657.65	632.99
41000	3710.28	1997.71	1431.34	1151.48	986.19	878.12	802.72	747.68	706.17	674.09	648.82
42000	3800.77	2046.44	1466.25	1179.57	1010.24	899.54	822.30	765.91	723.39	690.53	664.64
43000	3891.26	2095.16	1501.16	1207.65	1034.29	920.96	841.87	784.15	740.62	706.97	680.47
44000	3981.76	2143.88	1536.08	1235.74	1058.35	942.37	861.45	802.39	757.84	723.41	696.29
45000	4072.25	2192.61	1570.99	1263.82	1082.40	963.79	881.03	820.62	775.06	739.85	712.12
46000	4162.75	2241.33	1605.90	1291.91	1106.45	985.21	900.61	838.86	792.29	756.29	727.94
47000	4253.24	2290.06	1640.81	1319.99	1130.51	1006.63	920.19	857.09	809.51	772.73	743.77
48000	4343.74	2338.78	1675.72	1348.08	1154.56	1028.04	939.77	875.33	826.73	789.18	759.59
49000	4434.23	2387.51	1710.63	1376.16	1178.61	1049.46	959.34	893.57	843.96	805.62	775.42
50000	4524.73	2436.23	1745.54	1404.25	1202.66	1070.88	978.92	911.80	861.18	822.06	791.24
55000	4977.20	2679.85	1920.09	1544.67	1322.93	1177.97	1076.81	1002.98	947.30	904.26	870.37
60000	5429.67	2923.48	2094.65	1685.10	1443.20	1285.05	1174.71	1094.16	1033.42	986.47	949.49
65000	5882.14	3167.10	2269.20	1825.52	1563.46	1392.14	1272.60	1185.34	1119.53	1068.67	1028.61
70000	6334.61	3410.72	2443.75	1965.95	1683.73	1499.23	1370.49	1276.52	1205.65	1150.88	1107.74
75000	6787.09	3654.35	2618.31	2106.37	1803.99	1606.32	1468.38	1367.70	1291.77	1233.08	1186.86
80000	7239.56	3897.97	2792.86	2246.79	1924.26	1713.40	1566.27	1458.88	1377.89	1315.29	1265.98
85000	7692.03	4141.59	2967.41	2387.22	2044.53	1820.49	1664.16	1550.06	1464.00	1397.49	1345.11
90000	8144.50	4385.21	3141.97	2527.64	2164.79	1927.58	1762.06	1641.24	1550.12	1479.70	1424.23
95000	8596.97	4628.84	3316.52	2668.07	2285.06	2034.67	1859.95	1732.42	1636.24	1561.91	1503.36
100000	9049.45	4872.46	3491.07	2808.49	2405.32	2141.75	1957.84	1823.60	1722.36	1644.11	1582.48

Principal and Interest
Monthly Payment Amortization Table

15.50%

Term / Amount	12 Years	13 Years	14 Years	15 Years	16 Years	17 Years	18 Years	19 Years	20 Years	25 Years	30 Years
50	.77	.75	.74	.72	.71	.70	.69	.69	.68	.66	.66
100	1.54	1.50	1.47	1.44	1.42	1.40	1.38	1.37	1.36	1.32	1.31
200	3.07	2.99	2.93	2.87	2.83	2.79	2.76	2.73	2.71	2.64	2.61
300	4.60	4.49	4.39	4.31	4.24	4.18	4.14	4.10	4.07	3.96	3.92
400	6.14	5.98	5.85	5.74	5.65	5.58	5.52	5.46	5.42	5.28	5.22
500	7.67	7.47	7.31	7.17	7.06	6.97	6.89	6.83	6.77	6.60	6.53
600	9.20	8.97	8.77	8.61	8.48	8.36	8.27	8.19	8.13	7.92	7.83
700	10.74	10.46	10.23	10.04	9.89	9.76	9.65	9.56	9.48	9.24	9.14
800	12.27	11.95	11.69	11.48	11.30	11.15	11.03	10.92	10.84	10.56	10.44
900	13.80	13.45	13.15	12.91	12.71	12.54	12.41	12.29	12.19	11.88	11.75
1000	15.34	14.94	14.61	14.34	14.12	13.94	13.78	13.65	13.54	13.20	13.05
2000	30.67	29.87	29.22	28.68	28.24	27.87	27.56	27.30	27.08	26.40	26.10
3000	46.00	44.81	43.83	43.02	42.36	41.80	41.34	40.95	40.62	39.60	39.14
4000	61.33	59.74	58.44	57.36	56.48	55.74	55.12	54.60	54.16	52.79	52.19
5000	76.67	74.67	73.04	71.70	70.59	69.67	68.90	68.25	67.70	65.99	65.23
6000	92.00	89.61	87.65	86.04	84.71	83.60	82.67	81.89	81.24	79.19	78.28
7000	107.33	104.54	102.26	100.38	98.83	97.54	96.45	95.54	94.78	92.39	91.32
8000	122.66	119.47	116.87	114.72	112.95	111.47	110.23	109.19	108.32	105.58	104.37
9000	137.99	134.41	131.48	129.06	127.07	125.40	124.01	122.84	121.85	118.78	117.41
10000	153.33	149.34	146.08	143.40	141.18	139.33	137.79	136.49	135.39	131.98	130.46
11000	168.66	164.27	160.69	157.74	155.30	153.27	151.57	150.14	148.93	145.18	143.50
12000	183.99	179.21	175.30	172.08	169.42	167.20	165.34	163.78	162.47	158.37	156.55
13000	199.32	194.14	189.91	186.42	183.54	181.13	179.12	177.43	176.01	171.57	169.59
14000	214.65	209.07	204.52	200.76	197.66	195.07	192.90	191.08	189.55	184.77	182.64
15000	229.99	224.01	219.12	215.10	211.77	209.00	206.68	204.73	203.09	197.97	195.68
16000	245.32	238.94	233.73	229.44	225.89	222.93	220.46	218.38	216.63	211.16	208.73
17000	260.65	253.87	248.34	243.78	240.01	236.86	234.23	232.03	230.16	224.36	221.77
18000	275.98	268.81	262.95	258.12	254.13	250.80	248.01	245.67	243.70	237.56	234.82
19000	291.31	283.74	277.56	272.46	268.24	264.73	261.79	259.32	257.24	250.76	247.86
20000	306.65	298.67	292.16	286.80	282.36	278.66	275.57	272.97	270.78	263.95	260.91
21000	321.98	313.61	306.77	301.14	296.48	292.60	289.35	286.62	284.32	277.15	273.95
22000	337.31	328.54	321.38	315.48	310.60	306.53	303.13	300.27	297.86	290.35	287.00
23000	352.64	343.47	335.99	329.82	324.72	320.46	316.90	313.91	311.40	303.55	300.04
24000	367.97	358.41	350.59	344.16	338.83	334.40	330.68	327.56	324.94	316.74	313.09
25000	383.31	373.34	365.20	358.50	352.95	348.33	344.46	341.21	338.48	329.94	326.13
26000	398.64	388.27	379.81	372.84	367.07	362.26	358.24	354.86	352.01	343.14	339.18
27000	413.97	403.21	394.42	387.18	381.19	376.19	372.02	368.51	365.55	356.34	352.22
28000	429.30	418.14	409.03	401.52	395.31	390.13	385.79	382.16	379.09	369.53	365.27
29000	444.63	433.08	423.63	415.86	409.42	404.06	399.57	395.80	392.63	382.73	378.31
30000	459.97	448.01	438.24	430.20	423.54	417.99	413.35	409.45	406.17	395.93	391.36
31000	475.30	462.94	452.85	444.54	437.66	431.93	427.13	423.10	419.71	409.13	404.41
32000	490.63	477.88	467.46	458.88	451.78	445.86	440.91	436.75	433.25	422.32	417.45
33000	505.96	492.81	482.07	473.22	465.89	459.79	454.69	450.40	446.79	435.52	430.50
34000	521.29	507.74	496.67	487.56	480.01	473.72	468.46	464.05	460.32	448.72	443.54
35000	536.63	522.68	511.28	501.90	494.13	487.66	482.24	477.69	473.86	461.92	456.59
36000	551.96	537.61	525.89	516.24	508.25	501.59	496.02	491.34	487.40	475.11	469.63
37000	567.29	552.54	540.50	530.58	522.37	515.52	509.80	504.99	500.94	488.31	482.68
38000	582.62	567.48	555.11	544.92	536.48	529.46	523.58	518.64	514.48	501.51	495.72
39000	597.95	582.41	569.71	559.26	550.60	543.39	537.35	532.29	528.02	514.71	508.77
40000	613.29	597.34	584.32	573.60	564.72	557.32	551.13	545.94	541.56	527.90	521.81
41000	628.62	612.28	598.93	587.94	578.84	571.25	564.91	559.58	555.10	541.10	534.86
42000	643.95	627.21	613.54	602.28	592.96	585.19	578.69	573.23	568.63	554.30	547.90
43000	659.28	642.14	628.14	616.62	607.07	599.12	592.47	586.88	582.17	567.50	560.95
44000	674.61	657.08	642.75	630.96	621.19	613.05	606.25	600.53	595.71	580.69	573.99
45000	689.95	672.01	657.36	645.30	635.31	626.99	620.02	614.18	609.25	593.89	587.04
46000	705.28	686.94	671.97	659.64	649.43	640.92	633.80	627.82	622.79	607.09	600.08
47000	720.61	701.88	686.58	673.98	663.54	654.85	647.58	641.47	636.33	620.29	613.13
48000	735.94	716.81	701.18	688.32	677.66	668.79	661.36	655.12	649.87	633.48	626.17
49000	751.28	731.74	715.79	702.66	691.78	682.72	675.14	668.77	663.41	646.68	639.22
50000	766.61	746.68	730.40	717.00	705.90	696.65	688.91	682.42	676.95	659.88	652.26
55000	843.27	821.35	803.44	788.70	776.49	766.32	757.81	750.66	744.64	725.86	717.49
60000	919.93	896.01	876.48	860.40	847.08	835.98	826.70	818.90	812.33	791.85	782.72
65000	996.59	970.68	949.52	932.10	917.67	905.65	895.59	887.14	880.03	857.84	847.94
70000	1073.25	1045.35	1022.56	1003.80	988.26	975.31	964.48	955.38	947.72	923.83	913.17
75000	1149.91	1120.01	1095.60	1075.50	1058.85	1044.97	1033.37	1023.62	1015.42	989.81	978.39
80000	1226.57	1194.68	1168.64	1147.20	1129.43	1114.64	1102.26	1091.87	1083.11	1055.80	1043.62
85000	1303.23	1269.35	1241.68	1218.90	1200.02	1184.30	1171.15	1160.11	1150.80	1121.79	1108.84
90000	1379.89	1344.02	1314.72	1290.60	1270.61	1253.97	1240.04	1228.35	1218.50	1187.78	1174.07
95000	1456.55	1418.68	1387.76	1362.30	1341.20	1323.63	1308.93	1296.59	1286.19	1253.76	1239.30
100000	1533.21	1493.35	1460.79	1434.00	1411.79	1393.30	1377.82	1364.83	1353.89	1319.75	1304.52

15.75% Principal and Interest
Monthly Payment Amortization Table

Term Amount	1 Year	2 Years	3 Years	4 Years	5 Years	6 Years	7 Years	8 Years	9 Years	10 Years	11 Years
50	4.54	2.45	1.76	1.42	1.21	1.08	.99	.92	.87	.83	.80
100	9.07	4.89	3.51	2.83	2.42	2.16	1.98	1.84	1.74	1.66	1.60
200	18.13	9.77	7.01	5.65	4.84	4.32	3.95	3.68	3.48	3.32	3.20
300	27.19	14.66	10.52	8.47	7.26	6.47	5.92	5.52	5.22	4.98	4.80
400	36.25	19.54	14.02	11.29	9.68	8.63	7.89	7.36	6.95	6.64	6.40
500	45.31	24.43	17.52	14.11	12.10	10.78	9.86	9.20	8.69	8.30	8.00
600	54.37	29.31	21.03	16.93	14.52	12.94	11.84	11.03	10.43	9.96	9.60
700	63.43	34.20	24.53	19.75	16.93	15.09	13.81	12.87	12.17	11.62	11.19
800	72.50	39.08	28.03	22.57	19.35	17.25	15.78	14.71	13.90	13.28	12.79
900	81.56	43.96	31.54	25.40	21.77	19.40	17.75	16.55	15.64	14.94	14.39
1000	90.62	48.85	35.04	28.22	24.19	21.56	19.72	18.39	17.38	16.60	15.99
2000	181.23	97.69	70.07	56.43	48.38	43.11	39.44	36.77	34.75	33.20	31.97
3000	271.84	146.54	105.11	84.64	72.56	64.67	59.16	55.15	52.13	49.79	47.96
4000	362.46	195.38	140.14	112.85	96.75	86.22	78.88	73.53	69.50	66.39	63.94
5000	453.07	244.22	175.17	141.07	120.93	107.78	98.60	91.92	86.88	82.98	79.92
6000	543.68	293.07	210.21	169.28	145.12	129.33	118.32	110.30	104.25	99.58	95.91
7000	634.29	341.91	245.24	197.49	169.30	150.89	138.04	128.68	121.62	116.18	111.89
8000	724.91	390.75	280.27	225.70	193.49	172.44	157.76	147.06	139.00	132.77	127.87
9000	815.52	439.60	315.31	253.92	217.67	193.99	177.48	165.44	156.37	149.37	143.86
10000	906.13	488.44	350.34	282.13	241.86	215.55	197.20	183.83	173.75	165.96	159.84
11000	996.74	537.29	385.38	310.34	266.04	237.10	216.92	202.21	191.12	182.56	175.82
12000	1087.36	586.13	420.41	338.55	290.23	258.66	236.64	220.59	208.49	199.16	191.81
13000	1177.97	634.97	455.44	366.77	314.42	280.21	256.36	238.97	225.87	215.75	207.79
14000	1268.58	683.82	490.48	394.98	338.60	301.77	276.08	257.35	243.24	232.35	223.78
15000	1359.19	732.66	525.51	423.19	362.79	323.32	295.80	275.74	260.62	248.94	239.76
16000	1449.81	781.50	560.54	451.40	386.97	344.88	315.52	294.12	277.99	265.54	255.74
17000	1540.42	830.35	595.58	479.62	411.16	366.43	335.24	312.50	295.36	282.13	271.73
18000	1631.03	879.19	630.61	507.83	435.34	387.98	354.96	330.88	312.74	298.73	287.71
19000	1721.64	928.04	665.65	536.04	459.53	409.54	374.68	349.26	330.11	315.33	303.69
20000	1812.26	976.88	700.68	564.25	483.71	431.09	394.40	367.65	347.49	331.92	319.68
21000	1902.87	1025.72	735.71	592.47	507.90	452.65	414.12	386.03	364.86	348.52	335.66
22000	1993.48	1074.57	770.75	620.68	532.08	474.20	433.84	404.41	382.23	365.11	351.64
23000	2084.09	1123.41	805.78	648.89	556.27	495.76	453.56	422.79	399.61	381.71	367.63
24000	2174.71	1172.25	840.81	677.10	580.46	517.31	473.28	441.17	416.98	398.31	383.61
25000	2265.32	1221.10	875.85	705.32	604.64	538.87	493.00	459.56	434.36	414.90	399.60
26000	2355.93	1269.94	910.88	733.53	628.83	560.42	512.72	477.94	451.73	431.50	415.58
27000	2446.55	1318.79	945.92	761.74	653.01	581.97	532.44	496.32	469.10	448.09	431.56
28000	2537.16	1367.63	980.95	789.95	677.20	603.53	552.16	514.70	486.48	464.69	447.55
29000	2627.77	1416.47	1015.98	818.16	701.38	625.08	571.88	533.08	503.85	481.28	463.53
30000	2718.38	1465.32	1051.02	846.38	725.57	646.64	591.60	551.47	521.23	497.88	479.51
31000	2809.00	1514.16	1086.05	874.59	749.75	668.19	611.32	569.85	538.60	514.48	495.50
32000	2899.61	1563.00	1121.08	902.80	773.94	689.75	631.04	588.23	555.98	531.07	511.48
33000	2990.22	1611.85	1156.12	931.01	798.12	711.30	650.76	606.61	573.35	547.67	527.46
34000	3080.83	1660.69	1191.15	959.23	822.31	732.86	670.48	625.00	590.72	564.26	543.45
35000	3171.45	1709.54	1226.19	987.44	846.49	754.41	690.20	643.38	608.10	580.86	559.43
36000	3262.06	1758.38	1261.22	1015.65	870.68	775.96	709.92	661.76	625.47	597.46	575.41
37000	3352.67	1807.22	1296.25	1043.86	894.87	797.52	729.64	680.14	642.85	614.05	591.40
38000	3443.28	1856.07	1331.29	1072.08	919.05	819.07	749.36	698.52	660.22	630.65	607.38
39000	3533.90	1904.91	1366.32	1100.29	943.24	840.63	769.08	716.91	677.59	647.24	623.37
40000	3624.51	1953.75	1401.35	1128.50	967.42	862.18	788.80	735.29	694.97	663.84	639.35
41000	3715.12	2002.60	1436.39	1156.71	991.61	883.74	808.52	753.67	712.34	680.43	655.33
42000	3805.73	2051.44	1471.42	1184.93	1015.79	905.29	828.24	772.05	729.72	697.03	671.32
43000	3896.35	2100.29	1506.46	1213.14	1039.98	926.85	847.96	790.43	747.09	713.63	687.30
44000	3986.96	2149.13	1541.49	1241.35	1064.16	948.40	867.68	808.82	764.46	730.22	703.28
45000	4077.57	2197.97	1576.52	1269.56	1088.35	969.95	887.40	827.20	781.84	746.82	719.27
46000	4168.18	2246.82	1611.56	1297.78	1112.53	991.51	907.12	845.58	799.21	763.41	735.25
47000	4258.80	2295.66	1646.59	1325.99	1136.72	1013.06	926.84	863.96	816.59	780.01	751.23
48000	4349.41	2344.50	1681.62	1354.20	1160.91	1034.62	946.56	882.34	833.96	796.61	767.22
49000	4440.02	2393.35	1716.66	1382.41	1185.09	1056.17	966.28	900.73	851.33	813.20	783.20
50000	4530.63	2442.19	1751.69	1410.63	1209.28	1077.73	986.00	919.11	868.71	829.80	799.19
55000	4983.70	2686.41	1926.86	1551.69	1330.20	1185.50	1084.60	1011.02	955.58	912.78	879.10
60000	5436.76	2930.63	2102.03	1692.75	1451.13	1293.27	1183.20	1102.93	1042.45	995.76	959.02
65000	5889.82	3174.85	2277.20	1833.81	1572.06	1401.04	1281.80	1194.84	1129.32	1078.74	1038.94
70000	6342.89	3419.07	2452.37	1974.87	1692.98	1508.82	1380.40	1286.75	1216.19	1161.71	1118.86
75000	6795.95	3663.29	2627.53	2115.94	1813.91	1616.59	1479.00	1378.66	1303.06	1244.69	1198.78
80000	7249.01	3907.50	2802.70	2257.00	1934.84	1724.36	1577.60	1470.57	1389.93	1327.67	1278.69
85000	7702.08	4151.72	2977.87	2398.06	2055.77	1832.13	1676.20	1562.48	1476.80	1410.65	1358.61
90000	8155.14	4395.94	3153.04	2539.12	2176.69	1939.90	1774.80	1654.39	1563.67	1493.63	1438.53
95000	8608.20	4640.16	3328.21	2680.18	2297.62	2047.68	1873.40	1746.30	1650.54	1576.61	1518.45
100000	9061.26	4884.38	3503.38	2821.25	2418.55	2155.45	1972.00	1838.21	1737.41	1659.59	1598.37

Principal and Interest
Monthly Payment Amortization Table

15.75%

Term / Amount	12 Years	13 Years	14 Years	15 Years	16 Years	17 Years	18 Years	19 Years	20 Years	25 Years	30 Years
50	.78	.76	.74	.73	.72	.71	.70	.70	.69	.67	.67
100	1.55	1.51	1.48	1.46	1.43	1.42	1.40	1.39	1.38	1.34	1.33
200	3.10	3.02	2.96	2.91	2.86	2.83	2.80	2.77	2.75	2.68	2.65
300	4.65	4.53	4.44	4.36	4.29	4.24	4.19	4.15	4.12	4.02	3.98
400	6.20	6.04	5.92	5.81	5.72	5.65	5.59	5.54	5.50	5.36	5.30
500	7.75	7.55	7.39	7.26	7.15	7.06	6.98	6.92	6.87	6.70	6.63
600	9.30	9.06	8.87	8.71	8.58	8.47	8.38	8.30	8.24	8.04	7.95
700	10.85	10.57	10.35	10.16	10.01	9.88	9.78	9.69	9.61	9.38	9.28
800	12.40	12.08	11.83	11.62	11.44	11.29	11.17	11.07	10.99	10.72	10.60
900	13.95	13.59	13.31	13.07	12.87	12.71	12.57	12.45	12.36	12.06	11.93
1000	15.50	15.10	14.78	14.52	14.30	14.12	13.96	13.84	13.73	13.40	13.25
2000	30.99	30.20	29.56	29.03	28.59	28.23	27.92	27.67	27.46	26.79	26.50
3000	46.49	45.30	44.34	43.54	42.89	42.34	41.88	41.50	41.18	40.18	39.74
4000	61.98	60.40	59.12	58.06	57.18	56.45	55.84	55.34	54.91	53.58	52.99
5000	77.48	75.50	73.89	72.57	71.48	70.57	69.80	69.17	68.63	66.97	66.24
6000	92.97	90.60	88.67	87.08	85.77	84.68	83.76	83.00	82.36	80.36	79.48
7000	108.47	105.70	103.45	101.60	100.06	98.79	97.72	96.83	96.08	93.76	92.73
8000	123.96	120.80	118.23	116.11	114.36	112.90	111.68	110.67	109.81	107.15	105.97
9000	139.46	135.90	133.01	130.62	128.65	127.01	125.64	124.50	123.53	120.54	119.22
10000	154.95	151.00	147.78	145.14	142.95	141.13	139.60	138.33	137.26	133.93	132.47
11000	170.45	166.10	162.56	159.65	157.24	155.24	153.56	152.16	150.98	147.33	145.71
12000	185.94	181.20	177.34	174.16	171.53	169.35	167.52	166.00	164.71	160.72	158.96
13000	201.44	196.30	192.12	188.68	185.83	183.46	181.48	179.83	178.43	174.11	172.21
14000	216.93	211.40	206.89	203.19	200.12	197.57	195.44	193.66	192.16	187.51	185.45
15000	232.43	226.50	221.67	217.70	214.42	211.69	209.40	207.49	205.89	200.90	198.70
16000	247.92	241.60	236.45	232.21	228.71	225.80	223.36	221.33	219.61	214.29	211.94
17000	263.42	256.70	251.23	246.73	243.00	239.91	237.32	235.16	233.34	227.68	225.19
18000	278.91	271.80	266.01	261.24	257.30	254.02	251.28	248.99	247.06	241.08	238.44
19000	294.41	286.90	280.78	275.75	271.59	268.13	265.24	262.82	260.79	254.47	251.68
20000	309.90	302.00	295.56	290.27	285.89	282.25	279.20	276.66	274.51	267.86	264.93
21000	325.40	317.10	310.34	304.78	300.18	296.36	293.16	290.49	288.24	281.26	278.17
22000	340.89	332.20	325.12	319.29	314.48	310.47	307.12	304.32	301.96	294.65	291.42
23000	356.39	347.30	339.89	333.81	328.77	324.58	321.08	318.15	315.69	308.04	304.67
24000	371.88	362.40	354.67	348.32	343.06	338.69	335.04	331.99	329.41	321.43	317.91
25000	387.37	377.50	369.45	362.83	357.36	352.81	349.00	345.82	343.14	334.83	331.16
26000	402.87	392.60	384.23	377.35	371.65	366.92	362.96	359.65	356.86	348.22	344.41
27000	418.36	407.70	399.01	391.86	385.95	381.03	376.92	373.48	370.59	361.61	357.65
28000	433.86	422.80	413.78	406.37	400.24	395.14	390.88	387.32	384.31	375.01	370.90
29000	449.35	437.90	428.56	420.88	414.53	409.25	404.84	401.15	398.04	388.40	384.14
30000	464.85	453.00	443.34	435.40	428.83	423.37	418.80	414.98	411.77	401.79	397.39
31000	480.34	468.10	458.12	449.91	443.12	437.48	432.76	428.81	425.49	415.18	410.64
32000	495.84	483.20	472.89	464.42	457.42	451.59	446.72	442.65	439.22	428.58	423.88
33000	511.33	498.30	487.67	478.94	471.71	465.70	460.68	456.48	452.94	441.97	437.13
34000	526.83	513.40	502.45	493.45	486.00	479.81	474.64	470.31	466.67	455.36	450.37
35000	542.32	528.50	517.23	507.96	500.30	493.93	488.60	484.14	480.39	468.76	463.62
36000	557.82	543.60	532.01	522.48	514.59	508.04	502.56	497.98	494.12	482.15	476.87
37000	573.31	558.70	546.78	536.99	528.89	522.15	516.52	511.81	507.84	495.54	490.11
38000	588.81	573.80	561.56	551.50	543.18	536.26	530.48	525.64	521.57	508.94	503.36
39000	604.30	588.90	576.34	566.02	557.48	550.37	544.44	539.47	535.29	522.33	516.61
40000	619.80	604.00	591.12	580.53	571.77	564.49	558.40	553.31	549.02	535.72	529.85
41000	635.29	619.10	605.89	595.05	586.06	578.60	572.36	567.14	562.74	549.11	543.10
42000	650.79	634.20	620.67	609.55	600.36	592.71	586.32	580.97	576.47	562.51	556.34
43000	666.28	649.30	635.45	624.07	614.65	606.82	600.28	594.80	590.19	575.90	569.59
44000	681.78	664.40	650.23	638.58	628.95	620.93	614.24	608.64	603.92	589.29	582.84
45000	697.27	679.50	665.01	653.09	643.24	635.05	628.20	622.47	617.65	602.69	596.08
46000	712.77	694.60	679.78	667.61	657.53	649.16	642.16	636.30	631.37	616.08	609.33
47000	728.26	709.70	694.56	682.12	671.83	663.27	656.12	650.13	645.10	629.47	622.58
48000	743.75	724.80	709.34	696.63	686.12	677.38	670.08	663.97	658.82	642.86	635.82
49000	759.25	739.90	724.12	711.15	700.42	691.49	684.04	677.80	672.55	656.26	649.07
50000	774.74	755.00	738.90	725.66	714.71	705.61	698.00	691.63	686.27	669.65	662.31
55000	852.22	830.50	812.78	798.22	786.18	776.17	767.80	760.79	754.90	736.61	728.54
60000	929.69	906.00	886.67	870.79	857.65	846.73	837.60	829.96	823.53	803.58	794.78
65000	1007.17	981.50	960.56	943.36	929.12	917.29	907.40	899.12	892.15	870.54	861.01
70000	1084.64	1057.00	1034.45	1015.92	1000.59	987.85	977.20	968.28	960.78	937.51	927.24
75000	1162.11	1132.50	1108.34	1088.49	1072.06	1058.41	1047.00	1037.44	1029.41	1004.47	993.47
80000	1239.59	1208.00	1182.23	1161.05	1143.53	1128.97	1116.80	1106.61	1098.03	1071.44	1059.70
85000	1317.06	1283.49	1256.12	1233.62	1215.00	1199.53	1186.60	1175.77	1166.66	1138.40	1125.93
90000	1394.54	1358.99	1330.01	1306.18	1286.47	1270.09	1256.40	1244.93	1235.29	1205.37	1192.16
95000	1472.01	1434.49	1403.90	1378.75	1357.95	1340.65	1326.20	1314.09	1303.91	1272.33	1258.39
100000	1549.48	1509.99	1477.79	1451.31	1429.42	1411.21	1396.00	1383.26	1372.54	1339.29	1324.62

16.00% Principal and Interest
Monthly Payment Amortization Table

Term Amount	1 Year	2 Years	3 Years	4 Years	5 Years	6 Years	7 Years	8 Years	9 Years	10 Years	11 Years
50	4.54	2.45	1.76	1.42	1.22	1.09	1.00	.93	.88	.84	.81
100	9.08	4.90	3.52	2.84	2.44	2.17	1.99	1.86	1.76	1.68	1.62
200	18.15	9.80	7.04	5.67	4.87	4.34	3.98	3.71	3.51	3.36	3.23
300	27.22	14.69	10.55	8.51	7.30	6.51	5.96	5.56	5.26	5.03	4.85
400	36.30	19.59	14.07	11.34	9.73	8.68	7.95	7.42	7.02	6.71	6.46
500	45.37	24.49	17.58	14.18	12.16	10.85	9.94	9.27	8.77	8.38	8.08
600	54.44	29.38	21.10	17.01	14.60	13.02	11.92	11.12	10.52	10.06	9.69
700	63.52	34.28	24.61	19.84	17.03	15.19	13.91	12.98	12.27	11.73	11.31
800	72.59	39.18	28.13	22.68	19.46	17.36	15.89	14.83	14.03	13.41	12.92
900	81.66	44.07	31.65	25.51	21.89	19.53	17.88	16.68	15.78	15.08	14.53
1000	90.74	48.97	35.16	28.35	24.32	21.70	19.87	18.53	17.53	16.76	16.15
2000	181.47	97.93	70.32	56.69	48.64	43.39	39.73	37.06	35.06	33.51	32.29
3000	272.20	146.89	105.48	85.03	72.96	65.08	59.59	55.59	52.58	50.26	48.43
4000	362.93	195.86	140.63	113.37	97.28	86.77	79.45	74.12	70.11	67.01	64.58
5000	453.66	244.82	175.79	141.71	121.60	108.46	99.32	92.65	87.63	83.76	80.72
6000	544.39	293.78	210.95	170.05	145.91	130.16	119.18	111.18	105.16	100.51	96.86
7000	635.12	342.75	246.10	198.39	170.23	151.85	139.04	129.71	122.68	117.26	113.01
8000	725.85	391.71	281.26	226.73	194.55	173.54	158.90	148.24	140.21	134.02	129.15
9000	816.58	440.67	316.42	255.07	218.87	195.23	178.76	166.76	157.73	150.77	145.29
10000	907.31	489.64	351.58	283.41	243.19	216.92	198.63	185.29	175.26	167.52	161.44
11000	998.04	538.60	386.73	311.75	267.50	238.62	218.49	203.82	192.78	184.27	177.58
12000	1088.78	587.56	421.89	340.09	291.82	260.31	238.35	222.35	210.31	201.02	193.72
13000	1179.51	636.53	457.05	368.43	316.14	282.00	258.21	240.88	227.83	217.77	209.87
14000	1270.24	685.49	492.20	396.77	340.46	303.69	278.07	259.41	245.36	234.52	226.01
15000	1360.97	734.45	527.36	425.11	364.78	325.38	297.94	277.94	262.88	251.27	242.15
16000	1451.70	783.41	562.52	453.45	389.09	347.07	317.80	296.47	280.41	268.03	258.30
17000	1542.43	832.38	597.67	481.79	413.41	368.77	337.66	314.99	297.93	284.78	274.44
18000	1633.16	881.34	632.83	510.13	437.73	390.46	357.52	333.52	315.46	301.53	290.58
19000	1723.89	930.30	667.99	538.47	462.05	412.15	377.38	352.05	332.98	318.28	306.73
20000	1814.62	979.27	703.15	566.81	486.37	433.84	397.25	370.58	350.51	335.03	322.87
21000	1905.35	1028.23	738.30	595.15	510.68	455.53	417.11	389.11	368.04	351.78	339.01
22000	1996.08	1077.19	773.46	623.49	535.00	477.23	436.97	407.64	385.56	368.53	355.15
23000	2086.81	1126.16	808.62	651.83	559.32	498.92	456.83	426.17	403.09	385.29	371.30
24000	2177.55	1175.12	843.77	680.17	583.64	520.61	476.69	444.70	420.61	402.04	387.44
25000	2268.28	1224.08	878.93	708.51	607.96	542.30	496.56	463.22	438.14	418.79	403.58
26000	2359.01	1273.05	914.09	736.85	632.27	563.99	516.42	481.75	455.66	435.54	419.73
27000	2449.74	1322.01	949.24	765.19	656.59	585.68	536.28	500.28	473.19	452.29	435.87
28000	2540.47	1370.97	984.40	793.53	680.91	607.38	556.14	518.81	490.71	469.04	452.01
29000	2631.20	1419.94	1019.56	821.87	705.23	629.07	576.00	537.34	508.24	485.79	468.16
30000	2721.93	1468.90	1054.72	850.21	729.55	650.76	595.87	555.87	525.76	502.54	484.30
31000	2812.66	1517.86	1089.87	878.55	753.86	672.45	615.73	574.40	543.29	519.30	500.44
32000	2903.39	1566.82	1125.03	906.89	778.18	694.14	635.59	592.93	560.81	536.05	516.59
33000	2994.12	1615.79	1160.19	935.23	802.50	715.84	655.45	611.45	578.34	552.80	532.73
34000	3084.85	1664.75	1195.34	963.57	826.82	737.53	675.31	629.98	595.86	569.55	548.87
35000	3175.59	1713.71	1230.50	991.91	851.14	759.22	695.18	648.51	613.39	586.30	565.02
36000	3266.32	1762.68	1265.66	1020.26	875.46	780.91	715.04	667.04	630.91	603.05	581.16
37000	3357.05	1811.64	1300.82	1048.60	899.77	802.60	734.90	685.57	648.44	619.80	597.30
38000	3447.78	1860.60	1335.97	1076.94	924.09	824.29	754.76	704.10	665.96	636.55	613.45
39000	3538.51	1909.57	1371.13	1105.28	948.41	845.99	774.63	722.63	683.49	653.31	629.59
40000	3629.24	1958.53	1406.29	1133.62	972.73	867.68	794.49	741.16	701.02	670.06	645.73
41000	3719.97	2007.49	1441.44	1161.96	997.05	889.37	814.35	759.69	718.54	686.81	661.88
42000	3810.70	2056.46	1476.60	1190.30	1021.36	911.06	834.21	778.21	736.07	703.56	678.02
43000	3901.43	2105.42	1511.76	1218.64	1045.68	932.75	854.07	796.74	753.59	720.31	694.16
44000	3992.16	2154.38	1546.91	1246.98	1070.00	954.45	873.94	815.27	771.12	737.06	710.30
45000	4082.89	2203.35	1582.07	1275.32	1094.32	976.14	893.80	833.80	788.64	753.81	726.45
46000	4173.62	2252.31	1617.23	1303.66	1118.64	997.83	913.66	852.33	806.17	770.57	742.59
47000	4264.36	2301.27	1652.39	1332.00	1142.95	1019.52	933.52	870.86	823.69	787.32	758.73
48000	4355.09	2350.23	1687.54	1360.34	1167.27	1041.21	953.38	889.39	841.22	804.07	774.88
49000	4445.82	2399.20	1722.70	1388.68	1191.59	1062.91	973.25	907.92	858.74	820.82	791.02
50000	4536.55	2448.16	1757.86	1417.02	1215.91	1084.60	993.11	926.44	876.27	837.57	807.16
55000	4990.20	2692.98	1933.64	1558.72	1337.50	1193.06	1092.42	1019.09	963.89	921.33	887.88
60000	5443.86	2937.79	2109.43	1700.42	1459.09	1301.52	1191.73	1111.73	1051.52	1005.08	968.60
65000	5897.51	3182.61	2285.21	1842.12	1580.68	1409.97	1291.04	1204.38	1139.15	1088.84	1049.31
70000	6351.17	3427.42	2461.00	1983.82	1702.27	1518.43	1390.35	1297.02	1226.77	1172.60	1130.03
75000	6804.82	3672.24	2636.78	2125.53	1823.86	1626.89	1489.66	1389.66	1314.40	1256.35	1210.74
80000	7258.47	3917.05	2812.57	2267.23	1945.45	1735.35	1588.97	1482.31	1402.03	1340.11	1291.46
85000	7712.13	4161.87	2988.35	2408.93	2067.04	1843.81	1688.28	1574.95	1489.65	1423.87	1372.17
90000	8165.78	4406.68	3164.14	2550.63	2188.63	1952.27	1787.59	1667.60	1577.28	1507.62	1452.89
95000	8619.44	4651.50	3339.92	2692.33	2310.22	2060.73	1886.90	1760.24	1664.90	1591.38	1533.61
100000	9073.09	4896.32	3515.71	2834.03	2431.81	2169.19	1986.21	1852.88	1752.53	1675.14	1614.32

Principal and Interest
Monthly Payment Amortization Table

16.00%

Term Amount	12 Years	13 Years	14 Years	15 Years	16 Years	17 Years	18 Years	19 Years	20 Years	25 Years	30 Years
50	.79	.77	.75	.74	.73	.72	.71	.71	.70	.68	.68
100	1.57	1.53	1.50	1.47	1.45	1.43	1.42	1.41	1.40	1.36	1.35
200	3.14	3.06	2.99	2.94	2.90	2.86	2.83	2.81	2.79	2.72	2.69
300	4.70	4.59	4.49	4.41	4.35	4.29	4.25	4.18	4.18	4.08	4.04
400	6.27	6.11	5.98	5.88	5.79	5.72	5.66	5.61	5.57	5.44	5.38
500	7.83	7.64	7.48	7.35	7.24	7.15	7.08	7.01	6.96	6.80	6.73
600	9.40	9.17	8.97	8.82	8.69	8.58	8.49	8.42	8.35	8.16	8.07
700	10.97	10.69	10.47	10.29	10.13	10.01	9.90	9.82	9.74	9.52	9.42
800	12.53	12.22	11.96	11.75	11.58	11.44	11.32	11.22	11.14	10.88	10.76
900	14.10	13.75	13.46	13.22	13.03	12.87	12.73	12.62	12.53	12.24	12.11
1000	15.66	15.27	14.95	14.69	14.48	14.30	14.15	14.02	13.92	13.59	13.45
2000	31.32	30.54	29.90	29.38	28.95	28.59	28.29	28.04	27.84	27.18	26.90
3000	46.98	45.81	44.85	44.07	43.42	42.88	42.43	42.06	41.74	40.77	40.35
4000	62.64	61.07	59.80	58.75	57.89	57.17	56.57	56.07	55.66	54.36	53.80
5000	78.30	76.34	74.75	73.44	72.36	71.46	70.72	70.09	69.57	67.95	67.24
6000	93.95	91.61	89.70	88.13	86.83	85.76	84.86	84.11	83.48	81.54	80.69
7000	109.61	106.87	104.64	102.81	101.30	100.05	99.00	98.13	97.39	95.13	94.14
8000	125.27	122.14	119.59	117.50	115.77	114.34	113.14	112.14	111.31	108.72	107.59
9000	140.93	137.41	134.54	132.19	130.24	128.63	127.29	126.16	125.22	122.30	121.03
10000	156.59	152.68	149.49	146.88	144.72	142.92	141.43	140.18	139.13	135.89	134.48
11000	172.25	167.94	164.44	161.56	159.19	157.22	155.57	154.20	153.04	149.48	147.93
12000	187.90	183.21	179.39	176.25	173.66	171.51	169.71	168.21	166.96	163.07	161.38
13000	203.56	198.48	194.33	190.94	188.13	185.80	183.86	182.23	180.87	176.66	174.82
14000	219.22	213.74	209.28	205.62	202.60	200.09	198.00	196.25	194.78	190.25	188.27
15000	234.88	229.01	224.23	220.31	217.07	214.38	212.14	210.27	208.69	203.84	201.72
16000	250.54	244.28	239.18	235.00	231.54	228.68	226.28	224.28	222.61	217.43	215.17
17000	266.20	259.54	254.13	249.68	246.01	242.97	240.43	238.30	236.52	231.02	228.61
18000	281.85	274.81	269.08	264.37	260.48	257.26	254.57	252.32	250.43	244.61	242.06
19000	297.51	290.08	284.03	279.06	274.96	271.55	268.71	266.34	264.34	258.19	255.51
20000	313.17	305.35	298.97	293.75	289.43	285.84	282.85	280.35	278.26	271.78	268.96
21000	328.83	320.61	313.92	308.43	303.90	300.13	297.00	294.37	292.17	285.37	282.40
22000	344.49	335.88	328.87	323.12	318.37	314.42	311.14	308.39	306.08	298.96	295.85
23000	360.14	351.15	343.82	337.81	332.84	328.72	325.28	322.41	319.99	312.55	309.30
24000	375.80	366.41	358.77	352.49	347.31	343.01	339.42	336.42	333.91	326.14	322.75
25000	391.46	381.68	373.72	367.18	361.78	357.30	353.57	350.44	347.82	339.73	336.19
26000	407.12	396.95	388.66	381.87	376.25	371.59	367.71	364.46	361.73	353.32	349.64
27000	422.78	412.22	403.61	396.55	390.72	385.89	381.85	378.48	375.64	366.91	363.09
28000	438.44	427.48	418.56	411.24	405.20	400.18	395.99	392.49	389.56	380.49	376.54
29000	454.09	442.75	433.51	425.93	419.67	414.47	410.14	406.51	403.47	394.08	389.98
30000	469.75	458.02	448.46	440.62	434.14	428.76	424.28	420.53	417.38	407.67	403.43
31000	485.41	473.28	463.41	455.30	448.61	443.05	438.42	434.55	431.29	421.26	416.88
32000	501.07	488.55	478.36	469.99	463.08	457.35	452.56	448.56	445.21	434.85	430.33
33000	516.73	503.82	493.30	484.68	477.55	471.64	466.71	462.58	459.12	448.44	443.77
34000	532.39	519.08	508.25	499.36	492.02	485.93	480.85	476.60	473.03	462.03	457.22
35000	548.04	534.35	523.20	514.05	506.49	500.22	494.99	490.62	486.94	475.62	470.67
36000	563.70	549.62	538.15	528.74	520.96	514.51	509.13	504.63	500.86	489.21	484.12
37000	579.36	564.89	553.10	543.42	535.44	528.80	523.28	518.65	514.77	502.79	497.57
38000	595.02	580.15	568.05	558.11	549.91	543.10	537.42	532.67	528.68	516.38	511.01
39000	610.68	595.42	582.99	572.80	564.38	557.39	551.56	546.69	542.59	529.97	524.46
40000	626.34	610.69	597.94	587.49	578.85	571.68	565.70	560.70	556.51	543.56	537.91
41000	641.99	625.95	612.89	602.17	593.32	585.97	579.85	574.72	570.42	557.15	551.36
42000	657.65	641.22	627.84	616.86	607.79	600.26	593.99	588.74	584.33	570.74	564.80
43000	673.31	656.49	642.79	631.55	622.26	614.56	608.13	602.76	598.25	584.33	578.25
44000	688.97	671.75	657.74	646.23	636.73	628.85	622.27	616.77	612.16	597.92	591.70
45000	704.63	687.02	672.69	660.92	651.20	643.14	636.42	630.79	626.07	611.51	605.15
46000	720.28	702.29	687.63	675.61	665.68	657.43	650.56	644.81	639.98	625.09	618.59
47000	735.94	717.56	702.58	690.29	680.15	671.72	664.70	658.83	653.90	638.68	632.04
48000	751.60	732.82	717.53	704.98	694.62	686.02	678.84	672.84	667.81	652.27	645.49
49000	767.26	748.09	732.48	719.67	709.09	700.31	692.99	686.86	681.72	665.86	658.94
50000	782.92	763.36	747.43	734.36	723.56	714.60	707.13	700.88	695.63	679.45	672.38
55000	861.21	839.69	822.17	807.79	795.92	786.06	777.84	770.97	765.20	747.39	739.62
60000	939.50	916.03	896.91	881.23	868.27	857.52	848.55	841.05	834.76	815.34	806.86
65000	1017.79	992.36	971.65	954.66	940.63	928.98	919.27	911.14	904.32	883.28	874.10
70000	1096.08	1068.70	1046.40	1028.10	1012.98	1000.44	989.98	981.23	973.88	951.23	941.33
75000	1174.37	1145.03	1121.14	1101.53	1085.34	1071.90	1060.69	1051.31	1043.45	1019.17	1008.57
80000	1252.67	1221.37	1195.88	1174.97	1157.69	1143.36	1131.40	1121.40	1113.01	1087.12	1075.81
85000	1330.96	1297.70	1270.62	1248.40	1230.05	1214.82	1202.12	1191.49	1182.57	1155.06	1143.05
90000	1409.25	1374.04	1345.37	1321.84	1302.40	1286.27	1272.83	1261.58	1252.14	1223.01	1210.29
95000	1487.54	1450.37	1420.11	1395.27	1374.76	1357.73	1343.54	1331.66	1321.70	1290.95	1277.52
100000	1565.83	1526.71	1494.85	1468.71	1447.12	1429.19	1414.25	1401.75	1391.26	1358.89	1344.76

16.25% Principal and Interest
Monthly Payment Amortization Table

Term / Amount	1 Year	2 Years	3 Years	4 Years	5 Years	6 Years	7 Years	8 Years	9 Years	10 Years	11 Years
50	4.55	2.46	1.77	1.43	1.23	1.10	1.01	.94	.89	.85	.82
100	9.09	4.91	3.53	2.85	2.45	2.19	2.01	1.87	1.77	1.70	1.64
200	18.17	9.82	7.06	5.70	4.90	4.37	4.01	3.74	3.54	3.39	3.27
300	27.26	14.73	10.59	8.55	7.34	6.55	6.01	5.61	5.31	5.08	4.90
400	36.34	19.64	14.12	11.39	9.79	8.74	8.01	7.48	7.08	6.77	6.53
500	45.43	24.55	17.65	14.24	12.23	10.92	10.01	9.34	8.84	8.46	8.16
600	54.51	29.45	21.17	17.09	14.68	13.10	12.01	11.21	10.61	10.15	9.79
700	63.60	34.36	24.70	19.93	17.12	15.29	14.01	13.08	12.38	11.84	11.42
800	72.68	39.27	28.23	22.78	19.57	17.47	16.01	14.95	14.15	13.53	13.05
900	81.77	44.18	31.76	25.63	22.01	19.65	18.01	16.81	15.91	15.22	14.68
1000	90.85	49.09	35.29	28.47	24.46	21.83	20.01	18.68	17.68	16.91	16.31
2000	181.70	98.17	70.57	56.94	48.91	43.66	40.01	37.36	35.36	33.82	32.61
3000	272.55	147.25	105.85	85.41	73.36	65.49	60.02	56.03	53.04	50.73	48.92
4000	363.40	196.34	141.13	113.88	97.81	87.32	80.02	74.71	70.71	67.63	65.22
5000	454.25	245.42	176.41	142.35	122.26	109.15	100.03	93.39	88.39	84.54	81.52
6000	545.10	294.50	211.69	170.82	146.71	130.98	120.03	112.06	106.07	101.45	97.83
7000	635.95	343.58	246.97	199.28	171.16	152.81	140.04	130.74	123.74	118.36	114.13
8000	726.80	392.67	282.25	227.75	195.61	174.64	160.04	149.41	141.42	135.26	130.43
9000	817.65	441.75	317.53	256.22	220.06	196.47	180.05	168.09	159.10	152.17	146.74
10000	908.50	490.83	352.81	284.69	244.52	218.30	200.05	186.77	176.78	169.08	163.04
11000	999.35	539.91	388.09	313.16	268.97	240.13	220.06	205.44	194.45	185.99	179.34
12000	1090.20	589.00	423.37	341.63	293.42	261.96	240.06	224.12	212.13	202.89	195.65
13000	1181.04	638.08	458.65	370.10	317.87	283.79	260.07	242.79	229.81	219.80	211.95
14000	1271.89	687.16	493.93	398.56	342.32	305.62	280.07	261.47	247.48	236.71	228.25
15000	1362.74	736.24	529.21	427.03	366.77	327.45	300.08	280.15	265.16	253.62	244.56
16000	1453.59	785.33	564.49	455.50	391.22	349.28	320.08	298.82	282.84	270.52	260.86
17000	1544.44	834.41	599.77	483.97	415.67	371.11	340.09	317.50	300.51	287.43	277.16
18000	1635.29	883.49	635.06	512.44	440.12	392.94	360.09	336.17	318.19	304.34	293.47
19000	1726.14	932.58	670.34	540.91	464.58	414.77	380.09	354.85	335.87	321.25	309.77
20000	1816.99	981.66	705.62	569.37	489.03	436.60	400.10	373.53	353.55	338.15	326.07
21000	1907.84	1030.74	740.90	597.84	513.48	458.43	420.10	392.20	371.22	355.06	342.38
22000	1998.69	1079.82	776.18	626.31	537.93	480.26	440.11	410.88	388.90	371.97	358.68
23000	2089.54	1128.91	811.46	654.78	562.38	502.09	460.11	429.56	406.58	388.88	374.98
24000	2180.39	1177.99	846.74	683.25	586.83	523.92	480.12	448.23	424.25	405.78	391.29
25000	2271.24	1227.07	882.02	711.72	611.28	545.75	500.12	466.91	441.93	422.69	407.59
26000	2362.08	1276.15	917.30	740.19	635.73	567.58	520.13	485.58	459.61	439.60	423.89
27000	2452.93	1325.24	952.58	768.65	660.18	589.41	540.13	504.26	477.29	456.51	440.20
28000	2543.78	1374.32	987.86	797.12	684.64	611.24	560.14	522.94	494.96	473.41	456.50
29000	2634.63	1423.40	1023.14	825.59	709.09	633.07	580.14	541.61	512.64	490.32	472.80
30000	2725.48	1472.48	1058.42	854.06	733.54	654.90	600.15	560.29	530.32	507.23	489.11
31000	2816.33	1521.57	1093.70	882.53	757.99	676.73	620.15	578.96	547.99	524.14	505.41
32000	2907.18	1570.65	1128.98	911.00	782.44	698.56	640.16	597.64	565.67	541.04	521.71
33000	2998.03	1619.73	1164.26	939.46	806.89	720.39	660.16	616.32	583.35	557.95	538.02
34000	3088.88	1668.82	1199.54	967.93	831.34	742.22	680.17	634.99	601.02	574.86	554.32
35000	3179.73	1717.90	1234.83	996.40	855.79	764.05	700.17	653.67	618.70	591.77	570.63
36000	3270.58	1766.98	1270.11	1024.87	880.24	785.87	720.17	672.34	636.38	608.67	586.93
37000	3361.43	1816.06	1305.39	1053.34	904.70	807.70	740.18	691.02	654.06	625.58	603.23
38000	3452.27	1865.15	1340.67	1081.81	929.15	829.53	760.18	709.70	671.73	642.49	619.54
39000	3543.12	1914.23	1375.95	1110.28	953.60	851.36	780.19	728.37	689.41	659.40	635.84
40000	3633.97	1963.31	1411.23	1138.74	978.05	873.19	800.19	747.05	707.09	676.30	652.14
41000	3724.82	2012.39	1446.51	1167.21	1002.50	895.02	820.20	765.72	724.76	693.21	668.45
42000	3815.67	2061.48	1481.79	1195.68	1026.95	916.85	840.20	784.40	742.44	710.12	684.75
43000	3906.52	2110.56	1517.07	1224.15	1051.40	938.68	860.21	803.08	760.12	727.02	701.05
44000	3997.37	2159.64	1552.35	1252.62	1075.85	960.51	880.21	821.75	777.80	743.93	717.36
45000	4088.22	2208.72	1587.63	1281.09	1100.30	982.34	900.22	840.43	795.47	760.84	733.66
46000	4179.07	2257.81	1622.91	1309.56	1124.76	1004.17	920.22	859.11	813.15	777.75	749.96
47000	4269.92	2306.89	1658.19	1338.02	1149.21	1026.00	940.23	877.78	830.83	794.65	766.27
48000	4360.77	2355.97	1693.47	1366.49	1173.66	1047.83	960.23	896.46	848.50	811.56	782.57
49000	4451.62	2405.05	1728.75	1394.96	1198.11	1069.66	980.24	915.13	866.18	828.47	798.87
50000	4542.47	2454.14	1764.03	1423.43	1222.56	1091.49	1000.24	933.81	883.86	845.38	815.18
55000	4996.71	2699.55	1940.44	1565.77	1344.81	1200.64	1100.26	1027.19	972.24	929.91	896.69
60000	5450.96	2944.96	2116.84	1708.11	1467.07	1309.79	1200.29	1120.57	1060.63	1014.45	978.21
65000	5905.20	3190.38	2293.24	1850.46	1589.33	1418.94	1300.31	1213.95	1149.01	1098.99	1059.73
70000	6359.45	3435.79	2469.65	1992.80	1711.58	1528.09	1400.34	1307.33	1237.40	1183.53	1141.25
75000	6813.70	3681.20	2646.05	2135.14	1833.84	1637.23	1500.36	1400.71	1325.78	1268.06	1222.76
80000	7267.94	3926.62	2822.45	2277.48	1956.09	1746.38	1600.38	1494.09	1414.17	1352.60	1304.28
85000	7722.19	4172.03	2998.85	2419.83	2078.35	1855.53	1700.41	1587.47	1502.55	1437.14	1385.80
90000	8176.43	4417.44	3175.26	2562.17	2200.60	1964.68	1800.43	1680.85	1590.94	1521.67	1467.31
95000	8630.68	4662.86	3351.66	2704.51	2322.86	2073.83	1900.45	1774.23	1679.33	1606.21	1548.83
100000	9084.93	4908.27	3528.06	2846.85	2445.11	2182.98	2000.48	1867.61	1767.71	1690.75	1630.35

Principal and Interest
Monthly Payment Amortization Table

16.25%

Term Amount	12 Years	13 Years	14 Years	15 Years	16 Years	17 Years	18 Years	19 Years	20 Years	25 Years	30 Years
50	.80	.78	.76	.75	.74	.73	.72	.72	.71	.69	.69
100	1.59	1.55	1.52	1.49	1.47	1.45	1.44	1.43	1.42	1.38	1.37
200	3.17	3.09	3.03	2.98	2.93	2.90	2.87	2.85	2.83	2.76	2.73
300	4.75	4.64	4.54	4.46	4.40	4.35	4.30	4.27	4.24	4.14	4.10
400	6.33	6.18	6.05	5.95	5.86	5.79	5.74	5.69	5.65	5.52	5.46
500	7.92	7.72	7.56	7.44	7.33	7.24	7.17	7.11	7.06	6.90	6.83
600	9.50	9.27	9.08	8.92	8.79	8.69	8.60	8.53	8.47	8.28	8.19
700	11.08	10.81	10.59	10.41	10.26	10.14	10.03	9.95	9.88	9.65	9.56
800	12.66	12.35	12.10	11.89	11.72	11.58	11.47	11.37	11.29	11.03	10.92
900	14.25	13.90	13.61	13.38	13.19	13.03	12.90	12.79	12.70	12.41	12.29
1000	15.83	15.44	15.12	14.87	14.65	14.48	14.33	14.21	14.11	13.79	13.65
2000	31.65	30.87	30.24	29.73	29.30	28.95	28.66	28.41	28.21	27.58	27.30
3000	47.47	46.31	45.36	44.59	43.95	43.42	42.98	42.61	42.31	41.36	40.95
4000	63.29	61.74	60.48	59.45	58.60	57.89	57.31	56.82	56.41	55.15	54.60
5000	79.12	77.18	75.60	74.31	73.25	72.37	71.63	71.02	70.51	68.93	68.25
6000	94.94	92.61	90.72	89.18	87.90	86.84	85.96	85.22	84.61	82.72	81.90
7000	110.76	108.05	105.84	104.04	102.55	101.31	100.28	99.43	98.71	96.50	95.55
8000	126.58	123.48	120.96	118.90	117.20	115.78	114.61	113.63	112.81	110.29	109.20
9000	142.41	138.92	136.08	133.76	131.84	130.26	128.94	127.83	126.91	124.07	122.85
10000	158.23	154.35	151.20	148.62	146.49	144.73	143.26	142.04	141.01	137.86	136.50
11000	174.05	169.79	166.32	163.48	161.14	159.20	157.59	156.24	155.11	151.64	150.15
12000	189.87	185.22	181.44	178.35	175.79	173.67	171.91	170.44	169.21	165.43	163.80
13000	205.70	200.66	196.56	193.21	190.44	188.15	186.24	184.65	183.31	179.22	177.45
14000	221.52	216.09	211.68	208.07	205.09	202.62	200.56	198.85	197.41	193.00	191.10
15000	237.34	231.53	226.80	222.93	219.74	217.09	214.89	213.05	211.51	206.79	204.75
16000	253.16	246.96	241.92	237.79	234.39	231.56	229.22	227.25	225.61	220.57	218.39
17000	268.99	262.40	257.04	252.65	249.04	246.04	243.54	241.46	239.71	234.36	232.04
18000	284.81	277.83	272.16	267.52	263.68	260.51	257.87	255.66	253.81	248.14	245.69
19000	300.63	293.27	287.28	282.38	278.33	274.98	272.19	269.86	267.91	261.93	259.34
20000	316.45	308.70	302.40	297.24	292.98	289.45	286.52	284.07	282.01	275.71	272.99
21000	332.28	324.14	317.52	312.10	307.63	303.93	300.84	298.27	296.11	289.50	286.64
22000	348.10	339.57	332.64	326.96	322.28	318.40	315.17	312.47	310.22	303.28	300.29
23000	363.92	355.01	347.76	341.82	336.93	332.87	329.50	326.68	324.32	317.07	313.94
24000	379.74	370.44	362.88	356.69	351.58	347.34	343.83	340.88	338.42	330.85	327.59
25000	395.57	385.88	378.00	371.55	366.23	361.82	358.15	355.08	352.52	344.64	341.24
26000	411.39	401.31	393.12	386.41	380.87	376.29	372.47	369.29	366.62	358.43	354.89
27000	427.21	416.75	408.24	401.27	395.52	390.76	386.80	383.49	380.72	372.21	368.54
28000	443.03	432.18	423.36	416.13	410.17	405.23	401.12	397.69	394.82	386.00	382.19
29000	458.86	447.62	438.48	430.99	424.82	419.71	415.45	411.90	408.92	399.78	395.84
30000	474.68	463.05	453.60	445.86	439.47	434.18	429.78	426.10	423.02	413.57	409.49
31000	490.50	478.49	468.72	460.72	454.12	448.65	444.10	440.30	437.12	427.35	423.13
32000	506.32	493.92	483.84	475.58	468.77	463.12	458.43	454.50	451.22	441.14	436.78
33000	522.15	509.36	498.96	490.44	483.42	477.60	472.75	468.71	465.32	454.92	450.43
34000	537.97	524.79	514.08	505.30	498.07	492.07	487.08	482.91	479.42	468.71	464.08
35000	553.79	540.23	529.20	520.16	512.71	506.54	501.40	497.11	493.52	482.49	477.73
36000	569.61	555.66	544.32	535.03	527.36	521.01	515.73	511.32	507.62	496.28	491.38
37000	585.44	571.10	559.44	549.89	542.01	535.49	530.06	525.52	521.72	510.07	505.03
38000	601.26	586.53	574.56	564.75	556.66	549.96	544.38	539.72	535.82	523.85	518.68
39000	617.08	601.97	589.68	579.61	571.31	564.43	558.71	553.93	549.92	537.64	532.33
40000	632.90	617.40	604.80	594.47	585.96	578.90	573.03	568.13	564.02	551.42	545.98
41000	648.73	632.84	619.92	609.33	600.61	593.38	587.36	582.33	578.12	565.21	559.63
42000	664.55	648.27	635.04	624.20	615.26	607.85	601.68	596.54	592.22	578.99	573.28
43000	680.37	663.71	650.16	639.06	629.91	622.32	616.01	610.74	606.32	592.78	586.93
44000	696.19	679.14	665.28	653.92	644.55	636.79	630.34	624.94	620.43	606.56	600.58
45000	712.01	694.58	680.40	668.78	659.20	651.27	644.66	639.15	634.53	620.35	614.23
46000	727.84	710.01	695.52	683.64	673.85	665.74	658.99	653.35	648.63	634.13	627.87
47000	743.66	725.45	710.64	698.50	688.50	680.21	673.31	667.55	662.73	647.92	641.52
48000	759.48	740.88	725.76	713.37	703.15	694.68	687.64	681.75	676.83	661.70	655.17
49000	775.30	756.32	740.88	728.23	717.80	709.16	701.96	695.96	690.93	675.49	668.82
50000	791.13	771.75	756.00	743.09	732.45	723.63	716.29	710.16	705.03	689.28	682.47
55000	870.24	848.93	831.60	817.40	805.69	795.99	787.92	781.18	775.53	758.20	750.72
60000	949.35	926.10	907.20	891.71	878.94	868.35	859.55	852.19	846.03	827.13	818.97
65000	1028.46	1003.28	982.80	966.01	952.18	940.72	931.17	923.21	916.53	896.06	887.21
70000	1107.58	1080.45	1058.39	1040.32	1025.42	1013.08	1002.80	994.22	987.04	964.98	955.46
75000	1186.69	1157.63	1133.99	1114.63	1098.67	1085.44	1074.43	1065.24	1057.54	1033.91	1023.71
80000	1265.80	1234.80	1209.59	1188.94	1171.91	1157.80	1146.06	1136.25	1128.04	1102.84	1091.95
85000	1344.91	1311.98	1285.19	1263.25	1245.16	1230.16	1217.69	1207.27	1198.54	1171.77	1160.20
90000	1424.02	1389.15	1360.79	1337.56	1318.40	1302.53	1289.32	1278.29	1269.05	1240.69	1228.45
95000	1503.14	1466.32	1436.39	1411.86	1391.64	1374.89	1360.95	1349.30	1339.55	1309.62	1296.69
100000	1582.25	1543.50	1511.99	1486.17	1464.89	1447.25	1432.57	1420.32	1410.05	1378.55	1364.94

16.50% Principal and Interest
Monthly Payment Amortization Table

Term / Amount	1 Year	2 Years	3 Years	4 Years	5 Years	6 Years	7 Years	8 Years	9 Years	10 Years	11 Years
50	4.55	2.47	1.78	1.43	1.23	1.10	1.01	.95	.90	.86	.83
100	9.10	4.93	3.55	2.86	2.46	2.20	2.02	1.89	1.79	1.71	1.65
200	18.20	9.85	7.09	5.72	4.92	4.40	4.03	3.77	3.57	3.42	3.30
300	27.30	14.77	10.63	8.58	7.38	6.60	6.05	5.65	5.35	5.12	4.94
400	36.39	19.69	14.17	11.44	9.84	8.79	8.06	7.53	7.14	6.83	6.59
500	45.49	24.61	17.71	14.30	12.30	10.99	10.08	9.42	8.92	8.54	8.24
600	54.59	29.53	21.25	17.16	14.76	13.19	12.09	11.30	10.70	10.24	9.88
700	63.68	34.45	24.79	20.02	17.21	15.38	14.11	13.18	12.49	11.95	11.53
800	72.78	39.37	28.33	22.88	19.67	17.58	16.12	15.06	14.27	13.66	13.18
900	81.88	44.29	31.87	25.74	22.13	19.78	18.14	16.95	16.05	15.36	14.82
1000	90.97	49.21	35.41	28.60	24.59	21.97	20.15	18.83	17.83	17.07	16.47
2000	181.94	98.41	70.81	57.20	49.17	43.94	40.30	37.65	35.66	34.13	32.93
3000	272.91	147.61	106.22	85.80	73.76	65.91	60.45	56.48	53.49	51.20	49.40
4000	363.88	196.81	141.62	114.39	98.34	87.88	80.60	75.30	71.32	68.26	65.86
5000	454.84	246.02	177.03	142.99	122.93	109.85	100.74	94.12	89.15	85.33	82.33
6000	545.81	295.22	212.43	171.59	147.51	131.81	120.89	112.95	106.98	102.39	98.79
7000	636.78	344.42	247.84	200.18	172.10	153.78	141.04	131.77	124.81	119.45	115.26
8000	727.75	393.62	283.24	228.78	196.68	175.75	161.19	150.60	142.64	136.52	131.72
9000	818.71	442.83	318.64	257.38	221.27	197.72	181.34	169.42	160.47	153.58	148.18
10000	909.68	492.03	354.05	285.98	245.85	219.69	201.48	188.24	178.30	170.65	164.65
11000	1000.65	541.23	389.45	314.57	270.43	241.65	221.63	207.07	196.13	187.71	181.11
12000	1091.62	590.43	424.86	343.17	295.02	263.62	241.78	225.89	213.96	204.78	197.58
13000	1182.58	639.64	460.26	371.77	319.60	285.59	261.93	244.72	231.79	221.84	214.04
14000	1273.55	688.84	495.67	400.36	344.19	307.56	282.08	263.54	249.62	238.90	230.51
15000	1364.52	738.04	531.07	428.96	368.77	329.53	302.22	282.36	267.45	255.97	246.97
16000	1455.49	787.24	566.48	457.56	393.36	351.49	322.37	301.19	285.28	273.03	263.44
17000	1546.45	836.44	601.88	486.15	417.94	373.46	342.52	320.01	303.11	290.10	279.90
18000	1637.42	885.65	637.28	514.75	442.53	395.43	362.67	338.84	320.94	307.16	296.36
19000	1728.39	934.85	672.69	543.35	467.11	417.40	382.81	357.66	338.77	324.23	312.83
20000	1819.36	984.05	708.09	571.95	491.70	439.37	402.96	376.48	356.59	341.29	329.29
21000	1910.33	1033.25	743.50	600.54	516.28	461.33	423.11	395.31	374.42	358.35	345.76
22000	2001.29	1082.46	778.90	629.14	540.86	483.30	443.26	414.13	392.25	375.42	362.22
23000	2092.26	1131.66	814.31	657.74	565.45	505.27	463.41	432.96	410.08	392.48	378.69
24000	2183.23	1180.86	849.71	686.33	590.03	527.24	483.55	451.78	427.91	409.55	395.15
25000	2274.20	1230.06	885.11	714.93	614.62	549.21	503.70	470.60	445.74	426.61	411.61
26000	2365.16	1279.27	920.52	743.53	639.20	571.17	523.85	489.43	463.57	443.67	428.08
27000	2456.13	1328.47	955.92	772.12	663.79	593.14	544.00	508.25	481.40	460.74	444.54
28000	2547.10	1377.67	991.33	800.72	688.37	615.11	564.15	527.08	499.23	477.80	461.01
29000	2638.07	1426.87	1026.73	829.32	712.96	637.08	584.29	545.90	517.06	494.87	477.47
30000	2729.03	1476.08	1062.14	857.92	737.54	659.05	604.44	564.72	534.89	511.93	493.94
31000	2820.00	1525.28	1097.54	886.51	762.13	681.01	624.59	583.55	552.72	529.00	510.40
32000	2910.97	1574.48	1132.95	915.11	786.71	702.98	644.74	602.37	570.55	546.06	526.87
33000	3001.94	1623.68	1168.35	943.71	811.29	724.95	664.89	621.20	588.38	563.12	543.33
34000	3092.90	1672.88	1203.75	972.30	835.88	746.92	685.03	640.02	606.21	580.19	559.79
35000	3183.87	1722.09	1239.16	1000.90	860.46	768.89	705.18	658.84	624.04	597.25	576.26
36000	3274.84	1771.29	1274.56	1029.50	885.05	790.86	725.33	677.67	641.87	614.32	592.72
37000	3365.81	1820.49	1309.97	1058.09	909.63	812.82	745.48	696.49	659.70	631.38	609.19
38000	3456.78	1869.69	1345.37	1086.69	934.22	834.79	765.62	715.32	677.53	648.45	625.65
39000	3547.74	1918.90	1380.78	1115.29	958.80	856.76	785.77	734.14	695.35	665.51	642.12
40000	3638.71	1968.10	1416.18	1143.89	983.39	878.73	805.92	752.96	713.18	682.57	658.58
41000	3729.68	2017.30	1451.58	1172.48	1007.97	900.70	826.07	771.79	731.01	699.64	675.04
42000	3820.65	2066.50	1486.99	1201.08	1032.55	922.66	846.22	790.61	748.84	716.70	691.51
43000	3911.61	2115.71	1522.39	1229.68	1057.14	944.63	866.36	809.44	766.67	733.77	707.97
44000	4002.58	2164.91	1557.80	1258.27	1081.72	966.60	886.51	828.26	784.50	750.83	724.44
45000	4093.55	2214.11	1593.20	1286.87	1106.31	988.57	906.66	847.08	802.33	767.90	740.90
46000	4184.52	2263.31	1628.61	1315.47	1130.89	1010.54	926.81	865.91	820.16	784.96	757.37
47000	4275.48	2312.52	1664.01	1344.06	1155.48	1032.50	946.96	884.73	837.99	802.02	773.83
48000	4366.45	2361.72	1699.42	1372.66	1180.06	1054.47	967.10	903.56	855.82	819.09	790.30
49000	4457.42	2410.92	1734.82	1401.26	1204.65	1076.44	987.25	922.38	873.65	836.15	806.76
50000	4548.39	2460.12	1770.22	1429.86	1229.23	1098.41	1007.40	941.20	891.48	853.22	823.22
55000	5003.23	2706.13	1947.25	1572.84	1352.15	1208.25	1108.14	1035.32	980.63	938.54	905.55
60000	5458.06	2952.15	2124.27	1715.83	1475.08	1318.09	1208.88	1129.44	1069.77	1023.86	987.87
65000	5912.90	3198.16	2301.29	1858.81	1598.00	1427.93	1309.62	1223.56	1158.92	1109.18	1070.19
70000	6367.74	3444.17	2478.31	2001.80	1720.92	1537.77	1410.36	1317.68	1248.07	1194.50	1152.51
75000	6822.58	3690.18	2655.33	2144.78	1843.84	1647.61	1511.10	1411.80	1337.22	1279.82	1234.83
80000	7277.42	3936.19	2832.36	2287.77	1966.77	1757.45	1611.84	1505.92	1426.36	1365.14	1317.16
85000	7732.25	4182.20	3009.38	2430.75	2089.69	1867.29	1712.58	1600.04	1515.51	1450.46	1399.48
90000	8187.09	4428.22	3186.40	2573.74	2212.61	1977.13	1813.32	1694.16	1604.66	1535.79	1481.80
95000	8641.93	4674.23	3363.42	2716.72	2335.53	2086.97	1914.05	1788.28	1693.81	1621.11	1564.12
100000	9096.77	4920.24	3540.44	2859.71	2458.46	2196.81	2014.79	1882.40	1782.95	1706.43	1646.44

Principal and Interest   16.50%
Monthly Payment Amortization Table

Term Amount	12 Years	13 Years	14 Years	15 Years	16 Years	17 Years	18 Years	19 Years	20 Years	25 Years	30 Years
50	.80	.79	.77	.76	.75	.74	.73	.72	.72	.70	.70
100	1.60	1.57	1.53	1.51	1.49	1.47	1.46	1.44	1.43	1.40	1.39
200	3.20	3.13	3.06	3.01	2.97	2.94	2.91	2.88	2.86	2.80	2.78
300	4.80	4.69	4.59	4.52	4.45	4.40	4.36	4.32	4.29	4.20	4.16
400	6.40	6.25	6.12	6.02	5.94	5.87	5.81	5.76	5.72	5.60	5.55
500	8.00	7.81	7.65	7.52	7.42	7.33	7.26	7.20	7.15	7.00	6.93
600	9.60	9.37	9.18	9.03	8.90	8.80	8.71	8.64	8.58	8.39	8.32
700	11.20	10.93	10.71	10.53	10.38	10.26	10.16	10.08	10.01	9.79	9.70
800	12.79	12.49	12.24	12.03	11.87	11.73	11.61	11.52	11.44	11.19	11.09
900	14.39	14.05	13.77	13.54	13.35	13.19	13.06	12.96	12.87	12.59	12.47
1000	15.99	15.61	15.30	15.04	14.83	14.66	14.51	14.39	14.29	13.99	13.86
2000	31.98	31.21	30.59	30.08	29.66	29.31	29.02	28.78	28.58	27.97	27.71
3000	47.97	46.82	45.88	45.12	44.49	43.97	43.53	43.17	42.87	41.95	41.56
4000	63.95	62.42	61.17	60.15	59.31	58.62	58.04	57.56	57.16	55.93	55.41
5000	79.94	78.02	76.46	75.19	74.14	73.27	72.55	71.95	71.45	69.92	69.26
6000	95.93	93.63	91.76	90.23	88.97	87.93	87.06	86.34	85.74	83.90	83.11
7000	111.92	109.23	107.05	105.26	103.80	102.58	101.57	100.73	100.03	97.88	96.97
8000	127.90	124.83	122.34	120.30	118.62	117.24	116.08	115.12	114.32	111.86	110.82
9000	143.89	140.44	137.63	135.34	133.45	131.89	130.59	129.51	128.61	125.85	124.67
10000	159.88	156.04	152.92	150.38	148.28	146.54	145.10	143.90	142.90	139.83	138.52
11000	175.87	171.64	168.22	165.41	163.11	161.20	159.61	158.29	157.18	153.81	152.37
12000	191.85	187.25	183.51	180.45	177.93	175.85	174.12	172.68	171.47	167.79	166.22
13000	207.84	202.85	198.80	195.49	192.76	190.50	188.63	187.07	185.76	181.78	180.07
14000	223.83	218.45	214.09	210.52	207.59	205.16	203.14	201.46	200.05	195.76	193.93
15000	239.82	234.06	229.38	225.56	222.41	219.81	217.65	215.85	214.34	209.74	207.78
16000	255.80	249.66	244.68	240.60	237.24	234.47	232.16	230.24	228.63	223.72	221.63
17000	271.79	265.27	259.97	255.64	252.07	249.12	246.67	244.63	242.92	237.71	235.48
18000	287.78	280.87	275.26	270.67	266.90	263.77	261.18	259.02	257.21	251.69	249.33
19000	303.76	296.47	290.55	285.71	281.72	278.43	275.69	273.40	271.50	265.67	263.18
20000	319.75	312.08	305.84	300.75	296.55	293.08	290.20	287.79	285.79	279.65	277.03
21000	335.74	327.68	321.14	315.78	311.38	307.73	304.71	302.18	300.07	293.64	290.89
22000	351.73	343.28	336.43	330.82	326.21	322.39	319.22	316.57	314.36	307.62	304.74
23000	367.71	358.89	351.72	345.86	341.03	337.04	333.73	330.96	328.65	321.60	318.59
24000	383.70	374.49	367.01	360.90	355.86	351.70	348.24	345.35	342.94	335.58	332.44
25000	399.69	390.09	382.30	375.93	370.69	366.35	362.75	359.74	357.23	349.57	346.29
26000	415.68	405.70	397.60	390.97	385.51	381.00	377.25	374.13	371.52	363.55	360.14
27000	431.66	421.30	412.89	406.01	400.34	395.66	391.76	388.52	385.81	377.53	373.99
28000	447.65	436.90	428.18	421.04	415.17	410.31	406.27	402.91	400.10	391.51	387.85
29000	463.64	452.51	443.47	436.08	430.00	424.96	420.78	417.30	414.39	405.50	401.70
30000	479.63	468.11	458.76	451.12	444.82	439.62	435.29	431.69	428.68	419.48	415.55
31000	495.61	483.72	474.06	466.15	459.65	454.27	449.80	446.08	442.96	433.46	429.40
32000	511.60	499.32	489.35	481.19	474.48	468.93	464.31	460.47	457.25	447.44	443.25
33000	527.59	514.92	504.64	496.23	489.31	483.58	478.82	474.86	471.54	461.43	457.10
34000	543.57	530.53	519.93	511.27	504.13	498.23	493.33	489.25	485.83	475.41	470.96
35000	559.56	546.13	535.22	526.30	518.96	512.89	507.84	503.64	500.12	489.39	484.81
36000	575.55	561.73	550.52	541.34	533.79	527.54	522.35	518.03	514.41	503.37	498.66
37000	591.54	577.34	565.81	556.38	548.61	542.19	536.86	532.41	528.70	517.36	512.51
38000	607.52	592.94	581.10	571.41	563.44	556.85	551.37	546.80	542.99	531.34	526.36
39000	623.51	608.54	596.39	586.45	578.27	571.50	565.88	561.19	557.28	545.32	540.21
40000	639.50	624.15	611.68	601.49	593.10	586.16	580.39	575.58	571.57	559.30	554.06
41000	655.49	639.75	626.98	616.53	607.92	600.81	594.90	589.97	585.85	573.29	567.92
42000	671.47	655.35	642.27	631.56	622.75	615.46	609.41	604.36	600.14	587.27	581.77
43000	687.46	670.96	657.56	646.60	637.58	630.12	623.92	618.75	614.43	601.25	595.62
44000	703.45	686.56	672.85	661.64	652.41	644.77	638.43	633.14	628.72	615.23	609.47
45000	719.44	702.17	688.14	676.67	667.23	659.42	652.94	647.53	643.01	629.22	623.32
46000	735.42	717.77	703.44	691.71	682.06	674.08	667.45	661.92	657.30	643.20	637.17
47000	751.41	733.37	718.73	706.75	696.89	688.73	681.96	676.31	671.59	657.18	651.02
48000	767.40	748.98	734.02	721.79	711.72	703.39	696.47	690.70	685.88	671.16	664.88
49000	783.38	764.58	749.31	736.82	726.54	718.04	710.98	705.09	700.17	685.14	678.73
50000	799.37	780.18	764.60	751.86	741.37	732.69	725.49	719.48	714.46	699.13	692.58
55000	879.31	858.20	841.06	827.04	815.51	805.96	798.03	791.42	785.90	769.04	761.84
60000	959.25	936.22	917.52	902.23	889.64	879.23	870.58	863.37	857.35	838.95	831.09
65000	1039.18	1014.24	993.98	977.42	963.78	952.50	943.13	935.32	928.79	908.86	900.35
70000	1119.12	1092.25	1070.44	1052.60	1037.92	1025.77	1015.68	1007.27	1000.24	978.78	969.61
75000	1199.06	1170.27	1146.90	1127.79	1112.05	1099.04	1088.23	1079.21	1071.68	1048.69	1038.87
80000	1278.99	1248.29	1223.36	1202.97	1186.19	1172.31	1160.77	1151.16	1143.13	1118.60	1108.12
85000	1358.93	1326.31	1299.82	1278.16	1260.33	1245.57	1233.32	1223.11	1214.57	1188.51	1177.38
90000	1438.87	1404.33	1376.28	1353.34	1334.46	1318.84	1305.87	1295.06	1286.02	1258.43	1246.64
95000	1518.80	1482.34	1452.74	1428.53	1408.60	1392.11	1378.42	1367.00	1357.46	1328.34	1315.90
100000	1598.74	1560.36	1529.20	1503.71	1482.73	1465.38	1450.97	1438.95	1428.91	1398.25	1385.15

16.75% Principal and Interest
Monthly Payment Amortization Table

Term Amount	1 Year	2 Years	3 Years	4 Years	5 Years	6 Years	7 Years	8 Years	9 Years	10 Years	11 Years
50	4.56	2.47	1.78	1.44	1.24	1.11	1.02	.95	.90	.87	.84
100	9.11	4.94	3.56	2.88	2.48	2.22	2.03	1.90	1.80	1.73	1.67
200	18.22	9.87	7.11	5.75	4.95	4.43	4.06	3.80	3.60	3.45	3.33
300	27.33	14.80	10.66	8.62	7.42	6.64	6.09	5.70	5.40	5.17	4.99
400	36.44	19.73	14.22	11.50	9.89	8.85	8.12	7.59	7.20	6.89	6.66
500	45.55	24.67	17.77	14.37	12.36	11.06	10.15	9.49	9.00	8.62	8.32
600	54.66	29.60	21.32	17.24	14.84	13.27	12.18	11.39	10.79	10.34	9.98
700	63.77	34.53	24.87	20.11	17.31	15.48	14.21	13.29	12.59	12.06	11.64
800	72.87	39.46	28.43	22.99	19.78	17.69	16.24	15.18	14.39	13.78	13.31
900	81.98	44.40	31.98	25.86	22.25	19.90	18.27	17.08	16.19	15.50	14.97
1000	91.09	49.33	35.53	28.73	24.72	22.11	20.30	18.98	17.99	17.23	16.63
2000	182.18	98.65	71.06	57.46	49.44	44.22	40.59	37.95	35.97	34.45	33.26
3000	273.26	147.97	106.59	86.18	74.16	66.33	60.88	56.92	53.95	51.67	49.88
4000	364.35	197.29	142.12	114.91	98.88	88.43	81.17	75.89	71.94	68.89	66.51
5000	455.44	246.62	177.65	143.63	123.60	110.54	101.46	94.87	89.92	86.11	83.14
6000	546.52	295.94	213.18	172.36	148.32	132.65	121.75	113.84	107.90	103.34	99.76
7000	637.61	345.26	248.70	201.09	173.03	154.75	142.05	132.81	125.88	120.56	116.39
8000	728.69	394.58	284.23	229.81	197.75	176.86	162.34	151.78	143.87	137.78	133.01
9000	819.78	443.91	319.76	258.54	222.47	198.97	182.63	170.76	161.85	155.00	149.64
10000	910.87	493.23	355.29	287.26	247.19	221.07	202.92	189.73	179.83	172.22	166.27
11000	1001.95	542.55	390.82	315.99	271.91	243.18	223.21	208.70	197.81	189.44	182.89
12000	1093.04	591.87	426.35	344.72	296.63	265.29	243.50	227.67	215.80	206.67	199.52
13000	1184.13	641.19	461.87	373.44	321.34	287.39	263.80	246.65	233.78	223.89	216.14
14000	1275.21	690.52	497.40	402.17	346.06	309.50	284.09	265.62	251.76	241.11	232.77
15000	1366.30	739.84	532.93	430.89	370.78	331.61	304.38	284.59	269.74	258.33	249.40
16000	1457.38	789.16	568.46	459.62	395.50	353.71	324.67	303.56	287.73	275.55	266.02
17000	1548.47	838.48	603.99	488.34	420.22	375.82	344.96	322.54	305.71	292.77	282.65
18000	1639.56	887.81	639.52	517.07	444.94	397.93	365.25	341.51	323.69	310.00	299.27
19000	1730.64	937.13	675.05	545.80	469.65	420.04	385.55	360.48	341.67	327.22	315.90
20000	1821.73	986.45	710.57	574.52	494.37	442.14	405.84	379.45	359.66	344.44	332.53
21000	1912.81	1035.77	746.10	603.25	519.09	464.25	426.13	398.43	377.64	361.66	349.15
22000	2003.90	1085.09	781.63	631.97	543.81	486.36	446.42	417.40	395.62	378.88	365.78
23000	2094.99	1134.42	817.16	660.70	568.53	508.46	466.71	436.37	413.60	396.10	382.40
24000	2186.07	1183.74	852.69	689.43	593.25	530.57	487.00	455.34	431.59	413.33	399.03
25000	2277.16	1233.06	888.22	718.15	617.96	552.68	507.29	474.32	449.57	430.55	415.66
26000	2368.24	1282.38	923.74	746.88	642.68	574.78	527.59	493.29	467.55	447.77	432.28
27000	2459.33	1331.71	959.27	775.60	667.40	596.89	547.88	512.26	485.53	464.99	448.91
28000	2550.42	1381.03	994.80	804.33	692.12	619.00	568.17	531.23	503.52	482.21	465.53
29000	2641.50	1430.35	1030.33	833.06	716.84	641.10	588.46	550.21	521.50	499.43	482.16
30000	2732.59	1479.67	1065.86	861.78	741.56	663.21	608.75	569.18	539.48	516.66	498.79
31000	2823.68	1528.99	1101.39	890.51	766.27	685.32	629.04	588.15	557.46	533.88	515.41
32000	2914.76	1578.32	1136.91	919.23	790.99	707.42	649.34	607.12	575.45	551.10	532.04
33000	3005.85	1627.64	1172.44	947.96	815.71	729.53	669.63	626.10	593.43	568.32	548.66
34000	3096.93	1676.96	1207.97	976.68	840.43	751.64	689.92	645.07	611.41	585.54	565.29
35000	3188.02	1726.28	1243.50	1005.41	865.15	773.75	710.21	664.04	629.39	602.76	581.92
36000	3279.11	1775.61	1279.03	1034.14	889.87	795.85	730.50	683.01	647.38	619.99	598.54
37000	3370.19	1824.93	1314.56	1062.86	914.58	817.96	750.79	701.98	665.36	637.21	615.17
38000	3461.28	1874.25	1350.09	1091.59	939.30	840.07	771.09	720.96	683.34	654.43	631.79
39000	3552.36	1923.57	1385.61	1120.31	964.02	862.17	791.38	739.93	701.32	671.65	648.42
40000	3643.45	1972.89	1421.14	1149.04	988.74	884.28	811.67	758.90	719.31	688.87	665.05
41000	3734.54	2022.22	1456.67	1177.77	1013.46	906.39	831.96	777.87	737.29	706.09	681.67
42000	3825.62	2071.54	1492.20	1206.49	1038.18	928.49	852.25	796.85	755.27	723.32	698.30
43000	3916.71	2120.86	1527.73	1235.22	1062.89	950.60	872.54	815.82	773.25	740.54	714.92
44000	4007.80	2170.18	1563.26	1263.94	1087.61	972.71	892.83	834.79	791.24	757.76	731.55
45000	4098.88	2219.51	1598.78	1292.67	1112.33	994.81	913.13	853.76	809.22	774.98	748.18
46000	4189.97	2268.83	1634.31	1321.39	1137.05	1016.92	933.42	872.74	827.20	792.20	764.80
47000	4281.05	2318.15	1669.84	1350.12	1161.77	1039.03	953.71	891.71	845.18	809.42	781.43
48000	4372.14	2367.47	1705.37	1378.85	1186.49	1061.13	974.00	910.68	863.17	826.65	798.05
49000	4463.23	2416.79	1740.90	1407.57	1211.20	1083.24	994.29	929.65	881.15	843.87	814.68
50000	4554.31	2466.12	1776.43	1436.30	1235.92	1105.35	1014.58	948.63	899.13	861.09	831.31
55000	5009.74	2712.73	1954.07	1579.93	1359.51	1215.88	1116.04	1043.49	989.04	947.20	914.44
60000	5465.17	2959.34	2131.71	1723.56	1483.11	1326.42	1217.50	1138.35	1078.96	1033.31	997.57
65000	5920.60	3205.95	2309.35	1867.19	1606.70	1436.95	1318.96	1233.21	1168.87	1119.41	1080.70
70000	6376.04	3452.56	2487.00	2010.82	1730.29	1547.49	1420.42	1328.07	1258.78	1205.52	1163.83
75000	6831.47	3699.17	2664.64	2154.44	1853.88	1658.02	1521.87	1422.94	1348.69	1291.63	1246.96
80000	7286.90	3945.78	2842.28	2298.07	1977.47	1768.55	1623.33	1517.80	1438.61	1377.74	1330.09
85000	7742.33	4192.39	3019.92	2441.70	2101.06	1879.09	1724.79	1612.66	1528.52	1463.85	1413.22
90000	8197.76	4439.01	3197.56	2585.33	2224.66	1989.62	1826.25	1707.52	1618.43	1549.96	1496.35
95000	8653.19	4685.62	3375.21	2728.96	2348.25	2100.16	1927.71	1802.39	1708.35	1636.06	1579.48
100000	9108.62	4932.23	3552.85	2872.59	2471.84	2210.69	2029.16	1897.25	1798.26	1722.17	1662.61

Principal and Interest
Monthly Payment Amortization Table

16.75%

Term Amount	12 Years	13 Years	14 Years	15 Years	16 Years	17 Years	18 Years	19 Years	20 Years	25 Years	30 Years
50	.81	.79	.78	.77	.76	.75	.74	.73	.73	.71	.71
100	1.62	1.58	1.55	1.53	1.51	1.49	1.47	1.46	1.45	1.42	1.41
200	3.24	3.16	3.10	3.05	3.01	2.97	2.94	2.92	2.90	2.84	2.82
300	4.85	4.74	4.64	4.57	4.51	4.46	4.41	4.38	4.35	4.26	4.22
400	6.47	6.31	6.19	6.09	6.01	5.94	5.88	5.84	5.80	5.68	5.63
500	8.08	7.89	7.74	7.61	7.51	7.42	7.35	7.29	7.24	7.09	7.03
600	9.70	9.47	9.28	9.13	9.01	8.91	8.82	8.75	8.69	8.51	8.44
700	11.31	11.05	10.83	10.65	10.51	10.39	10.29	10.21	10.14	9.93	9.84
800	12.93	12.62	12.38	12.18	12.01	11.87	11.76	11.67	11.59	11.35	11.25
900	14.54	14.20	13.92	13.70	13.51	13.36	13.23	13.12	13.04	12.77	12.65
1000	16.16	15.78	15.47	15.22	15.01	14.84	14.70	14.58	14.48	14.18	14.06
2000	32.31	31.55	30.93	30.43	30.02	29.68	29.39	29.16	28.96	28.36	28.11
3000	48.46	47.32	46.40	45.64	45.02	44.51	44.09	43.73	43.44	42.54	42.17
4000	64.62	63.10	61.86	60.86	60.03	59.35	58.78	58.31	57.92	56.72	56.22
5000	80.77	78.87	77.33	76.07	75.04	74.18	73.48	72.89	72.40	70.90	70.27
6000	96.92	94.64	92.79	91.28	90.04	89.02	88.17	87.46	86.87	85.08	84.33
7000	113.08	110.42	108.26	106.50	105.05	103.86	102.86	102.04	101.35	99.26	98.38
8000	129.23	126.19	123.72	121.71	120.06	118.69	117.56	116.62	115.83	113.44	112.44
9000	145.38	141.96	139.19	136.92	135.06	133.53	132.25	131.19	130.31	127.62	126.49
10000	161.53	157.73	154.65	152.14	150.07	148.36	146.95	145.77	144.79	141.80	140.54
11000	177.69	173.51	170.12	167.35	165.08	163.20	161.64	160.35	159.27	155.98	154.60
12000	193.84	189.28	185.58	182.56	180.08	178.03	176.34	174.92	173.74	170.16	168.65
13000	209.99	205.05	201.05	197.78	195.09	192.87	191.03	189.50	188.22	184.34	182.71
14000	226.15	220.83	216.51	212.99	210.10	207.71	205.72	204.08	202.70	198.52	196.76
15000	242.30	236.60	231.98	228.20	225.10	222.54	220.42	218.65	217.18	212.70	210.81
16000	258.45	252.37	247.44	243.42	240.11	237.38	235.11	233.23	231.66	226.88	224.87
17000	274.60	268.14	262.91	258.63	255.11	252.21	249.81	247.80	246.13	241.06	238.92
18000	290.76	283.92	278.37	273.84	270.12	267.05	264.50	262.38	260.61	255.24	252.98
19000	306.91	299.69	293.84	289.06	285.13	281.88	279.19	276.96	275.09	269.42	267.03
20000	323.06	315.46	309.30	304.27	300.13	296.72	293.89	291.53	289.57	283.60	281.08
21000	339.22	331.24	324.77	319.48	315.14	311.56	308.58	306.11	304.05	297.78	295.14
22000	355.37	347.01	340.23	334.70	330.15	326.39	323.28	320.69	318.53	311.96	309.19
23000	371.52	362.78	355.70	349.91	345.15	341.23	337.97	335.26	333.00	326.14	323.25
24000	387.68	378.55	371.16	365.12	360.16	356.06	352.67	349.84	347.48	340.32	337.30
25000	403.83	394.33	386.63	380.34	375.17	370.90	367.36	364.42	361.96	354.50	351.35
26000	419.98	410.10	402.09	395.55	390.17	385.73	382.05	378.99	376.44	368.68	365.41
27000	436.13	425.87	417.56	410.76	405.18	400.57	396.75	393.57	390.92	382.86	379.46
28000	452.29	441.65	433.02	425.97	420.19	415.41	411.44	408.15	405.39	397.04	393.52
29000	468.44	457.42	448.48	441.19	435.19	430.24	426.14	422.72	419.87	411.22	407.57
30000	484.59	473.19	463.95	456.40	450.20	445.08	440.83	437.30	434.35	425.40	421.62
31000	500.75	488.97	479.41	471.61	465.21	459.91	455.53	451.87	448.83	439.58	435.68
32000	516.90	504.74	494.88	486.83	480.21	474.75	470.22	466.45	463.31	453.76	449.73
33000	533.05	520.51	510.34	502.04	495.22	489.58	484.91	481.03	477.79	467.94	463.79
34000	549.20	536.28	525.81	517.25	510.22	504.42	499.61	495.60	492.26	482.12	477.84
35000	565.36	552.06	541.27	532.47	525.23	519.26	514.30	510.18	506.74	496.30	491.89
36000	581.51	567.83	556.74	547.68	540.24	534.09	529.00	524.76	521.22	510.48	505.95
37000	597.66	583.60	572.20	562.89	555.24	548.93	543.69	539.33	535.70	524.66	520.00
38000	613.82	599.38	587.67	578.11	570.25	563.76	558.38	553.91	550.18	538.84	534.06
39000	629.97	615.15	603.13	593.32	585.26	578.60	573.08	568.49	564.65	553.02	548.11
40000	646.12	630.92	618.60	608.53	600.26	593.44	587.77	583.06	579.13	567.20	562.16
41000	662.28	646.69	634.06	623.75	615.27	608.27	602.47	597.64	593.61	581.38	576.22
42000	678.43	662.47	649.53	638.96	630.28	623.11	617.16	612.22	608.09	595.56	590.27
43000	694.58	678.24	664.99	654.17	645.28	637.94	631.86	626.79	622.57	609.74	604.33
44000	710.73	694.01	680.46	669.39	660.29	652.78	646.55	641.37	637.05	623.92	618.38
45000	726.89	709.79	695.92	684.60	675.30	667.61	661.24	655.95	651.52	638.10	632.43
46000	743.04	725.56	711.39	699.81	690.30	682.45	675.94	670.52	666.00	652.28	646.49
47000	759.19	741.33	726.85	715.03	705.31	697.29	690.63	685.10	680.48	666.46	660.54
48000	775.35	757.10	742.32	730.24	720.32	712.12	705.33	699.67	694.96	680.64	674.59
49000	791.50	772.88	757.78	745.45	735.32	726.96	720.02	714.25	709.44	694.82	688.65
50000	807.65	788.65	773.25	760.67	750.33	741.79	734.72	728.83	723.91	709.00	702.70
55000	888.42	867.51	850.57	836.73	825.36	815.97	808.19	801.71	796.31	779.90	772.97
60000	969.18	946.38	927.89	912.80	900.39	890.15	881.66	874.59	868.70	850.80	843.24
65000	1049.95	1025.24	1005.22	988.86	975.43	964.33	955.13	947.47	941.09	921.70	913.51
70000	1130.71	1104.11	1082.54	1064.93	1050.46	1038.51	1028.60	1020.36	1013.48	992.60	983.78
75000	1211.48	1182.97	1159.87	1141.00	1125.49	1112.69	1102.07	1093.24	1085.87	1063.50	1054.05
80000	1292.24	1261.84	1237.19	1217.06	1200.52	1186.87	1175.54	1166.12	1158.26	1134.40	1124.32
85000	1373.00	1340.70	1314.52	1293.13	1275.55	1261.04	1249.01	1239.00	1230.65	1205.30	1194.59
90000	1453.77	1419.57	1391.84	1369.19	1350.59	1335.22	1322.48	1311.89	1303.04	1276.20	1264.86
95000	1534.53	1498.43	1469.16	1445.26	1425.62	1409.40	1395.95	1384.77	1375.43	1347.10	1335.13
100000	1615.30	1577.30	1546.49	1521.33	1500.65	1483.58	1469.43	1457.65	1447.82	1418.00	1405.40

17.00% Principal and Interest
Monthly Payment Amortization Table

Term / Amount	1 Year	2 Years	3 Years	4 Years	5 Years	6 Years	7 Years	8 Years	9 Years	10 Years	11 Years
50	4.57	2.48	1.79	1.45	1.25	1.12	1.03	.96	.91	.87	.84
100	9.13	4.95	3.57	2.89	2.49	2.23	2.05	1.92	1.82	1.74	1.68
200	18.25	9.89	7.14	5.78	4.98	4.45	4.09	3.83	3.63	3.48	3.36
300	27.37	14.84	10.70	8.66	7.46	6.68	6.14	5.74	5.45	5.22	5.04
400	36.49	19.78	14.27	11.55	9.95	8.90	8.18	7.65	7.26	6.96	6.72
500	45.61	24.73	17.83	14.43	12.43	11.13	10.22	9.57	9.07	8.69	8.40
600	54.73	29.67	21.40	17.32	14.92	13.35	12.27	11.48	10.89	10.43	10.08
700	63.85	34.61	24.96	20.20	17.40	15.58	14.31	13.39	12.70	12.17	11.76
800	72.97	39.56	28.53	23.09	19.89	17.80	16.35	15.30	14.51	13.91	13.44
900	82.09	44.50	32.09	25.97	22.37	20.03	18.40	17.21	16.33	15.65	15.11
1000	91.21	49.45	35.66	28.86	24.86	22.25	20.44	19.13	18.14	17.38	16.79
2000	182.41	98.89	71.31	57.72	49.71	44.50	40.88	38.25	36.28	34.76	33.58
3000	273.62	148.33	106.96	86.57	74.56	66.74	61.31	57.37	54.41	52.14	50.37
4000	364.82	197.77	142.62	115.43	99.42	88.99	81.75	76.49	72.55	69.52	67.16
5000	456.03	247.22	178.27	144.28	124.27	111.24	102.18	95.61	90.69	86.90	83.95
6000	547.23	296.66	213.92	173.14	149.12	133.48	122.62	114.73	108.82	104.28	100.73
7000	638.44	346.10	249.57	201.99	173.97	155.73	143.06	133.86	126.96	121.66	117.52
8000	729.64	395.54	285.23	230.85	198.83	177.97	163.49	152.98	145.09	139.04	134.31
9000	820.85	444.99	320.88	259.70	223.68	200.22	183.93	172.10	163.23	156.42	151.10
10000	912.05	494.43	356.53	288.56	248.53	222.47	204.36	191.22	181.37	173.80	167.89
11000	1003.26	543.87	392.19	317.41	273.38	244.71	224.80	210.34	199.50	191.18	184.68
12000	1094.46	593.31	427.84	346.27	298.24	266.96	245.23	229.46	217.64	208.56	201.46
13000	1185.67	642.75	463.49	375.12	323.09	289.20	265.67	248.58	235.78	225.94	218.25
14000	1276.87	692.20	499.14	403.98	347.94	311.45	286.11	267.71	253.91	243.32	235.04
15000	1368.08	741.64	534.80	432.83	372.79	333.70	306.54	286.83	272.05	260.70	251.83
16000	1459.28	791.08	570.45	461.69	397.65	355.94	326.98	305.95	290.18	278.08	268.62
17000	1550.49	840.52	606.10	490.54	422.50	378.19	347.41	325.07	308.32	295.46	285.41
18000	1641.69	889.97	641.75	519.40	447.35	400.44	367.85	344.19	326.46	312.84	302.19
19000	1732.90	939.41	677.41	548.25	472.20	422.68	388.29	363.31	344.59	330.22	318.98
20000	1824.10	988.85	713.06	577.11	497.06	444.93	408.72	382.43	362.73	347.60	335.77
21000	1915.30	1038.29	748.71	605.96	521.91	467.17	429.16	401.56	380.86	364.98	352.56
22000	2006.51	1087.73	784.37	634.82	546.76	489.42	449.59	420.68	399.00	382.36	369.35
23000	2097.71	1137.18	820.02	663.67	571.61	511.67	470.03	439.80	417.14	399.74	386.14
24000	2188.92	1186.62	855.67	692.53	596.47	533.91	490.46	458.92	435.27	417.12	402.92
25000	2280.12	1236.06	891.32	721.38	621.32	556.16	510.90	478.04	453.41	434.50	419.71
26000	2371.33	1285.50	926.98	750.24	646.17	578.40	531.34	497.16	471.55	451.88	436.50
27000	2462.53	1334.95	962.63	779.09	671.02	600.65	551.77	516.28	489.68	469.26	453.29
28000	2553.74	1384.39	998.28	807.95	695.88	622.90	572.21	535.41	507.82	486.64	470.08
29000	2644.94	1433.83	1033.93	836.80	720.73	645.14	592.64	554.53	525.95	504.02	486.87
30000	2736.15	1483.27	1069.59	865.66	745.58	667.39	613.08	573.65	544.09	521.40	503.65
31000	2827.35	1532.72	1105.24	894.51	770.43	689.64	633.51	592.77	562.23	538.78	520.44
32000	2918.56	1582.16	1140.89	923.37	795.29	711.88	653.95	611.89	580.36	556.16	537.23
33000	3009.76	1631.60	1176.55	952.22	820.14	734.13	674.39	631.01	598.50	573.54	554.02
34000	3100.97	1681.04	1212.20	981.08	844.99	756.37	694.82	650.13	616.64	590.92	570.81
35000	3192.17	1730.48	1247.85	1009.93	869.85	778.62	715.26	669.26	634.77	608.30	587.60
36000	3283.38	1779.93	1283.50	1038.79	894.70	800.87	735.69	688.38	652.91	625.68	604.38
37000	3374.58	1829.37	1319.16	1067.64	919.55	823.11	756.13	707.50	671.04	643.06	621.17
38000	3465.79	1878.81	1354.81	1096.50	944.40	845.36	776.57	726.62	689.18	660.44	637.96
39000	3556.99	1928.25	1390.46	1125.35	969.26	867.60	797.00	745.74	707.32	677.82	654.75
40000	3648.20	1977.70	1426.11	1154.21	994.11	889.85	817.44	764.86	725.45	695.20	671.54
41000	3739.40	2027.14	1461.77	1183.06	1018.96	912.10	837.87	783.98	743.59	712.58	688.33
42000	3830.60	2076.58	1497.42	1211.92	1043.81	934.34	858.31	803.11	761.72	729.96	705.11
43000	3921.81	2126.02	1533.07	1240.77	1068.67	956.59	878.74	822.23	779.86	747.33	721.90
44000	4013.01	2175.46	1568.73	1269.63	1093.52	978.83	899.18	841.35	798.00	764.71	738.69
45000	4104.22	2224.91	1604.38	1298.48	1118.37	1001.08	919.62	860.47	816.13	782.09	755.48
46000	4195.42	2274.35	1640.03	1327.34	1143.23	1023.33	940.05	879.59	834.27	799.47	772.27
47000	4286.63	2323.79	1675.68	1356.19	1168.08	1045.57	960.49	898.71	852.41	816.85	789.06
48000	4377.83	2373.23	1711.34	1385.05	1192.93	1067.82	980.92	917.83	870.54	834.23	805.84
49000	4469.04	2422.68	1746.99	1413.90	1217.78	1090.07	1001.36	936.96	888.68	851.61	822.63
50000	4560.24	2472.12	1782.64	1442.76	1242.63	1112.31	1021.80	956.08	906.81	868.99	839.42
55000	5016.27	2719.33	1960.91	1587.03	1366.90	1223.54	1123.97	1051.69	997.50	955.89	923.36
60000	5472.29	2966.54	2139.17	1731.31	1491.16	1334.77	1226.15	1147.29	1088.18	1042.79	1007.30
65000	5928.31	3213.75	2317.43	1875.58	1615.42	1446.00	1328.33	1242.90	1178.86	1129.69	1091.25
70000	6384.34	3460.96	2495.70	2019.86	1739.69	1557.23	1430.51	1338.51	1269.54	1216.59	1175.19
75000	6840.36	3708.17	2673.96	2164.13	1863.95	1668.46	1532.69	1434.11	1360.22	1303.49	1259.13
80000	7296.39	3955.39	2852.22	2308.41	1988.21	1779.70	1634.87	1529.72	1450.90	1390.39	1343.07
85000	7752.41	4202.60	3030.49	2452.68	2112.47	1890.93	1737.05	1625.33	1541.58	1477.29	1427.01
90000	8208.43	4449.81	3208.75	2596.96	2236.74	2002.16	1839.23	1720.94	1632.26	1564.18	1510.95
95000	8664.46	4697.02	3387.01	2741.23	2361.00	2113.39	1941.41	1816.54	1722.94	1651.08	1594.90
100000	9120.48	4944.23	3565.28	2885.51	2485.26	2224.62	2043.59	1912.15	1813.62	1737.98	1678.84

Principal and Interest
Monthly Payment Amortization Table

17.00%

Term Amount	12 Years	13 Years	14 Years	15 Years	16 Years	17 Years	18 Years	19 Years	20 Years	25 Years	30 Years
50	.82	.80	.79	.77	.76	.76	.75	.74	.74	.72	.72
100	1.64	1.60	1.57	1.54	1.52	1.51	1.49	1.48	1.47	1.44	1.43
200	3.27	3.19	3.13	3.08	3.04	3.01	2.98	2.96	2.94	2.88	2.86
300	4.90	4.79	4.70	4.62	4.56	4.51	4.47	4.43	4.41	4.32	4.28
400	6.53	6.38	6.26	6.16	6.08	6.01	5.96	5.91	5.87	5.76	5.71
500	8.16	7.98	7.82	7.70	7.60	7.51	7.44	7.39	7.34	7.19	7.13
600	9.80	9.57	9.39	9.24	9.12	9.02	8.93	8.86	8.81	8.63	8.56
700	11.43	11.17	10.95	10.78	10.64	10.52	10.42	10.34	10.27	10.07	9.98
800	13.06	12.76	12.52	12.32	12.15	12.02	11.91	11.82	11.74	11.51	11.41
900	14.69	14.35	14.08	13.86	13.67	13.52	13.40	13.29	13.21	12.95	12.84
1000	16.32	15.95	15.64	15.40	15.19	15.02	14.88	14.77	14.67	14.38	14.26
2000	32.64	31.89	31.28	30.79	30.38	30.04	29.76	29.53	29.34	28.76	28.52
3000	48.96	47.83	46.92	46.18	45.56	45.06	44.64	44.30	44.01	43.14	42.78
4000	65.28	63.78	62.56	61.57	60.75	60.08	59.52	59.06	58.68	57.52	57.03
5000	81.60	79.72	78.20	76.96	75.94	75.10	74.40	73.83	73.35	71.89	71.29
6000	97.92	95.66	93.84	92.35	91.12	90.12	89.28	88.59	88.01	86.27	85.55
7000	114.24	111.61	109.47	107.74	106.31	105.13	104.16	103.35	102.68	100.65	99.80
8000	130.56	127.55	125.11	123.13	121.50	120.15	119.04	118.12	117.35	115.03	114.06
9000	146.88	143.49	140.75	138.52	136.68	135.17	133.92	132.88	132.02	129.41	128.32
10000	163.20	159.43	156.39	153.91	151.87	150.19	148.80	147.65	146.69	143.78	142.57
11000	179.52	175.38	172.03	169.30	167.05	165.21	163.68	162.41	161.35	158.16	156.83
12000	195.84	191.32	187.67	184.69	182.24	180.23	178.56	177.17	176.02	172.54	171.09
13000	212.15	207.26	203.30	200.08	197.43	195.24	193.44	191.94	190.69	186.92	185.34
14000	228.47	223.21	218.94	215.47	212.61	210.26	208.32	206.70	205.36	201.30	199.60
15000	244.79	239.15	234.58	230.86	227.80	225.28	223.20	221.47	220.03	215.67	213.86
16000	261.11	255.09	250.22	246.25	242.99	240.30	238.08	236.23	234.69	230.05	228.11
17000	277.43	271.04	265.86	261.64	258.17	255.32	252.96	250.99	249.36	244.43	242.37
18000	293.75	286.98	281.50	277.03	273.36	270.34	267.84	265.76	264.03	258.81	256.63
19000	310.07	302.92	297.13	292.42	288.55	285.36	282.71	280.52	278.70	273.19	270.88
20000	326.39	318.86	312.77	307.81	303.73	300.37	297.59	295.29	293.37	287.56	285.14
21000	342.71	334.81	328.41	323.20	318.92	315.39	312.47	310.05	308.03	301.94	299.40
22000	359.03	350.75	344.05	338.59	334.10	330.41	327.35	324.81	322.70	316.32	313.65
23000	375.35	366.69	359.69	353.98	349.29	345.43	342.23	339.58	337.37	330.70	327.91
24000	391.67	382.64	375.33	369.37	364.48	360.45	357.11	354.34	352.04	345.08	342.17
25000	407.99	398.58	390.96	384.76	379.66	375.47	371.99	369.11	366.71	359.45	356.42
26000	424.30	414.52	406.60	400.15	394.85	390.48	386.87	383.87	381.37	373.83	370.68
27000	440.62	430.46	422.24	415.54	410.04	405.50	401.75	398.64	396.04	388.21	384.94
28000	456.94	446.41	437.88	430.93	425.22	420.52	416.63	413.40	410.71	402.59	399.19
29000	473.26	462.35	453.52	446.32	440.41	435.54	431.51	428.16	425.38	416.97	413.45
30000	489.58	478.29	469.16	461.71	455.60	450.56	446.39	442.93	440.05	431.34	427.71
31000	505.90	494.24	484.79	477.10	470.78	465.58	461.27	457.69	454.71	445.72	441.96
32000	522.22	510.18	500.43	492.49	485.97	480.59	476.15	472.46	469.38	460.10	456.22
33000	538.54	526.12	516.07	507.88	501.15	495.61	491.03	487.22	484.05	474.48	470.48
34000	554.86	542.07	531.71	523.27	516.34	510.63	505.91	501.98	498.72	488.86	484.73
35000	571.18	558.01	547.35	538.66	531.53	525.65	520.79	516.75	513.39	503.23	498.99
36000	587.50	573.95	562.99	554.05	546.71	540.67	535.67	531.51	528.05	517.61	513.25
37000	603.82	589.89	578.63	569.44	561.90	555.69	550.55	546.28	542.72	531.99	527.50
38000	620.14	605.84	594.26	584.83	577.09	570.71	565.42	561.04	557.39	546.37	541.76
39000	636.45	621.78	609.90	600.22	592.27	585.72	580.30	575.80	572.06	560.75	556.02
40000	652.77	637.72	625.54	615.61	607.46	600.74	595.18	590.57	586.73	575.12	570.28
41000	669.09	653.67	641.18	631.00	622.64	615.76	610.06	605.33	601.39	589.50	584.53
42000	685.41	669.61	656.82	646.39	637.83	630.78	624.94	620.10	616.06	603.88	598.79
43000	701.73	685.55	672.46	661.78	653.02	645.80	639.82	634.86	630.73	618.26	613.05
44000	718.05	701.49	688.09	677.17	668.20	660.81	654.70	649.62	645.40	632.64	627.30
45000	734.37	717.44	703.73	692.56	683.39	675.83	669.58	664.39	660.07	647.01	641.56
46000	750.69	733.38	719.37	707.95	698.58	690.85	684.46	679.15	674.73	661.39	655.82
47000	767.01	749.32	735.01	723.34	713.76	705.87	699.34	693.92	689.40	675.77	670.07
48000	783.33	765.27	750.65	738.73	728.95	720.89	714.22	708.68	704.07	690.15	684.33
49000	799.65	781.21	766.29	754.12	744.14	735.91	729.10	723.45	718.74	704.53	698.59
50000	815.97	797.15	781.92	769.51	759.32	750.93	743.98	738.21	733.41	718.90	712.84
55000	897.56	876.87	860.12	846.46	835.25	826.02	818.38	812.03	806.75	790.79	784.13
60000	979.16	956.58	938.31	923.41	911.19	901.11	892.77	885.85	880.09	862.68	855.41
65000	1060.75	1036.30	1016.50	1000.36	987.12	976.20	967.17	959.67	953.43	934.57	926.69
70000	1142.35	1116.01	1094.69	1077.31	1063.05	1051.30	1041.57	1033.49	1026.77	1006.46	997.98
75000	1223.95	1195.73	1172.88	1154.26	1138.98	1126.39	1115.97	1107.31	1100.11	1078.35	1069.26
80000	1305.54	1275.44	1251.08	1231.21	1214.91	1201.48	1190.36	1181.13	1173.45	1150.24	1140.55
85000	1387.14	1355.16	1329.27	1308.16	1290.84	1276.57	1264.76	1254.95	1246.79	1222.13	1211.83
90000	1468.74	1434.87	1407.46	1385.11	1366.78	1351.66	1339.16	1328.77	1320.13	1294.02	1283.11
95000	1550.33	1514.59	1485.65	1462.06	1442.71	1426.76	1413.56	1402.59	1393.47	1365.91	1354.40
100000	1631.93	1594.30	1563.84	1539.01	1518.64	1501.85	1487.95	1476.41	1466.81	1437.80	1425.68

APPENDIX FOUR
REMAINING BALANCE FACTORS

To use the remaining balance tables start with the top line under the appropriate original term of the loan and then go down the table to the age of the loan for which you want the remaining balance.

All factors in the remaining balance tables are per a $100.00 loan amount so that a 30-year loan at a rate of 11 1/2% interest would have a remaining balance of $92.86 at the end of 25 years and of course, -0- at the end of 30-years. For a $10,000.00 loan, simply multiply the factor by 100, a $100,000.00 loan, multiply by 1,000 etc.

The factors also represent a percentage of the loan so that a $100.00 loan has 92.86% remaining at the end of 10-years, 84.77% at the end of 15-years and 45.03% at the end of 25-years.

A remaining balance at the end of 10-years for a loan so that a $100.00 loan has 92.86% remaining at the end of 10-years, 84.77% at the end of 25-years.

A remaining balance at the end of 10-years for a loan of $72,450.00 at 11.75% interest for a 30-year term would be $67,479.93 which is 724.50 x 93.14 or $72,450.00 x 93.14%. The factor of 724.50 was known by dividing $72,450.00 by 100. All factors are per $100.00 loan amounts.

7.00%

Age of Loan	1	2	3	4	5	6	7	8	9	10	15	20	25	30
1	0.	51.74	68.96	77.55	82.69	86.10	88.53	90.33	91.73	92.84	96.09	97.62	98.47	98.98
2		0.	35.69	53.48	64.13	71.20	76.22	79.97	82.86	85.16	91.90	95.07	96.83	97.89
3			0.	27.67	44.23	55.22	63.03	68.85	73.35	76.93	87.40	92.33	95.07	96.73
4				0.	22.88	38.08	48.88	56.93	63.16	68.10	82.58	89.40	93.18	95.47
5					0.	19.70	33.71	44.15	52.23	58.64	77.41	86.26	91.16	94.13
6						0.	17.44	30.45	40.50	48.49	71.87	82.88	88.99	92.69
7							0.	15.76	27.93	37.60	65.93	79.27	86.67	91.15
8								0.	14.45	25.93	59.55	75.39	84.17	89.49
9									0.	13.42	52.72	71.23	81.50	87.72
10										0.	45.39	66.77	78.63	85.81
11										0.	37.54	61.99	75.56	83.77
12										0.	29.11	56.87	72.26	81.58
13										0.	20.08	51.37	68.73	79.23
14										0.	10.39	45.47	64.94	76.72
15											0.	39.15	60.87	74.02
16											0.	32.38	56.51	71.12
17											0.	25.11	51.84	68.02
18											0.	17.32	46.83	64.69
19											0.	8.96	41.46	61.13
20												0.	35.69	57.30
21												0.	29.52	53.20
22												0.	22.89	48.80
23												0.	15.79	44.08
24												0.	8.17	39.02
25													0.	33.60
26													0.	27.78
27													0.	21.55
28													0.	14.86
29													0.	7.69
30														0.
35														
40														

7.25%

Age of Loan	1	2	3	4	5	6	7	8	9	10	15	20	25	30
1	0.	51.81	69.04	77.64	82.78	86.19	88.62	90.43	91.82	92.93	96.17	97.69	98.53	99.03
2		0.	35.77	53.61	64.27	71.35	76.38	80.13	83.03	85.33	92.05	95.21	96.95	97.99
3			0.	27.77	44.38	55.40	63.23	69.07	73.58	77.16	87.63	92.54	95.24	96.87
4				0.	22.99	38.25	49.09	57.18	63.42	68.38	82.87	89.67	93.42	95.67
5					0.	19.82	33.90	44.39	52.50	58.94	77.76	86.58	91.45	94.38
6						0.	17.56	30.65	40.76	48.79	72.26	83.27	89.34	92.99
7							0.	15.88	28.15	37.88	66.35	79.70	87.07	91.50
8								0.	14.58	26.16	60.00	75.87	84.63	89.89
9									0.	13.55	53.17	71.75	82.00	88.17
10										0.	45.83	67.32	79.18	86.31
11										0.	37.94	62.56	76.15	84.32
12										0.	29.46	57.45	72.89	82.17
13										0.	20.34	51.95	69.38	79.87
14										0.	10.54	46.03	65.62	77.39
15											0.	39.68	61.57	74.73
16											0.	32.85	57.21	71.87
17											0.	25.50	52.54	68.79
18											0.	17.61	47.51	65.48
19											0.	9.12	42.10	61.93
20												0.	36.29	58.11
21												0.	30.04	54.00
22												0.	23.32	49.58
23												0.	16.10	44.84
24												0.	8.34	39.73
25													0.	34.25
26													0.	28.35
27													0.	22.01
28													0.	15.20
29													0.	7.87
30														0.
35														
40														

Remaining Balance Factors
Original Term In Years

7.50%

Age of Loan

Age	1	2	3	4	5	6	7	8	9	10	15	20	25	30
1	0.	51.87	69.13	77.73	82.87	86.29	88.71	90.52	91.91	93.02	96.25	97.76	98.58	99.08
2		0.	35.85	53.73	64.42	71.51	76.55	80.30	83.20	85.50	92.21	95.34	97.06	98.08
3			0.	27.87	44.53	55.58	63.44	69.29	73.81	77.39	87.85	92.73	95.41	97.01
4				0.	23.10	38.42	49.31	57.42	63.68	68.65	83.15	89.93	93.64	95.86
5					0.	19.93	34.09	44.63	52.78	59.24	78.10	86.90	91.73	94.62
6						0.	17.68	30.85	41.02	49.09	72.64	83.64	89.67	93.28
7							0.	16.00	28.36	38.16	66.77	80.13	87.46	91.83
8								0.	14.71	26.38	60.44	76.34	85.07	90.28
9									0.	13.68	53.62	72.26	82.49	88.60
10										0.	46.26	67.87	79.72	86.79
11										0.	38.34	63.13	76.73	84.85
12										0.	29.80	58.02	73.50	82.75
13										0.	20.60	52.52	70.03	80.49
14										0.	10.69	46.59	66.29	78.05
15											0.	40.20	62.26	75.43
16											0.	33.32	57.91	72.60
17											0.	25.90	53.23	69.55
18											0.	7.90	48.18	66.26
19											0.	9.29	42.74	62.72
20												0.	36.88	58.91
21												0.	30.56	54.79
22												0.	23.76	50.36
23												0.	16.42	45.59
24												0.	8.52	40.44
25													0.	34.89
26													0.	28.92
27													0.	22.48
28													0.	15.54
29													0.	8.06
30														0.
35														
40														

7.75%

Age	1	2	3	4	5	6	7	8	9	10	15	20	25	30
1	0.	51.93	69.21	77.82	82.96	86.38	88.80	90.61	92.00	93.11	96.33	97.82	98.64	99.12
2		0.	35.94	53.85	64.56	71.66	76.71	80.46	83.36	85.66	92.36	95.47	97.17	98.17
3			0.	27.97	44.68	55.77	63.64	69.50	74.03	77.62	88.07	92.93	95.58	97.15
4				0.	23.20	38.59	49.52	57.66	63.95	68.93	83.44	90.18	93.86	96.04
5					0.	20.04	34.27	44.87	53.05	59.54	78.43	87.22	92.01	94.85
6						0.	17.80	31.05	41.28	49.40	73.03	84.01	90.00	93.56
7							0.	16.13	28.57	38.44	67.19	80.55	87.84	92.16
8								0.	14.84	26.60	60.88	76.81	85.50	90.65
9									0.	13.81	54.06	72.77	82.97	89.03
10										0.	46.70	68.41	80.25	87.27
11										0.	38.74	63.69	77.30	85.37
12										0.	30.15	58.60	74.11	83.31
13										0.	20.86	53.09	70.67	81.10
14										0.	10.84	47.15	66.95	78.70
15											0.	40.73	62.94	76.11
16											0.	33.79	58.60	73.31
17											0.	26.29	53.91	70.29
18											0.	18.20	48.85	67.03
19											0.	9.45	43.38	63.50
20												0.	37.47	59.70
21												0.	31.09	55.58
22												0.	24.19	51.14
23												0.	16.74	46.33
24												0.	8.69	41.15
25													0.	35.54
26													0.	29.49
27													0.	22.95
28													0.	15.88
29													0.	8.25
30														0.
35														
40														

Remaining Balance Factors
Original Term In Years

8.00%

Age of Loan	1	2	3	4	5	6	7	8	9	10	15	20	25	30
1	0.	51.99	69.29	77.91	83.06	86.47	88.90	90.70	92.09	93.19	96.40	97.89	98.69	99.16
2		0.	36.02	53.98	64.71	71.82	76.87	80.63	83.53	85.82	92.51	95.60	97.27	98.26
3			0.	28.06	44.83	55.95	63.84	69.72	74.25	77.84	88.29	93.12	95.74	97.28
4				0.	23.31	38.77	49.74	57.91	64.21	69.20	83.72	90.43	94.07	96.22
5					0.	20.16	34.46	45.11	53.33	59.84	78.77	87.53	92.27	95.07
6						0.	17.92	31.26	41.55	49.70	73.41	84.38	90.32	93.83
7							0.	16.25	28.79	38.72	67.60	80.97	88.21	92.48
8								0.	14.97	26.83	61.31	77.27	85.92	91.02
9									0.	13.95	54.51	73.27	83.45	89.44
10										0.	47.13	68.94	80.76	87.72
11										0.	39.15	64.25	77.86	85.87
12										0.	30.50	59.17	74.71	83.86
13										0.	21.13	53.67	71.30	81.69
14										0.	10.99	47.71	67.61	79.33
15											0.	41.25	63.61	76.78
16											0.	34.26	59.29	74.02
17											0.	26.69	54.60	71.03
18											0.	18.49	49.52	67.79
19											0.	9.62	44.02	64.28
20												0.	38.06	60.48
21												0.	31.62	56.36
22												0.	24.63	51.91
23												0.	17.07	47.08
24												0.	8.87	41.85
25													0.	36.19
26													0.	30.06
27													0.	23.42
28													0.	16.22
29													0.	8.44
30														0.
35														
40														

8.25%

Age of Loan	1	2	3	4	5	6	7	8	9	10	15	20	25	30
1	0.	52.05	69.37	77.99	83.15	86.56	88.99	90.79	92.18	93.28	96.48	97.95	98.74	99.21
2		0.	36.11	54.10	64.85	71.97	77.03	80.79	83.69	85.99	92.65	95.72	97.38	98.34
3			0.	28.16	44.98	56.14	64.05	69.93	74.47	78.07	88.50	93.30	95.89	97.41
4				0.	23.42	38.94	49.95	58.15	64.47	69.47	83.99	90.68	94.28	96.39
5					0.	20.27	34.65	45.35	53.60	60.13	79.10	87.83	92.53	95.28
6						0.	18.04	31.46	41.81	50.00	73.78	84.73	90.64	94.09
7							0.	16.38	29.00	39.00	68.01	81.38	88.58	92.78
8								0.	15.10	27.05	61.75	77.73	86.34	91.37
9									0.	14.08	54.95	73.77	83.91	89.84
10										0.	47.56	69.47	81.27	88.17
11										0.	39.55	64.80	78.41	86.36
12										0.	30.85	59.74	75.30	84.40
13										0.	21.40	54.23	71.93	82.27
14										0.	11.14	48.26	68.26	79.95
15											0.	41.78	64.28	77.44
16											0.	34.74	59.96	74.71
17											0.	27.09	55.28	71.75
18											0.	18.79	50.18	68.53
19											0.	9.78	44.66	65.04
20												0.	38.66	61.25
21												0.	32.14	57.14
22												0.	25.07	52.67
23												0.	17.39	47.82
24												0.	9.05	42.55
25													0.	36.83
26													0.	30.63
27													0.	23.89
28													0.	16.57
29													0.	8.62
30														0.
35														
40														

Remaining Balance Factors
Original Term In Years

8.50%

Age of Loan	1	2	3	4	5	6	7	8	9	10	15	20	25	30
1	0.	52.12	69.45	78.08	83.24	86.65	89.08	90.88	92.27	93.37	96.55	98.01	98.79	99.24
2		0.	36.19	54.22	64.99	72.13	77.19	80.95	83.85	86.15	92.80	95.84	97.47	98.42
3			0.	28.26	45.14	56.32	64.25	70.15	74.69	78.29	88.71	93.49	96.04	97.53
4				0.	23.52	39.11	50.17	58.39	64.73	69.74	84.26	90.92	94.48	96.55
5					0.	20.38	34.84	45.59	53.88	60.43	79.42	88.13	92.79	95.49
6						0.	18.16	31.66	42.07	50.30	74.16	85.09	90.94	94.34
7							0.	16.50	29.21	39.28	68.42	81.78	88.93	93.08
8								0.	15.23	27.28	62.18	78.18	86.74	91.71
9									0.	14.22	55.39	74.26	84.36	90.22
10										0.	48.00	69.99	81.77	88.60
11										0.	39.95	65.35	78.95	86.84
12										0.	31.19	60.30	75.88	84.92
13										0.	21.66	54.80	72.54	82.83
14										0.	11.29	48.81	68.90	80.56
15											0.	42.30	64.95	78.08
16											0.	35.21	60.64	75.39
17											0.	27.49	55.95	72.46
18											0.	19.09	50.85	69.27
19											0.	9.95	45.29	65.80
20												0.	39.25	62.02
21												0.	32.67	57.90
22												0.	25.51	53.43
23												0.	17.71	48.55
24												0.	9.23	43.25
25													0.	37.48
26													0.	31.20
27													0.	24.36
28													0.	16.92
29													0.	8.82
30														0.
35														
40														

8.75%

Age of Loan	1	2	3	4	5	6	7	8	9	10	15	20	25	30
1	0.	52.18	69.53	78.17	83.33	86.74	89.17	90.97	92.36	93.45	96.62	98.07	98.84	99.28
2		0.	36.28	54.35	65.14	72.28	77.35	81.11	84.01	86.31	92.94	95.96	97.57	98.50
3			0.	28.36	45.29	56.50	64.45	70.36	74.91	78.51	88.92	93.66	96.19	97.64
4				0.	23.63	39.28	50.38	58.63	64.98	70.01	84.53	91.16	94.68	96.71
5					0.	20.50	35.03	45.83	54.15	60.73	79.75	88.42	93.03	95.69
6						0.	18.28	31.86	42.33	50.60	74.53	85.43	91.24	94.58
7							0.	16.63	29.43	39.56	68.83	82.18	89.28	93.36
8								0.	15.36	27.50	62.61	78.62	87.14	92.04
9									0.	14.35	55.83	74.74	84.81	90.60
10										0.	48.43	70.51	82.26	89.02
11										0.	40.35	65.90	79.48	87.30
12										0.	31.54	60.86	76.45	85.43
13										0.	21.93	55.36	73.14	83.38
14										0.	11.44	49.36	69.54	81.15
15											0.	42.82	65.60	78.71
16											0.	35.68	61.30	76.06
17											0.	27.89	56.62	73.16
18											0.	19.39	51.50	69.99
19											0.	10.12	45.93	66.54
20												0.	39.84	62.77
21												0.	33.20	58.66
22												0.	25.95	54.18
23												0.	18.04	49.28
24												0.	9.41	43.95
25													0.	38.12
26													0.	31.76
27													0.	24.83
28													0.	17.26
29													0.	9.01
30														0.
35														
40														

Remaining Balance Factors
Original Term In Years

9.00%

Age of Loan	1	2	3	4	5	6	7	8	9	10	15	20	25	30
1	0.	52.24	69.61	78.26	83.42	86.84	89.26	91.06	92.44	93.54	96.69	98.13	98.88	99.32
2		0.	36.36	54.47	65.28	72.44	77.51	81.27	84.17	86.47	93.08	96.08	97.66	98.57
3			0.	28.46	45.44	56.68	64.65	70.57	75.13	78.73	89.12	93.84	96.33	97.75
4				0.	23.74	39.46	50.60	58.87	65.24	70.28	84.80	91.39	94.87	96.86
5					0.	20.61	35.22	46.07	54.42	61.02	80.07	88.71	93.27	95.88
6						0.	18.40	32.07	42.59	50.90	74.89	85.77	91.53	94.81
7							0.	16.75	29.64	39.84	69.23	82.57	89.62	93.64
8								0.	15.49	27.73	63.04	79.06	87.53	92.36
9									0.	14.49	56.27	75.22	85.24	90.96
10										0.	48.86	71.03	82.74	89.43
11										0.	40.76	66.44	80.00	87.75
12										0.	31.90	61.41	77.01	85.92
13										0.	22.20	55.92	73.74	83.92
14										0.	11.60	49.91	70.16	81.73
15											0.	43.34	66.25	79.33
15											0.	36.16	61.97	76.71
17											0.	28.29	57.28	73.84
18											0.	19.69	52.16	70.70
19											0.	10.29	46.56	67.27
20												0.	40.43	63.52
21												0.	33.72	59.41
22												0.	26.39	54.92
23												0.	18.37	50.01
24												0.	9.60	44.64
25													0.	38.76
26													0.	32.33
27													0.	25.30
28													0.	17.61
29													0.	9.20
30														0.
35														
40														

9.25%

Age of Loan	1	2	3	4	5	6	7	8	9	10	15	20	25	30
1	0.	52.30	69.69	78.34	83.51	86.93	89.35	91.14	92.53	93.62	96.76	98.18	98.93	99.35
2		0.	36.45	54.59	65.42	72.59	77.66	81.43	84.33	86.62	93.22	96.19	97.75	98.64
3			0.	28.55	45.59	56.87	64.85	70.79	75.35	78.95	89.33	94.01	96.47	97.86
4				0.	23.84	39.63	50.81	59.11	65.50	70.54	85.06	91.61	95.05	97.00
5					0.	20.73	35.41	46.31	54.69	61.32	80.39	88.99	93.51	96.06
6						0.	18.52	32.27	42.85	51.21	75.26	86.11	91.81	95.04
7							0.	16.88	29.86	40.12	69.63	82.95	89.94	93.91
8								0.	15.62	27.96	63.47	79.49	87.90	92.67
9									0.	14.62	56.71	75.70	85.66	91.31
10										0.	49.29	71.53	83.21	89.82
11										0.	41.16	66.97	80.52	88.19
12										0.	32.25	61.97	77.57	86.40
13										0.	22.47	56.48	74.33	84.44
14										0.	11.75	50.46	70.78	82.29
15											0.	43.86	66.89	79.93
16											0.	36.63	62.62	77.35
17											0.	28.70	57.94	74.51
18											0.	20.00	52.81	71.40
19											0.	10.46	47.18	67.99
20												0.	41.01	64.26
21												0.	34.25	60.16
22												0.	26.83	55.66
23												0.	18.70	50.73
24												0.	9.78	45.33
25													0.	39.40
26													0.	32.90
27													0.	25.78
28													0.	17.96
29													0.	9.39
30														0.
35														
40														

Remaining Balance Factors
Original Term In Years

9.50%

Age of Loan	1	2	3	4	5	6	7	8	9	10	15	20	25	30
1	0.	52.36	69.77	78.43	83.60	87.01	89.44	91.23	92.61	93.70	96.83	98.24	98.97	99.38
2		0.	36.53	54.72	65.56	72.74	77.82	81.59	84.49	86.78	93.35	96.30	97.84	98.71
3			0.	28.65	45.74	57.05	65.06	71.00	75.57	79.17	89.53	94.18	96.60	97.96
4				0.	23.95	39.80	51.02	59.35	65.75	70.81	85.32	91.84	95.23	97.14
5					0.	20.84	35.60	46.55	54.97	61.61	80.70	89.27	93.73	96.24
6						0.	18.64	32.48	43.11	51.51	75.62	86.44	92.08	95.25
7							0.	17.01	30.08	40.40	70.03	83.33	90.27	94.16
8								0.	15.75	28.18	63.89	79.92	88.27	92.97
9									0.	14.76	57.14	76.16	86.08	91.65
10										0.	49.72	72.04	83.67	90.21
11										0.	41.56	67.50	81.02	88.62
12										0.	32.60	62.51	78.11	86.87
13										0.	22.74	57.03	74.91	84.95
14										0.	11.91	51.01	71.39	82.84
15											0.	44.38	67.52	80.52
16											0.	37.10	63.27	77.97
17											0.	29.10	58.59	75.17
18											0.	20.30	53.46	72.09
19											0.	10.63	47.81	68.70
20												0.	41.60	64.98
21												0.	34.78	60.89
22												0.	27.27	56.39
23												0.	19.03	51.45
24												0.	9.96	46.01
25													0.	40.04
26													0.	33.47
27													0.	26.25
28													0.	18.31
29													0.	9.59
30														0.
35														
40														

9.75%

Age of Loan	1	2	3	4	5	6	7	8	9	10	15	20	25	30
1	0.	52.43	69.85	78.52	83.68	87.10	89.52	91.32	92.70	93.78	96.90	98.29	99.01	99.41
2		0.	36.62	54.84	65.71	72.89	77.98	81.75	84.65	86.94	93.49	96.41	97.93	98.77
3			0.	28.75	45.89	57.23	65.26	71.21	75.78	79.39	89.72	94.34	96.73	98.06
4				0.	24.06	39.97	51.24	59.59	66.01	71.07	85.58	92.05	95.41	97.27
5					0.	20.96	35.79	46.79	55.24	61.91	81.01	89.54	93.95	96.41
6						0.	18.76	32.68	43.37	51.81	75.97	86.76	92.35	95.46
7							0.	17.13	30.29	40.68	70.43	83.71	90.58	94.41
8								0.	15.88	28.41	64.31	80.34	88.63	93.26
9									0.	14.89	57.57	76.62	86.49	91.98
10										0.	50.15	72.53	84.12	90.58
11										0.	41.97	68.02	81.51	89.03
12										0.	32.95	63.06	78.64	87.33
13										0.	23.01	57.58	75.48	85.45
14										0.	12.07	51.55	71.99	83.38
15											0.	44.90	68.15	81.10
16											0.	37.58	63.91	78.59
17											0.	29.50	59.24	75.82
18											0.	20.61	54.10	72.77
19											0.	10.80	48.43	69.41
20												0.	42.19	65.70
21												0.	35.30	61.62
22												0.	27.72	57.12
23												0.	19.36	52.16
24												0.	10.15	46.69
25													0.	40.67
26													0.	34.04
27													0.	26.72
28													0.	18.67
29													0.	9.79
30														0.
35														
40														

Remaining Balance Factors
Original Term In Years

10.00%

Age of Loan	1	2	3	4	5	6	7	8	9	10	15	20	25	30
1	0.	52.49	69.93	78.60	83.77	87.19	89.61	91.40	92.78	93.87	96.97	98.35	99.05	99.44
2		0.	36.70	54.96	65.85	73.04	78.13	81.91	84.81	87.09	93.62	96.52	98.01	98.83
3			0.	28.85	46.04	57.41	65.46	71.42	75.99	79.60	89.92	94.50	96.85	98.15
4				0.	24.17	40.15	51.45	59.83	66.26	71.33	85.83	92.27	95.57	97.40
5					0.	21.07	35.98	47.03	55.51	62.20	81.32	89.80	94.16	96.57
6						0.	18.88	32.88	43.63	52.10	76.33	87.08	92.61	95.66
7							0.	17.26	30.51	40.96	70.82	84.07	90.88	94.65
8								0.	16.01	28.64	64.73	80.75	88.98	93.53
9									0.	15.03	58.01	77.08	86.88	92.30
10										0.	50.58	73.02	84.56	90.94
11										0.	42.37	68.54	82.00	89.43
12										0.	33.30	63.60	79.17	87.77
13										0.	23.29	58.13	76.04	85.93
14										0.	12.22	52.09	72.58	83.91
15											0.	45.42	68.76	81.66
16											0.	38.05	64.54	79.19
17											0.	29.91	59.88	76.45
18											0.	20.91	54.74	73.43
19											0.	10.98	49.05	70.09
20												0.	42.77	66.41
21												0.	35.83	62.33
22												0.	28.16	57.83
23												0.	19.69	52.86
24												0.	10.34	47.37
25													0.	41.30
26													0.	34.60
27													0.	27.20
28													0.	19.02
29													0.	9.98
30														0.
35														
40														

10.25%

Age of Loan	1	2	3	4	5	6	7	8	9	10	15	20	25	30
1	0.	52.55	70.01	78.69	83.86	87.28	89.70	91.49	92.86	93.95	97.03	98.40	99.09	99.47
2		0.	36.79	55.09	65.99	73.20	78.29	82.06	84.96	87.24	93.75	96.62	98.09	98.89
3			0.	28.95	46.20	57.60	65.65	71.63	76.21	79.82	90.11	94.65	96.97	98.24
4				0.	24.28	40.32	51.66	60.07	66.51	71.59	86.08	92.48	95.74	97.52
5					0.	21.19	36.17	47.27	55.78	62.49	81.62	90.06	94.37	96.73
6						0.	19.01	33.09	43.89	52.40	76.68	87.39	92.86	95.85
7							0.	17.39	30.73	41.24	71.21	84.43	91.18	94.88
8								0.	16.15	28.87	65.15	81.16	89.33	93.80
9									0.	15.17	58.44	77.53	87.27	92.61
10										0.	51.00	73.51	84.99	91.29
11										0.	42.77	69.06	82.47	89.82
12										0.	33.66	64.13	79.68	88.20
13										0.	23.56	58.67	76.59	86.41
14										0.	12.38	52.63	73.16	84.42
15											0.	45.94	69.37	82.21
16											0.	38.52	65.17	79.78
17											0.	30.31	60.52	77.08
18											0.	21.22	55.37	74.08
19											0.	11.15	49.67	70.77
20												0.	43.35	67.10
21												0.	36.35	63.04
22												0.	28.61	58.54
23												0.	20.03	53.56
24												0.	10.52	48.04
25													0.	41.93
26													0.	35.16
27													0.	27.67
28													0.	19.37
29													0.	10.18
30														0.
35														
40														

Remaining Balance Factors
Original Term In Years

10.50%

Age of Loan	1	2	3	4	5	6	7	8	9	10	15	20	25	30
1	0.	52.61	70.08	78.77	83.95	87.37	89.78	91.57	92.95	94.03	97.10	98.45	99.13	99.50
2		0.	36.87	55.21	66.13	73.35	78.44	82.22	85.11	87.39	93.88	96.72	98.16	98.94
3			0.	29.05	46.35	57.78	65.85	71.83	76.42	80.03	90.30	94.81	97.09	98.33
4				0.	24.38	40.49	51.88	60.30	66.77	71.85	86.33	92.68	95.90	97.64
5					0.	21.30	36.36	47.50	56.05	62.78	81.92	90.32	94.57	96.88
6						0.	19.13	33.29	44.15	52.70	77.03	87.70	93.10	96.04
7							0.	17.52	30.94	41.52	71.59	84.79	91.47	95.10
8								0.	16.28	29.10	65.56	81.56	89.66	94.06
9									0.	15.31	58.86	77.97	87.65	92.90
10										0.	51.43	73.99	85.42	91.62
11										0.	43.17	69.57	82.94	90.20
12										0.	34.01	64.66	80.19	88.62
13										0.	23.84	59.21	77.13	86.86
14										0.	12.54	53.16	73.74	84.91
15											0.	46.45	69.97	82.75
16											0.	38.99	65.79	80.35
17											0.	30.72	61.15	77.68
18											0.	21.53	56.00	74.73
19											0.	11.33	50.28	71.44
20												0.	43.93	67.79
21												0.	36.88	63.74
22												0.	29.05	59.24
23												0.	20.36	54.25
24												0.	10.71	48.71
25													0.	42.56
26													0.	35.73
27													0.	28.14
28													0.	19.72
29													0.	10.38
30														0.
35														
40														

10.75%

Age of Loan	1	2	3	4	5	6	7	8	9	10	15	20	25	30
1	0.	52.67	70.16	78.86	84.04	87.46	89.87	91.66	93.03	94.10	97.16	98.49	99.16	99.53
2		0.	36.96	55.33	66.27	73.50	78.60	82.37	85.27	87.54	94.00	96.82	98.23	99.00
3			0.	29.14	46.50	57.96	66.05	72.04	76.63	80.24	90.49	94.95	97.20	98.41
4				0.	24.49	40.67	52.09	60.54	67.02	72.11	86.57	92.88	96.05	97.75
5					0.	21.42	36.55	47.74	56.32	63.07	82.22	90.57	94.77	97.03
6						0.	19.25	33.50	44.41	53.00	77.37	88.00	93.34	96.22
7							0.	17.64	31.16	41.80	71.98	85.14	91.75	95.31
8								0.	16.41	29.33	65.97	81.95	89.98	94.31
9									0.	15.45	59.29	78.41	88.02	93.19
10										0.	51.85	74.46	85.83	91.95
11										0.	43.58	70.07	83.39	90.56
12										0.	34.36	65.19	80.68	89.02
13										0.	24.11	59.75	77.66	87.31
14										0.	12.70	53.70	74.30	85.40
15											0.	46.96	70.57	83.28
16											0.	39.47	66.41	80.91
17											0.	31.12	61.78	78.28
18											0.	21.84	56.62	75.35
19											0.	11.50	50.89	72.09
20												0.	44.50	68.47
21												0.	37.40	64.43
22												0.	29.49	59.94
23												0.	20.69	54.94
24												0.	10.90	49.37
25													0.	43.18
26													0.	36.29
27													0.	28.62
28													0.	20.08
29													0.	10.58
30														0.
35														
40														

Remaining Balance Factors
Original Term In Years

11.00%

Age of Loan	1	2	3	4	5	6	7	8	9	10	15	20	25	30
1	0.	52.73	70.24	78.94	84.12	87.54	89.96	91.74	93.11	94.18	97.22	98.54	99.20	99.55
2		0.	37.04	55.45	66.41	73.65	78.75	82.53	85.42	87.69	94.13	96.91	98.31	99.05
3			0.	29.24	46.65	58.14	66.25	72.25	76.84	80.45	90.67	95.10	97.31	98.49
4				0.	24.60	40.84	52.30	60.78	67.27	72.37	86.81	93.07	96.20	97.86
5					0.	21.54	36.74	47.98	56.59	63.36	82.51	90.81	94.95	97.16
6						0.	19.37	33.70	44.67	53.30	77.71	88.29	93.57	96.39
7							0.	17.77	31.38	42.08	72.36	85.48	92.03	95.52
8								0.	16.55	29.56	66.38	82.34	90.30	94.55
9									0.	15.59	59.71	78.84	88.38	93.47
10										0.	52.28	74.93	86.23	92.26
11										0.	43.98	70.57	83.84	90.92
12										0.	34.72	65.71	81.17	89.42
13										0.	24.39	60.28	78.19	87.74
14										0.	12.86	54.23	74.86	85.87
15											0.	47.47	71.15	83.79
16											0.	39.94	67.01	81.46
17											0.	31.53	62.39	78.87
18											0.	22.15	57.24	75.97
19											0.	11.68	51.49	72.74
20												0.	45.08	69.13
21												0.	37.92	65.11
22												0.	29.94	60.63
23												0.	21.03	55.62
24												0.	11.09	50.03
25													0.	43.80
26													0.	36.85
27													0.	29.09
28													0.	20.43
29													0.	10.78
30														0.
35														
40														

11.25%

Age of Loan	1	2	3	4	5	6	7	8	9	10	15	20	25	30
1	0.	52.80	70.32	79.03	84.21	87.63	90.04	91.82	93.19	94.26	97.28	98.59	99.23	99.57
2		0.	37.13	55.58	66.55	73.79	78.90	82.68	85.57	87.84	94.25	97.01	98.37	99.10
3			0.	29.34	46.80	58.32	66.45	72.45	77.05	80.66	90.85	95.24	97.41	98.56
4				0.	24.71	41.01	52.51	61.01	67.52	72.63	87.05	93.26	96.34	97.97
5					0.	21.65	36.93	48.22	56.86	63.64	82.80	91.05	95.14	97.30
6						0.	19.50	33.91	44.94	53.59	78.05	88.58	93.79	96.55
7							0.	17.90	31.60	42.36	72.73	85.82	92.29	95.72
8								0.	16.68	29.79	66.79	82.72	90.61	94.78
9									0.	15.73	60.14	79.26	88.73	93.74
10										0.	52.70	75.39	86.63	92.57
11										0.	44.38	71.07	84.27	91.26
12										0.	35.07	66.23	81.64	89.80
13										0.	24.66	60.81	78.70	88.16
14										0.	13.02	54.76	75.41	86.33
15											0.	47.98	71.73	84.29
16											0.	40.41	67.61	82.00
17											0.	31.93	63.01	79.44
18											0.	22.46	57.85	76.57
19											0.	11.86	52.09	73.37
20												0.	45.65	69.79
21												0.	38.44	65.78
22												0.	30.38	61.30
23												0.	21.36	56.29
24												0.	11.28	50.69
25													0.	44.42
26													0.	37.40
27													0.	29.56
28													0.	20.79
29													0.	10.97
30														0.
35														
40														

Remaining Balance Factors
Original Term In Years

11.50%

Age of Loan	1	2	3	4	5	6	7	8	9	10	15	20	25	30
1	0.	52.86	70.40	79.12	84.30	87.72	90.13	91.91	93.27	94.34	97.34	98.63	99.26	99.60
2		0.	37.21	55.70	66.69	73.94	79.06	82.83	85.72	87.99	94.37	97.10	98.44	99.14
3			0.	29.44	46.95	58.50	66.64	72.66	77.26	80.86	91.03	95.38	97.51	98.63
4				0.	24.82	41.18	52.72	61.25	67.77	72.88	87.29	93.45	96.48	98.06
5					0.	21.77	37.12	48.46	57.13	63.93	83.09	91.29	95.32	97.42
6						0.	19.62	34.11	45.20	53.89	78.38	88.87	94.01	96.71
7							0.	18.03	31.82	42.64	73.11	86.15	92.55	95.90
8								0.	16.82	30.02	67.19	83.10	90.91	95.00
9									0.	15.87	60.56	79.68	89.07	93.99
10										0.	53.12	75.85	87.01	92.86
11										0.	44.78	71.55	84.70	91.59
12										0.	35.43	66.74	82.11	90.17
13										0.	24.94	61.34	79.21	88.57
14										0.	13.18	55.28	75.95	86.78
15											0.	48.49	72.30	84.77
16											0.	40.88	68.20	82.52
17											0.	32.34	63.61	80.00
18											0.	22.77	58.46	77.17
19											0.	12.03	52.69	73.99
20												0.	46.22	70.44
21												0.	38.96	66.45
22												0.	30.82	61.97
23												0.	21.70	56.96
24												0.	11.47	51.33
25													0.	45.03
26													0.	37.96
27													0.	30.03
28													0.	21.14
29													0.	11.18
30														0.
35														
40														

11.75%

Age of Loan	1	2	3	4	5	6	7	8	9	10	15	20	25	30
1	0.	52.92	70.48	79.20	84.38	87.80	90.21	91.99	93.35	94.41	97.40	98.68	99.30	99.62
2		0.	37.30	55.82	66.83	74.09	79.21	82.98	85.87	88.13	94.49	97.19	98.50	99.19
3			0.	29.54	47.10	58.68	66.84	72.86	77.46	81.07	91.20	95.51	97.61	98.70
4				0.	24.93	41.36	52.94	61.48	68.01	73.13	87.52	93.63	96.61	98.16
5					0.	21.89	37.31	48.70	57.39	64.21	83.37	91.52	95.49	97.55
6						0.	19.74	34.32	45.46	54.19	78.71	89.14	94.22	96.86
7							0.	18.16	32.04	42.92	73.48	86.47	92.80	96.09
8								0.	16.95	30.25	67.59	83.47	91.20	95.22
9									0.	16.01	60.97	80.09	89.41	94.24
10										0.	53.54	76.30	87.39	93.14
11										0.	45.18	72.04	85.12	91.91
12										0.	35.78	67.25	82.57	90.52
13										0.	25.22	61.86	79.70	88.97
14										0.	13.35	55.80	76.48	87.21
15											0.	49.00	72.86	85.24
16											0.	41.35	68.79	83.03
17											0.	32.75	64.21	80.54
18											0.	23.08	59.07	77.75
19											0.	12.21	53.28	74.60
20												0.	46.78	71.07
21												0.	39.48	67.10
22												0.	31.27	62.63
23												0.	22.04	57.62
24												0.	11.66	51.98
25													0.	45.64
26													0.	38.51
27													0.	30.50
28													0.	21.50
29													0.	11.38
30														0.
35														
40														

Remaining Balance Factors
Original Term In Years

12.00%

Age of Loan	1	2	3	4	5	6	7	8	9	10	15	20	25	30
1	0.	52.98	70.56	79.28	84.47	87.89	90.29	92.07	93.43	94.49	97.46	98.72	99.32	99.64
2		0.	37.38	55.94	66.97	74.24	79.36	83.13	86.02	88.27	94.60	97.27	98.56	99.23
3			0.	29.64	47.25	58.86	67.03	73.06	77.67	81.27	91.38	95.65	97.71	98.77
4				0.	25.04	41.53	53.15	61.72	68.26	73.39	87.75	93.81	96.74	98.25
5					0.	22.00	37.50	48.93	57.66	64.50	83.65	91.74	95.65	97.66
6						0.	19.87	34.53	45.72	54.48	79.04	89.42	94.43	97.00
7							0.	18.29	32.26	43.20	73.84	86.79	93.05	96.26
8								0.	17.09	30.48	67.99	83.83	91.49	95.42
9									0.	16.15	61.39	80.50	89.73	94.48
10										0.	53.95	76.75	87.76	93.42
11										0.	45.58	72.52	85.53	92.22
12										0.	36.13	67.75	83.02	90.87
13										0.	25.50	62.37	80.19	89.35
14										0.	13.51	56.32	77.00	87.64
15											0.	49.50	73.41	85.71
16											0.	41.81	69.36	83.53
17											0.	33.15	64.80	81.08
18											0.	23.39	59.66	78.32
19											0.	12.39	53.87	75.20
20												0.	47.35	71.69
21												0.	40.00	67.74
22												0.	31.71	63.29
23												0.	22.37	58.27
24												0.	11.85	52.61
25													0.	46.24
26													0.	39.06
27													0.	30.97
28													0.	21.85
29													0.	11.58
30														0.
35														
40														

12.25%

Age of Loan	1	2	3	4	5	6	7	8	9	10	15	20	25	30
1	0.	53.04	70.64	79.37	84.56	87.97	90.38	92.15	93.50	94.56	97.52	98.76	99.35	99.66
2		0.	37.47	56.06	67.11	74.39	79.51	83.28	86.16	88.42	94.71	97.36	98.62	99.27
3			0.	29.74	47.41	59.04	67.23	73.27	77.87	81.48	91.55	95.77	97.80	98.83
4				0.	25.15	41.70	53.36	61.95	68.51	73.64	87.97	93.99	96.87	98.33
5					0.	22.12	37.69	49.17	57.93	64.78	83.93	91.96	95.81	97.77
6						0.	19.99	34.73	45.98	54.78	79.36	89.68	94.63	97.14
7							0.	18.42	32.48	43.48	74.21	87.10	93.28	96.43
8								0.	17.23	30.71	68.38	84.19	91.76	95.62
9									0.	16.29	61.80	80.90	90.05	94.71
10										0.	54.37	77.19	88.12	93.68
11										0.	45.97	72.99	85.93	92.52
12										0.	36.49	68.24	83.46	91.21
13										0.	25.77	62.89	80.67	89.72
14										0.	13.67	56.84	77.52	88.05
15											0.	50.00	73.95	86.15
16											0.	42.28	69.93	84.02
17											0.	33.56	65.39	81.60
18											0.	23.70	60.26	78.87
19											0.	12.57	54.46	75.79
20												0.	47.91	72.31
21												0.	40.51	68.38
22												0.	32.15	63.93
23												0.	22.71	58.91
24												0.	12.05	53.25
25													0.	46.04
26													0.	39.61
27													0.	31.44
28													0.	22.21
29													0.	11.78
30														0.
35														
40														

Remaining Balance Factors
Original Term In Years

Age of Loan	1	2	3	4	5	6	7	8	9	10	15	20	25	30

12.50%

Age of Loan	1	2	3	4	5	6	7	8	9	10	15	20	25	30
1	0.	53.10	70.72	79.45	84.64	88.06	90.46	92.23	93.58	94.63	97.57	98.80	99.38	99.67
2		0.	37.55	56.19	67.25	74.53	79.66	83.43	86.31	88.56	94.83	97.44	98.68	99.31
3			0.	29.84	47.56	59.22	67.42	73.47	78.07	81.68	91.72	95.90	97.89	98.89
4				0.	25.26	41.88	53.57	62.19	68.75	73.89	88.19	94.16	96.99	98.42
5					0.	22.24	37.88	49.41	58.19	65.06	84.20	92.18	95.97	97.88
6						0.	20.12	34.94	46.24	55.07	79.68	89.94	94.82	97.28
7							0.	18.55	32.70	43.75	74.57	87.41	93.51	96.59
8								0.	17.36	30.94	68.77	84.54	92.03	95.81
9									0.	16.43	62.21	81.30	90.36	94.93
10										0.	54.78	77.62	88.47	93.94
11										0.	46.37	73.45	86.32	92.81
12										0.	36.84	68.74	83.89	91.53
13										0.	26.05	63.40	81.14	90.08
14										0.	13.84	57.35	78.02	88.45
15											0.	50.50	74.49	86.59
16											0.	42.74	70.49	84.49
17											0.	33.96	65.97	82.11
18											0.	24.02	60.84	79.42
19											0.	12.75	55.06	76.37
20												0.	48.46	72.91
21												0.	41.02	69.00
22												0.	32.59	64.57
23												0.	23.05	59.55
24												0.	12.24	53.87
25													0.	47.44
26													0.	40.15
27													0.	31.90
28													0.	22.56
29													0.	11.98
30														0.
35														
40														

12.75%

Age of Loan	1	2	3	4	5	6	7	8	9	10	15	20	25	30
1	0.	53.17	70.79	79.54	84.73	88.14	90.54	92.31	93.66	94.71	97.63	98.84	99.41	99.69
2		0.	37.64	56.31	67.39	74.68	79.81	83.58	86.45	88.70	94.94	97.52	98.73	99.34
3			0.	29.94	47.71	59.40	67.62	73.67	78.28	81.88	91.88	96.02	97.97	98.95
4				0.	25.36	42.05	53.78	62.42	68.99	74.13	88.41	94.32	97.10	98.50
5					0.	22.36	38.07	49.65	58.46	65.34	84.47	92.39	96.12	97.98
6						0.	20.24	35.15	46.50	55.36	80.00	90.20	95.00	97.40
7							0.	18.69	32.92	44.03	74.93	87.71	93.74	96.74
8								0.	17.50	31.17	69.16	84.89	92.30	96.00
9									0.	16.57	62.62	81.68	90.66	95.15
10										0.	55.20	78.04	88.81	94.18
11										0.	46.77	73.91	86.70	93.09
12										0.	37.20	69.22	84.31	91.85
13										0.	26.33	63.90	81.60	90.44
14										0.	14.00	57.86	78.51	88.83
15											0.	51.00	75.02	87.02
16											0.	43.21	71.05	84.95
17											0.	34.37	66.54	82.61
18											0.	24.33	61.42	79.95
19											0.	12.94	55.61	76.93
20												0.	49.02	73.50
21												0.	41.53	69.61
22												0.	33.03	65.20
23												0.	23.39	60.18
24												0.	12.43	54.49
25													0.	48.03
26													0.	40.69
27													0.	32.37
28													0.	22.91
29													0.	12.18
30														0.
35														
40														

Remaining Balance Factors
Original Term In Years

13.00%

Age of Loan	1	2	3	4	5	6	7	8	9	10	15	20	25	30
1	0.	53.23	70.87	79.62	84.81	88.23	90.62	92.39	93.73	94.78	97.68	98.88	99.43	99.71
2		0.	37.72	56.43	67.53	74.83	79.95	83.73	86.60	88.84	95.04	97.60	98.79	99.38
3			0.	30.04	47.86	59.58	67.81	73.87	78.48	82.08	92.04	96.14	98.05	99.00
4				0.	25.47	42.22	53.99	62.65	69.24	74.38	88.63	94.48	97.22	98.57
5					0.	22.48	38.27	49.88	58.72	65.62	84.74	92.60	96.27	98.08
6						0.	20.37	35.35	46.75	55.66	80.31	90.45	95.18	97.53
7							0.	18.82	33.14	44.31	75.28	88.01	93.95	96.89
8								0.	17.64	31.41	69.55	85.23	92.55	96.17
9									0.	16.72	63.03	82.07	90.96	95.35
10										0.	55.61	78.47	89.14	94.42
11										0.	47.16	74.37	87.07	93.36
12										0.	37.55	69.71	84.72	92.15
13										0.	26.61	64.40	82.05	90.78
14										0.	14.17	58.36	79.00	89.21
15											0.	51.49	75.54	87.43
16											0.	43.67	71.59	85.40
17											0.	34.77	67.10	83.10
18											0.	24.64	62.00	80.47
19											0.	13.12	56.18	77.49
20												0.	49.57	74.09
21												0.	42.04	70.22
22												0.	33.47	65.82
23												0.	23.72	60.81
24												0.	12.63	55.11
25													0.	48.62
26													0.	41.23
27													0.	32.83
28													0.	23.27
29													0.	12.39
30														0.
35														
40														

13.25%

Age of Loan	1	2	3	4	5	6	7	8	9	10	15	20	25	30
1	0.	53.29	70.95	79.70	84.90	88.31	90.71	92.47	93.81	94.85	97.73	98.91	99.46	99.72
2		0.	37.81	56.55	67.67	74.97	80.10	83.87	86.74	88.97	95.15	97.67	98.84	99.41
3			0.	30.14	48.01	59.76	68.00	74.07	78.68	82.27	92.20	96.26	98.13	99.05
4				0.	25.58	42.40	54.20	62.88	69.48	74.62	88.84	94.64	97.33	98.64
5					0.	22.59	38.46	50.12	58.99	65.90	85.00	92.80	96.41	98.18
6						0.	20.49	35.56	47.01	55.95	80.62	90.70	95.36	97.64
7							0.	18.95	33.36	44.59	75.63	88.30	94.16	97.03
8								0.	17.78	31.64	69.93	85.56	92.80	96.34
9									0.	16.86	63.43	82.44	91.24	95.55
10										0.	56.02	78.88	89.46	94.65
11										0.	47.56	74.82	87.44	93.62
12										0.	37.90	70.18	85.13	92.44
13										0.	26.89	64.90	82.49	91.10
14										0.	14.33	58.86	79.48	89.58
15											0.	51.98	76.05	87.83
16											0.	44.13	72.13	85.84
17											0.	35.18	67.66	83.57
18											0.	24.96	62.56	80.98
19											0.	13.30	56.75	78.03
20												0.	50.12	74.66
21												0.	42.55	70.81
22												0.	33.91	66.43
23												0.	24.06	61.42
24												0.	12.82	55.71
25													0.	49.20
26													0.	41.77
27													0.	33.29
28													0.	23.62
29													0.	12.59
30														0.
35														
40														

Remaining Balance Factors
Original Term In Years

Age of Loan

13.50%

Age of Loan	1	2	3	4	5	6	7	8	9	10	15	20	25	30
1	0.	53.35	71.03	79.79	84.98	88.39	90.79	92.54	93.88	94.92	97.79	98.95	99.48	99.74
2		0.	37.89	56.67	67.81	75.12	80.25	84.02	86.88	89.11	95.26	97.74	98.89	99.44
3			0.	30.24	48.16	59.93	68.20	74.26	78.87	82.47	92.36	96.37	98.21	99.10
4				0.	25.69	42.57	54.41	63.11	69.72	74.87	89.05	94.80	97.43	98.71
5					0.	22.71	38.65	50.36	59.25	66.18	85.26	93.00	96.54	98.26
6						0.	20.62	35.77	47.27	56.24	80.93	90.94	95.53	97.75
7							0.	19.08	33.58	44.87	75.98	88.58	94.37	97.17
8								0.	17.91	31.87	70.31	85.89	93.04	96.50
9									0.	17.00	63.83	82.81	91.52	95.74
10										0.	56.42	79.29	89.78	94.87
11										0.	47.95	75.26	87.79	93.87
12										0.	38.26	70.66	85.52	92.73
13										0.	27.17	65.39	82.92	91.42
14										0.	14.50	59.36	79.95	89.93
15											0.	52.47	76.55	88.22
16											0.	44.59	72.66	86.27
17											0.	35.58	68.21	84.04
18											0.	25.27	63.13	81.48
19											0.	13.48	57.31	78.56
20												0.	50.66	75.22
21												0.	43.05	71.40
22												0.	34.35	67.03
23												0.	24.40	62.03
24												0.	13.02	56.32
25													0.	49.78
26													0.	42.30
27													0.	33.75
28													0.	23.97
29													0.	12.79
30														0.
35														
40														

13.75%

Age of Loan	1	2	3	4	5	6	7	8	9	10	15	20	25	30
1	0.	53.41	71.11	79.87	85.07	88.48	90.87	92.62	93.95	94.99	97.84	98.98	99.50	99.75
2		0.	37.98	56.79	67.94	75.26	80.39	84.16	87.02	89.25	95.36	97.82	98.93	99.47
3			0.	30.33	48.31	60.11	68.39	74.46	79.07	82.66	92.51	96.48	98.28	99.15
4				0.	25.80	42.74	54.62	63.34	69.96	75.11	89.26	94.95	97.53	98.78
5					0.	22.83	38.84	50.59	59.51	66.45	85.52	93.19	96.68	98.35
6						0.	20.75	35.97	47.53	56.53	81.23	91.17	95.69	97.86
7							0.	19.21	33.80	45.15	76.32	88.86	94.56	97.30
8								0.	18.05	32.11	70.69	86.21	93.27	96.66
9									0.	17.15	64.23	83.17	91.79	95.92
10										0.	56.83	79.69	90.09	95.08
11										0.	48.34	75.70	88.14	94.11
12										0.	38.61	71.12	85.91	93.00
13										0.	27.46	65.87	83.35	91.73
14										0.	14.66	59.86	80.41	90.27
15											0.	52.96	77.04	88.60
16											0.	45.05	73.18	86.69
17											0.	35.98	68.76	84.49
18											0.	25.59	63.68	81.97
19											0.	13.67	57.87	79.08
20												0.	51.20	75.77
21												0.	43.55	71.98
22												0.	34.79	67.62
23												0.	24.73	62.63
24												0.	13.21	56.91
25													0.	50.35
26													0.	42.83
27													0.	34.21
28													0.	24.33
29													0.	12.99
30														0.
35														
40														

Remaining Balance Factors
Original Term In Years

14.00%

Age of Loan	1	2	3	4	5	6	7	8	9	10	15	20	25	30
1	0.	53.47	71.18	79.95	85.15	88.56	90.95	92.70	94.03	95.06	97.89	99.02	99.53	99.77
2		0.	38.07	56.91	68.08	75.41	80.54	84.30	87.16	89.38	95.46	97.89	98.98	99.50
3			0.	30.43	48.46	60.29	68.58	74.66	79.27	82.85	92.67	96.59	98.35	99.19
4				0.	25.91	42.92	54.83	63.57	70.20	75.35	89.46	95.09	97.63	98.84
5					0.	22.95	39.03	50.83	59.77	66.73	85.77	93.38	96.80	98.43
6						0.	20.87	36.18	47.79	56.82	81.53	91.40	95.85	97.96
7							0.	19.35	34.02	45.43	76.66	89.13	94.76	97.43
8								0.	18.19	32.34	71.06	86.53	93.50	96.81
9									0.	17.29	64.63	83.53	92.05	96.10
10										0.	57.23	80.09	90.39	95.28
11										0.	48.73	76.13	88.48	94.35
12										0.	38.97	71.58	86.28	93.27
13										0.	27.74	66.36	83.76	92.03
14										0.	14.83	60.35	80.86	90.61
15											0.	53.44	77.53	88.97
16											0.	45.51	73.70	87.09
17											0.	36.38	69.30	84.93
18											0.	25.90	64.23	82.45
19											0.	13.85	58.42	79.59
20												0.	51.73	76.31
21												0.	44.05	72.54
22												0.	35.22	68.21
23												0.	25.07	63.23
24												0.	13.41	57.50
25													0.	50.92
26													0.	43.36
27													0.	34.67
28													0.	24.68
29													0.	13.20
30														0.
35														
40														

14.25%

Age of Loan	1	2	3	4	5	6	7	8	9	10	15	20	25	30
1	0.	53.54	71.26	80.04	85.23	88.64	91.02	92.77	94.10	95.13	97.94	99.05	99.55	99.78
2		0.	38.15	57.04	68.22	75.55	80.68	84.45	87.30	89.51	95.56	97.95	99.02	99.53
3			0.	30.53	48.61	60.47	68.77	74.85	79.46	83.04	92.82	96.69	98.42	99.23
4				0.	26.03	43.09	55.04	63.80	70.43	75.59	89.66	95.24	97.73	98.90
5					0.	23.07	39.22	51.06	60.03	67.00	86.02	93.56	96.93	98.51
6						0.	21.00	36.39	48.05	57.11	81.83	91.63	96.00	98.06
7							0.	19.48	34.24	45.71	77.00	89.40	94.94	97.55
8								0.	18.33	32.57	71.44	86.84	93.72	96.95
9									0.	17.44	65.02	83.88	92.31	96.27
10										0.	57.44	80.48	90.68	95.48
11										0.	49.12	76.56	88.81	94.57
12										0.	39.32	72.04	86.65	93.53
13										0.	28.02	66.83	84.17	92.32
14										0.	15.00	60.84	81.31	90.93
15											0.	53.92	78.01	89.33
16											0.	45.96	74.21	87.49
17											0.	36.79	69.83	85.36
18											0.	26.21	64.78	82.91
19											0.	14.03	58.97	80.09
20												0.	52.27	76.84
21												0.	44.55	73.10
22												0.	35.65	68.78
23												0.	25.41	63.81
24												0.	13.60	58.09
25													0.	51.49
26													0.	43.88
27													0.	35.12
28													0.	25.03
29													0.	13.40
30														0.
35														
40														

Remaining Balance Factors
Original Term In Years

14.50%

Age of Loan	1	2	3	4	5	6	7	8	9	10	15	20	25	30
1	0.	53.60	71.34	80.12	85.32	88.72	91.10	92.85	94.17	95.19	97.98	99.08	99.57	99.79
2		0.	38.24	57.16	68.35	75.69	80.83	84.59	87.43	89.64	95.65	98.02	99.06	99.55
3			0.	30.63	48.76	60.64	68.96	75.05	79.66	83.23	92.96	96.79	98.49	99.27
4				0.	26.14	43.26	55.25	64.03	70.67	75.83	89.86	95.37	97.82	98.95
5					0.	23.19	39.41	51.30	60.29	67.28	86.27	93.74	97.04	98.58
6						0.	21.13	36.60	48.31	57.40	82.12	91.85	96.15	98.15
7							0.	19.61	34.46	45.99	77.33	89.66	95.12	97.66
8								0.	18.47	32.81	71.80	87.14	93.93	97.09
9									0.	17.58	65.42	84.23	92.56	96.43
10										0.	58.04	80.87	90.97	95.67
11										0.	49.51	76.98	89.13	94.79
12										0.	39.67	72.49	87.01	93.77
13										0.	28.30	67.31	84.57	92.60
14										0.	15.17	61.32	81.74	91.24
15											0.	54.40	78.48	89.68
16											0.	46.41	74.70	87.87
17											0.	37.19	70.35	85.78
18											0.	26.53	65.32	83.37
19											0.	14.22	59.51	80.58
20												0.	52.79	77.36
21												0.	45.04	73.65
22												0.	36.09	69.35
23												0.	25.74	64.39
24												0.	13.80	58.66
25													0.	52.05
26													0.	44.40
27													0.	35.58
28													0.	25.38
29													0.	13.60
30														0.
35														
40														

14.75%

Age of Loan	1	2	3	4	5	6	7	8	9	10	15	20	25	30
1	0.	53.66	71.42	80.20	85.40	88.80	91.18	92.92	94.24	95.26	98.03	99.11	99.59	99.80
2		0.	38.32	57.28	68.49	75.84	80.97	84.73	87.57	89.77	95.75	98.08	99.10	99.58
3			0.	30.73	48.91	60.82	69.15	75.24	79.85	83.42	93.11	96.89	98.55	99.31
4				0.	26.25	43.44	55.46	64.25	70.91	76.06	90.05	95.51	97.90	99.01
5					0.	23.31	39.61	51.53	60.55	67.55	86.51	93.91	97.16	98.65
6						0.	21.25	36.80	48.56	57.68	82.41	92.06	96.30	98.24
7							0.	19.75	34.68	46.26	77.66	89.92	95.30	97.77
8								0.	18.61	33.04	72.17	87.44	94.14	97.22
9									0.	17.73	65.80	84.57	92.80	96.59
10										0.	58.43	81.24	91.24	95.85
11										0.	49.90	77.39	89.45	95.00
12										0.	40.02	72.94	87.37	94.01
13										0.	28.58	67.78	84.96	92.87
14										0.	15.34	61.80	82.17	91.55
15											0.	54.88	78.94	90.02
16											0.	46.86	75.20	88.24
17											0.	37.59	70.86	86.19
18											0.	26.84	65.85	83.81
19											0.	14.40	60.04	81.06
20												0.	53.32	77.87
21												0.	45.53	74.18
22												0.	36.52	69.91
23												0.	26.08	64.96
24												0.	13.99	59.23
25													0.	52.60
26													0.	44.92
27													0.	36.03
28													0.	25.73
29													0.	13.81
30														0.
35														
40														

Remaining Balance Factors
Original Term In Years

15.00%

Age of Loan	1	2	3	4	5	6	7	8	9	10	15	20	25	30
1	0.	53.72	71.49	80.28	85.48	88.88	91.26	93.00	94.31	95.33	98.08	99.14	99.60	99.81
2		0.	38.41	57.40	68.63	75.98	81.11	84.87	87.71	89.90	95.84	98.14	99.14	99.60
3			0.	30.83	49.06	61.00	69.34	75.43	80.04	83.61	93.25	96.99	98.61	99.35
4				0.	26.36	43.61	55.67	64.48	71.14	76.30	90.24	95.64	97.99	99.06
5					0.	23.43	39.80	51.77	60.81	67.82	86.75	94.08	97.27	98.72
6						0.	21.38	37.01	48.82	57.97	82.70	92.27	96.43	98.33
7							0.	19.88	34.91	46.54	77.99	90.17	95.46	97.87
8								0.	18.75	33.27	72.53	87.73	94.34	97.35
9									0.	17.87	66.19	84.90	93.03	96.74
10										0.	58.83	81.62	91.51	96.02
11										0.	50.29	77.80	89.75	95.20
12										0.	40.37	73.38	87.71	94.24
13										0.	28.87	68.24	85.34	93.13
14										0.	15.51	62.27	82.59	91.84
15											0.	55.35	79.39	90.34
16											0.	47.31	75.68	88.61
17											0.	37.99	71.37	86.59
18											0.	27.16	66.38	84.25
19											0.	14.59	60.57	81.53
20												0.	53.84	78.37
21												0.	46.02	74.71
22												0.	36.95	70.46
23												0.	26.42	65.53
24												0.	14.19	59.80
25													0.	53.15
26													0.	45.43
27													0.	36.48
28													0.	26.08
29													0.	14.01
30														0.
35														
40														

15.25%

Age of Loan	1	2	3	4	5	6	7	8	9	10	15	20	25	30
1	0.	53.78	71.57	80.37	85.56	88.96	91.34	93.07	94.38	95.39	98.12	99.17	99.62	99.82
2		0.	38.49	57.52	68.76	76.12	81.25	85.01	87.84	90.03	95.94	98.20	99.18	99.62
3			0.	30.93	49.22	61.17	69.52	75.62	80.23	83.79	93.39	97.08	98.67	99.38
4				0.	26.47	43.78	55.87	64.71	71.37	76.53	90.43	95.77	98.07	99.11
5					0.	23.55	39.99	52.00	61.07	68.09	86.99	94.25	97.38	98.78
6						0.	21.51	37.22	49.08	58.26	82.98	92.48	96.57	98.41
7							0.	20.02	35.13	46.82	78.32	90.42	95.63	97.98
8								0.	18.89	33.51	72.89	88.02	94.53	97.47
9									0.	18.02	66.57	85.23	93.26	96.88
10										0.	59.23	81.99	91.78	96.19
11										0.	50.67	78.21	90.05	95.39
12										0.	40.73	73.81	88.05	94.47
13										0.	29.15	68.70	85.71	93.38
14										0.	15.68	62.75	83.00	92.13
15											0.	55.82	79.83	90.66
16											0.	47.76	76.16	88.96
17											0.	38.38	71.88	86.98
18											0.	27.47	66.90	84.67
19											0.	14.77	61.10	81.99
20												0.	54.36	78.86
21												0.	46.51	75.23
22												0.	37.38	71.00
23												0.	26.75	66.08
24												0.	14.39	60.36
25													0.	53.70
26													0.	45.94
27													0.	36.92
28													0.	26.43
29													0.	14.21
30														0.
35														
40														

Remaining Balance Factors
Original Term In Years

15.50%

Age of Loan	1	2	3	4	5	6	7	8	9	10	15	20	25	30
1	0.	53.84	71.65	80.45	85.64	89.04	91.41	93.14	94.45	95.46	98.17	99.20	99.64	99.83
2		0.	38.58	57.64	68.90	76.26	81.40	85.15	87.97	90.16	96.03	98.26	99.22	99.64
3			0.	31.03	49.37	61.35	69.71	75.81	80.42	83.98	93.53	97.17	98.72	99.42
4				0.	26.58	43.96	56.08	64.93	71.61	76.76	90.62	95.90	98.15	99.15
5					0.	23.67	40.18	52.24	61.33	68.35	87.22	94.41	97.48	98.85
6						0.	21.63	37.43	49.34	58.54	83.26	92.68	96.70	98.49
7							0.	20.15	35.35	47.09	78.64	90.66	95.79	98.07
8								0.	19.03	33.74	73.24	88.30	94.72	97.58
9									0.	18.17	66.95	85.55	93.48	97.02
10										0.	59.62	82.35	92.03	96.35
11										0.	51.06	78.61	90.34	95.58
12										0.	41.08	74.24	88.38	94.68
13										0.	29.43	69.15	86.08	93.63
14										0.	15.85	63.21	83.40	92.40
15											0.	56.29	80.27	90.97
16											0.	48.21	76.62	89.30
17											0.	38.78	72.37	87.36
18											0.	27.79	67.41	85.08
19											0.	14.96	61.62	82.44
20												0.	54.87	79.35
21												0.	46.99	75.74
22												0.	37.80	71.54
23												0.	27.09	66.63
24												0.	14.58	60.91
25													0.	54.23
26													0.	46.45
27													0.	37.37
28													0.	26.77
29													0.	14.42
30														0.
35														
40														

15.75%

Age of Loan	1	2	3	4	5	6	7	8	9	10	15	20	25	30
1	0.	53.90	71.73	80.53	85.73	89.12	91.49	93.22	94.52	95.52	98.21	99.23	99.65	99.84
2		0.	38.66	57.76	69.03	76.40	81.54	85.28	88.10	90.28	96.11	98.32	99.25	99.66
3			0.	31.14	49.52	61.52	69.90	76.00	80.61	84.16	93.66	97.26	98.78	99.45
4				0.	26.69	44.13	56.29	65.16	71.84	77.00	90.80	96.02	98.22	99.20
5					0.	23.79	40.37	52.47	61.58	68.62	87.45	94.57	97.58	98.90
6						0.	21.76	37.63	49.59	58.82	83.53	92.88	96.82	98.56
7							0.	20.29	35.57	47.37	78.95	90.90	95.94	98.16
8								0.	19.17	33.98	73.60	88.58	94.90	97.70
9									0.	18.32	67.33	85.87	93.70	97.15
10										0.	60.01	82.70	92.28	96.51
11										0.	51.44	79.00	90.63	95.76
12										0.	41.43	74.67	88.70	94.89
13										0.	29.71	69.60	86.43	93.86
14										0.	16.02	63.68	83.79	92.67
15											0.	56.75	80.70	91.27
16											0.	48.65	77.09	89.64
17											0.	39.18	72.86	87.72
18											0.	28.10	67.92	85.49
19											0.	15.15	62.14	82.87
20												0.	55.38	79.82
21												0.	47.47	76.24
22												0.	38.23	72.06
23												0.	27.42	67.17
24												0.	14.78	61.45
25													0.	54.77
26													0.	46.95
27													0.	37.81
28													0.	27.12
29													0.	14.62
30														0.
35														
40														

Remaining Balance Factors
Original Term In Years

16.00%

Age of Loan	1	2	3	4	5	6	7	8	9	10	15	20	25	30
1	0.	53.97	71.80	80.61	85.81	89.20	91.56	93.29	94.58	95.58	98.25	99.25	99.67	99.85
2		0.	38.75	57.88	69.17	76.54	81.68	85.42	88.23	90.41	96.20	98.37	99.28	99.68
3			0.	31.24	49.67	61.70	70.08	76.19	80.79	84.34	93.80	97.35	98.83	99.48
4				0.	26.80	44.30	56.50	65.38	72.07	77.22	90.98	96.14	98.30	99.24
5					0.	23.91	40.57	52.70	61.84	68.88	87.68	94.73	97.47	98.96
6						0.	21.89	37.84	49.85	59.11	83.80	93.07	96.94	98.63
7							0.	20.42	35.79	47.65	79.27	91.13	96.09	98.25
8								0.	19.32	34.21	73.95	88.85	95.08	97.80
9									0.	18.46	67.71	86.18	93.90	97.27
10										0.	60.40	83.05	92.52	96.66
11										0.	51.82	79.39	90.90	95.93
12										0.	41.78	75.C9	89.01	95.09
13										0.	30.00	70.05	86.78	94.09
14										0.	16.19	64.14	84.18	92.93
15											0.	57.21	81.12	91.56
16											0.	49.09	77.54	89.96
17											0.	39.57	73.34	88.08
18											0.	28.41	68.42	85.88
19											0.	15.33	62.65	83.30
20												0.	55.88	80.28
21												0.	47.95	76.73
22												0.	38.65	72.58
23												0.	27.75	67.70
24												0.	14.98	61.99
25													0.	55.30
26													0.	47.45
27													0.	38.25
28													0.	27.46
29													0.	14.82
30														0.
35														
40														

16.25%

Age of Loan	1	2	3	4	5	6	7	8	9	10	15	20	25	30
1	0.	54.03	71.88	80.69	85.89	89.28	91.64	93.36	94.65	95.65	98.29	99.28	99.68	99.86
2		0.	38.83	58.00	69.30	76.68	81.82	85.55	88.36	90.53	96.29	98.43	99.31	99.70
3			0.	31.34	49.82	61.87	70.27	76.38	80.98	84.52	93.93	97.43	98.88	99.50
4				0.	26.91	44.48	56.70	65.60	72.30	77.45	91.16	96.26	98.37	99.28
5					0.	24.03	40.76	52.94	62.09	69.15	87.90	94.88	97.77	99.01
6						0.	22.02	38.05	50.10	59.39	84.07	93.26	97.06	98.70
7							0.	20.56	36.01	47.92	79.58	91.35	96.23	98.33
8								0.	19.46	34.45	74.29	89.12	95.25	97.90
9									0.	18.61	68.08	86.49	94.11	97.4C
10										0.	60.78	83.40	92.76	96.80
11										0.	52.20	79.77	91.17	96.10
12										0.	42.12	75.50	89.31	95.28
13										0.	30.28	70.49	87.13	94.31
14										0.	16.36	64.59	84.56	93.18
15											0.	57.67	81.53	91.84
16											0.	49.53	77.98	90.27
17											0.	39.97	73.81	88.43
18											0.	28.73	68.91	86.27
19											0.	15.52	63.15	83.72
20												0.	56.38	80.73
21												0.	48.42	77.22
22												0.	39.07	73.08
23												0.	28.09	68.23
24												0.	15.17	62.53
25													0.	55.82
26													0.	47.95
27													0.	38.69
28													0.	27.81
29													0.	15.02
30														0.
35														
40														

Remaining Balance Factors
Original Term In Years

16.50%

Age of Loan	1	2	3	4	5	6	7	8	9	10	15	20	25	30
1	0.	54.09	71.96	80.77	85.97	89.36	91.71	93.43	94.72	95.71	98.33	99.30	99.70	99.87
2		0.	38.92	58.12	69.44	76.82	81.95	85.69	88.49	90.65	96.37	98.48	99.34	99.71
3			0.	31.44	49.97	62.05	70.45	76.57	81.16	84.69	94.06	97.51	98.93	99.53
4				0.	27.03	44.65	56.91	65.82	72.52	77.68	91.33	96.37	98.43	99.32
5					0.	24.15	40.95	53.17	62.35	69.41	88.12	95.03	97.85	99.06
6						0.	22.15	38.26	50.36	59.67	84.34	93.44	97.17	98.77
7							0.	20.69	36.24	48.20	79.88	91.58	96.37	98.41
8								0.	19.60	34.68	74.63	89.38	95.42	98.00
9									0.	18.76	68.45	86.79	94.30	97.51
10										0.	61.16	83.74	92.99	96.94
11										0.	52.58	80.14	91.44	96.26
12										0.	42.47	75.91	89.61	95.46
13										0.	30.56	70.92	87.46	94.53
14										0.	16.53	65.04	84.93	93.42
15											0.	58.12	81.94	92.12
16											0.	49.97	78.42	90.58
17											0.	40.36	74.28	88.77
18											0.	29.04	69.40	86.64
19											0.	15.71	63.65	84.13
20												0.	56.88	81.17
21												0.	48.89	77.69
22												0.	39.49	73.58
23												0.	28.42	68.75
24												0.	15.37	63.05
25													0.	56.34
26													0.	48.44
27													0.	39.12
28													0.	28.15
29													0.	15.23
30														0.
35														
40														

16.75%

Age of Loan	1	2	3	4	5	6	7	8	9	10	15	20	25	30
1	0.	54.15	72.03	80.85	86.05	89.44	91.79	93.50	94.78	95.77	98.37	99.33	99.71	99.88
2		0.	39.01	58.24	69.57	76.96	82.09	85.82	88.62	90.77	96.45	98.53	99.37	99.73
3			0.	31.54	50.12	62.22	70.64	76.75	81.34	84.87	94.18	97.59	98.97	99.56
4				0.	27.14	44.82	57.11	66.05	72.75	77.90	91.50	96.48	98.50	99.35
5					0.	24.27	41.14	53.40	62.60	69.67	88.34	95.17	97.94	99.11
6						0.	22.28	38.47	50.61	59.95	84.60	93.62	97.28	98.83
7							0.	20.83	36.46	48.47	80.19	91.79	96.50	98.49
8								0.	19.74	34.92	74.97	89.63	95.58	98.09
9									0.	18.91	68.82	87.08	94.49	97.62
10										0.	61.55	84.07	93.21	97.07
11										0.	52.96	80.51	91.69	96.42
12										0.	42.82	76.31	89.90	95.64
13										0.	30.84	71.35	87.79	94.73
14										0.	16.70	65.49	85.29	93.65
15											0.	58.57	82.34	92.38
16											0.	50.40	78.85	90.88
17											0.	40.75	74.74	89.10
18											0.	29.35	69.88	87.01
19											0.	15.90	64.14	84.53
20												0.	57.37	81.61
21												0.	49.36	78.15
22												0.	39.91	74.08
23												0.	28.75	69.26
24												0.	15.57	63.57
25													0.	56.86
26													0.	48.92
27													0.	39.56
28													0.	28.49
29													0.	15.43
30														0.
35														
40														

Remaining Balance Factors
Original Term In Years

17.00%

Age of Loan	1	2	3	4	5	6	7	8	9	10	15	20	25	30
1	0.	54.21	72.11	80.93	86.13	89.51	91.86	93.57	94.85	95.83	98.41	99.35	99.73	99.88
2		0.	39.09	58.36	69.71	77.10	82.23	85.95	88.75	90.89	96.53	98.58	99.40	99.74
3			0.	31.64	50.27	62.40	70.82	76.94	81.53	85.05	94.31	97.67	99.02	99.58
4				0.	27.25	44.99	57.32	66.27	72.98	78.12	91.67	96.59	98.56	99.39
5					0.	24.39	41.33	53.63	62.85	69.93	88.55	95.31	98.02	99.16
6						0.	22.41	38.67	50.87	60.23	84.86	93.79	97.38	98.88
7							0.	20.97	36.68	48.75	80.49	92.00	96.63	98.56
8								0.	19.89	35.15	75.31	89.88	95.74	98.18
9									0.	19.06	69.18	87.37	94.68	97.73
10										0.	61.93	84.40	93.42	97.20
11										0.	53.34	80.88	91.94	96.56
12										0.	43.17	76.71	90.18	95.81
13										0.	31.13	71.78	88.10	94.93
14										0.	16.87	65.94	85.64	93.88
15											0.	59.02	82.73	92.64
16											0.	50.83	79.28	91.17
17											0.	41.14	75.19	89.42
18											0.	29.67	70.36	87.36
19											0.	16.08	64.63	84.92
20												0.	57.85	82.03
21												0.	49.83	78.61
22												0.	40.33	74.56
23												0.	29.08	69.76
24												0.	15.76	64.09
25													0.	57.37
26													0.	49.41
27													0.	39.99
28													0.	28.84
29													0.	15.63
30														0.
35														
40														

17.25%

Age of Loan	1	2	3	4	5	6	7	8	9	10	15	20	25	30
1	0.	54.27	72.19	81.01	86.21	89.59	91.94	93.64	94.91	95.89	98.45	99.37	99.74	99.89
2		0.	39.18	58.48	69.84	77.23	82.36	86.09	88.87	91.01	96.61	98.63	99.43	99.76
3			0.	31.74	50.42	62.57	71.01	77.12	81.71	85.22	94.43	97.74	99.06	99.60
4				0.	27.36	45.17	57.52	66.49	73.20	78.35	91.84	96.69	98.62	99.42
5					0.	24.51	41.52	53.86	63.10	70.19	88.76	95.44	98.10	99.20
6						0.	22.54	38.88	51.12	60.51	85.11	93.97	97.49	98.94
7							0.	21.10	36.90	49.02	80.78	92.21	96.75	98.63
8								0.	20.03	35.39	75.64	90.13	95.89	98.27
9									0.	19.20	69.54	87.65	94.86	97.83
10										0.	62.30	84.72	93.63	97.32
11										0.	53.71	81.24	92.18	96.71
12										0.	43.51	77.10	90.46	95.98
13										0.	31.41	72.20	88.42	95.12
14										0.	17.05	66.37	85.99	94.10
15											0.	59.46	83.11	92.88
16											0.	51.26	79.69	91.44
17											0.	41.53	75.64	89.74
18											0.	29.98	70.83	87.71
19											0.	16.27	65.11	85.30
20												0.	58.34	82.45
21												0.	50.29	79.06
22												0.	40.74	75.03
23												0.	29.41	70.26
24												0.	15.96	64.59
25													0.	57.87
26													0.	49.89
27													0.	40.42
28													0.	29.18
29													0.	15.83
30														0.
35														
40														

APPENDIX FIVE
DISCOUNT YIELD TABLE

The Discount Yield Table shows what the true interest or yield is after a loan has been discounted. A discount or points can be charged so that the true yield or interest is actually higher than that reported on the debt instrument. For example, amortgage note of $100,000 at an 11 1/2% rate for a 30-year term was sold for $95,000. The discount was 5% or 5 points and the true yield or interest would be raised to 12.18%. If this 30-year loan matured (paid out) in 12 years the yield would be approximately 1/2 the distance between the 10 and 15 year yields or 12.62%. FHA, VA and Conventional mortgages with a 30-year term are considered to have an average maturity of 12 years.

Discount Yield Table

Rate of Interest	Bid Price	5 Years	10 Years	15 Years	20 Years	25 Years	30 Years
9%	95	11.22	10.21	9.89	9.73	9.64	9.58
	96	10.76	9.96	9.70	9.58	9.51	9.46
	97	10.31	9.72	9.52	9.43	9.38	9.34
	98	9.87	9.48	9.35	9.28	9.25	9.23
	99	9.43	9.24	9.17	9.14	9.12	9.11
9⅛%	95	11.34	10.34	10.01	9.86	9.77	9.71
	96	10.89	10.09	9.83	9.71	9.63	9.59
	97	10.44	9.84	9.65	9.56	9.50	9.47
	98	9.99	9.60	9.47	9.41	9.38	9.35
	99	9.56	9.36	9.30	9.27	9.25	9.24
9¼%	95	11.47	10.47	10.14	9.99	9.90	9.84
	96	11.01	10.22	9.96	9.83	9.76	9.72
	97	10.56	9.97	9.78	9.68	9.63	9.60
	98	10.12	9.73	9.60	9.54	9.50	9.48
	99	9.68	9.49	9.42	9.39	9.38	9.36
9⅜%	95	11.60	10.60	10.27	10.11	10.03	9.97
	96	11.14	10.35	10.09	9.96	9.89	9.85
	97	10.69	10.10	9.90	9.81	9.76	9.73
	98	10.25	9.85	9.73	9.66	9.63	9.61
	99	9.81	9.61	9.55	9.52	9.50	9.49
9½%	95	11.73	10.73	10.40	10.24	10.16	10.10
	96	11.27	10.47	10.21	10.09	10.02	9.98
	97	10.82	10.22	10.03	9.94	9.89	9.85
	98	10.37	9.98	9.85	9.79	9.76	9.73
	99	9.93	9.74	9.67	9.64	9.63	9.62
9⅝%	95	11.86	10.85	10.53	10.37	10.28	10.23
	96	11.40	10.60	10.34	10.22	10.15	10.11
	97	10.94	10.35	10.16	10.07	10.01	9.98
	98	10.50	10.11	9.98	9.92	9.88	9.86
	99	10.06	9.86	9.80	9.77	9.75	9.74
9¾%	95	11.98	10.98	10.66	10.50	10.41	10.36
	96	11.52	10.73	10.47	10.35	10.28	10.23
	97	11.07	10.48	10.29	10.19	10.14	10.11
	98	10.62	10.23	10.10	10.04	10.01	9.99
	99	10.18	9.99	9.93	9.90	9.88	9.87
9⅞%	95	12.11	11.11	10.78	10.63	10.54	10.49
	96	11.65	10.86	10.60	10.47	10.40	10.36
	97	11.20	10.61	10.41	10.32	10.27	10.24
	98	10.75	10.36	10.23	10.17	10.14	10.11
	99	10.31	10.11	10.05	10.02	10.00	9.99
10%	95	12.24	11.24	10.91	10.76	10.67	10.62
	96	11.78	10.98	10.72	10.60	10.53	10.49
	97	11.32	10.73	10.54	10.45	10.40	10.37
	98	10.88	10.48	10.36	10.30	10.26	10.24
	99	10.43	10.24	10.18	10.15	10.13	10.12
10⅛%	95	12.37	11.37	11.04	10.89	10.80	10.75
	96	11.90	11.11	10.85	10.73	10.66	10.62
	97	11.45	10.86	10.67	10.57	10.52	10.49
	98	11.00	10.61	10.48	10.42	10.39	10.37
	99	10.56	10.37	10.30	10.27	10.26	10.25

Discount Yield Table

Rate of Interest	Bid Price	5 Years	10 Years	15 Years	20 Years	25 Years	30 Years
10¼%	95	12.49	11.50	11.17	11.02	10.93	10.88
	96	12.03	11.24	10.98	10.86	10.79	10.75
	97	11.58	10.99	10.79	10.70	10.65	10.62
	98	11.13	10.74	10.61	10.55	10.52	10.50
	99	10.69	10.49	10.43	10.40	10.38	10.37
10⅜%	95	12.62	11.62	11.30	11.15	11.06	11.01
	96	12.16	11.37	11.11	10.99	10.92	10.88
	97	11.70	11.11	10.92	10.83	10.78	10.75
	98	11.25	10.86	10.74	10.68	10.64	10.62
	99	10.81	10.62	10.55	10.52	10.51	10.50
10½%	95	12.75	11.75	11.43	11.27	11.19	11.14
	96	12.29	11.49	11.24	11.11	11.05	11.01
	97	11.83	11.24	11.05	10.96	10.91	10.88
	98	11.38	10.99	10.86	10.80	10.77	10.75
	99	10.94	10.74	10.68	10.65	10.63	10.62
10⅝%	95	12.88	11.88	11.56	11.40	11.32	11.27
	96	12.41	11.62	11.36	11.24	11.18	11.14
	97	11.96	11.37	11.17	11.08	11.03	11.00
	98	11.51	11.12	10.99	10.93	10.90	10.88
	99	11.06	10.87	10.81	10.78	10.76	10.75
10¾%	95	13.01	12.01	11.68	11.53	11.45	11.40
	96	12.54	11.75	11.49	11.37	11.30	11.26
	97	12.08	11.49	11.30	11.21	11.16	11.13
	98	11.63	11.24	11.11	11.06	11.02	11.00
	99	11.19	10.99	10.93	10.90	10.89	10.88
10⅞%	95	13.13	12.14	11.81	11.66	11.58	11.53
	96	12.67	11.88	11.62	11.50	11.43	11.39
	97	12.21	11.62	11.43	11.34	11.29	11.26
	98	11.76	11.37	11.24	11.18	11.15	11.13
	99	11.31	11.12	11.06	11.03	11.01	11.00
11%	95	13.26	12.26	11.94	11.79	11.71	11.66
	96	12.80	12.00	11.75	11.63	11.56	11.52
	97	12.34	11.75	11.56	11.47	11.42	11.39
	98	11.88	11.49	11.37	11.31	11.28	11.26
	99	11.44	11.25	11.18	11.15	11.14	11.13
11⅛%	95	13.39	12.39	12.07	11.92	11.84	11.79
	96	12.92	12.13	11.88	11.76	11.69	11.65
	97	12.46	11.87	11.68	11.59	11.54	11.52
	98	12.01	11.62	11.49	11.43	11.40	11.38
	99	11.56	11.37	11.31	11.28	11.26	11.25
11¼%	95	13.52	12.52	12.20	12.05	11.97	11.92
	96	13.05	12.26	12.00	11.88	11.82	11.78
	97	12.59	12.00	11.81	11.72	11.67	11.64
	98	12.14	11.75	11.62	11.56	11.53	11.51
	99	11.69	11.50	11.43	11.40	11.39	11.38
11⅜%	95	13.64	12.65	12.33	12.18	12.10	12.05
	96	13.18	12.39	12.13	12.01	11.95	11.91
	97	12.72	12.13	11.94	11.85	11.80	11.77
	98	12.26	11.87	11.75	11.69	11.66	11.64
	99	11.82	11.62	11.56	11.53	11.51	11.50

Discount Yield Table

Rate of Interest	Bid Price	5 Years	10 Years	15 Years	20 Years	25 Years	30 Years
11½%	95	13.77	12.78	12.46	12.31	12.23	12.18
	96	13.30	12.51	12.26	12.14	12.08	12.04
	97	12.84	12.25	12.06	11.98	11.93	11.90
	98	12.39	12.00	11.87	11.81	11.78	11.76
	99	11.94	11.75	11.69	11.66	11.64	11.63
11⅝%	95	13.90	12.90	12.58	12.44	12.36	12.31
	96	13.43	12.64	12.39	12.27	12.20	12.17
	97	12.97	12.38	12.19	12.10	12.06	12.03
	98	12.51	12.13	12.00	11.94	11.91	11.89
	99	12.07	11.87	11.81	11.78	11.77	11.76
11¾%	95	14.03	13.03	12.71	12.57	12.49	12.44
	96	13.56	12.77	12.51	12.40	12.33	12.30
	97	13.10	12.51	12.32	12.23	12.18	12.16
	98	12.64	12.25	12.13	12.07	12.04	12.02
	99	12.19	12.00	11.94	11.91	11.89	11.88
11⅞%	95	14.16	13.16	12.84	12.69	12.62	12.57
	96	13.69	12.90	12.64	12.52	12.46	12.43
	97	13.22	12.63	12.45	12.36	12.31	12.28
	98	12.77	12.38	12.25	12.19	12.16	12.15
	99	12.32	12.12	12.06	12.03	12.02	12.01
12%	95	14.28	13.29	12.97	12.82	12.74	12.70
	96	13.81	13.02	12.77	12.65	12.59	12.55
	97	13.35	12.76	12.57	12.49	12.44	12.41
	98	12.89	12.50	12.38	12.32	12.29	12.27
	99	12.44	12.25	12.19	12.16	12.14	12.13
12⅛%	95	14.41	13.42	13.10	12.95	12.87	12.83
	96	13.94	13.15	12.90	12.78	12.72	12.68
	97	13.48	12.89	12.70	12.61	12.57	12.54
	98	13.02	12.63	12.51	12.45	12.42	12.40
	99	12.57	12.38	12.31	12.29	12.27	12.26
12¼%	95	14.54	13.55	13.23	13.08	13.00	12.96
	96	14.07	13.28	13.03	12.91	12.85	12.81
	97	13.60	13.02	12.83	12.74	12.69	12.67
	98	13.15	12.76	12.63	12.57	12.54	12.53
	99	12.69	12.50	12.44	12.41	12.40	12.39
12⅜%	95	14.67	13.67	13.36	13.21	13.13	13.09
	96	14.19	13.41	13.15	13.04	12.98	12.94
	97	13.73	13.14	12.95	12.87	12.82	12.80
	98	13.27	12.88	12.76	12.70	12.67	12.65
	99	12.82	12.63	12.57	12.54	12.52	12.51
12½%	95	14.79	13.80	13.49	13.34	13.26	13.22
	96	14.32	13.53	13.28	13.17	13.11	13.07
	97	13.86	13.27	13.08	13.00	12.95	12.92
	98	13.40	13.01	12.88	12.83	12.80	12.78
	99	12.95	12.75	12.69	12.66	12.65	12.64
12⅝%	95	14.92	13.93	13.61	13.47	13.39	13.35
	96	14.45	13.66	13.41	13.30	13.23	13.20
	97	13.98	13.40	13.21	13.12	13.08	13.05
	98	13.52	13.14	13.01	12.95	12.92	12.91
	99	13.07	12.88	12.82	12.79	12.77	12.76

Discount Yield Table

Rate of Interest	Bid Price	5 Years	10 Years	15 Years	20 Years	25 Years	30 Years
12¾%	95	15.05	14.06	13.74	13.60	13.52	13.48
	96	14.58	13.79	13.54	13.42	13.36	13.33
	97	14.11	13.52	13.34	13.25	13.21	13.18
	98	13.65	13.26	13.14	13.08	13.05	13.03
	99	13.20	13.00	12.94	12.91	12.90	12.89
12⅞%	95	15.18	14.19	13.87	13.73	13.65	13.61
	96	14.70	13.92	13.67	13.55	13.49	13.46
	97	14.24	13.65	13.46	13.38	13.33	13.31
	98	13.78	13.39	13.26	13.21	13.18	13.16
	99	13.32	13.13	13.07	13.04	13.03	13.02
13%	95	15.31	14.32	14.00	13.86	13.78	13.74
	96	14.83	14.04	13.79	13.68	13.62	13.59
	97	14.36	13.78	13.59	13.51	13.46	13.44
	98	13.90	13.51	13.39	13.33	13.30	13.29
	99	13.45	13.26	13.19	13.17	13.15	13.14
13⅛%	95	15.43	14.44	14.13	13.99	13.91	13.87
	96	14.96	14.17	13.92	13.81	13.75	13.72
	97	14.49	13.90	13.72	13.63	13.59	13.56
	98	14.03	13.64	13.52	13.46	13.43	13.42
	99	13.57	13.38	13.32	13.29	13.28	13.27
13¼%	95	15.56	14.57	14.26	14.12	14.04	14.00
	96	15.09	14.30	14.05	13.94	13.88	13.85
	97	14.62	14.03	13.85	13.76	13.72	13.69
	98	14.15	13.77	13.64	13.59	13.56	13.54
	99	13.70	13.51	13.45	13.42	13.40	13.39
13⅜%	95	15.69	14.70	14.39	14.25	14.17	14.13
	96	15.21	14.43	14.18	14.07	14.01	13.98
	97	14.74	14.16	13.97	13.89	13.85	13.82
	98	14.28	13.89	13.77	13.71	13.69	13.67
	99	13.82	13.63	13.57	13.54	13.53	13.52
13½%	95	15.82	14.83	14.52	14.38	14.30	14.26
	96	15.34	14.55	14.31	14.19	14.14	14.10
	97	14.87	14.28	14.10	14.02	13.97	13.95
	98	14.41	14.02	13.90	13.84	13.81	13.80
	99	13.95	13.76	13.70	13.67	13.65	13.65
13⅝%	95	15.94	14.96	14.65	14.51	14.43	14.39
	96	15.47	14.68	14.43	14.32	14.27	14.23
	97	15.00	14.41	14.23	14.14	14.10	14.08
	98	14.53	14.15	14.02	13.97	13.94	13.92
	99	14.08	13.88	13.82	13.80	13.78	13.77
13¾%	95	16.07	15.09	14.77	14.63	14.56	14.52
	96	15.59	14.81	14.56	14.45	14.39	14.36
	97	15.12	14.54	14.35	14.27	14.23	14.21
	98	14.66	14.27	14.15	14.09	14.07	14.05
	99	14.20	14.01	13.95	13.92	13.91	13.90
13⅞%	95	16.20	15.21	14.90	14.76	14.69	14.65
	96	15.72	14.94	14.69	14.58	14.52	14.49
	97	15.25	14.67	14.48	14.40	14.36	14.33
	98	14.78	14.40	14.28	14.22	14.19	14.18
	99	14.33	14.13	14.07	14.05	14.03	14.03

Discount Yield Table

Rate of Interest	Bid Price	5 Years	10 Years	15 Years	20 Years	25 Years	30 Years
14%	95	16.33	15.34	15.03	14.89	14.82	14.78
	96	15.85	15.07	14.82	14.71	14.65	14.62
	97	15.38	14.79	14.61	14.53	14.48	14.46
	98	14.91	14.52	14.40	14.35	14.32	14.30
	99	14.45	14.26	14.20	14.17	14.16	14.15
14⅛%	95	16.46	15.47	15.16	15.02	14.95	14.92
	96	15.98	15.19	14.95	14.84	14.78	14.75
	97	15.50	14.92	14.74	14.65	14.61	14.59
	98	15.04	14.65	14.53	14.48	14.45	14.43
	99	14.58	14.39	14.33	14.30	14.28	14.28
14¼%	95	16.58	15.60	15.29	15.15	15.08	15.05
	96	16.10	15.32	15.08	14.97	14.91	14.88
	97	15.63	15.05	14.86	14.78	14.74	14.72
	98	15.16	14.78	14.66	14.60	14.57	14.56
	99	14.70	14.51	14.45	14.42	14.41	14.40
14⅜%	95	16.71	15.73	15.42	15.28	15.21	15.18
	96	16.23	15.45	15.20	15.09	15.04	15.01
	97	15.76	15.17	14.99	14.91	14.87	14.85
	98	15.29	14.90	14.78	14.73	14.70	14.69
	99	14.83	14.64	14.58	14.55	14.54	14.53
14½%	95	16.84	15.86	15.55	15.41	15.34	15.31
	96	16.36	15.58	15.33	15.22	15.17	15.14
	97	15.88	15.30	15.12	15.04	15.00	14.97
	98	15.42	15.03	14.91	14.86	14.83	14.81
	99	14.95	14.76	14.70	14.68	14.66	14.66
14⅝%	95	16.97	15.98	15.68	15.54	15.47	15.44
	96	16.49	15.70	15.46	15.35	15.30	15.27
	97	16.01	15.43	15.25	15.17	15.12	15.10
	98	15.54	15.16	15.04	14.98	14.96	14.94
	99	15.08	14.89	14.83	14.80	14.79	14.78
14¾%	95	17.10	16.11	15.81	15.67	15.60	15.57
	96	16.61	15.83	15.59	15.48	15.43	15.40
	97	16.14	15.55	15.37	15.29	15.25	15.23
	98	15.67	15.28	15.16	15.11	15.08	15.07
	99	15.21	15.01	14.95	14.93	14.91	14.91
14⅞%	95	17.22	16.24	15.94	15.80	15.73	15.70
	96	16.74	15.96	15.72	15.61	15.56	15.53
	97	16.26	15.68	15.50	15.42	15.38	15.36
	98	15.79	15.41	15.29	15.24	15.21	15.20
	99	15.33	15.14	15.08	15.05	15.04	15.03
15%	95	17.35	16.37	16.07	15.93	15.86	15.83
	96	16.87	16.09	15.84	15.74	15.68	15.66
	97	16.39	15.81	15.63	15.55	15.51	15.49
	98	15.92	15.54	15.42	15.36	15.34	15.32
	99	15.46	15.27	15.21	15.18	15.17	15.16
15⅛%	95	17.48	16.50	16.19	16.06	15.99	15.96
	96	16.99	16.22	15.97	15.87	15.81	15.79
	97	16.52	15.94	15.76	15.68	15.64	15.62
	98	16.05	15.66	15.54	15.49	15.46	15.45
	99	15.58	15.39	15.33	15.31	15.29	15.29

Discount Yield Table

Rate of Interest	Bid Price	5 Years	10 Years	15 Years	20 Years	25 Years	30 Years
15¼%	95	17.61	16.63	16.32	16.19	16.12	16.09
	96	17.12	16.34	16.10	16.00	15.94	15.92
	97	16.64	16.06	15.88	15.80	15.77	15.74
	98	16.17	15.79	15.67	15.62	15.59	15.58
	99	15.71	15.52	15.46	15.43	15.42	15.41
15⅜%	95	17.74	16.76	16.45	16.32	16.26	16.22
	96	17.25	16.47	16.23	16.12	16.07	16.05
	97	16.77	16.19	16.01	15.93	15.89	15.87
	98	16.30	15.91	15.80	15.74	15.72	15.70
	99	15.83	15.64	15.58	15.56	15.54	15.54
15½%	95	17.86	16.88	16.58	16.45	16.39	16.35
	96	17.38	16.60	16.36	16.25	16.20	16.17
	97	16.90	16.32	16.14	16.06	16.02	16.00
	98	16.42	16.04	15.92	15.87	15.84	15.83
	99	15.96	15.77	15.71	15.68	15.67	15.66
15⅝%	95	17.99	17.01	16.71	16.58	16.52	16.48
	96	17.50	16.73	16.49	16.38	16.33	16.30
	97	17.02	16.44	16.27	16.19	16.15	16.13
	98	16.55	16.17	16.05	16.00	15.97	15.96
	99	16.08	15.89	15.83	15.81	15.80	15.79
15¾%	95	18.12	17.14	16.84	16.71	16.65	16.61
	96	17.63	16.85	16.61	16.51	16.46	16.43
	97	17.15	16.57	16.39	16.32	16.28	16.26
	98	16.68	16.29	16.18	16.12	16.10	16.09
	99	16.21	16.02	15.96	15.94	15.92	15.92
15⅞%	95	18.25	17.27	16.97	16.84	16.78	16.74
	96	17.76	16.98	16.74	16.64	16.59	16.56
	97	17.28	16.70	16.52	16.44	16.41	16.39
	98	16.80	16.42	16.30	16.25	16.23	16.21
	99	16.34	16.15	16.09	16.06	16.05	16.04
16%	95	18.38	17.40	17.10	16.97	16.91	16.88
	96	17.89	17.11	16.87	16.77	16.72	16.69
	97	17.40	16.83	16.65	16.57	16.53	16.51
	98	16.93	16.55	16.43	16.38	16.35	16.34
	99	16.46	16.27	16.21	16.19	16.17	16.17
16⅛%	95	18.50	17.53	17.23	17.10	17.04	17.01
	96	18.01	17.24	17.00	16.90	16.85	16.82
	97	17.53	16.95	16.78	16.70	16.66	16.64
	98	17.06	16.67	16.56	16.50	16.48	16.47
	99	16.59	16.40	16.34	16.31	16.30	16.29
16¼%	95	18.63	17.66	17.36	17.23	17.17	17.14
	96	18.14	17.37	17.13	17.03	16.98	16.95
	97	17.66	17.08	16.90	16.83	16.79	16.77
	98	17.18	16.80	16.68	16.63	16.61	16.59
	99	16.71	16.52	16.46	16.44	16.43	16.42
16⅜%	95	18.76	17.78	17.49	17.36	17.30	17.27
	96	18.27	17.49	17.26	17.16	17.11	17.08
	97	17.78	17.21	17.03	16.95	16.92	16.90
	98	17.31	16.93	16.81	16.76	16.73	16.72
	99	16.84	16.65	16.59	16.56	16.55	16.55

Discount Yield Table

Rate of Interest	Bid Price	5 Years	10 Years	15 Years	20 Years	25 Years	30 Years
16½%	95	18.89	17.91	17.62	17.49	17.43	17.40
	96	18.40	17.62	17.38	17.28	17.24	17.21
	97	17.91	17.33	17.16	17.08	17.05	17.03
	98	17.43	17.05	16.93	16.89	16.86	16.85
	99	16.96	16.77	16.72	16.69	16.68	16.67
16⅝%	95	19.02	18.04	17.75	17.62	17.56	17.53
	96	18.52	17.75	17.51	17.41	17.37	17.34
	97	18.04	17.46	17.29	17.21	17.17	17.16
	98	17.56	17.18	17.06	17.01	16.99	16.98
	99	17.09	16.90	16.84	16.82	16.80	16.80
16¾%	95	19.14	18.17	17.87	17.75	17.69	17.66
	96	18.65	17.88	17.64	17.54	17.49	17.47
	97	18.16	17.59	17.41	17.34	17.30	17.29
	98	17.69	17.30	17.19	17.14	17.12	17.10
	99	17.21	17.03	16.97	16.94	16.93	16.93
16⅞%	95	19.27	18.30	18.00	17.88	17.82	17.79
	96	18.78	18.00	17.77	17.67	17.62	17.60
	97	18.29	17.72	17.54	17.47	17.43	17.41
	98	17.81	17.43	17.31	17.27	17.24	17.23
	99	17.34	17.15	17.09	17.07	17.06	17.05
17%	95	19.40	18.43	18.13	18.01	17.95	17.92
	96	18.90	18.13	17.90	17.80	17.75	17.73
	97	18.42	17.84	17.67	17.59	17.56	17.54
	98	17.94	17.56	17.44	17.39	17.37	17.36
	99	17.47	17.28	17.22	17.19	17.18	17.18
17⅛%	95	19.53	18.56	18.26	18.14	18.08	18.05
	96	19.03	18.26	18.03	17.93	17.88	17.86
	97	18.54	17.97	17.80	17.72	17.69	17.67
	98	18.06	17.68	17.57	17.52	17.50	17.49
	99	17.59	17.40	17.34	17.32	17.31	17.30
17¼%	95	19.66	18.68	18.39	18.27	18.21	18.18
	96	19.16	18.39	18.16	18.06	18.01	17.99
	97	18.67	18.10	17.92	17.85	17.82	17.80
	98	18.19	17.81	17.70	17.65	17.62	17.61
	99	17.72	17.53	17.47	17.45	17.44	17.43
17⅜%	95	19.78	18.81	18.52	18.40	18.34	18.31
	96	19.29	18.52	18.28	18.19	18.14	18.12
	97	18.80	18.22	18.05	17.98	17.94	17.93
	98	18.32	17.94	17.82	17.77	17.75	17.74
	99	17.84	17.65	17.60	17.57	17.56	17.56
17½%	95	19.91	18.94	18.65	18.53	18.47	18.45
	96	19.41	18.64	18.41	18.32	18.27	18.25
	97	18.92	18.35	18.18	18.11	18.07	18.06
	98	18.44	18.06	17.95	17.90	17.88	17.87
	99	17.97	17.78	17.72	17.70	17.69	17.68
17⅝%	95	20.04	19.07	18.78	18.66	18.60	18.58
	96	19.54	18.77	18.54	18.44	18.40	18.38
	97	19.05	18.48	18.31	18.23	18.20	18.18
	98	18.57	18.19	18.08	18.03	18.01	17.99
	99	18.09	17.90	17.85	17.82	17.81	17.81

Discount Yield Table

Rate of Interest	Bid Price	5 Years	10 Years	15 Years	20 Years	25 Years	30 Years
17¾%	95	20.17	19.20	18.91	18.79	18.73	18.71
	96	19.67	18.90	18.67	18.57	18.53	18.51
	97	19.18	18.61	18.43	18.36	18.33	18.31
	98	18.70	18.32	18.20	18.15	18.13	18.12
	99	18.22	18.03	17.97	17.95	17.94	17.93
17⅞%	95	20.30	19.33	19.04	18.92	18.86	18.84
	96	19.80	19.03	18.80	18.70	18.66	18.64
	97	19.31	18.73	18.56	18.49	18.46	18.44
	98	18.82	18.44	18.33	18.28	18.26	18.25
	99	18.34	18.16	18.10	18.08	18.07	18.06
18%	95	20.42	19.46	19.17	19.05	19.00	18.97
	96	19.92	19.16	18.93	18.83	18.79	18.77
	97	19.43	18.86	18.69	18.62	18.59	18.57
	98	18.95	18.57	18.46	18.41	18.39	18.38
	99	18.47	18.28	18.23	18.20	18.19	18.19
18⅛%	95	20.55	19.59	19.30	19.18	19.13	19.10
	96	20.05	19.28	19.06	18.96	18.92	18.90
	97	19.56	18.99	18.82	18.75	18.71	18.70
	98	19.07	18.70	18.58	18.54	18.51	18.50
	99	18.60	18.41	18.35	18.33	18.32	18.31
18¼%	95	20.68	19.71	19.43	19.31	19.26	19.23
	96	20.18	19.41	19.18	19.09	19.05	19.03
	97	19.69	19.11	18.94	18.87	18.84	18.83
	98	19.20	18.82	18.71	18.66	18.64	18.63
	99	18.72	18.53	18.48	18.45	18.44	18.44
18⅜%	95	20.81	19.84	19.56	19.44	19.39	19.36
	96	20.31	19.54	19.31	19.22	19.18	19.16
	97	19.81	19.24	19.07	19.00	18.97	18.96
	98	19.33	18.95	18.84	18.79	18.77	18.76
	99	18.85	18.66	18.60	18.58	18.57	18.56
18½%	95	20.94	19.97	19.69	19.57	19.52	19.49
	96	20.43	19.67	19.44	19.35	19.31	19.29
	97	19.94	19.37	19.20	19.13	19.10	19.08
	98	19.45	19.07	18.96	18.92	18.90	18.89
	99	18.97	18.78	18.73	18.71	18.70	18.69
18⅝%	95	21.06	20.10	19.82	19.70	19.65	19.62
	96	20.56	19.80	19.57	19.48	19.44	19.42
	97	20.07	19.50	19.33	19.26	19.23	19.21
	98	19.58	19.20	19.09	19.04	19.02	19.01
	99	19.10	18.91	18.86	18.83	18.82	18.82
18¾%	95	21.19	20.23	19.95	19.83	19.78	19.76
	96	20.69	19.92	19.70	19.61	19.57	19.55
	97	20.19	19.62	19.45	19.39	19.36	19.34
	98	19.70	19.33	19.22	19.17	19.15	19.14
	99	19.22	19.04	18.98	18.96	18.95	18.94
18⅞%	95	21.32	20.36	20.08	19.96	19.91	19.89
	96	20.82	20.05	19.83	19.74	19.70	19.68
	97	20.32	19.75	19.58	19.51	19.48	19.47
	98	19.83	19.45	19.34	19.30	19.28	19.27
	99	19.35	19.16	19.11	19.08	19.07	19.07

Discount Yield Table

Rate of Interest	Bid Price	5 Years	10 Years	15 Years	20 Years	25 Years	30 Years
19%	95	21.45	20.49	20.20	20.09	20.04	20.02
	96	20.94	20.18	19.96	19.86	19.82	19.81
	97	20.45	19.88	19.71	19.64	19.61	19.60
	98	19.96	19.58	19.47	19.42	19.40	19.40
	99	19.47	19.29	19.23	19.21	19.20	19.20
19⅛%	95	21.58	20.62	20.33	20.22	20.17	20.15
	96	21.07	20.31	20.08	19.99	19.95	19.94
	97	20.57	20.00	19.84	19.77	19.74	19.73
	98	20.08	19.71	19.60	19.55	19.53	19.52
	99	19.60	19.41	19.36	19.34	19.33	19.32
19¼%	95	21.70	20.74	20.46	20.35	20.30	20.28
	96	21.20	20.44	20.21	20.12	20.08	20.07
	97	20.70	20.13	19.97	19.90	19.87	19.86
	98	20.21	19.83	19.72	19.68	19.66	19.65
	99	19.73	19.54	19.48	19.46	19.45	19.45
19⅜%	95	21.83	20.87	20.59	20.48	20.43	20.41
	96	21.33	20.56	20.34	20.25	20.21	20.20
	97	20.83	20.26	20.09	20.03	20.00	19.98
	98	20.34	19.96	19.85	19.81	19.79	19.78
	99	19.85	19.67	19.61	19.59	19.58	19.57
19½%	95	21.96	21.00	20.72	20.61	20.56	20.54
	96	21.45	20.69	20.47	20.38	20.34	20.33
	97	20.95	20.39	20.22	20.15	20.13	20.11
	98	20.46	20.09	19.98	19.93	19.91	19.90
	99	19.98	19.79	19.74	19.71	19.70	19.70
19⅝%	95	22.09	21.13	20.85	20.74	20.69	20.67
	96	21.58	20.82	20.60	20.51	20.47	20.46
	97	21.08	20.51	20.35	20.28	20.25	20.24
	98	20.59	20.21	20.10	20.06	20.04	20.03
	99	20.10	19.92	19.86	19.84	19.83	19.83
19¾%	95	22.22	21.26	20.98	20.87	20.83	20.81
	96	21.71	20.95	20.73	20.64	20.60	20.59
	97	21.21	20.64	20.48	20.41	20.38	20.37
	98	20.71	20.34	20.23	20.19	20.17	20.16
	99	20.23	20.04	19.99	19.97	19.96	19.95
19⅞%	95	22.34	21.39	21.11	21.00	20.96	20.94
	96	21.84	21.08	20.86	20.77	20.73	20.72
	97	21.33	20.77	20.60	20.54	20.51	20.50
	98	20.84	20.47	20.36	20.31	20.30	20.29
	99	20.35	20.17	20.11	20.09	20.08	20.08
20%	95	22.47	21.52	21.24	21.13	21.09	21.07
	96	21.96	21.20	20.98	20.90	20.86	20.85
	97	21.46	20.90	20.73	20.67	20.64	20.63
	98	20.97	20.59	20.48	20.44	20.42	20.41
	99	20.48	20.29	20.24	20.22	20.21	20.21

APPENDIX SIX

Figure 1
Income Analysis—FHA

Monthly Income

a. Borrower's
   Base Pay $_____

b. Co-Borrower's
   Base Pay $_____

   _____ $_____

c. Minus Income Tax $_____

d. Total Net Income $_____

e. 38% Net Income $_____

   Housing Expense/
   Income Ratio _____%

   Housing Expenses cannot exceed
   38% of net income and total
   obligations cannot exceed 53%
   of net income.

f. 53% Net Income $_____

   Obligations/
   Income Ratio _____%

Monthly Payment

Mortgage Payment

g. P & I $_____

h. MIP $_____

i. Taxes $_____

j. Insurance $_____

k. Maintenance $_____

l. Utilities $_____

m. Total Housing
   Expense $_____

n. Recurring Charges
   Soc. Sec. $_____

   Obligations which
   exceed 12 months

   $_____

o. Total Recurring
   Obligations $_____

p. Total all
   Monthly Paymts. $_____

TOTAL NET INCOME (Line d) $_____

TOTAL MONTHLY PAYMTS. (Line p) – $_____

BALANCE FOR FAMILY SUPPORT $_____.__

REMAINING INCOME FOR FAMILY SUPPORT is a significant factor in determining whether the borrower will be approved. Consideration is given to the number of dependents in family and size of home being purchased.

Figure 2
Income Analysis—VA

Ratio Calculation

Gross Income		Housing & Debt Payment	
Veteran	$_____	P & I	$_____
Spouse	$_____	Taxes	$_____
Other	$_____	Insurance	$_____
Total	$_____ (A)	Food Ins.	$_____
		Other	$_____

Ratio

Total $_____ (B)

Divide (D) _____
                  debt payment

By (A) _____   Recurring
              Gross Income   Obligations $_____ (C)

= _____ %   Total $_____ (D)
              Ratio (E)

Residual Income

Total Income	$_____	Net Income	$_____
Less:		*Less:*	
Income Tax	$_____	Recurring	
SS/Retirement	$_____	Obligations (C)	$_____
Other	$_____	Monthly Paymt. (B)	$_____
Plus		Maint./Util.	$_____
Non-taxable	+_____	Residual Income	$_____ (F)
Net Income	$_____		

Ratio (E) should not exceed 41% without compensating factors.

If ratio is higher than 41% the RESIDUAL INCOME MUST BE AT LEAST 20% higher than shown on chart below:

Family Size	N/E	Midwest	South	West
1	411	399	409	443
2	646	627	643	697
3	786	763	781	847
4	873	848	868	941
5	951	924	946	1024
6	1026	999	1021	1099
7	1101	1074	1096	1174

Figure 3
Income Analysis—Conventional

Monthly Income

a. Borrower's Base Income $_____

b. Spouse's Base Income $_____

c. Other $_____

d. Total Effective Income $_____

e. 25% of Total Income $_____

   (Mo. Pmt./Income _____%)

f. 33% of Total Income $_____

   (Obligation/Income _____%)

Monthly Payments

First Mortgage Payments

g. P & I $_____

h. Taxes $_____

i. Haz. Ins. $_____

j. PMI $_____

k. Other $_____

l. Total Mortgage Payment $_____

m. Total of all other monthly payments extending beyond 10 months, including Alimony/Child Support if applicable $_____

n. TOTAL ALL PAYMENTS $_____

Figure 4
Home Loan Financial Analysis Form
Part 1
Cash Required

Type Loan	Lower of Sales Price or Value − Maximum Loan = Down Payment + Closing Cost + Escrow + Origination Fee + Any Cash Required for Mortgage Ins. + Discount Points = Required Cash Investment							
FHA								
VA								
95% Conventional								
90% Conventional								
80% Conventional								
Second Mortgage								
Wrap Around								
Assumption of Present Mortgage(s)								

Compare verifiable cash assets available for settlement to cash required for closing.

Figure 5
Home Loan
Financial Analysis Form
Part II
Monthly Payment

Type Loan	Interest Rate	Term	P & I	+ Taxes	+ Hazard Insurance	+ Mortgage Insurance	+ Condo or Association Dues	+ Flood Insurance	= Total Monthly Payment
FHA									
VA									
95% Conventional									
90% Conventional									
80% Conventional									
Second Mortgage									
Wrap Around									
Assumption of Present Mortgage(s)									

Compare verifiable monthly income to total monthly payment. Refer to the FHA, VA or conventional section for general guidelines of income to monthly house payment. After analyzing information provided in Part I and Part II, one should always consider the assumability feature, particularly in reference to any due-on-sale clause.

Figure 6
Four Ways to Determine Maximum Loan Amounts Using the FHA Section 203(b) Formula.

Begin by making a comparison between two totals. The first of two totals is the FHA appraised value plus FHA closing costs. The second total is the contract price plus the FHA closing cost the purchaser pays. The second total can also be the contract price, minus any concession items, plus the FHA closing cost paid by the buyer. Before you begin determining the loan amount you must choose the lower of the two totals. On each example below the first figure ($70,000) is termed the *acquisition cost*. The number below the $70,000 is the FHA closing cost paid by the buyer. The total of the acquisition cost and the FHA closing cost paid by the buyer is the *total acquisition*. Once you correctly determine the total acquisition, you simply use the short-cut formula shown below. In example I, the two totals would be the same. In example II, the total of the acquisition cost plus the FHA closing cost paid by the buyer (nothing) is the lower of the two totals. In example III, the total of the acquisition minus the concession is the lower of the two totals. In example IV, the total of the acquisition cost plus the FHA closing cost paid by the buyer (1/2) is the lower of the two totals. If you do not understand the meaning of the "lower of the two totals," go back and reread the first four sentences of this paragraph.

Total Acquisition Below $50,000

If the total acquisition is below $50,000, you simply multiply by 97% to determine the loan amount. A word of caution! If the total acquisition exceeds $50,000 by $1, you must use the 97% - 95% formula or the short-cut formula.

Assuming a sales price and FHA value of $70,000 and $1,800 for the FHA estimate of closing cost.

I. Purchasers are paying their own closing cost and prepaid items:

$70,000	$71,800	$25,000	$46,800	$24,250
+ 1,800	-25,000	× 97%	× 95%	+44,460
$71,800	$46,800	$24,250	$44,460	$68,710

Maximum Loan is $68,700
(Short-cut: $71,800 × 95% = $68,210 + $500 = $68,710 = $68,700)

purchaser's closing cost:

$25,000	$45,000	$24,250
× 97%	× 95%	+42,750
$24,250	$42,750	$67,000

,500 + $500 = $67,000)

ourchasers' closing cost and prepaid items:

;00	$25,000	$44,300	$24,250
)00	× 97%	× 95%	+42,085
00	$24,250	$42,085	$66,335

(Short -cut: $69,300 × 95% = $65,835 + $500 = $66,335 =$66,300)

*FHA can view prepaid items paid by the seller as a sales concession. In this example, the $700 is an estimate for prepaid items which is deducted from the sales price as a concession paid by the seller.

IV. Sellers are paying a portion of the closing cost:

$70,000	$70,900	$25,000	$45,900	$24,250
+ 900*	-25,000	× 97%	× 95%	+43,605
$70,900	$45,900	$24,250	$43,605	$67,855

Maximum loan is $67,850
(Short-cut: $70,900 × 95% = $67,355 + $500 = $67,855 =$67,850)

*In this example, we assumed the seller was paying one half of the purchaser's closing cost (FHA estimate is $1,800 divided by 2 = $900).

Figure 7
FHA Section 245 and VA GPM
Principal and Interest
Monthly Payment Amortization Factors per $1,000

Plan I—With increasing payment for 5 years at 2.50 percent each year

Int. Yr.	8.00	8.25	8.50	8.75	9.00	9.25	9.50	9.75	10.00	10.25	10.50	10.75	11.00	11.25
1	6.6651	6.8277	6.9918	7.1574	7.3244	7.4928	7.6625	7.8335	8.0057	8.1791	8.3537	8.5295	8.7063	8.8842
2	6.8317	6.9984	7.1666	7.3364	7.5075	7.6801	7.8541	8.0293	8.2058	8.3836	8.5626	8.7427	8.9240	9.1063
3	7.0025	7.1733	7.3458	7.5198	7.6952	7.8721	8.0504	8.2300	8.4110	8.5932	8.7767	8.9613	9.1471	9.3340
4	7.1775	7.3527	7.5294	7.7078	7.8876	8.0689	8.2517	8.4358	8.6213	8.8080	8.9961	9.1853	9.3757	9.5673
5	7.3570	7.5365	7.7177	7.9005	8.0848	8.2706	8.4580	8.6467	8.8368	9.0282	9.2210	9.4150	9.6101	9.8065

Plan II—With increasing payment for 5 years at 5.0 percent each year.

Int. Yr.	8.00	8.25	8.50	8.75	9.00	9.25	9.50	9.75	10.00	10.25	10.50	10.75	11.00	11.25
1	6.0579	6.2089	6.3613	6.5153	6.6706	6.8274	6.9856	7.1451	7.3059	7.4679	7.6312	7.7957	7.9613	8.1281
2	6.3608	6.5193	6.6794	6.8410	7.0042	7.1688	7.3349	7.5023	7.6712	7.8413	8.0128	8.1855	8.3594	8.5345
3	6.6789	6.8453	7.0134	7.1831	7.3544	7.5272	7.7016	7.8775	8.0547	8.2334	8.4134	8.5948	8.7774	8.9612
4	7.0128	7.1875	7.3640	7.5422	7.7221	7.9036	8.0867	8.2713	8.4575	8.6451	8.8341	9.0245	9.2162	9.4093
5	7.3634	7.5469	7.7322	7.9193	8.1082	8.2988	8.4910	8.6849	8.8804	9.0773	9.2758	9.4757	9.6771	9.8798

Plan III—With increasing payment for 5 years at 7.50 percent each year
Note: Plan III Factors also apply to the VA GPM Program.

Int. Yr.	8.00	8.25	8.50	8.75	9.00	9.25	9.50	9.75	10.00	10.25	10.50	10.75	11.00	11.25
1	5.5101	5.6500	5.7915	5.9344	6.0788	6.2246	6.3719	6.5204	6.6704	6.8216	6.9740	7.1277	7.2826	7.4387
2	5.9233	6.0738	6.2258	6.3795	6.5347	6.6915	6.8498	7.0095	7.1706	7.3332	7.4971	7.6623	7.8288	7.9966
3	6.3676	6.5293	6.6928	6.8580	7.0248	7.1934	7.3635	7.5352	7.7084	7.8832	8.0594	8.2370	8.4160	8.5964
4	6.8452	7.0190	7.1947	7.3723	7.5517	7.7329	7.9158	8.1003	8.2866	8.4744	8.6638	8.8548	9.0472	9.2411
5	7.3585	7.5454	7.7343	7.9252	8.1181	8.3128	8.5094	8.7079	8.9081	9.1100	9.3136	9.5189	9.7257	9.9342

Example: A Plan III mortgage amount of $65,750 at 10% rate would have a monthly principal and interest amount of $438.58 (6.6704 x 65.75). The P & I amounts for the succeeding years could be derived by either multiplying the factor times the loan amount or by simply adding 7.5% to the preceding year's monthly payment (7.1706 x 65.75 = $471.47 or $438.58 x 7.5% = $471.47).

Plan I—With increasing payment for 5 years at 2.50 percent each year

Int.	11.50	11.75	12.00	12.25	12.50	12.75	13.00	13.25	13.50	13.75	14.00	14.25	14.50	14.75
Yr.														
1	9.0631	9.2430	9.4238	9.6056	9.7882	9.9717	10.1560	10.2411	10.5269	10.7135	10.9008	11.0888	11.2775	11.4667
2	9.2897	9.4740	9.6594	9.8457	10.0329	10.2210	10.4099	10.5996	10.7901	10.0814	11.1734	11.3660	11.5594	11.7534
3	9.5219	9.7109	9.9009	10.0918	10.2837	10.4765	10.6701	10.8646	11.0599	11.2559	11.4527	11.6502	11.8484	12.0472
4	9.7600	9.9537	10.1484	10.2441	10.5408	10.7384	10.9369	11.1362	11.3364	11.5373	11.7390	11.9415	12.1446	12.3484
5	10.0040	10.2025	10.4021	10.6027	10.8043	11.0069	11.2103	11.4146	11.6198	11.8257	12.0325	12.2400	12.4482	12.6571
6	10.2541	10.4576	10.6622	10.8678	11.0744	11.2820	11.4906	11.7000	11.9103	12.1214	12.3333	12.5460	12.7594	12.9736

Plan II—With increasing payment for 5 years at 5.0 percent each year.

Int.	11.50	11.75	12.00	12.25	12.50	12.75	13.00	13.25	13.50	13.75	14.00	14.25	14.50	14.75
Yr.														
1	8.2960	8.4649	8.6348	8.8058	8.9777	9.1505	9.3243	9.4990	9.6745	9.8508	10.0279	10.2059	10.3845	10.5639
2	8.7108	8.8881	9.0666	9.2461	9.4266	9.6081	9.7905	9.9739	10.1582	10.3433	10.5293	10.7161	10.9038	11.0921
3	9.1463	9.3325	9.5199	9.7084	8.8979	10.0885	10.2800	10.4726	10.6661	10.8605	11.0558	11.2520	11.4489	11.6467
4	9.6036	9.7992	9.9959	10.1938	10.3928	10.5929	10.7940	10.9962	11.1994	11.4035	11.6086	11.8145	12.0214	12.2291
5	10.0838	10.2891	10.4957	10.7035	10.9124	11.1225	11.3338	11.5460	11.7594	11.9737	12.1890	12.4053	12.6225	12.8405
6	10.5880	10.8036	11.0205	11.2386	11.4581	11.6787	11.9004	12.1233	12.3473	12.5724	12.7985	13.0255	13.2536	13.4826

Plan III—With increasing payment for 5 years at 7.50 percent each year
Note: Plan III factors also apply to the VA GPM Program

Int.	11.50	11.75	12.00	12.25	12.50	12.75	13.00	13.25	13.50	13.75	14.00	14.25	14.50	14.75
Yr.														
1	7.5960	7.7543	7.9138	8.0743	8.2358	8.3983	8.5618	8.7263	8.8917	9.0580	9.2252	9.3933	9.5621	9.7318
2	8.1657	8.3359	8.5073	8.6798	8.8535	9.0282	9.2040	9.3808	9.5586	9.7374	9.9171	10.0978	10.2793	10.4617
3	8.7781	8.9611	9.1453	9.3308	9.5175	9.7053	9.8943	10.0843	10.2755	10.4677	10.6609	10.8551	11.0502	11.2464
4	9.4364	9.6332	9.8312	10.0306	10.2313	10.4332	10.6363	10.8407	11.0461	11.2528	11.4604	11.6692	11.8790	12.0898
5	10.1442	10.3556	10.5686	10.7829	10.9986	11.2157	11.4341	11.6537	11.8746	12.0967	12.3200	12.5444	12.7699	12.9966
6	10.9050	11.1323	11.3612	11.5916	11.8235	12.0569	12.2916	12.5277	12.7652	13.0040	13.2440	13.4852	13.7277	13.9713

Example: A Plan III mortgage amount of $65,750 at 12.25% rate would have a monthly principal and interest amount of $530.89 (8.0743 × 65.75). The P & I amounts for the succeeding years could be derived by either multiplying the factor times the loan amount or by simply adding 7.5% to the preceding year's monthly payment (8.6798 × 65.75 = $570.70 or $530.89 × 7.5% = $570.71).

Reprinted by permission, from Doris Sowell, *Fundamentals of Finance* © 1981.

Figure 8
FHA 245 MIP Factors for Condominum Loans

MIP Factors—For First Year Monthly Payment

	8.00	8.25	8.50	8.75	9.00	9.25	9.50
Plan I	.4167	.4168	.4169	.4170	.4171	.4172	.4173
Plan II	.4181	.4182	.4184	.4185	.4186	.4187	.4189
Plan III	.4194	.4195	.4197	.4199	.4200	.4202	.4203

	9.75	10.00	10.25	10.50	10.75	11.00	11.25
Plan I	.4174	.4174	.4175	.4176	.4177	.4178	.4178
Plan II	.4190	.4191	.4192	.4193	.4194	.4195	.4196
Plan III	.4204	.4206	.4207	.4209	.4210	.4211	.4212

	11.50	11.75	12.00	12.25	12.50	12.75	13.00
Plan I	.4179	.4180	.4180	.4181	.4182	.4182	.4183
Plan II	.4197	.4198	.4199	.4200	.4201	.4202	.4203
Plan III	.4214	.4215	.4216	.4217	.4218	.4220	.4221
Plan IV	.4184	.4184	.4185	.4186	.4186	.4187	.4187
Plan V	.4195	.4196	.4197	.4198	.4198	.4199	.4200

	13.25	13.50	13.75	14.00	14.25	14.50	14.75
Plan I	.4183	.4184	.4184	.4185	.4185	.4186	.4186
Plan II	.4203	.4204	.4205	.4206	.4206	.4207	.4208
Plan III	.4222	.4223	.4224	.4225	.4226	.4227	.4228
Plan IV	.4188	.4188	.4189	.4189	.4190	.4190	.4191
Plan V	.4200	.4201	.4202	.4202	.4203	.4203	.4204

To arrive at the monthly Mortgage Insurance Premium (MIP) determine the plan to be used and the interest rate. Locate the plan and interest on the above chart.

The MIP payment changes on an annual basis for the first five or ten years, however the change is insignificant, therefore we have shown only the first year's monthly MIP factor.

To determine the payment multiply the loan amount by the appropriate factor.

Reprinted, by permission from Doris Sowell *Fundamental of Finance* © 1981

*Refer to RSP™ section for lower rates.

Figure 9
FHA Section 245
Factors to Determine Loan Amounts and Highest Outstanding Balance

	8.00%	8.25%	8.50%	8.75%	9.00%	9.25%	9.50%
Plan I	.96998	.96943	.96889	.96837	.96777	.96679	.96586
Plan II	.95768	.95569	.95376	.95187	.95003	.94824	.94621
Plan III	.94087	.93792	.93505	.93224	.92951	.92684	.92424

	9.75%	10.00%	10.25%	10.50%	10.75%	11.00%	11.25%
Plan I	.96495	.96407	.96312	.96188	.96069	.95954	.95843
Plan II	.94401	.94186	.93979	.93777	.93580	.93388	.93201
Plan III	.92168	.91920	.91677	.91441	.91200	.90932	.90670

Highest Outstanding Balance Factors

	8.00%	8.25%	8.50%	8.75%	9.00%	9.25%	9.50%
Plan I	1000.0201	1000.5896	1001.1418	1001.6772	1002.3079	1003.3129	1004.2877
Plan II	1012.8612	1014.9708	1017.0324	1019.0469	1021.0152	1022.9385	1025.1491
Plan III	1030.9556	1034.1948	1037.3747	1040.4962	1043.5603	1046.5880	1049.5206

	9.75%	10.00%	10.25%	10.50%	10.75%	11.00%	11.25%
Plan I	1005.2331	1006.1499	1007.1468	1008.4360	1009.6867	1010.9001	1012.0773
Plan II	1027.5353	1029.8670	1032.1457	1034.3725	1036.5488	1038.6758	1040.7549
Plan III	1052.4189	1055.2642	1058.0575	1060.7999	1063.5966	1066.7321	1069.8097

Reprinted, by permission from Doris Sowell *Fundamentals of Finance* © 1981

Figure 9 (Continued)
FHA Section 245
Factors to Determine Loan Amounts and Highest Outstanding Balance *

	11.50%	11.75%	12.00%	12.25%	12.50%	12.75%	13.00%
Plan I	.95734	.95630	.95522	.95392	.95267	.95145	.95028
Plan II	.93020	.92843	.92671	.92502	.92306	.92115	.91929
Plan III	.90415	.90166	.89922	.89685	.89452	.89226	.89004
Plan IV	.93827	.93606	.93393	.93150	.92916	.92686	.92466
Plan V	.90706	.90413	.90094	.89778	.89471	.89175	.88887

	13.25%	13.50%	13.75%	14%	14.25%	14.50%	14.75%
Plan I	.94914	.94803	.94697	.94593	.94492	.94395	.94300
Plan II	.91749	.91572	.91401	.91233	.91070	.90911	.90756
Plan III	.88787	.88574	.88367	.88164	.87966	.87771	.87581
Plan IV	.92253	.92047	.91834	.91610	.91394	.91185	.90982
Plan V	.88608	.88338	.88706	.87822	.87545	.87274	.87012

Highest Outstanding Balance Factors

	11.50%	11.75%	12.00%	12.25%	12.50%	12.75%	13.00%
Plan I	1013.2195	1014.3277	1015.4743	1016.8540	1018.1930	1019.4929	1020.7547
Plan II	1042.7873	1044.7742	1046.7169	1048.6314	1050.8562	1053.0311	1055.1576
Plan III	1072.8307	1075.7964	1078.7082	1081.5673	1084.3752	1087.1331	1089.8422
Plan IV	1033.8188	1036.2553	1038.6198	1041.3283	1043.9734	1046.5419	1049.0358
Plan V	1069.3910	1072.8549	1076.6526	1080.4449	1084.4449	1087.7544	1091.2753

	13.25%	13.50%	13.75%	14.00%	14.25%	14.50%	14.75%
Plan I	1021.9798	1023.1694	1024.3247	1025.4470	1026.5373	1027.5968	1028.6266
Plan II	1057.2370	1059.2707	1061.2602	1063.2066	1065.1115	1066.9759	1068.8012
Plan III	1092.5039	1095.1195	1097.6900	1100.2169	1102.7012	1105.1441	1107.5468
Plan IV	1051.4571	1053.8076	1056.2509	1058.8317	1061.3389	1063.7745	1066.1403
Plan V	1094.7095	1098.0588	1101.3253	1104.5107	1108.0046	1111.4367	1114.7854

Reprinted, by permission from Doris Sowell *Fundamentals of Finance* © 1981

*Refer to RSP^{TM} Section for lower rates.

Figure 10
Principal and Interest

Monthly Payment Amortization Factors
per $1,000 from 8% to 19.5% In
1/2% Increments for 30-Year and 15-Year Loans

30 Years		15 Years	
Rate	*Factor*	*Rate*	*Factor*
8%	7.3376	8%	9.5565
8.5	7.6891	8.5	9.8474
9.0	8.0462	9	10.1427
9.5	8.4085	9.5	10.4422
10	8.7757	10	10.7461
10.5	9.1474	10.5	11.0540
11	9.5232	11	11.3660
11.5	9.9029	11.5	11.6819
12	10.2861	12	12.0017
12.5	10.6726	12.5	12.3252
13	11.0620	13	12.6524
13.5	11.4541	13.5	12.9832
14	11.8487	14	13.3174
14.5	12.2456	14.5	13.6550
15	12.6444	15	13.9959
15.5	13.0452	15.5	14.3399
16	13.4476	16	14.6870
16.5	13.8515	16.5	15.0371
17	14.2568	17	15.3900
17.5	14.6633	17.5	15.7458
18	15.0709	18	16.1042
18.5	15.4794	18.5	16.4652
19	15.8889	19	16.8288
19.5	16.2992	19.5	17.1947

Figure 11
FHA and VA P & I Factors—MIP Premium Factors for 221(d) (2), 203(k) & 234(c) (Condominiums)

Rate	Term	First	Last	Total Renewals	P & I
7.75	15	.4098	.0238	44.720	9.42
	20	.4126	.0215	62.589	8.21
	25	.4141	.0174	81.480	7.56
	30	.4150	.0156	101.474	7.17
8.00	15	.4099	.0247	44.975	9.56
	20	.4127	.0207	62.844	8.37
	25	.4142	.0196	82.142	7.72
	30	.4151	.0179	102.429	7.34
8.25	15	.4100	.0243	45.137	9.71
	20	.4128	.0201	63.121	8.53
	25	.4143	.0185	82.517	7.89
	30	.4152	.0153	102.769	7.52
8.50	15	.4102	.0254	45.415	9.85
	20	.4129	.0223	63.654	8.68
	25	.4143	.0179	82.938	8.06
	30	.4153	.0196	103.942	7.69
8.75	15	.4103	.0254	45.601	10.00
	20	.4130	.0224	63.984	8.84
	25	.4145	.0179	83.418	8.23
	30	.4153	.0185	104.454	7.87
9.00	15	.4104	.0254	45.791	10.15
	20	.4132	.0228	64.343	9.00
	25	.4146	.0184	83.946	8.40
	30	.4153	.0183	105.062	8.05
9.25	15	.4106	.0257	45.993	10.30
	20	.4133	.0236	64.728	9.16
	25	.4147	.0196	84.529	8.57
	30	.4154	.0190	105.760	8.23
9.50	15	.4107	.0261	46.207	10.45
	20	.4133	.0219	64.896	9.33
	25	.4148	.0213	85.177	8.74
	30	.4155	.0208	106.560	8.41

Rate	Term	First	Last	Total Renewals	P & I
9.75	15	.4108	.0267	46.432	10.60
	20	.4134	.0233	65.335	9.49
	25	.4148	.0190	85.388	8.92
	30	.4156	.0156	106.560	8.60
10.00	10	.4050	.0340	29.270	13.22
	15	.4052	.0341	46.668	10.75
	20	.4135	.0223	65.548	9.66
	25	.4149	.0221	86.148	9.09
	30	.4156	.0191	107.560	8.78
10.25	10	.4053	.0343	29.364	13.36
	15	.4111	.0283	46.920	10.90
	20	.4137	.0245	66.048	9.82
	25	.4149	.0208	86.460	9.27
	30	.4157	.0155	107.712	8.97
10.50	10	.4054	.0346	29.460	13.50
	15	.4113	.0278	47.052	11.06
	20	.4138	.0240	66.312	9.99
	25	.4150	.0200	86.820	9.45
	30	.4158	.0213	108.924	9.15
10.75	10	.4056	.0349	29.556	13.64
	15	.4113	.0291	47.328	11.21
	20	.4138	.0238	66.600	10.16
	25	.4151	.0198	87.228	9.63
	30	.4158	.0190	109.248	9.34
11.00	10	.4058	.0353	29.664	13.78
	15	.4115	.0288	47.496	11.37
	20	.4139	.0241	66.912	10.33
	25	.4152	.0202	87.684	9.81
	30	.4158	.0177	109.632	9.53
11.25	10	.4059	.0358	29.772	13.92
	15	.4116	.0288	47.664	11.53
	20	.4140	.0247	67.260	10.50
	25	.4153	.0211	88.200	9.99
	30	.4158	.0172	110.112	9.72

Rate	Term	First	Last	Total Renewals	P & I
11.50	10	.4061	.0364	29.880	14.06
	15	.4117	.0288	47.840	11.69
	20	.4141	.0256	67.630	10.67
	25	.4153	.0228	87.774	10.17
	30	.4159	.0175	110.673	9.91
11.75	10	.4062	.0362	29.941	14.21
	15	.4118	.0290	48.034	11.85
	20	.4142	.0270	68.035	10.84
	25	.4153	.0253	89.420	10.35
	30	.4159	.0188	111.341	10.10
12.00	10	.4063	.0368	30.055	14.35
	15	.4119	.0294	48.234	12.01
	20	.4143	.0250	68.157	11.02
	25	.4154	.0218	89.481	10.54
	30	.4160	.0214	112.122	10.29
12.25	10	.4065	.0368	30.129	14.50
	15	.4120	.0300	48.447	12.17
	20	.4143	.0272	68.619	11.19
	25	.4154	.0258	90.244	10.72
	30	.4160	.0255	113.014	10.48
12.50	10	.4067	.0376	32.250	14.64
	15	.4122	.0308	48.679	12.33
	20	.4144	.0258	68.790	11.37
	25	.4155	.0231	90.393	10.91
	30	.4161	.0172	112.647	10.68
12.75	10	.4068	.0376	30.327	14.79
	15	.4123	.0319	48.916	12.49
	20	.4145	.0289	69.315	11.54
	25	.4155	.0210	90.580	11.10
	30	.4161	.0232	113.743	10.87
13.00	10	.4069	.0377	30.409	14.94
	15	.4123	.0310	49.025	12.66
	20	.4146	.0283	69.539	11.72
	25	.4156	.0277	91.553	11.28
	30	.4161	.0163	113.485	11.07

Rate	Term	First	Last	Total Renewals	P & I
13.25	10	.4071	.0388	30.542	15.08
	15	.4124	.0324	49.288	12.82
	20	.4146	.0283	69.786	11.90
	25	.4157	.0276	91.845	11.47
	30	.4162	.0249	114.834	11.26
13.50	10	.4072	.0389	30.628	15.23
	15	.4125	.0319	49.417	12.99
	20	.4147	.0281	70.058	12.08
	25	.4157	.0267	92.199	11.66
	30	.4162	.0191	114.700	11.46
13.75	10	.4073	.0392	30.718	15.38
	15	.4127	.0338	47.706	13.15
	20	.4148	.0286	70.360	12.26
	25	.4158	.0271	92.595	11.85
	30	.4162	.0145	114.634	11.66
14.00	10	.4075	.0395	30.812	15.53
	15	.4128	.0336	49.659	13.32
	20	.4148	.0295	70.690	12.44
	25	.4158	.0284	94.055	12.04
	30	.4163	.0276	116.381	11.85
14.25	10	.4076	.0399	30.909	15.68
	15	.4128	.0336	50.019	13.49
	20	.4149	.0309	71.052	12.62
	25	.4158	.0305	93.572	12.23
	30	.4163	.0242	116.491	12.05
14.50	10	.4078	.0404	31.009	15.83
	15	.4129	.0338	50.193	13.66
	20	.4149	.0328	71.451	12.80
	25	.4158	.0227	93.256	12.43
	30	.4163	.0214	116.649	12.25
14.75	10	.4078	.0400	31.061	15.99
	15	.4130	.0342	50.382	13.83
	20	.4150	.0297	71.466	12.99
	25	.4159	.0261	93.886	12.62
	30	.4163	.0198	116.976	12.45

Figure 12
A History of FHA/VA Mortgage Rate Changes
May 7, 1968–December 19, 1988

Effective Date	Percent	Effective Date	Percent
May 7, 1968	6-3/4	October 12, 1981	16-1/2
January 24, 1969	7-1/2	November 16, 1981	15-1/2
January 5, 1970	8-1/2	January 25, 1982	16-1/2
December 2, 1970	8	March 2, 1982	15-1/2
January 13, 1971	7-1/2	August 9, 1982	15
February 18, 1971	7	August 24, 1982	14
August 10, 1973	7-3/4	September 24, 1982	13-1/2
August 25, 1973	8-1/2	October 12, 1982	12-1/2
January 22, 1974	8-1/4	November 15, 1982	12
April 15, 1974	8-1/2	May 9, 1983	11-1/2
May 13, 1974	8-3/4	June 7, 1983	12
July 5, 1974	9	July 11, 1983	12-1/2
August 14, 1974	9-1/2	August 1, 1983	13-1/2
November 24, 1975	9	August 23, 1983	13
January 21, 1975	8-1/2	November 1, 1983*	12-1/2
March 3, 1975	8	March 21, 1984	13
April 28, 1975	8-1/2	May 8, 1984	13-1/2
September 3, 1975	9	May 29, 1984	14
January 5, 1976	8-3/4	August 13, 1984	13-1/2
March 30, 1976	8-1/2	October 22, 1984	13
October 18, 1976	8	November 21, 1984	12-1/2
May 31, 1977	8-1/2	March 25, 1985	13
February 28, 1978	8-3/4	April 19, 1985	12-1/2
May 23, 1978	9	May 21, 1985	12
June 29, 1978	9-1/2	June 5, 1985	11-1/2
April 23, 1979	10	November 20, 1985	11
September 26, 1979	10-1/2	December 13, 1985	10-1/2
October 26, 1979	11-1/2	March 3, 1986	9-1/2
February 11, 1980	12	November 24, 1986	9
February 28, 1980	13	January 19, 1987	8-1/2
April 4, 1980	14	April 13, 1987	9-1/2
April 28, 1980	13	May 11, 1987	10
May 15, 1980	11-1/2	September 8, 1987	10-1/2
August 10, 1980	12	October 5, 1987	11
September 22, 1980	13	November 10, 1987	10-1/2
November 24, 1980	13-1/2	February 1, 1988	9-1/2
March 9, 1981	14	April 4, 1988	10
April 13, 1981	14-1/2	May 23, 1988	10-1/2
May 8, 1981	15-1/2	November 1, 1988	10
August 17, 1981	16-1/2	December 19, 1988	10-1/2
September 14, 1981	17-1/2		

* Starting December 1, 1983 the FHA Rate was Freed
    RSP #1 (5/88)

Figure 13
Common Adjustable Rate Mortgage Indices

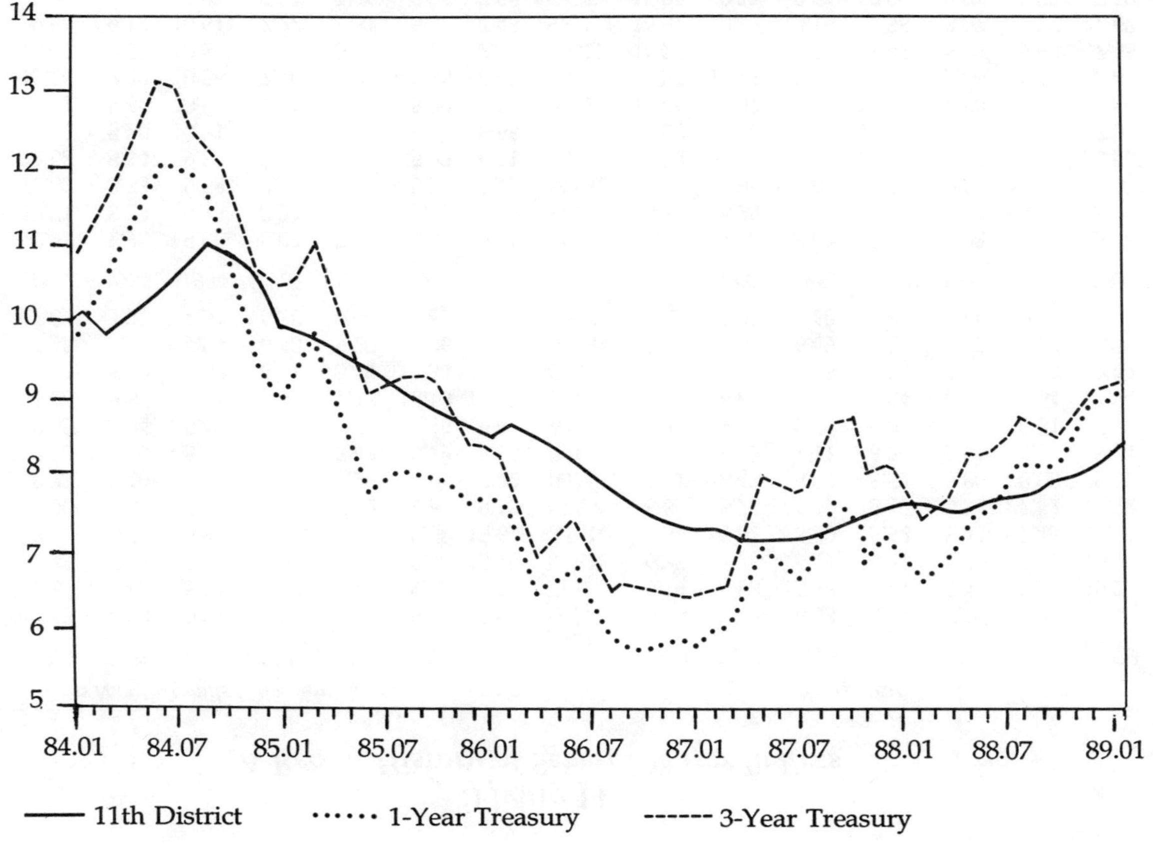

——— 11th District   •••••• 1-Year Treasury   - - - - - 3-Year Treasury

Figure 14
A Recent History of Several Major Indices

6 Month T-bills (Discount Basis)

	1973	1974	1975	1976	1977	1978	1979	1980
JAN	5.53	7.63	6.53	5.24	4.78	6.69	9.50	11.85
FEB	5.75	6.87	5.67	5.14	4.90	6.74	9.35	12.72
MAR	6.43	7.83	5.64	5.49	4.88	6.64	9.46	15.10
APR	6.53	8.17	6.01	5.20	4.79	6.70	9.50	13.62
MAY	6.62	8.50	5.65	5.60	5.19	7.02	9.53	9.15
JUN	7.23	8.23	5.46	5.78	5.20	7.20	9.06	7.22
JUL	8.08	8.03	6.49	5.60	5.35	7.47	9.19	8.10
AUG	8.70	8.85	6.94	5.42	5.81	7.36	9.45	9.44
SEP	8.54	8.60	6.87	5.31	5.99	7.95	10.13	10.55
OCT	7.26	7.56	6.39	5.07	6.41	8.49	11.34	11.57
NOV	7.82	7.55	5.75	4.94	6.43	9.20	11.86	13.61
DEC	7.44	7.09	5.93	4.51	6.38	9.40	11.85	14.77

	1981	1982	1983	1984	1985	1986	1987	1988
JAN	13.88	12.93	7.90	9.06	8.03	7.13	5.47	6.31
FEB	14.13	13.71	8.23	9.13	8.34	7.08	5.60	5.96
MAR	12.98	12.62	8.33	9.58	8.92	6.60	5.56	5.91
APR	13.43	12.68	8.34	9.83	8.31	6.07	5.93	6.21
MAY	15.33	12.22	8.20	10.31	7.75	6.16	6.11	6.53
JUN	13.95	12.31	8.89	10.55	7.16	6.28	5.99	6.76
JUL	14.40	12.24	9.29	10.58	7.16	5.85	5.86	6.97
AUG	15.55	10.11	9.53	10.65	7.35	5.58	6.14	7.36
SEP	15.06	9.54	9.19	10.51	7.27	5.31	6.57	7.43
OCT	14.01	8.30	8.90	10.05	7.32	5.26	6.86	7.50
NOV	11.53	8.32	8.89	8.99	7.26	5.42	6.23	7.76
DEC	11.47	8.23	9.14	8.36	7.09	5.53	6.36	8.24

1 Year Treasury

	1973	1974	1975	1976	1977	1978	1979	1980
JAN	5.89	7.42	6.83	5.81	5.29	7.28	10.41	12.06
FEB	6.19	6.88	5.98	5.91	5.47	7.34	10.24	13.92
MAR	6.85	7.76	6.11	6.21	5.50	7.31	10.25	15.82
APR	6.85	8.62	6.90	5.92	5.44	7.45	10.12	13.30
MAY	6.89	8.78	6.39	6.40	5.84	7.82	10.12	9.39
JUN	7.31	8.67	6.29	6.52	5.80	8.09	9.57	8.16
JUL	8.39	8.79	7.11	6.20	5.94	8.39	9.64	8.65
AUG	8.82	9.36	7.70	6.00	6.37	8.31	9.98	10.24
SEP	8.31	8.87	7.75	5.84	6.53	8.64	10.84	11.52
OCT	7.40	8.05	6.95	5.50	6.97	9.14	12.44	12.49
NOV	7.57	7.66	6.49	5.29	6.95	10.01	12.39	14.15
DEC	7.27	7.31	6.60	4.89	6.96	10.30	11.98	14.88

	1981	1982	1983	1984	1985	1986	1987	1988
JAN	14.08	14.32	8.62	9.90	9.02	7.73	5.78	6.99
FEB	14.57	14.73	8.92	10.04	9.29	7.61	5.96	6.64
MAR	13.71	13.95	9.04	10.59	9.86	7.03	6.03	6.71
APR	14.32	13.98	8.98	10.90	9.14	6.44	6.50	7.01
MAY	16.20	13.34	8.90	11.66	8.46	6.65	7.00	7.40
JUN	14.86	14.07	9.66	12.08	7.80	6.73	6.80	7.49
JUL	15.72	13.24	10.20	12.03	7.86	6.27	6.68	7.75
AUG	16.72	11.43	10.53	11.82	8.05	5.93	7.03	8.17
SEP	16.52	10.85	10.16	11.58	8.07	5.77	7.67	8.09
OCT	15.38	9.32	9.81	10.90	8.01	5.72	7.59	8.11
NOV	12.41	9.16	9.94	9.82	7.88	5.80	6.96	8.48
DEC	12.85	8.91	10.11	9.33	7.68	5.87	7.17	8.99

3 Year Treasury

	1973	1974	1975	1976	1977	1978	1979	1980
JAN	6.27	6.96	7.23	6.99	6.22	7.61	9.50	10.88
FEB	6.58	6.76	6.65	7.06	6.44	7.67	9.29	12.84
MAR	6.86	7.35	6.81	7.13	6.47	7.70	9.38	14.05
APR	6.78	8.05	7.76	6.84	6.32	7.85	9.43	12.02
MAY	6.83	8.27	7.39	7.27	6.55	8.07	9.42	9.44
JUN	6.83	8.15	7.17	7.31	6.39	8.30	8.95	8.91
JUL	7.54	8.41	7.72	7.12	6.51	8.54	8.94	9.27
AUG	7.89	8.66	8.16	6.86	6.79	8.33	9.14	10.63
SEP	7.25	8.41	8.29	6.66	6.84	8.41	9.69	11.57
OCT	6.81	8.00	7.81	6.24	7.19	8.62	10.95	12.01
NOV	7.00	7.61	7.46	6.09	7.22	9.04	11.18	13.31
DEC	6.81	7.24	7.44	5.68	7.30	9.33	10.71	13.65

	1981	1982	1983	1984	1985	1986	1987	1988
JAN	13.01	14.64	9.64	10.93	10.43	8.41	6.41	7.87
FEB	13.65	14.73	9.91	11.05	10.55	8.10	6.56	7.38
MAR	13.51	14.13	9.84	11.59	11.05	7.30	6.58	7.50
APR	14.09	14.18	9.76	11.98	10.49	6.86	7.32	7.83
MAY	15.08	13.77	9.66	12.75	9.75	7.27	8.02	8.24
JUN	14.29	14.48	10.32	13.18	9.05	7.41	7.82	8.22
JUL	15.15	14.00	10.90	13.08	9.18	6.86	7.74	8.44
AUG	16.00	12.62	11.30	12.50	9.31	6.49	8.03	8.77
SEP	16.22	12.03	11.07	12.34	9.37	6.62	8.67	8.57
OCT	15.50	10.62	10.87	11.85	9.25	6.56	8.75	8.43
NOV	13.11	9.98	10.96	10.90	8.88	6.46	7.99	8.72
DEC	13.66	9.88	11.13	10.56	8.40	6.43	8.13	9.11

5 Year Treasury

	1973	1974	1975	1976	1977	1978	1979	1980
JAN	6.34	6.95	7.41	7.46	6.58	7.77	9.20	10.74
FEB	6.60	6.82	7.11	7.45	6.83	7.83	9.13	12.60
MAR	6.81	7.31	7.30	7.49	6.93	7.86	9.20	13.47
APR	6.67	7.92	7.99	7.25	6.79	7.98	9.25	11.84
MAY	6.80	8.18	7.72	7.59	6.94	8.18	9.24	9.95
JUN	6.69	8.10	7.51	7.61	6.76	8.36	8.85	9.21
JUL	7.33	8.38	7.92	7.49	6.84	8.54	8.90	9.53
AUG	7.63	8.63	8.33	7.31	7.03	8.33	9.06	10.84
SEP	7.05	8.37	8.37	7.13	7.04	8.43	9.41	11.62
OCT	6.77	7.97	7.97	6.75	7.32	8.61	10.63	11.86
NOV	6.92	7.68	7.80	6.52	7.34	8.84	10.93	12.83
DEC	6.80	7.31	7.76	6.10	7.48	9.08	10.42	13.25

	1981	1982	1983	1984	1985	1986	1987	1988
JAN	12.77	14.65	10.03	11.37	10.93	8.68	6.64	8.18
FEB	13.41	14.54	10.26	11.54	11.13	8.34	6.79	7.71
MAR	13.41	13.98	10.08	12.02	11.52	7.46	6.79	7.83
APR	13.99	14.00	10.02	12.37	11.01	7.05	7.57	8.19
MAY	14.63	13.75	10.03	13.17	10.34	7.52	8.26	8.58
JUN	13.95	14.43	10.63	13.48	9.60	7.64	8.02	8.49
JUL	14.79	14.07	11.21	13.27	9.70	7.06	8.01	8.66
AUG	15.56	13.00	11.63	12.68	9.81	6.80	8.32	8.94
SEP	15.93	12.25	11.43	12.53	9.81	6.92	8.94	8.69
OCT	15.41	10.80	11.28	12.06	9.69	6.83	9.08	8.51
NOV	13.38	10.38	11.41	11.33	9.28	6.76	8.35	8.79
DEC	13.60	10.22	11.54	11.07	8.73	6.67	8.45	9.09

Figure 14 (Continued)

National Median Cost of Fun

	*1979	1980	1981	1982	1983	1984	1985	1986
JAN	—	8.09	9.50	11.44	10.14	9.89	9.75	8.50
FEB	—	8.29	9.82	11.26	9.75	9.73	9.40	8.29
MAR	—	7.95	10.24	11.37	9.72	9.73	9.36	8.35
APR	—	8.79	10.40	11.35	9.62	9.64	9.29	8.22
MAY	7.35	9.50	10.59	11.39	9.62	9.74	9.19	8.12
JUN	7.27	9.41	10.79	11.38	9.54	9.67	8.95	7.95
JUL	7.44	9.18	10.92	11.54	9.65	9.90	8.87	7.94
AUG	7.49	8.98	10.76	11.50	9.81	10.01	8.77	7.80
SEP	7.38	8.78	11.02	11.17	9.74	9.93	8.63	7.59
OCT	7.47	8.60	11.53	10.91	9.85	10.15	8.59	7.50
NOV	7.77	8.68	11.68	10.62	9.82	10.04	8.50	7.33
DEC	7.87	8.84	11.58	10.43	9.90	9.92	8.48	7.28

	1987	1988
JAN	7.22	7.12
FEB	7.02	7.11
MAR	6.99	7.13
APR	6.93	7.12
MAY	6.92	7.11
JUN	6.90	7.11
JUL	6.96	7.14
AUG	6.95	7.21
SEP	6.93	7.21
OCT	7.03	7.29
NOV	7.04	
DEC	7.11	

11th District Cost of Funds

	*1978	1979	1980	1981	1982	1983	1984	1985
JAN	6.49	7.25	8.76	10.45	11.95	10.46	10.03	10.22
FEB	7.10	7.92	9.65	11.16	12.34	10.42	10.17	10.16
MAR	6.51	7.42	8.86	10.95	12.14	9.87	9.98	9.98
APR	6.68	7.67	9.82	11.14	12.17	9.81	10.14	9.97
MAY	6.61	7.67	10.41	11.43	12.17	9.63	10.26	9.70
JUN	6.75	7.76	10.08	12.14	12.67	9.82	10.43	9.57
JUL	6.69	7.68	9.67	11.85	12.23	9.68	10.71	9.37
AUG	6.71	7.77	9.39	12.03	11.96	9.97	10.86	9.27
SEP	6.89	7.91	9.29	12.33	11.77	10.00	11.04	9.13
OCT	6.83	7.79	9.11	12.29	11.29	10.00	10.99	9.03
NOV	7.11	8.42	9.52	12.47	11.04	10.03	10.89	9.04
DEC	7.04	8.65	9.63	12.18	11.09	10.19	10.52	8.88

	1986	1987	1988
JAN	8.77	7.40	7.615
FEB	8.96	7.45	7.647
MAR	8.74	7.31	7.509
APR	8.59	7.25	7.519
MAY	8.44	7.22	7.497
JUN	8.37	7.27	7.618
JUL	8.20	7.28	7.593
AUG	8.02	7.28	7.659
SEP	7.90	7.39	7.847
OCT	7.72	7.44	7.828
NOV	7.60	7.56	7.914
DEC	7.51	7.65	

FHLBB Contract Rate

	1973	1974	1975	1976	1977	1978	1979	1980
JAN	7.53	8.47	9.32	9.07	8.84	8.95	10.08	11.78
FEB	7.55	8.53	9.19	9.03	8.80	8.99	10.14	12.30
MAR	7.54	8.47	9.07	8.92	8.76	9.04	10.22	12.56
APR	7.55	8.43	8.92	8.85	8.74	9.14	10.29	13.21
MAY	7.62	8.49	8.85	8.84	8.75	9.17	10.35	13.74
JUN	7.64	8.66	8.86	8.82	8.78	9.27	10.46	12.88
JUL	7.70	8.82	8.89	8.85	8.83	9.41	10.67	12.23
AUG	7.87	8.95	8.95	8.91	8.86	9.55	10.88	11.89
SEP	8.10	9.15	8.93	8.94	8.86	9.62	10.94	12.00
OCT	8.35	9.31	8.97	8.94	8.88	9.68	11.01	12.31
NOV	8.42	9.37	9.09	8.91	8.89	9.74	11.23	12.85
DEC	8.46	9.39	9.09	8.90	8.93	9.85	11.59	13.15

	1981	1982	1983	1984	1985	1986	1987	1988
JAN	13.24	15.37	13.04	11.70	12.09	10.40	9.19	8.92
FEB	13.73	15.22	12.88	11.73	11.90	10.46	8.89	8.84
MAR	13.91	15.07	12.61	11.69	11.72	10.24	8.80	8.84
APR	13.99	15.39	12.42	11.61	11.62	10.00	8.79	8.93
MAY	14.19	15.57	12.36	11.63	11.62	9.80	8.93	8.90
JUN	14.40	15.01	12.21	11.79	11.29	9.83	9.02	8.98
JUL	14.77	14.96	12.18	12.03	11.02	9.88	9.05	8.98
AUG	15.03	15.03	12.25	12.24	10.87	9.88	9.05	8.98
SEP	15.38	14.71	12.38	12.43	10.76	9.71	8.91	9.00
OCT	15.47	14.37	12.19	12.52	10.86	9.59	8.86	8.98
NOV	15.80	13.74	12.11	12.38	10.80	9.48	8.89	9.11
DEC	15.53	13.44	11.94	12.26	10.70	9.29	8.86	9.16

Source: Telerate
*Data not available prior to this date.

Figure 15
Comparable Sales Chart
(For requesting increase in appraised value)

Address of Comparable Properties	Area (Square Feet)	Number of Stories	Number of Rooms	Number of Baths	Type of Heat & Air Conditioning (if any)	Type of Construction	Age	Sales Price	Date of Sale (Month & Year)	Type of Financing	Other Amenities (if necessary list in Remarks)	Number of Fireplaces	Garage or Carport
Subject Property													
Sale #1 (address)													
Sale #2 (address)													
Sale #2 (address)													
REMARKS:													
Subject Property													
Sale #1 (address)													
Sale #2 (address)													
Sale #3 (address)													

Figure 16
Schedule of Real Estate

(To be used for loan processing of an individual with multiple ownership of rental properties)

Address	Mkt. Value	Mrtg. Bal.	Equity	Gross Rent	Mrtg. Pay	Income	Mortgagee Name Loan # & Mailing Address	Subdivision Name & Comments

I certify that the above named subdivisions are not "Contiguous" to each other, except as follows

_____

Figure 17
Should You Refinance That Costly Mortgage?

A rule of thumb is a 2% to 3% lower interest rate makes financing worthwhile. Eliminate guess work by using this formula for a more exact cost savings.

Refinance Worksheet

Present monthly payments .... $_____
*Number of months to pay .... ×_____
    Total payments .... $_____A

Payments at alternative
    lower rate .... $_____
*Number of months to pay............ ×_____
    Total payments .... $_____B

    Difference in total payments
    (A minus B) .... $_____C

Refinance costs:
    Any prepayment penalty .... $_____D
    Closing costs of new mortgage,
       including any "points" .... $_____E
    Added income taxes over term
       of mortgage because of
       reduced deduction from
       lower interest rate .... $_____F

    Total (D plus E plus F) .... $_____G

    Net savings over life
       of mortgage (C minus G) .... $_____

*NOTE: Number of months to pay should be for the period of time you expect to own the property and not the number of months required to retire the loan.

This worksheet can also be used in deciding which new loan is best for your needs.

Comparing an existing loan with an original balance of $60,000, a 30-year term and an interest rate of 12-1/2% interest to a $60,000 loan at 10-1/2% interest for 30 years. We will assume the 10-1/2% loan incurs closing cost of 4%, a discount of 4% and the mortgagor is in a 30% tax bracket. We will also assume that the mortgagor will live in the property for 10 years.

Refinance Worksheet

```
Present monthly payments ........... $  640.35
*Number of months to pay ........... ×    120
    Total payments  ..................................... $ 76,842 A


Payments at alternative
    lower rate  ...................... $  548.84
*Number of months to pay ........... ×    120
    Total payments  ..................................... $ 65,860.80 B


    Difference in total payments
    (A minus B) ...................................... $  10,981.20 C


Refinancing costs:
    Any prepayment penalty .......... $  -0-    D
    Closing costs of new mortgage
      including any "points"  ......... $  4,800   E (8%)
    Added income taxes over term
      of mortgage because of
      reduced deduction from
      lower interest ..................................... $  3,294.36  F


    Total (D plus E plus F) ............................. $  8,094.36  G


    Net savings over life
      of mortgage (C minus G)  ......................... $  2,886.84
```

**Line C × tax bracket = Line F
  e.g., $10,981.20 x 30% = $3,294.36

For information concerning the tax treatment of discount points see question 1.69.

This worksheet can also be used in deciding which new loan is best for your needs.

© 1st Quarter Packet.

Figure 18
FHA One-Time MIP Refund of Unearned Premiums

Factors in this figure are for determining refunds based on an interest rate of 12 %.

Unearned Premium Refund per Thousand Dollars
Term of Loan in Years

Policy Year	15	20	25	30
1	$21.80	$27.70	$34.00	$34.30
2	18.90	24.80	31.60	29.70
3	15.10	20.70	27.30	23.90
4	11.70	16.70	22.50	18.90
5	8.70	13.20	18.00	15.00
6	6.30	10.20	14.10	11.90
7	4.40	7.90	11.00	9.50
8	3.00	6.00	8.50	7.70
9	2.00	4.60	6.70	6.40
10	1.30	3.50	5.30	5.40
11	0.70	2.70	4.30	4.70
12	0.40	2.00	3.50	4.10
13	0.10	1.50	2.90	3.60
14	0.00	1.00	2.30	3.20
15		0.70	1.90	2.80
16		0.20	1.50	2.40
17		0.10	1.20	2.10
18		0.00	0.90	1.80
19			0.60	1.50
20			0.40	1.30
21			0.20	1.00
22			0.10	0.80
23			0.00	0.60
24				0.40
25				0.30
26				0.20
27				0.10
28				0.00
29				
30				

Figure 19
DD 214

2(NA) NOT APPLICABLE

CHARACTER OF SEPARATION	REPORT OF SEPARATION FROM THE ARMED FORCES OF THE UNITED STATES	DEPARTMENT
HONORABLE		ARMY

SEPARATION DATA

1 LAST NAME — FIRST NAME — MIDDLE NAME	2 SERVICE NUMBER	3 GRADE — RATE — RANK AND DATE OF APPOINTMENT	4 COMPONENT AND BRANCH OR CLASS
		PFC(T)28 AUG 53	AUS AMEDS

5 QUALIFICATIONS		6 EFFECTIVE DATE OF SEPARATION	7 TYPE OF SEPARATION
NA		DAY 1 MONTH OCT YEAR 54	REL FR ACT MIL SVC

SPECIALTY NUMBER OR SYMBOL	RELATED CIVILIAN OCCUPATION AND D O T NUMBER
NA	NA

8 REASON AND AUTHORITY FOR SEPARATION	9 PLACE OF SEPARATION
SR 615-360-5 SPN 04 SR 615-363-5 SEC III	CAMP KILMER NEW JERSEY

10 DATE OF BIRTH			11 PLACE OF BIRTH (City and State)	12 DESCRIPTION					
DAY 19	MONTH SEP	YEAR 30	NEW YORK NY	SEX MALE	RACE CAU	COLOR HAIR BROWN	COLOR EYES BLUE	HEIGHT 5'8"	WEIGHT 165

SELECTIVE SERVICE DATA

13 REGISTERED		14 SELECTIVE SERVICE LOCAL BOARD NUMBER (City County State)	15 INDUCTED		
YES X	NO	SELECTIVE SERVICE NUMBER .. #19 BRONX NY(BRONX)	DAY 4	MONTH NOV	YEAR 52

16 ENLISTED IN OR TRANSFERRED TO A RESERVE COMPONENT	COMPONENT AND BRANCH OR CLASS	COGNIZANT DISTRICT OR AREA COMMAND
YES X NO	TRANS ARMY RES AMEDS	NEW YORK MIL DIST

17 MEANS OF ENTRY OTHER THAN BY INDUCTION				18 GRADE — RATE OR RANK AT TIME OF ENTRY INTO ACTIVE SERVICE
ENLISTED NA	REENLISTED	COMMISSIONED	CALLED FROM INACTIVE DUTY	PVT-1

19 DATE AND PLACE OF ENTRY INTO ACTIVE SERVICE			20 HOME ADDRESS AT TIME OF ENTRY INTO ACTIVE SERVICE (St RFD City County and State)
DAY 4	NOV	YEAR 52 PLACE NEW YORK NY	

SERVICE DATA

STATEMENT OF SERVICE FOR PAY PURPOSES

	A YEARS	B MONTHS	C DAYS	25 ENLISTMENT ALLOWANCE PAID ON EXTENSION OF ENLISTMENT, IF ANY			
				DAY	MONTH	YEAR	AMOUNT
21 NET (NA) SERVICE COMPLETED FOR PAY PURPOSES EXCLUDING THIS PERIOD							
22 NET SERVICE COMPLETED FOR PAY PURPOSES THIS PERIOD	1	10	28	NA			
23 OTHER SERVICE (Act of 16 June 1942 as amended) COMPLETED FOR PAY PURPOSES	0	0	0	26 FOREIGN AND/OR SEA SERVICE			
24 TOTAL NET SERVICE COMPLETED FOR PAY PURPOSES	1	10	28	YEARS 0	MONTHS 8	DAYS 0	

27 DECORATIONS MEDALS BADGES COMMENDATIONS CITATIONS AND CAMPAIGN RIBBONS AWARDED OR AUTHORIZED

NATIONAL DEF SVC MEDAL

28 MOST SIGNIFICANT DUTY ASSIGNMENT	29 WOUNDS RECEIVED AS A RESULT OF ACTION WITH ENEMY FORCES (Place and date, if known)
1859 TOKYO GEN DISP 8128 AU	NONE

30 SERVICE SCHOOLS OR COLLEGES, COLLEGE TRAINING COURSES AND/OR POST GRAD COURSES SUCCESSFULLY COMPLETED	DATES (From)	MAJOR COURSES	31 SERVICE TRAINING COURSES SUCCESSFULLY COMPLETED
NONE			NONE

SAMPLE

INSURANCE AND PAY DATA

GOVERNMENT INSURANCE INFORMATION (A) Permanent plan premium must continue to be paid when due or within 31 days thereafter, or insurance will lapse (B) Term insurance not under waiver same as (A) above (C) Term insurance under waiver — premium payment must be resumed within 120 days after separation Forward premiums on NSLI to Veterans Administration District Office having jurisdiction over the area shown in Item 47 Forward premiums on USGLI to Veterans Administration Washington 25 D C (See VA Pamphlet 9-3) When paying premiums give full name, address, Service Number Policy Number(s), Branch of Service, date of separation Contact nearest VA office for information concerning Government Life Insurance

32A KIND & AMT OF INSURANCE & MTHLY PREMIUM	32B ACTIVE SERVICE PRIOR TO 76 APRIL 1951	33 MONTH ALLOTMENT DISCONTINUED	34 MONTH NEXT PREMIUM DUE
NONE INDEMNITY	YES NO X UNKNOWN	NA	NA

35 TOTAL PAYMENT UPON SEPARATION	36 TRAVEL OR MILEAGE ALLOWANCE INCLUDED IN TOTAL PAYMENT	37 DISBURSING OFFICER'S NAME AND SYMBOL NUMBER
NA	NA	NA

AUTHENTICATION

38 REMARKS (Continue on reverse)	39 SIGNATURE OF OFFICER AUTHORIZED TO SIGN
REL FR ACT MIL SVC & TRFD TO ARMY RES TO COMPL 8 YRS SVC UNDER MIL TNG & SV ACT MOP $300.00 BLOOD GROUP "A" NO DAYS LOST UNDER SEC 6(a)APP 2b MCM 1951	

PERSONAL DATA

40 V A BENEFITS PREVIOUSLY APPLIED FOR (Specify type) COMPENSATION PENSION INSURANCE BENEFITS ETC				CLAIM NUMBER
NA				

41 DATES OF LAST CIVILIAN EMPLOYMENT		42 MAIN CIVILIAN OCCUPATION	43 NAME AND ADDRESS OF LAST CIVILIAN EMPLOYER
FROM NA	TO NA	NONE 2-99.999	NONE

44 UNITED STATES CITIZEN	45 MARITAL STATUS	46 NON SERVICE EDUCATION (Years successfully completed)				MAJOR COURSE OR FIELD
YES X NO	MARRIED	GRAM MAR 8	HIGH SCHOOL 4	COL LEGE 4	DEGREE(S) BS	PHARMACY

47 PERMANENT ADDRESS FOR MAILING PURPOSES AFTER SEPARATION (St RFD City County and State)	48 SIGNATURE OF PERSON BEING SEPARATED

DD FORM 214 EDITION OF 1 JAN 50 IS OBSOLETE — INDIVIDUAL'S COPY (TO BE DELIVERED TO THE INDIVIDUAL BEING SEPARATED)

Figure 20

Certificate of Eligibility (Front)

Veterans Administration

9419365

Certificate of Eligibility

FOR LOAN GUARANTY BENEFITS

NAME OF VETERAN *(First, Middle, Last)*

SERVICE SERIAL NUMBER/SOCIAL SECURITY NUMBER

ENTITLEMENT CODE

4

BRANCH OF SERVICE

Air Force

DATE OF BIRTH

6/12/54

IS ELIGIBLE FOR THE BENEFITS OF CHAPTER 37, TITLE 38, U.S. CODE, AND HAS THE AMOUNT OF ENTITLEMENT SHOWN AS AVAILABLE ON THE REVERSE, SUBJECT TO THE STATEMENT BELOW, IF CHECKED.

☐ Valid unless discharged or released subsequent to date of this certificate. A certification of continuous active duty as of date of note required.

ADMINISTRATOR OF VETERANS AFFAIRS

(Signature of Authorized Agent)

NASHVILLE, TN. 37203

(Issuing Office)

FEB 19 1986

(Date Issued)

Figure 20 (Continued)
Certificate of Eligibility (Back)

DO NOT RITE ON THIS SIDE—FOR VA USE ...Y

LOAN NUMBER (include amount if direct loan)	ENTITLEMENT		DATE AND INITIALS OF VA AGENT
	USED	AVAILABLE	
	1810	OTHER	
LH-34358-TN	27,500		27,500	NONE	3-26-86 ℒ.

SAMPLE

NOTE: The figure shown as available entitlement represents the portion of a loan which may be guaranteed or insured by VA to a lender. For information about maximum loan amounts, see VA Pamphlets 26-4 and 26-71-1, or contact the nearest VA office for further information.

Available entitlement is subject to reduction if VA incurs actual liability or loss on the loan(s), if any, listed below, obtained by the veteran with the assistance of loan benefits derived from military service in WW II or the Korean conflict.

		REDUCED		
OUTSTANDING LOAN NUMBER(S)	DATE	INITIALS OF VA AGENT	ITEM	DATE	INITIALS OF VA AGENT

VA FORM **26-8320**
DEC 1980

SUPERSEDES VA FORM 26-8320, FEB 1979, WHICH WILL NOT BE USED.

Figure 21
Residential Loan Application (Front)

Residential Loan Application   **CONVENTIONAL**

| MORTGAGE APPLIED FOR | ☐ Conventional · ☐ FHA ☐ VA | Amount $ | Interest Rate % | No. of Months | Monthly Payment Principal & Interest $ | Escrow/Impounds (to be collected monthly) [☐ Taxes ☐ Hazard Ins ☐ Mtg Ins] |

Prepayment Option

Subject Property

| Property Street Address | | City | | County | State | Zip | No Units |

Legal Description (Attach description if necessary)   Year Built

Purpose of Loan ☐ Purchase ☐ Construction-Permanent ☐ Construction ☐ Refinance ☐ Other (Explain)

| Complete this line if Construction-Permanent or Construction Loan | Lot Value Data | Original Cost | Present Value (a) | Cost of Imps (b) | Total (a + b) | ENTER TOTAL AS PURCHASE PRICE IN DETAILS OF PURCHASE |
| Year Acquired | $ | $ | $ | $ | |

Complete this line if a Refinance Loan   Purpose of Refinance   Describe Improvements [ ] made [ ] to be made

| Year Acquired | Original Cost | Amt Existing Liens | | | Cost $ |
| | $ | $ | | | |

Title Will Be Held In What Name(s)   Manner In Which Title Will Be Held

Source of Down Payment and Settlement Charges

This application is designed to be completed by the borrower(s) with the lender's assistance. The Co-Borrower Section and all other Co-Borrower questions must be completed and the appropriate box(es) checked if ☐ another person will be jointly obligated with the Borrower on the loan, or ☐ the Borrower is relying on income from alimony, child support or separate maintenance or on the income or assets of another person as a basis for repayment of the loan, or ☐ the Borrower is married and resides, or the property is located, in a community property state.

Borrower				**Co-Borrower**		
Name		Age	School Yrs	Name		Age	School Yrs

Present Address	No. Years ___ ☐ Own ☐ Rent	Present Address	No. Years ___ ☐ Own ☐ Rent
Street		Street	
City/State/Zip		City/State/Zip	

Former address if less than 2 years at present address   Former address if less than 2 years at present address

Street		Street	
City/State/Zip		City/State/Zip	
Years at former address ☐ Own ☐ Rent		Years at former address ☐ Own ☐ Rent	

| Marital Status: ☐ Married ☐ Separated ☐ Unmarried (incl single, divorced, widowed) | DEPENDENTS OTHER THAN LISTED BY CO BORROWER NO / AGES | Marital Status: ☐ Married ☐ Separated ☐ Unmarried (incl single, divorced, widowed) | DEPENDENTS OTHER THAN LISTED BY BORROWER NO / AGES |

| Name and Address of Employer | Years employed in this line of work or profession? ___ years   Years on this job ___ ☐ Self Employed* | Name and Address of Employer | Years employed in this line of work or profession? ___ years   Years on this job ___ ☐ Self Employed* |

| Position/Title | Type of Business | Position/Title | Type of Business |

| Social Security Number *** | Home Phone | Business Phone | Social Security Number *** | Home Phone | Business Phone |

Gross Monthly Income				**Monthly Housing Expense**		**Details of Purchase**	
Item	Borrower	Co-Borrower	Total		Present	Proposed	Do Not Complete If Refinance
Base Empl Income	$	$	$	First Mortgage (P&I)		$	a Purchase Price $
Overtime				Other Financing (P&I)			b Total Closing Costs (Est.)
Bonuses				Hazard Insurance			c Prepaid Escrows (Est.)
Commissions				Real Estate Taxes			d Total (a + b + c) $
Dividends/Interest				Mortgage Insurance			e Amount This Mortgage ( )
Net Rental Income				Homeowner Assn Dues			f Other Financing ( )
Other† (Before completing, see notice under Describe Other Income below)				Other			g Other Equity ( )
				Total Monthly Pmt	$	$	h Amount of Cash Deposit ( )
				Utilities			i Closing Costs Paid by Seller ( )
Total	$	$	$	Total	$	$	j Cash Reqd For Closing (Est.) $

Describe Other Income

◇ B—Borrower   C—Co-Borrower

NOTICE: † Alimony, child support, or separate maintenance income need not be revealed if the Borrower or Co-Borrower does not choose to have it considered as a basis for repaying this loan

| | | Monthly Amount |
| | | $ |

If Employed In Current Position For Less Than Two Years, Complete the Following

B/C	Previous Employer/School	City/State	Type of Business	Position/Title	Dates From/To	Monthly Income
						$

These Questions Apply To Both Borrower and Co-Borrower

If a "yes" answer is given to a question in this column, please explain on an attached sheet.

	Borrower Yes or No	Co-Borrower Yes or No
Are there any outstanding judgments against you?	___	___
Have you been declared bankrupt within the past 7 years?	___	___
Have you had property foreclosed upon or given title or deed in lieu thereof in the last 7 years?	___	___
Are you a party to a law suit?	___	___
Are you obligated to pay alimony, child support, or separate maintenance?	___	___
Is any part of the down payment borrowed?	___	___
Are you a co-maker or endorser on a note?	___	___

	Borrower Yes or No	Co-Borrower Yes or No
Are you a US citizen?	___	___
If "no", are you a resident alien?	___	___
If "no", are you a non-resident alien?	___	___
Explain Other Financing or Other Equity (if any)		

*FHLMC/FNMA require business credit report, signed Federal Income Tax returns for last two years, and, if available, audited Profit and Loss Statement plus balance sheet for same period
**All Present Monthly Housing Expenses of Borrower and Co-Borrower should be listed on a combined base
***Optional for FHLMC

FHLMC 65 Rev 10/86   Fannie Mae Form 1003 Rev 10/86

Figure 21 (Continued)
Residential Loan Application (Back)

This Statement and any applicable supporting schedules may be completed jointly by both married and unmarried co-borrowers if their assets and liabilities are sufficiently joined so that the Statement can be meaningfully and fairly presented on a combined basis, otherwise separate Statements and Schedules are required (FHLMC 65A/FNMA 1003A). If the co-borrower section was completed about a spouse, this statement and supporting schedules must be completed about that spouse also.

☐ Completed Jointly ☐ Not Completed Jointly

Assets	Liabilities and Pledged Assets

Indicate by (*) those liabilities or pledged assets which will be satisfied upon sale of real estate owned or upon refinancing of subject property.

Description	Cash or Market Value	Creditors Name Address and Account Number	Acct Name if Not Borrower's	Mo. Pmt and Mos Left to Pay	Unpaid Balance
Cash Deposit Toward Purchase Held By	$	Installment Debts (Include revolving charge accounts)		$ Pmt/Mos	$
Checking and Savings Accounts (Show Name of Institutions (Account Numbers) Bank S & L or Credit Union					
Addr					
City					
Acct No					
Bank S & L or Credit Union					
Addr					
City					
Acct No					
Bank S & L or Credit Union					
Addr					
City		Other Debts Including Stock Pledges			
Acct No					
Stocks and Bonds (No./Description)		Real Estate Loans			
Life Insurance Net Cash Value					
Face Amount $					
Subtotal Liquid Assets		Automobile Loans			
Real Estate Owned (Enter Market Value from Schedule of Real Estate Owned)					
Vested Interest in Retirement Fund					
Net Worth of Business Owned (ATTACH FINANCIAL STATEMENT)					
Automobiles Owned (Make and Year)					
Furniture and Personal Property		Alimony/Child Support/Separate Maintenance Payments Owed to			
Other Assets (Itemize)		Total Monthly Payments		$	
Total Assets	$	Net Worth (A minus B) $		Total Liabilities	$

SCHEDULE OF REAL ESTATE OWNED (If Additional Properties Owned Attach Separate Sheet)

Address of Property (Indicate S if Sold, PS if Pending Sale or R if Rental being held for income)	Type of Property	Present Market Value	Amount of Mortgages & Liens	Gross Rental Income	Mortgage Payments	Taxes Ins Maintenance and Misc	Net Rental Income
		$	$	$	$	$	$
TOTALS →		$	$	$	$	$	$

List Previous Credit References

B—Borrower C—Co-Borrower	Creditor's Name and Address	Account Number	Purpose	Highest Balance	Date Paid
				$	

List any additional names under which credit has previously been received

AGREEMENT The undersigned applies for the loan indicated in this application to be secured by a first mortgage or deed of trust on the property described herein, and represents that the property will not be used for any illegal or restricted purpose, and that all statements made in this application are true and are made for the purpose of obtaining the loan. Verification may be obtained from any source named in this application. The original or a copy of this application will be retained by the lender, even if the loan is not granted. The undersigned ☐ intend or ☐ do not intend to occupy the property as their primary residence. I/we fully understand that it is a federal crime punishable by fine or imprisonment, or both, to knowingly make false statements concerning any of the above facts as applicable under the provisions of Title 18, United States Code, Section 1014.

Borrower's Signature _____ Date _____   Co-Borrower's Signature _____ Date _____

Information for Government Monitoring Purposes

The following information is requested by the Federal Government for certain types of loans related to a dwelling, in order to monitor the lender's compliance with equal credit opportunity and fair housing laws. You are not required to furnish this information, but are encouraged to do so. The law provides that a lender may neither discriminate on the basis of this information, nor on whether you choose to furnish it. However, if you choose not to furnish it, under Federal regulations this lender is required to note race and sex on the basis of visual observation or surname. If you do not wish to furnish the above information, please check the box below. (Lender must review the above material to assure that the disclosures satisfy all requirements to which the Lender is subject under applicable state law for the particular type of loan applied for.)

Borrower: ☐ I do not wish to furnish this information
Race/National Origin:
American Indian, Alaskan Native ☐   Asian Pacific Islander ☐
Black ☐   Hispanic ☐   White ☐
Other (specify) _____
Sex: Female ☐   Male ☐

Co-Borrower: ☐ I do not wish to furnish this information
Race/National Origin:
American Indian, Alaskan Native ☐   Asian Pacific Islander ☐
Black ☐   Hispanic ☐   White ☐
Other (specify) _____
Sex: Female ☐   Male ☐

To Be Completed by Interviewer

This application was taken by:
☐ face to face interview
☐ by mail
☐ by telephone

Interviewer _____
Name of Interviewer's Employer _____
Interviewer's Phone Number _____
Address of Interviewer's Employer _____

FHLMC Form 65 Rev. 10/86   REVERSE   Fannie Mae Form 1003 Rev. 10/86

Figure 22
Request for Verification of Employment

Form Approved
OMB No. 63R-1062

PRIVACY ACT NOTICE: This information is to be used by the agency collecting it in determining whether you qualify as a prospective mortgagor under its program. It will not be disclosed outside the agency without your consent except to your employer(s) for verification of employment and as required and permitted by law. You do not have to give us this information, but if you do not your application for approval as a prospective mortgagor may be delayed or rejected. The information requested in this form is authorized by Title 38, U.S.C., Chapter 37 (If VA); by 12 U.S.C.,Section 1701 et.seq. (If HUD/FHA) and Title 42 U.S.C., 1471 et.seq., or U.S.C., 1921 et.seq. (If U.S.D.A. FmHA).	VETERANS ADMINISTRATION, U.S.D.A. FARMERS HOME ADMINISTRATION, AND U.S.DEPARTMENT OF HOUSING AND URBAN DEVELOPMENT HOUSING - FEDERAL HOUSING COMMISSIONER **REQUEST FOR VERIFICATION OF EMPLOYMENT**

INSTRUCTIONS	LENDER: Complete Items 1 through 7. Have the applicant complete item 8. Forward the completed form directly to the employer named in Item 1.	EMPLOYER: Complete either Parts II and IV or Parts III and IV. Return form directly to Lender named in Item 2 of Part I.

PART I - REQUEST

1. TO: (Name and Address of Employer)	2. FROM: (Name and Address of Lender)	
3. I certify that this verification has been sent directly to the employer and has not passed through the hands of the applicant or any other interested party. (Signature of Lender)	4. TITLE OF LENDER	5. DATE
		6. FHA,VA, or FmHA NUMBER
7. NAME AND ADDRESS OF APPLICANT	I have applied for a mortgage loan and stated that I am/was employed by you. My signature in the block below authorizes verification of my employment information.	
	8. EMPLOYEE'S IDENTIFICATION	
	SIGNATURE OF APPLICANT	

PART II - VERIFICATION OF PRESENT EMPLOYMENT

EMPLOYMENT DATA	PAY DATA				
9. APPLICANT'S DATE OF EMPLOYMENT	12A. BASE PAY ☐ ANNUAL ☐ HOURLY ☐ MONTHLY ☐ WEEKLY ☐ OTHER (Specify)			FOR MILITARY PERSONNEL ONLY	
10. PRESENT POSITION				Type	Monthly Amount
				BASE PAY	$
11. PROBABILITY OF CONTINUED EMPLOYMENT				RATIONS	$
	12B. EARNINGS			FLIGHT OR HAZARD	$
	Type	Year to Date	Past Year		
	BASE PAY			CLOTHING	$
13. IF OVERTIME OR BONUS IS APPLICABLE, IS ITS CONTINUANCE LIKELY? OVERTIME ☐ Yes ☐ No BONUS ☐ Yes ☐ No	OVERTIME	$	$	QUARTERS	$
	COMMISSIONS	$	$	PRO PAY	$
	BONUS	$	$	OVERSEAS OR COMBAT	$
14. REMARKS (If paid hourly, please indicate average hours worked each week during current and past year)					

PART III - VERIFICATION OF PREVIOUS EMPLOYMENT

15. DATES OF EMPLOYMENT	16.SALARY/WAGE AT TERMINATION PER (YEAR) (MONTH) (WEEK)			
	BASE	OVERTIME	COMMISSIONS	BONUS
17. REASONS FOR LEAVING	18. POSITION HELD			

PART IV - CERTIFICATION

"Federal statutes provide severe penalties for any fraud, intentional misrepresentation, or criminal connivance or conspiracy purposed to influence the issuance of any guaranty or insurance by the VA Administrator, the HUD/FHA Commissioner, or the USDA Farmers Home Administrator."

19. SIGNATURE	20. TITLE OF EMPLOYER	21. DATE

Previous Editions are Obsolete

HUD-92004-g, vA-26-8497; FmHA-410-5 (12-79)

RETURN DIRECTLY TO SENDER

Figure 23
Request for Verification of Deposit

Form Approved
OMB No. 63R-1062

VETERANS ADMINISTRATION AND U.S. DEPARTMENT OF HOUSING AND URBAN DEVELOPMENT
HUD COMMUNITY PLANNING AND DEVELOPMENT
HUD HOUSING - FEDERAL HOUSING COMMISSIONER

REQUEST FOR VERIFICATION OF DEPOSIT

PRIVACY ACT NOTICE STATEMENT - This information is to be used by the agency collecting it in determining whether you qualify as a prospective mortgagor for mortgage insurance or guaranty or as a borrower for a rehabilitation loan under the agency's program. It will not be disclosed outside the agency without your consent except to financial institutions for verification of your deposits and as required and permitted by law. You do not have to give us this information, but, if you do not, your application for approval as a prospective mortgagor for mortgage insurance or guaranty or as a borrower for a rehabilitation loan may be delayed or rejected. This information request is authorized by Title 38, U.S.C., Chapter 37 (if VA); by 12 U.S.C., Section 1701 et-seq., (if HUD/FHA); and by 42 U.S.C., Section 1452b (if HUD/CPD).

INSTRUCTIONS

LENDER OR LOCAL PROCESSING AGENCY: Complete Items 1 through 8. Have applicant(s) complete Item 9. Forward directly to the Depository named in Item 1. DEPOSITORY: Please complete Items 10 through 15 and return DIRECTLY to Lender or Local Processing Agency named in Item 2.

PART I - REQUEST

1. TO (Name and Address of Depository)	2. FROM (Name and Address of Lender or Local Processing Agency)

I certify that this verification has been sent directly to the bank or depository and has not passed through the hands of the applicant or any other party.

3. Signature of Lender or Official of Local Processing Agency	4. Title	5. Date	6. Lender's Number (Optional)

7. INFORMATION TO BE VERIFIED:

Type of Account and/or Loan	Account/Loan in Name of	Account/Loan Number	Balance
			$
			$
			$
			$

TO DEPOSITORY: I have applied for mortgage insurance or guaranty or for a rehabilitation loan and stated that the balance on deposit and/or outstanding loans with you are as shown above. You are authorized to verify this information and to supply the lender or the local processing agency identified above with the information requested in Items 10 through 12. Your response is solely a matter of courtesy for which no responsibility is attached to your institution or any of your officers.

8. NAME AND ADDRESS OF APPLICANT(S)	9. SIGNATURE OF APPLICANT(S)

TO BE COMPLETED BY DEPOSITORY

PART II - VERIFICATION OF DEPOSITORY

10. DEPOSIT ACCOUNTS OF APPLICANT(S)

Type of Account	Account Number	Current Balance	Average Balance for Previous Two Months	Date Opened
		$	$	
		$	$	
		$	$	
		$	$	

11. LOANS OUTSTANDING TO APPLICANT(S)

Loan Number	Date of Loan	Original Amount	Current Balance	Installments (Monthly/Quarterly)	Secured by	Number of Late Payments within Last 12 Months
		$	$	$ per		
		$	$	$ per		
		$	$	$ per		

12. ADDITIONAL INFORMATION WHICH MAY BE OF ASSISTANCE IN DETERMINATION OF CREDIT WORTHINESS: Please include information on loans paid-in-full as in Item 11 above)

13. Signature of Depository Official	14. Title	15. Date

The confidentiality of the information you have furnished will be preserved except where disclosure of this information is required by applicable law. The completed form is to be transmitted directly to the lender or local processing agency and is not to be transmitted through the applicant or any other party.

Replaces Form FHA-2004-F, which is Obsolete   ☆U.S. Government Printing Office: 1981—341-466/4254   VA 26-8497a/HUD-92004-F-8234 (7-80)

Figure 24
HUD-1 Uniform Settlement Statement (Front)

A. Settlement Statement

U.S. Department of Housing and Urban Development

OMB No. 2502-0265 (Exp. 12-31-86)

B. Type of Loan

1. ☑ FHA 2. ☐ FmHA 3. ☐ Conv. Unins.   4. ☐ VA   5. ☐ Conv. Ins.

6. File Number	7. Loan Number	8. Mortgage Insurance Case Number

C. Note: This form is furnished to give you a statement of actual settlement costs. Amounts paid to and by the settlement agent are shown. Items marked "(p.o.c.)" were paid outside the closing; they are shown here for informational purposes and are not included in the totals.

D. Name and Address of Borrower	E. Name and Address of Seller	F. Name and Address of Lender

G. Property Location	H. Settlement Agent	
	Place of Settlement	I. Settlement Date

J. Summary of Borrower's Transaction		K. Summary of Seller's Transaction	
100. Gross Amount Due From Borrower		**400. Gross Amount Due To Seller**	
101. Contract sales price		401. Contract sales price	
102. Personal property		402. Personal property	
103. Settlement charges to borrower (line 1400)		403.	
104.		404.	
105.		405.	
Adjustments for items paid by seller in advance		**Adjustments for items paid by seller in advance**	
106. City/town taxes to		406. City/town taxes to	
107. County taxes to		407. County taxes to	
108. Assessments to		408. Assessments to	
109.		409.	
110.		410.	
111.		411.	
112.		412.	
120. Gross Amount Due From Borrower		**420. Gross Amount Due To Seller**	
200. Amounts Paid By Or in Behalf Of Borrower		**500. Reductions In Amount Due To Seller**	
201. Deposit or earnest money		501. Excess deposit (see instructions)	
202. Principal amount of new loan(s)		502. Settlement charges to seller (line 1400)	
203. Existing loan(s) taken subject to		503. Existing loan(s) taken subject to	
204.		504. Payoff of first mortgage loan	
205.		505. Payoff of second mortgage loan	
206.		506.	
207.		507.	
208.		508.	
209.		509.	
Adjustments for items unpaid by seller		**Adjustment for items unpaid by seller**	
210. City/town taxes to		510. City/town taxes to	
211. County taxes to		511. County taxes to	
212. Assessments to		512. Assessments to	
213.		513.	
214.		514.	
215.		515.	
216.		516.	
217.		517.	
218.		518.	
219.		519.	
220. Total Paid By/For Borrower		**520. Total Reduction Amount Due Seller**	
300. Cash At Settlement From/To Borrower		**600. Cash At Settlement To/From Seller**	
301. Gross Amount due from borrower (line 120)		601. Gross amount due to seller (line 420)	
302. Less amounts paid by/for borrower (line 220)	( )	602. Less reductions in amt. due seller (line 520)	( )
303. Cash ☐ From ☐ To Borrower		603. Cash ☐ To ☐ From Seller	

Principal & Interest: $_____
1/12 City Taxes: _____
1/12 County Taxes: _____
1/12 Hazard Insurance: _____
1/12 Mortgage Insurance: _____
1/12 Flood Insurance: _____
Adjustment: _____
_____
Total Monthly Payment: $_____

We acknowledge that the tax prorations contained herein are made in accordance with the best information available at the time of closing and if the actual taxes differ, the parties hereto agree to adjust the prorations between themselves at the time of receipt of the actual bills.

Previous Edition Is Obsolete

HUD-1 (3-86)
RESPA, HB 4305.2

Figure 24 (Continued)
HUD-1 Uniform Settlement Statement (Back)

L. Settlement Charges

700. Total Sales/Broker's Commission based on price $ @ % =	Paid From Borrower's Funds at Settlement	Paid From Seller's Funds at Settlement
Division of Commission (line 700) as follows:		
701. $ to		
702. $ to		
703. Commission paid at Settlement		
704.		
800. Items Payable In Connection With Loan		
801. Loan Origination Fee %		
802. Loan Discount %		
803. Appraisal Fee to		
804. Credit Report to		
805. Lender's Inspection Fee		
806. Mortgage Insurance Application Fee to		
807. Assumption Fee		
808.		
809.		
810.		
811.		
900. Items Required By Lender To Be Paid In Advance		
901. Interest from to @ $		
902. Mortgage Insurance Premium for months to		
903. Hazard Insurance Premium for years to		
904. years to		
905.		
1000. Reserves Deposited With Lender		
1001. Hazard Insurance months @ $ per month		
1002. Mortgage Insurance months @ $ per month		
1003. City property taxes months @ $ per month		
1004. County property taxes months @ $ per month		
1005. Annual assessments months @ $ per month		
1006. months @ $ per month		
1007. months @ $ per month		
1008. months @ $ per month		
1100. Title Charges		
1101. Settlement or closing fee to		
1102. Abstract or title search to		
1103. Title examination to		
1104. Title insurance binder to		
1105. Document preparation to		
1106. Notary fees to		
1107. Attorney's fees to		
(includes above items numbers:)		
1108. Title Insurance to		
(includes above items numbers:)		
1109. Lender's coverage $		
1110. Owner's coverage $		
1111.		
1112.		
1113.		
1200. Government Recording andd Transfer Charges		
1201. Recording fees: Deed $; Mortgage $; Releases $		
1202. City/county tax/stamps: Deed $; Mortgage $		
1203. State tax/stamps: Deed $; Mortgage $		
1204.		
1205.		
1300. Additional Settlement Charges		
1301. Survey to		
1302. Pest inspection to		
1303.		
1304.		
1305.		
1400. Total Settlement Charges (enter on lines 103, Section J and 502, Section K)		

I have carefully reviewed the HUD-1 Settlement Statement and to the best of my knowledge and belief, it is a true and accurate statement of all receipts and disbursements made on my account or by me in this transaction. I further certify that I have received a copy of HUD-1 Settlement Statement.

_____   _____

Borrowers   Sellers

The HUD-1 Settlement Statement which I have prepared is a true and accurate account of this transaction. I have caused or will cause the funds to be disbursed in accordance with this statement.

_____   _____

Settlement Agent   Date

WARNING: It is a crime to knowingly make false statements to the United States on this or any other similar form. Penalties upon conviction can include a fine or imprisonment. For details see: Title 18 U.S. Code Section 1001 and Section 1010

Figure 25
Perpetual Calendar

Select the desired year from the table below.
The number shown with each year tells you the calendar to use for that year.

Year		Year		Year		Year		Year		Year		Year		Year		Year	
1801	5	1824	12	1847	6	1870	6	1893	7	1916	14	1939	1	1962	2	1985	3
1802	6	1825	7	1848	14	1871	1	1894	1	1917	2	1940	9	1963	3	1986	4
1803	7	1826	1	1849	1	1872	9	1895	3	1918	3	1941	3	1964	11	1987	5
1804	8	1827	2	1850	2	1873	4	1896	11	1919	4	1942	4	1965	6	1988	13
1805	3	1828	10	1851	3	1874	5	1897	6	1920	12	1943	5	1966	7	1989	1
1806	4	1829	5	1852	12	1875	6	1898	7	1921	7	1944	14	1967	1	1990	2
1807	5	1830	6	1853	7	1876	14	1899	14	1922	1	1945	2	1968	9	1991	3
1808	13	1831	7	1854	1	1877	1	1900	2	1923	2	1946	3	1969	4	1992	11
1809	1	1832	8	1855	2	1878	3	1901	3	1924	10	1947	4	1970	5	1993	6
1810	2	1833	3	1856	10	1879	10	1902	4	1925	5	1948	12	1971	6	1994	7
1811	3	1834	4	1857	5	1880	12	1903	5	1926	6	1949	7	1972	14	1995	1
1812	11	1835	5	1858	6	1881	7	1904	13	1927	7	1950	1	1973	2	1996	9
1813	6	1836	13	1859	7	1882	1	1905	1	1928	8	1951	2	1974	3	1997	4
1814	7	1837	1	1860	8	1883	3	1906	2	1929	3	1952	10	1975	10	1998	5
1815	1	1838	2	1861	3	1884	10	1907	3	1930	4	1953	5	1976	5	1999	6
1816	9	1839	3	1862	4	1885	5	1908	11	1931	11	1954	6	1977	7	2000	14
1817	4	1840	11	1863	5	1886	6	1909	6	1932	6	1955	7	1978	8		
1818	5	1841	6	1864	6	1887	7	1910	7	1933	7	1956	8	1979	2		
1819	6	1842	7	1865	7	1888	8	1911	1	1934	1	1957	3	1980	10		
1820	14	1843	1	1866	1	1889	3	1912	9	1935	9	1958	11	1981	5		
1821	2	1844	4	1867	2	1890	4	1913	4	1936	4	1959	6	1982	6		
1822	3	1845	4	1868	14	1891	5	1914	5	1937	5	1960	7	1983	7		
1823	4	1846	5	1869	5	1892	6	1915	13	1938	6	1961	1	1984	1		

Figure 25 (Continued)
Perpetual Calendar

Figure 25 (Continued)
Perpetual Calendar

Figure 26
Important Dates
1989-1990-1991

Holiday	1989	1990	1991
New Year's Day	Sun/Jan 1	Mon/Jan 1	Tue/Jan 1
Martin Luther King, Jr. Day	Mon/Jan 16	Mon/Jan 15	Mon/Jan 21
Lincoln's Birthday	Sun/Feb 12	Mon/Feb 12	Tue/Feb 12
Valentine's Day	Tue/Feb 14	Wed/Feb 14	Thu/Feb 14
Washington's Birthday (Observed)	Mon/Feb 20	Mon/Feb 19	Mon/Feb 18
Ash Wednesday	Wed/Feb 8	Wed/ Feb 28	Wed/ Feb 13
Washington's Birthday	Wed/Feb 22	Thu/Feb 22	Fri/Feb 22
St. Patrick's Day	Fri/Mar 17	Sat/Mar 17	Sun/Mar 17
Palm Sunday	Sun/Mar 19	Sun/Apr 8	Sun/Mar 24
Good Friday	Fri/Mar 24	Fri/Apr 13	Fri/Mar 29
Passover	Thu/Apr 20	Tue/Apr 10	Sat/Mar 30
Easter Sunday	Sun/Mar 26	Sun/Apr 15	Sun/Mar 31
Mother's Day	Sun/May 14	Sun/May 13	Sun/May 12
Armed Forces Day	Sat/May 20	Sat/May 19	Sat/May 18
Victoria Day (Canada)	Mon/May 22	Mon/May 21	Mon/May 20
Memorial Day (Observed)	Mon/May 29	Mon/May 28	Mon/May 27
Memorial Day	Tue/May 30	Wed/May 30	Thu/May 30
Flag Day	Wed/Jun 14	Thu/Jun 14	Fri/Jun 14
Father's Day	Sun/Jun 18	Sun/ Jun 17	Sun/Jun 16
Canada Day (Canada)	Sat/Jul 1	Sun/Jul 1	Mon/Jul 1
Independence Day	Tue/Jul 4	Wed/July 4	Thu/Jul 4
Labor Day	Mon/Sep 4	Mon/Sep 3	Mon/Sep 2
Rosh Hashanah	Sat/Sep 30	Thu/Sep 20	Mon/Sep 9
Yom Kippur	Mon/Oct 9	Sat/Sep 29	Wed/ Sep 18
Columbus Day (Observed)	Mon/Oct 9	Mon/Oct 8	Mon/Oct 14
Thanksgiving Day (Canada)	Mon/Oct 9	Mon/Oct 8	Mon/Oct 14
Columbus Day	Thu/Oct 12	Fri/Oct 12	Sat/Oct 12
United Nations Day	Tue/Oct 24	Wed/Oct 24	Thu/Oct 24
Halloween	Tue/Oct 31	Wed/ Oct 31	Thu/Oct 31
Election Day	Tue/Nov 7	Tue/Nov 6	Tue/Nov 5
Veterans Day	Sat/Nov 11	Sun/Nov 11	Mon/Nov 11
Thanksgiving Day	Thu/Nov 23	Thu/ Nov 22	Thu/Nov 28
Hanukkah	Sat/Dec 23	Wed/Dec 12	Mon/Dec 2
Christmas Day	Mon/Dec 25	Tue/Dec 25	Wed/Dec 25

Figure 27
"Value" Can Be in the Eyes of the Beholder

READER SERVICE PROGRAM (RSP™)

Now from Mortgage Techniques, the company that brought you one of the most unique and informative books on real estate mortgages, comes a new Reader Service Program that will ensure your book as being the authority for FHA, VA and Conventional Loans.

Here's what we have to offer—*The Mortgage Manual* has been nationally acclaimed as one of the best real estate reference books available. Now there is a service to keep this truly remarkable book on a current and completely up-to-date status.

For just $15.95* per year you can subscribe to a service that will bring you the latest changes or additions to the various loan programs. This information will come in the form of stick-on replacement pages that can be placed in your notes section (the section you are currently in) or over the pages affected by recent changes. This method is similar to that used by a leading encyclopedia company. New editions will contain the changes or additions in the text, but there is no assurance as to printing dates for new editions as these dates will be governed completely by supply and demand. We think you'll agree that our Reader Service Program is an economical way to keep this truly wonderful book completely updated.

Rules that govern the Reader Service Program are as follows:

1. Membership is available for $15.95*. Each member will receive four up-dates for a single membership.
2. The obligation of RSP™ is to update *The Mortgage Manual.* Changes in the industry that affect answers to the questions in the book are the primary subject mattere covered by the updates.
3. New information that does not affect the answers in the book will be furnished as deemed feasible by Mortgage Techniques.
4. RSP™ members have the right to order duplicate up-date pages for $3.00* per package, plus a one-time handling fee of $2.50*.

The procedure for ordering duplicate updates is to simply wait and see what we have to offer in our updates and then place your order according to your need. If you think our news is necessary for each book you have purchased, just simply drop us a line with a check for the appropriate amount.

With the "Reader Service" (RSP™) program, your book should have a lifetime of 2 to 3 years. Not a bad investment when you compare the cost to the frequency of your use of the product which some of our customers claim to be several times each day.

To order, simply write to Mortgage Techniques, P.O. Box 17214, Memphis, TN 38187-0214.

Lenders who have purchased bulk orders of this book and have used them as gifts for customers should not overlook the opportunity of providing updates for those customers.

*Prices are subject to change without notice.

READER SERVICE PROGRAM

READER SERVICE PROGRAM

READER SERVICE PROGRAM

READER SERVICE PROGRAM

READER SERVICE PROGRAM

ACRONYMS

The reader should check the glossary for any definitions associated with these acronyms.

AACI—Accredited Appraiser Canadian Institute
AAE—Accredited Assessment Evaluator
ABA—American Bar Association
AC—Alternating Current, also Acre
A/C—Air Conditioning
ACC—Annual Contributions Contract
ACRS—Accelerated Cost Recovery Systems
ADT—Average Daily Traffic
AFA—Association of Federal Appraisers
AFM—Accredited Farm Manager
AGC—Associated General Contractors of America
AHS—Annual Housing Survey
AIA—American Institute of Architects
AIC—Appraisal Institute of Canada
AICPA—American Institute of Certified Public Accountants
AIHC—American Institute of Housing Consultants
AIP—American Institute of Planners
AIR—American Industrial Real Estate Association
AIREA—American Institute of Real Estate Appraisers
AITD—All-Inclusive Trust Deed
aka—Also known as
A/L—Assignment of Lease
ALDA—American Land Development Association

ALTA—American Land Title Association
A/M—Assignment of Mortgage
AMA—Affirmative Marketing Agreement
AMI—Alternative Mortgage Instrument
AML—Adjustable (or Alternative) Mortgage Loan. Refer to ARM
AMMINET—Automatic Mortgage Market Information Network.
AMO—Accredited Management Organization
AMPO—Amount to make the project operational
AMREX—American Real Estate Exchange
ANSI—American National Standards Institute
AOMA—Apartment Owners and Managers Association of America
APA—American Planning Association
APR—Annual percentage rate
ARC Accelerated remittance cycle
AREUEA—American Real Estate and Urban Economics Association
ARM—Adjustable Rate Mortgage
ARPS—Adjustable rate preferred stock
ARWA—American Right of Way Association
ASA—American Society of Appraisers
ASCP—American Society of Consulting Planners
ASREC—American Society of Real Estate Counselors
BAB—Build America Better Program
BBB—Better Business Bureau
BHC—Bank Holding Company
BIC—Broker-in-charge
BLM—Bureau of Land Management
BLS—Bureau of Labor Statistics
BMIR—Below market interest rate
BOCA—Building Officials and Code Administrators
BOMA—Building Owners and Managers Association
BOMI—Building Owners and Managers Institute
BOR—Bureau of Outdoor Recreation
BSPRA—Builder's and Sponsor's Profit and Risk Allowance
BTU—British thermal unit
CAE—Certified Assessment Evaluator

CAI—Community Associations Institute
CAIVR—Credit Alert Interactive Voice Response
CAM—Certified Apartment Manager
CARDS Certificates for Amortizing Revolving Debt
CARS Certificates for Automobile Receivables
CATS Certificates of Accrual on Treasury Securities
CBD—Central Business District
CBS—Concrete block and stucco
CC&R's—Covenants, conditions, and restrictions
CCIM—Certified Commercial Investment Member, affiliated with the NAR
CD—Certificate of deposit
CDR—Collateralized Depositary Receipt
CE—Certified Exchanger
CGL—Comprehensive, general liability insurance
CHUMS—Computerized Homes Underwriting Management Systems
CID—Commercial Investment Division
CJ—Certificate of Judgement
CMB—Certified mortgage banker
CMBS—Conventional mortgage-backed securities
CMO—Collateralized mortgage obligation
CO—Certificate of Occupancy
COF—Cost of funds
COLTS—Colorado, Oklahoma, Louisiana, Texas, States
CPA—Certified Public Accountant, designation awarded by the AICPA
CPI—Consumer Price Index
CPM—Certified Property Manager, affiliated with the NAR
CPR—Constant prepayment rate
CRA—Certified review appraiser, Community Reinvestment Act
CRB—Certified residential broker, affiliated with the NAR
CREA—Canadian Real Estate Association
CRV—Certificate of Reasonable Value
CSM—Certified shopping center manager
CUNA—Credit Union National Association
dba—Doing business as

DLIR—Department of Labor
and Industrial Relations
DLUM—Detailed land-use map
DP—Down payment
DRM—Direct reduction mortgage
EC—Extended coverage
ECOA—Equal Credit Opportunity Act
EIS—Environmental Impact Statement
EM—Earnest money
ENO (E&O)—Errors and omissions insurance
EPA—Environmental Protection Agency
ERISA—Employee Retirement Income Security Act
ESOP—Employee Stock Ownership Plan
FAR—Floor area ratio
FASB Financial Accounting Standards Board
FCA—Farm Credit Administration
FCRA—Fair Credit Reporting Act
FDIC—Federal Deposit Insurance Corporation
FFLS—Federal Farm Loan System
FHA—Federal Housing Administration
FHLB—Federal Home Loan Bank
FHLBB—Federal Home Loan Bank Board
FHLMC—Federal Home Loan Mortgage Corporation
(Freddie Mac)
FIA—Federal Insurance Administration
FICA—Federal Income Contributions Act
FLB—Federal Land Bank
FLBA—Federal Land Bank Association
FLI—Farm and Land Institute
FLIP—Flexible Loan Insurance Program
FMBA—Farm Mortgage Bankers Association
FmHA—Farmer's Home Administration
FMV—Fair market value
FNMA—Federal National Mortgage Association (Fannie Mae)
FPM—Flexible payment mortgage
FRM—Fixed-rate Mortgage
FRS—Federal Reserve System
FSBO—For sale by owner
FSLIC—Federal Savings and Loan Insurance Corporation

384

FTC—Federal Trade Commission
FY—Fiscal year
GAAP—Generally accepted accounting principles
GAO—General Accounting Office
GC—General contractor
GCR—Guest-car ratio
GEM—Growing equity mortgage
GLA—Gross leasable area
GMC—Guaranteed Mortgage Certificate
GNMA—Government National Mortgage Association (Ginnie Mae)
GPARM Graduated Payment adjustable rate mortgage
GPM—Graduated payment mortgage
GRI—Graduate, REALTORS(R) Institute
GRM—Gross rent multiplier
GSA—General Services Administration
GSE—Government Sponsored Enterprise
HAC—Housing Assistance Council
HAP—Housing Assistance Plan
HBA—Homebuilder's Association
HFA—Housing Finance Agency
HHFA—Housing and Home Finance Agency
HOW—Homeowner's Association
HUD—U.S. Department of Housing and Urban Development
IAAO—International Association of Assessing Officers
ICBO—International Conference of Building Officials
ICSC—International Council of Shopping Centers
IFA—Independent fee appraiser
IO— Interest only
IRC—Internal Revenue Code
IREM—Institute of Real Estate Management
IRS—Internal Revenue Service
J/T—Joint tenant
LIBOR London inter-bank offer rate
LOC—Letter of credit
LSR—Liveability-space ratio
Ltd.—Limited
LTVR—Loan-to-value ratio
LUI—Land-use intensity

LUL—Land-Use Law
LUMS—Land utilization marketing study
MAGIC—Mortgage Guaranty Insurance Company
MAI—Member, Appraisals Institute
MBA—Mortgage Bankers Association of America
MBB—Mortgage-backed bond
MBS—Mortgage-backed securities
MCC—Mutual Capital Certificate
MCC—Mortgage Credit Certificate
MGIC—See MAGIC
MGRM—Monthly gross rent multiplier
MGS—Mortgage-backed securities
MI—Mortgage insurance
mica—mortgage insurance companies of America
MIP—Mortgage insurance premium
MLS—Multiple Listing Service
MMC—Money market certificate of deposit
MMI—Mutual mortgage insurance
MPR—Minimum property requirement
MPS—Minimum property standards
MRB—Mortgage revenue bonds
MRS Mortgage-related security
MXD—Mixed-use development
n/a (n/A, N/A)—Not applicable
NAA—National Apartment Association
NAAO—National Association of Assessing Officers
NABM—National Association of Building Manufacturers
NACOR—National Association of Real Estate Corporate
    Executives
NAHB—National Association of Home Builders
NAHRO—National Association of Real Estate Corporate
    Executives
NAIFA—National Association of Independent Fee Appraisers
NAMSB—National Association of Mutual Savings Banks
NAR—National Association of Realtors
NARC —National Association of Regional Councils
NAREB—National Association of Real Estate Brokers
NAREE—National Association of Real Estate Editors

386

NAREIT—National Association of Real Estate Investment Trusts, Inc.

NARELLO—National Association of Real Estate Licensing Law Officials

NASD—National Association of Securities Dealers

NCUA—National Credit Union Association

NEPA—National Environmental Policy Act

NFCA—National Federation of Condominium Associations

NHP—National Housing Partnerships

NIFLB—National Institute of Farm and Land Brokers

NLA—Net leasable area

NOI—Net operating income

NOW—Negotiable order of withdrawal

NPA—National Parking Association

NSMA—National Second Mortgage Association

NSPE—National Society of Professional Engineers

NTO—National Tenants Organization

OAR—Overall rate of return, overall rate, overall (capitalization) rate

OBHC—One-Bank Holding Company

OCC—Office of Comptroller of Currency

OEO—Office of Economic Opportunity

OEQC—Office of Environmental Quality Control

OE&T—Operating expenses and taxes

OID—Original issue discount

OLISR—Office of Interstate Land Sales Registration

OL&T—Owners, landlords, and tenants public liability insurance

OSHA—Occupational Safety and Health Act

PA—Public accountant

PAC Bond—Planned Amortization Class Bond

PAM—Pledged account mortgage. Refer to *FLIP*.

PB—Principal Broker

PC—Participation Certificate or Partition Sales Certificate

PD—Property disposition

PHA—Public Housing Administration

P&I—Principal and interest

PITI—Principal, interest, and taxes, and insurance. What is in most cases the monthly house payment for FHA, VA, and conventional loans

PLAM—Price level adjusted mortgage

PMI—Private mortgage insurance

PMM—Purchase money mortgage

PO—Principal only

POC—Paid outside closing

PRD—Planned residential development

PSC—Participation sale certificate

PUD—Planned unit development

RAM—Reverse annuity mortgage

RAP—Regulatory accounting principles

REA—Rural Electrification Administration or Reciprocal easement agreement.

REEA—Real Estate Educators Association

REIT—Real estate investment trust

REMIC—Real estate mortgage investment conduit

REMT—Real estate mortgage trust

REO—Real estate owned

REPAC—Real Estate Political Action Committee

RESPA—Real Estate Settlement Procedures Act

RESSI—Real Estate Securities and Syndication Institute

RL—Rollover loan (Rollover, Rollover mortgage)

RM—Residential member

RNMI—REALTOR'S® National Marketing Institute

ROI—Return on investment

RRA—Registered review appraiser

RRM—Renegotiated (or Renegotiable) rate mortgage. Refer to *ARM*.

R/W—Right of way

SAM—Shared appreciation mortgage

SARA—Society of American Registered Architects

SBA—Small Business Adminstration

SBIC—Small Business Investment Company

SEC—Securities and Exchange Commission

SFD—Single family detached

SIR—Society of Industrial REALTORS®

S&L—Savings & Loan Association

SMSA—Standard Metropolitan Statistical Area
SRA—Senior realty appraiser (or Senior residential appraiser)
SREA—Senior real estate analyst (or appraiser)
SREA—Society of Real Estate Appraisers
SRPA—Senior real property appraisers
T/C—Tenant in common
T/E—Tenancy by entirety
TLTV—Total loan-to-value
TRUCS—Truck receivables underlying certificates
TSO—Timeshare ownership
UCC—Uniform Commercial Code
ULI—Urban Land Institute
ULSPA—Uniform Land Sales Practices Act
ULTA—Uniform Land Transaction Act
UPA—Uniform Partnership Act
URA—Urban Renewal Administration
URETSA—Uniform Real Estate Time Share Act
USGS—United States Geological Survey
VA—Veterans Administration
VRM—Variable rate mortgage
WAC—Weighted average coupon
WAM—Weighted average maturity
WCR—Women's Council of REALTORS®
W/W—Wall-to-wall
YTM—Yield to maturity

GLOSSARY

This Glossary is designed to give a one- or two-sentence definition of a real-estate-related term based on common usage. In nearly all cases, a single definition is given. For a more detail study of the terms, the author recommends the purchase of a book solely designed as a glossary.

AAA tenant—A prime tenant with the highest credit rating.

Abandonment—Property that is voluntarily given up by the owner. The property has been left and is not being maintained or advertised for sale or for lease. Taxes are not being paid.

Abatement—A reduction or termination of a debt. The reduction or termination can occur from an actual payment or from legal action.

Abode—A dwelling place which may or may not be a person's principal residence.

Abrogate—To terminate or repeal.

Absentee owner—An owner of income property who does not manage or reside at the subject property.

Absolute auction—An auction at which property is sold to the highest bidder regardless of a minimum price or the final bid price.

Absorption rate—A rate which serves as a forecast of how quickly properties can be sold or leased in a given area. For example, if a developer is able to lease 20% of the units available to the market in a given area for a given time, the absorption rate is 20%. This term is usually found in feasibility studies.

Abstract of title—A condensed history of the title of a property. An abstract of title should be a chronological history of all recorded instruments that affect the title of the subject property. In some states, an attorney will perform a title search using the abstract. He or she will then issue an opinion which can be used to obtain title insurance.

Abut—Connect or join. If two pieces of property touch each other, they are said to abut. Synonymous with adjoin.

Abutment—A load-bearing, vertical member of a structure. Examples of abutments would be a wall or a column.

Accelerated remittance cycle (ARC)—An option available to Freddie Mac's sellers and servicers which allows the lender to decrease the management and guarantee fee in return for remitting principal and interest payments early.

Acceleration clause—A clause in a note, bond, mortgage, or deed of trust that gives the lender the right to demand the remaining balance due and payable because of some event that has an adverse effect on the lender. Examples of an adverse effect are:
1. Failure to pay the PITI (Principal, Interest, Taxes, and Insurance),
2. Placing additional liens on the property without the consent of the lender, when said consent is required (FNMA requires their consent in certain cases),
3. Events that can affect the lender's security such as extreme abuse or deterioration of the improvement.

Acceptance—The consent or act of accepting an offer to enter into a contract. Acceptance is binding and legal when both seller and purchaser agree to the initial terms or after all counter offers have been made and are deemed acceptable by both parties.

Accession—The right of an owner to claim property that is added or joined to his or her property by natural means or by labor or material of another party.

Accessory building—A building or structure detached from but on the same property as a main building. Garages, storage buildings, and guest houses are examples.

Access right—Right of ingress and egress to and from one's property. This right can be implied or expressed.

Accident and health premium—A premium paid by a mortgagor for an insurance policy to ensure the continuance of mortgage payments in the event of the borrower's disability or illness.

Accommodation party—One who accommodates another by signing a note or a bill without receiving compensation.

Accretion—An addition to property by a gradual deposit of soil or an increase of exposed land by a permanent receding of the water.

Accrual method—For federal income tax purposes, it is an accounting method in which the taxpayer counts income and expenses when they are earned or applicable as opposed to counting income and expenses as they are received or paid (cash basis).

Accrued interest—Interest earned but not paid since the last due date. This term is used frequently in discussions of adjustable-rate mortgages that allow negative amortization. The accrued interest for these loans is the negative amortization.

Acknowledgment—A written certification or declaration stating that an execution of an instrument, such as a deed or note, is of a person's own free will. An acknowledgment is a declaration or certification that has been made before a notary public or other attesting officer.

Acoustical tile—Tile that has a sound-absorbing function or purpose.

Acquisition cost—As used by FHA, it is the cost to acquire the property. Please see the definition of Total Acquisition.

Acre—Land that measures 43,560 square feet. A lot 200' x 218' is 43,600 square feet.

Action to quiet title—A court action to establish ownership of real property. This court action usually acts to remove any interest or claim to title of real estate. The action results in removing any cloud on the title.

Act of God—An event which causes damage by nature such as a flood, earthquake, or winds; an occurrence which was not caused by man.

Actuary—A mathematical expert who calculates insurance risks and, therefore, the premiums to cover those risks.

Addendum—An agreement or list that is added to a contract or agreement or other document such as a letter of intent. FHA and VA require that an addendum be added to or incorporated in a sales contract, if it is written prior to the appraisal. This addendum is sometimes referred to as the "amendatory language."

Add-on interest—Interest added on to the amount of the loan on the front end or beginning of the loan repayment period. The balance is then paid by installment. This form of interest is much more expensive than simple interest as it is paid on the entire amount for the entire term of the loan.

Adjoin—Connect or join. If two pieces of property touch each other, they are said to adjoin. Synonymous with *abut*.

Adjoining—Contiguous or touching the subject property.

Adjudication—A court decision or judgment.

Adjustable-mortgage loan—See *Adjustable rate mortgage*.

Adjustable-rate mortgage (ARM)—A mortgage for which the interest rate adjusts and is not fixed. Refer to Questions 3.7 and 3.24 through 3.34.

Adjusted gross income—See *Effective gross income*.

Adjustable-rate preferred stock (ARPS)—Variable rate securities that can reduce a firm's interest rate risk.

Adjusted tax basis—The original cost of the property plus any adjustments or capital expenditures for the improvement of property minus the depreciation taken.

Ad litum—Legal term that describes a guardian appointed to prosecute or defend a lawsuit for a minor or an incompetent individual.

Administrator—A person appointed by an appropriate court of law to settle the estate of a person who died without a will (intestate). There are different classifications of administrators who serve specific duties.

Administratrix—A female administrator.

Ad valorem—A method of taxation based on a fixed proportion of property value; for example, real estate taxes collected at the rate of a specific dollar amount of appraised value or assessment.

Advance—A partial disbursement of funds in a construction loan.

Adverse possession—A method of acquiring title to property by the possession of the property for a statutory period of time in an open, notorious, continuous, exclusive, and adverse manner.

Aeolian soil—Soil that is composed of materials deposited by the wind.

Aesthetic value—The value attributable to beauty created by improvements and natural surroundings. A densely wooded lot could add aesthetic value to the property.

Affidavit—A written statement sworn to before a notary public or an officer with authority to administer an oath.

Affidavit of title—A sworn statement by a seller that the title being conveyed is free from any clouds or defects.

Affinity—Relationship other than by blood. It is a relationship by marriage or by a group for a specific purpose such as a club or an organization.

Affirmative marketing—A method used by HUD to assure minorities of a fair housing plan. Authority for the program began with Title VIII of the Civil Rights Act of 1968.

A-frame—A type of architecture commonly seen in vacation and resort housing, particularly in ski resort areas. It consists of a gable roof that extends down to serve as the exterior walls, with an abundant use of glass on the front and rear of the dwelling.

After-tax cash flow—Cash flow minus income taxes. Refer to *Cash flow*.

Agency—The relationship between an agent and a principal. Agencies can be specific or general.

Agent—A person who is authorized to represent or act for another person (the principal) in negotiations with third parties. The authority may be expressed or implied. See *Agency*.

Agrarian—Something that relates to land or its distribution or division.

Agreement of sale—Refer to *Contract*.

Air rights—The right to use the space or air above the ground but not the ground itself. Air rights can be sold or leased.

Alcove—A recessed room connected to a main or larger room.

Alienation—A voluntary transfer or conveyance of property.

All-inclusive trust deed (AITD)—A new deed of trust securing a balance due on an existing note plus new funds that are advanced. This technique is also known as a wraparound mortgage.

Allodial system—Ownership of land in which the owner has full and absolute dominion over the property. This system is the basis for our property rights in the United States.

Allotment—Reservation of funds for the purchase of mortgages within a specified time period.

Alluvium, alluvion, or alluvial—Soil deposited by accretion along the shore or bank of a river.

Alternative-mortgage instrument (AMI)—Pertains to a mortgage without a level payment.

Amenity—A natural or man-made feature that increases the value of property. Examples would be a view of a golf course or the ocean or a beautifully landscaped yard.

American Institute of Real Estate Appraisers (AIREA)—A member organization of the National Association of REALTORS® (NAR). Designations are MAI (Member of the Appraisal Institute) and RM (Residential Member).

Amendatory language—Refer to *Addendum*. For FHA, refer to Question 1.51; for VA, refer to Question 2.92.

Amortization—Loan amortization is the paying off of a debt or mortgage, usually by monthly payments. An amortization schedule can show the payment number, interest payment, principal payment, and unpaid principal balance.

Amount to make the project operational (AMPO)—An allowance that can be included in a HUD mortgage to provide a non-profit sponsor with required working capital to make a project operational.

Ampere—Measure of electrical current equal to the current produced by the force of one volt through the resistance of one ohm.

Ancillary—Something that is subordinate or auxiliary.

Annex—To attach or add; that which is added to something else.

Annual contributions contract (ACC)—Debt service payments made by HUD to public housing units or rent subsidies and administrative costs for the Section 8 Housing Assistance Payments Program.

Annual housing survey (AHS)—An annual census by HUD and the Census Bureau to study housing units and trends in the movement of owners and renters.

Annual percentage rate (APR)—A method for calculating an interest rate as it relates to the interest collected, discount points charged to either purchaser, seller or both, and certain costs related to closing and mortgage insurance premiums.

Annuity—An assured income for life or a given period of time. This term normally relates to the insurance industry but is sometimes used in comparison with certain kinds of high-quality income from real estate investments.

Antenuptial agreement—A property agreement between a man and woman prior to marriage.

Application—Refers to the process of applying for a home mortgage loan or the FNMA 1003 form as illustrated in Figure 20.

Appointments—Decorative items such as furnishings and equipment in a building.

Apportionment—A division of expenses, liabilities, responsibilities, or property among individuals.

Appraisal—An opinion of value. Normally, a written statement of an appraiser's opinion of value for a specific purpose of a described property on a given date.

Appreciation—An increase in the value of property.

Appropriation—The private taking and use of public property. Also, the dedication of public land to a use such as a public park or a school.

Appurtenance—Item attributable to the land such as improvements or an easement. Something that belongs to something outside of the property but is considered part of the property and as such transfers upon sale or other transfer. An example would be an easement.

Apron—Something that connects such as the entrance to a driveway or the concrete portion around a swimming pool.

Arbitrage—The buying and selling of mortgages, futures, contracts, or mortgage-backed securities in various markets for the purpose of creating a profit from the differences in price.

Arm's length transaction—A transaction between individuals who do not have a conflict of interest or reason for collusion. The parties are as strangers to each other.

Arrears—At the end of a period, interest on home mortgages is paid in arrears. Example: The interest for April is due May 1st as opposed to rent which normally is paid in advance. The term can also pertain to delinquent mortgage payments.

Artesian Well—A deep well in which water rises to the surface by natural pressure.

As-is—Property sold in its present condition with no warranties made as to the plumbing, heating, electricity, or infestation of termites.

Assemblage—Combining several pieces of property to make one large, attractive property.

Assessed valuation—The dollar amount on which real estate taxes are levied. If a property worth $100,000 is assessed for tax purposes at 50% of value, the assessed valuation is $50,000.

Assessment—The fair market value of property for tax purposes or an expense appropriated to a unit of a whole, such as a condominium assessment or an additional charge for improvement.

Assessor—Commonly referred to as a tax assessor, it is that individual charged with determining the fair market value for tax purposes. Tax assessors do not set the tax, they merely set the value for tax purposes.

Assign—The act of transferring rights or property to another.

Assignee—One who receives rights or property.

Assignment of mortgage—A transfer of a mortgage from one mortgagee to another. In some cases, FHA will accept an assignment of a mortgage to assist a qualified, distressed mortgagor.

Assignor—One who assigns rights or property.

Assumability—See Assumption of mortgage and due on sale explanation in FHA section.

Assumption of mortgage—A purchaser assumes a mortgage on the subject property. The seller is still liable unless a release of liability is obtained from the lender.

At risk—For income tax purposes, it is the limit of deductible loss which equals the cash amount invested plus the loan(s) for which the owner is personally liable.

Attachment—The actual taking of property into the custody of a court to serve as collateral for a judgement sought in a pending lawsuit.

Attest—An act of witnessing by observance and then signing to the fact.

Attorney-in-fact—An individual, not necessarily an attorney, who is authorized to act for another in a specific or general assignment. This individual has privileges afforded as under *power of attorney*.

Attornment—A tenant's formal recognition of a new landlord.

Attractive nuisance doctrine—A legal doctrine holding that a property owner must protect children from injuring themselves by an attractive danger such as a swimming pool. In adherence to this doctrine, a property owner should erect a fence around a swimming pool.

Auction—A sale of property to the highest bidder. See also *Absolute auction.*

Average life of a mortgage—A statistic used in determining the true yield of a mortgage. A 30-year mortgage is said to have an average life of twelve years; a 10 to 12-year mortgage has an average life of seven years. Investors base the yield of a mortgage on the average lief as opposed to the original term.

Avulsion—The sudden removal of land by action of a body of water.

Backfilling—The act of putting back dirt removed for construction. It is done to fill the gap between the foundation wall and yard so water will drain away from the house.

Backup contract—A contract which will replace a prior contract in the event of failure by the parties of the prior contract to perform or close.

400

Balloon payment—The final payment of a loan, said payment paying the loan off in full. "Balloons" are used many times with a long-term amortization period such as 30 years with the balance being paid in full at some pre-designated time, such as at the end of five or ten years. This final payment is referred to as the "balloon" or "bullet."

Baluster—The support for the rail in a staircase; one of a series of upright posts.

Bank holding company (BHC)—A corporation that owns interests in one or more banks.

Bankrupt—A corporation, firm, or person who files for relief from the courts and surrenders all assets. There are several chapters of bankruptcy; Chapter 7 covers liquidation of the debtor's assets, Chapter 11 covers reorganization of a bankrupt business, and Chapter 13 covers repayment of debts by individuals.

Baseboard—A board that runs along the base of the wall where it meets the floor.

Base line—A surveyor's term used to indicate an east-west line.

Basis—An unadjusted basis is the cost of the property minus the land value. An adjusted basis is cost plus capital spent to modify the improvements minus the land value. For the purposes of determining capital gain or loss, it is the total cost of the property compared to the price minus the costs of the sale.

Basis points—A term used in relationship to interest rates. One basis point is equal to one 100th of one percent. The difference between 9% and 9.5% is 50 basis points.

Basket provision—Regulatory authority permitting insurance companies, savings and loan associations, and mutual savings banks to put a small percentage of their total assets in investments not otherwise allowed by regulatory acts.

Batt—The strip of insulation placed between the studs of a wall or joists of a ceiling or floor.

Batten—A narrow board normally used to cover a joint or space between boards. Often referred to as a batten board.

Beam—A load-bearing support that can be made of wood, iron, stone, or other strong material.

Bearer bond—A coupon bond payable to the individual who has possession of the bond.

Bedrock—Solid rock upon which the foundation of a large building may be established.

Bedroom community—Residential area for commuters who work at a nearby large city or employment center. Also called *Suburb*.

Belly-up—A project, business, or venture that has failed is said to have gone "belly-up" (as a capsized ship).

Benchmark—A mark etched on a durable substance such as a rock or metal. It can be used to show elevation above sea level or to indicate a measure of quality or performance in an industry.

Beneficial estate—Equitable title or estate. A condition in which legal title has not yet passed. Examples would be a person who owns a valid sales contract or a person who has a contract for land.

Beneficiary—A person who receives a benefit from certain acts such as through a will or proceeds from an insurance policy. Also, a lender who possesses a deed of trust or a note as security for a loan.

Bequeath—The giving of property by a will.

Betterment—Improvement to real estate. Something that is more substantial than ordinary repairs.

Biannual—Biannual is an event that occurs twice a year.

Bid—The price offered to acquire real estate. The winning bid at a real estate auction would be the highest price.

Bid in—The lender states a price at a foreclosure sale which will covers the unpaid balance plus allowable costs; the lender is said to have bid in his price.

Biennial—Biennial is an event that occurs every two years.

Bilateral contract—A contract in which each party promises to perform an act in exchange for the other party's promise to perform.

Bill of sale—This instrument is used for the sale of personal property and not real property (real estate).

Binder—In real estate, this term is used frequently in connection with title insurance. A binder is a report on certain real estate as of a certain date. It is not the same as a title insurance policy, but it can be used to obtain a policy. A binder is less costly than a policy and it will often meet a lender's title insurance requirement of a short-term loan, such as a construction loan. A binder covers a specific time. In hazard insurance, it is an agreement to insure for a specific time. In real estate contract law, it is a preliminary agreement between the seller and purchaser.

Bird dog—Generally a person who hunts or seeks out a lead or possibility of a good buy for an investor or a prospect or listing for a broker or other person in sales.

Bi-weekly mortgage—A mortgage requiring 26 payments per year as opposed to a monthly payment. Each payment is only half the size of the required regular monthly payment and the resulting effect is quicker loan amortization and reduced interest cost.

Blacktop—A paving surface usually made of asphalt.

Blanket mortgage—A single mortgage used to secure a debt for money loaned on several properties such as the lots a builder owns in a subdivision.

Blended rate—This term has a dual meaning:

1. A first mortgage lender can use it in an advertisement to induce his mortgagors to refinance and pay off the old low-interest-rate first mortgage. The first mortgage lender could offer a 10% interest loan as compared to the going rate of 12% if the mortgagor will refinance the existing mortgage which is at 8%.

2. A second mortgage lender or a wrap-around lender will advertize to not pay off the old mortgage with the low rate and short term remaining, but instead,

place a second mortgage or wrap-around loan behind the first and have a blended rate at below-market interest rates for first mortgage loans.

Blighted area—Usually an inner city area in which property values are falling and buildings are deteriorating.

Blockbusting—An illegal practice of promoting panic selling in an all-white neighborhood because someone of a minority or ethnic background has moved into or is said to be moving into the neighborhood. The blockbuster will then try to gain illegally from depressed prices either by buying or listing the properties at far below market values.

Blue laws—Restrictions against certain activities on Sundays or other holidays.

Blue-sky laws—State laws to protect the public against fraud in the offer and sale of securities.

Board and batten—Siding which is batten boards nailed over cracks between wider boards.

Board of Adjustment—A government body that hears appeals concerning zoning matters. This board can grant zoning variances.

Board of Equalization—A government body that hears appeals concerning real estate tax assessments. This board can lower assessments which could, in turn, lower the real estate tax.

Board of REALTORS®—The local association of REALTORS® who belong to the State and National Association of REALTORS®.

Board of Review—Refer to Board of Equalization.

Boiler plating—Using form language for contracts, deeds or deeds of trust, and CC&R's.

Bona fide—Genuine, sincere, in good faith. The term can be used in a sentence such as: *A bona fide offer to purchase real estate.*

Bond—A formal certificate that evidences a debt and outlines the terms.

Book value—An accounting term used to indicate the value of a business as a whole or any asset, such as real estate. This value is that as shown by accounting records which is normally net after depreciation.

Boot—Something of value given to even the exchange of like properties. Parcel A is worth $100,000 and is exchanged for parcel B worth $80,000 and $20,000 in cash. The boot is the $20,000 in cash.

Boring test—Using samples obtained by boring deep holes in the ground to determine the strength of the subsoil for construction purposes.

Borough—A section of a city, similar to an incorporated village, which has control over local matters. New York City has five boroughs.

Bottom land—Low land situated near a body of water.

Bottom line—Expression used to signify the net result such as after-tax cash flow. Term that is also used to mean the end result or final consequence.

Breach of contract—Failure to perform according to the terms of a contract. The party who has not breached the contract can rescind the agreement and sue for damages or performance.

Breach of trust—Abuse of the responsibilities or authority as set forth in a trust agreement.

Break-even point—A point at which gross income will cover operating expenses and the debt service.

Bridge financing or bridge loan—Short-term mortgage financing between the end of one loan and the beginning of another. A bridge loan is usually based on the amount of equity in the borrower's current home with the proceeds going towards the purchase of a new home. The loan helps to "bridge" the gap between one home to another without the benefit of cash proceeds from the sale of a previous home. A bridge loan is sometimes referred to as a *swing loan.*

British thermal unit (BTU) —A unit used to measure the efficiency or capacity of heating or cooling systems. A unit of heat required to raise one pound of water one degree in Fahrenheit.

Broker—A properly licensed agent who, for a fee or valuable consideration, serves as an agent for owners in facilitating the sale or lease of their property. A broker can be incorporated or act as a partnership, but the salespeople hired by the broker must act as individuals. A broker usually works for the seller who pays his or her commission.

Buffer strip or zone—Land between two areas of different use such as commercial and residential.

Builder's and sponsor's profit and risk allowance (BSPRA)—Credit given by HUD/FHA insurance programs for services provided by the developer, said credit is used against the required equity contribution.

Builder's risk insurance—Used to protect builders against fire and special risks while they have houses under construction. It increases as the building progresses and terminates at completion of construction.

Building and loan association—A savings and loan association.

Building code—A code used by local authority to regulate and ensure quality of construction in the building industry.

Building line—A line established by law for city lots which serves to establish a minimum distance between the front of a building and the front of a lot or a minimum distance between the sides of a building and the sides of a lot.

Building permit—Permission in writing from local authority to erect, demolish, repair, or improve a specific building at a designated lot.

Bullet—See *Balloon payment.*

Bundle of rights—A theory adhering to the concept that when one buys real estate one buys all the rights inherent in that property except what is limited or reserved by the sale. The rights to sell, lease, mortgage, bequeath, enjoy, share, and restrict property are supported by the Bundle of Rights theory.

Bungalow—A small one- or one-and-one-half-story house. It normally has a front porch.

Business day—Monday through Friday excluding holidays. Also known as *working days*.

Buy-back agreement—A seller agreeing to buy back a property at a specific price for specific conditions. Normally used by builders as a sales inducement.

Buydown—Refer to Questions 1.21, page 21, 2.85, and 3.37-3.39.

Buyer's market—Economic conditions in which demand for housing is at a low level.

Buy-sell agreement—An agreement between parties to buy if one party leaves an entity, such as a partnership, and the departing partner agreeing to sell to the remaining party or parties. The agreement can provide for an option to buy or sell.

Caisson—A water-tight chamber for men to work in underwater or in an open excavation where there is danger of walls caving in.

Call—An option to buy a specific security at a specified price within a designated period; demand for payment.

Call provision—In a mortgage or deed of trust, it is the clause that allows the lender to accelerate payment of the secured obligation. In bonds, a call provision is the issuer's right to redeem the bond before maturity.

Cal-vet loans—Real estate loans to veterans in California at reduced interest rates.

Canadian rollover mortgage—An adjustable rate mortgage in which the terms are renegotiated every five years.

Candle—A measure of light intensity that is approximately equal to the intensity of light from a 7/8 inch sperm candle burning at the rate of 120 grains per hour.

Candle hour—A measure of light equal to one candle burning for one hour.

Candle power—Luminous intensity of a light expressed in candles.

Cantilever—The part of a structural member which extends beyond its support and is capable of supporting loads and resisting lateral pressure by virtue of its rigidity and material strength.

Cantilever bridge—A bridge supported by two cantilevered members extending out toward each other and connecting with each other or to a suspended span.

Cap—Refer to Question 3.28.

Capital—The net worth of a business or an individual; accumulated wealth used to produce goods or more wealth.

Capital asset—As defined by the IRS, it is an asset that can receive favorable tax treatment upon sale. Assets excluded would be inventory, property held for resale, or property used in a trade or business.

Capital expenditure—The cost of an improvement as distinguished from a repair. Said improvement would extend the useful life of a property or enhance its value.

Capitalization—The process of converting anticipated future income, such as from rent, into a present value.

Capitalization rate—The rate used to derive the capital value divided by an income stream. The formula is: annual income divided by capitalization rate equals value.

Cash flow—Net income minus debt twice equals cash flow.

Cash-on-cash return—Rate of return based on cash returned to the investor on his cash investment. It is the relationship of the cash returned to the cash invested.

Caulking, calking—Flexible putty used to seal a crack or seam in a building and thus prevent passage of air and moisture.

Cause of action—Grounds for initiating legal proceedings to seek legal relief from another.

Caveat emptor—Latin phrase which means "let the buyer beware." A doctrine that means the buyer should examine the property thoroughly to satisfy any doubts about the condition of the improvements. This belief is diminishing greatly in the eyes of the courts.

Certificates for amortizing revolving debt (CARDS)—Credit-card-backed securities which gives the owner a pro-rata share in a fixed pool of credit card accounts.

Certificate for automobile receivables (CARS)—Similar to a CMO, but backed by a pool of automobile loans.

Certificates of accrual on treasury securities (CATS)—An ownership in an investment backed by U.S. Treasury notes and bonds.

Certificate of claim—A contingent promise to reimburse an insured lender for certain costs arising from a foreclosure. It is contingent upon the proceeds from the foreclosure sale being sufficient to cover the lender's claim.

Certificate of commitment—Refer to Questions 2.70-72.

Certificate of completion—A document issued by an architect or an engineer certifying that a construction project has been completed in accordance with the terms, conditions, and approved plans and specifications.

Certificate of deposit (CD)—A written document provided by a financial institution to evidence a deposit and the rate of interest it shall earn.

Certificate of eligibility—Refer to Questions 2.4 through 2.6, 2.10, 2.11, and 2.19-20 and Figure 19.

Certificate of occupancy (CO)—Official document stating that a structure complies with the building code and may be occupied legally.

Certificate of reasonable value (CRV)—The VA appraisal. Refer to Questions 2.67 and 2.90.

Certificate of sale—A certificate issued to the buyer of real property at a judicial sale.

Certificate of title—An attorney's written opinion as to the status of the title to real property based on public records.

Certification—Refers to a statement used in loan processing. When a copy of a document is used, as opposed to the original, the lender must certify as to the authenticity. For example, a copy of a sales contract must have the following statement: "We hereby certify this to be a true and exact copy of the exhibit we have in our file," or "We hereby certify this to be a true and exact copy of the original". The "certification" statement must be signed by the lender.

I always advise my students to use an original, or a copy with original signatures. If you use a copy and two years later an auditor asks to see the original, be prepared to come up with that document.

Certified copy—A true copy of the original and certified or attested to that fact by the holder of the original.

Certified mortgage banker (CMB) —A professional designation awarded by the Mortgage Bankers Association of America to those in the industry who have demonstrated superior knowledge and skills in the field of real estate finance.

Chain of title—Refer to *Abstract of title.*

Change order—A form used by a builder to specify changes from the approved original plan.

Chattel—Personal property that is not permanently attached. Something other than real estate.

Chattel mortgage—A loan secured by personal property.

Cistern—A tank for storing rainwater.

Civil Rights Act of 1866—This act was the first federal law to prohibit any type of discrimination based on race.

Civil Rights Act of 1968—Title VIII prohibits discrimination in mortgage applications and loans on the basis of race or ethnic background.

Clapboard—A board used for exterior siding. A clapboard is a long, thin board with edges graduated in thickness from one end to the other. Clapboards overlap each other when in place.

Clearing account—A bank account kept by a mortgage banker for the deposit of mortgage payments which are later cleared out for transmittal to the investor. A clearing account can also be used for the deposit of escrow funds.

410

Clear title—Title that is free of any clouds and is considered marketable.

Closed-end mortgage—A fixed mortgage amount which cannot be increased.

Closed period—A portion in the term of a mortgage during which it cannot be prepaid.

Closing—The actual transfer of title from seller to purchaser. This term is also used to indicate a time for the transfer such as, "We will meet you at the closing."

Closing costs—All costs related to closing except the prepaid or escrow items. Some examples of closing costs are: loan origination fee, discount points, sales commission, attorney fees, charge survey, title insurance premiums, appraisal fee, credit report, termite report cost, lan amortization schedule cost, recording fees, document preparation fee, mortgage insurance premiums, the VA fee, and loan transfer or assumption fee.

Closing statement—An accounting of the debits and credits incurred at closing. All FHA, VA, and most conventional financing loans use a uniform closing or settlement statement commonly referred to as the HUD-1. See Figure 23.

Cloud on title—An existence of a claim or encumbrance that impairs the owner's claim for clear title, but usually can be removed by judicial procedure.

Cluster housing—A planned subdivision development with dwelling units grouped in close proximity and sharing an open space or other recreation areas such as swimming pool, tennis courts, etc.

CMO—Collateralized mortgage obligation. An amortizing debt instrument collateralized by mortgages or mortgage-backed securities and characterized by cash flow sizing techniques and differential allocation of cash flows to investors. A CMO provides payment predictability with respect to mortgages that are pooled and packaged into mortgage-backed securities (MBS).

Code—A set of laws or regulations governing subjects such as building regulations or codes and criminal laws or codes.

411

Code of ethics—A guideline of acceptable practices or behavior subscribed to by an organization such as the National Association of REALTORS®.

Codicil—Alteration of an existing will.

Coinsurance—For hazard insurance purposes, it is the requirement of insuring to a minimum percentage of value so that in the event of a loss the insured can collect the full benefit from the loss. For title insurance purposes and the sharing of risks by more than one insurance company.

Cold canvas—A door-to-door solicitation for a specific purpose such as listings for a REALTOR®. Agents use this method in establishing a farm area.

Collateral—Property that serves as security for a loan.

Collateralized depository receipt (CDR)—The instrument delivered in fulfillment of the Chicago Board of Trade GNMA-CRD, a popular GNMA futures contract.

Collateralized Mortgage Obligation—See *CMO*.

Collusion—An agreement between two or more parties to perform an illegal act.

Colonial architecture—A home of traditional design, usually two stories, with emphasis on details such as small window panes, balanced openings, shutters, and dormer windows.

Color of title—Title that appears to be good or clear but usually has a defect.

Colorado, Oklahoma, Louisiana, Texas, States (COLTS)—Starting in 1987, this term was commonly used in Secondary Marketing. Many Investors would not buy mortgage-related assets from these states because of their troubled economies caused by oil or energy-related industries.

Commercial bank—A lending institution that primarily issues consumer or short-term loans. These types of institutions offer checking accounts, credit cards, savings, and other consumer or business-related services. Commercial banks are an excellent source for construction loans.

412

Commercial paper—A short-term, unsecured note used to raise capital. Many second mortgage lenders use commercial paper as an excellent primary source for funds to be used for their lending purposes.

Co-mingled funds—Money that has been mixed into an account that would be deemed improper or illegal. For example, a broker is required to keep a separate account for earnest money received on deposit. It would be illegal or unlawful for the broker to mix those funds with his/her personal or business account. For financial institutions, the term "co-mingled funds" relates to money in a single account, but separately accounted for or owned.

Commitment—An agreement from a lender to a borrower specifying the terms and conditions of a loan.

Commitment fee—A deposit or a reservation fee paid for future use of money. Normally, the deposit or reservation is placed at the time the commitment is rendered.

Commitment letter—A written agreement outlining a future commitment by a lender to reserve funds for a borrower subject to terms and conditions.

Common areas—Reference to property used by owners or tenants. An example would be a courtyard or playground area.

Common elements—Those portions or areas of a condominium used by all of the owners. Examples of common elements would be tennis courts, swimming pools, recreational facilities, and parking areas.

Common law—A body of laws originating from common or customary practices that developed in England.

Community association—A group composed of property owners that serves to protect and maintain a neighborhood or commonly owned properties.

Community property—Ownership of property in common by husband and wife.

Community Reinvestment Act (CRA)—In 1978 Congress enacted CRA to encourage lenders to meet the credit needs of all their local communities. The main thrust of

413

Community property—Ownership of property in common by husband and wife.

Community Reinvestment Act (CRA)—In 1978 Congress enacted CRA to encourage lenders to meet the credit needs of all their local communities. The main thrust of the law requires lenders to display a CRA notice, maintain a public comment file, and delineate their local communities.

Co-mortgagor—An individual who joins in the mortgage loan and ownership of the property. A co-mortgagor is jointly and individually liable for the indebtedness.

Comparable—Properties that are similar or comparable to the subject property.

Comparable sales—Those sales that are used in the market approach to value.

Compensating balances—A practice used by banks in the absence of security or collateral for a loan. This method would require a borrower, as a condition for obtaining a loan, to maintain a minimum average balance in an account with the lending institution, said balance normally being a minimum of 20% of the loan amount.

Competent—Legally capable of entering a contract; includes being of legal age as well as mentally competent and not a substance abuser.

Completion bond—A bond used to ensure the completion of a contractor's work or performance.

Component depreciation—An accounting method used to depreciate individual parts or components of a structure or improvement. A practice of dividing components of a structure or improvement into separate depreciating schedules. Examples of components would be electrical, plumbing, heating, air conditioning, roofing, floor covering, and permanently attached appliances.

Compound interest—Interest paid on the balance plus accumulated unpaid interest.

Concessionary items/concessions—Items that are paid for or given by a seller to induce a buyer to purchase or lease

Condemnation—Property that is taken by the powers of eminent domain. A public authority or government can compensate an owner and take his property for a public use. Examples of public use would be parks, schools, streets, fire stations, and police stations. A second use of the term would be to designate a building or structure unfit for occupancy.

Condition—A qualification or restriction attached to the transfer of property. An example would be that a property can be used only for residential purposes and cannot be subdivided. A provision or stipulation in a sales contract which requires certain events to take place or be followed before a sale can close.

Conditional commitment—The FHA property appraisal. Refer to Question 1.46.

Conditional Sales Contract—Refer to *Contract for Deed.*

Condominium—A joint ownership of property improved by multiple dwellings.

Condominium association—An organization of condominium owners authorized to enforce the condominium bylaws.

Conduit—A channel or pipe used to convey and protect wires, water, or other materials. In the secondary mortgage market, the term is used to describe a flow of mortgages from the originating lender to the investor. a "conduit program" would be an investor approving lenders and setting forth guidelines by which loans will be purchased.

Conforming—In secondary marketing, this word implies that loan amounts and underwriting guidelines are in conformity to those used by agencies such as FHLMC and FNMA. In appraising, this word means that a subject property is in like use, as compared to other properties in the same area. Example: A commercial establishment would be in conforming use in a commercial area. On the other hand, a commercial building would be in a nonconforming use in a single-family neighborhood.

Consanguinity—Blood relationship as distinguished from legal relationship.

Conservator—A party appointed by court to act as a guardian for a legally incompetent individual (usually an adult) and ensure that his/her property is managed properly.

Consideration—Something of value given to make a contract legal and binding.

Constant—An equal annual payment, expressed in a percentage, that will reduce the principal and pay interest over the life of the mortgage.

Constant prepayment rate (CPR)—The rate at which the principal balance on a pool of mortgages is being paid down. The rate is stated on an annualized basis.

Construction loan—A short-term loan intended for the construction of an improvement, such as a house.

Constructive notice—Legal assumption that information is available to everyone by virtue of its being in the public records or published in a newspaper rather than delivering it in person to all concerned.

Consumer Credit Reporting Act—Federal law that protects consumers from abuse by parties using credit reports.

Consumer lending—Loans made for personal property, such as automobiles and appliances.

Consumer price index (CPI) A measure of changes in the cost of goods and services. This statistical information is furnished by the Bureau of Labor Statistics of the Department of Labor.

Contiguous—A word used to describe properties that touch each other; it is especially important when assembling small parcels to ascertain that property lines are actually touching. The term is used in connection with FHA investor loans. Refer to Question 1.32.

Contingency—Refer to *Condition*.

Contour map—A topographical map showing elevations of the land.

416

Contract—When used in the acquisition of real estate, it is a written agreement between two or more parties stating the contract or sales price and the terms or conditions of the sale. For a contract to be legal and binding, there must be an offer in writing, an acceptance, a legal purpose, a consideration, a description of the property, competent parties, and signatures of the parties involved. It is an agreement between two or more parties, enforceable by law, that creates or modifies a relationship. A contract can be written or oral and there must be an offer and acceptance. Real estate contracts must be in writing. Consideration, something of value, may be required in some states.

Contract for deed—Title to the property remains in the seller's name while the buyer receives equity title and possession of the property and assumes the obligation to purchase the property. When conditions of the contract are fulfilled, legal title passes to the purchaser.

Contract rent—The rent for a property as per an existing lease.

Convection—For heating purposes, it is natural and forced circulatory motion.

Conventional loan—A real estate mortgage not affiliated with FHA or VA.

Convertible standby commitment—A commitment from FNMA to purchase mortgages that can be converted to the same yield as offered in the most recent Free Market Auction.

Convey—To transfer title to real property from one party to another by an acceptable instrument.

Conveyance—The instrument (except a will) used to transfer title to real property.

Cooperating broker or sale—Sale in which two or more agents participate.

Cooperative—Ownership of real estate through stock in a corporation.

417

Cornice—Top course or ornamental crowning member of a wall where it meets the roof under the eaves.

Correlation—In the final steps of an appraisal, using the three approaches to value—cost, income, and market, it is the reconciliation of the three into a final estimate of value.

Correspondent—A lender whose normal practice is to sell all loans originated to a particular investor or a group of investors. Another similar meaning is an approved FHA lender that is not a fully licensed FHA mortgagee. The conditions of becoming a FHA approved correspondent are much less stringent as compared to a licensed FHA mortgagee.

Co-signer—An individual who lends his name and therefore his character and credit to another individual in hopes that it will help obtain credit. This term is not the same as co-mortgagor. The co-signer is liable for the loan, but does not share in the title.

Cost approach—One of the three approaches to value. It emphasizes the cost or replacement value of the permanent improvements.

Cost of funds (COF)—An index referring to the cost lenders pay for attracting funds.

Cost-of-Living Index—Refer to *Consumer Price Index.*

Cotenancy—A form of co-ownership of property such as tenancy-in-common, joint tenancy, tenancy-by-the-entirety, or other forms of co-ownership of property.

Counter offer—Refers to an alteration of an original offer to buy or sell real estate.

Coupon bond—Bearer bond; not registered in the name of the owner. A bond with coupons for each interest installment.

Coupon rate—Rate of interest paid on a bond.

Covenant—A promise written into a deed to perform or not perform certain acts, or the existence or nonexistence of certain facts.

Crawl space—Automatically implies a house built on a conventional foundation as opposed to a concrete slab; an area beneath the floor of a house big enough for a person to crawl in and make an inspection.

Creative financing—A term that has come to mean financing other than through traditional sources. Creative financing can take the forms of seller financing, wrap-around financing, balloon mortgages, sale/leasebacks, substitution of collateral, and other alternative mortgage instruments.

Cul-de-sac—A street that is closed at one end with a circular area big enough for cars to turn around.

Culvert—Underground ditch that carries drainage water, such as under a highway.

Current production—A term used to describe loans that have been originated within the past 12 months. Loans that have aged for over 1 year are sometimes referred to as "seasoned."

Curtsey—Common-law right of a husband to a life estate in all or part of his deceased wife's property. This right may not exist in some states and those which do recognize it may have different interpretations.

Custodian—A financial institution which holds specific documents, such as original notes, in trust for another institution. Frequently used in connection with mortgage backed securities, such as GNMA.

Custom builder—An individual who normally pre-sells houses as opposed to a builder who builds for the speculative market.

Daily price limits—The maximum number of points a contract is allowed to rise above or fall below the previous day's settlement price.

Damages—Compensation for an individual's injuries or damages to his/her property by another. Also a lessening

419

of the value of property remaining after part of it has been taken by eminent domain.

Damper—Adjustable device in a fireplace, stove, or furnace used to regulate the draft caused by the fire.

DD 214—Refer to Questions 2.7 and 2.8 and Figure 18.

Dealer—An individual who buys property for resale to the public in the regular course of business. The same person may also buy property as an investor. In the lending profession, a dealer is in the business of buying and selling mortgage-backed securities as a principal rather than as an agent.

Debenture—An unsecured, long-term debt instrument.

Debit—A charge or cost. For accounting purposes, in a two-column form, debits will be on the left, credits on the right.

Debt coverage ratio—A factor used to express the amount of difference between net operating income and the debt service.

Debt ratio—A term used to compare a mortgage payment to the borrower's income.

Debt service—The principal and interest payment due on a mortgage.

Debt instrument—A document that evidences a debt. A mortgage note is a debt instrument.

Debt service—Periodic mortgage payment consisting of principal and interest.

Decedent—A deceased person.

Deck—The flat, wooden surface of a roof or a patio.

Declaration—Formerly used in connection with a condominium. A declaration of condominium is also known as the master deed. This instrument requires the developer to meet certain state laws in describing the condominium project.

Declaration of trust—An instrument which identifies property held by a trustee for another individual.

Decree—An order or judgement of a court.

Dedication—Property or an easement that is transferred to the public for its use.

Deed—An instrument used to transfer ownership of property.

Deed-in-lieu of foreclosure—The owner deeds the property to the lender to avoid foreclosure.

Deed of trust—An instrument that transfers title to property to a trustee for the duration of a loan. When the debt is paid, the trustee conveys the title to the owner.

Deed restrictions—Restrictions or limitations to the use of property as noted in the deed.

De facto—Latin for "in fact."

Default—Failure to perform a legal obligation. In residential mortgages an owner who fails to pay the monthly payment is in default.

Defeasance—A provision in a mortgage which allows the debtor to reclaim property that has been foreclosed, if certain conditions are met.

Defective title—Title that is not clear.

Defendant—Party who is defending or denying in a legal action.

Deferred maintenance—Depreciation caused by failure to maintain property properly; also called curable physical depreciation.

Deficiency—In relationship to a mortgage, a deficiency is created when the highest bid at foreclosure sale is less than the outstanding balance plus foreclosure-related costs.

Deficiency judgement—A judgement allowing the lender to pursue any legal measure to recover a loss created by a deficiency.

Delinquency ratio—Number of loans past due in relationship to number of loans serviced.

Delivery—The handing over of legal documents so that the recipient becomes the owner of property described in said documents.

Demand note—A debt instrument that allows the lender to call the balance due at any time without prior notice.

De minimis PUD—See *Planned Unit Development (PUD)*

Demographics—Statistical information concerning population growth and trends.

Density—A measure of the number of dwelling units per component size of land, such as an acre.

Deposit—Money or an item of value placed in good faith to express the desire to abide by the terms of an agreement or contract. It is subject to being returned.

Depreciation—In relationship to real estate and federal income tax law, it is the assumption that permanently attached improvements lessen in value, regardless of market conditions to the contract.

Descent—The act of transferring property upon death according to state law. State laws which govern inheritance of property.

Description—In real estate this term commonly refers to the property address or its legal description.

Detached single-family dwelling—A house with yard space in the front, sides, and rear.

Development loan—A short-term loan used for the acquisition of land intended for developed building sites or improvements such as grading, streets, and utilities.

Devise—Real property given by a will.

Direct Endorsement—See Question 1.49.

Direct reduction mortgage—A mortgage, usually between individuals, requiring level payments of principal. Payment will vary as interest lessens with the declining balance.

Disbursement—Cash payment for a draw according to the terms and provisions of a loan, usually a construction loan.

Discharge of bankruptcy—The date a bankruptcy is finally discharged. This date is important for loan underwriting purposes since certain programs require a minimum amount of time to have transpired from the date of bankruptcy before an application can be considered for approval.

Disclaimer—A denial or rejection of an obligation or responsibility also, a denial of ownership in property.

Discount—The difference between par or 100% of the face value of a note for obligation and the actual bid price for said obligation. If a mortgage of $100,000 sells for $95,000, the discount is 5% or $5000. The purpose of discount is to increase the yield of a mortgage or debt instrument. Refer to Questions 1.20, 1.37, 1.38, and Question 10, page 154. Also, refer to the explanation in the Discount Yield Table.

Discount points—The amount of discount expressed as a point or a percentage. For example: A discount of five points would be 5% of the loan amount; one point equals 1% of the loan amount.

Discount rate—In commercial banking, it is the rate charged by the Federal Reserve to member banks for borrowed funds.

Disintermediation—The situation in which depositors are withdrawing funds from a savings and loan institution for the purpose of working their money at higher yields in other deposits or investments.

Dispossess—Refer to *Eviction.*

Distressed property—Term that denotes property in trouble due to one of several reasons such as: cost overrun, insufficient income, poor management, or any other conditions which affect the mortgagor's ability to repay the loan on a timely basis.

Documentary evidence—Written evidence in support of claim.

Domicile—The apparently permanent home of an individual. A person may have several residences but only one domicile.

Dormer—A dormer window projects from the slope of a roof and has an appearance of a house in itself.

Double whammy—The practice of exercising a due-on-sale clause and charging a prepayment penalty on the same loan.

Dower—Common-law right of a wife to part of her deceased husband's property. Refer to *Curtsey*.

Downspout—A part of a gutter system that is in a vertical position.

Downzoning—Land that is rezoned to a lesser use in terms of commercialism or density. An example would be a rezoning of multiple-family plan to single-family use.

Draw—In mortgage terms, it implies a cash payment from the lender to the contractor or builder according to the terms and conditions of a construction loan.

Drip cap—A projection over a door or window which forces rainwater to fall away from the building.

Drop siding—Exterior siding applied to the framing structure by the "tongue and groove" method.

Dry closing—The act of closing without distribution of funds. Reasons for delay in funding are normally unfulfilled conditions of loan approval or lack of a satisfactory final inspection of the subject property.

Dual contract—An illegal practice of an agreement between a seller and purchaser that is different from what is disclosed to a lender. Refer to Question 1.82 and the comments to that question.

Dual periods of eligibility—Refer to Question 2.14.

Ducts—Conduits used in heating and air conditioning systems.

Due date—The date upon which a mortgage payment is due. Payments made after the due date are delinquent even though they may not involve a delinquent fee.

Due-on-sale clause—A clause in a mortgage allowing the lender to call the mortgage due and payable upon resale of a subject property.

Duplex—A two-family dwelling.

Duress—Compulsion, force, or pressure forcing an individual to perform an act.

Dutch Colonial—An architectural style of home design which features a gable roof.

Dwelling—A person's residence. Commonly used to imply a single-family dwelling or a house.

Earnest money—A cash deposit that accompanies a sales contract as a show of good faith in abiding by the terms and conditions as set forth in the contract.

Earnest money contract—Refer to *Contract.*

Easement—A right in property that is less than a right in possession. This term is most commonly used to refer to a right that a party has in relationship to another party's property.

Eaves—The lower portion of a roof that projects out over the side walls of a building.

Ecology—A study which shows the impact of the environment with living things.

Economic depreciation—Loss of value in property that can be caused by changes in the neighborhood or zoning.

Economic life—That period of time in which a property has a useful life. For VA loans, the term of the loan is normally limited to the number of years of economic life as indicated on the VA appraisal or CRV.

Economic rent—The rent a property would normally bring if leased. In most loan underwriting circumstances, an investor with multiple properties can claim an economic rent on a unit which happens to be vacant at the time of loan application.

Effective age—An appraisal term used to describe the age of a property other than its actual age. For example, a fifty-year-old house that has been recently renovated and had the installation of new plumbing, electrical, furnace, kitchen appliances, cabinets, etc., may have an effective age of 15 years.

Effective gross income—Gross income minus a vacancy allowance and collection loss.

Egress—The right to exit a property.

Elevation—The height of land above sea level. In a set of blueprints, it is the drawings of sides of a structure. For example, a front elevation would show the appearance of the front of a building.

Eligibility—Refer to the answer to Questions 2.3-5, and 2.21.

Elizabethan architecture—A two- or two and one-half story home featuring steep roof slopes and structural framework of exposed half-timbered wood with plaster in between.

Emblement—A farmer's crop resulting from his labor. The farmer has a right to remove the crop even though it may not mature before the end of his tenancy.

Eminent domain—The right of public authority to take property back by an exercise of its powers of condemnation. The property taken must be for public use and the owner must be justly compensated.

Employee Retirement Income Security Act (ERISA)—This act regulates the investments made by pension and profit-sharing plans. The Act also regulates conduct of the fiduciaries associated with pension funds.

Empty nesters—A couple whose children have grown and established residences of their own. A term frequently used in marketing analyses to determine the demand for certain housing by couples categorized as empty nesters.

Encroachment—An overlapping or trespassing of a structure or construction on one property onto an adjoining property. For example, part of a building or a driveway of one property extending over onto the adjoining property is an encroachment.

Encumbrance—An outstanding claim or lien on a property. A property with a mortgage is said to be encumbered by a mortgage.

End loan—A permanent loan placed on a property at the end of development or construction.

426

Endorsement—When FHA loans are endorsed, this action insures the loan under the National Housing Act.

Enjoined—Forbidden or regulated by a court order.

Entitlement—Refer to the answer to Question 2.21.

Entity—A form of ownership which can be as a partnership, corporation, limited partnership, or an individual.

Equal Credit Opportunity Act (ECOA)—In 1975 a federal law was enacted to prohibit any lender from discriminating against any purchaser on the basis of race, sex, color, religion, national origin, marital status, age or receipt of public assistance.

Equitable title—Interest in a property that has yet to close.

Equity—Value minus indebtedness.

Equity of redemption—A right given to a property owner to reclaim property lost prior to a foreclosure. Statutory redemption is the right, given in some states, to redeem the property after foreclosure.

Erosion—The gradual waste or depletion of land through natural causes.

Escalator clause—A clause in a lease which requires an increase in rent due to increase in cost. Examples of increases in cost could be property taxes or an index such as the Cost-of-Living Index.

Escape clause—A clause in a contract allowing parties to amend or cancel an agreement. Refer to FHA and VA amendatory language found in the answer to Questions 1.51 and 2.92.

Escheat—The act of property reverting to the state in the event of an owner's dying without leaving a will (intestate) and having no legal heirs. Abandoned property also reverts to the state.

Escrow—A deposit of valuable considerations such as money or documents with an impartial third party. Items of value are placed in escrow to assure the successful compliance of an agreement such as a contract of sale.

Escrow account—For mortgage purposes, it is an account that a mortgagee maintains for the periodic payment of real estate fees and insurance premiums for the mortgaged property. An escrow account also is used for the separation of money between parties such as a seller and purchaser. Funds held in escrow are to be deposited in an account maintained solely for the safekeeping of money by an impartial third party.

Escrow analysis—Normally, a periodic accounting to determine if deposits in the escrow account are adequate to pay obligations when due.

Escrow overage or shortage—Funds that are in excess of or insufficient for the balance required for the successful function of the escrow account.

Escrow payment—The portion of the monthly payment applied to obligations other than the principal and interest required of the mortgage.

Estate—The interest a person has in real property. There are many different types of estates, each giving a different degree of ownership. For federal income tax purposes, it is the total value of both real and personal property an individual possesses at the time of his/her death.

Estop—Obstruct or prevent

Estoppel—A legal doctrine preventing one from asserting a contention because of prior facts and circumstances which are contrary to the present contention. If a person signs a certificate acknowledging a balance owned on a mortgage of $50,000, the Doctrine of Estoppel would prevent that person from later contending that the balance owed was only $25,000. The document signed by a party acknowledging the balance of a debt is termed an Estoppel Certificate.

Et al—Latin for "and others."

Ethics—Refer to *Code of ethics.*

Et ux—Latin for "and wife."

Et vir—Latin for "and husband."

428

Eviction—A legal proceeding for a landlord to regain possession of real property.

Evidence of title—Legal documents that support ownership of real property. Normally, a deed is evidence of title.

Exception—A term normally used in connection with title insurance for matters that are "excepted" from coverage against loss. Title insurance policies usually will make an exception to a public utility easement.

Exclusive agency—A written listing with a real estate broker giving a right to sell property for a specific time; if the owner sells the property, the broker is not entitled to a commission.

Exclusive listing—A written, exclusive right to sell property for a specific period of time. There are two types of exclusive listings—exclusive agency and exclusive right to sell.

Exclusive right to sell—A written listing agreement giving a broker the exclusive right to sell a specific property. The listing broker is entitled to a commission regardless of who sells the property.

Exculpatory clause—Clause in a mortgage which prevents personal liability of the borrower.

Exculpatory language—Language in a note meaning the same as nonrecourse. The creditor will seek satisfaction in the security for the debt, and not from personal liability on the part of the debtor.

Execute—To perform in such a way as to make a document legally valid.

Executor—An individual or trust company designated in a will to carry out the instructions for disposal of property. The roles of an executor and an administrator are similar. An executor is named in a will, and an administrator is appointed if a party dies without a will or intestate.

Executrix—A woman named as an executor.

Exemplary damages—Damages awarded to a plaintiff over and above that which was sought for compensations from an actual loss for injuries. The excess damages charge is

429

used as an example of the punishment that can be rendered because of gross or deliberate negligence.

Extended coverage (EC)—That part of a standard fire insurance policy that extends coverage to other perils such as wind, lightning, hail, etc. Coverage that is beyond what the normal policy affords.

Facade—Usually the front wall of a building.

Face interest—The amount of interest stated on a mortgage or a note.

Face value—The par value of an instrument such as a mortgage, bond, or note.

Fair Credit Reporting Act—Federal law, enacted in 1971, that requires a lender to disclose to a borrower the nature and source of credit information. This law gives an individual the right to examine his credit history and any other information which may be on file with a credit reporting agency, within established guideline.

Fair market rent—Refer to *Economic rent.*

Fannie Mae—A nickname for the Federal National Mortgage Association (FNMA).

Farm—Normally used to describe large acreage used for growing crops or certain animals or fish for sale. Commonly used by REALTORS® to describe a selected area in which a concentrated effort is made to obtain listings.

Farmers Home Administration (FmHA)—An agency of the U.S. Department of Agriculture which administers programs for farmers and rural home purchasers.

Farm Mortgage Bankers Association—The founding organization of the present Mortgage Bankers Association. The Farm Mortgage Bankers Association was founded in 1914 and changed its name to The Mortgage Bankers Association in 1923. Refer to *Mortgage Bankers Association.*

Fascia—Flat, horizontal board used to cover the ends of rafters.

430

Feasibility Study—The detailed study of the chances for success of a proposed project.

Federal Home Loan Bank Board (FHLBB)—A board established to charter and regulate federal savings and loans institutions. The Board also oversees the operations of FSLIC and FHLMC.

Federal Home Loan Mortgage Corporation (FHLMC)—A private corporation authorized by Congress, whose primary purpose is to establish a secondary market for conventional home loans. FHLMC is also known as "Freddie Mac" and the "Mortgage Corporation." Money for Freddie Mac is generated by the sale of participation certificates secured by pools of conventional mortgage loans.

Federal Housing Administration (FHA)—A division of the U.S. Department of Housing and Urban Development which was established under the provisions of the National Housing Act as approved on 27 June 1934. This government agency is the innovator of the long-term, amortized, minimum down-payment home mortgage common in today's market.

Federal Land Bank—A source of long-term mortgage loans for rural properties featuring a variable interest rate with a maximum loan-to-value ratio of 85%. There are twelve of these banks.

Federal National Mortgage Association (FNMA) (Fannie Mae)—A corporation which provides a secondary market for FHA, VA, and conventional loans. Fannie Mae is the nation's largest private investor in American home mortgages. With assets in excess of $90 billion, Fannie Mae is the third largest corporation in the United States. Although stock is now publicly owned, the president of the United States still has the authority to appoint five of the fifteen directors.

Federal Reserve System—The central federal banking system which provides service and regulates member commercial banks.

Federal Savings and Loan Association—A financial institution which is a member of the Federal Home Loan Bank System and the Federal Savings and Loan and Insurance Corporation.

Federal Savings and Loan Insurance Corporation (FSLIC) The government agency which insures deposits in savings and loan associations.

Federal Trade Commission (FTC)—Federal agency charged with the regulation of advertisements and promotions of companies engaged in interstate commerce.

Fee simple—Ownership of property that is believed to be unrestricted subject to certain powers such as police, eminent domain, or certain other restrictions for public benefit.

Felony—A crime punishable by imprisonment in a state or federal prison. A felony usually is punishable by imprisonment for one year or more.

Felt—Fibrous material used for sheathing on walls and roof. It is a highly absorbent insulation against heat, cold, and dampness.

FHA loan—A loan which is insured by the Federal Housing Administration.

FHA non-supervised lender—Refer to Question 1.52.

Fiduciary—One who acts in a financial role for the benefit of another.

Final endorsement—The date FHA endorses the loan for mortgage insurance purposes.

Financial Accounting Standards Board (FASB)—A private independent entity which sets standards for financial accounting and reporting. FASB gets its authority from the SEC.

Fire wall—A brick or incombustible wall built between buildings or part of a building whose main purpose is to stop the spreading of fire. The wall should rise three feet above roof level.

Firm commitment—For FHA purposes, it is the loan approval period. Refer to Question 1.46.

Fixture—Personal property for improvements that are permanently affixed to the property so as to become real property. Built-in dishwashers, ovens, and microwaves are fixtures.

Flashing—Non-corrosive metal used around angles or junctions in roofs and exterior walls to insulate against leaks. Flashing is used around chimneys, vents, dormer windows, or valleys between two sections of a roof.

Flexible Loan Insurance Plan (FLIP)—A graduated payment mortgage with a pledged account.

Flexible payment mortgage (FPM)—A loan which allows interest only for a specific period, then principal and interest sufficient to amortize the mortgage.

Floor area ratio—The ratio of total floor area of a building to the total area of a site.

Floor joist—The framing which supports the floor. The normal size for the floor joist is either 2" x 8" or 2" x 10".

Floor loan—A mortgage with an initial funding based upon completion of a project with additional funding occurring upon a specific condition, such as achievement of an occupancy level or a cash-flow requirement.

Floor plan—The layout or arrangement of rooms in a building.

Floor-to-ceiling loan—A loan used for construction of a project which can be increased upon reaching cash-flow or occupancy requirements.

Flue—A duct or pipe for the passage of air, smoke, or gases. Smoke passes through a flue in a chimney.

Footing—The base of a foundation wall. A footing distributes the weight of a superstructure over a greater area so as to prevent shifting or settling.

Foreclosure—The legal action allowing a mortgagee to sell a mortgagor's property in an attempt to satisfy the debt.

Forfeiture—Loss of money or valuable consideration due to failure to perform under the terms of an agreement.

Formica—A plastic material most commonly used for kitchen cabinet counters.

Forward commitment—A commitment by a lender to purchase or make a loan in the future.

Forward delivery—The delivery of mortgages or mortgage-backed securities in fulfillment of a cash transaction or a future transaction paid at an earlier date.

Foyer—Hallway or open area at the entrance of a building.

Franchise—The authorization or license to do business and operate under the methods of another.

Fraud—The intentional misrepresentation of facts or figures to purposely deceive another party, such as a creditor.

Freddie Mac—Nickname for Federal Home Loan Mortgage Corporation.

Freehold—Estate which is free of a time limitation.

French provincial—A style of French architecture which is distinguished by its hipped roof and dormer-type windows.

Front footage—The linear measurement along the front portion of a parcel which adjoins a major street or walkway.

Front money—Money needed to start a project that is generally furnished by the developer or owner as his/her capital contribution.

Frost line—The depth to which soil freezes.

Fully-indexed rate—An interest rate on an Adjustable Rate Mortgage which equals the index plus the margin.

Functional depreciation—A loss of value created by causes within the property such as a poor floor plan.

Functional obsolescence—Structure, equipment, or floor plan which has become inefficient because of innovative changes that have occurred since its construction.

Funding fee—See Question 2.76.

Furring—Narrow strips of wood used to level up a pad of a wall or floor. Also wood strips between a wall and plaster to provide air space.

Gable—A ridged roof, triangular in shape. Refer to roof types in figures.

Gambrel roof—A ridged roof with four slopes in total. Refer to roof types in figures.

Gap financing—Financing used by contractors to close the gap between the floor loan and the construction loan. Usually what is used is a second mortgage standby commitment.

Garnishment—A legal action enabling a creditor to have an employer withhold money to be used in payment of a debt.

Generally accepted accounting principles (GAAP)—An approach to accounting or reporting by which a true portfolio sale gives recognition to either a profit or a loss. These principles are issued by the AICPA.

General contractor—The general contractor or prime contractor is the party engaged either to construct or to supervise a construction project. A general contractor may hire other contractors, known as subcontractors.

Georgian—An architecture of formal, colonial style adapted from English design. This architecture is characterized by simple lines; balanced window openings, doors, and chimneys; and much ornamentation.

G.I. loan—A VA loan.

Gingerbread—Excessive ornamentation on a house. Used with Victorian-style houses.

Ginnie Mae—Nickname for Government National Mortgage Association.

Good-faith estimate—A good-faith estimate, or disclosure, of the settlement charges the mortgagor will incur at closing. A good-faith estimate of settlement charges is required by the Real Estate Settlement Procedures Act.

Government National Mortgage Association (GNMA)—A government agency authorized to guarantee payments to investors for mortgage-backed securities and to absorb the cost of low-interest-rate loans which are used to finance low-income housing. GNMA facilitates the movement of money into the mortgage market through pooling mortgages together in a minimum amount of $500,000 and allowing certificates in as low as $25,000 and in multiple denominations of $5,000 thereafter. These certificates can be sold to the public, as opposed to the shipping of individual mortgages to the ultimate investor. FHA, VA, and Farmer's Home Administration Loans are eligible for Ginnie Mae mortgage-backed securities.

Government Sponsored Enterprise (GSE)—A designation meaning a secondary marketing entity with government support, such as: GNMA, FNMA, FHLMC.

Grace period—A time period, after maturity, by which one can act without penalty, i.e. as in making a loan payment or redeeming a time deposit.

Grade—The elevation or ground level of a building site, or to prepare a smooth surface for a building site.

Graduated payment adjustable rate mortgage (GPARM) Most GPM loans are fixed-rate loans. With a GPARM, payments are graduated, but the interest rate is based on an adjustable-rate mortgage. These loans are normally used to lower the monthly payment, which helps the applicant qualify for the loan. These loans normally involve negative amortization.

Graduated payment mortgage (GPM)—Monthly payments of principal and interest are graduated so that amortization of the loan can take place within the term specified. These loans normally involve negative amortization. Refer to the FHA and VA GPM loans.

Grandfather clause—A term meaning to allow the continuance of a use or a practice that is now forbidden by new legislation; the practice or use being allowed under the old legislation.

Grantee—That party who is the recipient of property.

Grantor—That party who transfers title to another party.

Gross area—The square footage of a building as measured by the outside walls.

Gross rent multiplier (GRM)—A rule of thumb used to determine value by dividing the sales price by the gross rental income. If a property sells for $60,000 and the annual-gross-rent income is $10,000, the gross rent multiplier is 6. GRM also can be determined on a monthly basis.

Ground lease—A lease of the ground or land and none of the improvements.

Grout—A thin mortar used to fill joints between bricks or blocks.

Growing equity mortgage (GEM)—A structured prepayment of a mortgage. Mortgage payments increase, usually on an annual basis, for a specified period of time. After the period of increases, the payments level off and early prepayment of the mortgage is achieved. For more information on a GEM, refer to Questions 2.80-81 found on pages 104 and 105.

Guaranteed mortgage certificate (GMC)—The bond-like instrument issued by the FHLMC representing ownership in a large pool of residential mortgages. Principal is returned annually and interest is paid semi-annually.

Guaranty—Refer to Questions 2.21-22.

Guardian ad litem—The party appointed by a court to represent the interests of a minor or incompetent in a lawsuit.

Half-timbered—Walls with timber frames exposed for decorative purposes.

Hangout—The remaining balance of a loan when the term is beyond that of the lease.

Hard cost—The cost of land acquisition and improvement.

Headers—Double wood boards supporting joists, windows or doors so that the weight is transferred to the studs.

Hedging—In mortgage banking, it is the purchase or sale of mortgage futures contract to offset cash market transactions to be made at a future date.

Heir—An individual who inherits property.

Hereditament—Real property; property that can be inherited.

Hidden defect—Cloud on a title that is not found by a search of public records.

Highest and best use—An appraisal term used to describe the best use of a property. If a property is located in a residentially-zoned subdivision, its highest and best use would be as a residence.

Hip roof—A roof with four sides sloping upward to a ridge.

Holdback—A provision whereby money is withheld until certain performance is made.

Holder in due course—A doctrine allowing a person who acquires a bearer instrument in good faith to keep said instrument free of certain claims.

Hold harmless clause—A provision in a contract whereby a party is protected from claims.

Home Mortgage Disclosure Act—Legislation requiring disclosure of mortgage data to the public by depository institutions which make federally-related mortgages in a Standard Metropolitan Statistical Area, and have assets in excess of $10 million. The data will be information pertaining to the number of loans originated or purchased and the total dollar amount on an annual basis.

Homeowner's association—An organization of owners in a condominium, planned unit development or subdivision. The purpose of a homeowner's association is to enforce deed restrictions and manage common elements of their development.

Homeowner's Warranty Program (HOW)—An insurance program used by builders to give warranty against defects in the house for a specific period of time. Extended coverage is provided beyond the normal one-year warranty period for new homes.

438

Homestead—Laws in some states which protect a person's principal residence against judgments up to certain amounts.

Homestead exemption—Favorable treatment in some states for a person's principal residence in relationship to the assessed valuation.

Horizontal Property Act—Legislation allowing condominium ownership of property.

Housing and Urban Development (HUD)—An agency established by the Housing and Urban Development Act of 1965 and whose purpose is the implementation and administration of government housing and urban development programs.

Housing expense—An FHA term meaning the combination of principal, interest, taxes, insurance, maintenance, and utilities.

Hypothecate—To pledge property as collateral for a debt without giving up title or possession.

Immediate Delivery—The physical delivery of loans from the seller to the purchaser for immediate underwriting and purchase by the investor. Normally thought to be within 30 days from the date of the commitment letter.

Impound—Refer to *Escrow*.

Improved land—Property which has been developed either partially or fully with installation of utilities, roads, curbs, gutters, and buildings.

Improvements—An item permanently attached to raw land. Additions to a building or the building itself can be classified as an improvement.

Imputed interest—An interest rate which is stated by the Internal Revenue Service because the interest stated in the mortgage is unrealistically low or no interest is stated.

Inchoate—This term describes something that has begun, but is not yet completed. Some examples would be a lien that is going to be recorded, but has not actually been recorded yet; or a deed that has been signed and acknowledged, but has not yet been made a public record.

Income approach—One of the three approaches to value used in appraising real property. In the income approach, value is created by the income produced by the subject property. Cost and market are the other two approaches to value.

Incompetent—In real estate law, a person is deemed incompetent if he or she cannot fulfill the obligations of a contract due to reasons such as being a minor or mentally ill.

Indemnify—The act of insuring or protecting a person against loss or damage.

Indenture—An executed deed to which two or more parties having different interests enter into corresponding grants or obligations to each other.

Index—A benchmark or measure used to indicate a cost. Refer to Question 3.24.

Index lease—A lease with a rent adjusting to the movement of an index such as the Consumer Price Index or Cost-of-Living Index.

Infrastructure—Facilities and services of a community as it relates to providing transportation, water, sewer, and recreation or community services.

Ingress—The right to enter or have access is ingress.

Injunction—A court order requiring a person or a party to refrain from performing or to perform a certain action.

In personam—A Latin term meaning "against the person." A court action against a defendant.

In rem—A Latin term meaning against the thing. A court action against a property as opposed to an individual.

Insolvency—A condition in which a debtor is unable to pay his creditors.

Installment—A partial payment of a purchase price of a propety or a methodical repayment of a debt.

Installment sale—A method of sale in which the property owner accepts a mortgage as part payment and reports the principal collected in a taxable year as income.

Institutional lender—A financial institution which invests in mortgages for its own portfolio.

Instrument—A legal document containing some right or obligation.

Insurable interest—An interest in property either real or personal which would cause a loss if the interest were damaged or destroyed.

Insurable title—A title of such quality that title insurance can be obtained.

Insurance—In residential property, the term "insurance" is normally encountered in three different roles or types of coverage. Insurance is available for protection against damage to real property, which is commonly known as fire or hazard insurance. Insurance is also available to cover losses incurred from a foreclosure. This commonly is referred to as private (private mortgage for conventional loans) or mortgage insurance for FHA loans. Insurance also is available for payment of the mortgage in full in the event of the death of a mortgagor.

Interest—The cost for the use of money.

Interest only (IO)—A security which pays cash flows from the interest paid by an underlying pool of mortgages. An IO is an interest-only security backed by an underlying collateral, a mortgage pool. See *PO*.

Interest rate—The cost for the use of money expressed as a percentage of the sum of money borrowed or the rate of return from an investment in a mortgage.

Interim financing—This term is used to express a mortgage which is of a short term and generally used for construction financing.

Interstate Land Sales Act—Federal law which is administered by the Department of Housing and Urban Development which requires that promotional and advertising procedures, as well as disclosures, meet certain minimum requirements when land is sold on an interstate basis.

Inter vivos—A Latin term meaning between living persons.

Intestate—Legal condition of a person who dies without a will.

Intrinsic value—The value of a tangible asset as separated from the intangible word. The value of something in itself. For example: The value of actual silver used in a coin is the intrinsic value as opposed to the value of the coin in the marketplace.

Inverse condemnation—Litigation to seek a claim by a property owner against a governmental agency or municipality for damages created to the value of property which was taken by eminent domain proceedings and for which no compensation was paid.

Investor—In mortgage banking, the term "investor" commonly is used in two situations; an investor can mean the party who owns the mortgage or will soon become the owner of the mortgage, or the term can commonly apply to a party who owns a residence on a non-occupant owner basis or that party who is applying for a mortgage to own a residence on a non-occupant-owner basis.

Jalousies—Adjustable glass louvers in windows or doors so that the amount of light and air can be regulated and rain excluded.

Jamb—A vertical member or lining of a doorway or window. A door jamb or window jamb supports the horizontal member of the opening.

Jerry-built—A slang term meant to imply construction an inferior workmanship or quality.

Joint—In construction, this term means the point at which two objects or surfaces join or meet.

Joint and several liability—An obligation or liability from one or all of the borrowers to their lender. Under joint and several liability, a lender can sue one or all of the borrowers for satisfactory performance.

Joint tenancy—Ownership of property by two or more parties. Each party owns an undivided interest with the right of survivorship. In the event of death of one of the owners, the surviving owner(s) inherits the property.

Joint venture—An agreement between two or more parties to invest in a business or property.

Joist—The supporting boards of a floor or a ceiling. This term is commonly used in conjunction with what it supports such as "floor joist" or "ceiling joist."

Journeyman—Skilled worker who has learned the trade through an apprenticeship or a period of on-the-job training.

Judgement—A formal decision by a court of law. A judgment can result in a lien against property or a garnishment of wages so that a creditor can collect the debt. The term "judgment" is also seen in real estate as it applies to an appraiser's process in deciding the value of property.

Judicial foreclosure—This type of foreclosure takes place through court action as opposed to power of sale given to a trustee.

Junior mortgage—In general, a mortgage which is subordinate or behind a prior mortgage. A second mortgage would be an example of a junior mortgage.

Just compensation—Payment based on market value of the real estate taken in condemnation.

Jutty—A structure which sticks out into a body of water. Said structure could be a pier composed of rocks or pilings. In construction, this term can be used in reference to a protruding pad of a building such as a balcony or bay window.

Key lot—A lot that enjoys added value because of its strategic location.

Kickback—Payment made in return for a referral which resulted in business for the payer. The person or business being referred is unaware of the payment. It is generally illegal.

Kicker—In real estate financing, this term identifies something more than principal and interest being returned to the lender. Examples of kickers would be equity participation in the ownership of the property or participation in rentals received.

Kick plate—A metal strip at the lower edge of a door used to protect the finish.

Kiln—A large, oven-like chamber used to dry or harden materials such as lumber, brick, and lime. This term is heard in connection with the construction industry when one reads that lumber has been kiln-dried.

Kilo—This term is used to note one thousand such as a kilogram having one thousand grams, a kilovolt having one thousand volts or a kilowatt having one thousand watts.

King post—The middle post of a truss.

Kiting checks—Method by which a check is written against funds not on deposit on the date the check is written.

Knoll—A small, rounded hill.

Laches—The practice of delaying or being negligent in asserting one's legal rights.

Lag screw—A large, heavy, wood screw with a square head. There is no slot in the head.

Laminated—Layers of wood or other material bonded together to form a single unit.

Land—The surface of the earth extending down to the center and upward to the sky. In real estate, the term "land" includes surface, mineral, and air rights.

Land banking—The practice of acquiring land and holding it for future use.

444

Land contract—This term is synonymous with contract for deed and installment land contract. With a land contract, the purchaser is not given title to the property until the full price has been paid. The purchaser enjoys equitable title in that he has the right to possession, but the seller retains legal title. In the event of default, the seller can regain his property more quickly than with a mortgage.

Land lease—A lease in which only the ground is rented.

Landlocked—A lot that does not have access to a public thoroughfare except through an adjacent lot.

Landlord—A party who rents property. A landlord is a lessor.

Landmark—An identifying mark or monument serving to indicate the boundary for a tract of land.

Lap joint—The point of contact between two pieces of wood connected together by lapping one over the other.

Lap siding—The siding used for exterior finishes of a house or other structure. Each board overlaps another in a fashion similar to clapboard siding.

Latent defect—A hidden or concealed defect. One that is known by a seller but cannot be seen by a purchaser or easily discovered by an appraiser or property inspector.

Lath—Thin strips of wood or metal or other material used as the support or groundwork for slates, tiles, or plaster.

Law day—The day a note or a mortgage is due to be paid.

Lawful interest—The maximum interest rate allowed by law.

Lead-based paint—Paint that was commonly used up until the early 60s. At that time, medical research showed the paint to be harmful for ingestion by humans. VA and FHA have taken steps to prevent and solve the problems created by lead-based paint. See notes on page 145 in Property Inspection Checklist section.

Lean-to—A term used to describe a shed or building constructed against an outside wall of another building and having an inclined roof. The structure appears to lean to the attached building.

Lease—A contract involving payment of rent for possession of real estate for a specific period of time.

Leasehold—The estate or interest which a tenant has in the real estate.

Lease-purchase—A method of purchasing property through gradual payments above the required rental.

Leaves—The hinged, sliding, or detachable parts of a sliding door, window, tabletop, or shutters.

Legacy—A gift of money or personal property by will.

Legal age—That age by which a person can take title to real estate and is no longer considered a minor.

Legal description—A statement acceptable by real estate law for describing real estate.

Legal name—That name used by an individual for business purposes. Normally implies a person's full name.

Legal notice—Notice that conforms to practices required by law.

Legal tender—Payment that is deemed acceptable by law from a debtor to a creditor.

Lender option—Refer to Question 1.61.

Lessee—A party who rents property from another. A tenant.

Lessor—The party who rents property to a tenant or lessee.

Letter of credit (LOC) A written agreement by which a bank substitutes its credit for that of an individual or business. The bank issuing the Letter of Credit will honor drafts or other demands for payment upon compliance with conditions specified in the LOC.

Letter of intent—A written agreement outlining a party's intentions to perform certain actions connected with real estate. A letter of intent is not binding. It is merely to show the intentions of the parties involved.

Level payment mortgage—A mortgage requiring the same payment each month until the debt is amortized or paid.

446

Leverage—The practice of creating money by borrowing on real estate either by acquiring the subject property or other properties.

Levy—Assess, collect, or seize.

Liability—A debt, financial obligation, or potential loss.

Liability insurance—Protection against claims by third parties due to damages or injuries caused by the insured or his property.

Liable—Responsible or obligated.

Lien—A claim or charge against property thereby causing the property to be used as security for the payment of the claim or debt. A mortgage is a lien.

Lien theory—This theory treats the mortgage as a secured debt against property by which the owner retains title. This theory differs from the title theory which supports the belief that mortgage property is transferred to the lender or his representative such as a trustee and the title is not re-conveyed until the debt has been paid.

Life—The period of time improvements to a property are expected to have physical or economic utility.

Life estate—An estate in property of which the duration is the life of the person or party receiving the estate or interest.

Life tenant—A tenant who enjoys the use of property for his/her life.

Light—In appraisal terminology, the word "light" indicates a single window pane.

Limited partnership—A partnership consisting of one or more parties who serve as general partners and are liable for losses and responsible for the operation of the business. The limited partners are liable only to the extent of their investment, and they are passive in terms of their participation in the business operation.

Line of credit—The maximum dollar amount a bank will lend to one of its credit worthy customers without requiring a new, formal loan submission.

447

Lintel—A horizontal piece of board, stone, or steel positioned above a door or a window. Its purpose is to support the load above the opening.

Liquidated damages—A predetermined amount agreed upon in a contract that one party will pay to another in the event of a breach of the subject contract.

Liquidity—The degree of ease with which certain assets can be converted into cash.

Lis pendens—A recorded legal notice indicating that there is a pending suit affecting property within that jurisdiction.

Listing—This term can refer to:
1. the written contract between principal and agent, or
2. an agreement between the seller of property and a broker, or
3. a property that a broker has for sale.

Litigate—To dispute or contend in form of law; to settle a dispute or seek relief in a court of law; to carry on a suit.

Litigation—A lawsuit. Legal action, including all proceedings therein.

Littoral—Land bordering on a large body of water.

Livability—The quality of property to be used as a home.

Live load—The weight which a building is subject to due to people and fixtures that occupy its space. Another example would be the weight of moving traffic over a bridge as opposed to the weight of the bridge itself.

Load-bearing wall—A wall that is built to withstand a supporting weight. A load-bearing wall gives structural support.

Loan application—Document from a would-be borrower to a lender requesting a loan.

Loan commitment—An agreement to lend a specific amount of money over stated terms and conditions including time periods.

Loan correspondent—This word has come to take on two meanings. The first is as an originator of loans and a servicer of those loans, such as a mortgage banker. The second is as an agent for an FHA-approved mortgagee.

Loan coverage—That ratio in which the net operating income before depreciation exceeds the debt service. An example would be net income before depreciation of $400,000 as to debt service of $200,000 would result in a two-to-one loan coverage ratio.

Loan-to-value ratio (LTV)—The percentage amount borrowed in the acquisition or refinancing of property. An 80% loan-to-value ratio would require the loan to be no more than 80% of the lesser of the purchase price or the appraised value.

Lock box—A metal box put on the door of a listed property by the listing agent so showings can occur without the listing agent's being required to be at the property. REALTORS® have a key to the box, which contains a key to the house.

Lock-in—That period of time in which a loan cannot be prepaid. This term is also used to imply a period of time in which loan discount points or the interest rate are set at a specific amount or percentage.

London inter-bank offer rate (LIBOR)—An average of daily lending rates from several major London banks. LIBOR has been used as an index for Adjustable Rate Mortgages.

Long-term lease—A lease of ten years or more in duration.

Loss-payable endorsement—An endorsement to the property insurance policy specifying the lender as a payee in the event of property damage. This endorsement protects the lender's interest in the property in proportionate value to the loan outstanding.

Lot—A distinct portion of land.

Lot and block—A method for describing or finding a parcel of land.

Louver—Horizontal slats or fins over an opening allowing ventilation with the exclusion of rain or snow.

Luminous ceiling—A ceiling of translucent materials emitting light throughout its entire surface from fluorescent tubes above the ceiling. Usually made of glass or plastic.

Maintenance—The work required to keep a building in its proper operating condition.

Majority—The age at which an individual is no longer deemed a minor for conducting business affairs or a term used to describe more than half.

Mandatory commitment—An agreement by which the buyer and seller must perform, neither having the option to not perform as stated in the commitment. If performance is not possible, there are usually severe penalties to be paid by the defaulting party.

Mansard roof—A roof with two slopes on all four sides. Refer to roof types in figures.

Margin—1) In futures trading, it is the specific amount set by each exchange which both buyers and sellers are required to deposit as a guarantee assuring successful performance of a commitment to take delivery during a designated period of time. The funds are held by the clearing organization of the exchange. 2) The down payment required when borrowing funds for stock purchases. The Federal Reserve Board sets margins in stock purchases and the down payment is expressed as a percentage of the purchase price or market value. 3) The spread between the index and the rate. Refer to Question 3.25.

Margin call—The requirement for additional funds or collateral to serve as security for trading losses on outstanding positions which are subject to margin.

Marketable title—Title to real estate which is free from defect.

Market approach to value—The evaluation of property based on actual sales of comparable properties.

Market price—The amount paid for property in an actual market transaction.

Market rent—Rent attributable to a unit, if it were leased to the public.—Contract rent is the actual rent paid for a unit.

Market value—The price at which a willing seller would sell and a willing buyer would buy, neither being under duress.

Mark to the market—The daily adjustment of margin accounts to reflect the market gain or loss on the position relative to the daily settlement price.

Masonry—Walls built of brick, stone, concrete, tile, or similar materials.

Master deed—The conveyance document used for the sale of condominiums.

Master lease—A controlling lease by which subsequent leases are governed. A master lease could apply to an office building with subsequent leases pertaining to individual spaces in the building.

Master plan—Usually pertains to a zoning matter in which a developer submits a plan for the overall, long-term development of a property.

Maturity—The date on which a loan is due to be paid in full.

Mechanic's lien—A lien given by law to protect and secure the payment for labor or materials.

Meeting of the minds—A consent or agreement between parties of a contract.

Merchantable title—Refer to *Marketable title*.

Meridian line—A surveyor's term used to indicate a north-south line.

Metes and bounds—A description of property by identifying boundaries through their terminal points and angles.

Midanet—Mortgage Information Direct Access Network. Freddie's Mac's automated system which electronically transfers loan data and accounting reports.

Military clause—A clause found in a lease allowing a military tenant to terminate the lease in the event of transfer, dis-

451

charge, or other circumstances requiring the transfer of his or her residence.

Mill—One tenth of a cent. This term normally is used for tax rate purposes. One hundred mills would be a tax of ten cents per dollar of assessed valuation.

Mineral rights—Those rights associated with the sale of resources such as oil or gas coming from the subject property.

Minimum lot area—The smallest lot allowed in a subdivision upon which a building may be erected.

Minimum property standards—Standards written for minimum workmanship and quality of dwellings secured by loans insured by the Federal Housing Administration.

Mini-warehouse—A one-story building subdivided into cubicles for storage purposes.

Minor—A person who is not of legal age as specified by law. A person who has not reached his/her majority.

Misdemeanor—A crime usually punishable by imprisonment for one year or less. A misdemeanor is less serious than a felony.

Misnomer—A mistake in a name. If such a mistake occurs in a deed, it must be corrected.

Misrepresentation—A representation either unintentional or deliberate of an untrue set of facts. Misrepresentation also may be failure to disclose a set of facts which said failure would cause another party to act differently from what he or she would have if there had been disclosure of facts.

Miter—In usage by carpenters, a miter is the ends of two pieces of boards that are cut in such a way that when they are joined together an angular shape is produced.

Mitigation of damages—A reduction in damages. For example, a landlord may have a duty to find a replacement tenant for a tenant who has breached the lease unlawfully.

Mixed use—A combination of uses such as commercial and residential on one subject property or an area. Also known as mixed zoning.

Mode—The most frequent value in an array of numbers or a manner or method of doing something.

Modified pass-through—The required passing through of principal and interest collected to the investor of a mortgage-backed security. In a modified pass-through, principal and interest are paid to the investor regardless of whether or not the mortgage payment is made by the borrower.

Modular housing—Units constructed in a factory for assemblage on a building lot.

Moisture barrier—Treated material used to retard or prevent moisture or water vapor from seeping into or through walls or floors of a building.

Molding—A strip of decorative material usually required to cover gaps at wall junctions.

Month-to-month tenancy—In absence of any written agreement, a lease, either written or oral, is deemed to be on a month-to-month tenancy.

Monument—A visible marker, either natural or artificial, set at a point to determine boundaries for a survey of property.

Moratorium—A period of time in which certain activity is not allowed or required.

More or less—A phrase used to indicate a slight variation in the true size of real property. Approximately. Indicates that a measurement is not exact.

Mortar—A paste-like material made of lime and cement mixed with sand and water. Mortar is used as a bonding material for brick or stone.

Mortgage—A written instrument creating a lien upon real estate for the security of payment of a specified debt.

Mortgage-backed bonds—A bond that is backed by a pool of mortgages. The bond is a general obligation of the issuing institution.

Mortgage-backed Securities (MBS)—Securities or investments which represent an undivided interest in a pool of loans secured by mortgages or deed of trusts. Income from the underlying mortgages is used to pay off the bond or securities.

Mortgage banker—A party who originates, sells, and services mortgages. A mortgage banker is distinct from a mortgage broker in that servicing of the loans or collecting of the principal, interest, taxes, and insurance is performed.

Mortgage bankers association (MBA)—An organization composed of mortgage banking companies or other institutions which perform mortgage banking services. The address is: Mortgage Bankers Association, 1125 15th St. NW, Washington, D.C. 20005. The MBA was originally formed as a trade association in 1914 and was known as the Farm Mortgage Bankers Association. The present name of Mortgage Bankers Association began usage in 1923.

Mortgage broker—A party who originates and sells mortgages but does not service the loan.

Mortgage commitment—See *Loan commitment*.

Mortgage constant—The percentage ratio between annual debt service and the principal loan amount. Dividing of the annual debt service by the principal loan amount will equal the mortgage constant.

Mortgage correspondent—See *Loan correspondent*.

Mortgage credit certificate (MCC)—A non-refundable tax credit bearing from 10% to 50% of the interest paid on a home mortgage loan. There are qualifying restrictions such as limiting the program to first-time homebuyers with restricted income limits and sales prices.

Mortgage credit condition (MC)—An FHA condition of loan approval which must be fulfilled before closing or insurance of the loan.

454

Mortgagee—The lender. An easy way to distinguish mortgagee from mortgagor is—the word mortgagee has two "e's" in it, just like the word lender.

Mortgage Insurance (MI)—Policy which protects against default and consequent potential loss to lender. FHA deals in mortgage insurance. See *Private mortgage insurance.*

Mortgagee letters—Changes or announcements by HUD Central office.— You may want to call HUD Central in Washington, D.C. and ask to be placed on the mailing list, there is a nominal fee.

Mortgage life insurance—A diminishing term life insurance policy with the beneficiary being the mortgagee for the purpose of paying off the mortgage in the event of death of the insured.

Mortgage-related security (MRS) A generic term used to describe a variety of mortgage-related securities.

Mortgage revenue bonds (MRB)—Bonds issued by a public agency to create funds for housing. The bonds are retired by payments generated by the mortgage loans. These bonds are typically tax-exempt securities sold by state or municipal authorities for the purpose of raising capital for low interest rate mortgage loans to qualified individuals.

Mortgaging out—To obtain 100% or more financing for the acquisition of and any construction involved in the subject property.

Mortgagor—The borrower.

Mosaic—A combination of colored stones, glass, or glass arranged to form a decorative design.

Most-favored-tenant clause—A provision in a lease by which a tenant is assured that any negotiating concessions given to other tenants will also be given to him.

Mother Hubbard clause—A provision in a mortgage allowing a mortgagee not only to foreclose on a mortgage in default but also to foreclose on the mortgagor for any other mortgages that are owed to the mortgagee.

M roof—A twin, double-pitch roof.—See roof types in figures.

Mullion—That framing which divides the lights or panes of windows.

Multi-family housing—A residential structure with more than one dwelling unit.

Multiple listing—A joint effort by real estate brokers to pool together their listings so that all members of the Multiple Listing Service will have an opportunity to sell the listings.

Mutual Capital Certificate (MCC)—Equity certificates issued by mutual savings and loan banks and used to satisfy net worth and reserve requirements.

Mutual Mortgage Insurance Fund (MMI)—The FHA Insurance fund in which all mortgage insurance premiums are deposited and from which all losses are met.

Mutual savings banks—State-chartered savings institutions that are mutually owned by their investors. These institutions invest mainly in mortgages.

Name change—In conveying property, this is the setting forth of the present name of the seller and the name under which the seller acquired title if it is different. Also known as "name affidavit" and "one and the same."

Named-peril insurance—Protects those risks and perils as set forth in the insurance policy and no other as distinguished from an all-risk policy.

National Apartment Association (NAA)—An organization for owners, builders, and others involved in the multi-family housing industry. Address: National Apartment Association, 1825 K Street NW, Washington, DC 20006.

National Association of Corporate Real Estate Executives (NACORE)—Organization composed of parties dealing with buying, selling, and management of real estate owned by corporations. Address: National Association of Corporate Real Estate Executives, 7799 SW 62nd Avenue NW, South Miami, Florida 33143.

National Association of Home Builders (NAHB)—An organization for home builders and related industries. The address is: National Association of Home Builders, 15th and M Street NW, Washington, DC 20005.

National Association of Real Estate Brokers (NAREB)—An organization for minority real estate brokers and salespeople. Address: National Association of Real Estate Brokers, 9th Floor, Suite 900, 1101 Fourteenth Street NW, Washington, DC 20005.

National Association of Real Estate License Law Officials—NARELLO is an organization composed of commissioners from state real estate licensing agencies. Address: National Association of Real Estate License Law Officials, 2580 South 90th Street, Omaha, Nebraska 68124.

National Association of REALTORS® (NAR)—An organization composed of REALTOR® members. This organization has in excess of 600,000 members. Address: National Association of REALTORS®, 430 North Michigan Avenue, Chicago, Illinois 60611.

Negative amortization—Refer to Question 3.10.

Negative cash flow—The net loss after all operating expenses and debt service are paid.

Negotiable instrument—A written promise (check, stock, promissory note) to pay money. It is transferable from one person to another.

Negotiable order of withdrawal (NOW)—An instrument which represents a withdrawal from a savings account.

Negotiated-rate loan—Refer to Question 1.32.

Net effective income—An FHA term meaning gross income minus income taxes.

Net leasable area—Floor space which may be used by tenants for conducting their business. Usually excludes such areas as lobbies and space needed to house heating, cooling, or other equipment of a building.

Net lease—A lease by which the tenant can pay such items as taxes, insurance, and maintenance.

Net listing—A listing by which the broker's commission is the excess of the sales price over a net price as agreed with the seller. This practice is illegal in some states.

Net net—Net income after deducting insurance and maintenance expenses.

Net net net—Net income after deducting the cost of insurance, maintenance, and real estate taxes.

Net Operating Income (NOI)—Income after operating expenses have been deducted but prior to income taxes and debt service (principal and interest payments). This term is preferred over the term "net income" in reference to business operations.

Net worth—Excess of assets over liabilities.

Net yield—The return on investment after subtracting all expenses.

Net yield reporting—The servicer of loans passes through principal to the investor as collected and interest on a scheduled basis. The principal portion of a mortgage payment is remitted, if it has been paid.

Newel—An upright post at the top or bottom of a stairway, or at the landing turn, or at a point about which a circular stairway winds. A newel supports the handrail.

Next of kin—Persons who are related by blood.

Niche—A recess in a wall, usually for some decorative object.

Nominal loan rate—Face rate of interest.

Nominee—An entity or individual designated to represent another entity or individual.

Non-bearing wall—A wall which does not help to support the structure of a building.

Nonconforming loan—Normally usage of the word nonconforming implies loan amounts in excess of Freddie Mac and Fannie Mae regulations. Loans which do not meet standard underwriting guidelines as set forth by the agencies can also be described as nonconforming.

Nonconforming use—Usage that violates zoning regulations but is allowed to continue because it predates regulation it violates.

Nondisturbance clause or agreement—An agreement in which the mortgagee allows the lessee to continue occupancy under a lease in the event there is foreclosure of the mortgage. A nondisturbance agreement is effective providing the mortgage lien is recorded prior to the lease in question. A second meaning is the right of a seller to obtain mineral rights provided that the exploration of minerals will not conflict with surface operations or development.

Nonjudicial foreclosure—Power to sell property at foreclosure without court procedure. This foreclosure proceeding can be used by a trustee named in a deed of trust.

Nonnegotiable instrument—An instrument, such as a mortgage, which must be transferred by assignment.

Non-owner occupied A property which is not occupied by the owner is said to be non-owner occupied.

Nonperformance—Failure or refusal to act as agreed in a contract or other form of agreement.

Nonrecourse loan—A loan secured by property only. The holder of the note cannot seek liability from the debtor.

Nook—Commonly used to describe an obscure corner of a room or a portion of a house or a parcel of land.

Normal wear and tear—Deterioration or depreciation caused by the age and use of the property. A tenant is not responsible for damage caused by normal use.

Notarize—The act of a Notary Public in witnessing the authenticity of a signature.

Notary public—A person authorized to acknowledge certain documents such as contracts, mortgages, deeds, and affidavits, attest to the authenticity of signatures, and administer oaths.

Note—A written instrument, such as a mortgage, which acknowledges a debt.

Note rate—Refer to Question 3.19.

Notice—Official proclamation of a legal action or intent to take action.

Notice of default—Official notice to a defaulting party declaring a default has occurred.

Notice to quit—A phrase which can mean that a landlord wants a tenant to vacate or a tenant intends to vacate by a certain date.

Notorious possession—Openly occupying real estate owned by another and one of the requirements for gaining ownership of the real estate by adverse possession.

Novation—A substitution of a debt or a debtor based on the agreement of all parties.

Nuisance—Land usage that unreasonably interferes with the surrounding land activities.

Null and void—A phrase used to describe something that cannot legally be enforced.

Obligation bond—A bond executed by the borrower in excess of the loan amount. The bond serves as security for the lender against nonpayment of taxes, insurance premiums, or any unpaid interest.

Obligee—A noteholder, bondholder, mortgagee, or creditor.

Obligor—The debtor or mortgagor.

Obsolescence—Loss of value due to circumstances other than normal wear and tear, such as functional utility or economic or social changes.

Occupancy agreement—An agreement to permit a purchaser to occupy prior to closing. Rent usually is prorated on a daily basis.

Occupancy rate or level—A percentage of rental units which are currently occupied.

Offer—An agreement, promise, or expression of willingness to perform in a specific manner in relationship to entering a contract for the purchase of property.

Offer and acceptance—The required ingredients of a valid contract. A meeting of the minds on purchase price and terms.

Offering sheet—A one-page summary which helps an investor to evaluate a mortgage loan being submitted for purchase.

Office of Interstate Land Sales Registration (OILSR)—This office is a division of HUD and is responsible for accepting registrations of certain subdivisions sold in interstate commerce.

Off-site cost—Expenses related to construction which are incurred away from the site of construction. Examples would be extending roads, sewers, and water lines to the site.

Off-site improvements—Improvements made to the site such as access streets, curbs, sewers, and utility connections.

Ohm—The resistance of a circuit in which a potential difference of one volt produces a current of one ampere. The practical unit of electrical resistance.

Open and notorious—See *Notorious possession.*—A description of the use of property which is essential in establishing adverse possession.

Open-end commitment—A commitment to advance construction loan funds where there is no permanent mortgage takeout.

Open-end mortgage—A mortgage which allows future advances of principal upon agreement of the mortgagor and mortgagee.

Open house—The practice of showing a listing during hours which have been advertised to the public.

Open listing—A listing in which the real estate broker does not have an exclusive agency or an exclusive right to sell. A listing in which a number of brokers can sell the property.

Operating expenses—Expenses, such as taxes, insurance, and utilities, incurred in the maintenance of properties. Operating expenses do not include debt service or depreciation.

Operating ratio—The percentage relationship between operating expenses and effective gross income.

Opinion of title—A written opinion as to the validity of title, generally prepared by an attorney.

Option—An agreement to purchase or lease subject property for a specific period and specific terms within a specified time. A consideration is given to the owner who agrees to give this right for the specified time.

Optional delivery—An option of delivering loans under a loan purchase program.

Oral contract—An unwritten contract. Contract to purchase real estate must be in writing. Contracts to lease property for a period of one year or less need not be in writing. However, it is strongly recommended that all real estate contracts or leases be in writing.

Ordinances—Rules written by municipalities for governing the uses of land.

Ordinary and necessary business expense—Acceptable deductions for federal income tax purposes. Expenses incurred through the normal operation of a business.

Ordinary income—For federal income tax purposes, this income can be in the form of salaries, fees, commissions, dividends, interest, and other items not classified as capital gain.

Ordinary interest—Interest calculated on the exact number of days in the interest period with the base period being or having 360 days.

Ordinary loss—Loss that can be deducted against ordinary income.

Orientation—The positioning of a structure on a site relative to prevailing winds, exposure to the sun, and privacy from neighboring structures or traffic.

Original face—The original principal amount of a mortgage-backed instrument.

Original-issue discount (OID)—A debt instrument that is issued for less than its stated redemption price at maturity.

Origination fee—A charge by the lender to help defray or possibly cover the cost of originating a loan. Origination fees are not considered tax deductible.

Originator—A person who solicits loans for a lender.

Out of the money—Standby commitment or option contracts that do not offer as favorable a price as is currently available in the market.

Overage—For leasing purposes, it is the amount of rent over the base rent based on gross sales revenue.

Overall capitalization rate—See *Overall rate of return.*

Overall rate of return—Net operating income divided by the purchase price of property. Also known as overall capitalization rate.

Overhang—Extension of a roof beyond the exterior wall.

Overimprovement—Improvement to property exceeding the necessary level for the property to achieve its highest and best return.

Override—Commission or fee paid to a managerial person, rental in excess of a face amount, or a provision in a listing agreement protecting the listing broker's right to a commission for a specified period of time in excess of the initial agreement (in the event the owner sells property to a customer the broker had worked with during the time of the listing).

Owner/occupant—A person who lives in the property he owns.

Ownership form—Type of ownership of real estate such as partnership, corporation, limited partnership, joint tenancy, tenancy in common, Sub-Chapter S Corporation, tenancy in severalty, tenancy by the entireties, community property, and trust.

Package mortgage—A mortgage which includes personal properties such as appliances and carpeting.

Pad—A graded site for a residential use or the area utility connections for a mobile home.

Par—A price of 100% or the price at which the principal equals the sales price. It is the price of a mortgage without a discount charged.

Parity—A situation in which the cash and futures contracts are selling at equal yields.

Parity clause—A provision allowing a mortgage to secure more than one note; all are secured equally without any priority or preference.

Parking index—A ratio indicating the number of parking spaces to the gross leasable area or to the number of leasable units.

Parquet floor—Hardwood floor that is short pieces laid in a design or pattern.

Partial release—A provision in a mortgage allowing some of the property pledged as collateral to be free, provided specific payment is made. For example, a five-acre tract of land serves as collateral for a mortgage. The owner wishes to pay the mortgagee half of the balance owed in return for a partial release for one-half of the land (two and one-half acres) pledged as collateral.

Participation certificate (PC)—The Federal Home Loan Mortgage Corporation issues PC's which represent ownership in residential mortgages. The mortgages are conventional loans. The purchaser of a PC is guaranteed a pro-rata share of principal and interest. Principal is paid as collected.

Participation loan—A mortgage in which one lender (or more) shares in the ownership with the lead or originating lender.

Participation loan with subordination—The lead lender exposes his or her position to all of the losses from a foreclosure to the extent of his or her ownership in the mortgage.

Participation mortgage—A mortgage in which a lender shares in part of the income generated from the property or the proceeds resulting from a sale of the property.

Partition—Division of real property into separate parcels according to the owners' proportionate shares. Prior to a partition, two owners could own property together as tenants in common. After the partition, each owner could own one portion of the property.

Partition sale—The sale of property in accordance with a court decree for the purpose of achieving a partition of real estate.

Partnership—An association of two or more persons for business purposes.

Part performance—Performance of a contract which is less than full performance required.

Party wall—A wall built between two properties sewing as an exterior wall for each property. Each owner or part has a right to use the wall, and it serves as an easement on each adjoining property covered by the wall.

Passive investor—One who invests money and has no active role in the business or property.

Pass-through certificate—A certificate giving ownership in a pool of mortgages.

Patent—An instrument by which the government conveys title of its land to an individual.

Percentage lease—A lease providing for a percentage of sales payable to the lessor.

Percolation test—Test which measures the drainage characteristics of soil. This test is normally used to evaluate the feasibility of a septic tank as a waste disposal method for a home.

Per diem—Daily.

Per diem interest—Interest calculated on a daily basis. Normally heard at closing when the interest must be prorated.

Perfecting a lien—The legal procedure required to create a lien.

Perfecting title—Correcting any flaws or defects in a title so that a clear title can be obtained.

Performance bond—A bond issued by an insurance company to guarantee the performance of certain work. If said work is not performed, the insurer either will complete the work or pay damages according to the amount of the bond.

Permanent financing—Long-term mortgage, usually of ten years or more in duration.

Permanent mortgage—See *Permanent financing.*

Permissive use—The right to use property with the express or implied permission of the owner.

Personal property—Property that is not classified as real property or real estate. Examples are securities, cash, furniture, household items. Appliances not permanently attached to a structure are viewed as personal property.

Physical depreciation—The actual loss in value to property resulting from wear and tear caused by use or natural elements.

Piggyback loan—Two lenders participating in the same loan. The mortgage has one lender with a senior position of ownership and a lender with a junior interest.

Pilaster—A column or projection used to support a floor girder or stiffen a wall.

Pipeline—A term used by lenders to inventory the dollar amount of loan applications in process. A lender needs to inventory its pipeline for decisions pertaining to commitment coverage.

Pitch—The angle of the slope of a roof.

Plaintiff—A person who institutes a lawsuit.

Planned amortization class bond (PAC Bond)—A tranche of a CMO used to retire a CMO by a predetermined amortization schedule independent of the prepayment rate on the underlying collateral. The amortization of the other tranches may have to slowed down or accelerated to met the PAC schedule.

Planned unit development (PUD)—A zoning classification to allow development of a planned community. A PUD usually contains a mixture of land uses such as office and residential as well as common open spaces. It is a planned development which offers flexibility in the design of a subdivision. A PUD project can offer a mixture of land uses such as cluster housing, traditional single-family dwellings, common areas, and light commercial or office zoning.

A de minimis PUD is distinguished from a PUD by the increased quality and quantity of the common area amenities. Units in a de minimis PUD have part of their value tied to the amenities available in the common areas.

FNMA will no longer accept a de minimus PUD, but will take a PUD.

Plasterboard—Drywall, sheetrock, or gypsum board used for construction as a substitute for plaster.

Plat—A map or chart of a specific land area. A plat shows property with its precise location and boundaries.

Plat book—A book containing plats of properties according to public records.

Plates—Pieces of wood placed on wall surfaces as fastening devices. The bottom member of a wall is a sole plate and the top member is a rafter plate.

Pledged account mortgage (PAM)—A home mortgage in which cash is contributed to an account and pledged to the lender. Money is drawn periodically from the account to supplement the mortgage payments. The mortgage is a graduated payment mortgage and is also known as a FLIP mortgage.

Plenum—A chamber serving as a distribution area for heating or cooling systems.

Plot plan—A drawing showing the placement of improvements on a site with precise locations and dimensions.

Plottage value—The increase of value in land by assembling smaller properties into one large site.

Plumb—A term implying a true vertical position or a perpendicular position. A door or window frame with side members not in a true vertical position is not plumb or is "out of plumb".

Pointing—The filling up of joints in a masonry wall such as brick so that the appearance is more attractive and the wall has more support.

Points—See *Discount points*.

Police power—The right of any governmental body to enforce laws which promote the public health, morals, and safety and the welfare of the community. Examples of police power are condemnation, zoning, rent controls, housing codes, licensing requirements, and subdivision regulations.

Position—For lenders, a position is the relationship of mortgages and inventory to loan commitments from investors.

Positive carry—Yield from long-term investments is more than the cost of short-term borrowing.

Possession—The holding, control, and occupancy of property.

Power of Attorney—An instrument allowing a person to act as an agent for another person in a legal matter. For an explanation of VA Power of Attorney, refer to Question 2.42.

Power of sale—Authority given to a trustee under a deed of trust to sell property in the event of default or nonpayment by the mortgagor.

Preclosing—A meeting prior to formal closing in which documents are reviewed and signed and estimated prorations are made. Preclosings are used in the conversion of apartment units to condominium units.

Prefabrication—Construction of components for a home in a factory-like environment. Walls, doors, or trusses can be built in a factory and then delivered to a building site for assemblage of a building.

Premises—Land and improvements.

Premium—(1) The payment for an insurance policy or (2) the value a debt instrument or security has in excess of its face amount.

Prepaid interest—Interest paid before it is earned.

Prepaid items or expenses—Obligations paid in advance at a real estate closing. Examples of prepaid items would be the advance prepayment of premium for property insurance, real estate taxes, and prepaid mortgage interest. Per diem interest accrued also is classified as a prepaid item.

Prepayment clause—A clause in a mortgage giving the borrower the right to pay a mortgage off before it is due.

Prepayment penalty—A fee imposed by a lender for the prepayment of a mortgage.

Pre-sale—The sale of a proposed project before construction begins.

Prescription—Rights to property by adverse possession. A continued use of another person's property can result in adverse possession. The continued use is termed a "prescription."

Present value—The current worth of a sum of money due on a specific, future date.

Price—In reference to the purchase of mortgages and bonds, it represents the amount paid in relationship to the face value of the instrument. If a mortgage sells for par, it is considered to be 100. If the mortgage is discounted by 5%, the price is 95.

Price level adjustable mortgage (PLAM)—A mortgage in which the balance and monthly payment will increase or decrease in direct relationship with an index such as the Consumer Price Index or Cost-of-Living Index.

Primary market—A lender using his own funds to make money available in the form of a loan directly to a borrower.

Principal—(1) The amount of debt excluding interest. (2) The party who either will own or use the subject property. In a lease, both the lessor and the lessee are principals. In the sale of property, both the seller and purchaser are principals. (3) A party who employs an agent or broker on his behalf. The agent or broker is said to be working for the principal.

Principal only (PO) A security which pays cash flows from the principal paid by an underlying pool of mortgages. A PO is an principal-only security backed by an underlying collateral, a mortgage pool. See *IO*.

Principal residence—The dwelling which one uses most of the time as a residence. The place one classifies as one's home.

Private mortgage insurance (PMI)—Insurance written by a private company benefitting the mortgage lender in case of default.

Private offering—A real estate investment offered to a limited group of investors. This type of offering or sale normally is without the benefit of advertising or general promotion and is exempt from registration with the Securities and Exchange Commission and State Securities Registration laws.

Probate—Proving that a will is valid. This term also can be used to describe any action over which probate court has jurisdiction.

Proceeds—(1) The sum realized from sale of property, or (2) the sum given to a borrower by the lender.

Procuring cause—In real estate sales, this term is used to determine whether a real estate salesperson is the procuring cause of the sale, entitling him or her to a commission.

Pro forma statement—A statement forecasting future income, expenses, net income, and cash flow.

Promissory note—A written promise to pay a specified sum to a specified person for specified terms.

470

Property—In legal definition, it is the right to possession, enjoyment, and disposition of all things subject to ownership.

Property disposition (PD) A department within FHA vested with the sale of property acquired by FHA. PD manages and sells property acquired from FHA approved lenders. The FHA lenders acquire the properties through foreclosure then later convey the property to FHA. PD can sell property to the public by an auction or a sealed bid.

Property line—The recorded boundary of a parcel of land.

Property management—The management of property used as a business such as an apartment complex.

Property report—A disclosure required by the Interstate Land Sales Act for the sale of subdivisions consisting of 50 lots or more, unless exempted. The report is filed with HUD's Office of Interstate Land Sales Registration.

Prorate—To allocate between seller and purchaser his or her proportionate share of expenses or obligations such as real estate taxes or property insurance.

Prospectus—A descriptive statement disclosing the details of a proposed investment. A prospectus would give information that is contained in a pro forma statement. If a prospectus has yet to be approved by the SEC, it is termed a "red herring." If a prospectus need not be approved, it is termed a descriptive memorandum.

Proxy—A person who represents another or a document granting representation to another.

Public offering—The solicitation of the general public to buy investment units. Usually requires approval by the SEC.

Punch list—A list of items requiring correction. A purchaser or a lender may list items to be corrected before a closing can take place. This list would be termed a punch list.

Purchase money mortgage—A loan from a seller to a buyer to be used in the acquisition of subject property.

Put—An option to sell a specific security at a specified price within a designated period.

Quadruplex—Four-unit building.

Quarter round—Molding used to cover a joint. A cross section of the molding would equal approximately one-fourth of a circle.

Quiet enjoyment—The uninterrupted use and possession of property given to an owner or tenant.

Quiet title—A court action to settle a title dispute. A quiet title suit or action is for the purpose of removing a defect or a cloud on the title adverse to the owner's interest.

Quitclaim deed—A deed which conveys only the grantor's rights in the property without disclosing the nature of the rights and with no warranties of ownership. A deed by which the grantor releases to the grantee any interest or title in the property which the grantor possesses.

Radiant heating—Heating by the use of coils, pipes, or panels recessed in the ceilings, walls, or floors using electricity, hot water, steam, or hot air.

Radon—A gas that can be trapped in a closed space, such as a house. As accumulated trapped gas inside a home, radon is believed to cause lung cancer. (See *Property Inspection Checklist*, page 149.)

Rafter—A structural roof member spanning from an exterior wall to a center ridge board. Rafters are used to support the roof.

Raked joint—Joint between bricks from which mortar has been scraped or raked out to a specific gap while fresh.

Range lines—Parallel lines marking out land into six-mile strips known as ranges. Range lines are parallel to a principal meridian and are numbered east or west of the meridian in a Government Rectangular Survey.

Ratable property or estate—Real or personal property that is subject to being taxed by a governing body.

Rate cap—Refer to Question 3.28.

Rate of return—The return of an investment measured in a percentage. A 6% Certificate of Deposit has a rate of return of 6%.

Ready, willing, and able—Description of a buyer who is legally capable and financially able to consummate a purchase.

Real estate—Physical land and its permanently attached improvements.

Real Estate Investment Trust (REIT)—A trust which invests its money in real estate or mortgages. If the trust meets certain requirements, it is exempt from corporate income tax. When a trust distributes a minimum of 95% of its income to its shareholders, it is exempt from corporate tax, but the shareholders must include the income in their personal tax returns.

Real Estate Mortgage Investment Conduit—See *REMIC*.

Real Estate Mortgage Trust (REMT)—A form of REIT that buys and sells real estate mortgages.

Real Estate Owned (REO)—A term that implies real estate owned by a lending institution for investment purposes or property acquired through foreclosure.

Real Estate Securities and Syndication Institute (RESSI)—An institution of syndicators affiliated with the National Association of REALTORS®.

Real Estate Settlement Procedure Act (RESPA)—A federal law which governs mortgage applications for federally-related real estate loans on one- to four-family dwelling properties. The principal stipulations of the act concern an informational booklet given to the parties at loan application, a good-faith estimate of closing costs, and a uniform settlement statement.

Real property—The rights and interests stemming from the ownership of real estate. This term often is used to mean the same as real estate.

Realtist—A member of the National Association of Real Estate Brokers.

REALTOR®—A registered trade name used by professionals in real estate who subscribe to a code of ethics established by the National Association of REALTORS®.

Reappraisal lease—A lease in which the rental is re-appraised or revalued at periodic intervals by independent appraisers. If a lease stipulates that the annual rent will be 10% of the property value, the lease most likely will have a re-appraisal provision at periodic intervals.

Reassessment—The revaluation of property for ad valorem tax purposes.

Recapture clause—A clause in a contract permitting the grantor of an instrument the right to take that interest back under certain conditions. This clause normally is found in percentage leases. In percentage leases, the recapture clause allows the lessor to regain the premises if sales are below a certain minimum amount.

Recapture rate—In appraising, this term is used to describe the rate at which investment capital will be returned over a period of time.

Recasting— The process of changing the term of a mortgage. An existing mortgage with a 10-year remaining term could be recast by extending the term to 20 years and lowering the monthly payment.

Reciprocity—A mutual agreement to exchange privileges. Two states may agree to allow a person to sell real estate in either state if the licensee has a valid license in one of the two states.

Recission or right of recission—A 3 day business period (72 hours), during which time the borrower can cancel the transaction. During the recission period, funds are withheld pending the decision of the borrower. This regulation is part of the Truth in Lending Act, Regulation Z. Under certain emergency circumstances, this required can be waived.

Reclaim—To convert previously uncultivated areas such as swamps or low-lying areas into suitable land for cultivation purposes.

Recognized gain—Economic gain that is recognizable for tax purposes.

Reconciliation—In appraising, reconciliation is the final step of adjusting comparables to arrive at the final estimate of value.

Reconveyance—The conveying of title back to the original owner. When a mortgage is paid in full under a deed of trust, title is reconveyed from the trustee to the equity owner.

Recording—Making written instruments a part of public record.

Recourse—The right of a lender to claim assets from a mortgagor in default, in addition to the subject property serving as security.

Recovery fund—A fund set up by a state real estate commission for the purpose of reimbursing wronged persons who are unable to get compensation from brokers for fraudulent acts or misrepresentation. A fund to assure payment of uncollectible court judgments against parties with a real estate license.

Redemption period—A time period during which a former owner can reclaim foreclosed property or property which has been sold for taxes. The redemption period is established by state law.

Red herring—A preliminary prospectus which has not been approved by the Securities and Exchange Commission.

Rediscount rate—The rate of interest charged by the Federal Reserve Bank for loans to its member banks.

Redlining—The illegal practice of lending institutions of restricting the number of loans or the loan-to-value ratio in certain neighborhoods on the basis of race or ethnic background.

Reduction certificate—An instrument in which the lender acknowledges the remaining balance, rate of interest, and date of maturity for a mortgage.

Referral—The act of recommending the use of a certain broker. The person making the recommendation may receive a referral fee, if he is properly licensed.

Refinance—To pay off an existing loan with a new loan. Reasons for refinancing can be many. However, in most cases it is either to raise capital or to replace a mortgage with a new mortgage that provides a better rate of interest and possibly better terms.

Reformation—A legal remedy that can correct mistakes in written instruments so that the corrected instrument will set forth the true intentions of the parties.

Registrar—The person responsible for maintaining accurate, efficient records of instruments which can be recorded.

Regulation A—Special exemption from normal SEC registration of a security issue when the amount of the offering is less than 1.5 million.

Regulation D—A regulation of the Securities and Exchange Commission which outlines necessary conditions or requirements for a private offering exemption.

Regulation Q—Regulation allowing certain federal agencies to offer different interest rates on savings accounts in banks and savings and loan associations. This legislation is responsible for the gradual deregulation of federally-regulated banks and savings institutions. Deregulations include phasing out of deposit interest rates, authorization for interest-bearing checking accounts, and allowing savings and loan associations to become involved in consumer loans to a greater degree.

Regulation Z—Truth in Lending. Regulation that requires full disclosure in writing of all costs connected with the credit portion of a purchase, including the APR.

Regulatory accounting principles (RAP) Accounting principles required by regulation that allows savings institutions to elect annually to defer gains or losses on the sale of assets and amortize these deferrals over the average life of each loan group or the stated life of each security sold.

Reinstatement—To bring back or restore a past-due loan to a current status.

Reinsurance—The practice of an original insurer gaining additional insurance from another insurer.

Reissue rate—A reduced charge by a title insurance company, if another policy had recently been issued on the same property.

Release—The act of freeing real estate from a mortgage, lien, or other encumbrance.

Release clause—A clause permitting a mortgagor to pay off a portion of a mortgage and have that portion of the secured property released from the mortgage.

Release of liability—For VA loan purposes, it is an assumptor's being approved to assume a VA loan and therefore to relieve the veteran from liability to the VA. FHA has a similar program. Conventional loans may or may not offer a release of liability.

Reliction—Gradual withdrawal of water leaving dry land exposed.

Relocation clause—A provision in a lease giving the landlord the right to move a tenant within the building.

Remainder—In estate and real property, that which takes effect after the expiration of a preceding estate. After a life estate has expired, the remaining estate would be termed a remainder.

Remainder man—That person who is entitled to receive possession of property after the death of a life tenant.

REMIC—Real Estate Mortgage Investment Conduit. A REMIC is a tax selection which can be used for mortgage-backed securities, CMO's, commercial-backed financing, and other mortgage-related securities. In comparison to a CMO, a REMIC has the following advantages:

1. Clarification of tax treatment
2. Ability to treat a REMIC as a sale instead of a borrowing

3. Thrift institutions such as savings and loan associations can count REMIC investments as meeting their tax and regulatory requirements

In summary, mortgages sold though the REMIC method could bring better prices which could result in lower yields to the public.

Source: Dan Amerman—UMIC, Memphis, Tennessee

Remise—To give up, release, or quitclaim interest in a property.

Rendering—A perspective drawing of a project.

Renegotiable rate mortgage (RRM)—A mortgage in which the interest rate is re-adjusted periodically.

Rent-roll—A list of leases for a project in which the tenant's lease periods and security deposits are all listed. Rent-roll is also known as rent schedule.

Rent-up—The amount of time for leasing all of a new project.

Replevin—A legal procedure to recover personal property which has been unlawfully taken or withheld. If a landlord has taken a tenant's property unlawfully, the tenant can file a procedure known as a replevin to repossess the property taken.

Repurchase agreement—A simultaneous agreement between the seller and purchaser of mortgage-backed security in which the seller agrees to repurchase the securities at a specified future date and price.

Rescind—The act of withdrawing an offer or a contract. Regulation Z requires a three-day rescission period in which the consumer can rescind the transaction. The three days are known as a rescission period.

Rescission—Cancellation of a transaction or contract by operation of law or mutual consent.

Residential member (RM)—A designation of the American Institute of Real Estate Appraisers.

Residential service contract—A contract insuring the electrical, plumbing, heating, and air conditioning of a home for a specified period of time.

478

Residual—The remaining income or value after deducting fixed obligations; value of property which is left after its economic life is finished.

Respondeat superior—The doctrine of law that a principal is liable and responsible for the acts of an agent.

Restoration of eligibility or entitlement—Refer to Question 2.12.

Restraint on alienation—A restriction or condition on the right to transfer property.

Restriction or restriction covenant—A limitation to the use of the property which normally is conveyed in the deed. Subdivision restrictions or zoning ordinances.

Retainage—Money which has been earned by a contractor, but is withheld or retained until the project is completed and all obligations discharged by the contractor.

Retire—To pay off a debt.

Reverse annuity mortgage (RAM)—A mortgage in which the mortgagee pays a monthly payment to the mortgagor. This mortgage is for elderly people who do not want to sell or refinance their home, but want to withdraw money from their equity.

Reverse leverage—Negative cash flow.

Reverse repurchase agreement—A simultaneous agreement in which the purchaser of mortgage-backed securities agrees to resell them at a specified future date and price.

Reversion—The act of property reverting to the lessor, grantor, or owner after the estate period has expired. A reversion in a lease would be that the property reverts to the landlord after the lease has expired.

Revocation The act of recalling or terminating power of authority given to another through such acts as Power of Attorney, Agency, or Licensing Privileges.

Rider—An addendum or amendment to a contract.

Ridge—The peak or top horizontal edge of a roof.

Ridgeboard—The top horizontal board of a roof. Rafters are attached to it.

Right of first refusal—The right of a party to match or equal the terms of a proposed contract before the contract is executed. The party owning a first right of refusal has the first opportunity either to purchase or lease the property.

Right of survivorship—The right of a surviving joint tenant to the property of a deceased joint tenant.

Right-of-way—The usage of property that is similar to an easement. A right-of-way can be a trail, driveway, public road, or any type of access to the property.

Riparian—The rights of an owner of property located next to a body of water such as a lake or a river.

Risk of loss—In contract law, it is the exposure to chances of loss or injury to either buyer or seller.

Risk rate—Generally the rate of return required to attract capital to an investment.

Risk/reward ratio—The relationship between the degree of risk involved in an investment to the anticipated return.

Rollover—Renewal of loan at time of maturity. Also the reinvestment of proceeds from sale of one housing unit into another.

Rotunda—A circular room or building which usually is topped with a domed roof.

Row houses—Dwelling units that are attached by common walls. Also sometimes known as townhouses.

Royalty—Money paid to an owner of property for the extraction of natural resources such as gas or oil. Royalty also can mean a franchise fee.

Rule of 72—A method of calculating the amount of time it takes for money to double itself when compound interest is applied. Divide 72 by your interest rate. The result is the number of years it will take for your money to double.

Run with the land—An expression affecting the present and future use of a subject property.

Rurban—Land that is on the fringe of urban development. Land in between urban and rural area.

R-value—A measure of insulating value; the type and thickness of insulation in attics, walls, floors, doors, windows, or roofs can be measured by an R-value. The "R" refers to resistance to the flow of heat.

Safe harbor rule—An expression which generally means an area of safety from legislation or regulation pertaining to income tax.

Sale-leaseback—Real estate that is sold to a buyer who simultaneously leases the property back to the seller.

Sale and servicing agreement—An agreement setting forth the requirements of the seller, who sells loans and retains servicing, and the investor, who purchases the loans.

Salvage value—The value an asset will have at the end of its useful life.

Sandwich lease—A lease held by a lessee who has subsequently leased to a tenant. An example would be Owner A leases to Lessee B. Lessee B then subleases to Lessee C. Lessee B is the owner of a sandwich lease.

Sash—The movable part of a window. The framework containing glass in a window or door.

Satellite tenant—A tenant in a shopping center who is relatively small and dependent on the larger, or anchor, tenant to attract business.

Satisfaction—Payment of a debt such as a judgment.

Satisfaction of a mortgage—A written instrument acknowledging the full payment of a mortgage. When recorded, this document clearly shows satisfaction of the mortgage debt.

Scenic easement—An easement to preserve the property in its natural or undeveloped state.

Schematics—Preliminary drawings and sketches prepared for the planning stages of a project.

Seasoned loan—A loan which has been outstanding for a period of time. FHA requires a loan to be seasoned for twelve months before it is eligible to be considered for

481

refinancing purposes. Secondary marketing people normally refer to loans that are over one year old as "seasoned production."

Secondary financing—Second mortgages or junior liens.

Secondary mortgage market—A market for the sale and purchase of real estate mortgages.

Second home—A vacation home.

Section 8 Program—A rental subsidy program in which eligible families receive a certificate that entitles them to seek housing in the community and to have much of the rent paid either by HUD or a Public Housing Authority.

Security—(1) Real estate that serves as collateral for a debt or (2) documents that show evidence of ownership such as bonds, stocks, certificates, and mortgages.

Security deposit—A deposit paid for good faith in completion of the terms of a lease.

Security interest—The interest in real estate serving as collateral.

Seed money—Front-end funds required for a real estate transaction. Examples of front-end cost would be feasibility studies, appraisals, loan commitment fees, attorney fees, and accountant fees.

Seisin—The actual possession of real estate and its rights as if it were a freehold estate.

Seller-servicer—A lender approved to sell and service mortgages. Approval to sell and service loans is granted by the investor.

Seller's market—Economic conditions in which demand for housing is at a peak level.

Semi-detached dwelling—A dwelling that is attached to one wall of an adjoining dwelling.

Servicing—Lenders who collect mortgage payments and then disperse principal, interest, and in most cases, taxes and insurance.

Setback—The minimum distance required for a dwelling to be built from a curb or street.

Settlement—Synonymous with *Closing*.

Settlement requirements—The dollar amount of certified funds required to close a loan.

Settlement statement—Refer to *Closing statement*.

Severalty—Ownership of real property by an individual entity.

Severance damages—The loss in value arising from a condemnation procedure in which a partial taking by condemnation creates a loss in value of the subject property.

Shakes—Refers to individual shingles on a roof. Shakes can be used as roofing or siding material and are composed of split wood, preferably cedar.

Shared appreciation mortgage (SAM)—A residential loan with a favorable interest rate which entitles the lender to a share of the appreciation in property value.

Shared equity—Refer to Question 1.80.

Shared equity mortgage—A residential loan in which the lender shares in the equity of the property.

Sheathing—Wide boards, usually 4 x 8's that are nailed to studding or roofing rafters to serve as a base for the outer covering of the walls or roof.

Sheriff's deed—Deed for property that is sold by court order in connection with satisfaction of delinquent taxes or a judgment.

Shim—Thin piece of wood used for leveling or tightening a stair, window, etc.

Shipping—The process of sending a complete mortgage package to the investor.

Shoe molding—A thin strip of wood or quarter round located at the junction of the baseboard and floor board and used to conceal the joint.

Short rate—The calculation of the refund of unearned premium or the premium earned on a hazard insurance policy cancelled between anniversary dates based on a higher rate to compensate for the short term of the policy.

Sill plate—The lowest member of the house framing which sits on top of the foundation wall. The lowest horizontal element of a frame such as a window or door frame.

Single family detached (SFD)—A dwelling with no adjoining walls or common areas with another dwelling.

Sinking fund—A fund set aside to provide for the payment of a long-term debt such as a bond. For income property, the term "sinking fund" applies to a special fund set aside from earnings for future replacements required to maintain the improvements.

Site development cost—Engineering, architectural, and legal fees associated with a real estate project; costs which are in contrast to land and construction costs which are termed hard cost.

Skip deed—Process of obtaining a signed deed transferring title to an eventual purchaser. Deed is not recorded until a new purchaser becomes available. This process is often used by relocation service companies. Refer to Question 1.60, Paragraph 9, c.

Slab—Concrete floor or roof; any flat, horizontal concrete area.

Small Business Investment Companies (SBIC)—Private companies licensed and regulated by the Small Business Administration to provide small businesses with equity, capital, and long-term financing.

Soffit—The underside of any part of a structure, especially roofs or eaves.

Soft dollars—The amount of investment in real estate which qualifies for tax deductions in the year paid. Prepaid interest and any fees that are deductible in the year they are paid would qualify as soft dollars.

Solvent—A financial position meaning the ability to meet one's current financial obligations.

Spec house—A term referring to a newly-constructed house that was not custom-built or pre-sold. The house is constructed on the speculation that someone will purchase it.

Special warranty deed—A deed conveying special warranty of the title as compared to general warranties. In a special warranty deed, the grantor warrants title against claims held "by, through, or under the grantor." The grantor does not warrant against title defects occurring before he owned the property.

Specific performance—Court action requiring the completion of a contract according to its terms.

Spot loans—Single-family loans solicited on an individual basis versus a package basis.

Spot zoning—Zoning of a parcel of land on a specialized basis as opposed to a general or master plan.

Spread—(1) The difference between the cost of money and the average rate at which it can be loaned. (2) The difference between bid price and asking price. (3) The extension of a lien or an existing mortgage to additional with additional real estate serving as collateral.

Square footage—An area measured in square feet. Square footage as applied to residential real estate is the number of heated and livable square feet as measured by the outside walls.

Square root price—A general rule of thumb used to determine values of homes. With this method, the price of a home can be approximated by multiplying the heated square footage by a dollar amount. For example: A 2000 square-foot home with a $40/square-foot price should be valued at $80,000. To determine a square-foot price, simply divide the sales price by the heated square footage ($80,000 + 2000 = $40). Heated area should be used so that even comparisons of square feet can be made between homes that have carports or garages to homes that have none. The drawback to this rule of thumb is that it gives a false implication that houses are valued solely by square footage. A home with three bedrooms, two baths, den, living room, dining room, and kitchen will not appraise automatically for more than a comparable home with the same components because each room in the subject property is one foot and six inches larger than the

485

comparable property. Houses of similar room composition and locations will most likely appraise for the same value regardless of small differences in the square footage created by rooms being slightly longer or wider than comparable rooms of another house.

Standard Metropolitan Statistical Area (SMSA)—A designation given by the federal Office of Management and Budget (OMB) to counties containing at least one central city of 50,000 or more residents. It is the area of a central city and its surrounding suburbs including small jurisdictions.

Standby commitment—A commitment to purchase loans on specified terms with the understanding that the commitment will not be exercised unless there is no alternative.

Standby contract—An option to sell mortgage-backed securities for a specified amount of mortgages by or upon a specific date at a specific price.

Standby fee—A fee charged by a lender to provide a standby loan commitment. The standby fee is forfeited if the loan is not closed by a specified time.

Standing mortgage—A mortgage without amortization payments and requiring the entire loan balance due at maturity. Interest is paid at periodic intervals.

Start rate—The rate of interest for the first year on an adjustable rate mortgage.

Starts—The number of residential dwelling units for which construction has started within a specific period of time.

Statute of frauds—Old English law requiring certain contracts to be in writing before they are considered enforceable. Real estate contracts must be in writing to be considered enforceable.

Statute of limitations—A statutory period of time in which a claim can be enforced by a suit.

Step-down lease—A lease providing for specific decreases in rent at certain intervals.

Step-up lease—A lease providing for specific increases in rent at certain intervals.

486

Stipulation—The terms of a written contract.

Straight pass-through—A practice of passing through the principal and interest collected to the investor of a mortgage-backed security. The payment in a straight pass-through is contingent upon the borrower's remitting the principal and interest.

Straw man—A person who purchases property for another in order to conceal the eventual owner's identity.

Strict foreclosure—A foreclosure proceeding without a sale of the mortgaged property.

Stud—A term used in construction for boards or framing materials that are vertical with horizontal pieces attached. Studs usually are placed either 16" or 24" apart.

Subchapter S—An Internal Revenue code under which certain small corporations may eliminate income tax at the corporate level by electing to be treated as a partnership. The shareholders pay the income tax.

Subcontractor—A person or a company that contracts work under a developer or a general contractor.

Subdivision—Land divided into a number of parcels and held for sale or lease.

Subflooring—Boards or sheets of plywood that are nailed directly to floor joists and serve as a base for the finished covering such as carpet or hardwood flooring.

Subject property—That property which is the subject of an appraisal, sale, lease, or option. The property in question.

Subject to—An assumption of an existing mortgage without personal liability as it pertains to the new owner. The original mortgagor is held liable for any deficiency resulting from a foreclosure.

Sublease—A lessee executing a lease to a third party for the remaining portion of the original lease.

Submortgage—The use of a mortgage as security for obtaining another mortgage.

Subordination—The act of moving a prior mortgage into a secondary position subject to agreement with holder of the prior mortgage. An example would be a first mortgage becoming a second mortgage. Subordination can also apply to leases, other debt instruments, and other real estate rights.

Subordination agreement—A clause allowing a holder of a prior encumbrance to become junior to an existing or anticipated encumbrance.

Subrogation—The substitution of one person for another in reference to a claim or right for a debt.

Subsidy—Funds to lower the cost of housing by granting below-market interest loans or the reduction in the cost of land, labor, or material.

Substitution of entitlement—A veteran seller's entitlement is restored by a qualified veteran assumptor with sufficient remaining entitlement. Refer to Question 2.12.

Substitution of liability—Refer to *Release of liability*.

Successors and assigns—Phrase meaning to succeed to the rights of ownership by corporation as assigned by said corporation.

Sump pump—A pump used to dispose of moisture and liquids collected in a basement.

Surcharge—Additional rental for utility services such as lights, gas, or water.

Surety—One who guarantees or underwrites the performance of another.

Surrender—To give up rights in a lease by mutual agreement between lessor and lessee.

Survey—A drawing showing the measurements of a parcel of land as well as the improvements to the land, the process by which the land is measured, and its boundary lines ascertained.

Sweat equity—Refer to Question 1.79.

Swing loan—See *Bridge financing*.

Syndication—Sale of property to a group of investors.

Tacking—The additional time periods allowed in making a claim to squatter's rights to land. Term pertaining to adverse possession.

Tail—What GNMA will allow in terms of contract deliveries which are above or below the agreed upon principal balance.

Takedown—The drawing of funds which are committed by a lender per a previous agreement.

Takeout financing—Long-term permanent financing which allows for a short-term construction loan.

Tax deed—Deed that conveys property repossessed by the government for nonpayment of taxes.

Tax escalation clause—The provision in a lease requiring the tenant to absorb any increase in real estate taxes.

Tax-increment financing—The financing of urban renewal by a bond issue which will be serviced from anticipated additional tax revenues generated from the redevelopment or renewal project.

Tax-lien—A lien against property for the amount of unpaid taxes.

Tax stop clause—Refer to *Tax escalation clause.*

Teaser rate—A low initial rate on an Adjustable Rate Mortgage. The low rate is used to attract or "tease" the borrower into accepting a ARM mortgage. An ARM loan transfers risk from the lender to the borrower. Some lenders are very anxious to make ARM loans. Lenders will sometimes offer a very low rate for the first year, in hopes that the public will accept ARM loans and the rates will go up as adjustments are made.

Tenancy—The holding of real estate by either lease or title.

Tenancy at sufferance—Tenancy established when a tenant wrongfully holds over after the expiration of a lease.

Tenancy at will—Tenancy created when a person holds or occupies real estate with the permission of the owner for an indefinite period of time. It can be cancelled at any time by the landlord or the tenant.

Tenancy by the entirety—Ownership of real estate by a married couple which requires that one cannot sell real estate without the consent of the other and also maintains that, upon the death of a spouse, the real estate is then owned by the surviving spouse. Normally, a borrower will be asked at loan application if title is to be held in tenancy by the entirety or tenancy in common.

Tenancy for years—Tenancy created by a lease for a fixed term.

Tenancy in common—Ownership in real estate by two or more persons each owning an undivided interest without right of survivorship.

Tenancy in severalty—Ownership of property vested in one person or one legal entity.

Tenant—(1) One who is commonly referred to as the lessee under a lease. (2) One who holds exclusive possession of property such as a life tenant or tenant for years.

Tender—(1) An offer by a contracting party to perform his or her part of a contract. (2) Payment or deliverance of an amount due a creditor.

Tenements—Items permanently affixed such as buildings and improvements.

Tenure—(1) The manner in which ownership rights are possessed such as an owner of property or a tenant in property. (2) Holding or possessing anything; the right to possess and use property.

Term—The period of time in such documents as a lease or a mortgage.

Terms—The conditions and obligations of a mortgage, a lease, or other contract.

Testate—Term meaning leaving a valid will at death. A man who makes a valid will is a testator. A woman who makes a valid will is a testatrix.

Time is of the essence—Phrase in a contract which means delays are unacceptable and performance must be completed by specific dates as set forth in the contract.

Time share—Multiple ownership of a unit in a development whereby use of the ownership is for a specific time period.

Title—Documentation as to the rightful ownership of real property.

Title I—Refers to FHA loans which are second mortgages.

Title II— Refers to FHA loans which are first mortgages.

Title binder—Written evidence of temporary title insurance which must be replaced by a permanent title insurance policy after a limited time.

Title defect—A claim against property which clouds the title to the property and prohibits clear title.

Title exception—A condition of the property which title policy will not insure.

Title insurance—An insurance policy warranting the validity of title to real estate. Insures against losses arising through defects in title or any liens or encumbrances.

Title opinion—Refer to *Opinion of title.*

Title report—The current status of title as it pertains to any defects, liens, easements, or covenants. It is not the chain of title.

Title search—Investigation of public records to determine anything which might affect a title.

Title theory states—Doctrine in which the mortgagee holds legal title until the debt is paid in full. The borrower is said to have equitable title.

Toenail—Method of driving nails at an angle into corners and other joints so they will hold better.

Tongue-and-groove—Method of joining boards together in which the jutting edge of one board fits into a grooved edge of a similar board.

Torrens system—Title registration used to verify the ownership and encumbrances (except tax liens), without requiring an additional search of the public records.

Tort—A civil wrong or negligent act which is neither a crime nor a breach of contract, but creates damages to the wronged party.

Total acquisition—"Total Acquisition" refers to the lesser of, 1) the "cost to the purchaser," plus closing costs the purchaser is paying, or 2) the FHA estimate of value plus the FHA estimate of closing costs.—The "cost to the purchaser" normally means the sales price, any repairs the purchaser is paying for, and closing cost the purchaser pays, as per the FHA closing cost schedule. Refer to Question 1.12.

Total loan-to-value (TLTV) A percentage arrived by dividing debt by value. The sum of the debt is the outstanding loan balance of a first mortgage plus the original balance of junior financing (second mortgage). The value used is the current market value.

Total obligation—An FHA term meaning the summation of housing expense, insurance, Social Security, and obligations which exceed a twelve-month repayment period.

Townhouse—A two-story dwelling attached to similar units by party walls. Also known as row houses.

Tract—A parcel of land. Usually refers to a large piece of land such as might be subdivided.

Tract houses—Houses in a large-scale development which are similar in design.

Tract loan—A mortgage to a developer for land being subdivided.

Trade date—The date when parties enter into an agreement to purchase or sell mortgage-backed securities.

Transfer tax—Tax imposed by state or local governments when real estate is transferred from seller to purchaser.

Trap—A bend in a water pipe which traps water so that gases will not escape from the plumbing system into the house.

Tread—Horizontal portion of a step in a stairway.

Trim—Interior finishing pieces such as moldings, window casings, and hardware.

Triplex—Three-unit dwelling.

Truck receivables underlying certificate (TRUCS)—A security asset backed by heavy-duty truck receivables. This term was introduced by Mac Truck Receivables Corporation.

Truss—A rigid framework for spanning over load-bearing walls. It is formed by assembling various units and its purpose is to carry a load (such as floor truss and roof truss).

Trust—The fiduciary relationship under which legal title to property is held by a person or entity with the intention that such property be administered by the trustee for the benefit of another who is termed the beneficiary and who holds equitable title to the property.

Trust deed—Refer to *Deed of trust.*

Trustee—An individual who holds title to property in trust for another as security for performance of an obligation.

Turnkey project—A phrase meaning the contractor will completely finish a building project on behalf of the owner or purchaser. When the contractor is completely finished, all the owner needs to do is turn the key to a completed building.

Under-improvement—A development or building which is less than its highest and best use for the property location.

Underwriter—A person who makes an analysis of a submission as to the risk involved. Underwriters can be used in the insurance industry, by mortgage companies, and in the securities business. In the mortgage business, an underwriter is one who approves or rejects loan submissions. Loan underwriting can be described as "an exercise in the art of judgement."

Undivided interest—Interest in property which has not been divided or segregated.

Unearned increment—Increase in the value of real estate through an unrelated effort by the property owner. Examples would be population growth, commercial development, and other occurrences which increase the value of property.

Unencumbered property—Property that is free and clear of any liens or claims.

Uniform Commercial Code (UCC)—A code which attempts to unify all law related to commercial transactions.

Uniform settlement statement—Standard closing statement required by Housing Urban Development. Also known as HUD-1. Refer to Figure 23.

Unilateral contract—A contract which binds only one party.

Unimproved property—Raw land which has not been developed.

Up/On—Refers to a commitment fee that is divided into two parts. A portion of the fee is paid upon execution of the commitment, the remainder is paid upon delivery of the loans to the investor.

Upset price—The minimum asking price for auctioned property.

Usufructuary rights—Rights and interests to use, without damaging it, property that belongs to another.

Usury—The act of charging an interest rate greater than is permitted by state law.

VA automatic approval—Refer to Question 2.47.

Vacancy rate—A rate or factor expressed in a percentage which estimates the vacancies for a rental project.—If a vacancy rate is 5%, this implies that in a 100-unit apartment project, there will be five vacant units at all times.

VA eligibility—Refer to Question 2.19.

VA entitlement—Refer to Question 2.19.

VA guaranty—Refer to Question 2.19.

Valuable consideration—Items including money or those items that can support a contract.

Valuation condition (VC)—A condition of the FHA appraisal which must be met prior to closing or insurance of the loan.

Vapor barrier—Material used to prevent vapor or moisture from passing out of rooms into outside walls.

VA power of attorney—Refer to Question 2.42.

Variance—Permission granted from a governing authority to construct or conduct a usage of improvements that is contrary to code or law.

Vendee—A purchaser, usually of real estate.

Vendor—A seller, usually of real estate.

Veneer—Brick, thin sheets of wood, or other material serving as a cover for cheaper material on outside walls.

Verification of deposit—Refer to Figure 22.

Verification of employment—Refer to Figure 21.

Volt—Electromotive force which, when steadily applied to a conductor whose resistance is one ohm, will produce a current of one ampere.

Voluntary conveyance—Refer to *Deed in lieu of foreclosure.*

Wainscoting—Wood or other material different from the wall which is used to line the lower three or four feet of an interior wall.

Waiver—To give up or voluntarily abandon a claim, right, or privilege.

Warehouse line—Credit used by a lender to close loans and hold them until the mortgages are sold to the investor.

Warehousing—The practice of gathering real estate mortgages for later resale in the secondary market.

Warranty—A promise that certain facts or statements are true.

Warranty deed—A deed conveying title and containing a covenant from the grantor to the grantee that title is free and clear of encumbrances, other than any stated in the contract or deed.

Water table—The distance from natural ground water to the ground surface.

Watt—A measure of electrical power that is equal to the flow of one ampere caused by the pressure of one volt.

Watt-hour—A unit used to determine the basis of electric bills. A 75-watt light bulb burning for one hour will use 75 watts of electricity.

Weather stripping—Insulation by means of felt or metal placed around the interior opening of a door or window to keep out wind and rain.

Weep hole—One of a series of small holes in a retaining or foundation wall for permitting excess water to drain.

Weighted average coupon—The weighted average coupon (wac) of mortgage loans is calculated by multiplying the unpaid principal balance of each mortgage loan by the coupon of such mortgage loan (resulting in a "product" for each mortgage loan). The sum of the products divided by the sum of the unpaid principal balances equals the WAC. The WAC means the weighted average coupon of mortgage loans as a group. Please see the HP-12c Section for calculating a wac with an HP-12c.

Weighted Average Maturity—The weighted average remaining maturity of a group of mortgage loans is calculated by multiplying the unpaid principal balance of each mortgage loan by the number of months remaining to maturity of such mortgage loan (resulting in a "product" for each mortgage loan), adding the products so obtained for all of the mortgage loans, and dividing the sum of all the products by the aggregate unpaid principal balance of all the mortgage loans. The WAM is the weighted average remaining maturity of the applicable mortgage loans as a group. Please see the HP-12c Section for calculating a WAC with an HP-12c.

Whole loan—The sale or purchase of an entire loan as opposed to the sale or purchase in a participation or share of the loan.

Without recourse—A mortgage in which the lender will not pursue personal liability against the borrower. The lender's security is the real estate being financed.

Women's Council of REALTORS® (WCR)—An organization affiliated with the National Association of REALTORS®. It is said to be the largest women's retail organization in America. Betty Harrison was the 1986 president.

Workout—A mutual attempt by the mortgagee and mortgagor to assist in avoiding foreclosure or bankruptcy.

Wrap-around mortgage—A financing arrangement in which a new mortgage is placed in a junior position to a prior mortgage or mortgages. The wrap-around mortgage payment is a combination of all mortgage payments. An example would be a wrap-around mortgage in a third position. The mortgagor would make one payment to the wrap-around mortgagee who would then keep his proportionate payment and pay the mortgage payment to the first and second mortgagees.

Writ of execution—A court order authorizing an official to execute a decision such as eviction of a tenant or selling property. A writ to carry out the judgment or decree of a court.

Yield—(1) The amount of income returned from an investment expressed as a percentage. For example, discount points plus interest rates will equal the yield. (2) The productivity of farm lands.

Yield to maturity (YTM) The percentage return of an investment based on the loan's reaching its maturity. For real estate mortgages, yield is based on an average life of the loan (see *Discount Yield Table*, page 315). Yield to maturity disregards the average life concept.

Zero lot lines—A structure with at least one side resting directly on the lot's boundary line.

GLOSSARY INDEX
AND THESAURUS

A glossary defines terms. There are 1269 terms in this glossary. Many times we can think of a subject related to a term, but cannot remember the term. For example, you are searching for a term that means without personal liability, but you cannot recall the term. Where do you start looking? Look in this index for the subject liability and you will find two terms that mean without personal liability; exculpatory clause, and non-recourse.

Accounting—Accrual method, basis, capital, debt coverage ratio, financial accounting standards board (fasb), generally accepted accounting principles (GAAP), liquidity, pro-forma, regulatory accounting principles (RAP)

Add—Accession, accretion, annex, tacking

Adjoining—Abut, contiguous, party wall.

Agreement—Addendum, binder, contract, buy-back agreement, buy-sell agreement, collusion, commitment, dual contract, exclusive right to sell, lease, letter of intent, listing, loan commitment, mandatory commitment, meeting of the minds, month-to-month tenancy, mortgage, nondisturbance clause or agreement, novation, occupancy agreement, offer, option, reciprocity, repurchase agreement, reverse repurchase agreement, sale and servicing agreement, subordination agreement, surrender

Allocation—Apportionment, prorate

Appraiser organization or designation—American Institute of Real Estate Appraisers (MAI and RM), Society of Real Estate Appraisers, SRA, SREA, SRPA

Assign—Alienation, assignee, assignment of mortgage, assignor

Auction—Absolute auction, bid, bid-in, upset price, convertible standby commitment, property disposition (PD)

Auxiliary—Ancillary

Balloon—Bullet

Behind—Arrears

Board—Baseboard, batten, beam, board and batten, clapboard, cornice, fascia, floor joist, furring, headers, jamb, joist, king post, laminated, lintel, miter, molding, plates, rafter, ridgeboard, sheathing shim, shoe molding, sill plate, stud subflooring

Borrowing—Leverage

Buyer beware—Caveat emptor

Calling a loan—Acceleration clause, call provision, demand note, double whammy, due-on-sale clause

Column—Abutment

Combining properties—Assemblage

Condemnation—Eminent domain, inverse, just compensation, severance damages, unfit

Connect—Adjoin, abut

Construction loan—Disbursement, draw, short-term

Contract—Offer and acceptance, agreement of sale, conditional sales contract, acquisition, consideration, earnest money, oral contract

Conveyance—Alienation, instrument

Co-signer—Accommodation party, co-mortgagor.

Cost—Basis, acquisition, annual percentage rate (APR), bid in, capital expenditure, certificate of claim, closing costs, concessionary items/concessions, consumer price index (CPI), correlation, cost approach, cost of funds (COF), cost-of-living index, debit, deficiency, escalator clause, hard cost, income approach, index, index lease, interest, interest rate, net net net, off-site cost, origination fee, positive carry, price level adjustable mortgage (PLAM), Real Estate Settlement Procedure Act (RESPA), regulation Z, seed money, site development cost, spread, subsidy, total acquisition

Court decision—Adjudication

Cove—Cul-de-sac

Crop—Emblements

Damages—Exemplary, breach of contract, inverse condemnation, liability insurance, liquidated damages, mitigation of damages, severance damages, tort, condemnation.

Decorative items—Appointments

Dedication—Easement

Deed—All-inclusive trust deed, deed of trust, indenture, boiler plating, contract for deed, declaration, deed-in-lieu of foreclosure, deed restrictions, evidence of title, inchoate, master deed, quitclaim deed, sheriff's deed, skip deed, special warranty deed, tax deed, trust deed, warranty deed

Deposit—Earnest money, escrow, impound, certificate of deposit (CD), clearing account, commitment fee, kiting checks, security deposit, verification of deposit

Depreciation—Component, economic, functional, physical, deferred maintenance, normal wear and tear

Discount—Points, par, discount rate, original-issue discount (OID), rediscount rate.

Easement—Appurtenance, dedication

Electricity—Ampere, candle hour, candle power, conduit, kilo, ohm, volt, watt, Watt-hour

Eminent domain—Condemnation, fee simple, inverse condemnation.

Enter—Access right, ingress

Equity participation—Kicker

Escrow—Impound, clearing account, escrow analysis, escrow payment, escrow overage or shortage

Exit—Access right, egress.

Fact—De facto

Failure—Default, breach of contract, forfeiture, misrepresentation, nonperformance

Foreclosure—Certificate of claim, deed-in-lieu, defeasance, deficiency, equity of redemption, judicial, non-judicial, redemption, strict.

Foundation—Crawl space, footing, slab

Glass—Jalousies, luminous ceiling

Grout—Mortar

Guardian—*Ad litum*, conservator, guardian ad litum

Hallway—Foyer

Heating—British thermal unit, convection, radiant, plenum

History—Abstract, credit

Home—Abode, domicile, dwelling, principal residence

Husband—Curtesy, *et vir*

Improvement—Appurtenance, betterment, fixture, overimprovement

Income—Annuity, income approach, net operating income (NOI)

Insulation—Batt, felt, R-value, Weather stripping

Insurance—Accident and health premium, binder, builder's risk, exception, extended coverage, mortgage insurance, mortgage life, mutual mortgage insurance, named-peril, private mortgage, reissue rate, short rate, Federal Savings and Loan Insurance Corporation (FSLIC), Flexible Loan Insurance Plan (FLIP)

Integration—Affirmative marketing, blockbusting, redlining

Interest—Accrued interest, add-on interest, amortization, annual percentage rate, basis points, blended rate, compound, coupon, disintermediation, face, imputed, nominal, ordinary, per diem, Rule of 72, yield, equitable title, interest only (IO), prepaid, undivided

Judgment—Adjudication, decree

Lawsuit—Litigation

Lease—Absorption rate, net

Leave—Access right, egress

Liability—Attractive nuisance doctrine, exculpatory clause, non-recourse, recourse, release, subrogation

Life—Economic, effective, life estate, life tenant

Marriage—Antenuptial agreement

Mathematical statistics—Actuary

Mortar—Grout, raked joint

Mortgage—Adjustable rate, bi-weekly, blanket, bridge loan, Canadian rollover, chattel, closed end, CMO, debt instrument direct reduction, encumbrance, end loan, face, flexible loan insurance program, flexible payment, floor loan, floor-to-ceiling, gap, graduated payment, growing equity, hypothecate, inchoate, interim, junior, law day, level payment, lien, lien theory, title theory, novation, open end, package, participation, pledged account, price level adjusted, purchase money, recasting, reduction certificate, renegotiable rate, reverse annuity, shared appreciation, shared equity, standing, sub-mortgage, subordination, swing loan, wrap-around, growing equity mortgage (GEM), broker, banker, constant, correspondent, revenue bond

Mortgage Bankers Association—Farm Mortgage Bankers Association

Natural cause—Act of God

Notice—Constructive, legal, lis pendens, notice of default, Notice to quit

Opening—Louver, balanced window, door, chimney

Order—Decree, injunction, change order, writ of execution

Others—*Et al*

Overlapping—Encroachment

Ownership (also see *Title*)—Allodial system, entity, fee simple, joint tenancy, ownership form, severalty, tenancy by the entirety, tenancy in common, tenure, cotenancy, evidence of title, notorious possession, partnership, corporation, limited partnership, sub-chapter s corporation, trust, time share

Personal Property—Chattel, estate, fixture, legacy

Points—Discount, par, basis, daily price limits, yield

Possession—Adverse, attachment, notorious, prescription, tacking, Seisin, remainder man

Power of Attorney—Attorney-in-fact, VA power of attorney

Prepayment—Closed period, lock-in, constant prepayment rate (CPR), double whammy, growing equity mortgage (GEM), prepayment clause, prepayment penalty

504

Profit—Arbitrage, builder's and sponsor's profit and risk allowance (BSPRA)

Public property—Appropriation, eminent domain, escheat

Purchaser—Grantee, vendee

Putty—Caulking

Recess—Niche, nook, alcove

Recessed room—Alcove

Recognition—Attornment

Regulation—Basket provision, code, recession, regulation A, regulation D, regulation Q, regulation Z, regulatory accounting principals (RAP)

Relationship—Affinity, agency, agent, consanguinity, next of kin

Rent—Economic, contract, fair market, gross rent multiplier (GRM), lessee, lessor, market, overage, override, rent-roll, rent-up, Section 8 Program, step down lease, step-up lease, surcharge

Representative—Fiduciary, nominee, power of attorney, surety, trustee

Rock—Bedrock, jutty

Roof—Eaves, flashing, gable, gambrel, hip, mansard, M-roof, overhang, pitch, ridge, shakes, soffit, cornice, deck, dormer, sheathing, hipped, rafter, ridgeboard, domed, slab, truss

Sales—Absorption rate, bird dog, broker, buy back agreement, contract, commission, comparable, conditional, earnest money, Interstate Land Sales Act, market approach to value, overage, par, percentage lease, procuring cause, recapture clause, square foot price, total acquisition.

Sales contract—See *Contract*

Secondary—Subordination

Secondary marketing—Delivery, forward commitment, forward delivery, hedging, index, institutional lender, investor delivery, index institutional lender, investor, loan correspondent, maturity, modified pass-through, nonnegotiable instrument, offering sheet, pipeline, Real Estate Investment Trust (REIT), Real Estate Mortgage Investment Conduit (REMIC), tandby commitment, warehousing, whole loan, Conduit, Conforming, Federal Home Loan Mortgage Corporation (FHLMC), Federal National Mortgage Association (FNMA) (Fannie Mae), Government National Mortgage Association (GNMA), Government Sponsored Enterprise (GSE), Secondary mortgage market, seasoned production

Securities—Bearer bond, blue-sky laws, call, call provision, CMO, completion bond, coupon, face, holder in due course, margin, margin call, mark to market, maturity, modified pass-through, mortgage-backed securities, mortgage bonds, mortgage revenue bonds, mutual capital certificate, obligation bond, original face, original-issue discount, parity, participation certificate, pass-through certificate, prospectus, public offering, adjustable rate preferred stock (ARPS), certificates for amortizing revolving debt (CARDS), certificates of accrual on treasury securities (CATS), forward delivery, mortgage-related security (MRS), mortgage revenue bonds (MRB), Real Estate Securities and Syndication Institute (RESSI), repurchase agreement, reverse repurchase agreement

Security—Collateral, compensating balances, lien, security deposit, security interest, submortgage

Seller—Grantor, vendor, seller-servicer, seller's market

Side—Elevation, facade

Soil—Aeolian, agrarian, alluvial, alluvion, alluvium, avulsion, backfilling, boring test, erosion, frost line, percolation test, accretion

Staircase—Baluster, newel

Standard—Boiler plating

Stop—Abrogate, estop, estoppel

506

Subordinate—Ancillary

Survey—Base line, meridian line, range lines

Tax—Ad valorem, assessed valuation, assessment, assessor, at risk, board of equalization, mill, reassessment, adjusted tax basis, escalator clause, housing expense, net effective income, operating expenses, ordinary and necessary business expense, ordinary income, ratable property or estate, recognized gain, remic, safe harbor rule, subchapter s, tax deed, tax escalation clause, tax-increment financing, tax-lien, tax stop clause, transfer tax, deed

Tile—Acoustical tile, lath, masonry

Title—Abstract, action to quiet title, adverse possession, affidavit of title, beneficial estate, certificate of, chain of, cloud, color of, community property, co-tenancy, defective, equitable, estate, evidence of, land contract, opinion, quitclaim deed, special warranty deed, tax deed warranty deed, clear, contract for deed, convey, conveyance, deed of trust, equitable, hidden defect, insurable, lien, theory, marketable, patent, perfecting, reconveyance, skip deed, tenancy, tenancy by the entirety, binder, exception, insurance, report, search, Torrens system, trust, trustee

Transfer—Alienation, assign, assignment of mortgage, convey, closing, condition, dedication, deed, deed of trust, descent, grantor, restraint on alienation, skip deed, transfer tax.

Twice—Biannual, biennial, bi-weekly mortgage

Value—Aesthetic, amenity, book, boot, consideration, equity, intrinsic, salvage, ad valorem, appraisal, appreciation, assessment, capitalization rate, certificate of reasonable (CRV), correlation, cost approach to, depreciation, discount, estate, face, functional depreciation, gross rent multiplier (GRM), income approach to, inverse condemnation, judgement, just compensation, loan-to-value ratio (LTV), market approach to, market, mode, obsolescence, plottage, present, price, reconciliation, residual, severance damages, square foot price, total loan-to-value (TLTV), unearned increment

Village—Borough

Wall—Abutment, facade, fire, party, load bearing, masonry, niche, non-bearing.

Water—Artesian well, caisson, cistern, culvert, drip cap, littoral, moisture barrier, reliction, riparian, trap, water table, weep hole

Wife—Dower, et ux

Will—Administrator, administratrix, beneficiary, bequeath, codicil, devise, escheat, executor, executrix, heir, hereditament, intestate, legacy, probate, testate

Witness—Acknowledgment, affidavit, attest, notarize

THE TWO-MINUTE INDEX

This index is cross-referenced in such a manner that the reader should be able to find answers to questions in less than two minutes. The index in this book is the key to the use of the material in this book.

509

INDEX

512

Author Biography

Albert Santi began his real estate career in 1966, while he was finishing his senior year at Memphis State University. Since then he has served as a real estate appraiser, mortgage banker, FHA DE underwriter, mortgage credit examiner and secondary marketing specialist. He has participated in the sale of residential and commercial properties, with special emphasis on loan servicing portfolios. Albert Santi was part of the development of electronic transmission of loan data and the creation of the FHLMC Midanet program.

Santi has taught at Memphis State University, State Technical Institute of Memphis, the Institute of Financial Education (U.S. League of Savings and Loan Associations) and the Mortgage Bankers Association.

ORDER FORM

TO ORDER: Simply fill out the enclosed order card and mail or call us toll-free 1-800-776-2871 Monday through Friday (8:30-5:30 CST). You may also call 312-346-7985.

YES! Please send the following:

_____THE LENDING MANUAL $45.00

_____AMORT+Plus $89.95

_____HP-12C REAL ESTATE SEMINAR $14.95

_____60 MINUTE FINANCE SEMINAR $8.95

_ **READER SERVICE UPDATES**

_____The Mortgage Manual $15.95/yr. _____Mortgage Lending $20.95/yr.

_____**Please send me more information on bulk quantities of**
   THE MORTGAGE MANUAL

Payment: *Check or money orders are payable to Probus Publishing. Add $3.00 for postage and handling for the first book and $1.00 for each additional copy. Illinois residents add 7% sales tax. A signature must accompany all credit card orders.*

MasterCard/Visa/American Express accepted.

Credit Card # _____

Expiration Date _____

Signature _____

Name _____

Address _____

City State _____

Zip _____

Phone _____

Send all orders to:
Probus Publishing Company
118 North Clinton Street
Chicago, Illinois 60606